CAREER OPPORTUNITIES

in the

SPORTS INDUSTRY

FOURTH EDITION

SHELLY FIELD

Ferguson

An imprint of Infobase Publishing

Career Opportunities in the Sports Industry, Fourth Edition

Ferguson
An imprint of Infobase Publishing
132 West 31st Street
New York NY 10001

Library of Congress Cataloging-in-Publication Data

Field, Shelly.
  Career opportunities in the sports industry / Shelly Field. — 4th ed.
    p. cm.
  Includes bibliographical references and index.
  ISBN-13: 978-0-8160-7780-9 (hardcover : alk. paper)
  ISBN-10: 0-8160-7780-0 (hardcover : alk. paper)
1. Sports—Vocational guidance—United States. I. Title.
  GV734.F545F54 2010
  796'.02373—dc22   2009033846

Ferguson books are available at special discounts when purchased in bulk quantities for businesses, associations, institutions, or sales promotions. Please call our Special Sales Department in New York at (212) 967-8800 or (800) 322-8755.

You can find Ferguson on the World Wide Web at http://ferguson.infobasepublishing.com

Series design by Kerry Casey
Composition by Hermitage Publishing Services
Cover printed by Sheridan Books, Ann Arbor, Mich.
Book printed and bound by Sheridan Books, Ann Arbor, Mich.
Date Printed: March 2010

Printed in the United States of America

10 9 8 7 6 5 4 3 2 1

This book is printed on acid-free paper and contains 30 percent postconsumer recycled content.

This book is dedicated to my parents,
Ed and the late Selma Field,
and my sisters, Jessica and Debbie,
for their support, guidance, and love.

CONTENTS

ACKNOWLEDGMENTS

I would like to thank every individual, team, company, corporation, agency, association, and union that provided information, assistance, and encouragement for this book and its previous editions.

I acknowledge with appreciation my editor, James Chambers, for his continuing help and encouragement. I would also like to express my sincere gratitude to Sarah Fogarty, project editor for this book.

I also must thank Kate Kelly, who, as my initial editor, provided the original impetus for this book, and Neal Maillet, editor of an earlier edition of *Career Opportunities in the Sports Industry.*

I gratefully acknowledge the assistance of Ed Field for his ongoing support in this and every other of my projects. In addition, I must give special thanks to Dan Barrett, for his sports expertise, humor, and friendship.

Others whose help was invaluable include the following: American Football Coaches Association; American Hockey League; American League; Jim Baker; Dave Bamett; Ryan Barrett; Alan Barrish; Joyce Blackman; Steve Blackman; Simon Borg, Major League Soccer; Al Buongiome; Sue Cabot; Earl "Speedo" Carroll; Catskill Regional Medical Center, Harris, N.Y.; Anthony Cellini; Dr. Betsy Clark, Ladies Professional Golf Association; Dr. Jessica L. Cohen; Norman Cohen; Jan Cornelius; Crawford Memorial Library Staff; Meike Cryan; Mark DiRaffaele; Direct Mail/Marketing Association, Inc.; Direct Marketing Educational Foundation, Inc.; Elias Sports Bureau; Michelle Edwards; Scott Edwards; Cliff Ehrlich, Catskill Development; Lisa Estrada; Ernest Evans; Eddie Ferenz; Deborah K. Field, Esq; Gregg Field; Lillian (Cookie) Field; Mike Field; Robert Field; Selma G. Field; Finkelstein Memorial Library Staff; Pat Flemming; Paul Francis, Jr.; Clark Gaines; John Gatto; Shelia Gatto; Alex Goldman;; Sam Goldych; Gail Haberle; Kent Hastings; Darren Hawks; Larry Hazzard; Lillian Hendrickson; Allan Henry; Eric Holmes, Canadian Football League; Tom Hoover; Jay Horowitz; Joan Howard; International Association of Approved Basketball Officials; International Boxing Federation; Roland Johnson; Jimmy "Handyman" Jones; Don King Enterprises; Karen Leever; Mark Levin; Los Angeles Lakers; Los Angeles Laker Girls; Darcy Maccarone; Major Indoor Soccer League; John Manzi, Monticello Raceway; Edward P. Marion; Joe Mcilvaine, former v.p. of baseball operations, New York Mets; Phillip Mestman; Rima Mestman; Beverly Michaels, Esq.; Martin Michaels, Esq.; Larry Miller; Jay D. Moore, WNBA; Monticello Central High School Guidance Department; Monticello Central High School Library Staff; Monticello Central Middle School Library Staff; Monticello Raceway; Mike Moore, Sharon Morris; MSG Sports; National Association of Professional Baseball Leagues; National Basketball Association; National Football League; National Football League Players Association; National Hockey League; National League; New Jersey Athletic Commission; New York Mets; New York State Athletic Commission; New York Yankees; Ellis Norman; North American Judges and Stewards Association; Dorsey J. Parker; Professional Football Referees Association; Mel Pulliam; Doug Puppel; Harvey Rachlin; Ramapo Catskill Library System; Ross Richardson; Bob Rosen, statistician; Bob Saludares, Community Employment Training Center, Las Vegas,; Michael Seiter; Eva Shain; Frank Shain, professional ring announcer; Marjorie Snyder; John Sohigian, Orange County Choppers; Laura Solomon;

Bob Sparks; Ron Scott Stevens; Matthew E. Strong; Thrall Library Staff; United States Department of Labor; United States Professional Tennis Association; United States Trotting Association; Brian Vargas; Brian Anthony Vargas; Sarah Ann Vargas; Amy Vasquez; Pat Vasquez; WABC TV Sports; Kaytee Warren; Carol Williams; Chet Williams; John Williams; Mike Wimer, Major Indoor Soccer League; WCBS TV Sports; WNBA; WNBC TV Sports; and the Women's Sports Foundation.

My thanks also to the many people, companies, and organizations who provided information and material for this book who wish to remain anonymous.

HOW TO USE THIS BOOK

The first edition of *Career Opportunities in the Sports Industry* was published in 1991. Now, some 18 years later, the sports industry is more popular than ever.

It is no secret that most people love sports. Whether they want to participate in a sport or prefer to be spectators, or both, there is no question that the sports industry continues to explode.

Today, major sports figures commanding multi-million-dollar paychecks are the norm. Many also land lucrative endorsement deals. Baseball is the national pastime. Every year, the Super Bowl breaks spectator records, and a multitude of fans wait for March Madness and the Final Four, and the list goes on.

All you need to do is turn on the television and flip through the channels and, depending on the time of year, you will be able to see baseball, football, soccer, basketball, golf, auto racing, horse racing, tennis, boxing, bowling, hockey, wrestling, and more. In addition to scheduled programming and news, there are television networks and cable stations dedicated entirely to both sports in general and specific sports.

Thousands and thousands of people are currently working in the sports industry. There are many more who want to enter this exciting industry but have no idea how to go about getting a job in it. Some are hoping to become a major sports figure and command a multimillion-dollar salary. Others may want to work in the business end of the industry. Some are not sure what they want to do; they just want to work in some aspect of the sports industry. Many are not aware of career opportunities, where to locate them, or the training required to be successful in their quest.

Career Opportunities in the Sports Industry is the single most comprehensive source for learning about job opportunities in this growing field. Reading this book will give you an edge over other applicants.

It was written for anyone who aspires to work in the sports industry, whether just for a job or to create a career. It was written for anyone who dreams of succeeding in the sports industry. This book was . . . written for you!

The jobs discussed in this book cover careers in professional athletics and also those in the business, education, officiating, sales, recreation, and fitness aspects of the sports industry.

This industry offers an array of opportunities for people with a variety of skills and talents. It needs athletes, secretaries, receptionists, salespeople, publicists, trainers, business managers, scouts, statisticians, coaches, teachers, referees, judges, store managers, health and fitness personnel, nutritionists, webmasters, marketing people, and more. It needs special event coordinators, advertising directors, copywriters, Web content producers, sports anchors, color commentators—and the list goes on.

The trick to locating the job you want is developing your skills and using them to get you in the door. Once you have your foot in the door, you can climb the career ladder to success.

Read through this book and determine what careers you are qualified for or interested in. Learn what education, training, and skills are needed to enter your profession of choice. You can then work toward having an interesting, exciting, and financially rewarding career in the sports industry.

What's New in the Fourth Edition

The fourth edition of *Career Opportunities in the Sports Industry* is chock-full of updated information. Salaries, employment and advancement prospects, training and educational requirements, and unions and associations for each job profile were reviewed and updated when necessary. The information in every appendix has been updated as well, giving you the most up-to-date names, addresses, phone numbers, and Web sites of colleges and universities, sports officiating programs, workshops and seminars, trade associations, unions and other organizations, sports teams, promoters and promotion companies, boxing and wrestling sanctioning bodies, and cable and network sports departments. Brand-new sports career Web sites have been added. New books and periodicals complete the bibliography.

Two new appendixes have been added, including a directory of U.S. harness racing tracks and U.S. thoroughbred racing tracks.

While the first three editions of *Career Opportunities in the Sports Industry* were very comprehensive in their coverage of careers and key jobs, eight new job profiles have been added to this updated edition. This brings the total number of career opportunities to 85.

Sources of Information

Information for this book was obtained through interviews, questionnaires, surveys, and a variety of books, magazines, newsletters, television and radio programs, and Web sites. Some information came through personal experience working in the sports industry. Other data were obtained from business associates who work in various areas of sports.

Among the people interviewed were men and women who work in all aspects of the sports industry. These include individuals working in business and administration; amateur, collegiate, and professional athletics; colleges; newspapers; magazines; radio and television stations; Web sites; health and fitness clubs; spas; racetracks; boxing gyms; and sports medicine clinics. Also interviewed were

agents, managers, attorneys, publicists, marketing people, team managers, owners and other corporate and administrative personnel, association directors, physical therapists, nutritionists, coaches, referees, and judges. Professional sports teams were contacted as well as schools, colleges, personnel offices, unions, trade associations, etc.

Organization of Material

Career Opportunities in the Sports Industry is divided into 12 general employment sections. These sections are: Professional Athletes; Professional Sports Teams; Sports Business and Administration; Coaching and Education; Sports Officiating; Sports Journalism; Recreation and Fitness; Boxing and Wrestling; Racing; Wholesaling and Retailing; Sports Medicine; and Sports Web Jobs. Within each of these sections are descriptions of specific careers.

There are two parts to each job classification. The first part offers job information in chart form. The second part presents information in a narrative text. In addition to the basic career description, you will find additional information on unions and associations as well as tips for entry.

This edition features an expanded appendix. Nineteen updated appendixes are offered to help you locate information you might want or need to get started looking for a job in the field or to climb the career ladder if you are already working in the industry.

Physical and e-mail addresses (when available) are included so that you can send your résumés. You can also use these appendixes to assist you in locating internships or to obtain general information.

These appendixes include: college and university degree programs offering majors in sports administration; college and university degree programs offering majors in physical education; programs in sports officiating; workshops and seminars; trade associations and unions; a directory of Major League Baseball (MLB); a directory of National Association of Professional Baseball Leagues (NAPBL); a directory of National Basketball Association (NBA); a directory of Women's National Basketball Association (WNBA); a directory of National Football League (NFL); a directory of Canadian Football League (CFL); a directory of

National Hockey League (NHL); a directory of American Hockey League (AHL); a directory of Major League Soccer (MLS); a directory of U.S. Harness Racing Tracks; a directory of U.S. Thoroughbred Racing Tracks; boxing and wrestling sanctioning bodies; a directory of boxing and wrestling promoters and promotion companies; a directory of cable and network television sports departments; and sports career Web sites.

A bibliography of sports-related books and periodicals and a glossary are also included.

Whether you choose to be a professional athlete, a sports official, the general manager of a pro sports team, a coach, a sports reporter, or a sports industry attorney; whether you choose to be a jockey, prize fighter, golf pro, or sports statistician; whether you choose to be a physical education teacher, sports columnist, team public relations director, sports agent, or anything in between, a career in the sports industry can be both exciting and fulfilling.

Your career in the sports industry is waiting for you. You just have to go after it. Persevere and you will make it!

Shelly Field
www.shellyfield.com

INTRODUCTION

The sports industry is huge. Over the years it has turned into a multibillion-dollar business. Thousands and thousands of people work in the various facets of the industry. One of them can be you.

Millions of people enjoy sports in some manner, yet most don't seriously consider the possibility of working in this exciting industry. They might see others in some facet of the industry and think, "Wow, those people are lucky," or might even think, "I wish I could have a job like that," but don't know how to take that desire further.

It is an interesting concept to many that they can actually have a job doing something that they enjoy or work in an industry that they love. It's difficult for many to believe that they can be that lucky.

This book was written for everyone who loves sports and wishes they could be part of it. This book can help make that dream a reality!

While it is unrealistic to think that everyone can be a professional baseball, basketball, football, hockey, or soccer player, it is important to know that there are talented people who do fulfill that dream. The baseball, football, and hockey fields are full of people who have been successful. So are the basketball courts.

It is important to know that almost any talent you have can be applied to obtaining a job in the sports industry. The possibilities are endless. You can be anything from a professional athlete to a general manager of a sports team; you might become a coach, physical education teacher, referee, secretary, or receptionist in a major sports team organization office.

If you prefer, your job in the field of sports can be that of a physical therapist, sports journalist, color commentator, television sports anchorperson,

accountant, or attorney. You might want to work in sports marketing, sponsorship, or public relations. You might want to become a boxing judge, retail sports shop salesclerk, or an athletic equipment manufacturer's representative. You might want to become the webmaster for a sports team's Web site, the Web site content producer, or the Web site marketing director. The choice is yours.

What this all means is that the world of sports is all-encompassing. Every time you work out, attend a baseball game, watch a tennis tournament, play golf, put on a pair of running shoes, listen to the sports segment on the television or radio news, read about sports in the newspaper, or check out a sports-oriented Web site, you are dealing with some aspect of the sports industry.

As you read the various sections in this book searching to find the perfect job, keep in mind that every job can be a learning experience and a stepping-stone to the next level. I have given you the guidelines. You have to do the rest.

Within each section of this book you will find all of the information necessary to acquaint you with most of the important jobs in the industry. A key to the organization of each entry follows:

Alternate Titles

Many jobs in the sports industry have alternate titles. The duties are the same, only the name is different. Titles vary from company to company and team to team.

Career Ladder

The career ladder illustrates a normal job progression. Remember that in many parts of the sports industry there are no hard-and-fast rules. Job progression may not necessarily follow a precise order.

Position Description

Every effort has been made to give well-rounded job descriptions. Keep in mind that no two companies, teams, or organizations are structured exactly the same. Therefore, no two jobs will be alike.

Salary Ranges

Salary ranges for the job titles in this book are as accurate as possible. Salaries for jobs in the sports industry reflect many variables. These include the specific sport in which the individual is working, as well as his or her experience, responsibilities, and position. Earnings are also dependent on the specific team for which an individual works as well as its prestige and popularity.

It should be noted that earnings for athletes can vary dramatically and are dependent on a number of factors, including the specific sport as well as the individual's talent and popularity.

Employment Prospects

If you choose a job that has an EXCELLENT, GOOD, or FAIR rating, you are lucky. You will have an easier time finding a job. If, however, you would like to work at a job that has a POOR rating, don't despair. The rating only means that it may be difficult to obtain a job, not that finding one is totally impossible.

Advancement Prospects

Try to be as cooperative and helpful as possible in the workplace. Don't attempt to see how little work you can do. Be enthusiastic, energetic, and outgoing. Go that extra step that no one expects. Learn as much as you can. When a job advancement possibility opens up, make sure that you are prepared to take advantage of it.

A variety of options for career advancement are included. However, you should be aware that there are no hard-and-fast rules for climbing the career ladder in the sports industry. While work

performance is important, advancement in many jobs is based on experience, education, training, employee attitude, talent, and of course individual career aspirations.

Many companies promote from within. The best way to advance your career is to get your foot in the door and then climb the career ladder.

Education and Training

This section presents the minimum educational and training requirements for each job area. This does not mean that you should limit yourself. Try to get the best training and education possible.

A college degree or background does not guarantee a job in the sports industry, but it might help prepare a person for life in the workplace. Education and training also encompass courses, seminars, programs, on-the-job training, and learning from others. Volunteer work, internships, and even helping out in family businesses can look good on your résumé.

Special Requirements

This section covers any special licensing and credentials that may be required for a specific job.

Experience, Skills, and Personality Traits

This section indicates experience requirements as well as specific skills and personality traits necessary for each job. These will differ from job to job. Whatever type of career you want, having an outgoing personality helps. Networking is essential to success. Contacts are important in all facets of the business. Make as many as you can. These people are helpful in both obtaining a job and advancing your career.

Best Geographical Location

Jobs in the sports industry are located throughout the country. The greatest number of opportunities will be found in cities hosting major league, minor league, or collegiate sports teams.

Opportunities in sports-oriented journalism, television, and radio may be located both in large metropolitan areas and small rural towns.

The same is true of jobs in sports retailing, wholesaling, education, fitness, recreation, and sports medicine. Those interested in becoming professional athletes might have to relocate to areas where sports teams and sporting events are headquartered.

If you are creative in your job hunting, opportunities may be found almost anywhere in the country.

Unions and Associations

This section offers other sources for career information and assistance. Unions and trade associations offer valuable help in obtaining career guidance, support, and personal contacts. They may also offer training, continuing education, scholarships, fellowships, seminars, and other beneficial programs.

Tips for Entry

Use this section to gather ideas on how to get a job and gain entry into the area of the business in which you are interested.

When applying for any job, always be as professional as possible. Dress neatly and conservatively. Don't wear sneakers. Don't chew gum. Don't smoke or use heavy perfume or men's cologne.

Always have a few copies of your résumé with you. These, too, should look neat and professional. Have them typed and presented well, checked and rechecked for grammar, spelling, and content.

If asked to fill in an application, fill in the entire application even if you have a résumé with you. Print your information neatly.

Be prepared when applying for jobs and filling in applications. Make sure you know your Social Security number. Ask people in advance whether you can use them as references. Make sure you know their full names, addresses, and phone numbers. Try to secure at least three personal references as well as three professional references you can use.

The ability to go online, whether from your home computer or one in a school or public library, puts you at a great advantage. No matter which aspect of the industry piques your interest, you need to be computer literate. It is always a plus.

Many sports-oriented companies, teams, and other organizations today have Web sites that may be helpful in your quest for that perfect job. You can obtain information about companies and their current job opportunities. You can also read up on industry news or even check the classifieds from newspapers in different areas via their online version of the paper.

If you aspire to become a professional athlete, get the best training you can. Refine your skills and techniques. Talk with your coaches and instructors and ask for help. Most people are glad to provide it.

Use every contact you have. Don't get hung up on the idea that you want to get a job by yourself. If you are lucky enough to know someone who can help you obtain a job you want, take him or her up on it. You'll have to prove yourself at the interview and on the job. Nobody can do that for you. (Remember to send a thank-you note to the person who helped you as well as to the interviewer after the interview.)

Once you get your foot in the door, learn as much as you can. As noted previously, doing a little bit more than is expected will be helpful in your career. Be cooperative. Be a team player. Don't burn bridges; it can hurt your career. Ask for help. Network. Find a mentor.

I can't stress enough how critical it is to be on time for everything. This includes job interviews, phone calls, work, and meetings. People will remember when you're habitually late, and it will work against you in advancing your career.

Do not be afraid to pursue your dream job. You can have a career that will enable you to get up each morning, happy that you are going to work. The sports industry can be glamorous, exciting, and financially rewarding. Don't get discouraged during your job-hunting period. Everyone does not land the first job they apply for.

You may have to pay your dues in the minor leagues. You may have to knock on a lot of doors, send out a lot of résumés, and apply for a lot of jobs you don't get, but eventually you can find the job of your dreams.

Have faith and confidence in yourself. You will make it to the top eventually, but you must persevere. In many instances, the individual who didn't make it in the career he or she wanted is the one who gave up too soon and didn't wait that extra day.

You have already taken the first step by picking up this book. Have fun reading it. Use it. It will help you find a career that you will truly love. When you do get the job of your dreams, do someone else a favor and pass along the benefit of your knowledge.

I love to hear success stories about your career and how this book helped you. If you have a story and want to share it, go to www.shellyfield.com. I can't wait to hear from you!

Good luck.

Shelly Field

PROFESSIONAL ATHLETES

PROFESSIONAL BASEBALL PLAYER

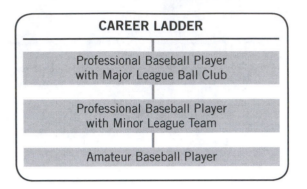

Position Description

It is the dream of many youngsters to grow up and play professional baseball. Most go on to other careers and forget their childhood dream. Some lucky young men (there are currently no successful professional leagues for women), however, get the opportunity to pursue their dream and become Professional Baseball Players.

The road to becoming a Pro Ballplayer is not easy. There are many pitfalls along the way. Competition is stiff in this industry. A lot of hard work is involved not only in becoming a Pro Player, but in staying in the pros as well. It is a long climb up the career ladder from an amateur baseball player to a Pro in the major leagues, but for those who love the sport, it is well worth it.

An individual usually begins his career by playing amateur baseball. He might be on a school, civic, nonprofit, or community team. Someone notices that he has more talent than the rest of the team members. It might be a coach, a physical education teacher, or someone just watching the game. Sometimes the individual begins to emerge as a star of the team. Over a period of time, a number of people will see a special talent in the player, a talent that the other athletes do not appear to possess.

By the time the individual reaches high school, it will be evident that he can play better than others on the team. He might have excellent pitching skills or be a harder hitter.

The next step toward becoming a Baseball Player entails getting the attention of someone in the pros to determine if the talent is really there. This process can be handled in a number of different ways. The individual's coach or another interested person may contact a professional team or a scout. The individual might contact these people himself. Also, some scouts travel throughout the country searching for talented young men who want to become Professional Ballplayers. Besides holding tryouts, they may visit schools, colleges, and other locations to talk to coaches, teachers, and players.

As noted previously, competition in this profession is fierce. Scouts may see hundreds of young men playing the game before they find one individual whom they feel will make it in the pros. When the scout does locate a talented player, he or she will bring him to the attention of a member of the baseball club, such as the director of minor league operations or the head scout.

The scout will then talk to the athlete and his family about the possibility of signing a contract to work with the team. In order to make an offer more acceptable, they may offer the athlete a full or partial scholarship to a college he would like to attend. A contract must then be negotiated and signed.

Athletes who are in college and want to turn pro may sign up for the draft. The draft is a system where teams get to choose athletes from a list of players who want to become professionals. The first team to choose from the list is the one that placed last in standings during the year. The next team to choose is the one that placed next to last, and so on. The team that won the championship gets last choice. If a team wants certain players who have already been chosen, the team may trade other players for them.

Baseball clubs have four different classes or levels of teams. The first three are called minor league clubs. They consist of the A team or rookie team; the AA team; the AAA, or "Triple A," team; and the major league club. While there are no hard-and-fast rules regarding which level club the novice Professional Baseball Player is assigned to, usually he begins to play with the rookie team. If, however, the individual is extremely talented, he might be assigned to play with any level.

Each major league ball club has a number of minor league affiliates. Therefore, if a Player is under contract to the New York Mets, he might be working with the Binghamton Mets, the Mets AA team.

While in the minor leagues, Baseball Players are trained to refine their skills while competing with other teams of the same stature. Players are expected to attend spring training and any other mandatory and regular training sessions.

After a season, if the Player is ready, he may move up from the rookie team to the AA team. After another, he may be assigned to play in the Triple A club. What every Professional Ballplayer aspires to is an assignment to play on a major league team. This is extremely difficult and does not happen to every Player. Many Players stay in the minor leagues for their entire career. It is important to remember that Players in the major league club may also be reassigned back to one of the minor league teams. As noted previously, there is no set rule for the level a Pro Ballplayer may be assigned to play.

Those playing in the minor leagues will not get even a fraction of the recognition or financial compensation that athletes in the major leagues do. These Players travel in buses from one area to another competing in games. Usually they do not stay in the most prestigious hotels or eat at the better restaurants. They do have the opportunity to learn and gain experience.

Every Ballplayer hopes eventually to be assigned to work in the major league team. During this period, he will be earning an excellent income for his efforts as well as gaining recognition as a Player. He may stay at this level for one or more years depending on his skills and talent.

Baseball Players must concern themselves with injuries that might prevent them from working or force them into early retirement. They must also worry about staying on top. At any time during their contract with one of the teams, the Pro Ballplayer may be traded to another team. While this may not bother some people, to others, the rejection can be an emotional strain.

Many major league Ballplayers work under tremendous stress and pressure for additional reasons. They must constantly stay at the top. Games or entire tournaments may depend on the actions of an individual, which adds to the stress level.

It is important to remember that individuals choosing baseball as a career will not have a choice of cities where they will be headquartered. They must move to the area where the team they are working with is located. Players also must travel extensively to away games during the playing season.

For most Players who make it to the major leagues, a career as a Professional Baseball Player is a dream come true. Many feel it is especially exciting to have thousands of fans cheering for them while they are working at a vocation that most people consider an avocation.

Salaries

Salaries for Pro Baseball Players vary greatly depending on the individual's skills, talents, experience level, and popularity. Other factors include the specific team and if it is in the majors or a minor league.

Earnings for Pro Baseball Players in the minor leagues start at $23,000 and go up from there. Earnings for Players in the major leagues are considerably more. The average Major League salary runs between $1.5 million and $2 million for everyday players. Very popular players with impressive records can command much more. Superstars like Alex Rodriguez (A-Rod) command $28 million or more.

Employment Prospects

Employment prospects are poor for those aspiring to be Pro Baseball Players. Competition is keen. If individuals have talent, however, they can make it in this profession.

While major league teams are located in major cities throughout the country, many minor league clubs are found in smaller cities.

Advancement Prospects

Advancement prospects for a Pro Player are largely dependent on the individual's skills, talents, drive, and determination. It takes hard work to train and play in this sport. Those who show they can do it and are good at what they do will move up. Advancement for Pro Players means that they move up a level in the types of clubs they play with. A rookie advances by moving to a team in the AA or AAA level. Each club has teams in each level. If a player shows potential, he will be moved to a higher level team to play. All Players hope to advance to an assignment to a major league team. Major league Players can advance their careers by improving their performance and command higher and higher salaries.

Education and Training

There are no formal educational requirements for Professional Ballplayers. This is not to say that Ballplayers are not educated. Many Players have college degrees from prestigious schools.

Individuals must be trained in the sport. Most formal training is obtained once the Player is under contract with a team, although Players who play ball in college may also obtain experience comparable to the minor leagues. During this period Players are trained by team coaches, trainers, and support staff to shape their talent and refine their skills.

Experience, Skills, and Personality Traits

Professional Baseball Players must love the sport. They should understand the rules, regulations, and policies of baseball. Individuals must be talented and skillful. It is useful for them to be team players and get along well with others.

The Players should be physically fit and energetic. They need to be motivated and confident as well as have the persistence, drive, and determination necessary to work their way to the top of the profession.

Individuals must be flexible in the geographic area they will have to live in during the playing season. Ball Players must also not mind traveling. They must also have the ability to deal with the stress and pressure that comes from working in this profession. Individuals who make it to the top must also be able to deal with the fame that usually follows.

A good sense of business is useful. While most individuals have someone to represent them, it is helpful to have a working knowledge of the business end of the industry.

Unions and Associations

Professional Ballplayers belong to a professional organization called the Association of Professional Ball Players of America (APBPA). They may also be members of the Major League Ball Players Association (MLBPA). These organizations work on behalf of Ballplayers to provide better conditions and also negotiate other parts of their contracts.

Tips for Entry

1. If you really want to become a Pro Baseball Player, you must practice and play at every opportunity.
2. If someone offers you constructive criticism, take it and try to improve your skills.
3. Try to find someone, such as a coach or a physical education teacher, who can help you in your career. If such people feel that you are talented, ask if they can contact a scout or a major league team recruitment official on your behalf.
4. If you cannot find anyone to act on your behalf, you might want to contact the recruitment office of one of the ball clubs. Tell them about yourself and learn what you should do to help your career progress.
5. If you or others feel that you have the talent, persevere. This is a difficult career to enter, but it can be done.

PROFESSIONAL BASKETBALL PLAYER

Position Description

For those who enjoy shooting baskets as a form of recreation, it is often hard to believe that there are actually people who get paid to do just that. Professional Basketball Players have the job of playing basketball for men's professional teams and earning a living at the game. Today, women can also play professionally for teams in the Women's National Basketball Association (WNBA).

Most Basketball Players began shooting baskets while they were youngsters. Basketball was their choice when it came to sports. Many played on their junior and varsity high school basketball teams. During this time, coaches, college scouts, and members of college alumni programs watched the young players. By the time they were juniors in high school, many potential Professional Basketball Players had been contacted by colleges or their representatives about the possibility of attending their school and playing on their basketball team.

Scouts and coaches look for a number of things. A very tall, athletic individual will usually catch their eye. There are, however, a number of shorter players. Those who score a lot of points on the court will generate the same interest. Scouts and other personnel may visit in person or obtain information from high school coaches, friends, acquaintances, or by reading sports articles in local newspapers.

Some students who appear to be very talented at the game are contacted by more than one college. Individuals must decide which college they want to attend. For many students, the decision is based not only on the academic standards of the school, but on the prestige of the school's basketball team. Strict regulations forbid scouts from offering and students from accepting incentives such as cars, money, and so on in order to attend a certain school and play on its basketball team.

Once a student is playing for a college team, he is usually not allowed to participate in the National Basketball Association (NBA) draft until graduation. However, there are some exceptions to the rule. For example, an exception might be granted if an individual could prove that staying in school was a financial hardship.

A good number of Professional Basketball Players go through the draft system. Individuals who intend to turn professional sign up to participate in the draft. Teams have the option of choosing their players from the draft.

Other Players who do not make it through the draft system and are not chosen can become free agents. These individuals usually hire an agent to represent them. The agent "shops around" for a team for the individual to play with. If the Player is talented and has a good record, he may be asked to go to a preliminary camp to see if his skills can be refined. If the camp visit works out satisfactorily, the individual becomes a member of the team.

Professional Basketball Players train at camps before the basketball season starts. Most basketball training camps and clinics start in the early fall. Individuals then play for the season, which begins in November and lasts about seven months.

Individuals must learn and adhere to the rules, regulations, and policies of the game. Individuals play either defensively or offensively, depending on their skills.

One of the best things about playing professional basketball is that it is always played on an inside court. Unlike players in baseball or football, Basketball Players do not have to concern themselves with the weather. It can be raining or snowing outside, but inside the weather is always perfect.

In addition to training, practicing, and playing games, Players may be expected to perform in exhibitions. They may participate for nonprofit causes or act as spokespeople for issues that are of concern to them individually or to the team.

Pro Players who make a name for themselves and perform well on the court may also be asked to endorse products in commercials or advertisements. Some Pro Players work with clothing or sports shoe companies developing lines of clothing and sneakers. Others endorse food products or sports-related products.

Individuals who are under contract to a team have to live in the area where the team is headquartered at least during the season. Professional Players train long hours. They must always stay in good physical shape. An injury to any part of the body could cut their career short. Professional Players must also continue to perform well in order to remain successful in their career.

Salaries

Earnings of Professional Basketball Players vary greatly depending on a number of factors. These include the experience level, skills, talents, and popularity of the individual player, as well as the specific team for which he or she is playing.

Players in the NBA Development League, for example, can earn from $25,000 to $50,000. Individuals playing in the Continental Basketball League (CBA) earn from $10,000 to $25,000 for the 30-game season.

Earnings for players in the NBA start at $300,000 for a rookie. From that point on, Professional Basketball Players can negotiate contracts that pay into the millions. There have been some NBA players who have negotiated contracts for more than $24 million.

It is important to note that basketball has a cap on salaries. This means that the team organization can spend only a certain amount of money for all of their team members. They can split the dollar amount any way they want but cannot go over the limit.

These salaries are for men playing in the NBA. Women playing professionally have considerably lower earnings. Men playing professional basketball can also earn millions of dollars in endorsements for various products such as shoes, clothing, toys, etc.

Employment Prospects

Employment prospects for Pro Basketball Players are poor. Each team hires only 15 players, and there are only a limited number of teams.

Some individuals who are talented but have not been able to find a position playing with the NBA have been fortunate to find work with other leagues, such as the Continental Basketball Association (CBA) or leagues that play in other countries.

Advancement Prospects

Advancement prospects for Professional Basketball Players are difficult to determine. Some individuals become superstars during their participation in the sport, while others are forgotten after their stint with a team. Advancement for Pro Basketball Players depends largely on their skills, talent, determination, popularity, and drive. Individuals who have those traits may become superstar Players demanding high earnings. They may also market themselves and obtain lucrative product endorsements.

Education and Training

There are no educational requirements for Professional Basketball Players. However, most individuals are graduates of the college they played for during their amateur days. Majors vary depending on the individual interests of the players.

Experience, Skills, and Personality Traits

The majority of Pro Basketball Players are at least six feet tall. Most are taller. There are exceptions, but these are limited. Individuals must be in excellent physical condition.

Pro Players should be very talented in the techniques and skills of the game. Being a team player is most helpful. As the individual will spend so much time on the court, a love of the game is necessary.

Unions and Associations

Individuals playing for teams in the National Basketball Association (NBA) are members of the NBA Players Association (NBAPA). This organization works on behalf of the Players in the NBA.

Tips for Entry

1. Attend basketball clinics, camps, seminars, and workshops to perfect and refine your skills.
2. Play every chance you get and practice as much as possible.
3. Talk to your coaches and physical education teachers about your aspirations and see if they can help or offer any advice.

PROFESSIONAL WOMEN'S BASKETBALL PLAYER

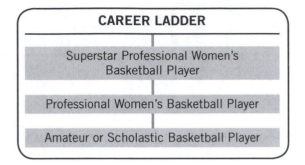
Position Description

Professional women's basketball is on the cutting edge of the sports industry challenging women's roles in professional sports. For many years, women played basketball on an amateur level in schools, colleges, and universities. With the creation of the Women's National Basketball League (WNBA) in 1997, women now have the opportunity to play basketball professionally.

Most Professional Women Basketball Players began their careers much like their male counterparts—shooting baskets as youngsters. Those who were lucky enough attended a high school where there was a girls' basketball team or a local community girls' team.

While the young women are still in high school, coaches, college scouts, and members of college alumni programs have the opportunity to watch them play. Many who show promise are contacted by colleges or their representatives regarding the possibility of attending their school and playing on their basketball team. In many cases, the young women, like their male counterparts, are offered scholarships to entice them to attend particular colleges.

Scouts and coaches look for a number of things in a basketball player. As most basketball players are tall, one of the first things to catch their eye are tall athletic women. Another thing which generates the interest of a scout or coach is a woman who scores a lot of points in a game.

Scouts and coaches often visit high schools in person to watch games. In some cases a high school coach will also contact a college coach or scout to tell them about a potential player. Sometimes scouts and coaches read articles in local newspapers about a specific team player. In many instances, talented young women are contacted by more than one college interested in having them attend and play on their team.

In these situations, individuals must decide which college they want to attend. Those aspiring to be Professional Women Basketball Players will often choose a school based on the prestige of the school's women's basketball team. It is important to note that there are strict regulations forbidding scouts from offering or students from accepting any incentives such as cars, money, etc., in order to attend a certain school or play on its team.

Just as the NBA holds a draft to choose potential players, so does the WNBA. Generally, women interested in turning professional sign up to participate in the draft. Teams then have the option of choosing their players from the draft.

Teams may choose their players from viewing the performance of individuals during school games. Sometimes the WNBA also holds a pre-draft camp for potential players from all over the country, so team coaches, managers, and scouts can evaluate players prior to the draft before choosing who they want.

Women who do not make it through the draft system and are not chosen to be on one of the WNBA teams can become free agents. These individuals usually hire an agent to represent them. The agent then shops around for a team for the woman to play with. Sometimes, if the Player has a good record, she may be asked to go to a preliminary camp to see if her skills can be refined. If the camp visit works out well, the individuals become a member of the team.

As part of the job, Professional Women's Basketball Players must attend training camps before the basketball season begins. These training camps generally start in the early fall. The women then are expected to play the season which begins in November and lasts about seven months.

Professional Female Basketball Players are expected to train, practice, and play games. Staying in good physical shape is mandatory. An injury to any part of the body could put their career to an end.

Additionally, they may be expected to perform in exhibitions. In some cases they might participate in not-for-profit causes. Some Players may additionally act as spokespeople for issues which are important to them individually or to their team. Professional Women's Basketball Players who attract a following and become popular may be asked to endorse products or appear in commercials or advertisements.

Once under contract to a team, Professional Women's Basketball Players are expected to live in the area where the team is headquartered during the season.

Salaries

Earnings of Professional Women's Basketball Players vary depending on a number of factors. These include the team the individual is playing for, as well as the experience level, skills, talents, and popularity of the woman.

Rookies earn a minimum of approximately $34,000 per season. What this means is that a Player would take home about $1,000 per game. While this sounds like a lot, it is nowhere close to what male players in the NBA earn. Female Players with more experience may earn between $50,000 and $100,000.

Many Players augment their salaries by securing endorsements for products or making personal appearances.

Employment Prospects

Employment prospects are poor for Professional Women's Basketball Players. There are currently only 13 teams within the WNBA and approximately 180 players. This doesn't mean that it is impossible to become a Professional Women's Basketball Player, just difficult. Scouts are always on the lookout for extremely talented women with extraordinary basketball skills.

Many women also go oversees to play professional basketball.

Advancement Prospects

Advancement prospects for Professional Women Basketball Players are dependent to a great extent on the skills, drive, determination, and popularity of the particular individual. Only some Players become superstars. Superstars can demand higher earnings or market themselves to obtain lucrative product endorsements.

Education and Training

There are no educational requirements for Professional Women's Basketball Players. Many individuals, however, are graduates of the college they played for during their amateur days.

Individuals often go through basketball training camps to learn skills necessary to the game.

Experience, Skills, and Personality Traits

Professional Female Basketball Players need to be very talented in the skills of the game. Being a team player is essential. The majority of Professional Women's Basketball Players are very tall.

Most individuals gained experience playing amateur basketball in school. A love of the sport is helpful.

Unions and Associations

Individuals playing for teams in the WNBA are members of the WNBA Players Association. This organization works on behalf of the Players in the WNBA.

Tips for Entry

1. Attend basketball clinics, camps, seminars, and workshops to refine and perfect your skills.
2. Play every chance you get and practice as much as possible.
3. Talk to your coaches and physical education teachers about your aspirations. Ask if they can offer any help or advice.
4. You can never tell who is watching your game. Play your best every time.

PROFESSIONAL FOOTBALL PLAYER

Duties: Playing football on a professional team

Alternate Title(s): Athlete; Pro Football Player

Salary Range: $325,000 to $28 million+

Employment Prospects: Poor

Advancement Prospects: Fair

Best Geographical Location(s) for Position: Cities hosting professional football teams

Prerequisites:

Education or Training—Football training

Experience—Experience playing amateur or collegiate football necessary

Special Skills and Personality Traits—Love of the sport; talented in skills and techniques of football; physically fit; aggressive; competitive; large and muscular body type

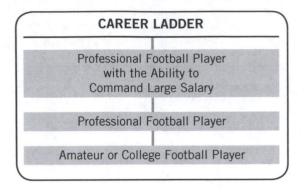

CAREER LADDER

Professional Football Player with the Ability to Command Large Salary

Professional Football Player

Amateur or College Football Player

Position Description

Football is one of the most popular sports today. Millions view professional football games on television and in person. Tickets to the annual Super Bowl are coveted.

Professional Football Players usually start their careers playing touch football as youngsters. (There are no female professional football leagues.) As they grow older they may try out for their junior high or high school team. Over time many individuals develop sufficient talent to obtain athletic scholarships to colleges that seek them out to play on their teams. Other individuals enroll in military academies and play on armed services teams.

Members of college teams generally must have at least a minimum passing grade to stay on the team. In addition to playing in games, schools that put a great deal of emphasis on their football program train their team members extensively in the sport. Athletes then have opportunities to refine their skills and learn everything there is to know about the game. They practice constantly. Players attend clinics and seminars to help them improve their skills and techniques until they are as close to perfect as possible.

Games and competitions help individuals hone their skills. Most colleges have tournaments against other schools. Some colleges belong to national collegiate conferences that organize tournaments.

Many college football games are televised by local, regional, and/or network television. This helps to bring the talented Players to the attention of pro teams. Scouts also travel to the various colleges seeking the very best Players. When individuals decide to turn professional, they sign up for a draft. This system gives professional teams the opportunity to choose new Players from people who are still amateurs. Only 336 Players are chosen from the draft each year. Players who are not drafted may become free agents and market themselves to any of the National Football League (NFL) teams. Others may try to become members of teams in the Canadian Football League (CFL).

Those who are lucky enough to be chosen will play professional football. Professional Football Players do not start right in playing with the team. Athletes attend training camps, which are usually held during the summer months. During this time they attend lectures and practice. They also compete against internal teams as they get ready for the football season. Individuals are assigned to do a specific job as part of the team. They may play offensively or defensively, depending on their skills.

Professional Football Players work actively for about six months of the year, during the football season. Individuals must constantly stay in shape, train, and exhibit talent or they will not be successful and their contracts may not be renewed. Players must move, at least during the season, to the area where the team is located. They must also travel to games held away from the home base.

The careers of Pro Football Players may be cut short due to injuries. Players who make it to the top, however, try to keep that worry in the back of their mind. What they try to concentrate on is the thought of being on a team that not only plays in the Super Bowl, but wins it as well.

Salaries

Salaries for Professional Football Players vary greatly depending on the individual and his skills, talent, experience, prestige, popularity, and the position he plays.

NFL Player salaries are regulated by a salary cap. What that means is there is a maximum amount each franchise can spend on the entire team of players. This salary cap is adjusted each season. Team owners can split that amount any way they choose.

The minimum annual salary any NFL team can pay a Professional Player is $325,000 for a rookie. One-year veterans are paid a minimum of $400,000 a year. Earnings go up considerably for those in demand. Professional Football Players may work out any financial contract that they can with their team. Some players have earnings in the millions. There are individuals who negotiate deals for $28 million or more. Many NFL Players also receive huge signing bonuses.

Interestingly enough, in football, no contracts are guaranteed. Signing bonuses, however, are. Football superstar Peyton Manning, for example, makes $10 million per year. His original contract was $40–50 million with a $20 million signing bonus. In 2008, Ben Roethlisberger, the quarterback for the Pittsburgh Steelers, had an annual paycheck of $27.7 million. In football, it all depends on the season.

Individuals may augment their income by securing endorsements for products or landing roles in television or the movies.

Employment Prospects

Employment prospects are poor for those aspiring to be Professional Football Players. However, talented individuals can make it into the pros if they show promise on their college team and stimulate interest in themselves by the professional teams.

Football Players who are still in college or getting ready to graduate who want to turn pro sign up to become part of the football draft. Professional teams send scouts around prior to the draft to determine who would be an asset to their team. Individuals then wait to be chosen. As noted previously, Players can also become free agents and market themselves to teams.

Advancement Prospects

Professional Football Players strive to be the best in their profession. Advancement prospects are determined mainly by the skills, talent, determination, and drive of the individual athlete. If he consistently performs well, other teams will want him under contract. When a demand is created, an individual's worth rises. He can then negotiate large salary contracts. The highlight of many Professional Football Players' careers is being a member of a winning Super Bowl team.

Individuals who become major football stars may also advance their careers by obtaining endorsements and movie and television deals.

Education and Training

Many professional athletes in other sports, such as baseball or boxing, come directly out of high school. Pro Football Players, however, usually stay amateur until they graduate from a four-year college.

Pro Football Players may have degrees in any subject. A Pro Football Player needs a good education to fall back on in case he is injured or cannot play for other reasons.

It is important for aspiring Football Players to attend a college or university that has a strong football program. In this way, they can make sure they obtain the necessary training, experience, and exposure to be picked up by one of the pro teams.

Experience, Skills, and Personality Traits

Usually Professional Football Players have played the game from the time they were youngsters. Individuals move up the ranks from high school through college and then to the professional level. Most people in this sport have a genuine love for the game.

A Professional Football Player, of course, must be extremely talented in the skills of the sport. Individuals must learn to be team players and to follow the rules of the game.

Football Players must be physically fit. Individuals should be competitive and aggressive. Most Football Players have large and muscular builds.

Because of the great number of injuries incurred when playing the game, the average playing life of a Football Player is only three and a half years. Players must be able to work with the knowledge that they may be injured at any time and that their career can be cut short.

Unions and Associations

Professional Football Players with the National Football League are members of the NFL Players Association (NFLPA). The NFLPA helps players maintain good working conditions and better contract negotiations. Individuals playing in Canada may be members of the Canadian Football League (CFL).

Tips for Entry

1. If you are interested in becoming a Professional Football Player, it is imperative to be on your college team. If you want to make it to the pros, you should try to attend a college that places a heavy emphasis on its football program.

2. Showing promise on a college team is one way to open the door to being successful as a pro.

3. Talk to your high school or college coach about your aspirations and ask for advice.

4. Keep yourself in good physical condition. You won't be able to play at all if you aren't.

5. Learn as much as your can about the sport. In addition to knowing the rules, regulations, and policies, read about its history, other players, teams, and so on.

PROFESSIONAL HOCKEY PLAYER

Position Description

Professional hockey is played on a special ice-skating rink that is surrounded by protective walls. Two teams compete against each other with both trying to place a hockey puck into the opponent's goal area. The Hockey Player plays the game while wearing ice skates. Teams are comprised of six players each. Hockey Players may hold offensive, defensive, or goalie positions. (Professional hockey currently has no women players.)

There is a great deal of teamwork involved in this sport. The game is classified as a contact sport much like football. While trying to make goals, players block those of the opposing side with their bodies. They may block another player with either their shoulders or hips.

Players must wear uniforms that include protective gear with shoulder pads, hip pads, helmets, and so on, similar to football players. They must be in top physical form or they will not be able to endure this sport.

Officials and referees in the game call fouls or penalties. Penalties can be called if a Player holds on to the puck too long, blocks another Player illegally, fights, or breaks any of the rules or regulations of the game. Penalties differ depending on the seriousness of the infraction. They can run the gamut of removing a Player from the team for a few minutes to removing him for the entire game.

Hockey Players can turn pro after graduating from high school or may remain amateurs while they are attending college. Those who turn pro right after high school often play in the minor leagues to gain experience. Individuals who attend or want to attend college may take part in the National Hockey League (NHL) draft. Players may be drafted before they attend college with the understanding that the team has an option on them after they graduate college. Individuals may also play college hockey and then take part in the draft.

Another path that aspiring Pro Hockey Players may take is to try to locate a team to play with outside of the United States. While they will usually not earn as much, many Players feel the experience and exposure will be worth it.

Individuals train during the fall. The regular playing season begins in October and continues through March. NHL playoffs for the Stanley Cup begin in late March or early April and go through May. Individuals who want to become Pro Players may have to relocate, at least for the playing season, to the team's home base. Players are expected to play in home games as well as travel to games held away from home.

Salaries

Salaries for Pro Hockey Players vary greatly. Factors determining earnings include whether the individual is playing in the minor leagues or with a major league team and its geographic location. Other factors include the Player's experience, expertise, skill in the game, and popularity. Individuals playing with minor league teams in this country may earn from $30,000 to $50,000. Players in the major leagues have salaries ranging from $300,000 to $10 million+.

Individuals who make a name for themselves and are popular with fans may also earn extra money endorsing products, appearing in commercials, and acting or making cameo appearances in movies or television.

Employment Prospects

Employment prospects for Professional Hockey Players are poor. Competition is tough for athletes in all sports, and hockey is no exception. However, as in all other sports, individuals who are extremely talented and skillful at hockey and have a great deal of drive and determination can break in.

Opportunities to play hockey may be located in the United States and Canada as well as Europe.

Advancement Prospects

Many Hockey Players advance their careers by moving from the minor leagues to the majors. Individuals may also climb the career ladder by landing a contract with a more prestigious team or by staying with the same team but commanding and receiving contracts for higher yearly earnings.

Advancement as an athlete in this sport, as in most others, depends on skills, talent, drive, and determination. The top spot a Pro Hockey Player can strive for is to be a member of the team that wins the Stanley Cup. Winning the Stanley Cup is to hockey what winning the World Series is to baseball.

Education and Training

There is no formal educational requirement to become a Pro Hockey Player. Some Players turn professional after finishing high school and others become Pros after college.

Individuals must, however, be able to skate expertly and know the skills and techniques of the sport. Much of top-notch talent comes from playing hockey and getting experience in the game at an early age. Many Pro Hockey Players refined their skills while playing on college teams.

Experience, Skills, and Personality Traits

Pro Hockey Players must be extremely skillful in the sport. Individuals must also be excellent ice skaters. They must know how to play well and know all the rules, regulations, and policies of the game. Successful Hockey Players have usually had a great deal of experience playing the game. Many started as young boys and became more experienced and skillful playing against others with the same interest.

Pro Players need to be competitive and aggressive. They should be team players. Individuals should have a lot of drive, determination, and perseverance if they want to make it in this sport. Pro Players need to be physically fit and have a lot of stamina.

Unions and Associations

Individuals playing for the National Hockey League are members of the NHL Players' Association (NHLPA). Those playing for other leagues are usually members of their players' associations.

Tips for Entry

1. Learn how to skate well. Take lessons to help you improve.
2. Talk to a coach or physical education teacher about your aspirations. Ask for advice.
3. Find an amateur hockey league to play with. If you are serious about this profession, you must start playing as early as you can and practice as much as possible.
4. Look for a college that offers hockey as one of its team sports. This will be a good way to refine your skills. Play in competition for the opportunity of being seen by scouts looking for talented individuals who are interested in turning pro.
5. Consider attending a hockey camp. These are usually held in the summer and can help you improve your skills and techniques.

PROFESSIONAL BOXER

CAREER PROFILE

Duties: Fighting in boxing bouts; learning and developing boxing skills

Alternate Title(s): Fighter; Pugilist

Salary Range: $200 to millions per bout, depending on individual's success

Employment Prospects: Good

Advancement Prospects: Fair

Best Geographical Location(s) for Position: Any location hosting boxing shows offers possibilities; Atlantic City, Las Vegas, and New York City are boxing capitals

Prerequisites:

    Education or Training—Training in boxing skills

    Experience—Experience as amateur boxer

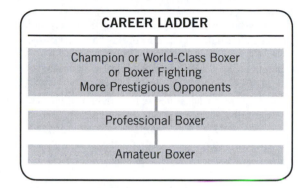

Special Skills and Personality Traits—Boxing skills; drive; determination; physically fit; patience; perseverance

Special Requirement—State licensing required

Position Description

In the last few years, boxing has become a multimillion-dollar business. Network and cable television stations pay huge amounts of money to obtain television rights to top fights. Promoters are paying extraordinary sums of money for the opportunity to stage fights.

Great numbers of fans pay fees to watch fights on pay-for-view stations. These fights are not televised on regular TV. Others pay admission to arenas, clubs, and bars to see fights on giant screens. Some boxing enthusiasts may pay up to $2,500 or more for a ringside seat at a championship event.

The sport of boxing has turned into an entertainment extravaganza. A number of the stars of the ring, the Boxers themselves, are also beginning to command purses in the multimillion-dollar range. It is no wonder then that so many young men want to become Professional Fighters. Boxing opens up opportunities of fame and fortune that most people can only dream about. While boxing is a male-dominated sport, women are now participating in it. (See Professional Woman Boxer, page 18.)

Those who aspire to be Professional Boxers start off as amateurs. During this time, the individual learns the rules and regulations of the game, such as round length, time between rounds, which blows are legal and illegal, and so on. The Boxer must also learn how to use all of the equipment in the gym to get into top physical condition. The Fighter may run, jump rope, use the heavy bag, punching bag, pads, perform aerobics exercises, and so on. Fighters who are not in perfect physical shape will not be able to perform well in the ring.

The Boxer must learn all the basic forms, styles, and blows used in boxing and to know when to use which blows. The Boxer must also be familiar with the defenses that can be used in the ring. Some Boxers instinctively know when to throw a left hook and when to throw a right uppercut. Others must work on skills to make them instinctive.

Amateur Boxers compete in competitions and tournaments gaining experience and skills against opponents in the ring. When they or their trainer feel they are ready, the individuals turn professional.

Boxers are classified in categories by their weight. Fighters must "make," or be, this weight at the official weigh-in to fight in the category.

Managers of Professional Boxers try to obtain matches for their Fighters with opponents of equal size, weight, and with an equal amount of experience and skill. An individual just starting out, usually has a match with another Boxer in the same weight category who either is just starting out or has had only two or three previous fights.

Pro Boxers move ahead in their career trying to advance to a level where they can become champions or world-class fighters. Depending on their skills, determination, drive, and the people working with them, they may fight only a few times or a great many times before achieving this goal.

As Boxers become more proficient and successful, they begin to receive more money to fight. They also may be rated by one of the boxing organizations that sanction fights. This is important because it helps them obtain opportunities to fight for championships. As individuals go through their career, they obtain a record of wins, losses, knockouts (KOs), and draws.

Boxers are usually licensed to fight by state athletic commissions. Either they are licensed by their own state, or they may receive a temporary permit from the state they are fighting in. Individuals are examined by a physician before a fight to make sure that they are physically fit to fight.

Boxers must travel often to other states or abroad to fight. Usually they are reimbursed for travel, room and board, and training expenses.

Boxers are expected to train, stay in good physical condition, and fight regularly. Most individuals have a manager who takes care of business, obtains fights, and watches out for the Boxer's interests. The manager receives a percentage of the Boxer's earnings in return for his or her services.

The Boxer has a trainer who usually works in his corner during a professional fight. As the Boxer becomes more successful, others are added to the team. These people might include promoters, attorneys, and publicists.

Although some individuals in their late thirties and early forties are still fighting, most Boxers retire at an earlier age. While they are pursuing their career, fighters must dedicate their life to boxing. Those who are successful can look forward to fame, fortune, and travel.

Salaries

Earnings vary enormously for Boxers, depending on their status and prestige in the boxing world. The money paid to Boxers for fighting is called a purse. There are Professional Fighters who receive a $200 purse for a bout; others receive multimillion-dollar purses.

Amateurs do not get paid. They fight in competitions to obtain experience in the ring and upgrade their status as fighters.

Professional Boxers beginning their careers may fight a four-round bout and receive $200 to $400. As they journey up the career ladder, individuals may earn $1,000 to $50,000 or more. Boxers on championship undercards (meaning they are not the main event) or those appearing on televised events may have larger purses. Individuals who can attract a great deal of pub-

licity and large audiences, such as champions, command the biggest purses of all. They may also receive percentages of money earned from ticket sales, promotional packages, television rights, and so on. Boxers may also be compensated very well for endorsing products and appearing in advertisements, on television shows, and in movies.

Employment Prospects

Prospects for individuals who want to be Boxers are excellent. Almost any healthy individual who wants to fight and is not afraid to get into the ring can become a Boxer. The problem is that many people want to become a Boxer in theory, but do not really want to fight.

A great many people decide that they want to be Boxers, find a gym, train, learn the skills, get in the ring with an opponent, and find that they never want to do it again. Individuals who have had training and experience in the ring and determine that they want to be involved professionally can turn pro. Individuals may fight on any type of fight card, or program, from small clubs to large arenas. If they are just starting out, they usually fight on the undercard of a main event. As the individual's career progresses, it is hoped that his position on the card will go up. All Fighters aspire to be the main attraction in a championship event.

Advancement Prospects

All Boxers begin their careers as amateurs. If they show promise, Boxers are entered into amateur competitions and tournaments, such as the Golden Gloves. When they are ready, they may move on to either the Olympics or turn pro. Many champions have come out of both the Golden Gloves and the Olympics.

Advancement prospects differ from person to person depending on a number of factors. These include how good a fighter the individual is, connections in the boxing industry, drive, determination, skill, and luck. Some individuals have become champions in as little as nine pro fights. Others have fought 100 times and still are at the same level. For example, some Boxers stay at the club level for their entire career. They fight in bouts on boxing shows and make a living but never really advance their career.

Others may move from the amateurs to the pros and quickly catch the eye of a promoter, moving up to become a world-class fighter. With more and more fights being televised, it is easier than ever for talented individuals to be seen by promoters, managers, or other industry people.

Education and Training

There is no formal educational requirement for Boxers. Fighters may have diverse educational backgrounds. Some individuals do not have a high school diploma, others are college graduates.

There is also no formal training program for Boxers. Most individuals begin their careers working out and training in gyms or youth programs. They are trained by either staff trainers or private trainers who feel that they show potential. Individuals usually train daily to become Professional Boxers. They may perform a variety of exercises and activities to become conditioned as well as to learn the skills and rules of the sport.

Special Requirements

Professional boxers are required to hold licenses from the athletic commissions of the states in which they fight.

Experience, Skills, and Personality Traits

Boxers need to be healthy and in good physical shape. They must want to fight in order to become successful. If an individual has drive and determination, he can learn the skills that are needed. Fighters who want to make it to the top must make a commitment to the sport. They will have to train hard daily. Individuals must live a healthy lifestyle, sleeping enough, eating nutritiously, and avoiding drugs and alcohol.

The Boxer should be able to take instruction and constructive criticism. Self-confidence, motivation, and the ability to deal with fear is necessary. A desire to be in the ring is mandatory. Patience and perseverance are helpful in attaining success.

Unions and Associations

Fighters living and/or fighting in states hosting athletic commissions must usually be associated with those organizations. In many states, the Boxer must be licensed to fight through state athletic commissions.

Boxers may also be associated with any number of organizations and trade associations or sanctioning organizations dedicated to the profession. These may include the International Boxing Federation (IBF), the International Boxing Association (IBA), the World Boxing Association (WBA), the World Boxing Organization (WBO), the World Boxing Federation (WBF), the International Boxing Hall of Fame (IBHF), the International Veteran Boxers Association (IVBA), or the National Veteran Boxers Association (NVBA).

Tips for Entry

1. Look for local gyms that train Boxers and spend some time in them.
2. Watch the various trainers, Boxers, managers, and so on. Talk to them and tell them you are interested in becoming a Boxer. Ask for advice and recommendations for a trainer or a program to become involved in.
3. Many Police Athletic Leagues (PAL), newspapers, boys' clubs, radio and television stations, and youth or community organizations sponsor boxing programs. These groups will help amateur Boxers begin their careers in the sport.
4. Contact your state's athletic commission if you have any questions about how to proceed or to check out credentials, qualifications, and reputations of trainers, managers, and so on. In states that have athletic commissions, these people usually must be licensed.
5. Read all you can about boxing. There are books and magazines about the history, skills, amateurs, professionals, current news, and so on. Learn as much as you can.
6. Contact trade associations to find out if they are holding seminars, workshops, or other meetings.

PROFESSIONAL WOMAN BOXER

CAREER PROFILE

Duties: Fighting in boxing bouts; learning and developing boxing skills

Alternate Title(s): Fighter; Pugilist

Salary Range: Difficult to determine due to nature of job

Employment Prospects: Fair

Advancement Prospects: Fair

Best Geographical Location(s) for Position: Any location hosting women's boxing shows offers possibilities; New York City, Las Vegas, Atlantic City, etc., are boxing capitals

Prerequisites:

Education or Training—Training in boxing skills

Experience—Amateur boxing experience

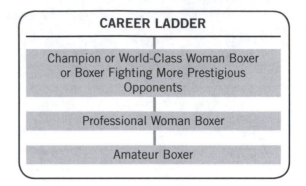

CAREER LADDER

Champion or World-Class Woman Boxer or Boxer Fighting More Prestigious Opponents

Professional Woman Boxer

Amateur Boxer

Special Skills and Personality Traits—Boxing skills; physical fitness; determination, drive; perseverance

Special Requirements—License required

Position Description

Many are not aware that women's boxing has a long history. While it has only recently come into vogue, women who are interested in becoming Professional Boxers owe a vote of thanks to those who helped pave the way.

It is reported that one of the first women's boxing matches in the United States occurred when two women fought for a silver butter dish in a New York City theater in 1876. In 1954 Barbara Buttrick became the first female Boxer to have her fight broadcast on national television.

Without women such as Caroline Svendsen, who in 1975 not only became the first woman to receive a documented boxing license in the United States, but also participated in a sanctioned boxing match in Carson City, Nevada, women's boxing might not be what it is today. Among others who helped pave the way were Pat Pineda, who in 1976 became the first woman to be licensed in the state of California, and Cathy "Cat" Davis, Jackie Tonawanda, and Marian "Lady Tyger" Trimiar, who had sued in New York State to receive boxing licenses.

The professional debut of Muhammad Ali's daughter, Laila "She-Bee Stingin" Ali in a fight against Jacqui Frazier, daughter of Joe Frazier, drew more than 100,000 pay-per-view buyers, helping to turn professional women's boxing into the sport it is today. While professional women's boxing is not the multimillion-dollar business that men's boxing is, it is on its way.

Those aspiring to be Professional Women Boxers generally start off as amateurs. During the amateur period, the women learn how to use the equipment in the gym as well as the rules and regulations of the game, and individuals also must get in top physical condition. Boxing is not easy and being in shape is essential.

Some women go into a gym to get in shape and decide they want to try their hand at boxing. Others have watched professional men's or women's boxing and go into the gym to prepare themselves for the career.

Fighters generally have a trainer to help get them in shape. They may train by running, jumping rope, using a heavy bag, punching bags, pads, performing aerobic exercises, or sparring with other fighters in a ring.

Women Boxers are expected to learn basic forms, styles, and blows used in the ring. They must know when to use which blow and when to use which defense. For some individuals, this is instinctive. For others, the skills must be learned and practiced until they become instinctive.

As amateurs, Women Boxers compete in competitions and tournaments. In this way they can gain experience and skills to fight effectively against other opponents in the ring. After a number of amateur bouts and when their trainer feels they are ready, the individuals turn professional.

Professional Women Boxers are classified in categories by their weight. Individuals may, for example, fight in categories such as lightweight, junior lightweight, bantamweight, middleweight, welterweight, light-heavyweight, heavyweight, etc. Before each professional fight, there is an official weigh-in where each fighter is weighed. At this time, the woman must be within the weight specifications for the specific weight classification in which she is fighting.

Professional Women Boxers generally have managers who try to obtain matches with opponents of equal size, weight, experience, and skill levels. For example, a good match for a woman who is just starting out professionally will be another woman who is also just starting out professionally or one who has only had two or three pro fights.

The manager also takes care of the Boxer's business and watches out for the Boxer's interests. The manager receives a percentage of the fighter's earnings in return for his or her services.

Once the Boxer goes professional, her trainer may also work in the corner during fights. The individual may also have cut men or women who try to repair any cuts or abrasions which occur during the fight.

The goal for Professional Women Boxers, as for their male counterparts, is advancing to a level where they can become champions. Some individuals achieve this goal quickly. For others it may take time. Some never get there. To a great extent, becoming a champion depends on the individual's skills, drive, determination, the people working with them, and, of course, luck.

Women Boxers are generally examined by a physician prior to a fight to make sure that they are physically fit to fight. Individuals must also be licensed to fight by state athletic commissions. In some cases they are licensed by their own state. In others they may receive a temporary permit from the state in which they are fighting.

As part of the job, Professional Women Boxers are expected to train, stay in good shape, and fight regularly. Boxers go through their career building a record of wins, losses, knockouts (KOs), and draws. As they become more proficient and successful, Boxers begin to receive more money to fight. They also may be rated by one of the women's boxing organizations that sanction fights. Those who are rated well obtain opportunities to fight for championships.

In order to take part in fights, Women Boxers must often travel to different states or other countries. In order to be successful in this sport, women, like men, must dedicate their lives to boxing while they are involved in the sport.

Professional Women Boxers have not yet experienced the tremendous fame and fortune their male counterparts garner. Those who are successful, however, can earn large sums of money and fame on a smaller level. For women who dream of becoming a Professional Boxer, the dream can now turn into reality.

Salaries

The money paid to Boxers for fighting is called a "purse." Purses vary tremendously for Professional Women Boxers depending on their status, prestige, experience, and skills. Professional Women Boxers currently are paid a minimum of $200 per round. The highest purse to date for a women in this position has been $1 million.

Earnings for Professional Women Boxers don't yet match the huge purses or earnings that their male counterparts sometimes command. Individuals also may receive percentages of money earned from ticket sales, promotional packages, television rights, etc. Some women receive additional compensation from endorsing products or doing personal appearances.

Employment Prospects

Prospects for those aspiring to be Professional Women Boxers are fair and improving all the time. Women's boxing is gaining new respect in the sports world and promoters are always looking for new, talented women interested in professional boxing.

Almost any woman who is healthy, fit, and wants to fight in the ring can. Some women find a gym, train, learn the skills, get in the ring with an opponent, and decide that they never want to do it again. Those who do come back may fight on a variety of types of fight cards or programs from small clubs to large arenas. Many casinos throughout the country are now also presenting boxing shows.

Advancement Prospects

All fighters, whether men or women, start out as amateurs. After participating in amateur competitions and tournaments such as the "Golden Gloves," if the women show promise they turn pro.

Advancement prospects are dependent on a number of variables, including the individual's talent, skills, drive, and determination. Luck and being in the right place at the right time and connections in the boxing industry also are important in career advancement.

Professional Women Boxers who are just starting out will usually fight on the undercard of a main event. As the individual gains experience and skills, her position should move up on the card. Some women move right up the career ladder and become champions. Others may fight on a club level for their entire career.

Education and Training

There are no formal educational requirements to become a Professional Woman Boxer. There are some Professional Boxers who are college graduates while others may not even hold high school diplomas.

There are no formal training programs for Professional Women Boxers. The path taken by most women aspiring to become Professional Boxers is finding a gym to work out and train with specific trainers or gym staff members.

Most individuals train daily to become Professional Women Boxers in order to learn the necessary skills and rules of the sport and become conditioned.

Special Requirements

Professional Women Boxers are required to hold licenses from each specific state's athletic commission in which they are fighting.

Experience, Skills, and Personality Traits

It is essential for Professional Women Boxers to be healthy and physically fit. It is also mandatory for the woman to want to fight in order to become successful in this sport. She must have drive, determination, commitment, and spirit. Patience and perseverance are useful in climbing the ladder to success as a champion.

Individuals must have the ability to take instruction and constructive criticism. Women must have a great deal of self-confidence and motivation to be in this sport. The ability to deal with fear is needed.

Unions and Associations

Like their male counterparts, Women Boxers fighting in states hosting athletic commissions must usually be associated with those organizations. Generally, the Boxer must be licensed to fight through the state athletic commissions.

There are also organizations and associations such as the International Female Boxers Association (IFBA) and the International Women's Boxing Federation (IWBF) among others that are dedicated to the profession.

Tips for Entry

1. Look for local gyms that train fighters (men or women) and spend some time there. Make sure it is something you want to do.
2. Watch the various trainers, fighters, managers, etc., at the gym. Talk to them and tell them that you are interested in fighting. Ask for advice and recommendations of trainers and other programs that might help.
3. Contact your state's athletic commission to check out credentials, qualifications, and reputations of trainers and managers.
4. Contact the various women's boxing associations to see if they are holding any seminars or workshops or can offer any advice.
5. Attend some live women's boxing events.

PROFESSIONAL SOCCER PLAYER

Duties: Playing either the indoor or outdoor variety of soccer professionally

Alternate Title(s): None

Salary Range: $20,000 to $25 million

Employment Prospects: Poor

Advancement Prospects: Poor

Best Geographical Location(s) for Position: Areas hosting professional soccer teams

Prerequisites:

Education or Training—No educational requirement; training in the sport of soccer

Experience—Experience as an amateur

Special Skills and Personality Traits—Complete knowledge of soccer rules and regulations; skilled in techniques of the sport; good one-on-one skills; team player; agile; quick reflexes; physically fit

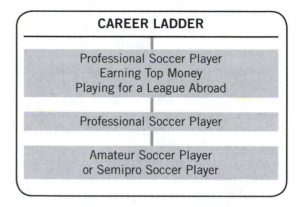

CAREER LADDER

Professional Soccer Player
Earning Top Money
Playing for a League Abroad

Professional Soccer Player

Amateur Soccer Player
or Semipro Soccer Player

Position Description

Many people in the United States became aware of soccer when Brazilian superstar Pelé signed a major money deal with the Cosmos, an American soccer team. For a sport to be financially viable today, it must be televised. Only very recently has soccer been able to capture the American public's sports imagination; for example, major games of the 1998 World Cup were aired on a major U.S. television network. Slowly, professional soccer is becoming a spectator sport in the United States.

Professional soccer is extremely popular overseas where live attendance makes it financially profitable. However, as the game is played extensively on the amateur and collegiate level here, there are athletes who turn pro in the sport in the United States. Some individuals get amateur training here and then seek work abroad. Some are even finding profitable work without leaving home. Those who play soccer in other countries can become major sports superstars. They also reap the rewards of huge salaries that players in this country do not receive.

There are two varieties of soccer. One is played outdoors on a soccer field and the other indoors in an arena.

Professional Soccer Players begin their careers as amateurs. Many play in amateur youth leagues.

Some gain experience playing on the high school level. In this country, most individuals begin by playing outdoor soccer and then make the transition to the indoor variety.

Teams recruit players in two ways. One is through the draft system. In the draft, amateur players who want to turn professional sign up to participate. The teams may then choose the players they want. The draft is for both high school and college seniors. Teams also conduct tryouts for those who do not take part in the draft.

Once a Soccer Player is chosen to play on a team, he attends training and practice sessions. If the Player shows that he will be an asset to the team, he is asked to stay. If not, he is let go.

Soccer Players who show great talent and skill in the sport may be lucky enough to be sought out by an international team. This is difficult, however, because of the intense competition. If an individual is chosen to be a member of an international team, he will have to relocate out of the country, at least for the playing season.

Salaries

Salaries for Professional Soccer Players in the United States are quite low in comparison to earnings in other professional sports. Individuals have annual earnings ranging from $20,000 to $400,000 or more. There are also a few players who have higher earnings—such as David Beckham who earned more than $25m—but these are few and far between. Individuals may earn more if they locate a position playing soccer for an overseas league.

Employment Prospects

Employment prospects are poor. There are only a limited number of teams to work with in this country. Many individuals try to obtain contracts with overseas leagues where more opportunities exist to play professionally.

Advancement Prospects

Advancement prospects are poor for Pro Soccer Players. Individuals may climb the career ladder by having a lot of talent and skill in the game. They will then be able to command the top salaries in the sport.

Other individuals who may be playing with a semi-pro league may advance their career by obtaining contracts with a professional team.

Still others climb the career ladder by going abroad to play with a foreign league.

Education and Training

There are no educational requirements to become a Professional Soccer Player. It is necessary, however, to be trained in the sport. Many individuals obtain this training by playing collegiate and amateur soccer while in college.

Those attending colleges hosting major soccer teams may have a better chance to refine their skills and techniques. They may also have a better opportunity to be seen playing the game.

Experience, Skills, and Personality Traits

Professional Soccer Players usually have obtained experience in the sport by playing on high school or college teams. Some may have gained experience by playing with a semiprofessional team before turning pro.

Individuals must have a full knowledge of the rules and regulations of soccer. They must be skilled in the techniques of the sport. Players should have good one-on-one skills and be team players.

To play the game successfully, Professional Soccer Players need quick reflexes and should be agile. Individuals should also be in excellent physical shape.

Unions and Associations

Professional Soccer Players may be members of Major League Soccer (MLS) or other professional leagues.

Tips for Entry

1. Since competition is so intense in this sport, you must be very talented. Play the game as often as possible. The more experience you have, the better your chances of being chosen to be a team member.
2. Learn to play soccer both indoors and outdoors. Understanding the different rules of the game will provide you with well-rounded training.
3. Try to attend a college that puts a heavy emphasis on its soccer team.
4. Consider attending a soccer camp to help refine your skills.
5. Contact the teams in the various soccer leagues to find out when they are holding tryouts. You can find the addresses in Appendix XIII.

LPGA TOUR PLAYER

CAREER PROFILE

Duties: Playing in golf events on the LPGA tour; practicing and honing skills

Alternate Title(s): Golf Professional; Golf Pro

Salary Range: $2,000 to $2.5 million+

Employment Prospects: Poor

Advancement Prospects: Fair

Best Geographical Location(s) for Position: Individuals must travel to tour locations both in the U.S. and at international sites

Prerequisites:

Education or Training—One to four years of collegiate golf, Futures Tour, LPGA Qualifying School; golf instruction; competitive golf experience

Experience—A great amount of experience playing golf as an amateur

Special Skills and Personality Traits—Excellent golf skills; dedication; ambition; ability to travel

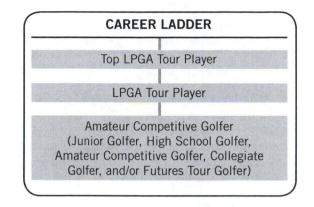

CAREER LADDER

Top LPGA Tour Player

LPGA Tour Player

Amateur Competitive Golfer
(Junior Golfer, High School Golfer,
Amateur Competitive Golfer, Collegiate
Golfer, and/or Futures Tour Golfer)

Position Description

Most people play golf on an amateur basis. For men and women who love the sport of golf and wish they could play all the time, there is a career opportunity in competitive professional golf. The PGA Tour generally hosts professional competitive golf for men, while the Ladies Professional Golf Association (LPGA) hosts competitive professional golf events for women.

An LPGA Tour Player is a woman who plays competitive golf on the LPGA tour. The LPGA sponsors an annual tour season of more than 35 tour events for women professional golfers. Those who win or typically place in the top 70 of an event will earn money for their performance.

Becoming a player on the LPGA tour is not easy. There are only a limited number of slots each year in which women can participate on the tour. Those interested in pursuing a career in this field must have excellent golfing skills and extensive competitive experience in addition to a great deal of drive and determination.

Every LPGA Tour member has a different story on how she got there. Some individuals starting playing golf when they were youngsters. Others started when they were older. The thing that they each have in common is a genuine love for the sport.

Before turning professional, the individual generally plays in a lot of competitive amateur events. As she gets more experience, she plays in more prestigious amateur tournaments.

In their quest to becoming LPGA Tour professionals, many women participate in the Futures Tour, "the official developmental tour of the LPGA." This women's golf organization is the largest international women's professional developmental tour in the world. One of the advantages to playing on this tour is that the top five players on the tour money list who play in at least six Futures events receive direct entry into the LPGA Tour for the following year. Those who are ranked sixth through 10th of the tour money list receive direct entry into the LPGA's Final Qualifying Event. Women who do not participate on the Futures Tour and earn one of the top slots must go through LPGA Qualifying School.

Individuals who garner a spot on the LPGA Tour still have a lot of work to do. Getting in is only half the job. One of the goals of the LPGA Tour Player is getting to the top of the career money list. This is accomplished by playing competitively.

In addition to playing in events, women must constantly practice to hone their skills. They may also take lessons from other golf pros.

For women who love to play golf, a career as an LPGA Tour Professional can be a dream come true.

Salaries

There is a tremendous range in earnings for LPGA Tour Professionals. Compensation is based on how well the individual does in golf events and the purse (or winning pot) for each event.

Top LPGA Tour Professionals may earn $2.5 million or more annually. There are others on the tour who may only earn $2,000 to $3,000 for the year. There are also women on the tour who earn everything in between.

Popular LPGA Tour Professionals who attract a following often augment earnings with lucrative endorsement deals.

Employment Prospects

Employment prospects are poor for individuals aspiring to work as LPGA Tour Professionals. There are a limited number of positions on the tour and competition is stiff. This does not mean that it is impossible to become a LPGA Tour Professional. It just means it is difficult.

Advancement Prospects

Advancement prospects for LPGA Tour Professionals are based on an individual's skills, drive, and determination. Career advancement for Tour Professionals means winning more events. Those who excel will become top money earners on the LPGA tour.

Education and Training

As noted previously, in order to qualify for a spot on the LPGA tour, individuals must generally go through Qualifying School. To be accepted in Qualifying School, women must be professional or amateur golfers who have demonstrated that they have an approved and authenticated USGA handicap of 3.4 or less. The purpose of Qualifying School is to determine who will be offered a position on the LPGA tour. To do this, women compete in stages playing rounds of golf. Those who win the final competitions are offered places on the tour.

Golf classes, seminars, and workshops will also be helpful in honing skills.

Experience, Skills, and Personality Traits

LPGA Tour Professionals need excellent golf skills. Drive, determination, and ambition are also essential. The flexibility to travel to play in events is necessary.

Individuals require a great deal of experience playing golf to be successful at this sport.

A typical career progression would include experience as a junior golfer and high school golfer, and experience in amateur competition (USGA, AJGA junior golf competitions), and the collegiate golf Futures Tour. The individual would then go on to become an LPGA Tour Player and hopefully a top LPGA Tour Player.

Unions and Associations

The premier organization for LPGA Tour Professionals is the Ladies Professional Golf Association (LPGA). This organization provides education and career support to members.

Tips for Entry

1. Play as much as you can. Practice, practice, practice.
2. If this is your career aspiration, start playing in tournaments now.
3. Find a golf pro and take lessons.
4. You should be aware that it can be very expensive to play professionally, with costs running between approximately $50,000 and $80,000 annually. As a result, many pros have sponsors and endorsement deals to augment earnings.
5. Subscribe to golf magazines and keep up with news, events, and happenings in the golf world.
6. To learn more about the LPGA, visit www.lpga.com and check out the many references about golf in general. The more you know about the sport, the more prepared you will be for a career in golf.

PROFESSIONAL SPORTS TEAMS

TEAM GENERAL MANAGER

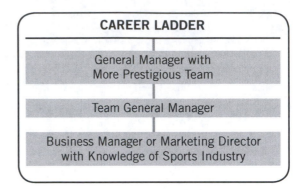

Position Description

All professional sports teams have General Managers. The General Manager of a professional sports team has an extremely important job. He or she is responsible for handling all of the day-to-day details of the team. The individual in this position has a lot of power and prestige. If things are going right for the team, the GM receives a share of the credit. If things do not go right for the team, the GM is often blamed and his or her position may be terminated.

It is important to remember that the sports industry is a multibillion-dollar business. Many of the qualifications required in any of the sports administration positions are similar to those that are important in any successful business venture. Responsibilities of the General Manager of a professional sports team are also much the same as they would be for any individual running a multibillion-dollar business.

Professional sports Team General Managers may work in any sport. The most common of these are basketball, baseball, football, soccer, and hockey. The GM may work with any of the major league teams or may work with various levels of minor league teams.

The GM will have varied duties depending on the size and prestige of the specific team. His or her main function is to oversee all aspects of the team's activities. Individuals working with smaller teams or those at various levels may be responsible for the actual day-to-day, operational functions. These duties might include operating the concessions and hiring the ticket takers, ushers, and other box office personnel. The GM might be responsible for all the publicity, press, and marketing of the team.

General Managers of larger, more prestigious major league teams usually are responsible for recommending, hiring, and supervising people to attend to these jobs. The extent of this hiring depends on how much leeway the team owner gives the Manager. A good GM surrounds him- or herself with the best people possible. This helps make the team a success, and the success will rub off on the GM.

The General Manager, for example, may recommend the hiring of the club secretary, assistant manager, marketing people, publicity people, trainers, and so on. The individual is also responsible for putting together a winning team. He or she may recommend the trading and drafting of team members. It is important that the GM stay up to date on the activities and background of all players in the sport. He or she needs almost a second sense regarding players and personnel.

The General Manager may decide, with the owner, salaries for team members and support personnel. As athletes become more and more popular and valuable, their salaries escalate.

The General Manager must help develop a team that is not only popular but also regularly draws fans to their events. Keeping the stadiums filled is important to professional sports teams. Popularity means money in the teams' pockets. It means the games will be sold out and good marketing prospects. It also means that successful television and radio contracts may be negotiated.

It is up to the General Manager to see that everything regarding the team and its organization is operating properly and efficiently. He or she must oversee everything, from the ticket takers and ushers to the moneymaking concessions, and must supervise all segments of all departments including the equipment manager, the players, publicity people, advertising, promotion and marketing, and anything and everything else relating to the team.

Depending on the team, the General Manager works closely with the owner and business manager. In some cases, when the GM works for a smaller minor league team, he or she might be called the business manager.

The General Manager must make sure that everything done by any member of the team and/or the support personnel works to make the team a success. The GM is directly responsible to the team owner. He or she works long hours trying to build a popular, successful team.

Salaries
Salaries for Team General Managers will vary depending on the sport, the team, its size and prestige, and the individual's expertise and experience.

Salaries can range from $25,000 to $50,000 plus for those working with minor league teams. Salaries for General Managers working for larger or major league teams may go to $3 million or more.

Employment Prospects
Employment prospects are fair for individuals willing to start working for lower salaries in the minor leagues. Some General Managers were athletes prior to obtaining this job. Most people, however, obtain this type of job by being familiar with business operations.

Advancement Prospects
A professional sports Team General Manager can advance his or her career by obtaining a position with another more prestigious team. To do this the individual must prove him- or herself thoroughly and build a track record of success. A great deal of this is determined by not only the individual's abilities but his or her drive to succeed.

Another way that a Team General Manager can advance his or her career is by building a team that emerges as a championship team. This usually makes the individual more valuable as a GM and increases his or her value both in prestige and money. This could happen, for example, if an individual is working with a baseball team that isn't expected to win in its league. The team surprises everyone and not only makes it to the finals but wins the big game.

Education and Training
Some individuals have become Team General Managers without a college degree. However, competition is so fierce for these jobs that a good education is extremely helpful.

Individuals aspiring to this type of career could major in sports or athletic administration. This relatively new degree is growing in popularity in colleges throughout the country. (A list of colleges and universities offering these degrees is in Appendix I.)

Other educational possibilities for General Manager positions might include majors in business or business administration, journalism, communications, and law. Seminars and other courses in sports administration, business, promotion, marketing, and publicity are also helpful.

Experience, Skills, and Personality Traits
The General Manager of a professional sports team needs a complete understanding of the sport he or she is working with. Enjoying the specific sport is certainly helpful. The individual literally sleeps, eats, and lives the sport. Team General Managers usually have moved through the ranks of team management to landing their jobs.

Good communications skills are necessary. The GM should be articulate in his or her speech and mannerisms. The ability to successfully negotiate is essential. A solid business background is also required. An eye for both marketing and business will boost the GM's opportunities for success.

The General Manager should have a lot of stamina and energy. He or she will be working long hours. The ability to deal with stress and tension is vital. The GM's job has more than its share of these tensions.

The individual should possess a great deal of self-confidence and be able to make sound decisions and judgments quickly. He or she also should be able to handle many details at one time without getting flustered.

Unions and Associations
There is no specific trade association for Team General Managers. Individuals may, however, belong to any number of professional trade associations related directly to their sport.

Tips for Entry

1. To become a Team General Manager, you will need to have a lot of luck, a great track record, and have to be in the right place at the right time. Be prepared.
2. Consider attending a college that offers a degree in sports administration. This will not only give you the training required but will help you make important contacts.
3. Attend seminars and workshops in sports management, business, marketing, and publicity.
4. Join sports-oriented trade associations and organizations. These groups will provide you with professional guidance and training, and help you make needed contacts.
5. If you are still in college, try to obtain an internship with a professional sports team. This too will provide you with a wealth of training and contacts.
6. Offer to manage an amateur or school sports team. This will help provide you with needed experience.
7. Apply for an office or clerical job with a professional team. This will get your foot in the door. Learn as you earn. Keep your ears open for new opportunities within the organization.

BUSINESS MANAGER

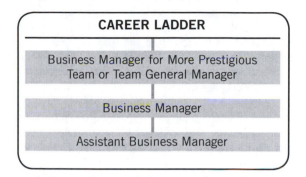

Position Description

The Business Manager of a professional sports team has many responsibilities. He or she works with the team general manager handling financial and business matters. In some professional teams, the Business Manager may also take on the duties of the general manager. Professional teams are structured in different ways. The Business Manager's duties depend on the specific structure of each team.

The Business Manager generally is responsible for handling the business of the team. He or she is, for example, required to make sure that there are signed contracts on file for every aspect and function of the team. These include contracts for athletes, coaches, trainers, as well as those for concessionaires, food service companies, rentals, and so on. If contracts are not signed, the Business Manager must contact the appropriate department or person to have them signed.

The Business Manager is responsible for obtaining bids for services used by the team. He or she may send out letters or make calls to advise suppliers that the team is seeking certain services. In this way, team management can be assured that the team obtains the best prices for required services. The individual may seek bids for things such as food service catering for the team and its support staff, hotels, motels, transportation, insurance, laundry service, and the like. Once the

Business Manager has decided on the most effective and economical supply company to use, he or she contacts the company and has contracts drawn up. After services have been rendered, the individual is responsible for obtaining bills and invoices, approving them, and making sure they are paid in a timely fashion.

In the same vein, the Business Manager may also be required to obtain bids for products used by the team, including office supplies, office equipment, training supplies and equipment, and other things. He or she always tries to find the most cost-effective companies to do the best job. The individual must get to know the various companies and their reputations. An organization that performs services late might be the least expensive but is not practical to use.

The Business Manager may be responsible for handling employment applications. After reviewing them, he or she may either distribute them to the appropriate department or personally respond. In teams that do not have a personnel director, the Business Manager may be responsible for handling advertising to fill positions as well as for conducting interviews.

Other personnel duties might include dealing with staff problems, responding to questions, and handling suggestions. The Business Manager must listen to individual problems and determine how to handle each. In some cases, the Business Manager deals with the difficulties personally. In other instances, he or she sends the individual to the appropriate person in the organization.

Dealing with general problems and complaints of patrons, fans, staff, associates, or others within or surrounding the team may also be one of the Business Manager's functions. He or she may be required to investigate problems which have been reported to him or her, and seek solutions or pass the responsibility on to the appropriate staff member.

Another function of the Business Manager may be to work with the stadium or arena hosting the team's events. The Business Manager must schedule the stadium when required for games, tournaments, or practice sessions. He or she might also schedule the use of rooms in the stadium for business meetings or other team events.

The Business Manager is required to keep track of all bills, invoices, charges, and so on, as well as all services rendered and products purchased. He or she must keep accurate records. In teams with larger business organizations, the Business Manager assigns duties to other staff members. In smaller organizations, he or she is responsible for handling all details.

In some teams, the Business Manager is in charge of collecting daily or weekly expenses and bills from personnel. The individual reviews, records, and sends them to the payroll department before filing them.

The individual works closely with the traveling secretary to work out travel arrangements for the team when it is playing away from the home base. Hotels, motels, transportation, food service, and so on must all be planned out before a team leaves home. The Business Manager may obtain bids on these services, recommend companies, hotels, bus lines, or other services, send out the actual contracts, and arrange for payments.

The Business Manager may be required to handle payroll responsibilities or may work with other departments, such as accounting, on the fiscal matters.

Depending on the specific team, sport, and organization, the Business Manager may also be responsible for arranging for training camps, rookie camps, drafts, and other meetings. The individual must oversee all the team's business, making sure that nothing is overlooked. The job is a great deal of work and responsibility. Most professional sports team Business Managers, however, do not seem to mind the 10- to 14-hour workdays.

Salaries

Salaries for team Business Managers vary depending on the sport, the team, its size and prestige, and the individual's expertise and experience.

Salaries can range from $27,000 to $65,000 plus for those working with minor league teams. Salaries for Business Managers working for larger or major league teams may go to $850,000 plus.

Employment Prospects

Employment prospects are fair for those aspiring to be Business Managers for professional sports teams. Individuals may, however, have to work for smaller, lesser-known teams in order to gain some experience.

Those seeking jobs as Business Managers with major league teams will find it difficult to break into the field without some experience and a track record of success.

Advancement Prospects

A Business Manager working for a professional sports team may advance his or her career by obtaining a job with a more prestigious team. This will result in higher earnings and more responsibilities.

The individual may also climb the career ladder by becoming a team general manager.

Education and Training

A minimum of a four-year college degree is preferred or recommended for most positions, although educational requirements may vary from job to job. Some professional teams do hire Business Managers without formal education but with on-the-job experience instead. Former athletes or support personnel are in this category.

Good choices for college majors might include business, business administration, sports administration, marketing, and liberal arts. Other educational possibilities may include majors in journalism, communications, and law. Seminars and courses in sports administration, business, promotion, and marketing will also be helpful.

Experience, Skills, and Personality Traits

A team Business Manager has to be highly organized and be able to deal with many projects at the same time. He or she must not get flustered. The Business Manager must be able to deal with the stress and tension on the job.

The more the individual knows about business, administration, and the sports industry, the better he or she will fare in obtaining and keeping this type of position. He or she should be poised and articulate with good communication skills.

The Business Manager must be good at dealing with people in a variety of situations. He or she must have the ability to solve problems and the foresight to try to avoid them. The individual should be self-confident and able to make sound decisions and judgments quickly.

Unions and Associations

There is no specific trade association for professional sports team Business Managers. Individuals may, however, belong to any number of professional trade associations that are related directly to their sport.

Tips for Entry

1. Consider attending a college that offers a degree in sports administration. This will not only give you the training required but will help you make important contacts within the sports industry.
2. Attend seminars and workshops in sports management, business, and marketing.
3. If you are still in college, try to obtain an internship with a professional sports team. This too will provide you with a wealth of training and contacts.
4. Offer to be the Business Manager for a school sports team. This will help provide you with experience.
5. Send your résumé and a cover letter to professional sports teams, inquiring about openings. Ask that your résumé be kept on file if there are no current openings. You might not get the job as Business Manager, but you might find an assistant's position open.
6. Openings may often be located online. Start searching some of the better-known job sites such as monster.com and hotjobs.com. Then check out sites specific to the sports industry.

DIRECTOR OF BASEBALL OPERATIONS

Duties: Coordinating the scouting, signing, and development of athletes for a baseball team

Alternate Title(s): Vice President of Baseball Operations

Salary Range: $52,000 to $1 milllion+

Employment Prospects: Poor

Advancement Prospects: Poor

Best Geographical Location(s) for Position: Cities hosting Major League Baseball teams

Prerequisites:

Education or Training—No formal educational requirement for some positions; four-year college degree may be preferred

Experience—Experience in game of baseball as athlete, scout, coach, trainer, and so on

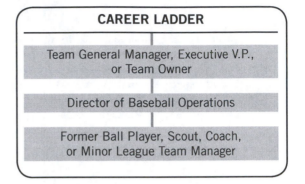

CAREER LADDER

Team General Manager, Executive V.P., or Team Owner

Director of Baseball Operations

Former Ball Player, Scout, Coach, or Minor League Team Manager

Special Skills and Personality Traits—Love of baseball; good with people; empathy; understanding; communications skills; ability to predict and project athletic talent

Position Description

The Director of Baseball Operations is responsible for coordinating the scouting, signing, and development of athletes for a baseball team. His or her contact with the athlete runs from the time a ball player is located by a scout, through his arrival on the team and entire stay.

This person, often called the vice president of baseball operations, is an integral force in the success of a team. He or she works on the personnel side of the team attempting to obtain the best possible athletes.

The goal of the Director of Baseball Operations is to secure athletes from the draft of high school seniors, junior college students, and juniors and seniors in four-year colleges. In drafting athletes at this stage, a lot of prediction and projection is required. It is often hard to tell how an athlete's skills and techniques can and will be developed. The Director works with scouts across the country and visits schools and colleges to try to locate the talent. He or she is also responsible for evaluating talented athletes that scouts have located.

The main function of the Director of Baseball Operations is to take an athlete from high school or college into the rookie leagues and through the ranks until the player is ready for the major league. In the process, he

or she may be traded and other athletes selected for the team.

When an athlete shows promise, the Director is responsible for trying to recruit him and getting him to sign a contract. In order to make an offer more attractive, the Director of Baseball Operations may offer a bonus to the player on signing. Bonuses might include additional monies and/or full college scholarships.

There are four different levels of baseball ranging from the rookies or class A team, to AA, AAA, and the major leagues. The Director of Baseball Operations determines which team the athlete will play with. As a rule, newer athletes are assigned to the rookie team first. After training and experience they move up the ranks of AA, AAA, and then, possibly, the major league team.

The Director is responsible for overseeing the development process of all the team's athletes. He or she helps take an athlete's raw talent, develop it, and bring out skills and techniques so that he will be ready to move up to play in the major leagues.

In some circumstances, the Director may feel that an athlete should be traded. This is a difficult situation for all concerned. The Director must explain the trade to the athlete and hope it is a good decision for the team. If, after the athlete has been traded, the individual turns out to be a superstar for a competing team, the Director may receive a lot of flack from upper management and from the fans. This type of job can have a lot of pressure. Other people frequently offer opinions to the Director on what he or she should not have done. This may happen in draft choices as well as trades. The Director will, however, be praised when he or she makes a good decision regarding team personnel.

The Director of Baseball Operations travels extensively. When not actively scouting, recruiting, and signing athletes, he or she often visits the affiliated minor league ball clubs. The Director may attend practice sessions or actual games. He or she talks with the athletes and makes sure that they are progressing satisfactorily. When not on the road, the Director is at home games for the major league team.

The Director of Baseball Operations usually supervises a number of other individuals, including the director of scouting, the director of minor league operations, and all the minor league managers.

Most Directors of Baseball Operations are very satisfied with their position. Many dreamed of working in baseball from the time they were youngsters. Now they can work at something they love.

Salaries

Earnings for a Director of Baseball Operations can vary dramatically. Variables may include the specific team and its popularity. Other factors include the experience and responsibilities of the individual. Annual salaries can range from $52,000 to $1 million or more.

Employment Prospects

Employment prospects are poor for individuals aspiring to be a Director of Baseball Operations. There are only a certain number of teams that offer such jobs. Additionally, people who are already in this position do not move out of it rapidly.

Individuals who are interested in this type of job may seek positions working in other sports. They must, however, know a great deal about any other sport in which they expect to participate.

Advancement Prospects

The Director of Baseball Operations is one of the top-ranking jobs in the sport. Individuals may advance their careers by becoming a team general manager, executive vice president, owner, or commissioner, but at this level prospects are limited. Most people who make it to this level of baseball are extremely satisfied with their position.

Education and Training

While there may be no formal educational requirement for this job, competition is fierce. Often the most qualified person gets the position. A college degree will help prepare an individual aspiring to be the Director of Baseball Operations for this position and for others he or she will have before and after.

Sports administration is one of the best possibilities as a college major. Individuals might also take courses in sports studies, communications, English, psychology, public relations, marketing, and business.

Experience, Skills, and Personality Traits

The Director of Baseball Operations must be fully knowledgeable about all aspects of the sport. To be successful and happy, he or she must love baseball. This job entails almost constant contact with the sport. Long hours are spent traveling, talking, and thinking baseball.

There are numerous career paths leading to this job. Some individuals were former ball players, scouts, or coaches. Others were team managers.

One of the most important attributes for a person in this position is the ability to deal with people well. The individual should be empathetic, understanding, and a good listener.

The Director of Baseball Operations needs good communications skills. He or she should be articulate and poised. An ability to write and a command of the English language are also necessary.

The ability to be a good judge of character and talent is essential in this field. The individual is responsible for meeting people who have raw, untapped talent. He or she must be able to judge not only if they are talented but if they have what it takes to make it playing professional ball.

The Director of Baseball Operations should not mind traveling. He or she might be on the road in various capacities for over half the year.

At times the Director of Baseball Operations may feel that everyone is pulling him or her in different directions. For example, when the Director makes a decision about a trade, others may not agree. The individual must be confident in his or her decisions. He or she must also have the ability to work under pressure in stressful situations.

Unions and Associations

There is no bargaining union for an individual employed as a Director of Baseball Operations, nor is there a specific trade association for people in this position. Individuals do, however, work closely with the players' union.

Tips for Entry

1. Be prepared to start at the bottom of the career ladder. The major problem in obtaining any job in professional baseball is entering the field. After you get in, you will have an easier time moving up the ladder. Try to locate a position in any capacity to help you get your foot in the door. Even if you have a four-year college degree, you may have to work in the mail room, as a clerk, or as a secretary. Once on the job, you will be able to move up as you learn and you will be on the spot when openings occur.

2. Try to obtain an internship with a professional sports team. Write to each team and inquire about the possibilities. This will help you gain hands-on experience and provide an avenue to make contacts.

3. Attend a college with a sports administration program. Many of these schools work directly with professional sports teams. Internships with the teams are available through cooperative programs.

4. Similar jobs are often available in other sports. If you are interested, contact other types of professional teams.

DIRECTOR OF MINOR LEAGUE OPERATIONS

CAREER PROFILE

Duties: Overseeing a baseball team's minor league operations; acting as liaison between minor league affiliates and major league club

Alternate Title(s): Minor League Director

Salary Range: $50,000 to $300,000+

Employment Prospects: Poor

Advancement Prospects: Poor

Best Geographical Location(s) for Position: Cities hosting major league ball clubs

Prerequisites:

    Education or Training—Educational requirements vary; see text

    Experience—Experience in some facet of baseball required

CAREER LADDER

Major League Team General Manager

Director of Minor League Operations

Other Position in Baseball such as Player, Coach, Manager of Minor League Team, etc.

Special Skills and Personality Traits—Familiarity with baseball; management and business skills; articulate; detail oriented; ability to work under stress; multilingual

Position Description

The Director of Minor League Operations oversees a baseball team's minor league operation. The job is much like that of the team general manager. The Director of Minor League Operations may have varied duties depending on the specific team and its requirements.

The individual is responsible for all of the ball club's minor league teams. He or she acts as a liaison between the minor league affiliates and the major league club. Much of the Director's job is administrative.

Minor league teams are often owned by private individuals and work under the auspices of the major league team. The Director of Minor League Operations must make sure that everything that the minor league club requires is available. For example, he or she must ensure that each team has adequate and satisfactory playing facilities.

The Director oversees the spring training of the minor league clubs. The individual checks into the housing, transportation, special foods, and so on needed by the team members. He or she also is responsible for ordering equipment required for the training camps and making sure it arrives on time and is in the correct location.

The Director of Minor League Operations is often responsible for hiring staff members necessary for the training and development of the team members. These people might include trainers, coaches, and others.

Another function of the individual is to oversee the movement of the players in the minor leagues. The Director of this department must know the strengths and weakness of each player in his or her clubs. He or she uses this information to determine where each athlete will play. There are different levels of teams in each league, ranging from A to AAA and up to the majors. The Director of Minor League Operations must decide which players belong in which league and what position they are best suited for.

One of the purposes of the minor league teams is to help develop and train talented athletes to play in the major leagues. The Director of Minor League Operations is responsible for handling problems with the players' development. Some athletes may, for example, require more individualized training or coaching. The Director must see to it that these situations are handled and taken care of in a timely fashion.

The Director may recommend the trading and drafting of team members. He or she works with the league's scouts in locating talent that will be an asset to the ball club. Depending on the specific position, the individual may recommend salaries for the team and its support personnel. He or she is also involved with contract negotiations.

In most cases, the Director of Minor League Operations works closely with the team's owner, business manager, and director of baseball operations. Sometimes the individual also assumes some of the duties of a business manager for the minor league clubs.

The Director of Minor League Operations uses his or her skills to ensure that the minor league teams are successful. He or she also works toward helping the athletes in the minor league system move up the ranks to the major league.

Depending on the situation, the individual may be directly responsible to the team owner or to the general manager.

Salaries

Salaries vary greatly for this position, depending on the specific duties, experience, and responsibilities of the Director of Minor League Operations. Individuals may earn from $50,000 to $300,000+ annually.

Employment Prospects

Employment prospects are poor. Only a limited number of teams in the country have this type of position, and competition is stiff. Those aspiring to become a Director of Minor League Operations may have more opportunities once they get their foot in the door of a professional sports team.

Advancement Prospects

Advancement prospects are poor for a sports team's Director of Minor League Operations. The next step up the ladder for most people in this profession would be to become a team general manager. However, as there is no one career path in the sports industry, individuals may also advance their careers in other jobs that have higher salaries and more prestige.

Education and Training

Competition is fierce for most jobs in the business end of the sports industry, and this position is no exception. While educational requirements may vary for this position, a minimum of a four-year college degree is recommended. Good majors might include business, business management, or sports administration.

Classes, seminars, and workshops in all aspects of business administration, management, sports administration, sports studies, and similar areas will prove useful.

It should be noted that educational requirements may be waived in lieu of experience. This may be the case when former pro athletes, coaches, or scouts apply for the job.

Experience, Skills, and Personality Traits

The Director of Minor League Operations needs to be familiar with almost every aspect of the sport. Individuals may have served in a number of different positions prior to obtaining the job of Director of Minor League Operations, from playing athletes to coaches or scouts.

Management and business skills are imperative in this position. The ability to successfully negotiate is essential. The individual must also be detail oriented. He or she is responsible for overseeing many ball clubs with a variety of different problems.

The Director of Minor League Operations should be articulate with good communications skills, both verbal and written. As many players now are coming from other countries, the ability to speak languages other than English is helpful. He or she must be self-confident and have the ability to make decisions and judgments quickly and efficiently.

The Director should have a lot of stamina and energy. He or she works long hours. An ability to deal with problems without becoming flustered is necessary as is the ability to deal well with stress and tension.

Unions and Associations

There is no specific trade association for the Director of Minor League Operations. The team the individual works for may belong to the National Association of Professional Baseball Leagues (NAPBL) or the International League of Professional Baseball Clubs (ILPBC).

Tips for Entry

1. The baseball commissioner's office offers training programs for those in the field of baseball. If you are interested in working in any facet of the sport, try to get involved with this program.
2. If you have not yet chosen a college, consider one that offers courses in sports administration. These courses are aimed at people interested in sports careers. Colleges with these majors also often offer internship programs with major sports teams.
3. If your college does not set up internships, you might want to contact the major sports teams yourself to see if you can work out an internship on your own.

4. Consider a clerical position or one as an administrative assistant with a professional sports team. It is an opportunity to learn the about the industry. As an added bonus, you will know when there are openings to apply for.

5. Get the best training you can in the management and business fields. These areas will prove useful when applying for a job as well as after obtaining one.

6. Send your résumé and a cover letter to each of the ball clubs you are interested in working with and inquire about assistant positions.

PROFESSIONAL SCOUT

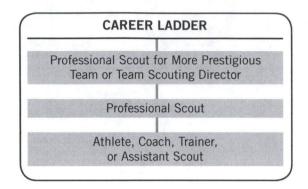

Special Skills and Personality Traits—Ability to evaluate athletes; persuasive; communications skills; articulate; multilingual

Position Description

Professional Scouts work for professional sports teams. They are responsible for finding talented athletes to play for their teams. These individuals usually specialize in a specific sport, such as baseball, football, hockey, basketball, or soccer.

A Professional Scout does a great deal of traveling. The individual must constantly be on the lookout for promising new talent. He or she may travel the country from coast to coast and abroad to seek out these people.

Scouts find promising athletes in a variety of ways. Word of mouth is one method. Someone might know the Scout and call to discuss a promising new prospect. The Scout may visit colleges and talk with coaches. The individual may also see potential professional athletes on televised amateur games or in live tournaments and other sports events.

Depending on the situation, the Scout may be responsible for actually signing an athlete or may just bring him or her to the attention of the team management. Some Scouts are authorized to negotiate and offer financial packages. Other Scouts are responsible for calling the team general manager or coach to make arrangements to bring the parties together for negotiation.

The Scout must evaluate possible new athletes for teams. To do this, the individual may talk to the athletes' former and current coaches, trainers, and others.

He or she also watches the individual in practice as well as in actual game competitions. The Scout may have a checklist of elements to look for. These things might include the athlete's talent, how he or she takes coaching instruction, interaction with the other members of the team, personal ego, and so on. Even though an athlete might be the best player in the world, the player will have little value if he or she does not cooperate with other members of the team. Scouts may also be interested in an athlete's psychological as well as physical makeup.

Some Scouts have other functions. For example, a Scout may be responsible for finding out which members of other professional teams are looking for a change. The Scout would then have to obtain relevant information about these players, such as any injuries the athletes have had, difficulties with team members, and so on.

Some Professional Scouts are responsible for watching the members of other teams to determine the competition's strengths and weaknesses.

The individual may be expected to make recommendations for both current and future athlete procurement. The Scout is required to report all of his or her activities to the team's general manager or head coach. He or she keeps the appropriate individual abreast of the status of all potential athletes. The Scout also reports on all geographic areas, specific games, tournaments, schools, and events visited on behalf of the team as well as coaches and other people he or she has talked with.

The Scout's workday is not the normal nine to five. The individual may be on the road traveling for a few days, weeks, or months until his or her mission is completed. The Scout is directly responsible to either the team's general manager or the head coach, depending on the specific situation.

Salaries

Salaries are dependent on the specific organization the individual Scout is working for. Earnings may also depend on the individual's experience and track record in the field.

Scouts may earn from $29,000 to $65,000 plus. Individuals working for major league teams may have annual salaries of $150,000 or more.

Employment Prospects

Employment prospects are fair for Professional Scouts and growing increasingly better. Almost every professional team has at least a couple of Scouts on their payroll. Most major teams employ a large number. Some teams employ 20 to 25 full-time Scouts in addition to a number of part-timers.

Employment may be found throughout the country in cities hosting professional sports teams. Positions may also be located with scouting pools and independent scouting agencies.

Advancement Prospects

Advancement prospects are fair for Scouts because the demand for fresh, talented athletes continues to grow. Individuals may climb the career ladder by locating a position with a more prestigious team. Others may advance by becoming a team's scout director.

Education and Training

While there may be no formal education requirement for many Professional Scout positions, a four-year college degree may prove useful. Individuals should consider attending a college that offers a degree in physical education, sports administration, or sports studies. These colleges will help the individual get a well-rounded education in addition to providing useful contacts and career guidance.

Many claim that an individual must have scouting in his or her blood to succeed. They feel the talent cannot be learned. Others feel that any individual with a complete understanding of a specific sport can gain sufficient experience.

Experience, Skills, and Personality Traits

Many Professional Scouts began their career as part-timers who worked full-time jobs in other professions. Other individuals were former athletes, coaches, or trainers. Scouts may come from all walks of life. What they have in common, however, is a complete understanding of the sport and an innate sense and ability to locate raw talent.

One of the most important qualifications a Professional Scout can have is the talent to evaluate athletes before they are superstars. This is difficult but can be attained with experience and background knowledge.

Professional Scouts should be personable, enthusiastic, and persuasive. After a Scout finds a talented athlete, he or she must be able to talk to the person and offer encouragement about the decision to sign up with the team.

The Scout must also be sympathetic and empathetic. At times, he or she may have to tell an athlete that he or she is not good enough to be signed to the team. This is a difficult situation for most people.

Professional Scouts need to have good communications skills. They should be articulate communicators and they should also maintain a professional appearance. As many players are now coming from other countries, the ability to speak languages other than English is helpful.

A Professional Scout needs to be able to keep a confidence on many levels. When the individual finally finds a potential athlete, he or she must not discuss publicly the subject until the person is signed with the team. If news gets out that a team is considering a specific athlete, other teams might step in and bid for the athlete.

Unions and Associations

Professional Scouts who work in the major leagues may belong to athletic organizations and associations relevant to the particular sport they are working with.

Tips for Entry

1. Attend a college offering degrees in sports administration studies or physical education. Many of these schools have intern programs with professional sports teams. See if you can be assigned to this area. Hands-on experience in school will be useful in obtaining a job later.
2. If your college does not offer internships, write to professional teams and ask about the possibilities of an internship. There may not be any financial

compensation, but the experience could pay off later with job possibilities.

3. Talk to coaches in colleges. Many will have contacts with professional teams.

4. Read the sports news regularly as well as periodicals specific to the sport you are interested in.

This will give you a good insight into the sports industry.

5. Try to find out when Scouts will be visiting your college or high school. See if you can arrange a meeting to talk about their career and any advice they can offer you.

MARKETING DIRECTOR

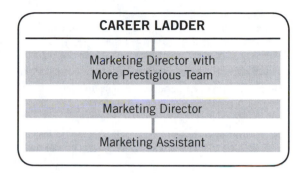

Position Description

The Marketing Director of a professional sports team is responsible for developing techniques of marketing a team, its name, and players' personalities. He or she may handle this in a variety of ways. The more successful and popular the team is, the easier the Marketing Director's job ultimately will be.

The individual is responsible for developing the concepts and campaigns that will decide how the team is to be marketed. In a sports team, the marketing department works in conjunction with the promotion, advertising, and public relations departments.

The Marketing Director decides how much and what type of advertising, promotion, public relations, and sales support will be most effective. He or she must develop sound, effective techniques to market both the team and its products.

Working with the promotion director, the individual might develop contests, promotions, giveaway programs, and so on. The Marketing Director constantly strives to expand and open up new markets. For example, the Director may find that offering a senior citizen's discount during afternoon games will help open up a new market. He or she might also find that reducing admission for adults bringing in children under 12 might also reach a different market. Everything the Marketing Director does is designed to bring more people to the stadium and to make the team popular and

exciting. It helps, of course, if the team is currently on a winning streak.

All marketing techniques are not accomplished in the stadium. The individual may develop personal appearance tours for the athletes, booking them as guests on television and radio shows or at autograph sessions in local malls. The Marketing Director may also arrange interviews with the press.

One of the important functions of the Marketing Director is to sell licenses to companies or organizations so that they can make licensed team products. In order to be sold legally, such products as mugs, glasses, T-shirts, hats, dolls, and so on bearing the team's name and logo must all be licensed.

The individual must decide which companies will be allowed to produce products to sell with the team logo emblazoned on them. He or she must also determine what companies will be associated with the team name.

Once permission is given to use the team logo, the Marketing Director makes sure that contracts are signed. He or she may also determine how the team will be compensated for the use of its name and/or logo. The team might receive a percentage of profits from each item sold or a flat fee for licensing.

The Marketing Director must plan, coordinate, and implement all of the team's marketing goals and objectives. He or she is expected to organize projects and become involved in promotions. Depending on the size of the marketing department, the individual may be responsible for everything or may assign duties to others working in the department.

The Marketing Director may be expected to write marketing campaign preliminary proposals or outlines for review by team management. The individual may also be responsible for writing memos or other informational data to keep other departments aware of the new marketing plans and campaigns that are undertaken.

The Marketing Director may be responsible for researching facts and data or may assign this task to an assistant. The individual might need demographic information about potential purchasers of team-licensed products, fans, patrons, and so on. He or she may also be interested in evaluating the effectiveness of certain advertising and promotions.

The Marketing Director may be required to write, design, or develop sales promotion letters or direct mail pieces in order to initiate new concepts, attract new fans, secure group sales, or reach other patron markets.

Where there is no director of public relations, the Marketing Director may be responsible for the preparation of promotional brochures, press releases, or newsletters. He or she may also be expected to attend trade shows and conventions on behalf of the team.

The Marketing Director works normal business hours most of the time but may have to work overtime on projects, special events, and promotions. He or she may spend a great deal of time working weekends or in the evenings when games, tournaments, and promotions are taking place.

Salaries
Salaries for Marketing Directors depend on a number of variables. These include the specific team the individual is working for and its prestige in the marketplace and media. Other factors affecting salaries are the individual's experience, responsibilities, and duties.

Earnings can range from $37,000 to $175,000 plus for a Marketing Director with a lot of experience, a great deal of responsibility, and working for a team that has a high visibility.

Employment Prospects
Employment prospects are poor for Marketing Directors of professional sports teams. Competition is fierce for these positions. There are only a limited number of professional teams, and once an individual obtains a job, he or she does not usually move on unless a better job opens up.

Advancement Prospects
Advancement prospects are dependent on the individual and his or her skills, drive, and determination. Those who are aggressive and productive will move up the career ladder.

One of the most common career paths for individuals in this field is to advance their career by moving into a similar position with a larger, more prestigious team.

Education and Training
A good education is necessary for individuals aspiring to be Marketing Directors of professional sports teams. A four-year college degree is the minimum requirement. Good choices for majors include marketing, public relations, communications, journalism, English, liberal arts, business, and sports administration.

Workshops and seminars in publicity and marketing will also prove useful.

Experience, Skills, and Personality Traits
The Marketing Director of a professional sports team needs to be creative and innovative. He or she should have excellent communication skills.

The ability to write well is essential. The individual should have a good command of the English language, spelling, and word usage. He or she must understand and have skills in marketing, public relations, and advertising.

The Marketing Director should be ambitious, aggressive, highly motivated, and energetic. He or she should be able to work under stress, handling many details and a variety of projects at one time.

Unions and Associations
Marketing Directors of professional sports teams may belong to trade associations relevant to the particular sport in which they work. They may also join general marketing, public relations, advertising, or promotion organizations, such as the American Marketing Association (AMA), the Association of National Advertisers (ANA), the Business/Professional Advertising Association (BPAA), the American Advertising Federation (AAF), Women In Communications (WIC), or the Public Relations Society of America (PRSA).

Tips for Entry
1. Try to find an internship with a professional sports team's marketing department. You probably will have to do a lot of clerical work, but it will be worth the experience. These opportunities are often located through your college placement office or directly through the team.

2. If you can get your foot into the door, it may be easier to move up the career ladder. A job as an assistant, trainee, or clerk in the marketing office will help you accomplish this. Once you are in, volunteer to do extra projects. Keep your eyes and ears open and learn as much as possible.

3. Consider obtaining some experience in a marketing field outside of the sports world. Send your résumé and cover letter to marketing firms or departments of stores, businesses, associations, and so on. If you learn the skills you will be able to work anyplace in any field.

4. Attend workshops and seminars in marketing, promotion, public relations, and sports administration. These will help give you additional expertise on subjects as well as give you a good opportunity to make contacts.

5. Send your résumé and a cover letter to professional sports teams inquiring about openings in the marketing department.

6. Job openings may be located on the Internet. Search popular career and job sites as well as sites specific to the sports industry.

7. Check out the Web sites of professional sports teams. Many list job openings.

MARKETING ASSISTANT

Duties: Assisting marketing director accomplish duties; helping develop campaigns; performing clerical and secretarial duties

Alternate Title(s): Assistant

Salary Range: $24,000 to $40,000+

Employment Prospects: Fair

Advancement Prospects: Fair

Best Geographical Location(s) for Position: Cities hosting professional sports teams

Prerequisites:

Education or Training—Minimum of four-year college degree

Experience—Experience in marketing, public relations, and promotion preferred but may not be required

CAREER LADDER

Marketing Coordinator, Assistant Marketing Manager, Assistant Marketing Director, or Marketing Director

Marketing Assistant

Marketing or Public Relations Intern or Entry Level

Special Skills and Personality Traits—Articulate; good writing skills; clerical and secretarial abilities; good communications skills; creative; marketing skills; aggressive; enthusiastic; ambitious; detail oriented

Position Description

The Marketing Assistant working in a sports team helps the marketing director accomplish his or her duties. Depending on the individual's experience level, he or she may be responsible for a wide range of functions, from performing secretarial or clerical duties to assisting with the development of the team's marketing plan.

The sports team's Marketing Assistant may help the director of the department develop and implement concepts and campaigns. The marketing department of a sports team works with the ticket sales, promotion, advertising, and public relations departments.

In teams with smaller budgets, such as a team with low visibility, one individual and an Assistant might be responsible not only for the marketing but also for the promotion, advertising, and public relations departments. While this type of job usually pays considerably less, the Assistant has the opportunity to work in all facets of marketing and will receive a well-rounded training.

The Marketing Assistant also works with the marketing director in the planning and coordination of all the team's marketing goals and objectives. If the individual has sufficient experience and expertise, he or she may be expected to help plan and organize projects and become involved in promotions.

If the Assistant is just a beginner, he or she takes on more clerical types of duties. The Assistant may be responsible for typing letters, reports, proposals, and memos. He or she may be required to make phone calls, answer the telephone, and take messages on behalf of the marketing director.

The Marketing Assistant may be expected to help coordinate and implement special events, promotions, and other programs that have been developed in the department. The individual often is responsible for working with other departments to ensure that marketing efforts and projects run smoothly.

The individual may develop or assist in the development and writing of sales promotion letters, direct mail pieces, brochures, press releases, and newsletters to help market the team. These might be used, for example, to attract new fans, patrons, or licensees interested in using team logos.

The Marketing Assistant may be responsible for helping the director handle the licensing of the team's name, logo, and likeness. He or she may be expected to field calls from potential companies interested in using the team's logo, do research on them, and send them information regarding the process. The individual may arrange meetings between the marketing director and interested companies to finalize agreements.

The Marketing Assistant is directly responsible to the team's marketing director. He or she works long hours, attending to regular business as well as working overtime during games, tournaments, championships, projects, special events, and promotions.

Salaries

A Marketing Assistant working for a professional sports team can earn between $24,000 and $40,000 plus annually. Salaries vary depending on the specific team and the individual's responsibilities and experience level.

Individuals with little or no experience in the field, or those working for sports teams with minimal popularity and visibility, average salaries on the low end of the scale. Marketing Assistants with more experience, greater responsibility, and working for teams with higher visibility may average annual earnings on the higher end of the salary scale.

Employment Prospects

Employment prospects are fair for Marketing Assistants. Opportunities may be located in the marketing departments of lesser-known professional teams as well as high-visibility major league teams.

Advancement Prospects

Advancement prospects are fair for Marketing Assistants. Individuals must work hard, be aggressive, driven, and highly motivated. Marketing Assistants can take a number of different paths in career advancement. Some may locate a similar position with a more prestigious team. This usually results in additional responsibilities and higher earnings. Others may become the department coordinator. Some individuals may climb the career ladder by landing a position as a professional sports team's assistant marketing manager or director or even marketing manager or director. This type of jump may occur if the individual is working with a smaller team. If the Marketing Assistant has a thorough knowledge of public relations, promotion, and advertising, he or she might also move on to become assistant director, assistant manager, director, or manager of any of those departments.

Education and Training

Competition is fierce in all facets of the sports industry. Those with the best education have the most opportunities both to obtain a position and be successful at it.

Most professional sports teams require that Marketing Assistants have at least a four-year college degree. Good choices for majors include marketing, public relations, advertising, business administration, liberal arts, communications, or sports administration.

Some colleges offer sports administration degrees. An advantage in going to such a college is that these colleges often work with professional sports teams to obtain internship programs for their students.

Experience, Skills, and Personality Traits

It is not necessary to know everything about sports to be a Marketing Assistant for a pro team. It does help, however, to have a general knowledge about the sport the team is associated with.

The Marketing Assistant should be articulate and have excellent communication skills. The ability to write well is necessary. The Marketing Assistant should have a good command of the English language and be able to spell well. Creativity in writing, speaking, and in developing ideas and concepts is helpful.

Those who want to succeed in this profession should be enthusiastic, ambitious, aggressive, highly motivated, and energetic. Marketing Assistants should be detail oriented with the ability to handle many details and a variety of projects at one time without getting flustered.

The Marketing Assistant should be able to perform clerical and secretarial duties, such as typing, filing, and handling phone calls. The ability to work with computers is a must.

Unions and Associations

Marketing Assistants working for professional sports may be members of a number of marketing, advertising, or public relations trade associations, such as the American Marketing Association (AMA), the Association of National Advertisers (ANA), the Business/Professional Advertising Association (BPAA), the American Advertising Federation (AAF), Women In Communications (WIC), or the Public Relations Society of America (PRSA). Individuals may also be members of organizations geared specifically toward the sport they are working with.

Tips for Entry

1. Send your résumé and cover letter to professional sports teams. Inquire about openings in the marketing department. Addresses of a number of pro teams are given in the Appendixes to help get you started.
2. Join trade associations. They offer continuing education, seminars, and internships. Attend their meetings. They will help you make valuable contacts.

3. Look for marketing seminars offered throughout the country. These will have educational value as well as offer the opportunity to make contacts.
4. Try to obtain an internship with a professional sports team. Many schools work with pro teams with their internship programs. If yours does not, contact teams directly to inquire about internship possibilities.
5. Job openings may be located on the Internet. Search popular career and job sites as well as specific sports teams' Web sites.

PROMOTION DIRECTOR

CAREER PROFILE

Duties: Setting up promotions for sports team; developing ideas to help sell seats in stadiums; arranging for personal appearances of team athletes

Alternate Title(s): Promotion Manager; Director of Promotion

Salary Range: $30,000 to $125,000+

Employment Prospects: Poor

Advancement Prospects: Fair

Best Geographical Location(s) for Position: Cities hosting professional sports teams

Prerequisites:

Education or Training—College degree or background may be preferred

Experience—Experience working in promotion, publicity, or public relations helpful but not always necessary

Special Skills and Personality Traits—Knowledge of promotion; creative; good writing skills; free to travel; articulate; ability to deal with a variety of people; energetic; organized; capable of dealing with many projects at one time

CAREER LADDER

```
Team General Manager, Promotion
Director, or Marketing Director for
Larger, More Prestigious Team

          Promotion Director

Press Agent, Publicist, or Sportswriter
```

Position Description

The Promotion Director working for a professional sports team is responsible for handling all of the promotions and special events used to bring the team to the attention of the public and make them more prestigious and popular. A sports team makes money and a profit by having fans come see the games. Through various promotions, the Promotion Director attempts to find ways to keep stadium seats filled.

The Promotion Director may have varied responsibilities, depending on the size of the team organization. In smaller organizations, the individual may be responsible for the team's public relations, publicity, and promotion. In larger organizations, such as major league teams, the individual usually is responsible for supervising publicists, public relations, and the promotions themselves. Depending on the staff size, he or she may work alone or may supervise one or two promotion representatives.

While a great many promotions occur during the game season, many take place throughout the year. Just because the team is not playing does not mean that the individual can stop developing and implementing promotional ideas.

The Promotion Director may come up with almost any type of promotion to boost ticket sales. For example, he or she might set up a promotion in a shopping mall where the team athletes sign autographs, take photos, and give out team memorabilia.

At times, he or she may arrange for the athletes to appear on television and radio talk, news, and variety shows. The Promotion Director might also set up personal appearances for athletes at nonprofit events. In many instances, the Promotion Director responds to the needs of charities and other nonprofit groups by arranging a variety of activities. He or she may have team athletes play in celebrity baseball or basketball games. The individual might set up hospital and prison appearances and the like. This type of event not only keeps the team in the public eye, but also is good public relations.

Depending on the sport, the Promotion Director might arrange for a number of team members to visit a Little League game or a Special Olympics event.

The Promotion Director is responsible for developing or working with fan associations, which in turn keep people interested in the team. He or she may have a fan appreciation day where fans receive lower-priced tickets, team memorabilia, and photos.

The Promotion Director is responsible for developing team-related giveaways, such as team hats, jackets, or T-shirts. He or she may also be in charge of coming up with merchandising ideas for items to sell that will keep the team's name in the public eye on a more consistent basis.

On occasion, the Promotion Director develops contests to promote the team. These contests may or may not run in conjunction with other tie-in companies. His or her main goal is to keep coming up with new and unique ideas to help make people know and like the team enough to spend money on stadium tickets.

The individual in this position works under constant pressure. His or her job performance is measured by the number of people buying ticket seats. The Promotion Director works long hours, both in the office and while at home trying to develop effective promotions and ideas. He or she also is usually on hand for all team games and events.

Depending on the team and the particular situation, the individual is responsible to the team manager or owner.

Salaries

Annual earnings for Promotion Directors of professional sports teams can range from $30,000 to $125,000 or more plus bonuses. The salaries vary greatly depending on a number of factors, including the sport, type of league involved, and the prestige, popularity, and success of the team with which the individual is working. Other variables include the individual's experience level and responsibilities.

Individuals working in this position often receive additional incentives or bonuses for filling stadium seats.

Employment Prospects

Employment prospects are poor for those seeking this position in a professional team. While most teams have a Promotion Director, he or she is usually hired from within the organization.

An individual may find it easier to enter the field by seeking work with a minor league or lesser-known team as a publicist. Then after obtaining some experience and proving him- or herself, the individual should seek employment with a major league team. People who have made contacts with others in sports teams as interns or trainees will have an easier time in their job hunt.

Advancement Prospects

Once they get their first job, advancement prospects are fair for Promotion Directors. While there is no set way for an individual to climb the career ladder in this field, one path is to become the team's general manager. Team owners often feel that if an individual can fill the stadium seats with fans consistently, he or she would be a good general manager. Another way for a Promotion Director to move up the career ladder is to become a Promotion Director with a more popular, prestigious team. There are some individuals who advance their career by becoming a team marketing director.

Education and Training

Most professional sports teams today generally prefer that their Promotion Directors hold a minimum of a four-year college degree. Good choices for majors for those seeking entry into this field include sports management, sports administration, marketing, communications, business, or a related field.

Colleges offering majors in sports management or administration often assist students in obtaining internships that in turn help the individual get his or her foot in the door with a sports team.

Experience, Skills, and Personality Traits

Promotion Directors need to be creative people. They must be able to see unique ways to promote the team as a whole as well as its individual players.

The Promotion Director of a sports team should be articulate with good communication skills, both verbal and written. The individual should be personable and easy to talk to. He or she deals with members of the team, management, and media. It is also important that the Promotion Director know how to follow through on projects so that they get done from beginning to end.

The individual should be energetic, because during promotions he or she works long hours. The Promotion Director must know how to arrange priorities and deal with them in a logical order and be able to assign tasks to others.

Unions and Associations

There are no unions or trade associations that Promotion Directors working in sports must belong to. Depending on what type of experience he or she entered the job with, however, the individual may belong to the National Sportscasters and Sportswriters Association (NSSA), the Public Relations Society of America (PRSA), Women In Communications (WIC), or the National Federation of Press Women (NFPW).

Tips for Entry

1. Try to get involved with an internship or training program with a major sports team. These can be located through colleges with sports administration programs or by directly contacting teams.
2. Promotion is promotion. If you know the basics and you are creative, you can promote anything in any area. Get experience in promotion and publicity even if it is not working in the sports

industry. For example, you might work with a public relations firm, a publicist, an advertising agency, or the like.

3. Consider working as a sportswriter or reporter for your school or local newspaper. This will help you make valuable contacts with those in the sports industry.

4. Try to work with a sports team in any capacity. Money should not be the most important factor at this point in your career. The experience will pay off financially later.

PUBLIC RELATIONS DIRECTOR

CAREER PROFILE

Duties: Handling the functions of the public relations department; supervising team publicists; handling special requests by fans or patrons; developing biographies, press kits, press releases, articles, etc.; dealing with the media

Alternate Title(s): Director of Public Relations; Public Relations Manager; PR Director; Director of PR

Salary Range: $38,000 to $150,000+

Employment Prospects: Poor

Advancement Prospects: Fair

Best Geographical Location(s) for Position: Cities hosting professional sports teams

Prerequisites:

   Education or Training—Four-year college degree required

   Experience—Experience working as publicist, sports information director, or sports journalist required

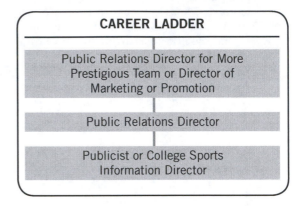

CAREER LADDER

Public Relations Director for More Prestigious Team or Director of Marketing or Promotion

Public Relations Director

Publicist or College Sports Information Director

Special Skills and Personality Traits—Public relations skills; writing skills; energetic; communication skills; creative; innovative; personable

Position Description

The Public Relations Director of a professional sports team is the individual in charge of the department dealing with the public. This means that the PR Director is responsible for handling the press, media, and public information.

In some organizations, the public relations department is large and the PR Director has team publicists working under him or her. In other teams, the individual is required to take charge of all duties. Responsibilities vary depending on the size of the department and the specific team. The individual may function in a number of different areas, including public relations, publicity, promotion, and/or marketing.

It is important to a team's management to keep the public informed and satisfied with the team. The PR Director is responsible for handling all problems that arise regarding the public. These difficulties can include anything from an unhappy fan to a patron who did not like the way a stadium employee dealt with a situation. The individual may answer letters and/or phone calls regarding problems and all types of situations.

The Public Relations Director may deal with usual fan requests, such as wanting to know how to obtain photographs of the team or of individual athletes, autographs, biographical information, game schedules, and

so on. The individual may take care of these projects, or assign an assistant, intern, or trainee to them.

Special requests of fans and patrons are always routed to the Public Relations Director. For example, the PR Director may be contacted by the family or friends of a 100-year-old fan to inquire if it would be possible to have a birthday card signed by the team. He or she may be called by a family member or physician to have a terminally ill child visited by a team member who may be the child's idol.

Some Public Relations Directors also organize team or individual athlete fan clubs. They may be responsible for developing the entire fan club or merely provide materials, such as biographies, press kits, and so on, to others who organize and run the clubs.

The Director of Public Relations is ultimately responsible for all publicity functions of the team. He or she may perform publicity tasks personally or supervise team publicists. The individual is responsible for developing and writing regular and special news announcements, press releases, feature stories, and articles.

The individual works with local, regional, and national media in print and broadcast press. He or she answers requests for interviews, photographs, and information as well as conducts press conferences about special events. The PR Director might even make suggestions for photo opportunities or feature stories to members of the media.

The PR Director is responsible for biographies, press kits, player rosters, stock photographs, statistical information, and other promotional and press information. He or she may also be responsible for producing media guides, daily programs, team newsletters, and other publications.

When team games are televised, especially those airing nationally, the PR Director may be responsible for providing clips of prior games for promotional purposes or clips of current games to news or sports directors.

Many professional sports teams have a promotion department. In those that do not, the PR Director may be required to handle promotional functions, including the development and implementation of ideas and campaigns. In teams with promotional departments, he or she may be responsible for publicizing the promotions.

The Public Relations Director may be required to handle community service projects, such as providing speakers to local groups, bestowing awards to local dignitaries and other honorees, becoming involved in community projects, and the like.

The Public Relations Director in a professional sports team works long hours, often late at night and on weekends. He or she may be responsible to the team's marketing director, general manager, or owner, depending on the structure of the organization.

Salaries

Salaries for Public Relations Directors working for professional sports teams can vary greatly from job to job depending on a number of factors. These include the specific sport and the prestige of the team for which the individual is working as well as the responsibilities, qualifications, and experience level of the individual. Salaries for this position range from $38,000 to $150,000 plus, with those on the lower end going to individuals working with lesser-known teams.

Employment Prospects

Employment prospects are poor for those aspiring to be Public Relations Directors of professional sports teams. Competition is fierce for these positions. It is more difficult to obtain positions with major-league and prestigious teams than with lesser-known and minor league teams.

Advancement Prospects

Advancement prospects are fair for the Director of Public Relations of a professional sports team. Individuals can take a number of different paths to climb the career ladder.

The PR Director may find a similar position with a more prestigious team. This will result in increased responsibilities and higher earnings. He or she may also become the director of marketing or promotion.

Education and Training

A minimum of a four-year college degree is necessary for most positions as Director of Public Relations for a professional sports team. Good choices for majors include public relations, communications, journalism, English, liberal arts, marketing, and business or sports administration.

Extra classes or seminars in writing, sports administration, marketing, public relations, and journalism can also be useful.

Experience, Skills, and Personality Traits

Some Public Relations Directors working in professional sports teams may have worked with the same or another team as a publicist or as a college sports information director before landing their current position. Others worked in journalism as sports reporters in either the print or broadcasting fields. Some individuals obtained experience handling public relations, publicity, or marketing in other fields before entering the sports industry.

Successful PR Directors are creative, innovative people. They are articulate and well groomed. Individuals must have good communications skills and be comfortable speaking on the phone or in person to large and small groups.

The PR Director should know enough about the sport to speak and write intelligently about it. A great many individuals are or become ardent fans of the sport and team they work with. The Director must be capable of planning and executing all public relations skills.

The PR Director must be able to communicate on all levels. He or she should be able to develop and write factual, concise, and interesting letters, press releases, copy, and feature stories.

Individuals should be energetic and be able to work on countless projects at the same time without becoming flustered. Supervisory skills may also be required.

Public Relations Directors working for sports teams should be persuasive and personable. They should not only be able to deal well with people, but enjoy it. This includes the general public as well as the media.

Unions and Associations

The Director of Public Relations working for a professional sports team may belong to a number of trade associations that provide educational and professional guidance as well as bring people with similar careers together. These might include the National Sportscasters and Sportswriters Association (NSSA), the Public Relations Society of America (PRSA), Women In Communications (WIC), and the National Federation of Press Women (NFPW). Individuals might also be members of organizations specific to the sport they are working in.

Tips for Entry

1. Join trade associations and attend their meetings, seminars, and conventions. This is a good way to obtain some extra continuing education and make important contacts.

2. Try to locate an internship in the public relations, promotion, or marketing department of a professional sports team. This will help you gain hands-on experience and get your foot in the door. Contact professional sports teams or see if your college sponsors an internship program.

3. Another good way of getting your foot in the door is to locate a job as an assistant or trainee in the PR department of a professional sports team. Write or call and inquire.

4. If you have some public relations experience, send your résumé and a cover letter to the various professional teams. Ask that your résumé be kept on file if there are no current job openings.

5. Get as much experience writing as possible. Think about writing a sports column or being a sports reporter for your school or local newspaper.

6. Check out job openings online. Start with some of the more popular sites such as hotjobs.com and monster.com and go from there.

7. Check out pro team Web Sites. Many list openings.

PUBLICIST

CAREER PROFILE

Duties: Creating public interest in team and players; creating publicity; preparing and writing press releases, press kits, informational sheets, and yearbooks; dealing with the media

Alternate Title(s): Sports Publicist; Team Publicist; Publicist

Salary Range: $27,000 to $100,000+

Employment Prospects: Fair

Advancement Prospects: Fair

Best Geographical Location(s) for Position: Cities hosting professional sports teams

Prerequisites:

Education or Training—Four-year college degree required

Experience—Sportswriter or reporter or experience in college sports information preferred

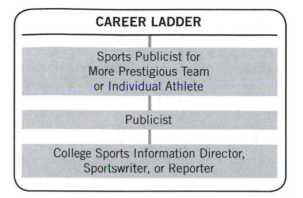

CAREER LADDER

Sports Publicist for More Prestigious Team or Individual Athlete

Publicist

College Sports Information Director, Sportswriter, or Reporter

Special Skills and Personality Traits—Understanding of the specific sport; public relations skills; good writing skills; articulate; ability to deal with media; energetic; ability to deal with many projects

Position Description

A professional sports team Publicist has an interesting job. The individual's main function is to publicize a professional team and its players. This creates public interest, which in turn makes people want to attend games and fill up stadiums and arenas. With the current interest in televised sports, increased popularity of a team or an athlete also means that the ownership can get more money and better deals for televised events.

The Publicist in this field might work with professional teams in any sport, including hockey, baseball, basketball, jai alai, soccer, football, or others. He or she might work with the major or minor leagues. In order to be effective in the job, it is important that the individual have an understanding of the sport in which he or she works.

The professional sports industry is a major force in the entertainment world. The professional sports team Publicist works with the sports news media daily. The individual deals with newspapers, magazines, television, cable networks, and radio stations. On the professional level, the sports team Publicist works with local, regional, and national media.

He or she knows the sports editors and calls to inform them of new deals being made by the team, new players, coaches, owners, managers, and so on. The professional sports team Publicist frequently receives

calls from the sports media asking specific questions or to request interviews with the players, coaches, trainers, or management.

The professional sports team Publicist or team Publicist, as he or she might be referred to, is responsible for setting up schedules of appearances for team members, coaches, managements, and owners. This could be for paid appearances or for appearances for nonprofit groups and charities. For example, a popular team member might be the national chairperson for an organization against teenage alcohol and drug abuse.

Professional teams receive many requests for public appearances, for either single athletes or the entire team. The Publicist has to decide which appearances to accept and which ones to reject. He or she must then write letters of regret with explanations that do not antagonize anyone to those requests that were not accepted.

The team Publicist arranges guest appearances on television and radio talk, variety, news, and sports shows for team members as well as print interviews. He or she also develops feature story ideas for both sports editors and the general media.

The Publicist must know everything that is happening, ranging from dates of games and scores to players' injuries. The individual prepares press releases on a regular basis with this information. When major events are occurring within the team, he or she may write releases more frequently. These press releases will be sent to sports media from a prepared media list.

The individual also prepares statistical informational sheets, injury data, and the like regularly. He or she is responsible for interviewing players, managers, coaches, and owners to obtain information for biographies, team yearbooks, press kits, and game programs.

The sports Publicist arranges and conducts press conferences. Major leagues usually hold more conferences than minor leagues. The individual may present press conferences weekly or even more frequently if a major event is taking place, such as a major trade or the signing of a popular athlete.

The sports Publicist is available for the media at games as well as at practice sessions. He or she must arrange for press passes, press credentials, and seating for members of the media. The individual also arranges locker room interviews. He or she is responsible for passing out press kits, biographies, and releases to press people at this time.

If the team the individual works for is traveling to another city, the sports Publicist phones media in that city to arrange interviews, appearances, and press conferences. The sports Publicist might also travel to the city ahead of time and take care of these tasks in person. In this manner, he or she gets to know the sports press from the other cities.

The individual in this job socializes frequently with sportswriters and reporters. He or she attends sports-related and social functions on behalf of the team. The sports team Publicist is always looking for a way to publicize his or her team and its members.

The sports team Publicist works long hours and many weekends. Activities sometimes slow down slightly during the sport's off-season. The individual in this position may be responsible to the team owners, general manager, or public relations director.

Salaries
Salaries vary from job to job depending on the team the individual works for. Salaries can range from $27,000 to $100,000 plus.

Variables include the sport, type of league the individual works with, and the team's popularity and success. Earnings also depend on the individual's experience level and responsibilities.

Individuals who work for minor league teams earn salaries at the lower end of the scale. Those working for major league teams earn from $40,000 to $100,000 plus.

Employment Prospects
Employment prospects are fair for professional sports team Publicists. Some teams have a professional sports team Publicist and an assistant publicist or a number of assistants. Individuals may have more luck finding jobs in the minor leagues and with lesser-known teams.

Advancement Prospects
Advancement prospects for professional team Publicists are good once an individual has held a job in this profession. The team Publicist may go on to work for another team in the sports industry or an individual athlete, or may go into sports marketing and endorsements. The individual might also start his or her own public relations or publicity company or find a job in a top agency. He or she might also become a press agent for people in other facets of the entertainment industry.

Things can change overnight in the sports industry. An individual may be working for a team that isn't very well known or doesn't have a lot of prestige. If the team wins unexpectedly, all of a sudden it might become popular, making the team Publicist position even more valuable.

Education and Training
The team Publicist usually must have a four-year college degree. The exception to this might be an individual who was a former professional athlete who has an understanding of sports, public relations, and publicity from working in the industry.

The sports team Publicist will find courses and seminars in public relations, publicity, marketing, journalism, English, writing, media exposure, sports studies, and physical education useful.

Experience, Skills, and Personality Traits
Professional sports team Publicists usually have had previous experience with the media. They often were sportswriters or reporters themselves. Some individuals in this position worked as college sports information directors before holding a job in professional sports.

The team Publicist must have a total understanding of the sport, the players, and the industry. He or she must also have a full working knowledge of how to use public relations and publicity tactics to promote the team. The individual should be a good writer with the ability to turn out factual, concise, and interesting press releases, biographies, yearbooks, and the like.

The ability to communicate well and speak articulately is essential. The individual must be comfortable speaking to large groups. He or she may often conduct press conferences.

The team Publicist should be personable. Sportswriters and reporters must like the individual and feel comfortable talking to him or her. A good working relationship between the team Publicist and the sports media is necessary.

The individual must be energetic. He or she must be able to work long hours, handle many details, and work on many different projects at one time.

Unions and Associations

The professional sports team Publicist does not belong to any union. However, he or she may belong to a number of trade associations, including the National Sportscasters and Sportswriters Association (NSSA), the Public Relations Society of America (PRSA), Women In Communications (WIC), and the National Federation of Press Women (NFPW).

Tips for Entry

1. Consider a summer or part-time job as a sports reporter for a local newspaper.

2. Work on your college newspaper. It is important to gain as much experience as possible writing.

3. Work in your college sports information office as an assistant or aide. This will give you a good overview of the job on an amateur level.

4. The professional sports team Publicist often has a number of assistants or trainees working with him or her doing the leg work and clerical work. Try to locate one of these positions.

5. An internship or summer job in the sports department of a local television station would also prove helpful. You will learn how sports reporters work and make some valuable contacts.

6. Job sites and professional sports team webpages may list job openings.

COMMUNITY RELATIONS DIRECTOR—SPORTS TEAM

CAREER PROFILE

Duties: Building and coordinating relationships between sports team and local agencies, civic groups, schools, community groups, political entities, and governmental agencies; promoting a positive image of sports team in community

Alternate Title(s): Community Affairs Director; Director of Community Relations; Community Services Director

Salary Range: $32,000 to $70,000+

Employment Prospects: Fair

Advancement Prospects: Fair

Best Geographical Location(s) for Position: Greatest number of positions located in areas hosting large numbers of professional sports teams.

Prerequisites:

Education or Training—Bachelor's degree usually required or preferred

Experience—Experience working in journalism, with sports teams, and with community and not-for-profit groups helpful

CAREER LADDER

Sports Team Public Relations Director or Community Relations Director for Larger, More Prestigious Sports Team

Sports Team Community Relations Director

Sports Team Community Relations Assistant Director or Public Relations Assistant Director or Journalism Position

Special Skills and Personality Traits—Creativity; people skills; good verbal and written communications skills; public speaking ability; organized; energetic

Position Description

Professional sports teams generally get involved in the community in which they are located. It is good public relations and good business. The individual in charge of handling community relations for a team is called the Community Relations Director.

He or she is responsible for building and coordinating the relationship between the team and local agencies, civic groups, schools, community groups, political entities, and governmental agencies. The Community Relations Director is expected to cultivate relationships with these groups.

One of the functions of the Community Relations Director is planning, designing, and executing programs to help the local community. Another is to promote a positive image of the sports team. While doing this, the Community Relations Director must always be sensitive to the local community and its needs.

The individual may, for example, develop a sponsorship program with an amateur Little League team, other local sporting events, cultural events, parades, and other community-related programs. The Community Relations Director—Sports Team might also develop programs to work with community groups such as the local chapter of the United Way, the Red Cross, children's charities, or area hospitals on specific projects. The idea is to keep the team's name in the public eye in a positive manner while helping the community.

Successful Community Relations Directors of sports teams have a good relationship with the people, businesses, and not-for-profit groups within the community. Their goal is to develop innovative community relations programs in which the sports team can take a leadership role.

In order to be part of the community, the Community Relations Director of a sports team often joins many of the not-for profit, civic, and community groups in the area. The Community Relations Director may be an active member of these groups or may serve on their board of directors and various committees.

The individual will frequently represent the team at community events. He or she may attend alone, with team owners, or other corporate or team administration people or even team members. The Community Relations Director may also be asked to speak at community functions, fund-raising events, and civic meetings.

It is important for the Community Relations Director to have a good working relationship with the media. This is helpful for many reasons. To begin with, the media is useful in helping spread the word about the team's community relations programs. The media is also beneficial in garnering positive press coverage when working on community events or fund-raisers or simply keeping the team's name in the public eye in a positive manner.

The Community Relations Director of a sports team is often called upon to make things happen. For example, a school may call the Community Relations Director if it wants to set up a meet and greet between team members and a specific class. He or she might also be called upon if an organization such as Make a Wish wants to create an experience for a child in their program. The Community Relations Director might be asked to find a way to have a day named for a prominent community citizen at the ball park or arena or might even be the one people call when they want to put their marriage proposal up in lights during halftime.

Sports teams are often asked by community and civic groups for donations. The Community Relations Director is expected to field all requests. The individual must then determine which requests can be met and then coordinate and distribute donations on behalf of the team to these community organizations.

The Community Relations Director must be sure that the team maintains a good public image at all times within the community. He or she may work in conjunction with the team's marketing and public relations directors in accomplishing this.

Salaries

Earnings for Community Relations Directors of sports teams can range from $32,000 to $70,000 or more annually. Factors affecting earnings include the specific team for which the individual works, its size, geographic location, and popularity. Other variables include the experience, reputation, and responsibilities of the Community Relations Director. Individuals working for popular, professional major league sports teams will earn more than their counterparts working for minor league teams.

Employment Prospects

Employment prospects are fair for Community Relations Directors of sports teams. Individuals may find employment throughout the country with major league and minor league sports teams. It should be noted that in smaller or minor league teams, the responsibilities of this position may be handled by the team's public relations director.

Advancement Prospects

Advancement prospects are fair for Community Relations Directors of sports teams. There are a number of different possibilities for climbing the career ladder depending on the individual's aspirations. Some individuals locate similar positions with larger or more prestigious sports teams. Others may land positions in the community relations area in industries outside of sports. Some Community Relations Directors are also promoted to positions as public relations or marketing directors for either the same or a more prestigious team.

There are some Community Relations Directors of sports teams who are offered positions as the director of not-for-profit organizations that they have been working with on behalf of the sports team.

Education and Training

Most sports teams require their Community Relations Directors to hold a minimum of a four-year college degree. Good possibilities for majors include English, public relations, journalism, marketing, sports administration, communications, or a related field.

Whatever major individuals pursue, classes in publicity, public relations, advertising, marketing, journalism, English, communications, writing, and related areas will be helpful in honing skills.

Seminars in public relations, dealing with community relations and not-for-profit groups, and publicity will also be useful.

Experience, Skills, and Personality Traits

Experience requirements vary depending on the specific team for which the individual works. Larger, more prestigious teams generally prefer their Community Relations Director to have more experience than those working for smaller teams.

Some Community Relations Directors of sports teams have worked with the team in various capacities previous to landing this job. Some were community relations assistant directors. Others worked in the public relations department. Some individuals also came out of journalism positions.

Community Relations Directors need to be outgoing, personable individuals with a lot of energy. They should like working with a variety of people. Enjoyment of the team's sport is an added bonus.

Individuals need to be articulate. The ability to speak comfortably in front of groups is necessary. Creativity and innovation are helpful. The ability to multitask without getting flustered and stressed is needed.

Unions and Associations

Community Relations Directors of sports teams may belong to a number of trade associations geared to the specific sport with which the individual is working. Individuals may also be members of local civic groups, not-for-profit organizations, and service clubs. Many Community Relations Directors also belong to the Public Relations Society of America (PRSA).

Tips for Entry

1. Positions are often advertised in the classified section of newspapers in areas hosting sports teams. Look under headings such as "Sports Teams," "Community Relations," "Community Affairs," or "Community Relations Director." Openings may also be listed under the name of the specific sports team.

2. Positions may also be located online. Start off by checking out some of the more popular generic career sites and then visit sites specific to the sports industry.

3. Don't forget to check out sports teams Web sites. Many post openings online.

4. Consider sending your résumé and a short cover letter to sports teams you might be interested in working with. You might get a call.

5. Join civic and not-for-profit groups and volunteer to be on committees. This will give you hands-on experience dealing with communities and look great on your résumé.

TICKET MANAGER

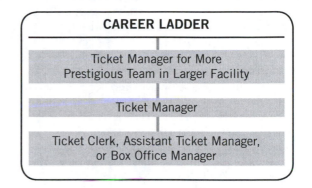

Position Description

Sports teams earn money for their owners in a number of ways. One method of obtaining income is selling television and cable rights to their games. Another income producer is selling items or licensing products emblazed with team logos. Still another important source of income for most sports teams are sales of tickets to their games.

The Ticket Manager is in charge of the department that handles ticket sales for scheduled team games. He or she has varied duties depending on the prestige and popularity of the team and the size of the ticket office.

Minor league teams and those with less fan-drawing power may have one individual in charge of ticket sales. He or she has the title Ticket Manager and is responsible for everything that occurs in the ticket office. Major league and other highly visible sports teams with a large fan following may have many people working in their ticket offices. In these instances the Ticket Manager oversees an entire office and staff.

An important function of the Ticket Manager is handling season ticket sales and fan seating requests. When the Ticket Manager receives requests for season tickets, he or she sends information to patrons on prices and available seat selections. The individual is responsible for compiling lists of season ticket holders and keeping the list up to date and in order. As many patrons purchase season tickets year after year, the Ticket Manager may also be responsible for communicating with fans and for regularly sending out brochures or flyers to them. He or she must keep track of every ticket subscription sold and the boxes or seats reserved.

Most stadiums have scheduled hours that patrons can purchase tickets prior to a game. If the individual is working a one-person ticket office, he or she is required to sell tickets personally. If the operation is larger, the Ticket Manager assigns sales duties to staff members working in the office. These individuals are responsible for selling the actual tickets, obtaining payment, and assigning seats.

The Ticket Manager must be aware of the various sections in the stadium and the pricing fees for tickets for each of these sections. In most stadiums the Ticket Manager has a layout chart of the seats. He or she marks off seats as they are purchased by fans. In some stadiums this chart is on a computer. In this manner, the Ticket Manager can see at a glance which seats are available and their location.

The Ticket Manager is also responsible for selling tickets the night or day of the event. Even if the individual is not personally selling the tickets, he or she generally is at the stadium for each game.

Handling group ticket sales is another function of the Ticket Manager. The individual is responsible for telling groups what the discounted price of tickets will be if they purchase them in blocks. He or she is also expected to arrange for the blocks of seats.

There is no room for error in the ticket office. All tickets must be accounted for. The Ticket Manager must keep track of each ticket sold by number and the payment received. Computerized ticket machines have made this task easier.

Individuals must be aware of how to put credit card purchases through the system and how to authorize ticket sales made by check. The Ticket Manager must also know how to spot counterfeit tickets.

The Ticket Manager is responsible for holding and dispersing tickets to fans who have purchased them prior to a game but have not picked them up. Another duty of the individual may be to give out complimentary tickets or passes that have been issued by team management, players, public relations, publicity, or marketing departments. These are often left at a "will call" window.

Ticket Managers must also deal with fans and patrons who have problems with their tickets and seating. These individuals might include people who have purchased tickets prior to the event and lost them, patrons who do not like the position of seats, or those who want to move to a different seat for other reasons. The Ticket Manager must remain calm and in control at all times and try to keep the fans as satisfied as possible.

Individuals in this position may be responsible to the business manager, comptroller, or general manager, depending on the structure of the particular team.

Salaries

Earnings for Ticket Managers can vary greatly. Variables include the responsibilities and experience of the individual, the size of the stadium, and the prestige of the team. While some stadiums can seat 1,500 people, others have seating capacities of more than 100,000. Ticket Managers responsible for ticket control in the 100,000-seater earn more than individuals handling smaller stadiums.

Ticket Managers working in smaller stadiums may earn approximately $27,000 per year, while individuals handling more responsibilities in larger stadiums may earn $70,000 or more.

Employment Prospects

Employment prospects are fair for Ticket Managers. Individuals may work for teams in a variety of sports. While positions may be located throughout the country, the prospects usually are better in cities hosting a large number of professional sports teams and having a number of stadiums.

Individuals may find employment working for professional major league teams, minor leagues, or colleges.

Advancement Prospects

There is no individual career path for Ticket Managers. The best prospects for advancement are for the person to locate a position with additional responsibilities and with a more prestigious team. This usually results in higher earnings.

Education and Training

As in many sports industry positions, educational requirements vary. Some positions may require an individual to have a four-year college degree. Others may require only some college experience. Still others may welcome individuals with a high school diploma and prior experience working in a box or ticket office.

Experience, Skills, and Personality Traits

A Ticket Manager must be a highly organized individual. He or she should be able to deal with many details at the same time. The Ticket Manager needs to be able to keep accurate records.

Bookkeeping and math skills are mandatory. A good memory is essential. As many box offices are now becoming computerized, it would be in the individual's best interests to have computer skills.

The Ticket Manager should have both verbal and written communication skills. He or she should also be a people person. At times the individual will have to deal with patrons who are unhappy with their seats or the prices. He or she should have the ability to remain cool and calm and be able to resolve disputes.

An ability to supervise and work well with others is necessary in this position.

Unions and Associations

There are no specific trade associations for Ticket Managers working with sports teams. Individuals may be members of organizations relevant to the particular sport they are working with.

Tips for Entry

1. Consider a summer or part-time job in a movie or theater ticket office. This will help you gain on-the-job experience.
2. Make sure that you have computer training and know how to work and feel comfortable with computer systems. Many offices are automated.

Computer literacy gives you an extra edge in the job market.

3. You may be able to gain experience in your college's activities or athletic department. See if you can locate a position working in the box office, doing clerical work in the activities office, or selling tickets to entertainment or sporting events.

4. Expect to start at the bottom of the career ladder in a professional sports team's box office. Take a job selling tickets to get your foot in the door. Learn as much as you can and wait for your opportunity to climb the career ladder.

5. Jobs in the box office may be advertised in the newspapers display or classified section in cities hosting arenas and domes. Look under heading classifications of "Box Office," "Tickets," "Sports," "Athletic Events," "Stadiums," or "Entertainment."

6. Call or write the personnel office of professional sports teams and inquire about openings in the box office or ticket department. Send your résumé and a cover letter requesting that it be held if there are no immediate openings.

7. Many professional sports teams offer internship programs. Request an assignment in ticket sales or the box office.

8. Search the Internet for job openings. Look on popular career and job sites as well as sites hosted by sports teams.

TRAVELING SECRETARY

Duties: Making travel arrangements for a professional sports team; moving the team around the country; dealing with crises and problems on the road; handling business affairs on the road

Alternate Title(s): Road Manager; Road Secretary

Salary Range: $29,000 to $125,000+

Employment Prospects: Poor

Advancement Prospects: Poor

Best Geographical Location(s) for Position: Cities hosting professional sports teams

Prerequisites:

Education or Training—Educational requirements vary; see text

Experience—Experience working with either professional sports teams or travel helpful but not always necessary

CAREER LADDER

Traveling Secretary for More Prestigious Team, Team Business Manager, or Other Administrative Position

Traveling Secretary

Traveling Secretary Intern, Professional Athlete, or Travel Agent or Escort

Special Skills and Personality Traits—Free to travel; enjoy traveling; articulate; ability to deal with a variety of people; energetic; organized; capable of dealing with many projects at one time; basic understanding of travel industry

Position Description

The Traveling Secretary working for a professional sports team is responsible for handling the operational details of the team when it is on the road. The individual makes sure that team members are as comfortable as possible and that their basic needs are met.

The Traveling Secretary is responsible for making travel arrangements for the team when it is on the road to other locations to play games. The individual is in charge of booking or chartering all buses, planes, and cars for the team. This includes transportation to get the players from a stadium to the airport, from the airport to the stadium, and to and from hotels. The Traveling Secretary either charters planes or books blocks of seats on commercial flights for the team. At times the individual also arranges for cars, limousines, or any other transportation needed to get players from point A to point B.

The Traveling Secretary must negotiate the best possible prices for the transportation as well as for hotels, motels, restaurants, and so on. He or she often must obtain price quotes from a number of different companies and is responsible for choosing the best one.

Another responsibility of the Traveling Secretary is to make sure that the entire team knows the correct meeting times and places for travel. He or she may fill

in forms or write letters or memos to alert team members of the dates, times, and locations of bus and plane travel.

The individual is ultimately responsible for making sure that all team members get where they are supposed to be on time with as little trouble as possible. For example, the Traveling Secretary is in charge of taking the team by bus to the airport so that they can fly to their destination. He or she is responsible for making sure that all their luggage gets on the plane. When the team arrives at the destination, the Traveling Secretary once again makes sure a bus is waiting to take the team either to the stadium or to the hotel. Once again, he or she must make sure that luggage gets off the plane and goes to the correct place.

The individual is responsible for making sure that each team member is assigned a hotel or motel room. He or she usually also makes arrangements for meals and distributes meal money to the team members.

The Traveling Secretary handles some of the work even before the team leaves town. A successful Traveling Secretary checks on details ahead of time, confirming that buses, planes, restaurants, and hotels are available at the right time. He or she should be able to deal with a crisis when it occurs. The individual must know what to do if a plane is late, luggage is lost, or hotel rooms are not available. He or she must also be able to deal with players who are late and miss planes or any other unexpected circumstance.

The Traveling Secretary goes with the team to all out-of-town games and to spring training sessions. He or she is responsible for moving the team throughout the country. In some situations, the individual also has additional responsibilities, such as managing the clubhouse or working with the team's ticket operation or sales campaign.

Depending on the situation and the team, the Traveling Secretary is usually responsible to either the team manager or the owner.

Hours are long. When the team travels, the individual works 24 hours a day. The job of Traveling Secretary can be rather stressful due to last-minute travel changes, people missing flights, and the like. Some people thrive on the excitement. Individuals have the opportunity of being with a sports team at all times, traveling around the country and seeing all the games of their favorite sport.

Salaries

Annual earnings for Traveling Secretaries can range from $29,000 to $125,000 or more plus benefit packages. The salaries vary greatly depending on a number of factors. These include the sport, type of league involved, and the prestige, popularity, and success of the team with which the individual is working. Other variables include the individual's experience level and responsibilities.

Employment Prospects

Employment prospects are poor. There is little turnover in this position. Once someone obtains a job, he or she seems to keep it for a long time.

While every sports team that moves around needs someone to make travel arrangements, many teams do not have an individual on staff with the job title Traveling Secretary. In many teams, the team managers, administrative assistants, or secretaries handle this job.

Most Traveling Secretary positions are held by those working in professional baseball. This is because teams in this sport move around the country more frequently and for longer periods of time than in other sports. As there are only 26 major league teams, jobs are quite limited.

Individuals may find it easier to break into this type of position working with smaller teams or minor leagues where they might also have additional responsibilities. In this way, they can obtain the needed experience as well as make important contacts.

Advancement Prospects

Advancement prospects are fair for the Traveling Secretary once he or she obtains a job. He or she may climb the career ladder by obtaining a position with a more prestigious team. Other Traveling Secretaries advance their careers by becoming a team's business manager or moving into another administrative position.

As in all jobs in the professional sports industry, it is difficult to determine the exact path of a career ladder. Depending on an individual's luck, perseverance, and qualifications, a Traveling Secretary can move to almost any position in a sports team once he or she gets a foot in the door.

Education and Training

Educational requirements for Traveling Secretaries vary from job to job. While most professional sports teams today generally prefer their Traveling Secretaries to hold a minimum of a four-year college degree, there are some teams that ask only for a high school diploma.

While a college degree may not be essential for every job, it certainly can't hurt. Competition is keen in the sports industry, and the better educated an individual is, the better his or her chances of success.

Good choices for majors for this type of position include sports management or administration or business. One of the perks of attending colleges offering majors in sports management or administration is that they often assist students in obtaining internships that in turn help the individual get his or her foot in the door with a sports team.

Experience, Skills, and Personality Traits

One of the most important traits for the Traveling Secretary to possess is the freedom and ability to travel. This is not the type of job for people who can't leave their home base or their family for extended periods of time. The individual must also enjoy traveling. The amount of time spent away from home usually depends on the sport. For example, Traveling Secretaries in the sport of baseball are probably away from home for longer periods of time than are those who work in football. It depends on the amount of time the team travels to other cities to play.

The individual should be personable and easy to talk to. He or she must deal with members of the team, management, and media as well as with people from hotels, motels, airlines, restaurants, and so on. Many people come to the Traveling Secretary with a variety of problems that they are having while on the road. These might be travel-related problems or those arising from being under pressure and away from home. The Traveling Secretary must be able to discuss the problems and try to come up with effective solutions.

The Traveling Secretary should be articulate with good communication skills. He or she will be talking to different people, making travel arrangements, and dealing with crises on the road.

The individual should have a command of math, good interpersonal skills, and understand the art of negotiation. He or she should know how to read maps, airline schedules, rental agreements, and have a basic understanding of the travel industry.

The Traveling Secretary must be very energetic. At times, he or she works long hours. When on the road, the individual is on call 24 hours a day. The Traveling Secretary must know how to arrange priorities and deal with them in a logical order.

The Traveling Secretary needs to be extremely organized and able to handle many varied details at one time. He or she must be able to remain unflustered even when a crisis arises.

Unions and Associations

Traveling Secretaries may be members of organizations relevant to the particular sports in which they are working.

Tips for Entry

1. Look for an internship or training program. These can be located through colleges with sports administration programs or by contacting teams directly.
2. Get experience making travel arrangements by getting a summer or part-time job with a travel agency.
3. Consider working as a travel escort or tour director for a tour group. It is important to obtain as much experience working with people and arranging travel plans as possible.
4. Volunteer to do the travel arrangements for an amateur or school sports team, local theater group, or band.
5. Try to work with a sports team in any capacity. Experience and contacts are very important in making it in this industry.
6. Look for jobs online. Start with some of the more popular sites such as monster.com and hotjobs.com and go from there.
7. Check out pro team Web sites. Many list openings.

EQUIPMENT MANAGER

CAREER PROFILE

Duties: Keeping equipment clean and repaired; transporting and securing the team's equipment when moving from game to game

Alternate Title(s): None

Salary Range: $27,000 to $65,000+

Employment Prospects: Fair

Advancement Prospects: Fair

Best Geographical Location(s) for Position: Cities hosting sports teams

Prerequisites:

Education or Training—Educational requirements vary; see text

Experience—Experience handling and repairing equipment specific to the sport

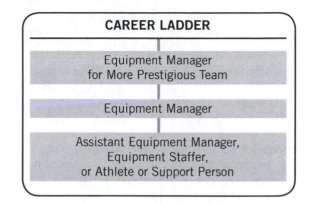

CAREER LADDER

Equipment Manager
for More Prestigious Team

Equipment Manager

Assistant Equipment Manager,
Equipment Staffer,
or Athlete or Support Person

Special Skills and Personality Traits—Ability to make minor equipment repairs; dependability; reliability; knowledge of sports equipment; detail oriented

Position Description

The team Equipment Manager is responsible for making sure that all the team's playing equipment is in shape and in proper working order. This type of position offers an individual who loves a specific sport but doesn't play well enough to become a star athlete the opportunity to feel like one of the team. He or she is required to attend practice sessions, games, and tournaments. If the team travels, the individual travels with them.

Before each game or practice session, the Equipment Manager is responsible for getting together all the equipment the athletes need to play. Equipment varies from sport to sport. The individual must check all the equipment and make sure that it is clean, in good shape, and ready for play.

If pieces of equipment are broken, the individual is responsible for either repairing them or making sure that they are repaired. If something is in poor condition and cannot be fixed, the Equipment Manager must replace it. Depending on the specific situation, he or she may just be responsible for reporting that a particular piece needs replacing or may be personally responsible for ordering or purchasing. The individual must be sure that the repair or replacement is made in time for practice and games.

During the games and/or practice sessions, if something breaks, the Equipment Manager is responsible for fixing it on the spot or having a substitute on

hand. The Equipment Manager hands out equipment to team members and coaches before each game or practice session. It is his or her duty to reclaim the equipment after each event. At this time, the Equipment Manager checks everything for wear and tear and determines how to handle any problems that may have developed.

The Equipment Manager is responsible for packing, transporting, and securing all equipment. When the team goes on the road for an "away" game, he or she travels with them carrying out the duties of the job. It is especially important for the team when it is away from home base that the Equipment Manager do his or her job professionally and correctly. It is often extremely difficult to obtain needed equipment in unfamiliar surroundings.

The Equipment Manager may deal with everyone related to the team, including athletes and support personnel. When anyone needs a specific piece of equipment or something needs repairing, he or she relies on the Equipment Manager. Depending on the specific situation, the Equipment Manager may work alone or may supervise assistants and other equipment staffers.

Equipment Managers work during all games and practice sessions as well as before and after each event collecting, cleaning, repairing, transporting, and securing all of the team's equipment. Individuals in this position may be responsible to the owner, general manager, field manager, or head coach.

Salaries

Earnings for Equipment Managers vary greatly depending on a number of variables. These include the specific team that the individual works for and its prestige and status. Other variables include the specific duties of the individual and his or her experience in the field.

As a rule, Equipment Managers working with professional teams earn more than those working with amateur and scholastic teams. Salaries for this position can run from $27,000 to $65,000 or more annually.

Employment Prospects

Employment prospects are fair for individuals willing to begin their careers as Equipment Managers with smaller, less prestigious teams. Opportunities occur less frequently for individuals seeking positions with better-known teams.

Employment possibilities may be located throughout the country with pro, semipro, amateur, and scholastic teams. Equipment Managers may have to relocate in order to find an opening in this field.

Advancement Prospects

Equipment Managers who want to climb the career ladder can usually advance by locating a similar position with a larger, more prestigious team. This, in turn, leads to higher earnings. Advancement prospects are determined by the drive and determination of the individual as well as his or her aptitude for the job. Some individuals advance their career by moving into other areas of sports administration.

Education and Training

Educational requirements for Equipment Managers vary from job to job. Some professional sports teams today prefer their Equipment Managers to hold a four-year college degree or at least have a college background. Other teams just ask applicants to have a high school diploma.

While a college degree may not be essential for every job, it certainly can't hurt. Competition is keen in the sports industry and the better educated an individual is, the better his or her chances of success.

Good choices for majors for this type of position include sports management or administration or business. One of the perks of attending colleges offering majors in sports management or administration is that they often assist students in obtaining internships that in turn help the individual get his or her foot in the door with a sports team.

Experience, Skills, and Personality Traits

A number of Equipment Managers landed their positions after actively playing on the team as an athlete. After retirement or injuries, the individual stayed with the team. Some Equipment Managers have worked themselves up from assistant equipment manager or other equipment staffer positions. Other Equipment Managers have had experience with the sport on a different level, such as coaching, training, or officiating. Still others have worked as sales representatives for sporting goods companies or as salespeople in retail shops.

Equipment Managers should have a complete understanding of the sport that they work with. Individuals also need a thorough working knowledge of all the equipment used in the particular sport and how it is used. It is essential that the individual know how to make at least minor repairs on the equipment used in the sport. The Equipment Manager should be reliable. When equipment is not in working condition, he or she must take care of the problem in a timely fashion.

The individual should also be detail oriented. He or she is responsible for making sure that all equipment is where it should be when it is required. The Equipment Manager must be able to know exactly what equipment is needed and how it is going to be packed and transported to the destination.

The Equipment Manager must also have the freedom to travel. He or she accompanies the team when it plays games away from their home turf.

Unions and Associations

Equipment Managers may belong to the Equipment Managers Association (EMA). This organization offers career guidance and support to individuals in this profession at both the amateur/scholastic level and in the pros. Individuals may also belong to organizations and trade associations directly related to the sport they are working with.

Tips for Entry

1. Volunteer to act as the Equipment Manager for one of your school's athletic teams. This is good experience and looks great on your résumé.
2. Consider attending a college offering a major in sports administration. These colleges usually coordinate internships that will help get your foot into the door of a professional team.
3. Learn everything you can about the particular sport you are interested in. Know the game, the rules, regulations, and, of course, the equipment required.

4. Try to locate internships or part-time jobs with sports teams, on the amateur level or in the pros. It doesn't matter if you can't find one in the specific sport that you're interested in. The important thing is to get experience and make contacts. Remember, always try to obtain letters of recommendation from the teams you work with.
5. Join relevant trade associations and attend their meetings. These too will help you make valuable contacts.
6. Consider getting a summer or part-time job in a sporting equipment shop. This will help familiarize you with sporting equipment.
7. Hang around sports teams, both the athletes and the support personnel. Get to know people. It's another way to make contacts.

INTERN

CAREER PROFILE

Duties: Working with a professional sports team to learn skills, get experience, and make contacts

Alternate Title(s): Trainee

Salary Range: $0 to $400+ a week or college credit

Employment Prospects: Fair

Advancement Prospects: Good

Best Geographical Location(s) for Position: Internships located throughout the country in cities that host professional sports teams

Prerequisites:

Education or Training—Undergraduate or graduate college student

Experience—College course work in subjects relevant to position the individual hopes to pursue or in sports administration

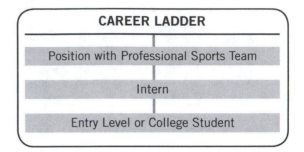

CAREER LADDER

Position with Professional Sports Team

Intern

Entry Level or College Student

Special Skills and Personality Traits—Eagerness; aggressiveness; desire to work in sports industry; good student; writing skills; communication skills; articulate; creative; innovative

Position Description

Most professional teams in baseball, football, hockey, basketball, and the like have Interns working with the team. An Intern works directly with a sports team, learning the business by gaining hands-on experience.

The individual obtains the necessary skills so that after graduation from college, he or she will be ready to enter the sports industry. The Intern is involved in actual work situations.

The Intern may work in just one specific area or may float from department to department in the team management. The individual may be assigned to or ask to work in various departments, including public relations, marketing, general management, equipment management, promotion, business, and player development.

The Intern's responsibilities vary depending on the specific internship program, the team, and the department he or she is working in. Most Interns work full time for a specified period, usually from six weeks to a school semester. In other situations, the Intern works during the specific team's season.

In most instances, professional teams find their Interns through colleges and universities that offer sports administration degrees. Part of the requirements necessary to graduate usually includes working as an Intern for a sports team or league.

Duties of the Intern depend on the department that they are assigned to. In some programs, the Interns are responsible for taking part in discussion groups, attending seminars, and completing specific projects as well as working with the team. In others, the individual is just required to fulfill his or her job-related functions. If the Intern is using the program to get school credit, he or she may be required to write a paper or do a project relating to the internship.

Interns learn how to perform tasks by actually doing them. He or she may start out with messenger duties, doing photocopying, collating, and the like. At the beginning, it might seem that working as an Intern for a sports teams is similar to performing the duties of a secretary. However, interning gives the individual needed experience in the field and a feel for how the entire industry works. As Interns learn more, they are usually allowed more leeway in their work activities.

One of the most important reasons to become an Intern is to get a foot in the door of the sports industry and make valuable contacts. A good number of Interns are hired after graduation by the team that they interned with.

Hours are usually long for Interns. The Intern who volunteers to do more than is asked is usually the one who is offered a job later. The more an Intern learns at this stage of his or her career, the better.

Interns are usually responsible to the head of the department they are working with. In other situations, a college faculty member may be responsible for Interns. The Intern often meets with supervisors to discuss problems and potential solutions of the job.

The whole idea of the internship program is to give the individual an overview of the sports industry and help him or her gain on-the-job experience. The Intern must grab every opportunity to learn as much as possible about the industry from experienced people who are working in the field.

Salaries

Compensation for Interns is usually low, if there is any monetary payment at all. Most Interns work for professional sports teams as a way of gaining experience, making important contacts, and fulfilling college requirements. College credit is often offered for the experience.

The Interns who do get paid may make a flat rate, such as $600 to $1,500, for the length of the internship. Others may be paid minimum wages or salaries up to approximately $400 plus weekly.

Employment Prospects

Employment prospects are fair for individuals who want to pursue internships with professional sports teams. While anyone can apply for an internship, most internships with major professional sports teams are given out through colleges that have sports administration degrees.

Advancement Prospects

Advancement prospects are good for Interns. Individuals who have successfully gone through intern programs usually have an easier time finding employment after graduation. Individuals who are eager to learn, aggressive, and helpful are often asked to return to the team after graduation. Other individuals find that with this added experience, coupled with contacts made during the internship, they have an easier time getting interviews and finding positions.

Education and Training

Interns working for sports teams are usually college students who are pursuing a career in the sports industry. Majors will differ depending on the specific career

choice. For example, an individual hoping to get into the publicity, promotion, or public relations field might have a major in public relations, English, or liberal arts. An individual hoping to be in some facet of the sports administration field might major in one of the sports administration programs currently being offered at colleges throughout the country.

Experience, Skills, and Personality Traits

One of the main reasons an Intern works for a sports team is to gain a degree of experience. He or she should learn as much as possible while on the job. This often means that the individual will be asked to perform menial or repetitive tasks. However, the experience value of this type of position is well worth the effort put in. Interns should be willing to do that extra amount of work without complaining.

The individual should be bright, aggressive, and articulate. He or she should have the ability to communicate well both verbally and on paper. The ability to follow instructions is imperative.

Unions and Associations

There are no specific unions or associations for Interns working with sports teams.

Tips for Entry

1. Write to professional sports teams and inquire about internships. Most have intern programs set up. In others you may have to create a position.
2. Start putting together a portfolio of your work. This will show initiative and illustrate your talents. For example, if you want to work in public relations, keep copies of all your press releases. If you are interested in box office management or promotion, volunteer your talents for school programs and build a portfolio of success stories.
3. Try to attend a college that has a sports administration or sports management program. Recruiters frequently visit these colleges, which have cooperative programs with professional sports teams.
4. Obtain letters of recommendations from professors and employers. These are a good addition to your résumé.
5. Internship programs are often available for minority students. If you are in this category, use them to your advantage.

CHEERLEADER

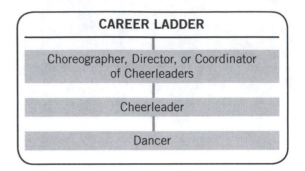

CAREER LADDER

Choreographer, Director, or Coordinator of Cheerleaders

Cheerleader

Dancer

Position Description

Cheerleaders for professional sports teams are individuals who cheer the team on and help excite the fans who have come to see a game or are watching it on television. The main function of Cheerleaders is to entertain the fans with routines during breaks in the game. Individuals may perform during quarter breaks, halftimes, and time-outs. As a rule, Cheerleaders for professional sports teams are women. They usually perform at basketball and football games.

Cheerleaders audition for spots on the squad. There is a great deal of competition for these positions. Depending on the specific team, there may be hundreds of applicants for each spot. For example, when the Los Angeles Lakers hold auditions for their cheerleaders, the Laker Girls, up to 600 women try out for the 15 openings.

Application procedures vary from team to team. Most include filling out a written application and résumé as well as an in-depth interview. All applicants must audition. Usually individuals audition first in groups. Then as the competitors are weeded out, they may also audition on their own. Auditions may take one or more days to complete.

The lucky individuals who are chosen to be Cheerleaders will attend orientation sessions where they learn what is expected of them. This includes information on rules, regulations, and policies that they must adhere to in order to stay a member of the cheerleading team. At this time, Cheerleaders also find out when they are expected at practice sessions and receive a schedule of games where they will be appearing.

Cheerleaders work hard learning the routines that have been choreographed for them. They may practice two or three times a week for three or four hours a session. The Cheerleaders must work together as a team to make everything run smoothly and for routines to appear perfect.

Individuals must be in good physical shape and well groomed at all times. They must look good out on the field. Cheerleaders are expected to perform at all games. They may put on shows anytime there is a game in their home stadium. Usually these occur during breaks in the game, such as halftimes.

Cheerleaders from some teams may also perform at other times. They may put on shows for charities, nonprofit events, public service, or television shows. Some teams like to showcase their Cheerleaders in an effort to publicize and promote the team and for other public relations reasons.

Most individuals who aspire to be Cheerleaders for professional sports teams do so for the excitement and the exposure. A number love the sport and want to be involved in the industry. Many hope that this exposure will lead to other jobs in the entertainment world, including dancing, singing, modeling, or acting in television, movies, or the theater.

There is a constant turnover of people in this profession. In some teams, individuals may have to try out for the season every year. In others, those who were members of the team and who performed well are asked back.

Cheerleaders are responsible to the coordinator or director in charge of the cheerleading team.

Salaries

It should be noted that cheerleading for a professional team is a part-time profession. Earnings for Cheerleaders vary from $35 to $350 plus per game depending on the team. Cheerleaders may earn additional money when performing in special appearances and promotions.

Generally, individuals feel that the experience and exposure gained is well worth the limited monetary returns.

Employment Prospects

Employment prospects are poor for individuals aspiring to be Cheerleaders for major league professional sports teams. Competition is keen. Cheerleaders usually have to audition every season. Individuals might find it easier to get their foot into the door by becoming a Cheerleader for a minor league team.

Advancement Prospects

Advancement prospects vary from individual to individual. Climbing the career ladder within the organization generally means becoming the director, coordinator, or choreographer of Cheerleaders.

Cheerleaders working with major league teams may get a great deal of recognition and move on to other areas of the entertainment industry. Many hope to be offered parts in television shows, movies, or commercials.

Others work with the team for a year or two and never get involved in anything else in the entertainment or sports industry. As most individuals who become Cheerleaders are dancers, many go on to other dancing roles.

Education and Training

Educational requirements vary depending on the team. Most major league teams interview individuals extensively before signing them up to be Cheerleaders. A college degree is not usually required. However, as noted previously, this is usually a part-time position. Educa-

tional requirements, therefore, depend on the individual's other occupation.

Cheerleaders do need training in dance skills. This may or may not be formal training.

Experience, Skills, and Personality Traits

As a rule, Cheerleaders are required to have extensive dance experience. The amount of experience differs with each team. Some teams require a minimum of eight years of dance experience.

Individuals must be able to follow, imitate, and remember dance routines. Knowledge of choreography may be useful.

Individuals should be energetic and physically fit. They need to be well groomed and have a pleasing appearance. Cheerleaders should be personable. They should have bubbly, exciting, and enthusiastic personalities. They need to be able to excite fans and entertain them.

Cheerleaders should be comfortable performing in front of large audiences. Individuals represent the team when they are working as well as when they are off the field. They should know how to carry themselves. Good verbal communications are imperative.

Unions and Associations

There is no specific trade association for Cheerleaders working with professional sports teams. Individuals may belong to associations related to various forms of dancing or choreography.

Tips for Entry

1. Take as many types of dance, aerobics, and choreography classes and workshops as you can. This will get you used to following other people's routines.
2. Watch the routines of dancers and cheerleaders and try to follow them. Then practice as much as you can.
3. Contact professional sports teams to find out whom you need to talk to or when they will be holding auditions for Cheerleaders.
4. Bring a résumé with you to auditions as well as an 8-by-10-inch glossy photograph of yourself if you have one. Remember to find out ahead of time what to wear or bring to the audition.
5. Most professional sports teams require their Cheerleaders to be at least 18 years old.
6. Persevere. If you do not make the cheerleading squad the first time, you can try again next year.

SPORTS BUSINESS AND ADMINISTRATION

PROFESSIONAL SPORTS AGENT

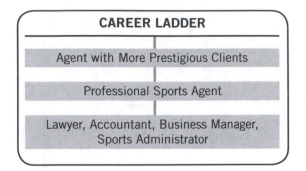

CAREER LADDER

Agent with More Prestigious Clients

Professional Sports Agent

Lawyer, Accountant, Business Manager, Sports Administrator

Position Description

A Professional Sports Agent works on behalf of professional athletes much as a booking agent works with entertainers. The individual in this position acts as an athlete's representative. When Agents work for athletes in this capacity, the athlete is called the client. The Agent tries to secure the best possible financial and benefit package for his or her client.

The Professional Sports Agent may function in a number of different ways for his or her client. To begin with, the Agent must locate a team for the client to work with. Usually by the time an athlete acquires an Agent, at least one if not more teams are bidding for the athlete's services.

Almost everyone is aware of athletes who receive huge salaries and contracts. These million-dollar salaries are usually the result of an Agent's work. The Agent acts as an intermediary and negotiator between the athlete and the team owner or general manager. He or she negotiates the best possible salary and contract for the athlete.

Some athletes retain their Agent to do other types of work. For example, the individual may also act as a financial Agent. He or she may recommend various investments to the athlete in order to help the individual build a solid financial base and secure tax advantages.

Agents may also locate product endorsements for their clients. Product endorsements mean that the athlete appears in an advertisement or commercial or endorses a product or service for a company. Many people respect the ideas and opinions of their sports idols. Obtaining a sports superstar's endorsement can mean an increase in product sales. As a result, the business of endorsements can be quite lucrative for the athlete. A part of the Agent's duties in this area is to make sure that the products endorsed will not harm the athlete's image but fit in with it. For example, most athletes will not endorse any brand of cigarette. It would ruin their health-conscious, athletic image.

Sports Agents may work for a variety of clients. They may, for instance, represent athletes, sports officials, coaches, managers, and members of sports-oriented organizations and trade associations. Most Sports Agents have more than one client. Agents must be sure, however, that they do not represent conflicting parties. Agents may also work with law firms, business management companies, certified public accountants, and management firms that specialize in sports.

Most athletes who have attained superstar status find that an Agent can represent them better than they themselves can. Agents who have both law and accounting backgrounds are familiar with contracts, legal problems, laws, and tax implications.

Sports Agents often do a great deal of socializing within the sports industry. Through these activities, they can keep up with the sports scene. Sports Agents do not work a nine-to-five day. They may go into the office early in the morning and stay late attending meetings and negotiating sessions.

Sports Agents are usually responsible directly to their clients. If the Agent is working for a firm, he or she may be responsible to the company's owner, manager, or director.

Salaries

It is difficult to determine earnings for Sports Agents. Most are paid on a percentage basis—generally a percentage of the client's income. Depending on the specific arrangements, the Agent may obtain a percentage of the client's negotiated salary alone or of all monies generated. The individual might receive a percentage of monies earned from endorsements, autobiographies, investments, and the like.

Percentages also vary from 5% to 20%. Most agents receive an average of 10%.

Instead of charging a percentage, some Agents charge clients on an hourly rate for services rendered. This can range from $200 to $600 an hour or more. Other Agents may charge their clients a flat fee; some use a combination of methods.

Some Sports Agents working for companies or firms receive a set salary or a salary plus either a commission from all clients they bring in to the agency or a percentage of monies earned by specific clients.

Successful Agents may have earnings ranging from $200,000 to $10 million or more. It must be kept in mind that many major athletes currently receive multibillion-dollar contracts for their services. Ten percent of this amount can make a Sports Agent very wealthy.

Employment Prospects

Individuals who aspire to be Sports Agents and who are highly qualified through a solid educational background will have a fair chance at locating a position. Although jobs may be located throughout the country, the best bet for finding a position of this type is in the major entertainment capitals, such as New York or Los Angeles.

Individuals may find a position with a law firm that specializes in the representation of athletes, a talent agency that has star athletes among its clients, or a business management firm.

Aspiring Agents may also find their own clients and be self-employed, running their own agency.

Advancement Prospects

Advancement prospects are fair for individuals who have a lot of drive, determination, and skill. Agents climb the career ladder by obtaining either more clients or more prestigious ones. Those who build a track record for themselves by negotiating better contracts or endorsements will find clients coming to them.

Education and Training

The most successful Agents in the sports field are those who have prepared themselves thoroughly for the job. An undergraduate college background is necessary. Graduate work, such as law school, will help immensely. Good majors include accounting, business, or sports administration. A law degree is even better.

Seminars and workshops in different facets of sports administration, business, and entertainment law can be useful. There are also a number of courses and seminars specifically geared toward Sports Agents.

Special Requirements

While individuals do not need to be certified to become Sports Agents, they do need to be certified to represent athletes from either the National Basketball Association (NBA), the National Football League (NFL), Major League Baseball (MLB), or the National Hockey League (NHL). Each league provides its own certification and requirements.

Experience, Skills, and Personality Traits

Professional Sports Agents must be excellent negotiators. Much of the job revolves around negotiation. Sales ability is another good attribute. The individual in effect is selling his or her client's services, talent, and image.

Most Agents are aggressive in a nonthreatening way. They must work constantly to obtain more money for their clients, better contracts, endorsements, and the like.

Agents should be able to work under extreme pressure and deal well with stress. Many clients have big egos and think they are worth more money than they receive. The Agent must be able to work under these conditions and still keep plugging away.

Unions and Associations

There are no specific trade associations for Sports Agents. Depending on their background, individuals may belong to either law and/or accounting organizations, which will provide seminars and professional guidance.

Tips for Entry

1. Try to obtain an internship working with a professional team in any administrative capacity. This will help you get hands-on experience in the field and help you make important contacts.
2. See if you can find a part-time or summer job working with a Professional Sports Agent. It doesn't matter if the financial compensation is limited. The experience will be worth it.
3. If you can't locate a Sports Agent, consider working with a booking agent, a business manager, or literary agent. Working with individuals whose job it is to sell someone else's talents will give you an idea of how the business works.
4. Attend relevant workshops and seminars. These will give you needed training and help you make contacts.

SPORTS STATISTICIAN

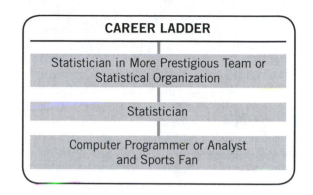

CAREER LADDER

Statistician in More Prestigious Team or
Statistical Organization

Statistician

Computer Programmer or Analyst
and Sports Fan

Position Description

A Sports Statistician collects data and analyzes and
interprets it. The Statistician's job is to count how many
times something takes place and keep track of all the
figures. While the actual job has been around for some
time, it is becoming more visible with the emergence of
computers.

Anyone who has watched an athletic event on television has probably seen the work of Statisticians. Baseball box scores are an example of statistics gathered by
a Statistician. The number of punches a fighter throws
at an opponent and the number that have landed are
examples of boxing statistics.

Many commentators and announcers use these statistics, or "stats," when discussing the progress of a particular game. As an event progresses, the Statistician updates
the game statistics and the various players' activities.

Statisticians may have varied duties depending on
their specific work situation. At the bottom work level,
the Statistician gathers raw data. He or she may then
move up the career ladder and program the data into a
computer or analyze it.

Statisticians working for a sports team or a private
sports statistics bureau may gather information and
figures on each player in a game as well as for the
entire team. This information may then be fed to the
announcer who is commenting on the game. Statistics
may also be given to the press and the rest of the media.
This is how most daily newspapers get the statistical

data they print about games. Information may also be
given to fans in game programs.

The Statistician also gathers statistics for the entire
playing season. This information may be used in a
number of ways. The publicity department may use
the data in a media book for fans and the press. The
information may also be used to determine the value
of each player. This is important in deciding who might
be traded and what kind of financial contract an athlete
should be awarded.

The player relations committee uses statistical analysis to determine what skills a team will lose if a certain player is traded. This analysis also helps determine
what playing assets a team will receive if it signs a new
athlete.

As noted previously, most of the professional Sports
Statistician's work is done on computers. The Statistician must know what to look for in the game and then
must know how to input the information into the computer. He or she may then analyze this data.

Football statistics are compiled and analyzed to
ascertain the statistics for each league for the year. Boxing Statisticians may show the stats of a fighter throw-
ing hundreds of punches in a bout but landing only a
small percentage of punches. In the same vein, a baseball Statistician may show one player hitting the ball a
great number of times but never getting a run. Another
ball player may have fewer hits but ones that are more
important to the game.

Statisticians are used for a variety of reasons. Some coaches feel that being aware of statistical information can help team members play better. Knowing a competitor's statistics can help them plan offense and defense. Fans are also interested in the numbers and like to know much of the trivia that goes with the game.

Individuals may work directly for sports teams, for television or radio stations or wire services, or for private statistician organizations. Sports Statisticians may work in almost any sport—baseball, football, hockey, boxing, basketball, and others.

Statisticians usually specialize in one or two sports. Individuals must have a complete knowledge of the sport that they will be gathering and compiling statistics in.

Statisticians working with sports teams are usually part of the publicity department. Those working for private companies may work with sportswriters, announcers, or directly with professional teams.

Salaries

Salaries for Statisticians may range from $25,000 to $95,000 plus depending on a number of factors. Variables include the type of organization the individual works for, its prestige, size, and location. Other variables include the duties, skills, and experience level of the Statistician.

Generally, those who are responsible for just gathering the raw data for statistics are paid less than those who do the computer programming and analysis.

Employment Prospects

Employment prospects are fair for full-time Sports Statisticians. Individuals may find work with professional teams, semiprofessional teams, television or radio stations, wire services, sports-oriented Web sites, or private sports statistical organizations.

Positions with network television and radio stations are usually located in cities where the networks are headquartered, such as New York or Los Angeles. Smaller cities offer opportunities for local or regional broadcasting.

Advancement Prospects

Advancement for a Statistician may mean he or she locates a similar position with a more prestigious team or private statistical organization. This is often difficult, but not impossible. Individuals must exhibit a great deal of skill, drive, and determination to move ahead and be successful in this profession.

Some Statisticians advance their careers by locating a position in sports-oriented public relations, publicity,

journalism, or broadcasting. Becoming a Statistician may give them entry into that field.

Education and Training

Most Statisticians are required to have at least a two-year degree. Many positions require a four-year college degree. Good course choices for those aspiring to be Statisticians are math, computer science, and technology. Classes in various sports studies may also be helpful.

Those who wish to advance their career into another field may be wise to take communications courses, English, journalism, public relations, and sports administration.

Experience, Skills, and Personality Traits

To be successful today, Sports Statisticians need to have a total working knowledge of computers. Individuals should know how to perform data entry as well as how to program and analyze data.

Statisticians should have analytical minds. Individuals need to have good math and arithmetic skills. The ability to add a list of numbers quickly and accurately is essential.

A knowledge and understanding of the sport that the individual is working in is necessary. Statisticians who are experts in more than one sport may find additional opportunities for work.

Unions and Associations

There is no specific trade association for Sports Statisticians. Individuals may, however, belong to organizations specific to the sport and situation they are working in. For example, Statisticians working in the baseball field may belong to the Baseball Writers Association of America (BBWAA). Other individuals may belong to the National Sportscasters and Sportswriters Association (NSSA), the Professional Football Writers of America (PFWA), the Professional Hockey Writers' Association (PHWA), or any other relevant organization.

Tips for Entry

1. Practice doing stats for your school sports teams. It will give you good hands-on experience.
2. Take as many computer courses as you can. This will help you get a step ahead of others competing for jobs.
3. Know everything there is to know about the sport you want to work in. Read books and periodicals about the game, its history, rules, and regulations.

4. Send your résumé to sports teams, wire services, and professional sports teams. Ask that it be kept on file if there are no current openings. Keep checking back. Don't wait for them to call you.
5. Job openings may be advertised in the classified section of newspapers in areas hosting professional sports teams or television stations. Look under headings such as "Professional Sports Team," "Pro Sports Team," "Sports," "Statistician," or "Television Sports Statistician."

SPORTS INDUSTRY PUBLICIST

CAREER PROFILE

Duties: Creating positive, exciting image for athletes; developing and writing press releases, press kits, informational sheets, and feature stories; handling media

Alternate Title(s): Sports Publicist; Publicist; Sports-Oriented Publicist

Salary Range: $25,000 to $200,000+

Employment Prospects: Fair

Advancement Prospects: Fair

Best Geographical Location(s) for Position: Large cities hosting many professional sports teams and sports events

Prerequisites:

Education or Training—Four-year college degree required for most positions

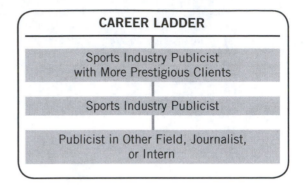

CAREER LADDER

Sports Industry Publicist with More Prestigious Clients

Sports Industry Publicist

Publicist in Other Field, Journalist, or Intern

Experience—Public relations, publicity, or journalism experience preferred

Special Skills and Personality Traits—Public relations skills; communication skills; articulate; creative; detail oriented

Position Description

The main function of a Publicist specializing in the sports industry is to create a positive, exciting image for an individual athlete, team, or sports-related event. The Publicist must create and develop methods to get the client's name better known and keep the individual's image in the spotlight.

A growing number of athletes in a variety of sports have become superstars. While this is due in part to their athletic talents, an exciting, diversified image is a great help. There have always been a few sports figures capable of drawing a great deal of recognition. Today the number is increasing. Part of this fame and superstardom may be attributed to an athlete's Publicist.

A Publicist in the sports industry may work for a public relations or publicity firm specializing in sports figures or an entertainment-oriented firm that handles sports stars. Individuals may also be self-employed and have one or more sports-oriented clients.

Professional athletes use the services of a private Publicist or publicity firm for a number of reasons. Individuals who are part of a team often want more publicity centered on them, and this requires more attention than they can obtain from the team publicist. Another reason for personal publicity may be that athletes who are recognized personalities can demand higher salaries. They may also be picked up to do lucra-

tive advertising product endorsements or might even diversify into acting.

After obtaining a client, one of the first things the Publicist does is to determine with the individual what type of image he or she would like to attain. The Publicist must also learn about the public's current perception of the client. The individual can then work on developing strategies and a publicity campaign to achieve the goals set forth.

Most Publicists try to keep their client's name and face in front of the public in a positive manner and as often as possible. Since the athlete may be visible only from an athletic standpoint, the Publicist has to come up with other interesting ways to have his or her client viewed.

This can be achieved in any of a number of ways, depending on the creativity of the Publicist. Publicists use promotions and publicity campaigns to attract attention. They may, for example, have the athlete appointed as the national chairperson of a major charity event. They may exploit a budding dating relationship between an athlete and another superstar. They constantly try to develop ideas to help bring the athlete's face and image to the attention of the media and public. This creates public interest in the athlete and helps push him or her to superstardom.

The professional sports industry is a major force in the entertainment world. As a result, the media usually follow stories and news developments about athletes.

The Publicist working in the sports industry works with the sports news media, advising them of new developments in the athlete's career. He or she also deals with newspapers and magazine editors and producers and reporters for television, cable, and radio stations outside the sports industry.

The Publicist arranges print interviews and guest appearances on television and radio talk, variety, news, and sports shows for clients. He or she also develops feature story ideas for both sports editors and the general media. When the Sports Industry Publicist sets up appearances and interviews for clients, he or she often accompanies them.

Sports Industry Publicists frequently receive calls from the sports media asking specific questions or requesting interviews with the athlete. If the athlete has already attained superstar status, the Publicist acts as a buffer between the individual and the media. He or she decides which interviews will be beneficial and which will not.

The Publicist also determines which public appearances the client will accept and which to reject. In rejecting requests, he or she must write letters of regret with explanations that do not antagonize anyone.

Another function of the Publicist is to write and develop press releases, biographies, informational sheets, and press kits, on a variety of subjects and then send them to the media from a prepared media list. This list includes names and addresses of editors, writers, producers, etc., in both the general press and sports-oriented media.

The Sports Publicist also arranges and conducts press conferences when important events are occurring in the athlete's life. He or she must be sure to schedule these conferences only when special events are occurring. If not, the press will not attend after the first conference. The individual may also arrange for press passes, press credentials, and seating for members of the media when the athlete is playing.

Publicists work long hours. Most of the time their job does not stop when they leave the office. They often think about campaign strategies and new ideas for clients, even at home. Individuals may also have late meetings and attend weekend and evening events. The Publicist may be responsible to his or her supervisor or directly to the client, depending on the situation.

Salaries

Salaries for Sports Industry Publicists vary greatly depending on a number of variables. These include the type of job setting the individual is working in and his or her experience level and responsibilities. Earnings may also depend on the specific clients and their publicity needs.

Salaries can range from $25,000 to $200,000 plus. Individuals with limited experience earn between $25,000 and $40,000. Those who have a proven track record and a great deal of responsibility have salaries ranging from $40,000 to $100,000 or more. Publicists working with one or more superstar clients can earn $200,000 and more a year.

Employment Prospects

Employment prospects are fair for Sports Industry Publicists. Individuals may work for athletes in any sport. They may work on their own or for sports-oriented public relations and publicity firms. Publicists may also be retained to handle the publicity for sports-related events. Positions may be located throughout the country. Individuals do, however, have an easier time in larger cities hosting many different sports teams and events.

Advancement Prospects

Advancement prospects for Sports Industry Publicists are fair. An individual can advance his or her career in this profession by obtaining more prestigious clients. Publicists who are creative and build their clients' image will have no problem advancing.

Some Publicists working for firms may climb the career ladder by opening their own firm. This move means that the individual has to obtain his or her own clients.

Should the athlete a Publicist is working with become an overnight superstar as a result of unexpectedly winning a tournament or championship, the Publicist's image is boosted along with the athlete's.

Education and Training

Individuals aspiring to work as Sports Industry Publicists should obtain a minimum of a four-year college degree. Good choices for majors include public relations, marketing, English, liberal arts, communications, journalism, and sports administration.

Additional courses, workshops and seminars in writing, marketing, media exposure, publicity, public relations, and sports marketing are also useful.

Experience, Skills, and Personality Traits

Publicists working in the sports industry may have worked in public relations or publicity or marketing in other fields prior to attaining their current job. Individuals might also have worked as journalists in either broadcast or print media. Others interned or had assistant positions working with full-fledged Sports Publicists, public relations firms, or professional teams.

The Sports Industry Publicist should have at least a basic understanding of the sport that the client plays and the industry. This will make it easier to talk and write about the field.

The Publicist must have excellent writing skills. He or she needs to be able to write creative, factual, concise, and interesting press releases, biographies, fact sheets, and feature stories. The individual needs to be able to implement a full range of public relations and publicity tactics to promote his or her clients.

Creative people usually make the most successful Publicists. There are hundreds of Publicists pushing their clients. The ones who develop creative strategies and campaigns are the ones who get the press.

The Publicist needs the ability to communicate well verbally. He or she must be as comfortable speaking to a large group of people as he or she is speaking to one person on the phone.

Publicists need to be nonthreateningly aggressive and persuasive. Individuals should also be likable and personable. Reporters and journalist should be comfortable talking to the Publicist. The better the relationship that the Publicist has developed with the media, the more press he or she will be able to obtain for a client.

Sports Industry Publicists must be detail oriented. They work on a great many projects at one time. Individuals also need the ability to deal with celebrities without being starstruck.

Unions and Associations

Sports Industry Publicists may belong to a number of trade associations that provide education, training, and professional guidance. These might include National Sportscasters and Sportswriters Association (NSSA), the Public Relations Society of America (PRSA), Women In Communications (WIC), and the National Federation of Press Women (NFPW). Individuals may also belong to organizations that are specific to their client's sport.

Tips for Entry

1. Work on your school newspaper to get experience writing.
2. Contact public relations firms for summer or part-time jobs. Hands-on experience will be helpful for the training aspect and look good on your résumé.
3. Try to locate an internship with a professional sports team or a public relations firm specializing in entertainment or sports industry PR.
4. Consider a summer or part-time job as a sports reporter for a local newspaper. Obtain as much experience writing as you can.
5. Join trade associations and attend their meetings. They will help you make valuable contacts and may offer assistance locating a job.
6. Openings may be advertised in the classified section of newspapers in areas hosting professional sports teams.
7. Job openings may be located online via the Internet. Check out any of the major career sites on the Web. Type in keywords such as "sports" and "sports publicist."

ACCOUNT EXECUTIVE FOR SPECIAL-RISK INSURANCE (SPORTS, ATHLETICS, AND RECREATION)

CAREER PROFILE

Duties: Writing special-risk policies for health clubs, spas, gymnastics schools, karate and judo schools, exercise clubs, athletes, sports complexes, etc.; pricing policies; typing policies; answering phone calls; providing insurance certificates

Alternate Title(s): Assistant to Producer

Salary Range: $25,000 to $85,000+

Employment Prospects: Fair

Advancement Prospects: Good

Best Geographical Location(s) for Position: Positions may be located throughout the country

Prerequisites:

    Education or Training—High school diploma minimum requirement; some positions may require college background or diploma

    Experience—Experience in insurance helpful

    Special Skills and Personality Traits—Knowledge of insurance industry; knowledge of athletics, sports, and/or recreational clubs or schools; selling skills; pleasant personality; communication skills; phone skills

    Special Requirements—Licensing may be required in some states

CAREER LADDER

```
Producer in Special-Risk Insurance
            |
Account Executive for Special-Risk
Insurance in Sports or Athletics
            |
Secretary to Account Executive
or Account Executive
in Other Facet of Insurance Industry
```

Position Description

Every company that opens for business stands the risk of having people injure themselves while on their property. Most companies buy liability and/or comprehensive insurance policies to make sure they are covered financially in case of an accident. Sports facilities such as exercise clubs, spas, gymnastics schools, health clubs, and dance and exercise schools need insurance too. In most instances, insurance on these types of facilities are called special-risk policies. Other special-risk policies in sports may be written for sports teams, individual athletes, athletic events, sports arenas, and coliseums.

The person who helps sell and write this type of insurance is called the Account Executive. He or she works in the special-risk division of an insurance agency. This division may specialize specifically in the sports industry or may handle a variety of special-risk needs, depending on the size of the organization.

The Account Executive works with an individual called the producer. Together the two will write insurance policies. Special-risk policies may be purchased for a number of different reasons. Facilities such as health clubs, exercise or dance schools, and the like may buy property and casualty insurance. This means that the facility is covered for liability and related coverage in case of an accident or injury that was either directly or indirectly their fault. Having coverage means that if an accident occurs, the policy pays for costs incurred as a result of the accident. Professional sports teams may buy an insurance policy for their players in case they are injured, incapacitated, or die. Sports complexes may buy a special policy for an outdoor event in case it rains. Organizations running golf tournaments with large prizes, such as a new car for making a hole in one, may even purchase a special policy that covers costs if a player actually does make the hole in one. The policy pays for the car if the prize is won.

When an individual needs this type of policy, he or she calls an insurance agency that handles special-risk policies. The Account Executive talks with the individual, asks questions regarding the requirements of the policy, and secures information about the facility, athlete, or event being covered. The Account Executive may also ask the person to fill in forms or questionnaires in order to acquire as much information as possible.

The Account Executive and/or the producer then work on pricing the policy. This may be done in a number of ways depending on the situation, including using a percentage of gross sales and square footage of a facility. In special-risk policies for athletes, factors determining the price or premium might include the athlete's earnings, health, and duties within the scope of his or her job. The Account Executive and/or producer may then use published rates or simplified rates to calculate the cost of a policy. This price, which is called a premium, is then quoted to the individual. Premiums on high-risk policies can be expensive, depending on the specific risk involved. In insurance, the word *risk* refers to the probability that an accident or injury might occur as well as what the costs to take care of it if it did occur would be.

The Account Executive may have other duties and responsibilities, depending on the specific job. He or she is expected to answer phone calls and talk to new customers as well as established accounts. The individual is responsible for pricing policies, either with the producer or on his or her own, depending on the structure of the company and the Account Executive's experience. The Account Executive is required to type new price quotes for customers and renew quotes as they come due.

One of the functions of the Account Executive is to talk to customers and answer questions. Customers may want explanations of why the premium is priced the way it is, what they are covered for, or how to handle a claim. Account Executives, therefore, must understand as much as possible about the policy and what is being insured.

Most Account Executives working in this field generally learn as they go from their superiors. Knowledge of health clubs, gymnastics schools, exercise clubs, karate schools, spas, or whatever facet of the recreation or sports industry the individual is working with is essential.

As the Account Executive gains experience and knowledge in both the sports field and the insurance industry, he or she learns more about pricing policies, special risks, and how to make sound judgments.

The Account Executive is called upon when customers need endorsements or additions to their policies. These endorsements may be required for any number of reasons where additional risks might be added to current policies. Additions may include the installation of new equipment, such as a swimming pool, or a major event being planned. The Account Executive also is expected to supply customers with certificates proving that they are insured. These may be necessary before a spa, club, or school opens up or before tickets can be sold to an event.

The Account Executive usually has normal working hours. He or she may work overtime when projects and special work must be completed. The individual usually is directly responsible to the producer he or she works with.

Salaries

Salaries for Account Executives working in special-risk situations vary depending on their experience level, responsibilities, drive, and determination. In addition to the regular salaries, many individuals earn bonuses when they bring in extra clients or write policies above those that they are expected to handle. Annual earnings can range from $25,000 to $85,000 plus.

Employment Prospects

Employment prospects in special-risk insurance in the sports, athletic, and recreational fields are fair and are improving every day. With more health and fitness clubs opening around the country as well as schools specializing in gymnastics, judo, karate, and the like, there will be a greater need for insurance. Athletes are also receiving record salaries and teams need to protect their investments.

Individuals may have to relocate in order to find a company handling special-risk sports insurance.

Advancement Prospects

Advancement prospects are good for individuals who are experienced and learn the business. The next step up the career ladder for most individuals is to become an insurance producer.

Individuals may stay in the facet of the industry handling special-risk policies in the sports, recreation, and athletic fields or may move into selling policies in unrelated areas.

Education and Training

Educational requirements vary from job to job and state to state. A high school diploma is the minimum requirement in most jobs. Some positions may require a college background or degree. Once on the job, individuals generally will receive either on-the-job training or be sent to special classes.

Special Requirements

Depending on the specific state requirements and the individual's duties, he or she may also be required to obtain an insurance agent's license or insurance broker's license. These are obtained by completing educational requirements from an approved insurance school. In some situations, continuing education, workshops, and seminars may also be necessary.

Experience, Skills, and Personality Traits

The individual in this type of job must be familiar with the insurance business. Most, but not all, individuals working in special-risk insurance have had experience in other facets of the industry. Knowledge of the sports, fitness, and health industries is also useful. For example, an individual who must quote a price on a policy for a health club will be able to do a better job if he or she knows the types of accidents that can occur in that type of facility.

Account Executives must be personable, pleasant, and easy to talk with. They need sales skills. What they do, in essence, after pricing a policy is sell it. A customer who feels more comfortable with the person he or she is talking to is more likely to purchase a policy with the company.

Communication skills, both verbal and written, are necessary. The Account Executive also should have good phone skills. A great deal of his or her work is done via the telephone.

Typing and/or word processing skills are other important skills for the Account Executive. The individual should be detail oriented and be able to deal with many different projects without getting flustered.

Unions and Associations

There are no trade associations specific to Account Executives handling special-risk insurance in the sports, recreation, and athletic fields. Individuals may, however, be members of groups such as the National Health Club Association (NHCA) and/or national and state insurance associations.

Tips for Entry

1. If you are still in school, consider a part-time or summer job working in an insurance agency. It doesn't matter what department you work in as long as you obtain experience.
2. Contact your state to find out what type of licensing requirements are required for agents and brokers in your area.
3. Talk to your local insurance agent to find out if he or she can recommend a company that handles special risk policies in the sports industry.
4. Insurance agencies may advertise openings in the newspaper's classified or display section. While the position may not be in special-risk policies, it may give you valuable experience and the opportunity to make important contacts. Look under heading classification of "Insurance," "Selling," "Special Risk," "Brokers," or "Agents."
5. Many insurance agencies have their own training programs. This will help you get your foot in the door of the insurance industry. You can then move on to special-risk departments.
6. Job possibilities may be located online via the Internet. Check out the major career and job sites on the Web to get started on your search. Type in keywords or categories such as "insurance," "sports," or "athletics."

SPORTS EVENT COORDINATOR

Duties: Handling the logistics necessary to put together a sporting event; overseeing details of a sporting event

Alternate Title(s): Event Coordinator

Salary Range: $27,000 to $130,000+

Employment Prospects: Fair

Advancement Prospects: Fair

Best Geographical Location(s) for Position: Areas hosting many facilities, such as arenas, stadiums, and coliseums

Prerequisites:

Education or Training—Four-year college degree required for most positions

Experience—Experience in event coordination, publicity, public relations, or marketing helpful

CAREER LADDER

Sports Event Coordinator at Larger, More Prestigious Facility or Sports Event Producer

Sports Event Coordinator

Publicist, Special Event Coordinator, Intern, or College Student

Special Skills and Personality Traits—Detail oriented; organized; good written and verbal communication skills; ability to foresee problems; coordination and planning skills

Position Description

The Olympic Games, the Super Bowl, and the World Series are major events in the world of sports. Other popular events might include the Kentucky Derby or a heavyweight championship fight. These events are not thrown together haphazardly. Each detail is worked out ahead of time to make sure things will go smoothly. The individual hired to do this is called the Sports Event Coordinator.

Sports Event Coordinators handle the logistics necessary when putting together a sporting event. Their main function is to oversee all the details that make the show a success.

Some Sports Event Coordinators work directly for the facility. Others are employed by promoters. They may work in a variety of situations and facilities from arenas, auditoriums, stadiums, and coliseums to hotels and resorts.

Many facilities hold diverse events on their premises throughout the year, including concerts, ballets, operas, symphonies, circuses, trade shows and conventions, and sporting events. Each type of show requires special considerations to ensure that it will be successful. Individuals may be responsible just for the coordination of sporting events or may be expected to handle the coordination of all events hosted in the specific arena or venue. Duties vary depending on the situation in which each individual works.

The Sports Event Coordinator may specialize in the coordination of programs in one specific sport or many. Opportunities might include coordination of amateur, scholastic, or professional events in tennis, bowling, or golf tournaments, marathons, dog or cat shows, boxing or wrestling events, or auto or motorcycle racing. Other opportunities might occur in baseball, hockey, football, soccer, basketball, and swimming.

One of the first things the Sports Event Coordinator must do is determine the scope of the event. He or she must find out how popular a program might be and the intended audience. If the Coordinator is working in a facility that regularly holds such events, this will be easier. Football and baseball stadiums, for example, usually have an idea of which games are going to be well attended before the event. The individual must know ahead of time if the facility will be large enough to handle the intended crowd. If it is not, he or she may be expected to search for a larger arena.

Once this has been accomplished, the individual must develop a plan of action. He or she works with the promoter, box office and ticket manager, public relations and marketing people, security, staff members, judges, officials, and others. The Coordinator may meet with the various department heads or directors to find out what possible problems might occur and how to head them off.

For some events that are bigger than usual, more rest room facilities, security, and food concessions than are normally required may have to be added. The individual must constantly try to foresee problems and situations that might occur and deal with them ahead of time. In this manner, things will probably go smoothly the day of the event.

The Coordinator is responsible for making sure that there is sufficient parking for the anticipated crowd. He or she may also develop routes to assist fans entering and exiting the stadium. While doing this, the Coordinator may work with the local police department and local media advising them of crowd situations, potential traffic tie-ups, and the like.

Depending on the particular situation, the Sports Event Coordinator may be expected to monitor what people in other departments are doing. He or she may supervise the public relations, advertising, and marketing efforts as well as work with the media. At times, the individual may function as a public relations person. He or she may call the media and arrange interviews, articles, feature stories, photo opportunities, and broadcasts. The Coordinator may have to set up and execute press conferences, cocktail parties, luncheons, and dinners. In other situations, the Coordinator may act as an intermediary between all the departments to make sure everything that is supposed to get done is completed.

The Coordinator may have additional duties depending on the specific event he or she is working with. For example, the Event Coordinator in a major boxing show is often responsible for making sure that a number of sets of new boxing gloves are delivered to the stadium. He or she must also make sure that a regulation scale is available at the prefight weigh-in. Those coordinating marathons must deal with the details of getting runners their identifying numbers, starting the race, checkpoints, finish lines, winners, and prizes. Those working in tennis may be responsible for officials, seating arrangements, and opponents. Each sport has its own set of special details to contend with.

In some cases, the Coordinator may be expected to handle transportation, food, and accommodations for athletes, officials, support staff, and other members of the production team. He or she is responsible for checking out all the little details that make the difference between a successful event and an unsuccessful one.

The individual may be expected to review what might be considered small things, such as checking on the temperature of the arenas and/or the playing or competing area. While this might seem insignificant to some, a playing area that is too hot or too cold may dramatically affect the way a team plays. The Coordina-

tor may also be responsible for making sure that there are a sufficient number of dressing rooms for the competitors and staff members and that they are properly equipped.

If the event is to be televised, the Coordinator works with the television production people, helping them to set up cameras and obtain the proper electric, lighting, and sound. He or she may or may not be responsible for coordinating any interviews or other media opportunities.

The Coordinator may be responsible for checking to see that the correct medical personnel and equipment are on hand and that all personnel are stationed in the correct locations. The individual is expected to do the same with the security people.

One of the most important functions of the Sports Event Coordinator is dealing with problems as they occur. Problems might arise at any time, from the inception of the idea of the promotion through the conclusion of the event. The individual must be able to deal with a variety of situations in a calm, cool, and collected manner.

This is an ideal type of situation for individuals who are both capable of and enjoy taking control of a situation. The Coordinator works with a sporting event from the very beginning to the very end. Hours are long in this type of job. The Sports Event Coordinator is expected to be present at all events. In addition to regular daytime hours, individuals may work in the evenings and on weekends.

The individual is often judged by his or her last event. If it is a success, the Coordinator is deemed successful; if it is a failure, so may be the Coordinator in the eyes of his or her superiors. The Sports Event Coordinator may be responsible to the promoter, facility general manager, or owner, depending on the structure of organization.

Salaries

Earnings for Sports Event Coordinators vary from job to job depending on a number of factors. These include the geographic location of the arena, its prestige, and the type of events presented. Other variables may include whether the individual is working directly for the arena or for a promoter and his or her responsibilities and experience level.

Sports Event Coordinators have salaries ranging from $27,000 to $130,000 plus depending on the specific job. Individuals just starting out with little experience or those working for smaller arenas are on the lower end of the pay scale. Those working in more prestigious venues or for promoters of major events are on the higher end.

Employment Prospects

Employment prospects are fair for individuals willing to start in this profession in smaller facilities. Jobs may be located throughout the country in arenas, stadiums, auditoriums, and coliseums. Positions may also be located at larger hotels and resorts that regularly host sporting events. Sports promoters may offer other employment possibilities.

Advancement Prospects

Advancement prospects depend on the individual's drive, determination, and how well he or she handles the job. Those who coordinate events that run smoothly and successfully will climb the career ladder by locating similar positions at facilities hosting more prestigious events.

Education and Training

A minimum of a four-year college degree is required for most positions in facilities. Good choices for majors include sports administration or management, business administration, communications, marketing, and public relations.

Jobs with sports promoters may have varied educational requirements, ranging from a high school diploma up to a college degree.

Experience, Skills, and Personality Traits

The first and foremost skill a Sports Event Coordinator must have is the ability to handle many details at one time. He or she must also be totally organized. The individual should have the ability to supervise others and delegate responsibility.

The Coordinator needs to be articulate and have good verbal communication skills. He or she needs to be able to deal with a variety of people on different levels. The individual must know how to write well and have a good grasp of the English language.

Event Coordinators need to have an understanding of the event or sport they are working with. The ability to foresee problems and deal with them is necessary. Individuals should have excellent planning and coordinating skills. A knowledge of public relations, marketing, and business will be useful.

Experience in publicity, special-event promotion, marketing, and public relations is useful in helping the individual not only obtain a job but to be successful. This experience may result from an internship in the sports industry or from working in either a related or an unrelated field.

Unions and Associations

Sports Event Coordinators may belong to associations and organizations that are directly related to the sport or sports in which they are working. These might include the National Association of Athletic Marketing and Development Directors (NAAMDD). Individuals might also belong to trade associations, such as the Public Relations Society of America (PRSA). These organizations may offer ideas, seminars, guidance, trade journals, and professional support.

Tips for Entry

1. Try to locate an internship in a major sports facility. This will help you obtain hands-on experience and offer you an opportunity to make important contacts.
2. Take courses and workshops in event coordination, sports marketing, and public relations. These will give you continued education in the field and ways of making contacts.
3. Send a letter with your résumé to the personnel directors of facilities requesting an interview. Ask that your résumé be kept on file even if a position is not currently available.
4. Obtain experience by volunteering to coordinate sports programs and events for your school.
5. Positions may be advertised in the classified or display sections of newspapers. Look under the heading classifications of "Sports," "Athletics," "Facilities," "Coordination," or "Coordinator."
6. You might also locate openings via the Internet. Check out the major career and job sites on the Web to get started on your search. Type in keywords such as "sports," "athletic events," or "event coordination."

SPORTS INFORMATION DIRECTOR (COLLEGE, UNIVERSITY)

CAREER PROFILE

Duties: Publicizing team and players; writing press releases; providing media with information about team; responding to media questions; preparing biographies, press kits, and yearbooks; arranging press conferences and press briefings

Alternate Title(s): Collegiate Sports Information Director; Sports Information Manager

Salary Range: $28,000 to $150,000+

Employment Prospects: Fair

Advancement Prospects: Fair

Best Geographical Location(s) for Positions: Positions located throughout the country; areas that have colleges and universities with large sports teams hold the most opportunities

Prerequisites:

Education or Training—Four-year college degree required for most positions

CAREER LADDER

Sports Information Director in Larger, More Prestigious Institution or Professional Sports Team Publicist

↑

Sports Information Director

↑

Sports Information Assistant, Public Relations, Media, or Journalism Position, or Entry Level

Experience—Experience in journalism, public relations, professional sports, or related area

Special Skills and Personality Traits—Good writing skills; personable; articulate; knowledge of sports; ability to deal with media

Position Description

The Sports Information Director works with collegiate athletic teams publicizing both the team and its players. The individual may work with one particular sports team or may be required to handle the press and publicity functions for all sports played at the college.

The Sports Information Director has a number of different writing responsibilities. He or she is required to write press releases on a variety of subjects. These might include upcoming games, new additions to the team, coaches, interesting stories on players, and the like. The Sports Information Director may also be required to send scores of games to the media. At times, the individual writes feature stories and articles for use by either the general media or specialized publications.

The Sports Information Director sends press releases, scores, and feature stories to all local media, including newspapers, magazines, other written publications, and television and radio stations. He or she is expected to look for additional avenues to distribute this information. If the individual is working with a school whose team merits regional or national publicity, he or she also sends information to sports editors in

these areas. He or she might also send press releases to media in a player's hometown.

The Sports Information Director is responsible for interviewing each athlete and coach in order to prepare biographies about the players, the team, and the coaches. Depending on the size of the school and its emphasis on sports, this information may be put together like a press kit in a folder, as a press guide in a booklet, or in the form of a yearbook. It may also contain statistics and records about the team, photographs of the players, coaches, and so on. The information is valuable to the Sports Information Director when writing press releases and feature stories or when answering media questions.

The Sports Information Director may be expected either to take photographs or arrange for a professional photographer. This depends on the size and budget of the college. Photos of single players and of players together as a team are needed. Game photos might also be required. If the individual is working in a situation where media coverage includes television, he or she might also arrange for video clips of the team.

The Sports Information Director is responsible for arranging, coordinating, and implementing press conferences and press briefings. Depending on the situation, these might be either formal affairs or informal events. The individual sends invitations to media informing them of the time, date, and location of the conference as well as the reason. Press conferences may be held for a number of reasons. A valuable new player might have transferred to the school and its team, a player might have been injured during a game and is hospitalized, or a new coach from a prestigious school might have been hired. There must be a real reason for a press conference. Otherwise, the next time one is scheduled, the media might not show up.

The Sports Information Director's relationship with the media is important. A good working relationship with these people helps make his or her job easier and more effective. The individual usually gets to know the sports reporters, editors, and journalists. Many areas have collegiate sports reporters or sports sections devoted entirely to the collegiate scene.

If the Sports Information Director has a good, honest relationship with the media, when the team needs some publicity, he or she can just pick up a phone. Conversely, the sports media people frequently need a story and should feel comfortable calling the Sports Information Director for suggestions.

The individual is responsible for responding to inquiries from the general public and the media. In some situations the Sports Information Director cannot answer a specific question at a given time or must say "No comment." This might be because of a delicate situation or a promise of confidentiality. The individual must explain the situation to the media without breaking confidentiality and while keeping the relationship intact.

The individual is responsible for collecting articles, newspaper and magazine clippings, and stories about the team. Copies of radio or television stories might also be collected. He or she may perform this function, assign the task to an assistant, or hire a media clipping service.

The Sports Information Director is especially busy on days of games. He or she must make sure that the press received passes to get in, are seated in good seats, and receive the latest press information. The individual also answers any questions they might have.

The Sports Information Director also sees to it that any school or local dignitaries have received complimentary passes and arranges for their seating. After the game, he or she may arrange a press conference.

The individual in this job works long hours, often at night and on weekends. The Sports Information Director is usually expected to attend all team games.

Depending on the structure of the school, he or she may be responsible to the sports director, the athletic director, or the president of the college.

Salaries

Salaries for Sports Information Directors vary greatly depending on a number of variables, including the size of the college or university, its enrollment, budget, and the amount of emphasis the school puts on sports. Compensation also is dependent on the experience level of the individual and his or her responsibilities.

Salaries can range from $28,000 to $150,000 or more annually for full-time Sports Information Directors. Those working in smaller schools or those with limited experience receive earnings on the lower end of the scale. Individuals working in large colleges and universities with major sports programs earn the higher salaries.

Employment Prospects

Larger schools may employ more than one individual in the Sports Information Department. A college may hire one director and an assistant director. Schools may also hire a Sports Information Director for football, one for basketball, and one for other sports.

Smaller schools usually have only one Sports Information Director. In very small colleges, the position may be only part time. Some small colleges don't employ anyone for this job, instead assigning the task to the college public affairs or public relations office. Other schools leave the sports information functions to the coaches.

Individuals who are willing to relocate to find a position, to work in a small school, or to take a part-time position have fair employment prospects.

Advancement Prospects

Advancement prospects vary depending on the manner in which the individual wants to climb the career ladder. He or she may find a position as a Sports Information Director in a larger, more prestigious school. This will result in increased earnings, responsibilities, and visibility.

The Sports Information Director might climb the career ladder by locating a position with a professional team. He or she might also work in public relations or publicity in another industry.

Education and Training

While there are rare cases of a high school graduate getting this job, the majority of these positions require a minimum of a four-year college degree. In order to be prepared for a position as a Sports Information Director, the individual should take courses in public relations, publicity, marketing, journalism, English, writing, sports studies, and physical education.

A number of seminars available throughout the country on obtaining publicity, writing press releases, and securing media exposure would also prove useful.

Experience, Skills, and Personality Traits

The individual in this type of job must enjoy sports. He or she has to watch games, work with coaches, and interact with players. It is also useful if the Sports Information Director has a knowledge of the various sports he or she is publicizing.

The Sports Information Director needs the ability to write well. He or she prepares press releases, booklets, leaflets, biographies, and feature stories. A good grasp of the English language is needed as is good spelling, word usage, and grammar.

The individual should be energetic. He or she works long hours. The Director should also be personable and enjoy dealing with people.

The Sports Information Director needs to be articulate with the ability to communicate well. A pleasant phone manner is essential. The ability to speak before groups of people is often necessary.

The individual should be able to work on many different projects at once and deal with details without getting flustered. He or she should have or be able to develop a good working relationship with the media.

Unions and Associations

The Sports Information Director working in a college or university usually belongs to a number of trade associations that provide forums for those in the same industry. The best known in this field is the College Sports Information Directors of America (CoSida). The Sports Information Director might also be a member of the National Sportscasters and Sportswriters Association.

Individuals might also be members of a number of other public relations trade associations, including the Public Relations Society of America (PRSA), Women In Communications (WIC), and the National Federation of Press Women (NFPW).

Tips for Entry

1. Get experience working with the media. Volunteer to do publicity for a nonprofit group.
2. Consider a summer or part-time job writing for a newspaper.
3. If your school doesn't have a Sports Information Department, offer to do publicity on school sports teams. See if you can write a column for your school or local paper on the college sports scene.
4. If your school does have this department, see if you can become an intern, trainee, an aide, assistant, or typist. Working in this department in any capacity will give you valuable hands-on experience and be useful for your résumé.
5. Join trade associations. Attend their meetings and subscribe to trade journals. These organizations will keep you abreast of trends in the industry.
6. Jobs may be advertised in the classified section of newspapers in areas where colleges with major athletic departments are located.
7. Positions might also be found on the Web sites of colleges and universities with major athletic departments or via a search through an online career or job site.
8. Check out job sites on the Internet. Start with traditional sites such as hotjobs.com and monster.com. Then surf the Net for other opportunities.

ATHLETIC PROGRAM FUND-RAISING AND DEVELOPMENT DIRECTOR

Duties: Raising funds for college athletic department to support intercollegiate sports programs; creating and developing fund-raising programs; implementing programs; cultivating potential donors

Alternate Title(s): Athletic Development Director; Director of Athletic Fund-raising

Salary Range: $29,000 to $150,000+

Employment Prospects: Fair

Advancement Prospects: Fair

Best Geographical Location(s) for Position: Positions may be located throughout the country

Prerequisites:

Education or Training—Minimum of four-year college degree for most positions

Experience—Experience in fund-raising and development

CAREER LADDER

Athletic Department Fund-raising and Development Director at Larger College with More Prestigious Sports Program

Athletic Program Fund-raising and Development Director

Fund-raising, Public Relations, or Marketing Assistant, or College Student

Special Skills and Personality Traits—Good interpersonal skills; aggressive; organizational skills; communication skills; creativity; interest in intercollegiate sports programs

Position Description

Running a college's athletic program is expensive. There are a number of ways a school can pay for their programs. Most schools charge for tickets to intercollegiate events. Funds from these programs, however, usually do not go very far if the school does not have a major facility to house events. Some colleges make money for their athletic programs by selling television rights to their games. Still others hire individuals to raise funds. The person in this position is called the Athletic Program Fund-raising and Development Director.

The individual's main function is to raise money for the college's athletic department and its programs. While this is not an easy job because so many organizations vie for funds from the public, many people take a special interest in their college's intercollegiate athletic program.

Responsibilities in this type of job vary from position to position. The main goal at most schools is to raise sufficient income to fund not only the current athletic programs but future ones as well.

The Athletic Program Fund-raising and Development Director is responsible for developing programs

that raise funds to keep the institution's athletic programs solvent. The individual is expected to find ways to raise money not only for large capital campaigns, such as new buildings, but also for other programs of the department, such as athletic scholarships.

The Director has to create and develop these programs and is responsible for their implementation. Programs to raise money differ from college to college, depending on the emphasis the administration and boards place on their athletic department.

Some Athletic Program Fund-raising and Development Directors run special events or organize huge annual fund-raising dinners, auctions, and dances to raise money. They may also develop and implement annual giving or sustaining campaigns. Most Athletic Program Fund-raising and Development Directors look for benefactors from within their alumni and school booster clubs.

In many instances, the Athletic Program Fund-raising Director works alongside the college's director of development. In other cases, the individual may be responsible for all fund-raising and development activities at the school.

The individual may also work with other departments to help attain athletic program fund-raising goals. For example, he or she might also deal with the public relations or public information department.

The Athletic Program Fund-raising and Development Director may be responsible for finding volunteers to help do the "leg work," or the running around necessary to make a project successful. The individual, for example, may organize a phone-a-thon where he or she can use volunteers to phone alumni and request donations.

The Athletic Program Fund-raising and Development Director is responsible for cultivating potential donors. To do this, he or she might attend luncheons, dinners, meetings, parties, and other affairs on behalf of the athletic department. The Director may also be expected to speak to groups of people about the athletic programs and department.

The Athletic Program Fund-raising and Development Director seeks annual gifts and endowments from individuals and corporations and tries to locate sponsorship for various projects the athletic department hopes to undertake. The individual might try to locate corporations willing to donate a number of athletic scholarships every year so that the college can attract talented athletes to the school.

The Director is expected to handle a great deal of paperwork. This could include reports describing the progress of varied fund-raising projects, press releases, and publicity programs to promote other fund-raising events. Other writing responsibilities may include creating direct mail pieces, advertising copy, fliers, fund-raising letters, invitations, speeches, and brochures.

The individual is responsible for keeping accurate records of donor activities and resource development. He or she may also develop and write newsletters advising patrons of new athletic programs undertaken at the school, athletic events, new athletes, coaches, and the like.

The Athletic Program Fund-raising and Development Director works long hours finding ways to keep the athletic program at the college running not only for the present but in the future as well. He or she works closely with the school's athletic director, coaches, and athletes.

The Athletic Program Fund-raising and Development Director is expected to attend to day-to-day office activities and social obligations to cultivate potential donors. The individual must also be familiar with everything that is happening in the athletic department.

Salaries
Annual earnings for Athletic Program Fund-raising and Development Directors can range from $29,000 to $150,000 or more, depending on a number of factors. These include the experience of the individual and his or her responsibilities. Other variables affecting salaries include the school's size, location, prestige, and the emphasis it puts on its athletic program.

Employment Prospects
Employment prospects are fair for college Athletic Program Fund-raising and Development Directors. As money gets tighter, more colleges will begin to hire people for these positions.

Individuals, however, may have to relocate to find a position. Small colleges usually do not hire a special person for this job. Instead they rely on the services of the college's director of development. Those aspiring to become an Athletic Program Fund-raising and Development Director must locate schools that emphasize intercollegiate sports programs.

Advancement Prospects
Advancement prospects for Athletic Program Fund-raising and Development Directors are fair. Individuals can climb the career ladder by locating positions in larger schools with more prestigious athletic programs. Some individuals advance their career by moving into corporate fund-raising.

Education and Training
Most positions for Athletic Program Fund-raising and Development Directors require a four-year college degree. Good choices for majors include marketing, public relations, sports administration, communications, and liberal arts.

Seminars and symposiums on fund-raising, development, and marketing will be useful.

Experience, Skills, and Personality Traits
For some people, the job of Athletic Program Fund-raising and Development Director is an entry-level position. Other individuals worked previously in public relations, fund-raising, development, or marketing at amateur, collegiate, or professional sports or in another industry entirely.

Athletic Program Fund-raising and Development Directors should be fairly aggressive and have good organizational skills. Individuals in this position must also have good interpersonal skills and the ability to deal well with volunteers.

Athletic Program Fund-raising and Development Directors need good verbal and written communications skills. Creativity is helpful in developing fund-raising letters, brochures, and mailings. The Athletic

Program Fund-raising and Development Director should also be capable of keeping accurate financial records and be adept at working with figures.

Individuals should have an interest in intercollegiate sports as well as an understanding of them. A great deal of their success in raising funds will come from talking to others interested in the same sporting subjects.

Unions and Associations

There is no specific organization that Athletic Program Fund-raising and Development Directors should belong to. Individuals may, however, be members of the National Society of Fund Raising Executives (NFRE).

Tips for Entry

1. Join a couple of nonprofit organizations with causes you are interested in. Volunteer to be on the fund-raising committee. This will provide useful experience and be important for your résumé.

2. If you are still in college, volunteer to do fund-raising for your school's athletic program.

3. Look for internships with either a college athletic program or a nonprofit organization. The internship will give you valuable hands-on experience and offer you the opportunity to make valuable contacts.

4. You might consider sending a copy of your résumé and a short cover letter to a number of colleges with strong athletic programs.

5. College placement offices often know of openings.

6. Surf the Net looking for openings. Start with some of the better-known job sites such as monster.com and hotjobs.com. Then check out other general job sites as well as those specializing in sports and education.

SPORTS FACILITY MANAGER

CAREER PROFILE

Duties: Overseeing activities and operations of sports venue; supervising staff

Alternate Title(s): Venue Manager; Arena Director; Director of Facility Operations; Stadium Manager; Stadium Director

Salary Range: $28,000 to $125,000+

Employment Prospects: Fair

Advancement Prospects: Fair

Best Geographical Location(s) for Position: Cities hosting professional, collegiate, and amateur sports teams

Prerequisites:

Education or Training—College degree preferred

Experience—Extensive related experience in marketing, sales, ticket sales, or facility management

CAREER LADDER

Sports Facility Manager of Larger, More Prestigious Facility or Director of Facility Operations

Sports Facility Manager

Assistant Sports Facility Manager

Special Skills and Personality Traits—Business skills; communication skills; sales ability; organization; ability to handle crises effectively; ability to multitask; supervisory skills; detail oriented

Position Description

Sports facilities, arenas, and stadium are the locations where sports events are attended. The operation of each of these venues offers a number of interesting career opportunities. One of the top jobs in a sports facility is that of the Sports Facility Manager. He or she is the individual responsible for overseeing the activities and operations of sports venues.

Facility sizes differ depending on the specific team and sport. Some facilities are large, hosting a number of different types of sporting events as well as events in other areas of the entertainment industry. Other facilities are smaller or may just host the games of one sport.

The Sports Facility Manager has a great many responsibilities. Duties will depend on the specific size and structure of the sports facility. The Facility Manager is responsible for the financial business of the venue. He or she is expected to make sure that the facility is as financially viable as possible. The individual may work with the accountants, business managers, marketing people, team management, or other business people to develop strategies and ideas to fulfill this goal. Within the scope of the job, the Facility Manager will also be responsible for developing budgets and running the sports facility within budget

In the case of multi-event facilities, the Facility Manager may be in charge of "selling" the facility to make sure it is booked as many days as possible. He or she

may deal with promoters of various types of events to do this. In single-event facilities such as baseball stadiums, the Facility Manager may be expected to develop ideas to generate additional monies.

The individual is often in charge of determining the best concessions for the sports facility, the best concession mix, the most viable food vendors, where vendors should be located, etc. He or she may be responsible for negotiating contracts with vendors and concessions. This is all important in generating as much income as possible for the sports venue.

The Sports Facility Manager is responsible for hiring and supervising staff. Staff may include security, maintenance personnel, groundskeepers, electricians, sound and light people, etc. In some facilities, the individual may work with a human resources manager. The Sports Facility Manager is responsible for directing the activities of the facility employees to insure the most efficient operations. He or she must also assure that all union rules and regulations are being met.

The individual may also be expected to retain consultants and private contractors. The facility may, for example, retain outside contractors to plow snow, handle lawn service, do electrical work or handle heating and ventilation projects.

In some facilities the Manager is responsible for advertising, marketing, and public relations on his or her own. In others, the individual will work with either the public relations firm or advertising agency handling these duties for the facility or with the team's P.R., marketing, and/or advertising people. Most Facility Managers also have a good working relationship with the media. This is helpful in getting good press coverage for the facility.

The Sports Facility Manager is expected to keep the venue clean and in good working condition. He or she is responsible for making sure repairs are made when required and for keeping the facility as safe as possible.

In running any facility, problems occur, crises happen, and situations must be dealt with. The Manager is ultimately responsible for handling all these situations. The individual who can do this effectively without getting flustered will be successful.

Salaries

Earnings for Sports Facility Managers can range from approximately $28,000 to $125,000 or more. Variables affecting earnings include the size, location, and prestige of the specific facility, as well as the experience, qualifications, and responsibilities of the individual. Earnings are also reflected in the amount of staff the Manager supervises. Those working in facilities hosting major league and professional sporting events will generally earn the highest salaries.

Employment Prospects

Employment prospects are fair for individuals aspiring to work as Facility Managers. Individuals may find employment in a variety of facilities or arenas hosting sporting events. Many larger facilities also host other entertainment events as well. While positions may be located throughout the country, the largest number of opportunities will be found in major cities.

Advancement Prospects

Advancement prospects for Sports Facility Managers are fair. The most common advancement path for individuals is to move into similar positions in larger, more prestigious facilities. Others move up to positions as director of facility operations or vice president of facility operations.

This is an interesting position. Some individuals do not want to move up to a bigger facility. Instead, they prefer to either add another facility to their management portfolio or expand the opportunities they already have in the facility they are currently working. In a larger, more prestigious sports facility, the responsibilities of some Managers are more specific. Smaller facilities, such as those hosting minor league teams, may mean that the Facility Manager has more control in making major decisions for the facility.

Education and Training

While education requirements vary from job to job, most positions require or at least prefer a minimum of a bachelor's degree. Good majors for this type of position include sports administration, finance, business, recreation management, marketing, or liberal arts.

Courses, workshops, or seminars in accounting, bookkeeping, business communications, marketing, public relations, and writing are helpful.

Experience, Skills, and Personality Traits

Facility Managers need an array of skills to be effective at their job. Individuals should have the ability to supervise employees and delegate responsibility. Communication skills, marketing skills, and business skills are also required.

Successful Facility Managers will be organized, detail oriented, have the ability to multitask, and be able to handle crises calmly and effectively. Customer service skills are mandatory.

The ability to read and understand contracts and the riders which often accompany them is necessary. The individual should also be knowledgeable about the sports industry and facility affairs.

Experience in facility management, marketing, ticket sales, or sponsorship is helpful. Some individuals came to this position from other positions within sports teams such as marketing, sponsorship, ticket sales, or concession management.

Unions and Associations

Sports Facility Managers may belong to a number of organizations which provide professional guidance and support. These include the International Association of Auditorium Managers (IAAM) and the Association of Higher Education Facility Officers (AHEFO.)

Tips for Entry

1. Look for an internship in a sports facility. Learn as much as you can and do more than is expected of you.
2. It's easier to break into this field at a smaller facility. Get some experience under your belt and apply for positions at larger, more prestigious facilities.
3. Openings may be listed on sports team or facility Web sites. Check them out.

4. Jobs may also be advertised in the classified section of newspapers. Look under heading classifications including "Facility Manager," "Sports Facility Manager," "Sports Venue Manager," "Facility Management," etc. Look under the names of the specific sports teams or facilities.

5. Send your résumé with a short cover letter to facilities you might be interested in working with.

6. Check out openings online. Start with traditional job sites such as monster.com and hotjobs.com and go from there.

ATTORNEY—SPORTS INDUSTRY

Duties: Handling legal matters for clients in sports industry; handling contractual matters; negotiating contracts; negotiating deals; providing legal advice and counsel; helping put together a sports superstar team; litigating

Alternate Title(s): Lawyer

Salary Range: $65,000 to $1 million+

Employment Prospects: Fair

Advancement Prospects: Good

Best Geographical Location(s) for Position: Positions may be located anywhere; more opportunities may exist in cities with larger numbers of professional sports teams

Prerequisites:

Education or Training—Law degree

Experience—Experience requirements vary from job to job; see text

Special Skills and Personality Traits—Negotiation skills; knowledge of sports industry; ability to read and understand contracts; focused; organized; ver-

bal and written communications skills; analytical mind; flexibility

Special Requirements—Must pass the bar exam and be licensed in the specific state in which individual works

CAREER LADDER

Attorney at Larger, More Prestigious Sports-Oriented Company, Partner in Law Firm Handling Sports Industry Clients, or Attorney in Private Practice Handling Large Roster of Prestigious Clients in Sports Industry
Attorney—Sports Industry
Law School Student, or Attorney in Other Specialty

Position Description

While there are Attorneys who have general practices handling a variety of legal issues, a good number of Attorneys specialize in specific fields. A popular specialty for many is sports and entertainment law. Sports and entertainment Attorneys are the individuals who handle the legal needs of those in the sports and entertainment industries.

While all Attorneys go through law school, pass a bar exam, and are admitted to the bar in the state or states in which they work, there are often differences in each specialty. Those who specialize in sports and entertainment law need a full understanding of the sports and entertainment industries and issues that affect them.

Attorneys specializing in the sports industry understand the unique needs of professional and amateur athletes. The sports industry has a wide variety of situations that require the services of Attorneys. There are agreements, contracts, and negotiations. There are copyrights, trademarks, sponsorships, and endorsements . . . and, of course, there are always lawsuits.

Specific responsibilities of Attorneys working in the sports industry will be dependent on the employment situation they are in. Those working with sports teams may, for example, have different responsibilities than those working for sports-oriented companies or sports agents. Those working with sports promoters may have different responsibilities from those working in sports-oriented law firms.

No matter where an Attorney specializing in the sports industry works, he or she is above all responsible for protecting the rights of his or her client.

A great many of the responsibilities of Attorneys working in the sports industry often revolve around contracts. Depending on the specific situation, individuals might negotiate and prepare contracts or review those others have written that they want people to sign.

Attorneys may, for example, review a contract for an amateur athlete getting ready to go pro. They might also be responsible for negotiating contracts for professional athletes signing with teams. Some Attorneys negotiate huge endorsement deals for their superstar sports clients.

Attorneys working for sports promoters may be expected to prepare the contracts for sporting events or review the contracts written by others. Attorneys working for sports teams may prepare and write contracts for the athletes, coaches, and team administrators and executives. Some Attorneys negotiate and prepare contracts for sponsorship deals for sports venues. Others may handle negotiations and contracts for televising or broadcasting of sporting events.

Whether actually preparing a contract or reviewing a contract, the Attorney must always be sure that all points that were agreed upon are actually in the document and that the specific wording is clear. Missing one point can literally cost one side or the other thousands upon thousands of dollars.

Contracts in the sports industry have their own language and can often be quite complicated. The individual is responsible for explaining all points to his or her client and making sure that each point is understood. The Attorney is additionally expected to make sure each contract he or she prepares reflects the points that the client has asked for and approved.

Attorneys must review each contract carefully whether or not he or she has actually written it. In some cases, after looking over a contract, an individual might find that an athlete is giving up more than he or she needs to or that the contract does not accurately reflect what the athlete or other client has indicated he or she wants. In these situations, the wording might need to be changed.

Attorneys working for sports teams may prepare and write contracts for the athletes, coaches, and team administrators and executives. Because contracts are often amended and changed by the other party, the Attorney will be responsible for reviewing the amended contracts for changes each time they are made. As noted previously, the change of even one word, if not correct, might potentially mean the loss of thousands of dollars to a team or athlete.

Attorneys working with sports promoters and promotion companies may either prepare contracts for athletes who appear at their shows or review contracts prepared by either the individual or his or her manager, agent, or Attorney. Depending on the situation, a sports promoter might sign athletes from various sports, including boxing, wrestling, skating, and so on. Each athlete who is signed for a sporting event or show needs a contract stating what each side will be responsible for and receive in return.

Many superstar athletes earn extra income by doing personal appearances. In these situations, their Attorney may negotiate not only the monies to be paid to appear but may specify additions they might want or require along with the basic appearance contract. These additional items may be added to the contract in the form of a rider. Riders may be simple one-page documents or may be longer depending on the complexity. Riders might state, for example, that the sports star requires specific types of foods and drinks, specific types of air and ground transportation, and specific types of security.

The Attorney must be sure that each point the sports star asks for is in writing in the contract and/or the rider. He or she must also be sure that the contract is signed by both parties in order for the contract to be valid.

Some Attorneys apply for copyrights or for trademarks on behalf of a sports team, sports star, or other client. Attorneys might additionally handle copyright or trademark infringement suits when necessary.

Sometimes sports stars find it is necessary to call Attorneys to handle situations where a tabloid or television show allegedly slanders them. In other situations, the athlete may be accused of a crime. The Attorney may take care of these situations or refer them to another specialist.

Attorneys can be useful at every stage of an athlete's career. At the beginning, the Attorney often can bring the athlete to the attention of people important to his or her career. Attorneys specializing in the sports industry can often cut through the red tape to get his or her client to the right people. Once the athlete is established, the Attorney is often instrumental in negotiating deals with teams and for endorsements and sponsorships. If, during the athlete's career, there are any legal matters needing attention, Attorneys handle those as well.

Attorneys specializing in the sports industry may also help athletes put together their management team, including managers, agents, business managers, publicists, accountants, and so on. They may also secure endorsements, sponsorships, licensing opportunities, and more.

Attorneys working with sports teams may handle the team's legal matters as well as labor relations and contract negotiations.

Salaries

Earnings for Attorneys specializing in the sports industry can vary dramatically. Individuals just starting out may earn $65,000 annually; others with a great deal of experience working for a prestigious law firm, a major sports team, or other sports industry company can earn $500,000 or more. Some Attorneys specializing in the sports industry earn $1 million or more annually.

Some lawyers specializing in the sports industry are paid a salary. Others earn income dependent upon contracts negotiated. Depending on the specific employment situation, these might include player's salaries, endorsements, sponsorships, public appearances, etc. Earnings for Attorneys who are in private practice are based to a great extent on amount and type of work they perform.

Employment Prospects

Employment prospects are fair for qualified individuals aspiring to work as Attorneys specializing in the sports and entertainment industries. Individuals may work for or be retained by athletes, teams, sports leagues, conferences, and educational institutions. They may work on behalf of sports organizations or athletes on the professional level as well as in amateur, collegiate, and Olympic sports areas.

Some individuals are employed by or are partners in law firms specializing in the sports and entertainment industries. Some may be employed by law firms that include sports or entertainment as their specialties. Others may be employed directly by sports teams, sports agencies, sports promotion companies, and sports venues.

Some very successful sports superstars also keep an Attorney on staff. Attorneys may also freelance or be hired on a retainer. Many individuals open their own firms.

Jobs and opportunities may be located throughout the country. The greatest number of opportunities, however, will exist in areas where there are larger numbers of professional sports teams.

Advancement Prospects

Advancement prospects are fair for Attorneys working in the sports industry. Individuals can climb the career ladder in a number of ways depending on their career aspirations. Some find similar positions in larger or more prestigious sports-oriented companies or teams. Those employed at law firms specializing in the sports and entertainment industries may find positions at larger or more prestigious law firms. Others may get more prestigious clients or may become partners. Some individuals strike out on their own and build their practice with a large roster of clients.

Education and Training

Attorneys are generally required to have a four-year college degree and then go through three years of law school. Law schools must be approved by the American Bar Association (ABA). In order to apply for these law schools, applicants must first take the Law School Admission Test (LSAT). In order to practice, individuals must pass a written bar exam and be admitted to the bar of the particular state in which they wish to practice.

Those aspiring to work in the sports industry should make sure they take courses geared toward the sports and entertainment industries. These courses might include contracts, tax law, business law, sports law, and intellectual property and copyright law.

There are a number of law schools that offer special programs or at least a large number of classes in sports and entertainment law, including UCLA, USC, NYU, Columbia, Stanford, Loyola, and California Western. It should be noted that most industry professionals suggest attending the best law school possible, whether or not they have sports or entertainment law specialties.

Sports and entertainment law conferences and symposiums will prove useful both for the educational opportunities and the ability to make valuable contacts.

Special Requirements

Attorneys specializing in the sports industry, like all other Attorneys, need to pass the bar exam for the state or states in which they will be practicing and be licensed and/or registered in the state in which they will be practicing.

Experience, Skills, and Personality Traits

Experience requirements for Attorneys specializing in the sports industry vary from job to job. Large law firms or major league sports teams may want their Attorneys to have three to five years or more of experience in sports or entertainment law. A smaller firm or minor league team may just require a year or two.

All Attorneys, whether specializing in the sports industry or not, need to have good written and verbal communications skills. The ability to think analytically and objectively is essential. Individuals additionally need to be responsible, organized, and professional with the highest standard of ethics.

Attorneys specializing in the sports industry need a full knowledge of all aspects of the industry. An understanding of the special legal issues that face athletes, sports teams, and others in the industry is also essential.

All Attorneys are privy to sensitive information. This can be especially true in the sports industry. The ability to keep this information confidential is essential. The ability to show discretion is critical. The individual must also be extremely trustworthy.

Unions and Associations

Attorneys specializing in the sports industry may be members of the American Bar Association (ABA) and specific state bar associations. Both the ABA and some state bar associations have sections or divisions devoted to sports or entertainment law. There are also professional organizations such as the Sports Lawyers Association (SLA) and the International Association of Entertainment Lawyers (IAEL) that bring together attorneys in the sports and entertainment industry to share knowledge and information.

Tips for Entry

1. Get involved in the sports industry even if it is not in the legal end. If you're still in school, find an internship with your college sports department, a professional sports team, or a sports facility. You want to be able to demonstrate an understanding and knowledge of the sports industry when you are ready to go after that perfect job.
2. Once you have some college under your belt, you might also consider an internship or job as a paralegal at a law firm that specializes in the sports or entertainment industry.
3. If you have your law degree, have passed the bar and have a great deal of experience in the sports industry, yet still haven't found that perfect job, contact a large law firm that doesn't yet have a sports or entertainment specialty and see if they are interested in adding one.
4. Send your résumé with a short cover letter to professional sports teams, law firms, sports promotion companies, sports facilities, and so on. You might get lucky.
5. Positions in this field may be advertised in the newspaper classified section in areas hosting professional sports teams, sports agents, sports venues, etc. Look under headings such as "Sports Industry Attorney," "Entertainment Industry Attorney," "Sports Team Attorney," "Attorney," "Legal Affairs-Sports Team," "Legal Affairs-Sports," "Sports Law," etc.
6. Check traditional job sites such as monster.com and hotjobs.yahoo.com, as well as job sites specific to the sports industry.

EXECUTIVE DIRECTOR—SPORTS INDUSTRY TRADE ASSOCIATION

communications skills; understanding of specific area of sports industry in which trade association is associated

Position Description

The sports industry, like other industries, has a large number of trade groups, associations, and organizations geared at promoting their particular industry segment. These trade associations cover a wide array of areas, including those dealing with sporting goods, sports-related products, services, and activities. Some associations target specific sports. Others encompass employees, employers, and educators who work in various areas of the sports industry. There are player associations for various sports, trade associations for coaches, trainers, managers, and the list goes on.

The individual in charge of overseeing the operations of a trade association is called the Executive Director. In some instances, he or she may also be called the Trade Association Director.

Trade associations generally are not-for-profit organizations. These groups bring together individuals in a similar field, support their members, represent their interests, provide them with business support, and often give them a voice in government. Depending on the specific organization, trade associations may also provide educational guidance and professional support to its members, as well as access to benefits.

Executive Directors of associations in the sports industry can have a variety of responsibilities depending on a number of factors. These include the specific organization, its mission, size, structure, prestige, and budget. In smaller organizations, the Executive Director may handle everything alone, perhaps with the help of committees of volunteers and interns. In larger trade associations, the Executive Director may have a large staff and assistants who help handle the various duties.

The Executive Director of a sports-oriented trade association generally works under the direction of a board of directors. Together they establish the direction that the trade association will go as well as the organization's policies.

The Executive Director is heavily involved in the budget and finances of the association. One of the responsibilities of the individual is often the preparation of the annual budget. Depending on the size and structure of the organization, this may be difficult because many of these organizations work with limited monies.

In order to help increase the funds of the association, the Executive Director is often responsible for fund-raising. The individual may develop, implement, and execute a number of special events during the year to raise needed money. These events may include dinners, membership drives, auctions, galas, golf tournaments, and more. If the association is large, there may be a fund-raising director who handles this function.

Grants are another source of funds that trade associations depend on to sustain themselves. The Executive Director is responsible for locating grants from federal, state, or local agencies as well as from private industry. He or she must then write and prepare the grant application. In some situations, the Executive Director oversees either a staff grant writer or a consultant who is expected to find and write these grants. If successful in securing a grant, the Executive Director is responsible for assuring that all rules and regulations of the grant are adhered to. A grant administrator may be assigned this task as well.

The Executive Director is often expected to solicit donations from the corporate world and private donors. In order to be effective at this task, the individual needs to be comfortable asking for money. Some people are very good at this. Others find it difficult or embarrassing. Gaining a comfort level in this type of task helps ensure the success of the organization's Director.

The Executive Director is expected to either personally handle or oversee the association's public relations and advertising. This may include public relations and advertising efforts directed toward the public as well as internally within the organization's membership. As part of this responsibility, press releases, calendar schedules, and newsletters must be developed and prepared. In addition, brochures, leaflets, and booklets must be developed and designed to promote the organization. In smaller organizations, the Executive Director may handle these tasks alone. In larger organizations, the Executive Director is responsible for overseeing the public relations and publications department and staffers.

The Executive Director is responsible for finding ways to increase the organization's membership. Depending on the size and structure of the organization, the individual may work with a membership director or handle the task alone. The Director will often speak at industry events, do media interviews, and send out membership materials among other things in order to get the organization better known and increase membership.

Many trade associations depend on the help of volunteers within their membership. The Executive Director is responsible for coordinating the efforts of all volunteer groups and committees within the association's membership.

A major function of many Executive Directors is scheduling conferences, conventions, and other educational and networking activities. The individual is expected to either handle these activities and events alone, or delegate the duties to a committee or conference coordinator.

The Executive Director of the trade association must be the champion of the organization. He or she is expected to attend meetings and events on behalf of the association. This may include industry events as well as community meetings. The individual will often be the liaison between the association and community groups, often serving on boards of community and civic organizations.

Other responsibilities of the Executive Director of a trade association in the sports industry might include:

- Developing new membership drives and handling membership applications and renewals
- Supervising staff
- Dealing with issues significant to the associations
- Attending industry meetings, conferences, and conventions on behalf of the association
- Determining the types of programs the association will undertake

Salaries

Earnings for Executive Directors of trade associations within the sports industry can range from approximately $26,000 to $150,000 or more depending on a number of factors. These include the size, structure, prestige, and budget of the specific trade association. Other factors affecting earnings include the responsibilities, professional reputation, and experience of the individual.

Employment Prospects

Employment prospects are fair for individuals seeking positions as Executive Directors of trade associations in the sports industry. Individuals may find employment in a wide array of areas of the industry depending on their interests. These might include associations dealing with sports-related products, services, and activities. There are also a variety of associations for almost every sport. Some associations encompass players, managers, agents, coaches, trainers, and more. There are associations that are geared to those working in arenas and other sports facilities. Some trade associations include employees, employers, and educators who work in the sports industry. There are associations for those who work in the wholesale and retail areas of the sports industry as well as those who manufacture sporting goods. There are also trade associations for those who are involved in pro sports, collegiate sports, and amateur sports, and the list goes on.

Some organizations are larger than others. Opportunities may be located throughout the country. It should be noted that indivuduals may need to relocate for positions.

Advancement Prospects

Advancement prospects are fair for Executive Directors of trade associations in the sports industry. Individuals may climb the career ladder in a number of ways. Many Executive Directors advance their careers by successfully building the trade organization they work with into a larger, more prestigious association. This generally results in increased responsibilities and earnings. Others climb the career ladder by finding similar positions at larger or more prestigious associations either in the sports industry or in a totally unrelated industry.

There are some individuals who make a name for themselves in the industry and end up being offered a coveted position with a sports team, a superstar athlete, or even the corporate end of the sports industry.

Education and Training

Most trade associations in the sports industry require or prefer their applicants to have a minimum of a four-year college degree. There may, however, be smaller associations that may accept an applicant with an Associate degree or even a high school diploma coupled with experience.

Courses, seminars, and workshops in fund-raising, grant writing, public relations, business, management, presentation skills, and the sports business and administration will be useful in honing skills and making new contacts.

Experience, Skills, and Personality Traits

Experience requirements depend, to a great extent, on the size, structure, and prestige of the specific trade association. Individuals seeking positions with prestigious sports industry associations generally are required to either have a minimum of three years' experience working with trade associations or working at a high-level corporate job within the industry. Experience in public relations, journalism, fund-raising, grant writing, and working with not-for-profit organizations will also be helpful.

It must be noted that there are some individuals who have limited experience in the business areas but land jobs in this field after successful careers as pro athletes or in some cases even well-known college athletes. While the experience level is different, these individuals generally have a great deal of clout in the industry and enough contacts to be successful.

Executive Directors of trade associations in the sports industry need to be creative visionaries. They need to be able to think outside of the box. Individuals must be well spoken with excellent verbal and communication skills. An understanding of grant writing is usually necessary as is the ability to develop and adhere to budgets. People skills are essential. Management and supervisory skills are also crucial.

An understanding and knowledge of the specific area of the sports industry that the association serves is essential.

Unions and Associations

Individuals interested in a career as an Executive Director of a trade association may want to contact the Center for Association Leadership. They might also join other professional associations within the sports industry in order to make contacts.

Tips for Entry

1. Get experience working with not-for-profit organizations by volunteering with a local civic or community organization.
2. Look for job openings in the classified sections of newspapers. Heading titles might be under key words such as "Trade Association," "Trade Association Executive Director," "Executive Director," "Sports Industry Trade Association," or "Association Executive." Jobs may also be advertised under the name of specific sports industry organizations.
3. Read trade publications specific to the sport or area in which you are interested in working. They often advertise openings.
4. Openings may be listed on the Web sites of specific trade associations.
5. Network as much as you can in the industry. Go to conferences, conventions, and educational seminars and workshops to meet industry insiders.
6. Offer to do the publicity or fund-raising for a local not-for-profit organization. It does not matter if the organization is related to the sports industry or not. If you can do publicity or fund-raising for one organization, you can do it for any type of group.

ADVERTISING ACCOUNT EXECUTIVE—SPORTS-ORIENTED PUBLICATION

Duties: Selling advertising space in sports-oriented periodical or newspaper; meeting with clients; writing orders; developing advertising promotions

Alternate Title(s): Salesman; Saleswoman; Sales Rep; Sales Executive

Salary Range: $23,000 to $125,000+

Employment Prospects: Good

Advancement Prospects: Good

Best Geographical Location(s) for Position: Positions may be located throughout country

Prerequisites:

Education or Training—Educational requirements vary; high school diploma, minimum requirement; college degree or background may be preferred or required; see text

Experience and qualifications—Experience requirements vary from job to job; see text

Special Skills and Personality Traits—Sales skills; personable; pleasantly aggressive; motivated; strong

desire to succeed; organized; ability to work unsupervised; ability to deal with discouragement; verbal and written communication skills

Special Requirements—Driver's license and reliable automobile may be required for many positions

CAREER LADDER

Advertising Account Executive at More Prestigious Sports-Oriented Publication, Advertising Sales Manager, or Marketing Director

↑

Advertising Account Executive— Sports-Oriented Publication

↑

Sales Assistant, Advertising Sales Rep Trainee, or Entry-Level Position

Position Description

There are many sports-oriented publications in existence today. Some are newspapers. Others are magazines, periodicals, or online publications. Some are geared toward consumers. Others are trade publications directed toward industry professionals. These publications specialize in almost every area of the sports industry. Some publications are in print form, while others are digital with online access.

Sports publications, like other publications, earn money in a number of ways. Print publications sell subscriptions and single copies. Online publications may sell access to their site. The majority of earnings for many sports publications, however, comes from the sale of advertising.

Individuals who sell advertising for sports-oriented publications are called Advertising Account Executives. They may also be referred to as sales reps, salesmen, saleswomen, or sales executives.

The main responsibility of Advertising Account Executives working for sports-oriented publications is to sell advertising space for those publications. The individual may be assigned accounts or may be expected to find potential advertisers on his or her own. Depending on the specific publication, Account Executives may be assigned accounts with national advertisers, local advertisers, or a combination of the two. They might deal with clients themselves or may deal with the client's advertising agency.

Advertising Account Executives selling advertising for sports-oriented publications may use a variety of methods to sell ads. Some set up meetings and go to visit potential advertisers in person. Others call or write potential advertisers.

In an effort to solicit both new and established advertisers, many Account Executives also use the Internet to prospect for potential advertisers. Many individuals now send out e-mail blasts to potential clients. Some Account Executives e-mail reader surveys or even articles to potential clients on how advertising in the particular publication has increased another advertiser's business. Individuals may also e-mail advertisers about special promotions and sales the publication may be having.

Account Executives selling advertising space in sports publications that are well known often have an easier time than their counterparts selling for lesser-recognized publications. The main reason for this is because they are selling a known commodity. In these situations, potential advertisers may be more aware of the demographics of the people who read the specific publication and have an idea what placing an ad or series of ads in the magazine might do for their business. On the other hand, if the publication is new or not very well known, the Advertising Account Executive generally needs to find ways to prove the importance of advertising in the publication to potential advertisers.

Many publications have advertisements inviting potential companies to advertise. Sometimes, these potential advertisers may simply contact the publication to get information about advertising opportunities. They may inquire about the publication, demographics, and/or advertising rates. Depending on the structure of the publication and its advertising department, calls may go directly to a sales manager who in turn will refer them to the appropriate Account Executive or may go to an Account Executive specifically assigned to handle these calls.

The Advertising Account Executive sends out advertising information and rate kits. This may be done via traditional mail, a delivery service, or through e-mail. These kits may contain things such as rate cards, informational facts sheets on the publication, demographics, testimonials from other advertisers, and copies of the publication. They may also contain information on the publication's special issues and promotions.

The Advertising Account Executives must have a complete knowledge of the publication. He or she must know the demographics of the publication's readers, how long the publication has been in existence, the products and services of other advertisers, and competing publications. This information can help the Advertising Account Executive illustrate how advertising in his or her publication can benefit a potential advertiser.

Many Account Executives selling advertising for sports-oriented publications develop advertising campaigns for their clients. They may develop monthly or even annual advertising campaigns designed to increase the client's business. In order to do this, the Account Executives must become familiar with client's products and/or services as well as that of the competition. After clients place orders for advertisements and campaigns are implemented, Account Executives are expected to monitor the effectiveness of the campaigns.

Account Executives frequently brainstorm with clients or their advertising agencies to develop effective advertising ideas. Generally, the more effective ads and advertising campaigns are, the more advertising customers will purchase in the future.

Advertising Account Executives often schedule appointments with potential clients to discuss advertising needs. It is essential that the Advertising Account Executive be aware of all the publication's advertising promotions as well as its rates, discounts, and advertising packages. He or she must also be able to fully explain all of these to advertisers so they know exactly what they are getting.

One of the ways to be successful as an Advertising Account Executive is to not only find ways to sell an advertiser one advertisement, but to build a lasting business relationship. He or she can do this by explaining promotions, putting together the best package possible, and servicing the account. The Advertising Account Executive must continually check with clients to be sure they are happy with their ads and are being billed properly. It is critical in this line of work to maintain a good ongoing business relationship. Staying in contact is key.

Obtaining new accounts is an essential part of the job for Account Executives selling advertising for sports-oriented publications. Individuals may spend a great deal of time calling new accounts, traveling to meet potential advertisers, and arranging for follow-up meetings. Sometimes an Account Executive sells an ad or advertising campaign to a client in one meeting. In other situations, it may take a number of meetings. It all depends on the needs of the potential advertiser and the selling skills of the Account Executive.

In order to get new business, the individual may make what are known as cold calls to potential advertisers. These calls may be made to people who have not yet advertised in the publication or those who have not advertised for an extended time period. After identifying him- or herself and the publication, the Account Executive attempts to set up an appointment to tell the potential advertiser more about the publication's advertising opportunities, promotions, and specials. Not every call will result in an appointment. The Advertising Account Executives must have the ability to accept rejection without taking it personally.

In order to entice new advertisers to try advertising in the publication, the Advertising Account Executive may offer a variety of promotions and discounts. The individual may also offer specials, promotions, and discounts to established accounts in order to tempt them to advertise more often or to commit to a major advertising campaign.

Sometimes these promotions are developed by the sales manager or the publication's marketing manager. In other cases, the Account Executive may help develop marketing and advertising ideas and campaigns for current or potential customers, designed to help increase their business. These may include sweepstakes or co-op ads among others. For example, the Account Executive may help develop an advertising campaign for a soft drink company and a major league sports team. He or she might develop a promotion for an advertising campaign for a sports fitness company and a major car manufacturer so readers could enter a sweepstakes and win prizes. In many instances, these types of promotions are developed in conjunction with the client's marketing department or advertising agency.

Account Executives must constantly call on businesses and companies that might buy advertisements. Depending on the specific sports publication, these might include any business or service that will benefit by having an advertisement in the periodical or newspaper. It is important to note that even though the publication is sports-oriented, the client does not have to be in the sports industry. Instead, the advertiser's particular product or service just needs to appeal to those reading the sports publication. For example, those reading a sports magazine may be interested in soft drinks, automobiles, televisions, vacations, etc. They might be interested in a specific brand of clothing or antiperspirant. Any of these products might, therefore, be good advertisers for a particular sports publication.

The Advertising Account Executive is usually assigned a sales territory in which to work. This means that he or she has a certain locality or area in which to sell ads. The individual usually sells only in his or her territory. Territories can be large or small or might even refer to a specific type of client. For example, an Account Executive might be responsible for soliciting ads from fitness company manufacturers or sports teams.

Depending on the size of the publication, the Account Executive might be responsible for actually writing the ads, acting as a copywriter, or even designing and laying out advertisements.

Many sports-oriented publications develop special issues designed to attract advertisers. They may, for example, have special issues when someone in the sports industry wins a huge award, a new or large sports venue opens for the season, or to celebrate a major sporting event. The Account Executive may call clients to discuss the special promotions the publication is running to see if they would like to participate in the issue and buy advertising space.

While Advertising Account Executives work under the direction of sales managers, much of their day is often spent working on their own. It is up to them to sell as many ads as possible. Often the job is not nine to five . . . especially if advertisers are on the other side of the country. The individual may find that he or she has to make a sales call to a client at eight in the morning or eight at night. The Account Executive may need to set up lunch meetings or dinners. No one watches what the Account Executive does all day. It is up to him or her to organize his or her time and efforts effectively. The bottom line is how much advertising can he or she sell.

Sometimes the Advertising Account Executive works in the field. At other times, the individual might be in the office, helping clients decide where, when, and how their advertising dollar would be best spent. The Account Executive also spends a great deal of time on the phone, locating potential clients or telling current customers about the status of their advertisements.

Advertising Account Executives working for all publications are expected to keep accurate records of advertisements sold, billings, and so on, and those working for sports-oriented publications are no exception. Individuals are responsible for writing orders and making sure each order gets to the appropriate department at the publication.

The most successful Account Executives continually find ways to generate revenue for the publication by looking for and negotiating a broad range of advertising deals and opportunities.

Salaries

Earnings for Advertising Account Executives working for sports-oriented periodicals or newspapers can vary tremendously. There are some individuals who have annual earnings of $23,000 and others who have annual earnings of $125,000 or more.

Individuals may be paid in a number of different ways. Some are paid a straight salary. Others receive a small salary plus commissions. Still others receive commissions alone. Advertising Account Executives also often receive bonuses when they meet or exceed sales projections.

Factors affecting earnings include the popularity, prestige, and size of the specific publication. As the majority of Advertising Account Executives receive at least part of their income from commission, other variables include the sales ability and motivation of the individual.

Motivated Advertising Account Executives selling advertising for well-known sports publications will earn the highest commissions. The greatest thing about selling on a commission is that the sky is the limit on earnings.

Employment Prospects

As advertising is one of the main methods in which publications make money, employment prospects are always good for talented, motivated individuals who can sell.

Jobs and opportunities may be located throughout the country in areas hosting sports-oriented magazines and newspapers. Individuals may work for local, regional, or national sports-oriented newspapers, consumer magazines, and trade publications.

Advancement Prospects

Advancement prospects are good for motivated Account Executives selling advertising for sports-oriented publications. Individuals may climb the career ladder by locating a similar position at a larger or more prestigious sports-oriented publication, being assigned a bigger or better territory, or getting bigger accounts. These situations offer the Account Executive the opportunity for increased earnings and responsibilities.

Some individuals also advance their careers by being promoted to the position of sales manager or advertising director of the sports-oriented publication. Still others become marketing directors for either the same or a similar publication.

Education and Training

Educational requirements vary for Advertising Account Executives working for sports-oriented publications. Some publications just require their Account Executives to hold a high school diploma. Others require or prefer their Account Executives to have a college background or degree.

Whatever the requirements, courses, workshops, and seminars in selling, salesmanship, advertising, public speaking, and related areas will be useful.

Special Requirements

Depending on the specific situation, Advertising Account Executives may need a driver's license and a reliable automobile.

Experience, Skills, and Personality Traits

Experience requirements for Account Executives selling advertising for sports-oriented publications vary from job to job. In some situations, this may be an entry-level position. Others require or prefer applicants to have anywhere between three to five years of sales experience.

A full working knowledge and understanding of the area of the sports industry in which the publication is targeted are necessary to adequately explain the benefits of advertising to potential advertisers. Account Executives should be motivated individuals with a strong desire to succeed.

They need excellent communications skills, both verbal and written. Individuals should also be responsible, organized, and have the ability to multitask without getting flustered. As a great deal of the job is accomplished on the telephone, good phone skills are vital. Exceptional sales skills are essential to success in this type of job. Individuals also need to be personable and pleasantly aggressive.

Math skills are necessary. Account Executives will need the ability to quickly and correctly figure out prices and costs for various advertising packages. The ability to use a computer and be familiar with various software is also necessary.

It is very important to understand that every prospect will not buy an ad. Account Executives must have a thick skin and learn not to take rejection personally. The ability to deal with discouragement is critical.

Unions and Associations

Advertising Account Executives selling for sports-oriented publications often belong to trade associations geared toward the area of the sports industry in which the publication is directed. In order to make important contacts, individuals also generally belong to business and civic groups in their area. Account Executives may also belong to the International Newspaper Advertising and Marketing Executives (INAME).

Tips for Entry

1. If you are still in school, see if you can find an internship in the advertising department of a sports-oriented trade magazine, periodical, or newspaper. You will learn a lot and make valuable contacts.

2. If you can't find an internship with a sports-oriented publication, any publication will be good training, give you great experience, and look good on your résumé when job hunting.

3. Consider sending your résumé and a short cover letter to sports-oriented trade magazines, periodicals, and newspapers. You can send it to the human resources department as well as to the advertising sales manager. Be sure to ask that your résumé be kept on file if there are no current openings.

4. Look for seminars and workshops on sales techniques. Whether or not these are geared specifically toward the sports industry, these courses will helpful in honing selling techniques.

5. Positions may be advertised in the classified section of newspapers under headings such as "Advertising," "Sports Trades," "Account Executive-Sports," "Salesperson," "Sales," or "Account Executive." Don't forget to look under specific names of sports-oriented publications.

6. Most sports-oriented magazines, publications, and newspapers also advertise openings in their own publication on their Web sites. Check them out.

7. Check traditional job sites such as monster.com and hotjobs.yahoo.com, as well as job sites specific to sports or publishing industries for openings.

COACHING AND EDUCATION

COACH OR MANAGER
(PROFESSIONAL SPORTS TEAM)

Position Description

The Coach or Manager working with a professional sports team has an important job. He or she is greatly responsible for the way a professional team plays for the season. The Coach at the pro level has one main function: to train, motivate, and work with team members to help them compete at the highest level.

Professional teams usually have a number of Coaches, although each has only one Head Coach. Baseball teams typically have a Manager who heads the team and a number of Coaches who function as assistants. The exact number depends on the specific sport and team. All Coaches work together trying to get their team prepared to play competitively for the season.

Depending on the specific sport, there may be a number of different types of Coaches working with the team. In addition to the Head Coach or Manager there will be assistants, strength coaches, pitching coaches, athletic trainers, and so on. The Coach works with other team personnel in his or her job. Coaches may work in any professional sport, including baseball, basketball, hockey, soccer, and football.

Professional Coaches do not have to coach more than one sport or more than one team. Their only responsibility is to the one team they have been hired to work with.

Coaches working with pros also do not have to teach players basic skills. By the time athletes make it to the pros, they are usually exceptionally talented players. Most are the cream of the crop in the particular sport they are competing at. Depending on the sport, individuals will come to the team through drafts, agents, and scouts. While the Coach is not solely responsible for choosing team members, his or her input is expected.

The Head Coach or Manager for the pro team is responsible for scheduling practice sessions and meetings. He or she is responsible for determining how frequently practices are held and the duration of each. Practices are devoted to refining the skills of both individual athletes and the team as a whole.

Coaches involved with pro sports must devise strategies and develop game tactics. They discuss team strategies and how they will be implemented. They also talk about problems with the way the team plays and potential solutions. In some instances, Coaches may use visuals to help train the players. They may view videotapes of their own games, practice sessions, or even games of the competition.

Coaches must motivate their players and teach them how to play as a team. They must make their players aware of the best ways to play the game as well as the route to winning.

The Head Coach or Manager attends all of his or her team's games, at home or away. During a game, he or she may change strategies, give signals, and call time-outs to talk to team members. He or she must be aware of everything that is happening in the game. The Coach or Manager may also decide who will play during a certain portion of the game and which players will go in as substitutes. He or she must know the strengths and weaknesses of all the team's players in order to determine which athlete should be out on the field or on the court when.

Before a game and during halftime, the Coach or Manager usually gives pep talks to the team and may offer advice to athletes regarding playing tactics. After a game, a Coach offers suggestions for the next competition.

In many instances, the Head Coach or Manager is expected to regulate the actions of the team members when they are not in actual playing situations. The team management or the individual Coach may have rules and regulations regarding what the athletes can and cannot do on their off time. For example, team members may have curfews when in training and during the playing season. Sports teams expect their athletes to refrain from substance abuse. The Manager or Coach can keep an athlete who fails to adhere to the rules from playing in a game or penalize him or her in some other manner.

Coaches work long hours preparing the team for competitions. In addition to attending the team's games and regular training sessions, Coaches must be at all practice sessions and training camps.

Coaches work closely with all members of the team and the organization. They are usually responsible to the team's general manager. Winning a game means that the individual's job is secure for the moment. Losing a game means the Coach or Manager could be replaced.

For Coaches who attain this level in the sport, there is usually a great deal of professional satisfaction, a lot of glamour working with high-visibility professional teams, and major financial remuneration.

Salaries

Coaches working on the pro level have a wide salary range. Earnings can vary from $35,000 for one Coach to $10 million or more for others. Earnings depend on a number of variables including the individual's qualifications, experience, and responsibilities. Other influencing factors include the specific sport he or she is coaching as well as the prestige of the team.

Employment Prospects

Employment prospects are poor for Coaches or Managers aspiring to work with pro teams. There are only a limited number of professional teams in any specific sport. However, individuals who have made a name for themselves coaching on the college level may be able to break in.

Individuals may find opportunities with minor league teams as well as major league teams.

Advancement Prospects

Advancement prospects for Coaches working in the professional leagues depend greatly on the performance of the individual. If he or she has built up a team dramatically, or if the team has won a number of competitions, the individual may climb the career ladder rapidly. Advancement prospects also are determined by the sport and the level at which the individual is currently in his or her career. If, for example, the Coach is working with a prestigious team, career advancement might include a major financial contract.

An individual working with a minor league team may move up to coach a major league team. Individuals may also become team managers.

Education and Training

Educational requirements vary for Coaches. As a great many individuals work their way through the college and university ranks, many have four-year college degrees. Others do not. While a degree may not be a requirement, it may be useful when the individual is on the job as well as when he or she moves on to other careers after coaching.

Individuals often participate in coaching seminars, workshops, and symposiums in their specific sport. These may be offered through trade associations or other organizations.

Experience, Skills, and Personality Traits

Pro Coaches should have a complete understanding of the sport that they are working with. Many individuals in this profession are former athletes or college coaches. Most Coaches in the pros held assistant coach positions before becoming a Head Coach. Most baseball Managers are former players, minor league managers, or major league coaches.

Especially at the pro level, Coaches must be able to motivate their team. The Coach must also be able to get the athletes to pull together and work as a team. This is often difficult to do when athletes begin to shine on their own as the team superstar. It is, however, a necessary task. Individuals must have excellent communications skills in order to explain styles and techniques.

Coaches should be calm individuals. Getting excited, yelling, and screaming does not serve any purpose. They must be able to deal well with people on all levels, from the owner of the team and players to the referee on the playing field.

The Head Coach or Manager works with a staff of assistants. He or she must therefore have supervisory skills. The individual must also be extremely organized and detail oriented.

It is important for the Coach working in the pros to be able to work with pressure and stress. He or she must constantly deal with the possibility that the team may lose. There is not a great deal of job stability for pro Coaches. If the team is winning, everyone is happy. If the team loses more than once, management often puts the blame on the Coach. He or she can be replaced at any time.

Unions and Associations

Coaches may belong to trade associations and other organizations relevant to the sport they coach. These associations offer professional guidance, support, training, and education.

Tips for Entry

1. Positions for Coaches working in the professional leagues are very rarely advertised in newspapers or trade journals. These are the kind of jobs you have to be at the right place at the right time for.
2. If you aspire to be a Coach for a pro team, you should first make a name for yourself either as an athlete or as a coach for a university or college hosting prestigious sports programs and teams. Once you have the educational background you need, try to obtain a position coaching for a college team and work your way up from there. You must rise in the ranks to become a Coach in the pros.
3. Get experience coaching by volunteering to coach local youth teams.
4. Another way to obtain experience coaching is by getting a summer job as a sports counselor or coach at a camp.

COACH (COLLEGE, UNIVERSITY)

CAREER PROFILE

Duties: Coaching college athletic teams; choosing team members; developing game strategies

Alternate Title(s): Head Coach; Assistant Coach

Salary Range: $25,000 to $4 million+

Employment Prospects: Good

Advancement Prospects: Fair

Best Geographical Location(s) for Position: Positions may be located throughout the country

Prerequisites:

Education or Training—Minimum of four-year college degree required for most positions

Experience—Experience as athlete helpful but not always necessary

Special Skills and Personality Traits—Knowledge of sports; teaching and coaching skills; physically fit; ability to motivate; detail oriented

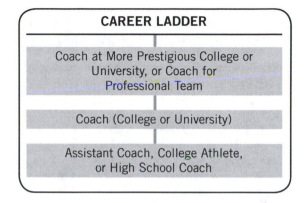

CAREER LADDER

Coach at More Prestigious College or University, or Coach for Professional Team

Coach (College or University)

Assistant Coach, College Athlete, or High School Coach

Position Description

The Coach of a college or university is responsible for coaching one or more of the school's sports teams. In larger colleges the individual may coach one specific sport. In smaller schools he or she may be required to coach all sports. Coaches have varied duties depending on the school they are working at, the size of the athletic department, and the emphasis put on the sports program.

Coaches are ultimately responsible for getting athletic teams ready to play competitively in games, tournaments, and championships. One of the main duties of the Coach is to put together a team of the best athletes available in the specific sport. He or she runs tryout sessions at the beginning of each season and invites the outstanding and most promising athletes to be part of the team.

In some situations, the Coach recruits students to play on the team from within the school. He or she may also have the responsibility of scouting high schools throughout the country to recruit athletes for the college team who are especially talented in a sport. The Coach may work with the college and offer young men and women athletic scholarships in an effort to entice them to attend and play on the school's teams. In larger schools the individual may pass this responsibility on to an assistant coach.

Once the athletes have all tried out, the Coach must choose the players of the team. The individual must evaluate each athlete's assets, drawbacks, and skills to determine who will be of greatest value to the team. He or she may do the evaluations alone, or may work with other coaches, instructors, and college personnel. The Coach then decides the position each athlete is best suited for.

The Coach sets times for the team to have practice sessions and meetings. He or she must determine how frequent practices will be and the duration of each session. Practices are devoted to developing the skills of both individual athletes and the team as a whole.

The individual discusses team strategies and methods of implementation. He or she also talks about any problems with the way the team plays and potential solutions.

The Coach works with other personnel in his or her college and opposing schools to schedule games, meets, tournaments, and championships. He or she is responsible for putting scheduled events on the calendar and notifying team members and others of the dates. The individual may also be responsible for scheduling practice areas, gym space, and transportation when games are played away from home base.

Coaches must motivate their players and teach them how to play as a team. They must make their players aware of the best techniques to play the game, the route to winning, and the rules of good sportsmanship.

In some colleges, the Coach might have additional duties. He or she may work as a physical education instructor. In this position, he or she is responsible for teaching duties as well. The Coach may be required to develop budgets, order equipment, keep it repaired and accounted for, and so on.

The Coach generally attends all of his or her team's games, at home or away. He or she is the leader of the team. During a game, the Coach may change strategies, give signals, and call time-outs to talk with team members. He or she must be aware of everything that is happening.

Before a game and during halftime, the Coach usually gives pep talks to the team and may offer advice to athletes regarding playing tactics. After a game, the Coach offers suggestions for improvement that might be helpful for the next game.

Athletes often look upon the Coach as a good friend, teacher, or father or mother figure. Many athletes go to their Coach with athletic and personal problems. He or she works long hours, preparing the team for potential victories, attending games, and dealing with members of the team, faculty, and administration. Losing a game is an indication that the Coach has to work a bit harder with the team. Winning an important tournament or championship generally gives the individual a great deal of satisfaction.

Salaries

Coaches' salaries vary widely depending on a number of variables, including the size, location, and prestige of the college or university and its emphasis on sports and athletic programs. Earnings are also dependent on the qualifications, experience, and duties of the individual. Salaries may range from $25,000 to $4 million plus for coaches working in colleges and universities. Coaches may also receive liberal fringe benefit packages.

Earnings of individuals coaching in small two-year schools or those with limited experience are on the lower end of the scale. Coaches working in large universities with strong emphasis on sports programs, such as those belonging to the National Collegiate Athletic Association (NCAA), receive higher earnings. These schools often derive large amounts of money from selling television rights to their games. They therefore can afford to pay Coaches higher salaries.

Employment Prospects

Employment prospects are good for Coaches working in colleges and universities. Positions may be located throughout the country. Individuals may, however, have to relocate to find a suitable position.

Coaches may work in junior colleges, community colleges, state schools, and private colleges and universities. Prospects become more difficult for those aspiring to Coach for NCAA teams.

Advancement Prospects

Advancement prospects differ widely for Coaches depending on a number of variables. The most prominent factor to consider is the level the Coach is currently at in his or her career. Other factors include the drive and determination of the individual and his or her coaching skills and contacts in the field.

College Coaches climb the career ladder by obtaining a similar position in a larger, more prestigious school. Coaches working in small junior or community colleges have the best advancement prospects. Individuals may also move up the next rung on the career ladder by locating a position as an assistant coach in a larger school.

The most coveted positions in amateur coaching are found in colleges that are members of the NCAA. These schools put a great deal of emphasis on sports activities and their sports teams. As noted previously, individuals in these positions usually receive higher salaries than other collegiate coaches. As games are televised, the Coach gets a lot of exposure, which helps when trying to advance into the pros.

Education and Training

As a rule, colleges require their Coaches to have at least a four-year college degree. A graduate degree is helpful. One of the best choices for a major is physical education. The only exception to this rule may be as well-known professional athlete who has turned to coaching as a career.

Courses, workshops, and symposiums in coaching, sports, administration, and so on are useful.

Experience, Skills, and Personality Traits

College Coaches need complete understanding of the sport (or sports) that they are coaching. Many individuals in this profession were college athletes prior to their entry in this career.

Coaches should be in good physical shape. They should also be able to provide information about health, nutrition, and fitness to their team. This is especially important now, when alcohol and drug abuse is so widespread.

A Coach should be able to motivate the athletes both individually and as a group. He or she is responsible for the athletes pulling together and working as a team. The Coach should be the type of person the team could look up to as a leader.

He or she needs the ability to deal with a variety of people in all situations. It is important that the Coach keep a level head and remain calm at all times.

The individual in this position must be able to handle many details at once. If the Coach is working with a staff, he or she must also have supervisory skills.

Unions and Associations

Coaches may belong to trade associations and other organizations relevant to the sport or sports they coach. These associations offer professional guidance, support, training, and education.

Some of these might include the American Baseball Coaches Association (ABCA), the American Football Coaches Association (AFCA), the American Hockey Coaches Association (AHCA), the American Swimming Coaches Association (ASCA), the College Swimming Coaches Association of America (CSCA), the Intercollegiate Tennis Coaches Association (ITCA), the National Association of Collegiate Gymnastics Coaches (NACGC), and the National Interscholastic Swimming Coaches Association of America (NISCA).

Others might be the National Soccer Coaches Association of America (NSCA), the National Wrestling Coaches Association (NWCA), the United States Cross Country Coaches Association (USCCCA), the United States Women's Track Coaches Association (USWTCA), the Women's Basketball Coaches Association (WBCA), and the various National Collegiate Athletic Association Coaches Associations (NCAACA).

Tips for Entry

1. Volunteer to coach local youth teams, such as Little League.
2. Consider a summer job as a sports counselor or coach at a camp.
3. Job openings may be advertised in the display or classified sections of newspapers. Look under heading classifications of "Coaching," "College," "Sports," "Athletics," or "Teaching."
4. Positions may also be advertised in trade journals.
5. Keep in close touch with your college's placement office. They are often advised of job openings.
6. State schools may publish lists of job opportunities in special bulletins. Write and inquire.
7. Join trade associations. These organizations provide a wealth of information for additional training as well as career guidance.
8. Search the major job and career sites on-line to see if there are openings in this field. There are also a number of sports sites on the Web hosting jobs in sports.

COACH (HIGH SCHOOL)

CAREER PROFILE

Duties: Coaching one or more of a high school's athletic teams; choosing team members; developing game strategies; teaching physical education

Alternate Title(s): Head Coach

Salary Range: $27,000 to $80,000+

Employment Prospects: Good

Advancement Prospects: Fair

Best Geographical Location(s) for Position: Positions located throughout the country

Prerequisites:

Education or Training—Minimum of a four-year college degree required for most positions

Experience—Student teaching experience may be required

Special Skills and Personality Traits—Teaching and coaching skills; enjoy working with young adults; ability to motivate; understanding; personable

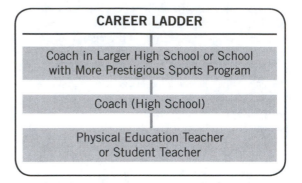

CAREER LADDER

Coach in Larger High School or School with More Prestigious Sports Program

Coach (High School)

Physical Education Teacher or Student Teacher

Position Description

A high school's Coach is often credited with the school's winning teams. Coaches working in high schools are responsible for coaching one or more of the school's sports teams. In larger schools the individual may coach one specific sport. In smaller schools, he or she may be required to coach all sports. These may include basketball, hockey, skiing, football, wrestling, soccer, and swimming, depending on the school's sports programs. High School Coaches are usually part of the teaching staff of the school.

Coaches working in secondary or high schools may work at public, private, or parochial institutions. They have varied duties depending on the school and the size of the athletic department. In many high schools, Coaches are also responsible for teaching physical education classes. They may also teach health or other related courses.

In larger schools hosting many different types of sports programs, it is unrealistic to believe that a single individual has sufficient time to coach all the teams. Therefore, the Head Coach often has to locate additional suitable Coaches. He or she is then responsible for supervising the athletic teams and the other Coaches.

A team's Coach is the person responsible for getting the entire team ready to play competitively in games, tournaments, and championships. He or she is responsible for putting together each team with the best athletes available in the school. The Head Coach works with the athletic director, head of the department, principal, and/or superintendent developing the athletic programs and deciding which sports the school actively participates in.

At the beginning of each school year, the Coach schedules tryout sessions for the specific sports. He or she may put announcements in the school paper, on the bulletin board, or in the gym. He or she may also personally invite athletes who show promise in selected sports to the tryouts.

The Head Coach and other school Coaches choose the members of the various teams once the athletes have all tried out. After the team members have been notified, practice sessions are scheduled. During these sessions, the Coach determines the positions each athlete is best suited for. The Coach informs team members of times and duration of practices. He or she also is responsible for letting team members know the rules, regulations, and policies of the school.

One of the main functions of the High School Coach is to help athletes develop their skills. He or she is also responsible for helping the members learn about good sportsmanship and teamwork.

The Coach must develop game strategies and methods for integrating them into the team. He or she also discusses problems with team plays and offers solutions.

In some situations, the Head Coach may be responsible for scheduling games, meets, tournaments, and championships with coaches from other schools. In other instances, this may be handled by the athletic director, head of the department, or other school personnel. The Head Coach is responsible for putting these athletic events on. No matter who sets up the programs, the Coach is responsible for making sure that his or her team is aware in advance of the event scheduled.

The Coach is also responsible for arranging for practice areas, gym space, and transportation when games are played away from the home school. He or she may also be required to plan for locker rooms or meals for competing teams coming to play at the school.

In addition to teaching skills and developing strategies, the Coach must be able to motivate his or her team and teach them how to work together. He or she must often offer words of praise and encouragement.

Depending on the specific responsibilities of the individual, he or she may be required to develop budgets, order equipment, keep it in repair, and so on. The Coach is responsible for making sure that the gym and all playing and athletic areas are neat, clean, and safe. If there is a problem, he or she must call a school maintenance person to deal with the difficulty.

The Coach attends all of his or her team's games, at home or away. Team members often look to their Coach, as the leader of the team, for guidance. During a game, the Coach may change strategies, give signals, and call time-outs to talk to team members. He or she must be aware of everything that is happening.

Before a game and during halftimes, he or she usually gives pep talks to the team and may advise athletes on playing tactics. After a game, the Coach offers a review and suggestions for the next game.

Coaches are aware that a player with problems can affect an entire team. Team members usually have great respect for High School Coaches. Team members often come to the Coach with both personal and athletic problems. The Coach's door must always be open to talk to a team member.

An important function of a High School Coach is to help students with athletic talent attain sports scholarships. To do this, he or she may call or write a recommendation to colleges offering these programs for school athletes. During the course of his or her work, the High School Coach may also contact professional sports teams and organizations to evaluate the talent of specific athletes.

After long hours of training, practice, and motivation, every Coach gets an enormous amount of pleasure seeing his or her team win. It is also gratifying to know he or she helped an athlete become a major force in a collegiate sports team or a superstar professional athlete.

Salaries

The salaries of High School Coaches can vary greatly. The reasons include the size, geographic location, and type of school the Coach is working at as well as the school's emphasis on sports and athletic programs. Coaches working in public schools may receive different salaries from their counterparts in private or parochial institutions.

Earnings for Coaches are also dependent on their qualifications, educational background, experience, and responsibilities. They may be employed as physical education teachers and also be responsible for all coaching duties.

Salaries may range from $27,000 to $80,000 plus for individuals working in high schools. The higher earnings are usually awarded to Coaches with a great deal of experience and responsibilities and who work in large cities.

Employment Prospects

Employment prospects are good for Coaches working in high schools. Positions may be located throughout the country. Coaches may work in public, private, or parochial schools. Individuals with the most opportunities are those who have highly diversified talents and who coach a variety of subjects. In a great many high schools, Coaches also must teach physical education. Some schools may offer part-time coaching positions.

Advancement Prospects

Advancement prospects are fair for High School Coaches. Most Coaches advance their careers in ways similar to other school teachers.

Individuals may move up the career ladder in a number of ways. The first is to locate a job in a more prestigious school or district that puts a strong emphasis on the sports programs. This will lead to higher earnings and greater job prestige for the individual.

Another method of career advancement occurs when an individual obtains additional education or gains seniority. In many school systems, compensation is directly related to the amount of education an individual has and the number of years he or she has been working.

Coaches who consistently have winning teams are also in demand in school systems that emphasize their sports programs.

Education and Training

High School Coaches working full time in most school systems are required to have minimum of a four-year college degree. A master's degree may be required for some positions. One of the best choices for a major is physical education. As most High School Coaches are part of the teaching staff, education degrees are usually mandatory.

Courses, workshops, and symposiums in coaching, sports, and administration are useful.

Experience, Skills, and Personality Traits

As noted previously, High School Coaches are usually part of the teaching staff. As a result, most have had experience with student teaching prior to a job appointment.

High School Coaches should enjoy working with young adults. Teaching and coaching skills are necessary. A complete knowledge and understanding of the sport (or sports) being coached is necessary. Coaches must be positive and able to motivate others. Teaching the skills of a sport is one part of the job; getting a team to implement the skills is another.

Coaches should be personable, understanding, and likable. They should be leaders whom team members can look up to.

First aid skills are helpful for Coaches in case of injuries or emergencies in the gym, practice area, or games.

Unions and Associations

Coaches working in high school settings may be members of local or national teachers' unions, depending on the school. Two of the largest of these bargaining unions are the National Educators Association (NEA) and the National Federation of Teachers (NFT). Organizations such as these work on behalf of teachers to help them obtain benefits, better working conditions, and higher salaries.

Coaches may also belong to any number of sports associations offering seminars, conferences, booklets, and career guidance. Some of these might include the American Baseball Coaches Association (ABCA), the American Football Coaches Association (AFCA), the American Hockey Coaches Association (AHCA), the American

Swimming Coaches Association (ASCA), the National Federation Interscholastic Coaches Association (NFICA), and the National Interscholastic Swimming Coaches Association of America (NISCA).

Others might be the National Soccer Coaches Association of America (NSCA), the National Wrestling Coaches Association (NWCA), the National Youth Sports Coaches Association (NYSCA), the United States Cross Country Coaches Association (USCCCA), the United States Women's Track Coaches Association (USWTCA), and the Women's Basketball Coaches Association (WBCA).

Tips for Entry

1. Jobs openings for High School Coaches are often advertised in the display or classified sections of newspapers. Look under heading classifications of "Coaching," "Sports," "Athletics," or "Teaching."
2. Many schools are now hiring Coaches for summer programs. This is a good way to obtain experience and get your foot in the door of a school system.
3. Volunteer to coach local youth teams, such as Little League teams.
4. Consider a summer job as a sports counselor or coach at a camp.
5. Coaching positions may also be advertised in trade journals.
6. Keep in close touch with your college's placement office. They are often advised of openings.
7. Send your résumé and a cover letter to schools. Ask that your résumé be kept on file if no opening is currently available.
8. Join trade associations. Trade journals usually offer career guidance, and the association meetings will help you make important contacts.
9. Search Internet job Web sites for possible openings.

ATHLETIC DIRECTOR (SECONDARY SCHOOL)

Position Description

The Athletic Director working in an educational setting has varied responsibilities depending on his or her situation. The individual is ultimately responsible for running the school system's athletic and sports programs.

Much of the work of the Athletic Director is supervisory and administrative. The individual works with other administrative personnel in the school system to plan and execute as broad a program as possible. His or her goal is to provide a full physical education program for all students in the school.

One of the main responsibilities of the Athletic Director is to develop, administer, and supervise the entire curriculum of physical education for the school or district, depending on the situation.

He or she assists in the recruiting, interviewing, and recommending of qualified people to work in the athletic department. The Athletic Director also is responsible for both supervising and evaluating people on the athletic staff. In certain positions, the individual is in charge of the orientation of the athletic staff and their in-service education.

The Athletic Director is responsible for coordinating and supervising the various physical education teachers, instructors, and coaches as well as all the teams and sports.

Depending on the situation, the Athletic Director is responsible for preparing the physical education budget for supplies. He or she either specifies requirements for the purchase of the supplies and equipment or supervises an individual in the department who handles this job. Once equipment and supplies are purchased, the Athletic Director is responsible for making sure that the supplies arrive in good shape or are replaced.

The Athletic Director is responsible for appraising, previewing, and recommending new materials and textbooks for use within the physical education department. He or she is required to work with the staff promoting the various physical fitness programs in the school as well as developing new upgraded programs. At times, the individual reviews and evaluates the programs that currently exist in the school.

The Athletic Director often meets with the school superintendent or director to inform him or her of the progress of the physical education and sports programs and recommend necessary changes.

The individual advises the superintendent if and when the school needs new facilities, such as athletic fields or tennis courts. He or she also must work with building and grounds personnel and other staff when assigning the physical education facilities for extracurricular use. The Athletic Director is responsible for the total organization and scheduling of all interscholastic athletic activities.

At the same time, he or she fosters good school-community relations by making sure that the community is aware of the accomplishments of the various school teams. This might include calling the press about winning teams or assigning someone to take care of this particular duty.

An important part of the job of the Athletic Director is to individualize physical education activities for students who have special needs and talents. For example, the AD might set up special competitions for students who are physically or mentally handicapped.

During competitions and games with other schools, the Athletic Director is responsible for arranging transportation for the home team to other schools. When another team comes to compete at his or her school, the AD must make arrangements for their needs, such as providing lockers, refreshments, and so on.

The individual must see to it that all insurance programs that cover school athletes or athletic programs are provided and administered. The Athletic Director must cooperate with school nurses, physicians, and office personnel to make sure that all reports are filed and claims made. He or she must make sure that all school athletes take physical exams before they participate in sports programs.

The Athletic Director either personally keeps records or assigns someone to the task of recording the results of all contests, competitions, awards, and scholarships. At intervals, he or she is usually required to plan and supervise recognition programs for outstanding school athletes.

The Athletic Director is in charge of directing all in-school and extracurricular sports and athletic programs. He or she attempts to obtain support from both the school athletic teams and nonparticipating sports fans. The individual is also required, at times, to present programs to local community groups.

The Athletic Director works long hours. He or she often develops programs or attends school events after normal school hours and on weekends.

In smaller schools, the Athletic Director may also teach physical education and/or coach one or more sports. In larger schools, the individual does not have any teaching or coaching responsibilities, which frees up his or her time to administer programs.

Depending on the specific situation, the Athletic Director is responsible to either the school superintendent or the school director.

Salaries

Annual earnings for Athletic Directors working in education vary greatly depending on a number of factors. These include the size and location of the school the individual is working for, whether it is a private or public school, and the school's emphasis on sports programs. Compensation is also dependent on the experience level and duties of the Athletic Director.

Salaries can start at $30,000 in a small private school system or may go up to $85,000 plus annually in large schools that put a great emphasis on their school's sports program.

Employment Prospects

Employment prospects are good for Athletic Directors. Individuals must, however, be willing to relocate to areas that need people in this position.

Jobs are available throughout the country in a variety of school systems. Individuals may look in both the public and private sector for employment.

Advancement Prospects

Advancement prospects are fair for Athletic Directors working in education. Individuals can move up the career ladder by obtaining a similar position in a larger school system with a more prestigious sports program. This will, in turn, usually lead to higher earnings.

Depending on the professional goals of the individual, he or she may also move into other supervisory positions in the school system or may move into a similar position in a large college.

Education and Training

Athletic Directors working in education require a minimum of a four-year college degree. Most positions require a graduate degree. Depending on the school system and the state in which the individual plans on working, the Athletic Director usually needs to major in education and/or physical education. He or she may also be required to take classes in administration.

Experience, Skills, and Personality Traits

Athletic Directors need supervisory and administrative skills. Individuals in this type of position should be able to prepare budgets and schedules and know how to keep to them.

The Athletic Director needs excellent interpersonal skills. He or she will be dealing with other school personnel, students, and parents. Good communication skills, both written and verbal, are necessary.

Individuals should have a keen interest in physical education and athletics and enjoy working with youth. They should, furthermore, be energetic and enthusiastic.

Athletic Directors working in an educational setting usually need teaching experience. However, this is not always true. Often, private schools do not require experience in the educational field; instead, they opt for expertise in sports and/or administration.

Unions and Associations

Athletic Directors who started out as teachers or instructors or currently teach may belong to a union, such as the American Federation of Teachers, which negotiates on behalf of teachers. Others who work in private schools may not.

Individuals may belong to various local groups or associations related to sports they may coach. They may also be involved with the American Alliance for Health, Physical Education, Recreation and Dance.

Tips for Entry

1. Get experience by volunteering to run local sports programs for area youth.
2. Consider working as a recreation director or assistant in a summer program in your area.
3. Work with local Little League teams. The experience will be helpful later in your career and look good on your résumé.
4. Positions as Athletic Directors are often advertised in local newspaper display and classified sections. Look under heading classifications of "Education," "Athletics," and "Sports."
5. Jobs may also be advertised in educational magazines and journals.
6. Try to attend a school with a sports management or administration program. These schools offer help in job placement.
7. Search the major career and job sites online. You might find openings advertised. Keywords might include "education," "athletic director," or "sports."

PHYSICAL EDUCATION INSTRUCTOR (COLLEGE)

Position Description

Physical Education Instructors working in schools of higher education may work in junior, community, or four-year colleges and universities. They may work in private institutions or state or public schools. Responsibilities vary with the specific job. Instructors may also be called teachers, coaches, or professors.

Individuals may teach required physical education classes as well as elective subjects to college students. Most colleges now provide a tremendous variety of courses for students to select from in order to fulfill their physical education requirements. Thus, those who teach college physical education now may have the opportunity to teach and participate in some of their favorite sports.

Individuals may instruct classes in almost any sport, including archery, badminton, bowling, tennis, racquetball, golf, wrestling, swimming, boxing, aerobics, dance, and exercise, to name a few. Instructors may also teach team sport classes.

Individuals may have mixed classes or may be responsible solely for classes for women or men. Unlike teaching in elementary or secondary schools, those working in most college situations usually do not decide what types of sports should be taught. Rather, individuals are assigned specific courses to teach. They must then determine how to teach each course. Instructors may spend an entire semester teaching a specific class in one sport.

In some states there are minimum, state-mandated physical education and fitness requirements that must be followed. An example of this might be a state university that requires that students be capable of passing a basic swimming test before graduation. In these situations, the Instructor may be expected to help students attain this goal. This may include teaching classes in the subject as well as giving private instruction to students who require it.

Depending on the type and level of class that an individual is teaching, he or she may have to individualize the training. In a beginning golf course, all students would probably be on the same level of expertise. However, in an intermediate tennis course, for example, students may be at a number of different levels. The Teacher may be expected to give one-on-one instruction. Instructors must be adept at working with individuals of all levels of skill, even if they are in the same class.

Physical Education Instructors working on the college level may have a variety of students, including some who are taking classes just to meet graduation requirements and others who are taking electives because they like to be involved in sports. Some students may also be heavily involved with the college's athletic programs.

Instructors must help the students set realistic goals and help them attain them. Many college Instructors are responsible for assisting a student who has the ability to turn professional. The Instructor might contact scouts, professional teams, or other useful people to achieve this goal.

Depending on the size of the college's sports department, the Physical Education Instructor may also have coaching duties. He or she may be expected to put together one or all of the college's sports teams in addition to coaching them throughout the playing season.

The individual is required to handle paperwork, including grading exams and other student work. He or she is expected to evaluate student progress in classes and assign a mark. In some colleges, this may be a letter or number grade. In others, it may be a pass or fail evaluation.

The Phys. Ed. Instructor is also responsible for reporting any accidents that occur in the gym or during games. He or she may be required to fill in insurance reports and forms about the accident. The individual may also be responsible for making sure that any required medical forms are filled in for students in his or her classes.

The Instructor is expected to keep the gym, lockers rooms, and other sports-oriented areas safe, neat, and in working order. If equipment needs to be fixed or replaced, he or she must report the problem to the head of the department or maintenance and make sure it is taken care of.

College Instructors may teach during the regular school season or work throughout the year. Hours may vary depending on teaching schedules. Instructors are expected to prepare for classes and teach as well as schedule regular hours to meet with students. Individuals also have to attend college faculty meetings. If they are involved in coaching or working with students participating in tournaments, games, or competitions, Instructors are also expected to attend these events.

Physical Education Instructors usually are responsible to either the head of the department or the athletic director, depending on the structure of the school.

Salaries

Earnings for Physical Education Instructors working on the college level vary greatly depending on a number of factors. These include the specific college, its geographic location, and the emphasis it puts on its athletic and sports programs. Other variables include the individual's education, responsibilities, skills, and his or her seniority.

Salaries can range from $27,000 to $75,000 plus. Compensation is usually augmented by liberal fringe benefit packages. Those working at two-year schools with little or no experience earn salaries on the bottom end of the scale. Individuals working at schools with prestigious athletic programs earn salaries toward the top.

Employment Prospects

Employment prospects are good for Physical Education Instructors on the college level. Individuals may find it easier to break into the profession by locating a position in a two-year school. While individuals may have to move to other areas to locate specific jobs, employment may be found in almost every area in the country.

Most colleges, even small ones, have more than one Physical Education Instructor. Many, especially those that put a great deal of emphasis on their sports and athletic program, have much larger departments.

Advancement Prospects

Advancement prospects are fair for Physical Education Instructors on a college level. Individuals might advance their careers by locating a position at a larger or more prestigious college or university. This usually results in increased earnings.

Some Phys. Ed. Instructors climb the career ladder by becoming head of the department, assistant athletic director, or athletic director at either his or her school or at another institution. Others advance by becoming coaches for more prestigious schools.

Education and Training

A minimum of a four-year college degree is required to teach in any college. However, most four-year colleges and universities require a master's degree or a doctorate. The most common degree for this type of position is one in physical education.

Experience, Skills, and Personality Traits

College Physical Education Instructors should enjoy working with adults. They should also like sports, athletics, and teaching. Most Instructors are sports fans.

Some Instructors have taught in high schools prior to obtaining a college-level job. Others landed their position after graduate school. Some individuals working in two-year schools located their job after graduating from a four-year school with a degree in physical education.

Individuals should have a knowledge of sports and athletics. While they need not be star athletes, they should know the rules, regulations, and skills of the sports they will be teaching. Having expertise in one if not more sports is necessary. The more the individual knows about specific sports or athletics, the easier he or she will find a job.

Instructors should be able to teach on a number of different levels of expertise. Patience and motivation are useful skills for those aspiring to be successful at their job.

The Phys. Ed. Instructor should have good communication skills. He or she must be able to explain directions, rules, and regulations to students. Writing skills are necessary for handling paperwork connected with the job.

Unions and Associations

Physical Education Instructors may belong to a bargaining union that helps them obtain better benefits, working conditions, and salaries. This depends on the specific school and position.

College Instructors may be members of organizations specific to the sports they are teaching or any number of other sports associations that offer seminars, conferences, booklets, and career guidance.

The college or university that the individual works for may also belong to the National Association of Collegiate Directors of Athletics (NACDA), the National Association of Intercollegiate Athletics (NAIA), the National Collegiate Athletic Association (NCCA), the National Junior College Athletic Association (NJCAA), or any of the collegiate conference organizations.

Tips for Entry

1. Keep in touch with your college's placement office. These offices receive notices of other colleges that need to hire Instructors.

2. Certain employment agencies specialize in locating positions for people in education. Check these out. They are usually located in major cities. Keep in mind that some agencies charge the employer a fee to find a suitable employee, while others charge the employee. Make sure you find out costs in advance.

3. Positions in education are often advertised in the display or classified section of the newspaper. Look under heading classifications of "College," "University," "Community College," "Junior College," "Instructor," "Physical Education," "Gym," "Teacher," "Professor," or the names of specific sports such as "Tennis Instructor," "Golf Instructor," and so on.

4. Get letters of recommendation from several of your professors at college.

5. Many state colleges have newsletters advising people of openings within the system. Contact state colleges to look into this.

6. It is sometimes easier to get your foot in the door by teaching at a local college part time. You then have experience on your résumé that may make it easier to obtain a full-time job.

7. Check out online job and career sites to see if there are any advertised openings. Search keywords such as "sports," "education," "college," and "athletics."

PHYSICAL EDUCATION TEACHER (SECONDARY SCHOOL)

CAREER PROFILE

Duties: Developing activities for gym classes; teaching sports; following mandated physical education and fitness requirements; coaching

Alternate Title(s): Phys. Ed. Teacher; Phys. Ed. Instructor; Gym Teacher; P.E. Teacher

Salary Range: $25,000 to $70,000+

Employment Prospects: Good

Advancement Prospects: Good

Best Geographical Location(s) for Position: Positions may be located throughout the country

Prerequisites:

Education or Training—Minimum of four-year college degree in physical education; many schools may require master's degree

Experience—Student teaching experience usually required

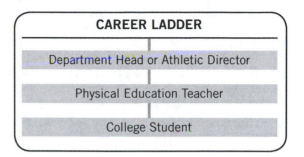

CAREER LADDER

Department Head or Athletic Director

Physical Education Teacher

College Student

Special Skills and Personality Traits—Enjoys sports; likes teaching; knowledge and understanding of sports games and rules; personable

Special Requirements—Teaching certificate or license

Position Description

Physical Education Teachers working in secondary schools can work in junior high or high schools and in public, private, or parochial institutions. Their duties vary depending on the type of job they are hired for.

A secondary school Physical Education Teacher might teach boys, girls, or mixed gym classes. The individual usually must develop activities for each class and decide what sports should be taught to which students. Some states mandate minimum physical education and fitness requirements that the Physical Education Teacher must follow.

It is up to the Physical Education Teacher to help each student attain the best possible fitness. In some schools, he or she may be required to develop sports programs for students with disabilities.

The Phys. Ed. Teacher or gym teacher, as he or she may be called, should be able to help students set realistic physical fitness goals and then help students reach them. Successful Teachers in this field will help all students, even those who don't seem to have any real interest in fitness or sports, attain a fitness level and have fun participating in activities. Good Phys. Ed. Teachers make even nonjoiners want to be involved in sports.

The individual often has to handle paperwork and produce documentation. For example, the Physical Education Teacher is responsible for reporting both verbally and in writing any accidents that occur in the gym or during games. The individual usually is responsible for documenting students' progress in various sports and for reporting these on grade sheets, report cards, or during parent-teacher conferences.

Depending on the size and structure of the phys. ed. department, the individual may be required to plan budgets for the department, write up requests for equipment, and order supplies. This usually occurs in smaller schools where there is no head of the department or where the Teacher acts as the department head.

Physical Education Teachers may be responsible for putting together school sports teams. In some schools the individual is required to act as the coach for the various teams. In others he or she is responsible for finding coaches for the different sports teams.

The teacher is responsible for keeping the gym, locker rooms, and other sports-oriented areas neat and safe. If equipment needs to be fixed or replaced, he or she usually is responsible for reporting the problem and following up on it.

In certain situations, the Physical Education Teacher may also be responsible for teaching other subjects, such as health, hygiene, and/or sex education classes.

Gym teachers may be responsible to the head of the department, athletic director, assistant principal, principal, or headmaster, depending on the particular school system.

Individuals usually work normal school hours. Phys. Ed. Teachers have to put in extra time to plan classes, write up reports, attend meetings and other educational sessions, and attend school-sponsored sporting events. P.E. Teachers who also coach work longer hours.

Many people enjoy the flexibility of teaching in a school system because schools are usually closed during holidays and the summer months.

Salaries

Salaries for Physical Education Teachers vary greatly depending on a number of variables. These include the type of school (private, parochial, public) and geographic location as well as the education, responsibilities, and seniority of the individual.

Salaries can range from $25,000 to $70,000 plus. Compensation is usually augmented by liberal fringe benefit packages. Physical Education Teachers can earn additional monies by coaching and teaching summer school.

Employment Prospects

Employment prospects are good for Physical Education Teachers who wish to work in secondary schools. While individuals may have to relocate to find specific jobs, employment may be found in almost every geographical area in the country.

Teachers also have the option of working in junior high schools or high schools, and public, private, or parochial institutions. Most secondary schools have at least two or more Physical Education Teachers on staff.

Advancement Prospects

Advancement prospects are good for Physical Education Teachers. Many individuals who stay at the same school for a number of years have the opportunity to be tenured. Usually tenured teachers cannot be fired or let go from their position. After teaching for a number of years, salaries usually rise. The individual might advance his or her career by locating another position at a larger school that pays more.

The Physical Education Teacher might also be promoted to head of the physical education department,

assistant athletic director, or athletic director at either his or her school or at another institution.

Education and Training

A minimum of a four-year college degree is usually required in most teaching positions. It is common for individuals seeking positions such as this to have a degree in education with a major in physical education. Some schools might also require a graduate degree.

Experience, Skills, and Personality Traits

Individuals who teach usually go through some type of student teaching experience while still in college. This helps prepare them for the job when they graduate.

Physical Education Teachers working in secondary schools should not only like sports but enjoy teaching and working with young adults. While all Phys. Ed. Teachers do not have to be terrific athletes, they should have a complete understanding of sports.

Successful teachers in all fields should be easygoing, understanding, and personable. Individuals should also have a knack for teaching.

Special Requirements

Individuals teaching in public schools are required to be licensed by the state in which they work.

Unions and Associations

Depending on the school, Physical Education Teachers may or may not belong to a bargaining union such as the National Educators Association (NEA) or the National Federation of Teachers (NFT). Organizations such as these work on behalf of teachers to help them obtain better benefits, working conditions, and salaries.

Teachers may also belong to any number of sports associations that offer seminars, conferences, booklets, and career guidance.

Tips for Entry

1. Certain employment agencies specialize in locating positions for teachers. Check these out. They are usually located in major cities.
2. Keep in touch with your college's placement office. These offices receive notices of schools that need to hire teachers.
3. Get letters of recommendation from several of your professors at school as well as your student teaching supervisor.
4. Apply for summer school positions. These are often easier to obtain and they help get your foot in the door of a school system.

5. Positions in education are often advertised in the classified or display section of the newspaper. The Sunday newspaper is one of the big days for advertising education jobs.

6. If you are interested in working in a specific area, write to the local newspaper and order a short-term subscription. In this way you will be able to keep track of all the job offerings. You can also generally see many of the ads online.

PHYSICAL EDUCATION TEACHER (ELEMENTARY SCHOOL)

CAREER PROFILE

Duties: Developing activities for gym classes; teaching physical education classes; instilling concepts of good sportsmanship

Alternate Title(s): Phys. Ed. Teacher; Gym Teacher; P.E. Teacher

Salary Range: $25,000 to $70,000+

Employment Prospects: Good

Advancement Prospects: Good

Best Geographical Location(s) for Position: Positions may be located throughout the country

Prerequisites:

Education or Training—Minimum of a four-year college degree in physical education; many schools may require a master's degree

Experience—Student teaching experience usually required

Special Skills and Personality Traits—Enjoys sports; likes teaching; flair for working with children; knowledge of sports and athletics; understanding

Special Requirements—Teaching license required to teach in public schools

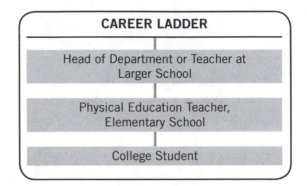

CAREER LADDER

Head of Department or Teacher at Larger School

Physical Education Teacher, Elementary School

College Student

Position Description

Physical Education Teachers working in elementary schools work with children. In some schools the Physical Education Teacher is responsible for all the school's gym classes. In others the individual might be responsible only for either the boys' or the girls' gym classes.

The Physical Education Teacher is also referred to as the P.E. or gym teacher. His or her duties vary depending on the specific job.

In some job situations, the P.E. Teacher is required to develop activities for each class. If the Teacher is working in a state where minimum physical education and fitness requirements are mandated, he or she must develop activities that follow the state guidelines. In other schools, the head of the department may develop specific activity rosters, and the individual gym teacher is required to put the activities into motion on a class level.

Physical Education Teachers must try to help each child attain the best fitness level possible. Elementary school gym teachers may have the added responsibility of assessing the needs of young students in their care and developing programs that help them gain coordination and confidence.

When teaching younger children, the individual must often deal with problems that Phys. Ed. Teach-

ers working with older students might not encounter. While all students must learn good sportsmanship, younger students often have a harder time dealing with such a concept. These problems could include a youngster losing a game, not being chosen for a team, and so on. The gym teacher must be able to deal with temper tantrums, crying, and other problems.

The P.E. Teacher must develop or teach sports programs for students with physical or emotional disabilities.

Physical Education Teachers working with young children must have a great deal of patience. They must explain games, sports, and rules in a manner in which youngsters can understand. They must be able to help children set realistic physical fitness goals and then help them reach those goals.

Successful Teachers in the physical education field need to be able to draw all children into participating and having fun.

The Teacher is required to report both verbally and in writing any accidents that occur in the gym. The individual should know and be able to practice basic first aid techniques. He or she should also be able to know when a child has the wind knocked out of him or her and when a child is seriously hurt.

Depending on the grade level and school, the Phys. Ed. Teacher might be responsible for documenting students' progress in various sports and for reporting these on grade sheets, report cards, or during parent-teacher conferences.

In some schools, the individual may be required to plan budgets for the department, write up requests for equipment, and order supplies. In other situations, the Teacher passes requests on to the head of the department.

The Gym Teacher must make sure that the gym, locker rooms, and other sports-oriented areas are neat and safe. If any equipment needs to be fixed or replaced, he or she usually must report the problem to the head of the department or the proper authority and follow up on the repair order.

Elementary School Physical Education Teachers may be responsible to the head of the department, assistant principal, principal, or headmaster, depending on the particular school system.

Individuals usually work normal school hours. In addition, they also have to put in extra hours writing reports, planning classes, and attending meetings. Most teachers have holidays and summers off.

Salaries

Salaries for Physical Education Teachers working in elementary schools can range from $25,000 to $70,000 or more. The variation in earning depends on whether the individual is working in a private, public, or parochial school, the size of the school system, and its geographic location. Salaries are also dependent on the education, responsibilities, and seniority of the individual. Earnings for most Elementary School Physical Education Teachers are augmented by liberal fringe benefit packages.

Employment Prospects

Employment prospects are good for Elementary School Physical Education Teachers. Almost every elementary school in the country has at least one Phys. Ed. Teacher on staff.

Teachers have the added benefit of being employable throughout the country.

Advancement Prospects

Advancement prospects are good for Elementary School Physical Education Teachers. Individuals who stay at the same school in the same position for a number of years have the opportunity to be tenured. Usually tenured teachers cannot be fired or let go from their position. This gives the individual a great amount of job stability.

Elementary School Phys. Ed. Teachers who wish to climb the career ladder may do so in a number of ways. Some individuals advance their career by locating a position in a larger school district that offers a higher salary. Other individuals seek promotion to the position of head of the physical education department.

Education and Training

A minimum of a four-year college degree is usually required in most teaching positions. It is common for individuals seeking positions such as this to have a degree in education with a major in physical education. Some positions might additionally require a graduate degree.

Seminars and classes in early childhood education as well as physical education are helpful.

Special Requirements

Individuals teaching in public schools are required to hold a teaching license or other credential. Credentials differ from state to state. Information may be obtained by contacting the specific state's department of education.

Experience, Skills, and Personality Traits

Elementary School Physical Education Teachers obtain experience by student teaching while in college. As a rule, the individual tries to do his or her student teaching in a situation simulating the general age group he or she wishes to work with after graduation.

Elementary School Physical Education Teachers must enjoy teaching and have a flair for working with children. They should have a good working knowledge of sports and athletics.

P.E. Teachers should be easygoing, understanding, compassionate, and personable.

Unions and Associations

The National Educators Association (NEA) and the National Federation of Teachers (NFT) are two of the bargaining unions that Elementary School Phys. Ed. Teachers may belong to. These organizations work on behalf of teachers to help them obtain better benefits, working conditions, and salaries. Teachers at some schools may not be members of any union.

Physical Education Teachers may also belong to any number of sports associations that offer educational and career guidance.

Tips for Entry

1. Volunteer time as a coach for a youngsters baseball, basketball, or football team. This will help you gain experience working with children.

2. Get letters of recommendation from several of your professors at school as well as your student teaching supervisor.

3. Certain employment agencies specialize in locating positions for teachers. Check these out. They are usually located in major cities. Check to find out who pays the employment agency fee. In some situations it is the school; in others, it is the teacher.

4. Keep in touch with your college's placement office. These offices receive notices of schools that plan on hiring teachers.

5. Apply for summer school positions. These are often easier to obtain, and they help get your foot in the door of a school system.

6. Positions in education are often advertised in the display or classified section of the newspaper. The Sunday newspaper is one of the big sources for advertised education jobs.

7. If you are interested in working in a specific area, write to the local newspaper and order a short-term subscription. This way, you will be able to keep track of all the job offerings.

8. Consider a summer position working in a town or city youth recreation department. This is another good way to gain valuable experience.

9. Search online for job openings. Type in keywords such as "teaching" or "physical education," into job or career search sites.

SPORTS OFFICIATING

PRO BASEBALL UMPIRE

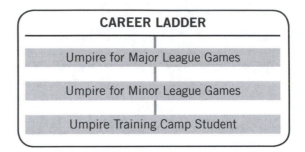

Position Description

Umpires are the individuals who officiate at baseball games. Without them, a baseball game would not run smoothly. The individual's main function is to make sure that all rules and regulations of the game are followed and the game proceeds smoothly. Umpires participate in all professional baseball games, from those conducted in the minor leagues on up to the majors.

There are usually four Umpires in each professional baseball game. One stands behind home plate and the other three stand near each base. Depending on the situation, the Umpires take turns officiating in each position from game to game. Special games, such as World Series games, may use additional Umpires.

Umpires must know all the rules and regulations of the sport. They are responsible for calling fouls, balls, and strikes. Individuals in this position are also the ones who make the call on whether a player is safe or out on a play at a base. The Umpire standing behind home plate calls the pitches as fouls, balls, and strikes. The Umpire is also responsible for making sure the pitcher has a supply of balls when needed. Safe and out calls are made by the Umpire standing nearest the base where the action is occurring. These Umpires are also responsible for making calls regarding balls hit to the outfield.

Umpires must keep their eyes on the ball and the action on the field at all times. There is no time for day-dreaming in this position. Looking away for even one second can mean missing important action.

A familiar scene in professional baseball is that of an athlete or a manager arguing with an Umpire over a decision. This arguing usually is in vain, as the Umpire's decision is final. If the Umpire's decision is not popular with the fans, he must also be able to deal with the booing that follows.

Umpires in professional baseball may have to travel a great deal in their jobs. They may be away from their home base for a third of the year during the baseball season. Individuals are assigned to officiate at a number of games in an area and then move on to another location. Umpires are usually treated well during their travels. Travel and lodging expenses are paid for as part of the job. Umpires are not allowed to fraternize with athletes, as this may lead to a conflict of interest during a game.

Individuals may work during afternoon games, evening games, and on weekends. Hours can be long. The Umpire is expected to be on the field for the entire game, which can take three hours or more. The individual also has to deal with the climate. Umpires may work on extremely hot or cold days, or in the rain.

Umpires in professional baseball are employed by the National League (NL) and the American League (AL). These leagues work under the auspices of the Baseball Commissioner's office.

PRO BASEBALL UMPIRE

CAREER PROFILE

Duties: Officiating at professional baseball games; calling balls, strikes, and fouls; making out and safe calls; settling disputes on the field

Alternate Title(s): Ump; Official

Salary Range: $25,000 to $350,000+

Employment Prospects: Poor

Advancement Prospects: Fair

Best Geographical Location(s) for Position: Cities hosting professional baseball teams

Prerequisites:

    Education or Training—Training at approved umpire school

    Experience—Experience officiating in the minor leagues

CAREER LADDER

Umpire for Major League Games

Umpire for Minor League Games

Umpire Training Camp Student

Special Skills and Personality Traits—Knowledge of rules, regulations, and policies of baseball; physically fit; good eyesight; ability to deal with stress and pressure; calm, cool, and collected; ability to travel

Position Description

Umpires are the individuals who officiate at baseball games. Without them, a baseball game would not run smoothly. The individual's main function is to make sure that all rules and regulations of the game are followed and the game proceeds smoothly. Umpires participate in all professional baseball games, from those conducted in the minor leagues on up to the majors.

There are usually four Umpires in each professional baseball game. One stands behind home plate and the other three stand near each base. Depending on the situation, the Umpires take turns officiating in each position from game to game. Special games, such as World Series games, may use additional Umpires.

Umpires must know all the rules and regulations of the sport. They are responsible for calling fouls, balls, and strikes. Individuals in this position are also the ones who make the call on whether a player is safe or out on a play at a base. The Umpire standing behind home plate calls the pitches as fouls, balls, and strikes. The Umpire is also responsible for making sure the pitcher has a supply of balls when needed. Safe and out calls are made by the Umpire standing nearest the base where the action is occurring. These Umpires are also responsible for making calls regarding balls hit to the outfield.

Umpires must keep their eyes on the ball and the action on the field at all times. There is no time for day-

dreaming in this position. Looking away for even one second can mean missing important action.

A familiar scene in professional baseball is that of an athlete or a manager arguing with an Umpire over a decision. This arguing usually is in vain, as the Umpire's decision is final. If the Umpire's decision is not popular with the fans, he must also be able to deal with the booing that follows.

Umpires in professional baseball may have to travel a great deal in their jobs. They may be away from their home base for a third of the year during the baseball season. Individuals are assigned to officiate at a number of games in an area and then move on to another location. Umpires are usually treated well during their travels. Travel and lodging expenses are paid for as part of the job. Umpires are not allowed to fraternize with athletes, as this may lead to a conflict of interest during a game.

Individuals may work during afternoon games, evening games, and on weekends. Hours can be long. The Umpire is expected to be on the field for the entire game, which can take three hours or more. The individual also has to deal with the climate. Umpires may work on extremely hot or cold days, or in the rain.

Umpires in professional baseball are employed by the National League (NL) and the American League (AL). These leagues work under the auspices of the Baseball Commissioner's office.

SPORTS OFFICIATING

Salaries

There is a large salary range for Umpires, depending on a number of variables. The most prominent variable is the level class the individual is officiating in. Those working in the minor leagues earn less than those in the majors. Umpires officiating at Class A games earn less than those doing the same job in AAA games. Individuals may earn annual salaries from $25,000 to $350,000 plus, depending on the level of game they are officiating at and their experience. Umpires may also earn more when officiating at major tournaments, such as the World Series.

Employment Prospects

Employment prospects are poor for those aspiring to be Umpires for professional baseball teams in the major leagues. Those who work in the minor leagues will have a better chance of getting their foot in the door.

Advancement Prospects

Advancement prospects are fair for Umpires officiating at professional baseball games if they have drive, determination, experience, and are skilled at what they do.

Individuals may climb the career ladder by being assigned to a position officiating for games between teams in a higher class. There are four classes in baseball, three in the minor leagues and one in the major leagues. The lowest class is A, which is where the rookies usually start to play; the next is AA; AAA follows. The major leagues are the highest level. Most Umpires aspire to work in the majors. A great accomplishment for the individual is to officiate during the World Series.

Education and Training

There is no formal educational requirement for Umpires. Individuals must, however, be thoroughly trained in the skills of officiating. This is usually accomplished at an Umpire training camp or school. After attending Umpire school, those who meet requirements go on to another training program. Individuals who complete this program are chosen to begin their careers as Umpires in the minor leagues.

Experience, Skills, and Personality Traits

After attending umpire school, Umpires usually start off officiating at minor league games. As they obtain more experience, they move through the ranks of the minor leagues. Talented individuals may then land positions in the major leagues.

Umpires need to know all the rules, regulations, and policies of the sport. They must be able to make calls on balls, strikes, and fouls. Individuals should be in good physical condition. They must be able to stand for long periods of time while watching the game. Good eyesight is essential.

Umpires should be able to deal with stress and pressure. As a rule, whatever decision the Umpire makes, one side is unhappy and disagrees. Umpires must be able to make quick decisions and accurate, consistent, and fair judgments. Individuals must be able to work in a situation where others disagree with their decisions and judgments. Umpires must be calm, cool, and collected at all times.

Umpires must be able to travel away from the home base for a good portion of the year. It also helps to like traveling and living out of a suitcase.

Unions and Associations

Umpires work with the National League (NL) and American League (AL). Individuals also work with the Office for Baseball Umpire Development (OBUD). This organization holds development programs for Umpires and maintains standards within the industry.

Tips for Entry

1. If you are interested in being an Umpire, you must go to an Umpire training school. The names of these schools can be located in the Appendixes section. Contact them to find out application procedures.
2. Watch Umpires at professional games live or on television. This will give you some insight into how they make their calls.
3. Volunteer to act as Umpire for youth games or Little League. This will help you determine if you want to make a career commitment to the profession.
4. You might want to talk to an Umpire, either amateur or professional, to get insight into the career.

AMATEUR/SCHOLASTIC BASEBALL UMPIRE

CAREER PROFILE

Duties: Officiating at baseball games; controlling the game; making calls; interpreting plays

Alternate Title(s): Ump; Baseball Official; Official

Salary Range: 0 to $350+ per game

Employment Prospects: Good

Advancement Prospects: Fair

Best Geographical Location(s) for Position: Positions located throughout the country

Prerequisites:

Education or Training—No formal educational requirement; some schools and colleges may require official training or certification

Experience—Experience playing or watching baseball needed

Special Skills and Personality Traits—Thick skinned; ability to deal with stress and tension; knowledge of game of baseball; ability to deal with others; fair; consistent; even tempered

CAREER LADDER

Umpire for College or University Games

Umpire for Junior High School or High School Games

Little League Umpire or Entry Level

Position Description

Baseball Umpires working in amateur or scholastic situations are responsible for officiating at the games. Individuals may officiate at various levels, from Little League through junior high school, high school, and college.

The Umpire, ump, or game official, as he or she may be called, is responsible for controlling the baseball game. Each game may have two or three Umpires. One is always positioned behind home plate. The others may be out in the field or at the bases. Together they try to make sure that each game is played fairly and consistent with the rules of the sport. In order to accomplish this, the Umpire must know the rules, regulations, and policies to the letter and be able to interpret them. One of the biggest mistakes an Umpire can make is not being consistent in his or her calls.

Many Umpires learn how to officiate by watching others do the same job. Others feel more comfortable performing their duties after attending clinics, workshops, and seminars on officiating and interpretation. Still others read and depend on rule books put out by associations and leagues.

Before each game the Umpire holds a pregame conference with the captains and/or coaches of both teams. During this conference or meeting, the individual goes over the rules, regulations, and policies that must be adhered to. Any questions by either side are discussed at this time. The Official also is given a line-up for each team.

The Umpire is the individual who calls out the familiar "play ball" at the beginning of each game. Once that call is made, he or she watches the game and each play carefully. He or she guides and controls the game from the beginning to the end.

One of the functions of the Umpire is to call pitches as balls, strikes, and fouls. The individual is responsible for making decisions and interpreting rules during the game. In the game of baseball, whatever the Umpire's decision, it stands. He or she is totally responsible for what happens on the field.

The Umpire's decision or call, however, is often controversial. Both sides may try to get him or her to change the call. Umpires, too, may disagree with each other. Individuals must remain calm, cool, and collected during these situations. They must also be able to handle unruly fans.

Baseball Umpires may work anytime a game is scheduled. They may officiate at a weekday afternoon game, an evening game, or on the weekends. Individuals must have the flexibility to fit into this type of schedule.

Salaries

As this is a part-time profession, individuals are paid on a per-game basis. In some amateur situations the

Umpire does not get paid at all. In others, such as in Little League games, he or she may receive $10 to $20 for acting as Umpire. The individual might be paid a fee of $25 to $250 in a high school or college game. Umpires working at tournaments or games hosted by the National Collegiate Athletic Association (NCAA) may receive $350 or more.

Employment Prospects

Employment prospects are good for individuals who are qualified and fully trained. It should be noted that the majority of amateur and scholastic Umpires and officials perform in this field as an avocation, not a vocation. Those aspiring to officiate in the sport full time must usually move up to the professional level.

Positions may be located throughout the country.

Advancement Prospects

Advancement prospects are fair for the Baseball Umpire. As the individual gains experience officiating at games, he or she may move up the career ladder by officiating at more prestigious games. For example, the Umpire may begin his or her career officiating at Little League games and move up to working at junior high school games. After a while, the individual may climb the career ladder by officiating at high schools, colleges, and universities. The top level an Umpire can reach is officiating in the professionals at a major league game.

Education and Training

There is no formal educational requirement for Baseball Umpires in an amateur or scholastic setting. Usually, however, people perform this job in addition to having a full-time career in either a similar or a totally different field. Educational backgrounds of Umpires vary; some hold high school diplomas while others have doctorates.

Officials for some local games may just need a complete knowledge of the game, its rules, and regulations. Others officiating at many high schools and college games must have some sort of training from a baseball officiating camp, clinic, or seminar.

Experience, Skills, and Personality Traits

Umpires working in baseball must be very thick skinned. No matter what decision the Umpire makes or how fair it seems, someone is usually not happy. Individuals who want to be friends with everyone should not be Umpires. There is a lot of stress and tension in this job. Individuals must understand that at the begin-

ning and be able to deal with it without getting flustered. They should also be able to take criticism without letting it get to them personally.

The Umpire must have a total knowledge of baseball and all its rules, regulations, and policies. He or she must be diplomatic and firm. The individual must have the ability to make good, consistent, and quick judgments in game situations and stick to them. He or she should be confident in his or her decisions.

Communication skills are important. The Umpire must also have the ability to deal well with others, including officials who may have their own point of view about a call as well as players and fans.

The individual should be fair and consistent in his or her judgments. This is not the time to take sides. It is imperative that the Umpire be calm and even tempered and not lose his or her head during a call.

Most Umpires love the game. They may have been amateur ball players or may watch baseball every chance they get.

Unions and Associations

One of the major associations for Amateur and Scholastic Baseball Umpires is the National Association of Leagues, Umpires and Scorers (NALUS). Individuals may also be members of the Amateur Baseball Umpires' Association (ABUA), Little League Baseball (LLB), or Pony Baseball (PB).

Tips for Entry

1. Learn about the game of baseball as completely as possible. Know all the rules, regulations, and policies.
2. You can often get experience by volunteering your services as an Umpire to work with children's and other nonprofit organizations.
3. Take training courses, seminars, workshops, and clinics in umpiring. These courses will help keep you up on the newest rules as well as give you additional opportunities to make contacts.
4. Read rule books and training manuals on the subject. These will help you learn more about being a good Umpire.
5. Watch Umpires in action in both amateur and professional baseball. This will give you insight into the profession and teach you how other Umpires perform their job.
6. Positions are often advertised in the newspaper classified section. Look under headings such as "Umpire," "School Baseball," or "Amateur Sports."

PRO FOOTBALL REFEREE

CAREER PROFILE

Duties: Officiating at professional football games; making sure rules and regulations are followed; calling fouls and imposing penalties

Alternate Title(s): Official; Ref

Salary Range: $700 to $10,000+ per game

Employment Prospects: Poor

Advancement Prospects: Fair

Best Geographical Location(s) for Position: Areas hosting professional football teams

Prerequisites:

Education or Training—No formal educational requirements; training in refereeing and officiating game necessary

Experience—Experience as a varsity college football referee necessary

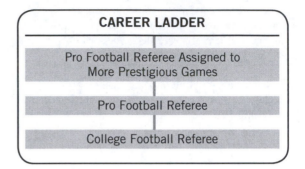

Special Skills and Personality Traits—Total knowledge of rules and regulations of pro football; fair; consistent; self-confident; ability to control emotions; calm, cool, and collected; thick skinned

Special Requirements—Licensing required

Position Description

Football Referees working in the pros are responsible for officiating at football games for professional teams. While high school games usually employ four Officials and colleges may use five or six, each professional game utilizes the services of seven Officials. Each individual is responsible for a specific officiating position on the field. For example, the person may officiate as a Referee, a headline judge, an umpire, line judge, backfield judge, or a side judge. An individual usually handles one position during a playing season. The Referee may stay in that position or request a change for the next season.

The main function of all Football Referees is to referee the game and make sure all the rules and regulations are followed. Individuals call fouls as they occur and impose penalties on players. The Referee is also expected to decide disputes within the game's framework according to the established regulations.

The main difference between officiating in professional and amateur or scholastic games is that if an individual makes a mistake in a call in a scholastic game, most people involved in football will never know about it. If the same mistake occurs in a pro game, the entire industry might learn about it. It could be televised, sportscasters might comment on it, and sports reporters would probably write about it in newspaper sports sections.

As pro football is usually played only once a week in an area, Pro Football Referees also work only once a week. Games may take place during the evenings or on weekends. The playing season is about four months.

Salaries

Earnings for Professional Football Referees can range from $700 to $3,000 a game. Individuals officiating at major games such as the playoffs or the Super Bowl may earn $10,000 or more for refereeing the game. The major factor affecting the differences in salary levels is the individual's experience. As football games are not played every day of the week, most Professional Football Referees hold down full-time jobs in addition to refereeing. These other jobs may be in sports-related fields or may be in areas totally out of the sports industry.

Employment Prospects

Employment prospects are poor for Professional Football Referees. There are many more individuals who want to officiate at games than there are games. This is not to say that a Football Ref cannot break into the pros. If the individual is good at the job, obtains a great deal of experience, and is willing to persevere, an opportunity may eventually open up.

Advancement Prospects

Once an individual makes it into officiating in the pros, advancement will mean that the Ref is assigned to officiate at more prestigious games. Being assigned to work in the Super Bowl, for example, would be a step up the career ladder for most individuals. Advancement is attained mostly by being skilled at the job and by obtaining additional experience.

Education and Training

There is no formal educational requirement to become a Pro Football Referee. Some individuals on the job have a high school diploma; others have gone through law school. As noted, most individuals have another job in addition to working as a Referee. Educational requirements, therefore, depend on the individual's other occupation.

Special Requirements

At the beginning of a Football Referee's career, the individual must go through a licensing procedure administered by the Professional Football Referees Association. Usually this involves reading rule, regulation, and policy books; attending training sessions; and taking an examination.

Experience, Skills, and Personality Traits

In order to become a Pro Football Referee, an individual must move up the ranks. Most Refs start working in the midget games, then go on to officiate at junior high and high school games. At that point, those aspiring to work in the pros begin officiating at college football games. An individual must have at least ten years' experience refereeing varsity college football before applying to the National Football League (NFL) to move into the pros. By this time, the Referee knows all the rules and regulations of the game. It is also preferred that Pro Referees be over the age of 35. This gives them sufficient time to gain needed experience in the game.

After individuals apply to work pro games, they are asked to submit a schedule of college games where they will be officiating. Retired NFL officials, called observers, then scout the various college referees and observe the way they handle themselves, their job, and the

game. It may take from two to four years from the time college Refs fill in applications until the NFL decides they are ready. At that time psychological tests are given to the individual to make sure that they are mentally and emotionally prepared for refereeing important pro games.

Referees must be fair people. They need the ability to make quick, accurate judgments. Individuals should be self-confident and sure of their decisions.

Referees must be able to control their own emotions, especially when others have lost control. Individuals should be even tempered and able to deal with situations in a calm, cool, and collected manner.

Referees should be able to command respect for their judgment and work. Individuals must realize that they are not in these positions to be liked but to be respected and to keep the game fairly regulated. As in all officiating positions, it is important that Referees be thick skinned. Many of the calls and decisions they make will make someone unhappy.

Unions and Associations

Professional Football Referees belong to the Professional Football Referees Association. This organization works on behalf of the Referees to keep the standards of the profession high and provides professional and educational guidance and support.

Tips for Entry

1. Get as much experience refereeing games as you can. Start by volunteering to officiate at youth or community games. Go on to junior high school, high school, and so on. The more experience you have, the better you will be.
2. See if there is a chapter of your state's interscholastic athletic association near you and attend meetings. They can help you in many ways by offering information and training in officiating, guidance, and support.
3. Talk to a few football Referees working your school's games. Most will be happy to share their experience and knowledge.
4. Local school and college football coaches often will help you get into officiating.

AMATEUR/SCHOLASTIC FOOTBALL REFEREE

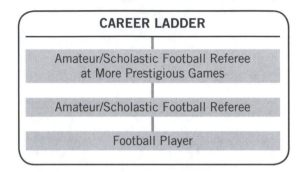

Position Description

An Amateur/Scholastic Football Referee is responsible for officiating at amateur and/or scholastic football games. The individual's main function is to make sure that the rules and regulations of the game are followed. He or she is also required to decide disputes according to the established regulations of the game.

These rules are usually set up in a guide or regulation book. The individual must study these books and know every regulation and policy to the letter. Football Refs must be aware when a player has committed a violation and how it affects the play. He or she must then decide whether or not to call a violation or let it go. It is important for the Ref to be consistent in calling all violations. He or she can show no favoritism to either team. While a Referee is not the most popular person at a game, a fair individual earns the respect of most teams.

Amateur/Scholastic Football Referees may work in a variety of settings. They may referee junior or varsity high school football games, college games, or games in any other amateur situation. Many Amateur Football Referees also serve various community youth football programs. Refs who have a great deal of experience may officiate at championship games.

Depending on the specific situation, an individual may obtain a position as an Amateur Football Referee just by knowing the game and rules of football. Other positions may require that an individual is licensed, has passed examinations, and has received formal training from a football official's association.

While the Referee must have a thorough knowledge of the rules and regulations, he or she must also know how to interpret them. He or she must be able to do this quickly, consistently, and confidently. There is no room for indecision as an Amateur Football Official.

The Ref should also keep abreast of rule and policy changes as they occur. Many Amateur Referees belong to local and state organizations that advise them of these changes. Individuals may be required to attend a number of meetings put on by these associations to help individuals improve their technique and offer a solid knowledge of the game.

Amateur/Scholastic Football Referees may work irregular hours. Games may take place during late afternoons, evenings, and on weekends. There can be a great deal of stress in this type of position. No matter what the call on a violation is, one side is usually upset. When a championship is on the line, there can be even more stress. The Ref must have the ability to know he or she is right and stick with that decision even though people are yelling, screaming, and in some cases, calling names.

Salaries

Compensation for Amateur Football Referees varies depending on a number of things, including the geographic location, the individual's experience, and the type of game he or she is officiating at. Fees for Refs working on a per-service basis will range from $10 to $25 per game for individuals officiating at midget or junior high games; $25 to $50 per game for those officiating at the high school level; and $50 to $1,000 or more for Referees officiating at college games.

Employment Prospects

Employment prospects are good for part-time Amateur and Scholastic Football Referees in the midget, junior high, and high school levels. Many areas are in desperate need of trained officials. It may become more difficult for individuals to find employment officiating in varsity college settings.

Advancement Prospects

For an Amateur Football Referee to achieve career advancement, he or she has to move up to a higher level of the sport. For example, the Referee officiating at junior high school games moves up to officiating at high school games. The individual at the high school level may advance to the junior college level and then to varsity college football. Refs who know the rules and regulations and are consistent and fair to both sides have a good chance at climbing the career ladder.

Education and Training

There is not usually any formal educational requirement to get a job as an Amateur Football Referee. Training requirements vary from position to position. In certain situations, the only requirement is that the individual understand amateur football and its rules and regulations.

Those hoping to advance, however, should try to obtain some type of amateur football officiating training. Many state and/or local amateur football associations hold training and interpretation meetings and seminars. At these seminars individuals can learn how to improve their officiating techniques as well as attain a greater knowledge of the rules and regulations of amateur football.

Special Requirements

Certain associations also require that their officials take annual examinations in order to be certified as Amateur Football Referees.

Experience, Skills, and Personality Traits

Many Amateur Football Referees have had personal experience playing the game themselves. Others have worked as coaches. The individual must have a total understanding and knowledge of the game and the rules. He or she will be making decisions based on these rules.

The Amateur Football Referee must be physically fit. He or she moves back and forth on the field in order to view the game. The Ref must be decisive and confident. The individual must be able to make a decision quickly according to the rules and regulations of the game and have confidence in the decision.

Even in amateur games, tempers on both sides often flare. It is important that the individual be even tempered and able to speak calmly and articulately.

Unions and Associations

Amateur and Scholastic Football Referees may belong to a number of associations that provide training and educational guidance and bring those interested in the sport on this level together. These might include the National Association of Sports Officials and the NFHS Officials Association. Individuals might also work with schools that are members of the National Association of Intercollegiate Athletics and/or the National Collegiate Athletic Association.

Tips for Entry

1. These positions are often advertised in the local newspaper classified sections. Look under heading classifications of "Sports Official," "Football," "Amateur Sports," "Scholastic Sports," or "Referee."
2. Many schools are in need of part-time officials. Call all the high schools and colleges that host football teams to check out their needs.
3. While it is not always necessary, try to obtain training from a state or local football officials association. This will put you a step above someone who doesn't have the proper training.
4. Join sports-oriented associations and organizations. This will help you build contacts.

AMATEUR/SCHOLASTIC BASKETBALL REFEREE

CAREER PROFILE

Duties: Officiating at amateur and scholastic basketball games; enforcing game rules and regulations; mediating court and other game disputes

Alternate Title(s): Official; Ref

Salary Range: $25 to $1,000+ per game

Employment Prospects: Good

Advancement Prospects: Good

Best Geographical Location(s) for Position: Positions may be located throughout the country

Prerequisites:

Education or Training—Training requirements vary; see text

Experience—College conference games require officiating experience

Special Skills and Personality Traits—Physically fit; self-confident; good judgment; knowledge of rules and regulations of amateur basketball; ability to deal with stress

Special Requirements—Certification may be required for some positions

CAREER LADDER

Amateur/Scholastic Basketball Referee for More Prestigious Games

Amateur/Scholastic Basketball Referee

Basketball Player, Fan, or Entry Level

Position Description

Amateur or Scholastic Basketball Referees are responsible for officiating at amateur and scholastic basketball games. The function of the Ref is to enforce rules and regulations of the game. Most basketball games have two Referees officiating. Together, the two make judgments about disputes that occur during the game.

Amateur Basketball Referees may work in a variety of settings. They may officiate at an area youth league game or at a small junior or varsity high school event. Individuals may also officiate at small college games as well as schools belonging to the National Collegiate Athletic Association. Despite the setting, Referee duties are usually very similar. He or she must make sure that the rules and regulations of the game are adhered to.

The individual usually has to study rule and regulation books provided by one of the amateur and scholastic basketball associations. It is extremely important that the Ref know and understand the rules, policies, and regulations of the game. Without total knowledge of this information, he or she is not able to make correct calls. This can cause a great many difficulties.

Depending on the situation, the Amateur Basketball Referee must usually attend a good number of seminars and workshops to improve his or her officiating skills, keep up with rule changes, and continually learn more about the game. This is especially true of individuals who officiate at larger schools and colleges holding major tournaments and championships.

Most Amateur and Scholastic Basketball Referees do not consider officiating as their main source of income. They work games part time while holding other full-time jobs in related or unrelated areas.

Refereeing offers individuals the opportunity to work in the sport and make money too. Hours are usually irregular. Games may be played anytime, from early Saturday morning to a weekday evening. The individual needs to have flexibility in his or her main job to be able to referee at games.

This is not the type of job to have if you want everyone to like you. Making an unpopular call in a hometown crowd is not easy, but often necessary. Like most refereeing positions, Amateur Basketball Refs may also be put under a great deal of stress and tension. Individuals must have the ability to deal with these situations.

Salaries

Amateur and Scholastic Basketball Referees are usually paid on a per-game basis. Salaries vary depending on the type of game the individual is officiating at and his or her experience. Individuals can earn from $25 to $75 for officiating at a high school basketball game. Compensation for officiating at college games can range from $40 to $1,000 or more, with the larger earnings going to individuals working important tournaments and championships.

Employment Prospects

Employment prospects for Amateur and Scholastic Basketball Referees are good. It must be kept in mind, however, that most people who officiate at amateur games have another profession. This work might be in sports or in a totally different field.

Employment possibilities are located throughout the country in small schools and colleges that have basketball teams. As individuals gain training and experience, they may also find opportunities to officiate at larger colleges and those belonging to the National Collegiate Athletic Association. Jobs may also be found with area youth organizations.

Many colleges now have active men's and women's basketball teams. While a woman can officiate at a man's basketball game and vice versa, the addition of women's teams adds more work opportunities to the sport.

Advancement Prospects

Amateur and Scholastic Basketball Referees can advance their careers by officiating at more prestigious games, championships, and tournaments. Individuals who are good at what they do can make a name for themselves and climb the career ladder.

Education and Training

Educational and training requirements vary depending on the specific position. For example, while a high school Basketball Referee might just be required to know the game and its rules, an individual aspiring to become a Basketball Referee for a college game might need some sort of certification. Generally, this certification is mandatory to officiate in National Collegiate Athletic Association games.

This certification and training can be obtained by attending classes, seminars, camps, and workshops sponsored by various basketball organizations and associations. Officiating skills may also be taught in classes at colleges offering majors in sports administration and physical education. Colleges that have intensive sports programs may also offer training programs.

Special Requirements

Individuals officiating at certain college games generally need some sort of certification. For those officiating at NCAA games, certification is mandatory. As noted previously, this certification can be obtained by attending classes, seminars, camps, and workshops sponsored by various basketball organizations and associations.

Experience, Skills, and Personality Traits

Basketball Referees, both professional and amateur, must be in extremely good physical condition. They generally run back and forth checking out plays during the entire game.

Individuals in officiating capacities must possess total self-confidence in themselves and their decisions. Basketball Refs should be able to act quickly and calmly. Good judgment is a must. They need to be even tempered and articulate. Successful Basketball Referees do not yell and scream and are not easily shaken.

Amateur Basketball Referees must have a total understanding of the game and knowledge of all rules and regulations. While the Amateur Basketball Referee does not need to have played the game, he or she should certainly at least enjoy the sport.

Most college conference games are worked by individuals who have had a great deal of officiating experience.

Unions and Associations

Amateur Basketball Referees may belong to a number of local, state, and national associations that provide training, certification, and professional guidance. These include the National Federation of State High School Associations (NFSHSA), the International Association of Approved Basketball Officials (IAABO), the U.S.A. Basketball (USAB), the Eastern College Basketball Association (ECBA), and the Eastern Women's Amateur Basketball League of the AAU (EWABL/AAU).

Tips for Entry

1. Contact associations to find out when they are holding training sessions.
2. Apply for admission at a "summer camp" seminar for Basketball Referees. (Check the Appendix section for seminar information.) Seminars such as these will train you, give you confidence, and help you make contacts in the industry.

. Amateur Basketball Referee positions are often advertised in the local newspaper display and classified sections. Look under such heading classifications as "Basketball," "Sports," "Officiating," "Referee," or "School Athletics."

4. Call schools and colleges that host basketball teams and inquire about their officiating needs.

5. Volunteer your services for area youth basketball games. This will give you experience and help make important contacts.

SPORTS JOURNALISM

SPORTSWRITER

Duties: Reporting news in the sports world; writing articles and feature stories on sporting events; attending games, tournaments, activities, and other sports-related events

Alternate Title(s): Sports Reporter; Beat Writer

Salary Range: $22,000 to $2 million+

Employment Prospects: Fair

Advancement Prospects: Fair

Best Geographical Location(s) for Position: Positions may be located throughout the country

Prerequisites:

Education or Training—Minimum of two-year college degree required; most positions require four-year college degree

Experience—Writing experience necessary

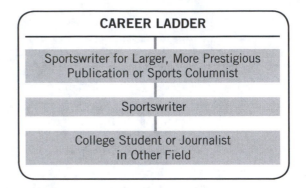

CAREER LADDER

Sportswriter for Larger, More Prestigious Publication or Sports Columnist

Sportswriter

College Student or Journalist in Other Field

Special Skills and Personality Traits—Excellent writing skills; good communication skills; basic knowledge of sports; enjoy attending sporting events; articulate; personable; dependable

Position Description

Sportswriters work for newspapers, magazines, and other periodicals. They also write for sports-oriented Web sites and the sports section of other sites. They are responsible for reporting news in the sports world, keeping the fans informed about scores, and writing both routine stories and feature articles on sports. Individuals may work for small local newspapers, larger metropolitan publications, or regional or national magazines.

Depending on the type of publication they work for, Sportswriters may write specifically about just one sport or may write stories on a variety of sports. A Sportswriter may cover a baseball game one day, a boxing match that night, and a golf tournament the next morning.

While good writers can often research almost any subject, it is helpful for a Sportswriter to both enjoy sports and know something about the field. Much of his or her time is spent attending games, tournaments, and matches, and talking to people in the sports industry.

When attending games and other sports events, the Sportswriter often sits in a special press section or press box with other Sportswriters, columnists, sportscasters, and photographers from other media.

Before the event, the team public relations person or publicist may pass out press releases, biographies, press kits, and other background information. The Sports-

writer looks these over and decides what information to use in his or her story.

In addition to attending and watching events, the Sportswriter is responsible for talking to athletes, team players, coaches, and managers in order to gather material for articles. He or she may do this before an event, after it, or both. The Sportswriter also keeps track of scores, game highlights, and fan reactions.

The Sportswriter or Sports Reporter, as he or she may be called, is responsible for writing an article reporting the events in whichever game he or she is assigned. He or she might write a number of articles on events leading up to a specific game, the athletes, reactions after a game, and so on.

In certain situations, the Sportswriter writes the story or outlines it at the arena where the event is taking place and calls it in on the phone or faxes the article directly to the editor.

At times, the Sportswriter is responsible for developing sports-related feature stories for the publication. Subject matter could be anything from a hometown ballplayer making it in the big leagues, to a story on the winner of a local marathon, or an interview with a sports hero.

Sportswriters are expected to attend press conferences scheduled by sports teams and any other sports-related groups.

In areas that host professional sports teams, larger newspapers may assign an individual working in the sports department to cover the day-by-day activities of a specific team. These people are known as Beat Writers. The Sportswriters in these positions must report the news of every game played by that team.

Beat Writers are responsible for turning in a standard amount of copy about their assigned team even when there is little to write about. It is imperative that they build a good working relationship with the players, coaches, managers, etc., on the team they are covering. The Sportswriters can then turn to these people when they need extra copy or to obtain comments and/or quotes regarding the team or other related topics.

Sportswriters working for small local newspapers often are responsible for reporting news on school, college, and other amateur sports as well as professional sports. They may have additional writing and reporting responsibilities outside the sports field.

For an individual who loves being around sports, the job of a Sportswriter is ideal. He or she is paid to attend and watch ball games, boxing matches, wrestling tournaments, golf tournaments, horse races, and the like. The Sportswriter has the opportunity to meet athletes, team members, and coaches, and often socializes with them. In this way, he or she learns what is happening first in the sports world.

The individual in this position often works long, irregular hours. He or she may work at night and on weekends. The Sportswriter is usually responsible to the sports editor of the publication. In smaller newspapers, he or she may be responsible directly to the editor of the paper.

Salaries

Salaries for Sportswriters vary greatly from job to job. Variables include the type of publication the individual is working for, its location, and his or her experience and responsibilities.

Sportswriters just starting out or those writing for local weeklies may earn salaries ranging from approximately $22,000 to $26,000 or more. Those who work for daily newspapers or monthly magazines may earn from $27,000 to $100,000 plus, depending on their experience and following. There are a small number of Sportswriters with their own columns or a large following who command salaries of $2 million or more.

Employment Prospects

Employment prospects are good for Sportswriters. Almost every newspaper throughout the country has at least one Sportswriter. Many of the larger newspapers have an entire sports department on staff. There are also a number of local, regional, and national magazines and periodicals that need Sportswriters.

Individuals can often enter the field of sportswriting by working at local and regional newspapers. Prospects get more difficult as the individual advances his or her career.

Advancement Prospects

Advancement prospects are fair for Sportswriters. The next step up the career ladder for individuals is to find a position writing in a larger, more prestigious newspaper or magazine. The higher the career level the individual reaches, the more difficult advancement becomes.

For example, after gaining some experience, those working for a weekly newspaper usually have no problem finding a job reporting sports in a daily paper. Individuals working in dailies have to locate positions in larger daily papers. Sportswriters working for newspapers in large cities often seek employment writing for national sports magazines.

Education and Training

While there are still a number of old-time Sportswriters hired years ago without a college background on staff at various papers throughout the country, most publications currently hiring expect some type of college background. Depending on the position, newspapers or magazines usually require a minimum of at least a two-year degree; most seek graduates of a four-year degree program.

Good choices for majors include journalism, English, public relations, and liberal arts. Any additional courses in writing are helpful as are those in sports studies, physical education, and the like.

Experience, Skills, and Personality Traits

A Sportswriter needs to write well. He or she should have a good command of the English language, grammar, and be able to spell well. The individual should be able to write crisp, clean, informative copy. He or she should be able to spot an interesting story and to develop creative, unique angles for other articles.

The individual needs to be dependable and able to write quickly and meet deadlines. He or she may attend a game at night and have the story in for the early-morning edition. The Sportswriter should have a basic understanding of the sport he or she is writing about. An interest in sports is helpful.

The individual should be articulate with good verbal communication skills. He or she should be friendly, personable, and easy to get along with and talk to.

Unions and Associations

Depending on the publication, Sportswriters may belong to local bargaining unions. Individuals might also belong to a trade association called the National Sportscasters and Sportswriters Association. This organization provides a forum for those in the industry and offers professional guidance and support.

Tips for Entry

1. Look for freelance assignments. Try to come up with an interesting story or a new angle on an old story. Then call, write, or visit the sports editor of your local newspaper and see if they might be interested. You may have to write on spec, which means that you will have to come up with an idea, write the story, submit it, and see if the newspaper wants it. If they do use it, you will be paid. If they don't, you will at least have gained some experience.

2. Part-time positions are often available, especially in weekly newspapers and some of the smaller dailies.

3. Look in the display or classified section of newspapers under heading classifications of "Sportswriter," "Journalist," "Sports," "Reporter," or "Writer."

4. Get as much writing experience as you can. Become a member of your college's newspaper. If you can find a summer or part-time job working at a newspaper, take it, even if it isn't in the sports department. The experience will be worth it.

5. Offer to cover school sports for your local newspaper. You may not get paid very much (or not at all), but you will have a sportswriting job to put on your résumé.

6. Many newspapers and magazines offer internships or training programs. Ask for at least part of your training to be in the sports department.

7. Begin to put together a portfolio of your best work. When one of your stories or articles appears in a school or local newspaper, cut it out and have it photocopied, making sure the name of the publication and date are included. You can also include good writing pieces that you have done for college. These can help illustrate your talents when applying for a job.

8. Search for a position on the Internet. Go to a job or career site and type in keywords such as "sports reporter," "sportswriter," or "reporter."

9. Check out sports-oriented Web sites. Many advertise their openings on their own sites.

SPORTS COLUMNIST

CAREER PROFILE

Duties: Writing a sports column on a regular basis for a publication

Alternate Title(s): Columnist

Salary Range: $23,000 to $2 million+

Employment Prospects: Fair

Advancement Prospects: Fair

Best Geographical Location(s) for Position: Positions may be located throughout the country

Prerequisites:

Education or Training—Most positions require a four-year college degree

Experience—Writing experience necessary

Special Skills and Personality Traits—Excellent writing skills; good communication skills; creative; enjoy sports; articulate; ability to work under pressure; personable

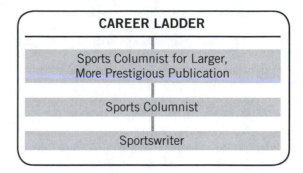

CAREER LADDER

Sports Columnist for Larger, More Prestigious Publication

Sports Columnist

Sportswriter

Position Description

Sports Columnists may work for newspapers, magazines, or other periodicals. They may also work for sports-oriented Web sites or the sports section of other Web sites. Their main responsibility is to write a column on a regular basis on some facet of the sports industry. These columns usually have a title. The Sports Columnist has a byline, often accompanied by a head-and-shoulder photograph of the individual.

Individuals may write their column daily, once a week, biweekly, or monthly, depending on the publication. If they are very successful and popular, Sports Columnists may have their columns syndicated. This means that the column is bought and published by more than one publication. The writings of Sports Columnists may appear in small local newspapers, larger metropolitan publications, and regional or national magazines and papers.

While sportswriters, as a rule, are responsible for reporting the sports news as it happens, the work of Sports Columnists usually reflects the writer's opinion in some way. Sports Columnists may write about one specific event and their feelings on the subject or may cover a number of newsworthy subjects on which they have varied opinions.

One of the main differences between a general sportswriter and a Sports Columnist is that the former is usually assigned stories by editors while the latter must develop ideas for his or her column. Sports

Columnists use their columns to write feature stories about athletes, sports events, specific sports, and the like. They constantly have to come up with and develop unique story ideas and feature articles about sports.

Depending on the type of publication they work for, Sports Columnists may write about just one sport or may create columns on sports in general. For example, Sports Columnist and newscaster Howard Cosell is remembered by many for his stories about the boxing world.

Sports Columnists spend a lot of time on the phone talking to people who are in the sports industry. These might include athletes, team owners, fighters, other sportswriters, sportscasters, and public relations and publicity people. They also often attend and watch sports-related events, from games and tournaments to boxing matches. The emergence of cable television has greatly increased the number of sports events that can be watched. If an individual cannot be at an event or watch it on television, he or she can videotape it for later reference.

The Sports Columnist also spends a great deal of time talking to athletes, team players, coaches, and managers in person. Part of the job may include traveling to where these important sports figures and the sporting events are.

As a rule, Sports Columnists are totally sports oriented. They are the type of people who would watch sports, talk sports, and know about sports whether or not they worked in the industry.

When attending live events, Sports Columnists usually sit in a special press section or press box with other sportswriters, sportscasters, and photographers. They also attend a great many press conferences, press parties, and dinners.

For those who love everything about sports, a Sports Columnist job is the ideal occupation. The individual is paid to talk and socialize with people he or she admires, attend sporting events and parties, and then give his or her opinion in a column.

Although the Sports Columnist may write only one column a week or one a day, he or she still works long, irregular hours gathering information for the piece. The individual in this position may be responsible to the sports editor or directly to the editor or publisher of the publication.

Salaries

Earnings of Sports Columnists can range greatly from person to person, depending on a number of variables. These include the size and type of publication the individual is working for and its location. Other variables include the experience and responsibilities of the individual as well as how popular and well known he or she is.

Sports Columnists just starting out or those writing for local weeklies may earn salaries ranging from $23,000 to $25,000 or more. Those who work for daily newspapers or monthly magazines may earn from $28,000 to $2 million plus. The syndication of a column by a major publication can also lead to earnings well over $1 million for a popular Sports Columnist.

Employment Prospects

Employment prospects are fair for Sports Columnists. In many smaller papers, the publication's sportswriter also is the Sports Columnist. Opportunities exist at almost every level from small, local newspapers to regional and national magazines and periodicals.

Individuals can often enter the field more easily by seeking a Sports Columnist position at a small local paper.

Some individuals may also write sports columns for sports-oriented websites on the Internet.

Advancement Prospects

Advancement prospects are fair for Sports Columnists. It is necessary to build a strong following in order to climb the career ladder. The next step for most Sports Columnists is to locate a position with a larger, more prestigious newspaper or magazine. The higher the career level the individual reaches, the more difficult advancement becomes.

Some Sports Columnists advance their careers by offering their column for syndication. This in turn leads to additional exposure in more publications and higher earnings.

Education and Training

Most publications today expect a sportswriter or Sports Columnist to have a four-year college degree. While there are a number of Sports Columnists who may not have a degree, they are either very well known or have built up a following as a retired athlete, sportscaster, commentator, and so on.

Good choices for majors for this career might include journalism, English, public relations, and/or liberal arts. Any additional courses in writing as well as those in sports studies and physical education would be helpful.

Experience, Skills, and Personality Traits

A Sports Columnist should have a good command of the English language and grammar and be able to spell well. He or she should be able to write crisply, clearly, and concisely. The ability to develop creative angles is imperative.

The individual should have a keen interest in sports. Contacts with athletes and those involved in the sports industry are necessary to get scoops on information.

The individual needs good communication skills, verbally as well as on paper. While there are some Sports Columnists whom athletes don't particularly like, those seeking to enter the field should be friendly, personable, and easy to get along with and talk to.

Unions and Associations

Depending on the publication and other writing responsibilities, Sports Columnists may belong to local bargaining unions. Individuals might also belong to a trade association called the National Sportscasters and Sportswriters Association. This organization provides a forum for those in the industry and offers professional guidance and support.

Tips for Entry

1. Look in the display or classified section of newspapers under heading classifications of "Sports Columnist," "Sportswriter," "Journalist," "Sports," "Reporter," or "Writer."
2. Get as much writing experience as you can. Become a member of your college's newspaper.

If you can find a summer or part-time job working at a newspaper, even if it isn't in the sports department, take it. The experience will be worth it.

3. Offer to cover school sports for your local newspaper. You may not get paid very much (or not at all), but you will have a sportswriting job to put on your résumé.

4. Many newspapers and magazines offer internships or training programs. Ask for at least part of your training to be in the sports department.

5. Begin to put together a portfolio of your best work. When one of your stories or articles appears in a school or local newspaper, cut it out and have it photocopied, making sure the name of the publication and date are included. You can also include good writing pieces that you have done for college. These examples can help illustrate your talents when applying for a job.

6. Write a sports column on spec for your local or school newspaper. Develop an interesting, unique angle to vent your opinion. Call, write, or visit the sports editor to see if the paper might be interested. Even if they don't use it, you will have made an important contact.

7. Part-time positions are often available, especially in weekly newspapers and some of the smaller dailies.

TELEVISION SPORTSCASTER

Duties: Reporting sports news to television audience; anchoring the sports desk on news programs; determining what information should go into a sportscast; providing color commentary during games

Alternate Title(s): Sports Reporter; Announcer

Salary Range: $25,000 to $8 million+

Employment Prospects: Fair

Advancement Prospects: Fair

Best Geographical Location(s) for Position: Positions may be located throughout the country

Prerequisites:

Education or Training—College degree required for most positions; see text

Experience—Broadcast and writing experience necessary

Special Skills and Personality Traits—Clear speaking voice; writing skills; communication skills; knowledge of sports; articulate; dependable

CAREER LADDER

```
┌──────────────────────────────────────┐
│ Sportscaster at Larger, More         │
│ Prestigious Station or Sports        │
│ Director                             │
└──────────────────────────────────────┘
              │
┌──────────────────────────────────────┐
│ Television Sportscaster              │
└──────────────────────────────────────┘
              │
┌──────────────────────────────────────┐
│ College Student, Desk Assistant,     │
│ Sportswriter, Sports Journalist, or  │
│ Professional Player                  │
└──────────────────────────────────────┘
```

Position Description

Television Sportscasters are responsible for reporting the sports news on television. They may work for local, regional, or national television stations. Individuals may also work for public or cable television stations.

The Television Sportscaster keeps fans informed about game scores as well as happenings in the sports world. A Television Sportscaster usually reports on all sports.

He or she usually is responsible for anchoring the sports desk on news programs. Depending on the job, the number of daily newscasts, and the size of the sports department, the individual may report sports news for all the station's newscasts, or may have specific spot. For example, the Sportscaster may anchor the sports desk on the nightly news or the midday report.

Television Sportscasters often go out into the field to cover the sports action. The individual may attend games, tournaments, matches, and bouts in a variety of sports. The Sportscaster may be required to interview athletes, managers, officials, or fans about specific events.

Most Sportscasters are avid sports fans who both enjoy sports and know a great deal about the industry. Sportscasters are fortunate to work in an environment they love. They attend sports events and interview people in the sports industry.

When attending games and other sports events, the Sportscaster may sit in a special press section or press box with other Sportscasters, writers, columnists, photographers, and press people. The Sportscaster may also be out on the field commenting on the game. Before or after games, he or she may do locker room interviews.

On occasion, the Sportscaster may be responsible for developing feature pieces on sports-related subjects or events. These features might cover a variety of areas. The Sportscaster may be required to develop the piece, research, interview, and also act as commentator.

The individual may write his or her own copy for the news report or may just read copy prepared by a writer. This usually depends on a number of variables, including the size of the sports department and the specific station and the writing talent of the Sportscaster.

Sportscasters may attend press conferences scheduled by sports teams and any other sports-related groups or may use videotaped sections of the conference during his or her broadcast. The individual may also read and review wire service reports to determine what is relevant for news broadcasts.

Individuals may also be responsible for announcing the play-by-play action and doing color commentary. Many of the Sportscasters who do this are former athletes with good communication skills.

Sportscasters working for small local stations often are responsible for reporting professional sports developments as well as news about school, college, and other amateur sports levels.

The work hours of a Sportscaster are difficult to determine. The individual may be required to attend luncheons, press parties, and conferences in the afternoon, attend sports events during the evening and on weekends, and still put together a sports spot for the television station. The Sportscaster is usually responsible to the sports director, news director, or the station manager.

Salaries

The salaries for Sportscasters vary greatly from job to job. Variables include the type of market the individual is working in, the specific station, and its location. Earnings also depend on the experience level, prestige, and duties of the individual.

Sportscasters who are working for local stations or those just beginning their career in television may have annual earnings from $25,000 to $29,000 or more. Individuals with more experience and those working in larger markets may earn between $30,000 and $85,000 or more. Sportscasters who have developed a large following and are working in a major market may have earnings of $250,000. There are individuals who work for nationwide media or do the commentary for major league games who can earn $8 million or more. These positions, however, are extremely limited.

Employment Prospects

Employment prospects are fair for Sportscasters who are willing to work on a local or regional level. As individuals aspire to work in larger markets, prospects become poorer.

Sportscaster hopefuls may find it easier to break into the industry on a small, local level and work their way up.

Advancement Prospects

Advancement prospects are fair for Sportscasters. Individuals who want to climb the career ladder find a position with a larger, more prestigious station. Unfortunately, it takes some time to achieve success in this industry. The higher the career level the individual reaches, the more difficult advancement becomes.

Another way for a Sportscaster to climb the career ladder is by becoming the sports director of a larger television station. However, many Sportscasters may not opt for this type of career advancement, as these positions may not always afford the individual an opportunity to be an on-air personality.

Education and Training

Competition is keen for positions as Sportscasters. Those with the best education will be better prepared for jobs. A four-year college degree with a major in communications is a good choice. A minor in sports administration or physical education might be helpful. Other possibilities for majors include journalism, English, or even liberal arts.

Courses, workshops, and seminars in writing, sports, and television are useful. Educational requirements may be waived in certain situations such as when a station snags a former top athlete to do the color commentary.

Experience, Skills, and Personality Traits

Sportscasters come from a variety of backgrounds. Some individuals land a position with a local station right after graduation from college. Others worked in sports as radio announcers or newspaper sportswriters. Many come up the ranks from areas of the television broadcasting industry such as television sportswriter, desk assistant, and others.

A Sportscaster needs a good, clear speaking voice. A command of the English language is necessary. The ability to write well is helpful. Individuals should be articulate and poised and be comfortable in front of a camera.

Dependability is necessary. No one will wait for a Sportscaster who doesn't appear for a live broadcast. The Sportscaster should have a basic understanding of the sport. An interest in sports is helpful but not always required.

The Sportscaster should have the ability to develop an on-air personality in order to build a viewer following.

Unions and Associations

Sportscasters may belong to a number of different bargaining unions depending on the specific position they hold and station they are working for. These might include the American Federation of Television and Radio Artists (AFTRA) or the Writers Guild of America (WGA). Individuals might also belong to trade associations, such as the National Sportscasters and Sportswriters Association (NSSA), the American Sportscasters Association (ASA), and the Radio Television News Directors Association (RTNDA).

Tips for Entry

1. Work with your college television station even if you can't get into the sports department. Hands-on experience will be useful.

2. If your college does not have a television station, work on the radio station. Try to get as much experience working in broadcasting as you can.
3. Job availabilities may be located in the newspaper's display or classified section. Look under heading classifications of "Broadcasting," "Sportscaster," "Television," "Journalist," "Sports," "Reporter," or "Sportswriter."
4. Get experience writing. Most Sportscasters must write their own copy—at least at the beginning.

Become a member of your college's newspaper. If you can, find a summer or part-time job working at a newspaper even if it isn't in the sports department. The experience will be worth it.
5. Look for a summer or part-time job at a local or cable radio station.
6. Many television stations and associations offer internships or training programs. Internships will give you on-the-job training and the opportunity to make important contacts.

RADIO SPORTSCASTER

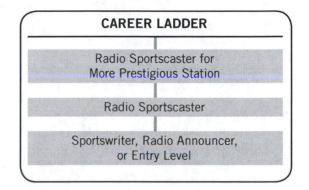

Position Description

Radio Sportscasters are responsible for reporting the sports news and events on the radio. They may work for local, regional, or network radio stations. Individuals may also work for public radio.

In addition to music and talk formats, there are a number of radio stations whose format is totally sports related. This type of station arrived on the scene when people began to prefer listening to music on FM stereo radio. Owners of AM stations had to try to maintain a listening audience and save their stations. Many owners opted for talk radio. As talk radio became more popular, so did entire formats dedicated to sports talk.

Radio Sportscasters working at sports talk stations may have different duties and responsibilities depending on their job description. They may serve as a sports reporter, host a sports-oriented talk show, perform as a color commentator for sporting events, and interview sports personalities.

While those working at sports radio stations will have more specific duties, Sportscasters on music, general talk format, or news stations may have more general responsibilities.

Music-oriented radio stations may have only a small sports department. Individuals working there may be expected to perform more varied functions. These Sportscasters usually are responsible for reporting current sports news, developments, and scores. Sportscast-

ers may be responsible for national sports news as well as local developments. Those working in smaller local stations may also be required to report school, college, and amateur sports news.

Most Radio Sportscasters do not specialize in just one sport, but instead report on all sporting events. However, some individuals may specialize in reporting on one sport, such as baseball or boxing. This usually occurs as the Sportscaster gains a larger following and prestige. Other individuals comment on games, tournaments, and matches as they occur in order to help listeners follow the action.

The Radio Sportscaster may be expected to anchor the sports reports during all newscasts in his or her shift. He or she may get one- to six-minute spots to do this. The individual may also be responsible for longer sports spots during the nightly news or the midday or morning report.

Many Radio Sportscasters have scheduled shows one or more times a week during which they may discuss all aspects of sports, receive call-ins, or have special in-studio guests.

In some situations, the Radio Sportscaster may go into the field to cover the sports action. The individual may attend games, tournaments, matches, and bouts in a variety of sports. The Sportscaster may be expected to interview athletes, managers, officials, or fans about specific events.

Individuals may attend press conferences scheduled by sports teams and any other sports-related groups. They may also obtain audio sections of the conference from other reporters who were at the press conference to use during their broadcast.

Sportscasters can obtain their information first-hand or may get it from the wire services. Organizations such as United Press International (UPI) and Associated Press (AP) have large news and sports staffs as well as freelance individuals who report all the up-to-the-minute developments. These reports go over a wire or Teletype and are printed out in thousands of news rooms and television and radio stations throughout the world. Most newspapers, magazines, and television and radio stations pay for this service, which they use daily in reporting the news, weather, and sports.

Radio Sportscasters usually are fans who enjoy sports and know a great deal about them. Individuals may get to attend games and other sports events as part of their job. They can also be out on the field commenting on the game. Before or after games, Radio Sportscasters often do locker room interviews.

On occasion, the Sportscaster is responsible for developing feature pieces on sports-related subjects or events. These features might cover a variety of areas. The Sportscaster may be required to develop the piece, research, and interview, or just act as commentator.

A great number of Radio Sportscasters write their own copy for the sports report. Some individuals, however, just read copy prepared by another writer. This usually depends on the size of the sports department, the specific station, and the writing talent of the Radio Sportscaster.

Radio Sportscasters usually work shifts. Individuals can be assigned to the early-morning, late-morning, afternoon, drive, evening, or night shift. Hours vary. In some stations shifts are three hours long, while in others individuals may work eight. Most of the time they are preparing for a sportscast, not actually on the air. Sportscasters may attend a slew of events when not on the air, such as games, tournaments, sports-oriented luncheons, press parties, and conferences. The Radio Sportscaster is usually responsible to the sports director, news director, or station manager.

Salaries

Earnings for Radio Sportscasters vary greatly from job to job. Variables include the type of market the individual is working in, the specific station, and its location. Other factors determining income include the Sportscaster's experience level, prestige, following, and duties.

Sportscasters who are working for local stations or those just beginning their careers in radio may have annual earnings from $24,000 to $27,000 or more. Individuals who have more experience and those working in larger markets may earn between $35,000 and $85,000. Radio Sportscasters who have developed a large following and are working in a major market may earn $100,000 plus. Some individuals working for radio networks or national cable stations earn $1 million a year or more. These people, however, are in the minority.

Radio Sportscasters may also augment their income by writing sports columns for papers or magazines.

Employment Prospects

Employment prospects are good for Radio Sportscasters who are willing to work on a local or regional level. When individuals aspire to work in larger markets, prospects become dimmer. Openings may be located throughout the country.

It is easier to break in to the industry on a small, local level and work up from there. Many smaller stations hire individuals with little or no experience. While the salaries in these situations are usually very low, the experience is worth the opportunity.

Advancement Prospects

Advancement prospects are fair for Radio Sportscasters. After obtaining some experience, a Radio Sportscaster may advance his or her career by locating a position with a larger, more prestigious station. This, in turn, usually leads to higher earnings. The higher the career level the individual reaches, the more difficult advancement becomes. It is not easy to break into the major market radio stations, but it can be done.

A Radio Sportscaster may also climb the career ladder by becoming the sports director of the same or a larger station.

Education and Training

Most radio stations, even small local ones, require a minimum of a four-year college degree. While any major may be acceptable, good choices might be communications, journalism, liberal arts, broadcasting, or English.

Courses, workshops, and seminars in writing, sports, broadcasting, radio, and communications are useful.

Experience, Skills, and Personality Traits

In some stations, the Radio Sportscaster can be an entry-level position. In others, he or she must have had experience working at another station. A great majority of Radio Sportscasters worked on college radio stations while in school. Many also were sportswriters.

The Radio Sportscaster needs to have a clear speaking voice. The ability to write well is most helpful. Individuals should be articulate and poised and be comfortable in front of a microphone.

Most but not all Radio Sportscasters are fans of at least one, if not more, sports. A basic understanding of the industry is helpful.

Unions and Associations

Sportscasters may belong to a number of different bargaining unions depending on the specific position they hold and the station they are working for. Some of the organizations offer individual membership, while others offer membership to the radio station. These groups often have seminars, conferences, and educational training for people working in radio. They also may provide trade journals, printed materials, and job guidance. Some of these organizations might include state broadcasting associations, the National Association of Broadcasters (NAB), the Radio and Advertising Bureau (RAB), or the National Association of Broadcast Employees and Technicians (NABET).

Other organizations Sportscasters might be members of include the American Federation of Television and Radio Artists (AFTRA) or the Writers' Guild of America (WGA), the National Sportscasters and Sportswriters Association (NSSA), the American Sportscasters Association (ASA), and the Radio Television News Directors Association (RTNDA).

Tips for Entry

1. Try to get as much experience working in broadcasting as you can. Work with your school radio station even if you can't get into the sports department. Hands-on experience will be useful.

2. Job openings are often advertised in the newspaper's display or classified section. Look under heading classifications of "Broadcasting," "Sportscaster," "Radio," "Announcer," "Sports," "Reporter," or "Sportswriter."

3. Many local stations advertise on their own station when there is an opening.

4. Make a demo tape and send it with your résumé and a cover letter to radio station owners, managers, or personnel directors. Look in the yellow pages of the phone book under "Radio" to find the stations available in an area.

5. Get experience writing copy. Become a member of your college newspaper. If you can, find a summer or part-time job working at a newspaper even if it isn't in the sports department. The experience will be worth it.

6. Many radio stations and associations offer internships or training programs. Internships will give you on-the-job training and the opportunity to make important contacts.

SPORTS PHOTOGRAPHER

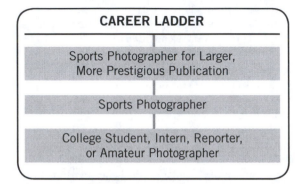
Position Description

A professional Sports Photographer has an interesting and varied job. He or she is responsible for taking photographs of sports-related events and people. The individual may work for a magazine or newspaper as a photojournalist. He or she might also work for an advertising agency, public relations firm, sports complex, sports team, specific individual, or as a freelance Sports Photographer.

Responsibilities depend on the individual's work situation and assignment. No matter what the responsibilities are, however, the individual's main function is taking active, creative sports photos.

Sports Photographers must be able to tell a complete story with their photos. This might be accomplished with one picture, or a photo essay or montage might be required to describe a story.

Individuals working in small or weekly publications often are responsible for all photography. This could include sports-related as well as nonsports-related pictures. Individuals working in these types of publications might also have some writing responsibilities in addition to acting as the paper's Sports Photographer.

The Sports Photographer attends tournaments, games, matches, and events where athletes might show up, such as charity balls and nightclubs. Depending on the situation in which he or she works, the individual

may be responsible for taking photographs of one sport or all sporting events in the area.

Individuals who work for major publications often travel to events, matches, and games. For example, a Sports Photographer working for a boxing magazine would be required to go to locations in which the major boxing matches were held.

The Sports Photographer working for a publication usually has intimate access to an event. He or she is right up there with the athletes taking pictures. For those who enjoy sports, this is an ideal situation.

The individual often works with a sports reporter on a project. Together the two develop stories for the sports page, section, or entire magazine.

Sometimes the Sports Photographer must be able to develop his or her own photographs. At other times the Photographer is just responsible for taking the photographs and turning in the exposed rolls of film.

The Sports Photographer may also be responsible for writing his or her own photo captions. Sometimes he or she is just required to obtain the information to match the photo. Someone else, such as a reporter, for example, is responsible for writing the caption.

Sports Photographers must go to a variety of sporting events. As many of these activities take place at night or weekends, these Photographers often work irregular hours. The Sports Photographer may be responsible to the sports editor or head editor, depending on the publication he or she is working for.

Salaries

Compensation for Sports Photographers varies widely. Salaries depend on the size, location, and prestige of the publication that the individual works for. Salaries are also dependent on the qualifications, skills, and experience of the Photographer.

Individuals working at smaller, local newspapers might have annual incomes ranging from $25,000 to $29,000 or more. Those working at larger publications may have earnings ranging from $27,000 to $45,000. Successful Sports Photographers working for major publications may have annual salaries of $200,000 plus.

Freelance Sports Photographers sell single photographs of sport-related events to publications and wire services. Pictures can command prices of $10 to $2,500 and up.

Employment Prospects

Employment prospects are fair for those aspiring to be Sports Photographers. Depending on their skills, experience, and qualifications, individuals might work for small weekly newspapers, larger daily newspapers, sports-oriented magazines, advertising agencies, public relations firms, sports complexes, specific athletes, sports teams, wire services, or they may be self-employed. Entry into the field is easier in the smaller, weekly publications.

Jobs are available throughout the country. Positions for major publications are often located in major cities where sports teams play and events take place.

Advancement Prospects

Advancement prospects are fair for Sports Photographers. A number of variables control the advancement process, including talent, contacts, and being in the right place at the right time.

Climbing the career ladder for most Sports Photographers can mean that they must locate positions with larger, more prestigious publications. This, in turn, leads to higher salaries.

Education and Training

Educational requirements vary from job to job. An impressive portfolio of photos may help an individual with a limited education land a job. However, many publications require or prefer their staff to hold college degrees.

As many Sports Photographers also function as journalists, courses in writing, journalism, and English are helpful. Courses or seminars in photography and darkroom techniques are useful.

Experience, Skills, and Personality Traits

The most important skill of a Sports Photographer is the ability to take impressive, interesting, and unique photographs of sporting events and athletes.

Many Sports Photographers worked on their high school or college newspaper getting experience. Others enjoyed attending sporting events and found that they could capture a moment in time on film.

Individuals often have to write their own captions to photos. They should have good communication skills, written and verbal.

The Sports Photographer should be creative. Nobody wants to see the same picture that has been taken by others. He or she also needs that innate ability to feel when something special is going to occur or to know when something will turn into a unique, interesting picture. These are the types of photos everyone, including major editors and publishers, will remember.

Most successful Sports Photographers genuinely love sports and sports-related activities. While this isn't a job requirement, it certainly helps.

Unions and Associations

There is no specific bargaining union for Sports Photographers. However, individuals may be members of various unions depending on where they are employed.

Sports Photographers may belong to trade associations, such as the National Federation of Press Women (NFPW), the National Press Club (NPC), or the National Press Photographers Association (NPPA).

Tips for Entry

1. Work on your school newspaper. Try to write articles, reports, and captions besides taking photographs. This will help give you experience in all fields of journalism.
2. Put together a portfolio of your best work. Try to take photographs of a variety of sports in different types of situations. Make sure your portfolio is neat, clean, and creative.
3. Consider working during the summer or part time at your local hometown newspaper. Work in any department you can to gain experience.
4. Many newspapers and magazines offer internship programs for journalists and photojournalists.

5. Positions as Sports Photographers are often advertised in the classified or display section of the newspaper. Look under heading classifications of "Photographer," "Sports Photographer," "Sports," or "Photojournalist."

6. Write to publications you are interested in working with and ask to set up an interview to see your portfolio. Always include a copy of your résumé.

7. You might also consider calling the personnel directors of larger publications or the editor in smaller publications to determine if an interview can be scheduled.

8. Take sports-oriented photographs and try to sell them on spec to local newspapers.

9. If your photos are of interest to a national audience, you might also consider trying to sell them to major publications or Web sites.

RECREATION AND FITNESS

SPORTS AND FITNESS PROGRAM COORDINATOR

CAREER PROFILE

Duties: Developing and implementing sports and fitness programs for a variety of facilities; evaluating programs; supervising staff

Alternate Title(s): Sports Program Coordinator; Recreation Specialist; Recreation Supervisor; Fitness Coordinator

Salary Range: $24,000 to $125,000+

Employment Prospects: Fair

Advancement Prospects: Good

Best Geographical Location(s) for Position: Positions may be located throughout the country

Prerequisites:

Education or Training—College degree required or preferred for most jobs

Experience—Experience working as recreation staffer or physical education teacher may be preferred

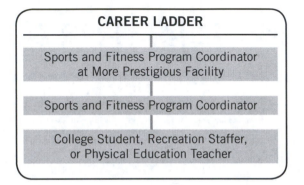

Special Skills and Personality Traits—Coordination skills; organized; detail oriented; knowledge of sports, fitness, and health; supervisory skills; communications skills; understanding of group dynamics; knowledge of exercise and/or dance

Position Description

Sports and fitness programs are regularly sponsored by communities, nonprofit groups, recreational facilities, and schools. Recently business and industry management has begun to recognize that healthy, fit employees are of increased value in the workplace. Executives have begun implementing employee sports and fitness programs within the corporate structure. The person who develops and implements such activity programs is called a Sports and Fitness Program Coordinator.

Sports and Fitness Program Coordinators are also known as recreation specialists or supervisors. The individual's main function is to assess the needs of the people who will be taking part in the program and develop its structure. Programs differ depending on individual group needs. Responsibilities, too, vary depending on the size and structure of the particular program.

Sports and Fitness Program Coordinators may work in a variety of settings, from community organizations and nonprofit groups to town, county, city, or state parks; schools; resorts; hotels; health clubs; and in major industries and businesses. Individuals may work with children, teenagers, adults, seniors, and those with special needs.

The first thing most Sports and Fitness Program Coordinators must do is to evaluate the program that is in use or to develop a new one. In performing this task, the individual must assess the needs of the people who will be participating. Sometimes the Program Coordinator must develop a budget. In others, he or she is given a budget to follow.

If the program is set up for company employees, it must accommodate their work schedule. The program must also take into account the various ages, fitness levels, and lifestyles of participants. Program Coordinators must determine what types of activities and functions will be most useful. Sports and Fitness Program Coordinators in most business companies, for example, must develop programs that can fit into an active, busy lifestyle. The Coordinator may develop a program that includes group lectures on nutrition, dieting clubs, and exercise, dance, and aerobics classes. He or she may also set up a gym area and hire exercise, nutrition, and fitness instructors. The individual may be responsible for recommending equipment, pricing, obtaining bids, and purchasing. Another responsibility in this work situation may be to make employees aware of the program, get them involved, and monitor the success.

Individuals working in other types of situations can run small programs or large ones. These can run the gamut from exercise and fitness classes for community sports camps to city sports teams, tournaments, and the coordination of year-round recreational facilities.

Once the programs have been determined, the Coordinator may be expected to put in purchase orders for sporting equipment, make sure it arrives, and teach staff members how to use it. He or she may also be responsible for interviewing and hiring staff members to teach and instruct classes and supervise programs, sporting events, tournaments, and facilities.

The Coordinator is responsible for overseeing the work of each instructor, leader, and staff member. He or she is required to keep each staff member abreast of all programs. The individual may be expected to teach staff sporting, fitness, and recreational skills. In some situations, he or she may run regular workshops for these people. The Coordinator must explain goals and requirements of the program to all employees and see to it that they are met.

Sports and Fitness Coordinators need to keep up on the newest trends. They may be required to take classes, workshops, and seminars to accomplish this. Individuals must find ways to introduce the new trends to program participants.

Other functions of the Sports and Fitness Coordinator may include writing reports and handling paperwork on a variety of things, such as the success and/or failures of the program, proposals, budgets, and accidents or injuries.

The Coordinator must know how to motivate both staff members and people involved in the various programs. The individual is responsible for coordinating all the support personnel necessary to make programs work. He or she acts as the intermediary when other people need to be involved in a project.

The Coordinator is also expected to handle problems related to the program. These might include situations such as complaints by participants about a facet of the program, a staff member, or an activity. It is the Coordinator's job to look into all problems, respond to them accordingly, and report them to the appropriate people.

Salaries

Salaries for Sports Program Coordinators can range from $24,000 to $125,000 and up depending on the specific job and the individual's responsibilities and experience level.

Coordinators with little or no experience may earn between $24,000 and $27,000 plus annually. Individuals with more experience and responsibilities may have annual salaries between $26,000 and $55,000 or more. Salaries are highest for Sports Program Coordinators running larger sports and fitness programs and those working in corporate and industry situations.

Employment Prospects

Employment prospects are fair and getting better. There are opportunities to work in this type of position in various settings throughout the country.

With the rise in health insurance and medical costs, it pays for companies to keep their employees healthy and physically fit. Job opportunities will be especially plentiful in corporate industry settings as more companies try to keep up with this trend.

Advancement Prospects

Advancement prospects are good. Individuals can climb the career ladder by locating positions in more prestigious settings and by obtaining jobs with more responsibilities. Those who are good at their job and have the determination and drive to get better can easily accomplish this. Individuals should constantly try to improve their skills by attending workshops, seminars, training sessions, and classes.

Education and Training

Educational requirements for Sports Program Coordinators vary from job to job. Most positions require a minimum of a four-year college degree. Good choices for majors include physical education, recreation, or sports administration.

Classes, workshops, seminars, and training sessions in exercise, sports administration, fitness, business, and specialized sports will be useful to the individual in both obtaining a job and being successful at it.

Experience, Skills, and Personality Traits

Sports Program Coordinators must be able to work well with people in all lifestyles. Supervisory skills are mandatory for most positions.

Coordinators must be able to initiate and develop programs or work with those put together by others. They must be organized and detail oriented. The ability to work on many different projects at once without getting flustered is necessary.

Individuals should have good communication skills, both verbal and written. They are often expected to develop and draw up proposals for programs. At times, the Sports Program Coordinator may have to speak in public to groups to drum up support for a program or to get people interested.

The Coordinator should have a total knowledge of health, fitness, and sports. The more the Coordinator knows about individual sports and fitness programs, the more effective he or she can be.

The ability to instruct others is necessary. He or she should understand group dynamics. The individual must also be able to work with people who have special needs regarding fitness and sports. First aid skills are helpful to the Coordinator when injuries occur and in emergency situations.

Many individuals have obtained these positions right after graduation from college. Others worked as recreation staffers or physical education teachers prior to assuming their current Sports and Fitness Program Coordinator job.

Unions and Associations

Sports Program Coordinators may belong to a number of organizations relevant to the type of facility in which they work. They may also be members of the American Alliance for Health, Physical Education, Recreation and Dance (AAHPERD), the National Association for Sport and Physical Education (NASPE), the National Dance Association (NDA), and the National Employee Services and Recreation Association (NESRA).

Tips for Entry

1. Volunteer your services to the sports and fitness programs of a local community group for children or senior citizens.
2. Jobs are often advertised in the classified section of the newspaper. Look under heading classifications of "Recreation," "Fitness," "Sports," "Athletics," or "Sports Programs."
3. Get experience working in a local health club as a manager, exercise specialist, or exercise instructor.
4. Many community groups use part-time or freelance people in this field. Call or write and inquire.
5. Send your résumé with a cover letter to nonprofit organizations hosting children's and seniors' programs as well as to industry and businesses. You may be able to create a position where there is none yet open.
6. Check out openings online. Start with some of the more popular sites such as monster.com and hotjobs.yahoo.com and go from there.

PERSONAL TRAINER

CAREER PROFILE

Duties: Guiding clients on a one-to-one basis in an exercise and fitness regime; assisting individuals attain utmost level of fitness

Alternate Title(s): Individual Trainer; Trainer

Salary Range: $25 to $2,000+ a session

Employment Prospects: Fair

Advancement Prospects: Fair

Best Geographical Location(s) for Position: Positions may be located throughout the country

Prerequisites:

Education or Training—No educational requirement; training in exercise, fitness, health, and nutrition helpful

Experience—Experience working in gym, health club, spa, etc., preferred

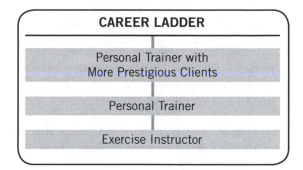

CAREER LADDER

Personal Trainer with More Prestigious Clients

Personal Trainer

Exercise Instructor

Special Skills and Personality Traits—Energetic; physically fit; health conscious; understanding of nutrition, fitness, and exercise; enthusiastic

Special Requirements—Voluntary certification is available for Personal Trainers

Position Description

Personal Trainers can lead very exciting lives depending on who their clients are. Personal Trainers may have clients who are well-known movie stars, executives in Fortune 500 companies, or just ordinary people who are extremely interested in their fitness.

A Personal Trainer is responsible for helping a person, on a one-on-one basis, attain his or her utmost level of fitness. The Personal Trainer has varied duties and responsibilities, depending on the individual client.

This type of career is usually more like being self-employed than holding a full-time job. While a job in an exercise salon or gym may last from nine to five, Personal Trainers may have a much longer day. They not only work with people to get them or keep them in shape, but they must also find clients to work with. They may do this in a number of ways. One way is advertising for clients in newspapers, magazines, on radio, or television. Or Trainers might begin by working as exercise instructors in a gym and impress a number of patrons who in turn request private sessions. The best way for Personal Trainers to gain clients is by word of mouth. If people are happy with their Trainer, they will usually tell their friends. This method can build a highly successful business for the Personal Trainer.

One of the first responsibilities of the Personal Trainer is to assess the client to find what physical shape he or she is currently in. The Trainer must also determine what the client expects of training sessions. Does he or she want to lose weight, firm up, become more physically fit? The Trainer must make sure that the client is medically able to go through the particular program decided on.

The Personal Trainer meets with the client on a regular basis. The two go through an exercise routine that the Trainer has tailored specifically for the client.

The Personal Trainer begins by instructing the person on how to do each exercise correctly. He or she may then exercise with the individual or may just offer encouragement to help the client continue with the exercise routine. As the client is paying the Personal Trainer for individualized instruction, he or she is less likely to put off a workout.

In some instances the Personal Trainer also develops a diet regime for the client. This might be to lose weight or to help the individual improve his or her eating habits.

A Personal Trainer's hours are irregular. He or she may have one client or many. Training times may range from one hour per client to three or four hours for those training for a specific reason, such as an athletic event or a movie role.

Personal Trainers may schedule training sessions in a variety of locations. The sessions may take place in the client's home or place of business. The Personal

Trainer might also train individuals in private or public gyms. Some Personal Trainers own mobile gyms, which they bring to the client's home or business.

Personal Trainers working with well-known athletes, movie stars, or other celebrities may travel with the individual around the world. While this seems like fun and may serve as a short holiday, the Personal Trainer who does this often loses out developing a clientele at home. He or she may schedule from three to five training sessions a day with other clients. Being on the road means that he or she can't take care of those commitments.

Personal Trainers are responsible to their clients. If a client is not happy with the training and workouts, he or she usually looks for another Trainer.

Salaries
It is extremely difficult to determine the earnings of Personal Trainers due to a number of variables. Compensation depends on the number and kind of clients the individual has. For example, if the Personal Trainer is working with major television or movie stars, he or she is usually able to charge more than an individual working with nonstars.

Earnings are also dependent on the amount the Personal Trainer charges each client and his or her geographic location, experience, and responsibilities.

Personal Trainers can earn from $25 to $2,000 plus a session. Those earning the higher figure usually work for stars and celebrities. An average fee for a session in a large city could range from $60 to $100 or more per hour.

Employment Prospects
Employment prospects are fair for Personal Trainers. As noted previously, Personal Trainers must usually find their own clients. If the individual is aggressive, knowledgeable, and good at what he or she does, there should be no problem getting started as a Personal Trainer.

Advancement Prospects
Advancement prospects are fair for Personal Trainers. To climb the career ladder in this profession, an individual must get more clients, charge more for his or her services, or find additional prestigious clients who can pay more.

Keeping clients happy and satisfied with their workout regime will lead to good word-of-mouth advertising. Personal Trainers may also advance their careers by opening up their own gyms or health clubs.

Education and Training
While there are no specific educational requirements for Personal Trainers, it is important that the individual know as much as possible about exercise and physical fitness. Some Personal Trainers have degrees in physical education, exercise physiology, exercise biochemistry, exercise science, and the like.

Some individuals have no formal training at all. Others received training in private gyms or health clubs by head instructors and by manufacturers of exercise equipment.

Personal Trainers should keep up on the newest trends in exercise, health, and nutrition. More and more classes and seminars on these subjects are being offered throughout the country.

Special Requirements
Personal Trainers may obtain voluntary certification giving them the designation of Certified Personal Trainer. A number of different organizations certify Personal Trainers. These might include the American College of Sports Medicine (ACSM), the American Council on Exercise (ACE), the International Fitness Professionals Association (IFPA), the National Academy of Sports Medicine (NASM), the National Council on Strength and Fitness (NCSF), and the National Federation of Professional Trainers (NFPT). Each of these organizations has different requirements to become certified and provides different certifications.

Experience, Skills, and Personality Traits
Personal Trainers should be energetic, physically fit people. They should like to exercise, be health conscious, and understand nutrition and fitness. They should also be personable, likable, and enthusiastic.

As Personal Trainers, they must not only obtain clients but also keep them. Individuals should have a basic knowledge of business. They should know how to advertise, charge people, do bookkeeping, and purchase equipment.

They should also be familiar with first aid procedures in case a client injures him- or herself.

Unions and Associations
Personal Trainers may belong to a number of different organizations, including the American Council on Exercise (ACE), the International Fitness Professionals Associations (IFPA), National Council for Certified Personal Trainers (NCCPT), and the National Federation of Personal Trainers (NFPT). These organizations provide professional support and guidance to members.

Individuals may also belong to local health, fitness, and nutritional organizations.

Tips for Entry

1. Work in a local gym or health club. This will help you make important contacts as well as give you valuable training.

2. If you are considering college, try to find one with a program geared toward fitness, nutrition, or exercise.

3. If you are currently in college, volunteer to work with any of the sports teams to learn how they train for a season.

4. Volunteer to run exercise or fitness sessions for a local organization, such as a boys' club, girls' club, or senior citizens' center. It will be good experience.

5. Look in the newspaper display or classified section under heading classifications such as "Exercise," "Fitness," "Instructor," or "Personal Trainer."

6. Many exercise and fitness machine manufacturers look for representatives. They offer training and then either give you a job or ask you to be a company representative in a certain area. This is good for learning how to use various machines and equipment. It also opens up opportunities to make more contacts in the fitness world.

7. You might attempt to get clients by advertising your services in a local newspaper or circular.

AEROBICS INSTRUCTOR

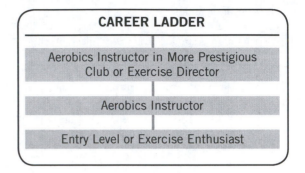

Position Description

With the current trend toward physical fitness and health, gyms, fitness centers, spas, and health clubs are becoming ubiquitous. The Aerobics Instructor's function is to lead classes for individuals or groups in aerobics and other forms of exercise. Individuals may work in private health clubs, gyms, schools, and elsewhere.

The Aerobics Instructor is responsible for helping the patrons of a club or gym perform the exercises in a safe manner. It is important that he or she know the correct methods for doing the various exercise routines. The individual is responsible not only for teaching classes but for helping make the club a productive, fun place for the patrons. If people do not have a good time at the gym, they often do not return.

Many Aerobics Instructors utilize dancing routines as part of their exercise program. These individuals must develop routines, choose music, and put the entire production together.

Depending on the size of the club and the responsibilities of the Instructor, he or she may have additional duties. For example, the individual may teach club or gym members how to use the different types of equipment. He or she must, therefore, have a complete understanding not only of how each piece of equipment is used correctly, but what its benefits are.

In some health clubs, spas, or gyms, the Aerobics Instructor is responsible for putting together personal fitness programs for members. He or she might prescribe the number, type, and level of aerobics classes necessary to attain the best physical fitness with the least amount of strain for a new member.

The Aerobics Instructor must understand the fitness level of most people in the class. If not, class members may become so exhausted and strained that injuries may occur, or they may become so tired they lose interest in the class. The Aerobics Instructor may teach various levels of classes for people who are at different fitness levels.

In some health clubs and gyms, the Aerobics Instructor is the one who initially assesses the patrons to find what physical shape they are in. If the patron is not in good physical shape, or in specific age categories, the Aerobics Instructor may be required to determine if he or she is medically able to go through the selected programs. In other gyms, an exercise specialist, the receptionist, or the club manager may handle this. Some clubs require statements from physicians before allowing patrons to participate in programs.

The Aerobics Instructor begins by instructing the class on how to perform each exercise correctly. He or she may then stand in front of the class and exercise with them or may just offer encouragement.

Hours may be irregular for Aerobic Instructors. Individuals may work a variety of shifts, depending on the specific gym or spa. Usually, however, Aerobics Instructors work a set number of hours. Individuals are responsible to the gym or spa owner or general manager.

Salaries

Earnings for Aerobics Instructors depend on the specific spa or gym, its location and prestige, and the experience and duties of the individual.

Some Aerobics Instructors earn little more than the minimum wage. Others earn a great deal more. Annual compensation can range from $24,000 to $36,000 plus. Aerobics Instructors working in prestigious spas in major cities usually earn even higher salaries.

Employment Prospects

Employment prospects are excellent for Aerobics Instructors. Job possibilities may be located in almost every part of the country. The better trained an individual is, the more opportunities there are for obtaining a good position.

Individuals can work in a variety of environments, from schools to gyms and franchise clubs to exclusive spas. They may work in male, female, or coed situations.

Advancement Prospects

Advancement prospects are fair for Aerobics Instructors. There are a number of ways of climbing the career ladder. The most common way is for the Aerobics Instructor to locate a position in a larger or more prestigious club or spa. Another method of career advancement is for the individual to become an exercise director, specialist, or club manager.

Aerobics Instructors who provide stimulating, exciting workouts build a following. When Instructors are in demand, they can often command higher salaries.

Education and Training

While there are no specific educational requirements for Aerobics Instructors, it is important that the individual have as much exercise training as possible. Courses, seminars, or workshops in exercise physiology, exercise biochemistry, and exercise science will be useful. A number of colleges currently offer programs in exercise and fitness.

Other training may be obtained on the job at spas and gyms. In some work situations an Aerobics Instructor must go through the gym's instructor training program before being hired. Manufacturers and representatives of exercise equipment companies are also good possibilities for training. These businesses often teach instructors about the correct use of their equipment.

Certain trade associations and organizations provide members with training in aerobics, dance, and exercise. Many of these organizations are now also beginning to offer certification.

Aerobics Instructors must keep up with the newest exercise trends. More and more classes and seminars on this subject are being offered nationwide. Basic first aid courses can also prove valuable to Instructors.

Experience, Skills, and Personality Traits

Aerobics Instructors need to be in top physical shape. They should be energetic and enjoy exercising. Individuals should like being around and teaching people. Aerobics Instructors should be personable and have enthusiastic personalities.

The individuals should also be familiar with first aid procedures in case a patron injures him- or herself.

Unions and Associations

Aerobics Instructors may belong to a number of trade associations providing educational guidance, training, and professional support. These might include the International Dance-Exercise Association (IDEA), or the Aerobics and Fitness Association of America (AFAA). Individuals might also belong to local fitness and health-oriented organizations.

Tips for Entry

1. If you are considering college, try to locate a school with a program geared toward fitness, exercise, and nutrition.
2. Volunteer your services running exercise sessions for local nonprofit organizations, such as boys' clubs, girls' clubs, and senior citizens' centers. This will provide good hands-on experience.
3. Positions for Aerobics Instructors are advertised in the the newspaper display or classified section under heading classifications such as "Aerobics," "Spa," "Health Club," "Gym," "Exercise," "Fitness," or "Instructor."
4. Many exercise and fitness machine manufacturers look for representatives. They provide training and may then either offer you a job or ask you to serve as a company representative in a certain territory. This is an excellent chance to learn how to use various machines and equipment. It also opens up opportunities to make contacts in the fitness world.
5. Send your résumé and a cover letter to spas, health clubs, and gyms. Ask that your résumé be kept on file if there are no current openings.
6. Write to the corporate headquarters of health industry and exercise franchise operations and chains. These spa and club organizations often offer training and job placement.

HEALTH CLUB MANAGER

Position Description

More and more health and fitness clubs are springing up around the country. All of these clubs need managers. Health Club Managers are responsible for running the facilities in a safe, efficient manner. They also help make the club a productive, fun place for patrons to visit.

Health clubs usually offer a number of services for those who want to maintain a healthy, fit lifestyle. Most facilities have exercise machines, aerobic conditioning equipment, and classes. Some health clubs also have running tracks and tennis, handball, and racquetball courts. Depending on the club, it might also offer spa facilities, such as pools, steam rooms, and whirlpools.

The Health Club Manager is an administrative member of the club staff. Working with the rest of the personnel, he or she coordinates employee efforts to create a well-run facility.

Responsibilities of the Health Club Manager vary from job to job depending on the structure of the club. In smaller clubs, the Manager usually has more varied duties. In larger clubs, he or she can assign certain tasks to an assistant manager.

In some situations, the Health Club Manager is responsible for hiring and firing personnel, including the receptionist, assistant manager, exercise directors, and aerobics instructors. The individual is also responsible for hiring lifeguards, masseurs or masseuses, and attendants for the pool and locker room. To do this the Manager may call employment agencies, write and place advertisements, and make phone calls to qualified people to find staff members.

Once staff members are hired, the Manager is responsible for making sure that they are trained properly and are aware of club rules and regulations. He or she may be required to hold classes or seminars for new staff members. If the Manager finds that one of the staff is not performing the job correctly, he or she must either correct the situation or discharge the staff member.

The Manager must check that all staff members who need to be licensed, such as lifeguards, have current licenses. If medical exams are required before hiring, he or she is responsible for making sure that examinations have been performed.

One of the major responsibilities of the Health Club Manager is to take care of the day-to-day problems that might occur in the club. If, for example, there is a disagreement between a patron and a staff member, the

Health Club Manager must straighten it out and keep the patron happy.

If an accident occurs in the club, the Manager must call health care personnel, notify the owner of the club and the insurance company, and possibly write a report about the accident.

In some instances the Manager is responsible for doing payrolls, bookkeeping, and record keeping. In other clubs, this responsibility is handled by a bookkeeper or the club owner.

In some health clubs, the Manager greets new or prospective patrons and shows them around the club in hopes of signing them up. In other clubs, this duty is given to receptionists or salespeople.

Another function of the Health Club Manager is to make sure that the physical club facility is kept safe, clean, and neat. He or she must make sure that all equipment is in proper working order. If something is broken, he or she arranges to have it repaired or replaced.

The Health Club Manager is often required to schedule exercise and aerobics classes. To do this, he or she must get to know the hours of the greatest patron influx. The Manager must keep up with everything that is happening in the club.

In some clubs, the Manager is responsible for advertising to bring in new members. He or she must get prices on the various media and decide on the type of ads, their frequency, and possible areas for placement. At times, the Manager may also be required to develop promotions to bring in new members. For example, he or she may try to bring in a new group of members, such as pregnant women. In such cases, the Manager might schedule classes for pregnant women, run special programs, and offer special prices for those attending. In a similar vein, the Manager may decide that bringing singles together would be the method to attract additional members and schedule "singles" exercise parties. The more members a club can attract, the more successful the club will be.

The Health Club Manager must be accessible to members. Some Managers float around the club talking to patrons. In this way, they can see what problems exist and what services members are most satisfied with. In other clubs, the Manager might send out questionnaires.

The Health Club Manager may be required to fill in for staff members who call in sick or work at positions that have not yet been filled. If the individual is filling in for an exercise instructor, he or she must be aware of the newest exercise techniques.

The Health Club Manager is usually responsible directly to the owner of the club. The Health Club Man-

ager may work varied hours depending on when the particular club is the busiest. He or she may have to work overtime when the club is extremely busy or when there is a problem, such as a staff member calling in sick.

Salaries

Salaries vary greatly for Health Club Managers. Variables include the size, type, geographic location, and prestige of the health club. Another important salary consideration is whether the facility is public, private, or part of a chain.

Compensation also is dependent on the education, experience, and responsibilities of the individual. Annual earnings may run from $25,000 to $65,000 or more. Salaries on the lower end of the scale go to individuals with little experience who work in smaller local clubs. Many Health Club Managers also receive bonuses for bringing in and signing up new members.

An additional benefit for the Health Club Manager is that he or she is usually allowed to use club facilities at no cost.

Employment Prospects

Employment prospects are excellent for Health Club Managers. More and more clubs are opening every day all over the country. Positions may be found in almost every geographical location. There is also a need for Health Club Managers in clubs on cruise lines, casino hotels, and resort hotels and spas.

Advancement Prospects

Advancement prospects are fair for Health Club Managers. Individuals who wish to stay in this field usually climb the career ladder by seeking the same type of position in a larger, more prestigious club. This, in turn, generally leads to higher earnings. Other individuals try to advance their careers by starting up and owning their own health club.

Education and Training

Educational requirements vary depending on the specific job. Some health clubs demand that their staff be college graduates, while others just require high school diplomas. Other clubs require the individual to go through one of their own training programs.

Business or management classes are helpful in a career as a Health Club Manager. Classes in various facets of exercise and nutrition might also be useful.

Special Requirements

Health Club Managers generally need to be certified in CPR. Many clubs are now requiring their Managers to also hold automated external defibrillator (AED) certification.

Experience, Skills, and Personality Traits

The Health Club Manager should be able to coordinate details, activities, and personnel. He or she needs to be able to supervise others in a strong yet friendly way. Self-confidence, composure, and good grooming are attributes in this type of job. The individual should also be articulate and have excellent communications skills, both in person and on the phone.

The Health Club Manager should be personable, friendly, and easy to get along with. He or she should be a people person.

The individual should be able to solve problems without losing his or her cool. The ability to deal with stress is necessary.

Most Health Club Managers are physically fit themselves and are equally interested in helping others attain a high fitness level. An understanding and knowledge of fitness and exercise is usually required.

Unions and Associations

There is no specific bargaining union for Health Club Managers. Individuals may, however, be working in a situation where all employees are unionized, such as a hotel or resort club or spa.

Health Club Managers may belong to the Association for Fitness In Business (AFFIB). This group provides educational support and career guidance to its members.

Tips for Entry

1. Positions for Health Club Managers are often advertised in newspaper display or classified sections. Look under heading classifications of "Health," "Health Club," "Management," "Fitness," "Spas," or "Sports."

2. If you don't have enough experience to manage a health club or can't find the position you want, try to get your foot in the door in some other way. For example, become the club's desk receptionist or a salesperson until a job opens up. In this way, you will be gaining experience and working in the health club atmosphere.

3. Look in the yellow pages of the phone book under "Health Club," "Spas," and the like. Send your résumé with a short cover letter to the owner inquiring about a job. Ask that your résumé be kept on file if a job is not currently available.

4. You might also consider calling the clubs listed in the yellow pages and ask to set up an interview.

5. If you are interested in working for a health club that is a part of a chain, write to their main office. Many companies offer training programs and then will place you in a job with the company.

6. Many hotels and resorts have health clubs that require Managers. Remember to check these when job hunting.

7. Remember to check out job possibilities on the Internet. Go to a career site and type in keywords such as "health club," "fitness," or "spas."

HEALTH CLUB ASSISTANT MANAGER

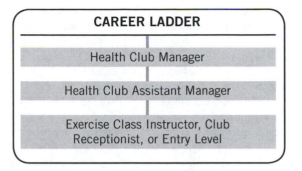

Position Description

Most health clubs in the country utilize the services of both a manager and an Assistant Manager. The time and work involved in running an operation usually makes this mandatory. The Assistant Health Club Manager is responsible for helping the manager run the facility. He or she assists in making sure the club is safe, productive, and enjoyable for patrons. The individual also is responsible for handling the duties of the club manager when he or she is not available.

Many clubs prefer to have the manager working one shift and an Assistant Manager working another so that the facility is always in the hands of a professional administrator. Some facilities also have more than one Assistant on staff.

The Assistant Manager has varied duties. He or she may be expected to offer input when other staff members are hired. The individual may also assist the manager in interviewing job applicants or reviewing applications. As new staff members join the club, the Assistant Manager may be responsible for helping the manager with training duties. The manager may also assign the Assistant to projects, such as checking

that staff members who require licensing are properly licensed and that paperwork is current and on file.

Individuals may be expected to handle a variety of paperwork. This can include anything from writing an accident report or recording staff hours for payroll to keeping track of money resulting from patron's fees. Assistant Managers may also be required to help the manager bill patrons who have not paid their membership fees. They may also be involved in sending out promotional material for the club.

The Assistant Manager is responsible for taking care of routine matters that occur when the manager is not on duty. These developments might include such areas as staff members calling in sick, broken equipment, or problems regarding patrons. Responsibilities regarding the handling of nonroutine difficulties may vary depending on the specific job. As a rule, if there is a major problem, the Assistant must contact the manager or club owner to get some direction on how it should be handled.

The individual assists the manager of the club in keeping the facility safe, clean, and neat. He or she is expected to routinely check all equipment to make sure it is in working order. The Assistant must also make sure that showers are working, towels are available, and everything is functioning correctly in the spa and sauna areas.

The Assistant Manager may be responsible for greeting prospective patrons on behalf of the manager. He or she may give patrons a tour of the club and may offer trial passes to use the facilities for the day. The individual is also expected to answer questions about club facilities, staff members' qualifications, and fee schedules. Depending on the facility, the Assistant Manager might also be responsible for demonstrating the correct use of various exercise machines. He or she might introduce new or potential members to other staff members and patrons to make them feel more comfortable at the club.

In many health clubs, especially smaller ones, the Assistant Manager may be required to teach exercise and aerobics classes. The individual must keep up with the latest techniques in exercise, dance, and aerobics. The Assistant may teach classes on a regular basis or just when other instructors are unavailable.

The Assistant Health Club Manager is directly responsible to the club manager. The individual may work various hours depending on the specific shift he or she is assigned. Assistant Managers are expected to work overtime when needed. This may occur when the manager cannot be at the club, when other staff members call in sick, or when the club is extremely busy and needs additional help.

Salaries

Assistant Health Club Managers may earn salaries that range from $22,000 to $37,000 or more. Factors affecting the range include the size, type, prestige, and geographical location of the facility. Other factors include the experience and responsibilities of the individual.

In some health clubs, staff members who bring in new patrons are awarded bonuses. Generally, individuals working in clubs in major cities earn more than those working in similar-sized clubs in other areas.

Employment Prospects

There are excellent employment opportunities for Assistant Health Club Managers. Individuals may work in health and fitness clubs that are privately owned or that are part of a chain. Assistant Managers may also work in hotels, resorts, spas, or cruise ships. Job openings may be located throughout the country.

Advancement Prospects

Advancement prospects are good for Assistant Health Club Managers. The next step up the ladder is either to locate a similar position in a larger, more prestigious club or to become a full-fledged club manager. As a great many managers move to other positions, there are frequent opportunities for advancement.

Education and Training

Educational requirements vary for Assistant Managers depending on each job. Some clubs prefer that their staff be college graduates or at least have a college background, while others require only a high school diploma. Many clubs, such as those that are part of nationwide chains, have their own training programs for staff members.

Classes in business, management, exercise, nutrition, and fitness are helpful both in attaining a job and for career advancement.

Special Requirements

Health Club Assistant Managers generally need to be certified in CPR. Many clubs are now requiring their Assistant Managers to also hold automated external defibrillator (AED) certification.

Experience, Skills, and Personality Traits

The Assistant Manager of a health club should have many of the skills that a full-fledged manager would have. Supervisory, business, and administrative skills are necessary. The individual should also be able to coordinate and handle many details and projects.

The Assistant Manager should be able to take control of a situation or problem and handle it. He or she should be self-confident and composed at all times.

Individuals in this position need good communication skills. They should be able to speak comfortably on a one-on-one basis as well as in front of groups and on the telephone. Assistant Health Club Managers should be personable and easy to get along with. They also should be service oriented.

Assistant Health Club Managers should look healthy and physically fit. Individuals should also be able to teach exercise, aerobics, and fitness classes.

Many Assistant Managers started their careers in health and fitness working as exercise or aerobics class instructors. Others held jobs as club receptionists. If individuals have a business or fitness background, this can also be an entry-level position.

Unions and Associations

Assistant Health Club Managers do not usually belong to any type of bargaining union. If, however, they are working in a club located in a resort or hotel that is unionized, they may be members.

Individuals may belong to health and fitness associations, such as the Association for Fitness in Business (AFFIB). This organization offers educational support and career guidance to its members.

Tips for Entry

1. The easiest way to find a job in this area is to look in the newspaper. Openings are usually advertised in display or classified sections under heading classifications of "Health," "Health Club," "Exercise Salon," "Management," "Fitness," "Spas," or "Sports."

2. Many clubs post signs on their windows or inside advertising job openings.

3. You might also consider taking a day to visit the various clubs in your area to see if they have openings. Bring your résumé with you and ask the receptionist about job possibilities. If there are openings, he or she will usually direct you to the club manager or ask you to fill out a job application.

4. If cold-call visiting to locate a job is not your style, you might want to send your résumé with a short cover letter to clubs in your area. You can find their names and addresses by looking in the yellow pages of the phone book under "Health Clubs," "Spas," and the like. Remember to request that your résumé be kept on file if a job is not currently available.

5. Job openings may be located on the Internet. Go to a job or career site and type in keywords such as "health clubs," "fitness," or "spas."

6. Be creative when looking for a job. Consider working for a health club or spa in a hotel, resort, or cruise ship.

7. Many health and fitness clubs and spas are chains or franchises. These businesses often offer training programs and then place you in a job at one of their facilities. If you are interested in this approach, write to the chain or franchise's main office.

TENNIS DIRECTOR

Duties: Organizing tennis program for a facility; bringing in new members; giving lessons; operating a pro shop; maintaining courts; scheduling lessons, tournaments, and court time

Alternate Title(s): Director of Tennis

Salary Range: $24,000 to $125,000+

Employment Prospects: Good

Advancement Prospects: Good

Best Geographical Location(s) for Position: Positions may be located throughout the country

Prerequisites:

    Education or Training—No formal educational requirement for some positions; others require or prefer a four-year college degree or background; training in tennis necessary

    Experience—Experience in business, management, and tennis needed

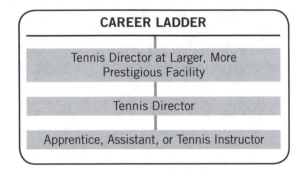

CAREER LADDER

Tennis Director at Larger, More Prestigious Facility

Tennis Director

Apprentice, Assistant, or Tennis Instructor

    Special Skills and Personality Traits—Skilled tennis player; business and marketing skills; communication skills; organizational skills; ability to teach all levels of tennis; detail oriented; supervisory skills

    Special Requirements—Voluntary certification available

Position Description

Tennis has always been a popular sport. With the current fitness trend hitting the country, it has become even more popular. Where once indoor courts were the exception, today thousands are located throughout the country. They can be found in various facilities, including country clubs, racquet clubs, resort hotels, and health and fitness clubs. There are even a couple of indoor tennis courts in the upper portion of Grand Central Station in New York City. The person who is in charge of the tennis program at these facilities is called the Tennis Director.

The individual in this position has varied duties depending on the specific job. His or her main function is to organize the tennis program for the facility. This responsibility is all-encompassing. The individual is responsible for everything from bookkeeping duties and staffing responsibilities to day-to-day facility operation.

The Tennis Director is expected to obtain members. To accomplish this, the individual may run various promotions or advertisements aimed at bringing new members into the facility. Once they are in, the Director must find ways to retain this membership. Many areas offer a number of tennis facilities. The Director, therefore, must develop ways to obtain and retain

patrons. A particular tennis club may, for example, have a well-known tennis pro teaching, or the club may be known for its posh surroundings or very helpful staff members.

The Director is also expected to develop tennis programs. These may include instructional workshops and seminars and tournaments for various levels of players. He or she may organize tournaments for juniors and seniors.

Most Tennis Directors are responsible for the operation of the pro shop. In some facilities, the Tennis Director owns the shop. In others, he or she just manages it. A pro shop is a small store within a tennis facility where people can purchase tennis equipment, supplies, and clothing. The individual receives a commission on sales made in the shop. He or she acts as the buyer, keeps stock in place, and recommends tennis equipment.

Court maintenance is another important function of the Tennis Director. He or she must see to it that courts are in perfect condition, clean, and safe. If they are not, the individual directs a maintenance person to fix the problem. The Tennis Director also is responsible for making sure all tennis racquets are in good shape. If not, he or she sees to it that they are repaired. The Tennis Director may do this him- or herself or may have an assistant or other staff member take care of repair. In addition to taking care of the club's racquets, the Director may also repair or have repaired patrons' racquets.

The individual must know how to schedule. The Director has a certain number of courts to fill, and he or she must know how to utilize them to the best advantage. For example, if the courts are always busy in the mornings and afternoons, but not the evenings, the Director may offer a discount for patrons willing to play at night.

The Tennis Director may be expected to do public relations work for the facility. He or she may write press releases on events held there and on special promotions, tournaments, and new professional tennis instructors. The individual may also invite the media to cover events or do feature stories.

Another major function of the Tennis Director is to provide instructions to patrons. The Director may give lessons him- or herself or may have a staff of tennis teachers and instructor professionals. The Director must schedule lessons for those who are interested. He or she may develop group lesson schedules and programs for those who have various levels of tennis playing skill.

The Tennis Director may work long hours. As he or she is ultimately responsible for every aspect of the organization of the tennis program, the individual may often have to work at night and on weekends as well as regular hours.

Salaries

Earnings can vary greatly for Tennis Directors depending on a great many factors. Some of these include the geographic location, prestige, and size of the facility. Other factors include the individual's experience and responsibilities. Another factor might be whether the facility is open year-round or is seasonal. This might occur if the Director is working in a facility with outdoor courts in a geographical area with cold winters. Earnings are also dependent on the amount of sales generated in the pro shop and the number of lessons taught.

Salaries for Tennis Directors may range from $24,000 to $85,000 plus. Some individuals who run programs in very large or prestigious facilities earn $125,000 and over annually.

Employment Prospects

Employment prospects are good for Tennis Directors who are skilled in their profession. Individuals may work in any type of tennis and racquet club, tennis and swimming club, exercise facility, spa, resort, camp, country club, or hotel. They may work in indoor, outdoor, or dual facilities. Job openings may be located throughout the country.

Positions in summer camps may not be year-round, running only from June through August.

Advancement Prospects

Advancement prospects are good for Tennis Directors. Individuals may advance their careers by locating similar positions in larger or more prestigious facilities. This will result in additional responsibilities and higher earnings.

Education and Training

Educational requirements vary for Tennis Directors. Some facilities require a college background or degree, while others do not. As a rule, most successful Tennis Directors do have a four-year college degree. As individuals are responsible for administering the tennis program, a degree or background in business or marketing is useful. A number of colleges currently offer degrees in tennis programming.

Individuals might also choose a college that places a heavy emphasis on its school's tennis team. In this way they will obtain training, experience, and participate in competitive tennis situations.

Special Requirements

Voluntary certification is available for Tennis Directors through the U.S. Professional Tennis Association (USPTA).

Experience, Skills, and Personality Traits

The Tennis Director should have a full range of business and marketing skills. He or she should have good communication skills, both verbal and written.

The Tennis Director needs supervisory skills as well. He or she administrates the entire tennis program. Therefore, the individual usually has a number of people working under him or her, including instructors, maintenance people, bookkeepers, and others.

The individual should be extremely organized. He or she must also know a great deal about scheduling. This comes in handy when scheduling lessons, court time, and tournaments.

The Tennis Director should know how to play tennis well. It is not necessary, however, for the Tennis Director to be a world-class player. It is more important that the individual is able to teach and communicate the methods and techniques of the sport. The individual must also be able to teach a variety of levels of players, from beginners through advanced.

Some positions may require or prefer certification.

Some individuals come out of college with a business or marketing degree and know a great deal about the sport. These people may locate a job as a Tennis Director right away. Other people obtain experience in the industry as assistants, interns, teachers, or tennis instructor professionals before becoming Tennis Directors.

Unions and Associations

The largest and oldest association in the professional tennis industry is the U.S. Professional Tennis Association (USPTA). This organization provides valuable help, professional guidance, and support as well as continuing education. It also licenses and certifies professionals working in the tennis industry.

Tips for Entry

1. If you aspire to be a successful Tennis Director, consider one of the colleges with a major in professional tennis management. Ferris State University in Big Rapids, Michigan, is one of these schools. Contact them for more information.
2. You might also consider attending a college with a strong tennis team.
3. Join the USPTA. It is very helpful to those involved in the tennis industry. It offers classes, manuals, booklets, seminars, conferences, and other guidance and support. It is well worth getting involved with.
4. Get a part-time or summer job working in a local tennis club, tennis camp, or other tennis facility. This will provide you with good on-the-job experience.
5. Speak to a Tennis Director of a large facility to see if he or she might consider becoming your mentor.

TENNIS TEACHING PROFESSIONAL

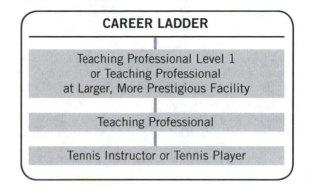

Position Description

With tennis and racquet clubs becoming more popular throughout the country, a growing number of people want to learn how to play the sport or to refine their skills. The individual who can help accomplish this goal is called either a Tennis Instructor or a Teaching Professional. Teaching Professionals differ from Tennis Instructors in that they pass through a certification program, whereas Instructors may have no professional training.

As with the Tennis Instructor, the main function of the Teaching Professional is to give tennis lessons to those interested in the sport. He or she, however, is also trained in other facets of the tennis industry, which makes him or her a more valuable asset to a club, resort, or organization. In many instances, the Teaching Professional may assume many of the duties of a tennis director.

The Teaching Professional is certified by the U.S. Professional Tennis Association (USPTA). To be certified, the individual must pass an examination developed by the organization. The organization also holds courses and seminars to help prepare individuals for certification. For example, the individual is trained in merchandising and business. He or she may also be educated on court maintenance, racquet repair, and pro shop operation. The individual must know and demonstrate to those administering the exam the various techniques and shots used in the sport. He or she also has to demonstrate teaching abilities.

Teaching Professionals are expected to offer instruction in both private and group lessons. They also must be able to teach tennis techniques on all levels, from beginner to experienced. In many circumstances, individuals are responsible for a junior development program at the tennis facility.

The Teaching Professional might be expected to schedule lessons for his or her students as well as reserve court time. In some instances, the individual may also be responsible for racquet repair.

Depending on the specific job, the Teaching Professional often is expected to run tournaments for students and other players to participate in. He or she must know how to develop the tournaments, schedule court times for players, and divide the tournament for different skill or age levels. At the tennis director's request, the individual may also be responsible for obtaining players to participate as well as for handling public relations.

In some situations, the Teaching Professional also is expected to operate the pro shop. In these cases, he or she may recommend tennis equipment, clothing, shoes, and the like to patrons.

Many Teaching Professionals work at year-round indoor tennis courts. Others may work part of the year in one location and the rest in another section of the country. Individuals who love to play tennis and to teach and enjoy the sport can have a very fulfilling career.

Salaries

Earnings may vary greatly for Teaching Professionals in tennis depending on a number of variables. These may include the facility the individual is working at, its prestige, size, and location. Other factors determining earnings include the experience, skills, drive, determination, and responsibilities of the Teaching Professional. Individuals may earn between $23,000 and $95,000 plus annually.

Teaching Professionals may be paid a salary in addition to being entitled to all money they earn giving lessons. The average cost of a tennis lesson is between $25 and $50 per hour. The Teaching Professional may also earn a commission of proceeds from pro shop revenue.

Employment Prospects

Employment prospects are good for those trained in the sport and skilled in business. Individuals may work in a variety of settings, including resort hotels, tennis clubs, racquet clubs, exercise facilities, spas, tennis camps, country clubs, and hotels. Facilities may be indoors, outdoors, or dual. Jobs may be located throughout the country.

Advancement Prospects

Teaching Professionals who are certified may advance their career by obtaining continuing education in the field. There are three levels of professional, ranging from the highest level, Professional 1, through Professional 3. There is also a Master Professional certification. Those who advance their level of certification have an easier time locating similar positions in larger or more prestigious facilities. This results in increased responsibilities and higher earnings.

Education and Training

Some tennis instructors have no training whatsoever. They are self-taught, skilled in the sport, and like to teach. Teaching Professionals, however, go through a certification program offered by the USPTA. The association gives a two-day examination that includes a written test as well as actual demonstrations. Prior to the test the USPTA offers training to assist individuals so that they will be able to pass the test. Once an individual is certified, he or she may take a variety of continuing education classes to help refine techniques in tennis, teaching, and business skills.

Special Requirements

Voluntary certification is available for Tennis Teaching Professionals through the USPTA (United States Professional Tennis Association).

Experience, Skills, and Personality Traits

The Tennis Teaching Professional must have good tennis skills. He or she need not, however, be a world-class tennis player. Individuals good enough to play on the tournament circuit usually do so for a while because they can make more money doing that. The Teaching Professional must be an excellent instructor. He or she must be able to show students techniques and communicate ways of performing them. The individual must be able to teach people in all levels of the sport. He or she must also be equally adept at teaching groups and individual students.

Teaching Professionals who attain success usually have good business and marketing skills. They are extremely organized and detail oriented. They know how to schedule classes, court time, and tournaments.

Individuals should enjoy working with people of all ages and at all levels of tennis. They should be pleasant, articulate, and well groomed. Communication skills are necessary.

Unions and Associations

The most prominent association in this field is the USPTA. The USPTA certifies Teaching Professionals, provides continuing education, and offers job guidance and support for those in the field.

Tips for Entry

1. Join the USPTA. The organization will be useful to you in getting your career started.
2. Attend tennis camps, seminars, workshops, and classes. The more techniques you learn from others, the more you will be able to teach to students.
3. Volunteer to teach tennis to a nonprofit or youth group in your area. It will be good on-the-job experience.
4. Positions are often advertised in the newspaper display or classified sections. Look under heading classifications of "Tennis," "Pro," or "Sports Instruction."
5. You might also consider sending your résumé and a cover letter to tennis clubs, health clubs, resorts, or hotels. Ask that your résumé be kept on file if there is no current opening.

GOLF PRO

CAREER PROFILE

Duties: Running a club, course, or resort's golf program; providing lessons; managing a pro shop; overseeing a golf course; recommending golf equipment

Alternate Title(s): Golf Professional; Pro; PGA Pro

Salary Range: $25,000 to $150,000+

Employment Prospects: Good

Advancement Prospects: Fair

Best Geographical Location(s) for Position: Positions located throughout the country; areas hosting a great many resort hotels may offer additional opportunities

Prerequisites:

Education or Training—Minimum of high school diploma; completion of PGA or LPGA training

Experience—Experience as an assistant pro or apprentice may be required

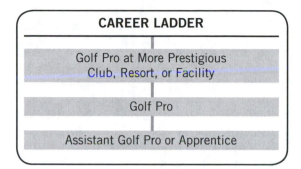

CAREER LADDER

Golf Pro at More Prestigious Club, Resort, or Facility

Golf Pro

Assistant Golf Pro or Apprentice

Special Skills and Personality Traits—Excellent golf skills; good teacher; personable; business and administrative skills; knowledge of first aid; positive attitude

Special Requirements—PGA or LPGA certification required

Position Description

Golf is an extremely popular sport in this country and in other nations as well. Millions of people play regularly, and a great many business deals are developed and finalized on golf courses.

The Golf Pro is the individual responsible for running a golf course and a program for a facility. He or she may work at a driving range, a public golf course, a private golf club, a golf hotel, or a resort hotel. Individuals may have varied duties depending on the specific job. The Pro is expected to be an expert on everything from the skills of the sport and course maintenance to the type of equipment that golfers should use.

One of the main functions of the individual is to help people interested in playing the sport develop their skills. To do this, the Pro often offers private or group lessons to patrons of the golf facility. He or she is usually paid a fee by the golfers for this instruction. Individuals may take one or more lessons over a period of time in hopes of improving their golf game. As golfers begin to see their game improve, they generally seek additional instruction. The Pro must be able to give lessons to all levels of people, from beginners to advanced players. The Pro is expected to schedule his or her own lessons as well as those of any other instructors at the course. The individual must also set fees for lessons. As a rule, the Pro is paid a higher fee for services than the other instructors.

In many golf clubs, the Pro may be responsible for hiring additional instructors, assistant pros, and the other personnel necessary to run the golf program successfully. He or she may be expected to advertise for openings, interview applicants, and talk with the press. Depending on the size and structure of a gold club, the Pro may also have to hire personnel for the food concessions, groundskeeping, maintenance, and pro shop, as well as caddies.

The Pro is responsible for the supervision and administration of staff members working under him or her. He or she is expected to schedule staff hours and make sure that enough personnel are on each shift to take care of the club patrons.

Another responsibility many Pros assume is running and managing of the pro shop. Here golfers can buy clubs, bags, balls, and other equipment for the game as well as golf clothes. In many cases, the Pro must do the buying for the shop, determining what brands of equipment and how much to purchase. He or she may be responsible for keeping track of inventory, invoices, pricing merchandise as it comes in, and displaying it in a pleasing manner, or assigning this duty to another staff member. People often patronize the shop to get the Pro's opinion and recommendation on the brand or type of clubs or other equipment to purchase.

The Pro is responsible for making sure that the course is in good shape. If there are dangerous or unsightly areas in need of repair, he or she is expected to have them taken care of in a timely manner.

If there is an emergency, accident, injury, or sick player in the club or on the course, the Pro is expected to call for an ambulance or medical personnel. He or she may administer first aid in emergencies. If there has been an accident, the Pro must fill out an accident report and notify the club or course owner or manager.

Other responsibilities of the Pro might include selling club memberships, obtaining greens fees, registrations, and renting equipment and golf carts.

Golf Pros are often asked to take part in charity events and golf tournaments to help raise money for worthwhile community causes. They may help put together players, find sponsors for prizes, and so on. Individuals may also find celebrity golfers to play in the tournament as well as play themselves.

Being a Golf Pro is the perfect job for those who enjoy the game. Pros have the opportunity to perfect their skills while helping others learn to perfect theirs. Pros working in the Midwest or eastern part of the country usually cannot work full time, because of the cold, snowy winters. Individuals who want to work full time must find a similar type of job in a warmer climate for the winter months. This is a drawback for some and a plus for others who like to travel.

Salaries
Earnings for Golf Pros vary greatly depending on a number of variables. These include the determination, drive, and personality of the individual as well as his or her skills, responsibilities, and experience level. Other factors include the location where the Pro is working and whether the individual has a recognized name in the golfing industry.

Pros often make a salary for running the golf program and managing the pro shop. They may earn commissions from sales of golf equipment, clothing, and shoes, and additional money by giving lessons.

Individuals may work part of the year in one section of the country and the balance of the time in another section. Earnings can range from $25,000 to $150,000 and up depending on the specific individual. Hourly rates for teaching golf skills to individuals may range between $30 and $250 plus.

Employment Prospects
Employment prospects are fair for individuals who are good at the sport. Golf Pros can work throughout the country. Pros in geographic areas that are cold and snowy in winter will have to move to warmer climates to continue working.

Individuals may work in a variety of settings, including driving ranges, community-owned golf courses, other public courses, private clubs, and luxurious resort hotels. Pros may also work for specific golf resorts.

While Pros can work throughout the country, more jobs may be located in areas in which many resort hotels are located.

Advancement Prospects
A Golf Pro can advance his or her career by locating a position at a more prestigious location. This usually results in higher earnings. For example, an individual working at a driving range might climb the career ladder by landing a job at a private golf club. Pros who run large pro shops and give lessons can increase their earnings.

Education and Training
There is no formal educational requirement to become a Golf Pro. Individuals, however, must usually go through a course of study offered by the Professional Golfers' Association (PGA) or Ladies Professional Golfer's Association (LPGA). The training offers courses in a number of areas of use to the Pro in his or her career.

Individuals must pass the training course in order to be approved and certified as a PGA Pro. PGA Pros also must serve as apprentices or assistants before becoming full-fledged Pros.

Special Requirements
In order to become PGA or LPGA certified pros, individuals must take approved courses through the PGA or LPGA.

Experience, Skills, and Personality Traits
The Golf Pro must be extremely talented and really enjoy the sport. He or she must know everything there is to know about golf. Many Pros began their career as professional golfers playing in tournaments. Some were top celebrities in their field. Others did not become household names but played in tournaments, enjoyed the sport, and want to work in it.

Pros need to be good teachers. They need the ability to instruct beginners through advanced golfers in the skills of the sport. Individuals should have a lot of patience and perseverance.

Pros must be personable and get along well with people. In order to be successful, the Pro must make people feel comfortable and confident. He or she must motivate them and help them enjoy the game.

As Golf Pros may be responsible for running the golf program, they must have both administrative and supervisory skills. A knowledge of business and management is needed.

Sales ability is required, especially if the Pro is paid a commission on golf equipment sold in the shop. It is also necessary for the Pro to sell his or her own skills in teaching.

Knowledge of first aid is helpful in cases of injury, sickness, or emergencies on the course.

Unions and Associations

The major trade association in the field of golf is the PGA. This organization provides training, support, certification, and professional guidance to those interested in golf.

Individuals might also belong to other organizations promoting the sport, such as the Ladies Professional Golf Association (LPGA).

Tips for Entry

1. Consider getting a part-time or summer job as a golf caddy. A caddy moves the golfer's equipment from hole to hole on the course. Being a caddy is an excellent way to work in the sport as you learn about the game.

2. If you are qualified, send your résumé and a cover letter to resort hotels, private golf clubs, or public courses. Ask that your résumé be kept on file if there are no current openings.

3. Play golf at various courses. Keep your ears open. You might hear of a job possibility. It will also help you make contacts that can, in turn, lead to a job offer.

4. Jobs openings may be located in trade magazines.

5. Positions may also be advertised in newspaper display or classified sections. Look under heading classifications of "Pro" or "Golf."

LIFEGUARD

Duties: Keeping water area safe for swimmers; saving the lives of swimmers; overseeing activities at a pool or beach

Alternate Title(s): None

Salary Range: $10 to $28+ per hour; $20,000 to $39,000+ annually

Employment Prospects: Good

Advancement Prospects: Fair

Best Geographical Location(s) for Position: Positions may be located throughout the country

Prerequisites:

Education or Training—No formal educational requirement

Experience—No experience necessary

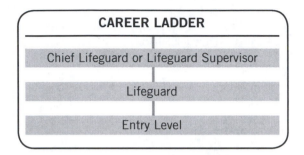

CAREER LADDER

Chief Lifeguard or Lifeguard Supervisor

Lifeguard

Entry Level

Special Skills and Personality Traits—Excellent swimmer; strong; physically fit; good eyesight; knowledge of lifesaving techniques; reliable; dependable; enjoy working with people

Special Requirement—Individuals must hold a Red Cross Advanced Lifesaving Certificate

Position Description

Lifeguards have important jobs. Their presence in certain situations often means the difference between life and death. Lifeguards may work in a variety of settings, including public pools, private pools, lakes, or the ocean. They may work indoors or outdoors. Responsibilities of each individual vary depending on the specific job. The Lifeguard's main function, however, is to keep the water area safe for swimmers.

Individuals working at a pool have different duties from Lifeguards at the seashore. Those working in a pool setting are responsible for keeping the area around the pool hazard-free. The individual watches patrons using the facility. If they begin to play rough, in or out of the water, the Lifeguard instructs them to calm down.

When on duty, the Lifeguard must keep his or her eyes on the water at all times. The individual must be alert. Daydreaming, reading, or trying to handle any other activity might mean a potential drowning.

The Lifeguard at the pool may also be expected to check the pool temperature periodically and regulate it as necessary. He or she may also be required to check on the amount of chlorine and other chemicals used in the pool to keep the water clean and safe. When necessary, the Lifeguard is expected to disperse additional chemicals into the water.

In many job situations, the Lifeguard is required to teach swimming lessons. He or she may instruct on a one-on-one basis or offer group classes to various levels of swimmers.

Lifeguards working at lakes or at the seashore do not have to check water temperatures. Depending on where they are working, however, they may be required to check water for bacteria or chemical contamination, shark infestation, etc.

It is difficult to stare into the ocean or large lakes for hours on end. Therefore, individuals working in these types of settings usually do so in groups. One Lifeguard watches the water for an hour and then takes a break or attends to other duties. Another Lifeguard then takes his or her place.

Large stretches of beach are usually divided into sections. Each section has a Lifeguard station or tower. These look like very tall chairs that hover high above the beach. From those seats, Lifeguards can watch activities in the water.

The Lifeguard must make sure that swimmers stay in designated areas. Many beaches also have rules and regulations that patrons must follow. Some areas, for example, do not allow glass containers on the beach. The Lifeguard must enforce all the rules of the beach. If the individual sees an infraction, he or she usually tells the people and gives warnings.

When a swimmer has a problem, the Lifeguards jump into action. They are responsible for rapidly reaching the individual and trying to save him or her. They may do this by running to the water, swimming out to the person in trouble, and bringing him or her back to shore. In some instances, Lifeguards may also take a boat to save a swimmer. Lifesaving can be difficult if the drowning person becomes hysterical and disoriented. Rough surf and tides can also make swimming out to the individual difficult. Lifeguards may also assist boaters in need of assistance.

Lifeguards working on the beach often have lifesaving drills. One individual acts as the victim while others handle lifesaving duties.

Once a Lifeguard brings the distressed swimmer back to shore, he or she may have to perform cardiopulmonary resuscitation (CPR) or other first aid. All Lifeguards must know CPR. Often there is no time to wait for an ambulance.

Lifeguards may perform other functions, such as helping lost children find their parents, treating minor first aid problems, handling lost-and-found duties, and providing directions.

Salaries

Earnings vary for Lifeguards depending on the specific job. Variables include the individual's responsibilities and experience as well as place of employment.

Lifeguards may be compensated in a number of ways. Individuals may receive an hourly rate, a weekly salary, or may earn a set amount for a season.

Lifeguards may earn between $10 and $28 plus an hour. Individuals who are paid salaries can earn between $20,000 and $39,000 plus annually. This is common in areas such as California and Florida, where Lifeguards work year-round on the beaches.

Lifeguards who teach swimming may also earn a fee for each lesson.

Employment Prospects

Employment prospects are good for Lifeguards. Individuals may work at indoor or outdoor pools. They may obtain positions in public or private settings. Many communities, cities, park services, and states hire Lifeguards.

Lifeguards may also work in camps, hotels, resorts, spas, clubs, or on cruise ships. Positions are also available at beaches on private or public lakes, or at the ocean.

Advancement Prospects

Lifeguards can advance their careers by becoming a supervising lifeguard or a chief lifeguard. Advancement is usually attained by seniority and by demonstrating supervisory abilities. Lifeguards can also advance their careers by obtaining positions at more prestigious or exciting locations.

Education and Training

There are usually no formal educational requirements needed to become a Lifeguard. Individuals must, however, be certified. The agency that ordinarily is responsible for setting certification requirements is the state's Department of Health. Requirements can vary from state to state.

The organization that provides certification is the American Red Cross. To obtain this certification, Lifeguards must take courses and pass tests in lifeguarding, first aid, and cardiopulmonary resuscitation and basic life support (CPRBLS). The American Red Cross sponsors these courses throughout the country.

Special Requirements

Lifeguards must hold a Red Cross Advanced Lifesaving Certificate.

Experience, Skills, and Personality Traits

The most important skill a Lifeguard should possess is the ability to be an excellent swimmer. The individual should also be a fast swimmer and a quick runner. The Lifeguard probably will be required to take a swimming speed test. He or she should also be strong and physically fit. Good eyesight is necessary.

Lifeguards need to be skilled in lifesaving techniques. A working knowledge of CPR and first aid are imperative. Individuals should enjoy working near the water, and if working outside, enjoy the sun.

Lifeguards must be reliable and dependable. They need supervisory skills. The ability to take control of a situation is essential. Individuals must be able to work under intense, stressful conditions.

Unions and Associations

There is no specific trade association for Lifeguards. If, however, an individual is working as a city or state employee, he or she may be a member of a local municipal union. Most Lifeguards are members of their local chapter of the American Red Cross.

Tips for Entry

1. You need to be an excellent swimmer to be a Lifeguard. Take swimming lessons.
2. Contact your local chapter of the American Red Cross for information on certification classes and continuing education.
3. Positions are often advertised in the local newspaper's display or classified section. Look under heading classifications of "Lifeguard," "Pool," "Lake," "Summer Employment," "Seaside," or "Ocean."

4. Jobs may be located in state parks or recreation departments. Cities and local communities also frequently hire Lifeguards.

5. You might consider writing to camps, hotels, resorts, spas, or clubs with swimming pools.

Send a copy of your résumé with a short cover letter. They may call you for an interview.

6. Jobs may be located on the World Wide Web. Search popular job sites, newspaper classifieds, or hotel and resort career opportunities.

BOXING AND WRESTLING

MATCHMAKER

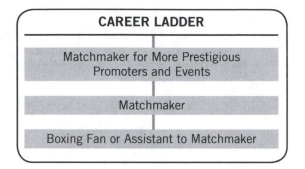

Position Description

A Matchmaker works in the field of boxing. His or her main function is to place two opponents together in the ring for a professional fight. The Matchmaker's job is to initiate good, entertaining, and competitive bouts.

In most instances, Matchmakers are hired by the promoter of a fight. The promoter may instruct the individual about which specific fighters he or she wants on the card, or program. In other situations, the promoter leaves the choice of fighters to the Matchmaker.

The Matchmaker must first determine what the purse, or earnings, will be for the fighters and/or the fight. For example, if the purse is to be $800 for a fighter, the Matchmaker would not be able to have a heavyweight champion on the card.

Sometimes fighters can earn multimillion-dollar purses. This usually occurs in major and championship fights. The Matchmaker must work within the budget the promoter sets for a fight and come up with the most exciting, competitive fighters available.

In addition to paying the fighters their purse, the Matchmaker may also be required to develop budgets for training, traveling expenses, food, and lodging for some of the fighters and their retinue. These expenses must be added into the event budget.

In order for the Matchmaker to be successful in arranging fights, he or she needs to have as much information as possible about as many fighters as possible. The Matchmaker must be familiar with managers, their fighters, fight records, amateur experience,

fight styles, weights, statures, and so on. Matchmakers also must know how and where to locate this information. Just putting together two junior middleweights in a ring does not necessarily make a good fight. For example, one opponent might be making his professional debut, while the other might be a seasoned pro. It would probably be a better fight if the two opponents both had some experience fighting professionally.

In order to be completely aware of fight industry information, the Matchmaker must constantly ask questions. In making decisions, he or she must then weigh the answers and consider who was the information source.

After finding two fighters who are competitively matched and who will agree to a purse, the Matchmaker works with the promoter to have contracts drawn up and signed. These contracts usually specify the date and location of the fight, the agreed-upon purse, the number of rounds, and the weight the fighters are expected to be for the match.

Matchmakers are licensed in the states that have athletic governing bodies. In some states, in order to become licensed as a Matchmaker, the individual must first have a contract with a promoter to do the matchmaking. This can be a catch-22 situation because one cannot be initiated without the other in place.

Matchmakers may work long hours doing the necessary research to put together good matches. Keep in mind that the individual usually is contracted to put together the entire fight card. This might run seven to 10 different bouts.

The Matchmaker works under a great deal of stress. He or she is responsible directly to the fight promoter. The individual must both please the promoter and put together a good fight card. This might be difficult if the promoter also has promotional ties to fighters he or she wants on the card.

Salaries

Salaries vary depending on the Matchmaker and how successful or in demand he or she is. Earnings may be based on specific boxing promotions, a flat fee, an annual salary, or any combination of these systems.

Individuals working full time and receiving weekly paychecks may earn from $25,000 to $300,000 plus.

Employment Prospects

Almost any individual who can find a promoter to hire him or her as a Matchmaker can find employment once. Some people think that anyone can promote and put together a successful boxing event. But Matchmakers who don't know what they are doing and put together an uncompetitive, unexciting show will not work in the profession again.

Employment prospects are fair for Matchmakers who are good at what they do. Most of the more established promoters in the country have had the same Matchmakers working with them for years. On the other hand, new promoters crop up all the time. An individual who is qualified as a Matchmaker might be able to build a relationship with a promoter who is just starting out.

While most of the major boxing matches are held in Atlantic City, Las Vegas, and New York, many other locations are beginning to host boxing events. This will give those starting out additional opportunities to break into the profession.

Advancement Prospects

It is important to note that there is no logical job progression in boxing. Individuals can get lucky in any facet of this business and jump to the top of the industry.

Matchmakers climb the career ladder by working with more prestigious fight promoters. Advancement prospects could include matchmaking fights for television or cable or championships.

Those who are good at what they do can advance quickly.

Education and Training

There are no formal educational requirements for Matchmakers. Individuals must learn from watching others and personal experience. Some in the industry say that good Matchmakers learn how to make good fights by osmosis. If that is true, individuals pursuing a career in this field should watch and analyze as many fights as possible. Trying to find a skilled, expert Matchmaker to apprentice with might also be helpful.

Special Requirements

Matchmakers may be required to hold a state license. This license is generally obtained through either the state's athletic or boxing commission.

Experience, Skills, and Personality Traits

Successful Matchmakers have an extensive background in boxing as well as other sports. As a rule, individuals in this profession spend a lot of time watching and absorbing boxing events. A Matchmaker needs almost a sixth sense when it comes to fighters. He or she should either have or develop the ability to know when two boxers could put on a very exciting show.

It helps if the Matchmaker has a good memory. In this way, he or she will remember facts and data about fighters. The individual should be personable. Matchmakers want managers and fighters to talk to them honestly.

Being a good salesperson helps when the Matchmaker is trying to get opponents to fight each other.

Unions and Associations

There is no Matchmaker union in boxing. Individuals may belong to the various sanctioning bodies, such as the World Boxing Association (WBA), the World Boxing Council (WBC), the World Boxing Organization (WBO), and the International Boxing Federation (IBF). Matchmakers may also be affiliated with any of the state athletic commissions.

Tips for Entry

1. Find a gym where fighters train. Get to know the various fighters, managers, trainers, and promoters who visit. Make contacts. They might be able to guide you to helpful people in the industry.
2. Read boxing magazines and record books. This will help you to begin to know about fighters and their records.
3. Attend live fights and watch them on television. Get the feel for the way the fighters are matched up.
4. Try to obtain a job working as an assistant, secretary, or clerk for a promoter or Matchmaker. This will give you good hands-on experience.

BOXING REFEREE

CAREER PROFILE

Duties: Officiating during a boxing match; enforcing rules of the sport; giving eight counts; stopping fights; making sure that a fighter is not seriously injured

Alternate Title(s): Ref; Official

Salary Range: $150 to $25,000+ per show

Employment Prospects: Fair

Advancement Prospects: Fair

Best Geographical Location(s) for Position: Positions may be located throughout the country; major boxing capitals are Las Vegas, New York City, and Atlantic City

Prerequisites:

Education or Training—No formal educational requirement; training in boxing officiating is necessary

Experience—Experience officiating in amateur bouts is required

CAREER LADDER

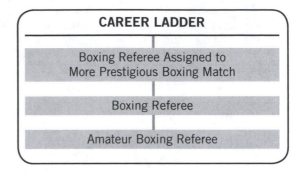

Boxing Referee Assigned to More Prestigious Boxing Match

Boxing Referee

Amateur Boxing Referee

Special Skills and Personality Traits—Enjoy sport of-boxing; know rules and regulations of game; self-confident; ability to work under pressure; physically fit

Special Requirements—State licensing may be required

Position Description

The Referee in professional boxing is the individual who stays in the ring with the boxers during a bout. The individual in this position is responsible for enforcing the rules of the match. While doing this, the Referee tries to keep the bout running smoothly. One Referee is present in each boxing match, and individuals may officiate during one or more bouts.

One of the first duties of the Referee is to inspect both fighters' gloves. This is done to make sure that none of the gloves have been altered in any way. The individual must be sure that all glove padding is intact and that no substances have been put on the gloves.

Before a bout begins, the Referee explains the rules and regulations to the fighters and their "seconds." (Seconds are those people in the corner with the fighter between rounds. A second may be the fighter's manager or trainer.) The Referee goes over the rules fully in the fighters' dressing rooms prior to the fight. Just before the bout starts, the individual calls both fighters and their seconds to the center of the ring and reviews the rules again briefly.

Once the fight has begun, the Referee follows the fighters around the ring making sure that they are adhering to the rules. The individual warns the fighters if they are delivering illegal punches, such as low blows, rabbit punches, punching on a break, or striking

when a fighter is down on the canvas. If, after a couple of warnings, one of the fighters persists in the illegal punches, the Referee may call a time-out. The individual may then tell the judges to take points away from that fighter.

The Referee commands the fighters to break, or take a step apart, when they are in a clinch. The individual also keeps close watch on the actions of both fighters to see that they are fighting back.

When a fighter is getting hit, the Referee must watch the individual's eyes and the way he breathes to be sure he is trying to defend himself. One of the most important responsibilities of the Referee is to make sure that neither fighter is injured badly. This requires the Referee to have some basic medical knowledge and is often difficult to do. If it seems that a fighter is stunned or injured, the Referee may either end the fight or give the individual a standing eight count. The Referee might also call a time-out so that the ringside physician can inspect the fighter.

The Referee has the power to stop a fight at any time for a number of reasons. He or she may do this if, as mentioned previously, one fighter is injured too badly to compete or will sustain permanent injuries if he continues. A Referee may also stop the bout if one fighter outclasses another so that the fight is not one-sided. Another reason to end a bout is if one boxer is not fighting to the best of his ability or appears to be in there only for the money. Under some circumstances, the Referee may also stop a fight if a boxer commits a major foul against another boxer while in the ring, such as an intentional low blow, head butt, or thumbing.

The major reasons Referees stop fights are KOs (knockouts) and TKOs (technical knockouts). Fights end when a boxer cannot come out of his corner at the beginning of a round or when he is knocked down and cannot get up before the referee counts to 10. Some states specify the number of times a fighter can be knocked down during a round or during a fight before the Referee must stop the fight.

The Referee may be responsible for momentarily stopping the fight to have a fighter's gloves taped back up, grease wiped off his face or body, or to have a mouthpiece that was knocked out washed and replaced.

When one fighter is knocked down, the Referee must send the opponent to a neutral corner. At the same time, he or she counts to 10 over the knocked-down fighter. So that no extra time is given to the downed boxer the Referee picks the count from the timekeeper, who begins counting as soon as the knockdown occurs. The downed fighter must take a count of eight even if he gets up before that.

At the end of the count, the Referee asks the fighter if he is okay and can continue fighting. If, in the Referee's opinion, the fighter cannot go on, he or she stops the fight (a technical knockout). This is a judgment call. Many times the fighter and his handlers do not agree. However, the decision of the Referee is final.

When the fight has ended, the Referee stands between the two contestants while the decision of the judges is read. When the winner is announced, the Referee holds up the winning fighter's hand and arm.

Salaries

Referees in professional boxing are paid by the promoter of the event. They are compensated on a per-event basis. Annual salaries depend on the number of shows they officiate as well as the type of show and the sanctioning organization.

Individuals may earn from $150 to $25,000 plus per show for their refereeing duties. Higher fees usually go to well-known referees working high-profile fights.

Employment Prospects

Employment prospects are fair for individuals who are trained and licensed. Referees are usually assigned to bouts by the state's athletic commission. Individuals may officiate at fights in their state or may get authorization to work in other states or countries.

Advancement Prospects

Advancement prospects are fair for Referees who are consistent, concerned with the safety of fighters, fair, and skilled in their jobs. Referees advance their careers by being assigned to officiate at more prestigious and world-class fights. Most Referees aspire to officiate at a major world championship fight.

At the beginning of a Referee's professional career, the individual usually officiates at four-round matches. The Referee then officiates at matches that go six rounds. After being reviewed by other officials or members of a state commission, the Referee may go on to officiate at matches of eight or more rounds.

Education and Training

There is no formal educational requirement necessary to become a Referee. Some individuals in this profession have a high school diploma, while others hold master's and doctoral degrees. Referees are required to attend classes, study rule books, and pass tests before being assigned bouts.

Special Requirements

In states hosting athletic commissions, Referees are usually required to be licensed. In order to become licensed, individuals may have to take written, oral, and medical examinations. Many states also require mandatory seminars and workshops and continuing education programs for Referees. Licensure is obtained through the state athletic commission or the boxing commission.

Experience, Skills, and Personality Traits

Professional Boxing Referees must enjoy the sport of boxing and also know a great deal about it. They must know all the rules and regulations. Referees must not only know the illegal blows but be able to recognize them too.

Referees must be adept at watching the "looks" of fighters. They must know when a boxer is hurt and when he cannot fight any longer. Some basic medical knowledge may be necessary for this task. Individuals must be self-confident. They will often make judgment calls. Everyone will not agree. Referees must consider the safety of the fighters above all else.

The Referee may work under stressful conditions. When the champ is losing, it is not easy to stop a championship fight.

Referees usually officiate in amateur bouts to obtain experience before moving into the pros. Individuals must referee a certain number of rounds in amateur competitions before becoming a Referee in the pros.

Individuals move around the ring quickly and constantly follow the fighters. In most states, Referees must undergo an annual medical examination to make sure that they are physically fit and in good shape.

Unions and Associations

Referees may be members of their state's athletic commission as well as any of the sanctioning organizations in boxing. They may also be members of various trade associations. Some of these include the International Boxing Federation (IBF), the North American Boxing Federation (NABF), the World Boxing Association (WBA), and the World Boxing Organization (WBO). Individuals may also contact USA Boxing for more information.

Tips for Entry

1. Watch professional boxing either on television or live. Try to get a feel for the way the Referee works.
2. Read all about boxing. There are numerous books in the library on the subject as well as a great number of boxing magazines and periodicals.
3. If your state has an athletic commission, write to them inquiring about licensing.
4. Look for an amateur boxing club in your area and talk to the individuals administering the program about your aspirations. There usually will be someone who can help you with your career goals.

PROFESSIONAL BOXING JUDGE

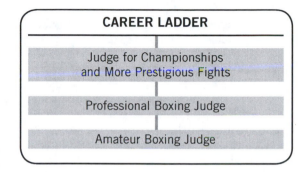

CAREER LADDER

Judge for Championships and More Prestigious Fights

↑

Professional Boxing Judge

↑

Amateur Boxing Judge

Position Description

A Professional Boxing Judge is responsible for judging professional boxing matches. Bouts are judged by three official Judges. In some areas, a referee may also judge the fight from inside the ring. However, this is becoming less common.

Fights may be scored in a number of ways, including the point system or the round system. Fights in some states use a combination of the two.

Judges in states having an athletic commission must be licensed. Professional Judges may also be licensed by boxing sanctioning organizations. Individuals are required to apply for their license and take written and/or oral examinations, pass physical exams, and pay licensing fees. Officials may be required to attend workshops, seminars, and training sessions covering the rules and regulations of the specific state they are being licensed in. Judges in most states are prohibited from having any financial interest in fighters or promotional companies.

The Judges at a professional fight are chosen from a list of qualified individuals. Judges are usually selected by the athletic commissioner or his or her deputies in states having athletic commissions. They may also be chosen by the sanctioning organization in fights authorized by the major sanctioning groups.

The Judges are assigned a ringside seat to view the fight. Individuals are usually stationed at opposite sides of the ring so that each gets an unrestricted view of the action.

The Judge watches the fight and scores each round on an official scorecard. The fighters are given points or rounds for specific actions, such as clean hitting and ring generalship. Boxers also score points from the Judges by fighting aggressively and defensively. In most states, Judges are required to write down their scores in ink or indelible pencil so that there can be no question of anyone changing the scores. Sometimes the Judge is required to give a brief written explanation of why he or she scored each round in the way that he or she did.

The Judge must be aware of all moves a boxer makes. The individual must also know what major fouls can occur in the ring, including low blows, intentional head butting, and not paying attention to the referee's warnings and instructions. Other fouls might include a fighter hitting an opponent who is down on the mat or other unsportsmanlike conduct in the ring. The Judge must also listen and watch the referee. At times, the referee takes points away from fighters because of an infraction or foul in the ring. When the referee indicates to the Judge that a point is being taken away in a round, the individual must mark it on his or her scorecard against the appropriate fighter.

While watching the fight, the Judge must keep his or her attention on the fighters at all times. It only takes a split second for action to occur in boxing. To score each round accurately, a Judge cannot miss anything.

After the fight is over, the Judge must tally up his or her scorecard and turn it over to the ring announcer.

The individual usually does this even in the event of a knockout (KO) or technical knockout (TKO).

A Judge may score one or more fights during a boxing show. He or she may be responsible to the state athletic commission, if there is one in the host state, or to the organization that sanctioned the fight.

Judges may have the opportunity to travel extensively both in the country and abroad to fulfill their duties.

Boxing is becoming more popular now than ever before. With coverage on network, local, and cable television, a growing number of bouts are being promoted. Many individuals are also promoting small, local bouts. This is good news for Professional Judges, as each bout requires their services.

Salaries
Professional Boxing Judges are paid by the promoter of the event and compensated on a per-show basis. Individuals may judge one or more fights on the fight card. Earnings vary depending on whether the individual is judging a main event or a preliminary bout. Earnings in major championship fights may also depend on the total fight receipts and the organization sanctioning the fight.

Fees may range from $150 to $5,000 or more per bout. Fees rise considerably for individuals judging major media events sanctioned by the boxing governing organizations.

Employment Prospects
Employment prospects are fair and are becoming better. There has been a rise in the number of fights promoted throughout the country in both live and televised events. National, regional, and cable TV are buying not just major championship fights but also run-of-the-mill events. On any given day, boxing can usually be viewed on at least one channel.

Individuals who have the best prospects are those who are fully trained, experienced, and licensed.

Advancement Prospects
Advancement prospects are fair for Professional Boxing Judges who exhibit skills, fairness, and professionalism in their work. Individuals may move up the career ladder by being selected to judge a larger number of fights.

The next step up for most individuals is to be assigned to judge a major fight. Each state's athletic commission may make different rulings about when an individual can be assigned to a championship bout. Depending on the state, individuals may have to judge professionally for over two years before they can be assigned as officials in an important heavyweight title fight.

Education and Training
While there is no formal educational requirement to become a Professional Boxing Judge, individuals may have to be licensed.

Special Requirements
In order to obtain licensing, individuals generally need to go through a number of classes, workshops, and seminars designed to teach them how to properly judge boxing matches. Individuals may also be required to read rule books and take and pass exams. Licensing is mandatory in states hosting athletic commissions and in fights sanctioned by the major sanctioning organizations, such as the World Boxing Association (WBA), the International Boxing Council (IBC), the World Boxing Council (WBC), and the International Boxing Federation (IBF).

Depending on the organization doing the licensing, the Professional Boxing Judge may have to take and pass a written and/or oral examination. Judges may also be required to attend seminars and workshops sponsored by boxing organizations.

Experience, Skills, and Personality Traits
In addition to being aware of all the rules and regulations of the sport of boxing, individuals must display good judgment. It is often difficult to determine who is more aggressive or more defensive in a very close fight. This know-how comes with training and experience.

Most individuals work as amateur judges before becoming Professional Boxing Judges. Judges must have confidence in their abilities and their decisions. They must be fair and exhibit total professionalism.

It is important that Professional Judges enjoy boxing and can deal with injuries and accidents occurring in the ring. If a Judge is squeamish, he or she will not be able to concentrate on the fight.

Unions and Associations
Boxing Judges may belong to state athletic commissions, the International Boxing Federation (IBF), the North American Boxing Federation (NABF), the WBA, the WBC, the World Boxing Organization (WBO), or the Boxing Officials Association (BOA). These organizations offer training, educational guidance, and support, and bring together those interested in the sport.

Tips for Entry
1. Contact your state's athletic commission and request information about becoming a Professional Boxing Judge. Many commissions hold training sessions. (If your state does not have an

athletic commission, contact one of the states that do, such as New York, New Jersey, or Nevada.)

2. If your state has an athletic commission, get licensed.

3. Obtain as much training as possible. The better trained you are, the better your chances will be of being a good Judge.

4. Get experience. Most Professional Judges get their experience working with the amateurs. Contact an amateur boxing association such as the Golden Gloves to get information.

5. Attend live boxing shows and watch boxing on television. Try to score fights and see how your scorecard stacks up against the Judges'.

6. Learn as much as you can about the sport of boxing. Read books, periodicals, and so on.

7. Find the local gyms where boxers train in your area. Spend some time there and make contacts.

8. Join relevant associations. These groups often provide training as well as help individuals make contacts.

BOXING MANAGER

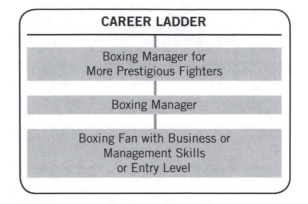

Position Description

A Boxing Manager is responsible for shaping and developing the career of professional fighters. Some Managers may start out with amateur fighters who are planning on turning professional. Others, who were fighters themselves or involved in some phase of the profession, build a reputation for themselves as Boxing Managers. Experienced professional fighters then seek out their services.

In states that have an athletic commission governing boxing, Managers must be licensed. Boxing Managers usually have a contractual agreement with fighters they represent. These Managers are responsible for keeping the sport and the fighters clean of any improprieties.

The Boxing Manager, as a rule, only signs fighters he or she feels have potential. The Manager is an integral force in the life and success of a fighter. He or she helps put together the best possible team to work with the fighters.

A good Manager supervises and oversees the fighter's entire career. In return the fighter pays the Manager a percentage of monies earned. The money earned for fights is called the purse. The Boxing Manager often invests money in the fighter to help him or her keep financially stable until money begins to come in. For example, the Manager may pay for boxing equipment, supplies, and clothing. He or she may pay gym and training expenses. Some Managers may even pay the fighter's room and board.

The Manager may be responsible for locating a trainer for the fighter. If a fighter already has a trainer, the Manager decides if he or she is suitable. The individual may also be required to find promoters, publicists, sparring partners, business managers, and the like.

Boxing or Fight Managers must carefully monitor the progress of their fighters. They must know when the fighter is ready for a fight and what type of challenger is suitable. For instance, a fighter who has had just two professional fights usually contracts for a three- or four-rounder. The boxer who has had 10 or 15 pro fights might contract for a 10- or 12-rounder.

The Manager is responsible not only for finding good matches for his or her fighter but for negotiating deals and getting contracts signed. If the Manager is not an attorney, he or she may retain one to work with the team. In this way, it is hoped that the fighter will be protected legally.

The Manager has to make sure that the fighter is trained and ready for a fight at the contracted weight. He or she works with the boxer's trainer to do this.

As fighters begin to rise in the ranks, the Manager works with publicists, public relations people, and the media setting up interviews, television spots, and obtaining written press coverage.

Once the Manager has built up the fighter and his image, personal endorsements and advertisements for the fighter might develop. This will make the fighter an even bigger box office draw when there is a fight.

Many Boxing Managers represent more than one fighter. Some represent entire boxing camps. This situation is good for both the Manager and the fighters. The Manager can earn money from a number of fighters. He or she may also be able to use some of the fighters in the camp as sparring partners. One of the greatest benefits, however, is that when one boxer gets a shot at a big fight, some of the others in the training camp will have a better opportunity to get placed on the undercard (the bouts that precede the main event).

While a Boxing Manager may work very hard and possibly never represent a champion, most Managers feel their fighters are the best and will eventually have the opportunity for a championship bout. It can be very exciting for the Manager to know that he or she has helped someone make it to the top of the profession.

Salaries

Salaries for Boxing Managers are impossible to determine. Earnings depend on many things, including the number of fighters a Manager has under contract, the purse they receive for each bout, and the number of matches each boxer fights annually. Earnings may also be dependent on other factors, such as management contract inclusions. Some Managers receive a percentage of all the fighters' earnings, including television or public appearances, movies, publishing deals, and commercial endorsements.

Most but not all Boxing Managers receive 33⅓% of the fighter's purse. As noted previously, some also receive a percentage of other income.

Most Managers handle more than one fighter. These individuals receive percentages of every fighter's purse. Managers representing champions who are fighting multimillion-dollar fights may earn many thousands of dollars each time their fighter gets in the ring. It must be noted that not all boxers become world-class fighters. Some boxers get matches in local clubs and receive only minimal purses throughout their careers.

Employment Prospects

Employment prospects are good. Almost anyone can be a Boxing Manager. The only real requirements are that the Manager must find a boxer to represent and that he or she must be licensed in states that have athletic commissions. Boxing Managers may find potential fighters to represent in any part of the country or world.

Boxing Managers must remember that just because they have a contract with a fighter, the money will not automatically roll in. The Manager must work constantly to secure matches for his or her fighters and move them up the ranks.

Advancement Prospects

Advancement prospects are fair for Boxing Managers. The only way to advance in this position is to acquire more prestigious fighters who can command larger purses. Sometimes Managers sign contracts with fighters who have already made it. Generally, however, Managers work with fighters over a period of time. Eventually the fighter begins to get better fights, televised fights, or a chance at a championship.

Education and Training

There is no formal educational requirement for Boxing Managers. Some Managers who have been quite successful hold high school diplomas. Others have degrees in business or law. A background in either certainly cannot hurt.

Individuals who are representing boxers can benefit from taking courses or seminars in marketing, public relations, business, and boxing.

Special Requirements

Managers who are licensed by state athletic commissions may have to complete individual state training requirements. These requirements may include an annual seminar, symposium, or workshop.

Experience, Skills, and Personality Traits

Successful Boxing Managers should either have contacts in the boxing world or have the ability to make them. A great fighter may never have the opportunity of being seen by others if the Manager does not know how to obtain good fights.

The Manager should be articulate and have good communication skills, both verbal and written. The individual will be calling promoters to obtain fights for the boxers he or she represents. He or she may also be talking to the media.

The Manager needs to be persuasive and aggressive. These are many Managers in the fight world trying to push their fighters to the forefront of the industry. The individual must be persuasive enough to have promoters and media give his or her fighters a chance.

While it is not essential to personally know how to box, Managers should have a basic understanding of the industry. He or she will then be able to choose the best support team to help develop a fighter's career.

Negotiation skills are a good asset when negotiating the fighter's contracts and purses. Business skills are essential.

Unions and Associations

Boxing Managers may be members of any of the state athletic commissions, sanctioning organizations, or boxing trade associations. These might include the International Boxing Federation (IBF), the World Boxing Association (WBA), the World Boxing Organization (WBO), the World Boxing Federation (WBF), the International Boxing Hall of Fame (IBHF), the International Veteran Boxers Association (IVBA), and the National Veteran Boxers Association (NVBA).

Tips for Entry

1. Join state athletic associations and commissions. These organizations regulate the boxing world and offer training and support. (Not all states have athletic commissions. However, if your fighter is working in a state that does, you will usually have to be licensed by that state.)

2. Become a member of as many boxing trade associations as you can. These will help you make valuable contacts and provide support.

3. Read books and periodicals about boxing. Keep up on the latest news in the industry.

4. Watch live and televised boxing. This too will help keep you up with the news in the boxing business as well as with the progressive fighters.

5. Many Boxing Managers pick up new fighters while they are still amateurs and ready to turn pro. This is a good way to get into the business. However, it takes judgment, a background in the profession, and often funding to maintain the boxer until fights are obtained and purses earned.

BOXING TRAINER

CAREER PROFILE

Duties: Developing talents of fighters; teaching boxers skills, punches, blocks, and forms; building confidence of boxer

Alternate Title(s): Trainer

Salary Range: Impossible to determine earnings

Employment Prospects: Good

Advancement Prospects: Fair

Best Geographical Location(s) for Position: Positions may be located throughout the country

Prerequisites:

Education or Training—No formal educational requirement; complete knowledge about sport of boxing

Experience—Experience in one or more facets of boxing

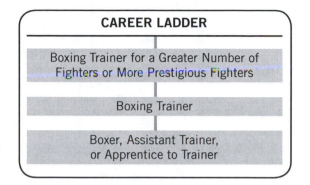

Special Skills and Personality Traits—Ability to motivate and instill confidence in fighters; boxing knowledge and skills; energetic; first aid skills

Special Requirements—State licensing may be required

Position Description

A Boxing Trainer develops the talents of fighters. The Trainer is responsible for teaching a fighter the skills of the sport. A good Trainer can take a fighter with drive and determination but only mediocre boxing skills and turn him or her into a world-class fighter.

Many Trainers may start their careers as amateur boxers. After a few rounds in the ring, individuals may realize that they do not have what it takes to become a professional boxer, nor do they want to be one. However, they may still be fascinated with the sport. After spending time in the gym with other boxers, trainers, and managers, they realize that a career as a Boxing Trainer could keep them working in boxing and out of the range of an opponent's gloves. Other individuals get their start as Trainers through friends who are boxers, by participating in youth programs, or by going to the gym to work out, etc. All Trainers have a love of the sport and a respect for the two opponents who get in the ring to fight.

Boxing Trainers work in the gym. The gym may be located in a variety of settings, from a city building to a rustic training camp. A gym may even be set up for a championship fight in a luxurious hotel anyplace in the world.

Most boxing gyms have either a boxing ring or something suitably equivalent plus the equipment required to train the fighters, including a heavy bag, mirrors, punching bag, jump ropes, medicine balls, etc. The Trainer will often have additional equipment for fighters who do not have their own, such as boxing gloves, hand wraps, stop watches, pads, etc. The Trainer must know how to use and take care of each piece of equipment.

Trainers may work for one or more fighters. If the fighter is a professional, the Trainer may be retained by the fighter's manager. Some Trainers work for a specific gym and help anyone who does not have a personal Trainer. Other Trainers work for boxing camps or boxing management or promotional organizations. Each Trainer has a different job style.

Basically, the Trainer teaches a fighter how to use all the equipment in the gym. He or she shows the fighter how to wrap hands before putting on gloves and how to use a jump rope, heavy bag, punching bag, pads, etc. If the fighter is new to the game the Trainer explains the rules and regulations of the sport, such as round length, time between rounds, legal blows, illegal blows, and mandatory counts.

The Trainer works to condition the fighter so that he or she is in top physical condition. This conditioning is accomplished by having the fighter jog, do aerobic exercises, jump rope, and perform other strengthening exercises. Fighters who are not in excellent physical shape usually do not perform well in the ring.

The Trainer is responsible for instructing the fighter on all the basic forms and styles used in boxing. He or she she also teaches the fighter the basic punches used in the sport. These blows include the left jab, straight right, left hook, combination, and uppercut. It is important that the fighter know how and when to use these punches. The fighter must also be familiar with the defenses he or she can use in the ring.

A successful Trainer can help the fighter know when to throw a left hook to the body or a right cross to the chin. He can teach when to use a shoulder block and when to bob and weave.

Once a Trainer has taught the fighter the basic skills, punches, and blocks, he or she puts the fighter in the ring for a sparring session with an opponent. Boxers spar to practice and perfect their skills against opponents in the same weight category. During sparring sessions, the Trainer watches carefully to see what skills he or she must work on with the fighter. During an actual bout, the Trainer stays with his or her boxer ringside, making suggestions as the fight proceeds.

The Trainer may also use video equipment to illustrate to the boxer his or her strong and weak points. Videos of potential opponents' bouts are also used by the Trainer to study styles.

Many fighters use the same Trainer from the time they are amateurs up through the ranks of professional boxing. Others change Trainers when they lose a fight. Trainers have a difficult, stressful job. They must often be hard on fighters in order to have them attain success in the ring. As fighters become more successful it is often difficult to motivate them to train and stay in shape.

Trainers may be responsible to different people depending on the specific situation. Those working directly with fighters may be responsible to either the fighter or his or her manager. Individuals working for gyms or management organizations will be responsible to the owner or general manager.

Salaries

It is impossible to determine the annual salaries for Boxing Trainers. Earnings are based on a number of variables, including the amount the fighter is earning for a fight, the frequency of his or her bouts, and the number of other fighters the Trainer is working with.

Earnings for most individuals are usually based on the amount of money the boxer receives for a fight. The Trainer may earn a percentage of the money or purse, ranging from 5% to 20% with most receiving 10%.

For a championship fight, with a multimillion-dollar purse, the Trainer can expect to do very well financially.

There are some Trainers who receive a set salary from a boxing management or promotional company to work full time with the company's fighters. A fighter may also pay a Trainer a set amount to get him ready for an upcoming fight. There are also Trainers who work part time in boxing and hold full-time jobs in other professions.

Employment Prospects

Employment prospects are good for talented Trainers. Individuals may find employment throughout the country. Trainers may work with individual fighters or for management companies, promotional organizations, boxing gyms, and athletic organizations.

Advancement Prospects

Boxing Trainers may advance their career in a couple of ways. The next step up the ladder for a Boxing Trainer is the opportunity to either train a champion or someone fighting a current champion. Trainers may also develop a fighter over the years until they become championship material.

As Trainers usually receive a percentage of the fighter's purse, any individual who either trains a number of winning fighters or trains more prestigious fighters will advance both their career and their earnings.

Education and Training

There is no formal educational requirement for Boxing Trainers. Individuals usually pick up their training skills through either watching or apprenticing with other Trainers. Some pick up skills working with amateur fighters. Many Trainers use what they learned as boxers themselves to teach other fighters.

Seminars and workshops offered by state athletic commissions, boxing organizations and associations, and sanctioning groups are very useful to Trainers.

Special Requirements

In states with athletic commissions, Trainers must often be licensed. Depending on the state, the individual may have to fill out a form or may have to take a written or oral examination.

Experience, Skills, and Personality Traits

Boxing Trainers need to know everything possible about boxing and fighters. Individuals must be totally familiar with basic blows, forms, and defenses. They also should know all the rules of the sport.

Trainers should have the ability to instill confidence in their fighters. They should be good teachers and know how to get ideas across and motivate others.

Trainers should be energetic and physically fit themselves. They should be health conscious, and have a good understanding of nutrition and fitness. Individuals must also know basic first aid procedures in case a fighter is injured during a training session or a bout.

Unions and Associations

Boxing Trainers may belong to state athletic commissions, sanctioning organizations, and trade associations, including the International Boxing Federation (IBF), International Veterans Boxers Association (IVBA), National Veteran Boxers Associations (NVBA), North American Boxing Federation (NABF), World Boxing Association (WBA), and World Boxing Organization (WBO).

Tips for Entry

1. Find the local gyms in your area that cater to training fighters. Spend time in them and try to make some contacts. Strike up a relationship with one or two of the Trainers and see if they can offer you some suggestions about getting into the field.

2. You might consider finding an amateur boxing club and offering to work with their fighters and staff. This should help you learn the business as you make contacts. When someone wants to turn pro, you can help.

3. Read all you can about all facets of boxing. There are a number of books on training and the sport of boxing that may help you.

4. Watch as much boxing as you can, both live and on television, to pick up boxing techniques.

5. Join local amateur boxing clubs, state athletic associations, sanctioning organizations, and any other relevant trade associations. These groups may provide training, professional guidance, and seminars, and they bring together people interested in the sport.

RING ANNOUNCER

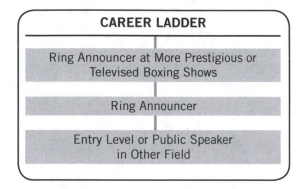

CAREER LADDER

Ring Announcer at More Prestigious or Televised Boxing Shows

Ring Announcer

Entry Level or Public Speaker in Other Field

Position Description

A Ring Announcer in the field of boxing is the master of ceremonies for the entire boxing show. He or she is responsible for announcing all pertinent information to the public. During a fight, the only announcement the public may hear that is not made by the Ring Announcer is the referee's instructions to the fighters before each bout.

Ring Announcers are usually required to arrive at the boxing event a few hours before a fight to gather and prepare information on the various matches. The individual works closely with the promoter of the show gathering information before the event. To begin with, the Announcer must secure the names of all fighters who will be on the boxing card. He or she must find out their weights, hometowns, the color of the trunks they will be wearing, and which corner each will be fighting out of.

After gathering the information, the Ring Announcer writes down all information to be used when making the announcements in the ring. He or she always verifies everything to make sure the data are correct.

At the beginning of the event, the Ring Announcer may introduce celebrities in the audience or the promoter or copromoters of the fight. In championship fights, the individual may also be responsible for introducing an entertainer who sings the national anthem. In certain states, the Ring Announcer may not introduce any person who is not directly related to the sport of boxing without permission from the athletic commission.

The Ring Announcer announces the name, weight, hometown, and color of the trunks of the opponents. He or she may also give the audience other information about the fighters, such as their professional record, the championship belts held, who the champion is and who the challenger is, and so on.

Each round of a professional fight is three minutes long with a one-minute rest period. The Ring Announcer, or M.C., tells the audience how many rounds the fight is scheduled for. This varies from fight to fight. Championship fights are usually 12 rounds. A knockout (KO) or technical knockout (TKO) can end a fight in the first round.

The Ring Announcer also tells the audience what organization is sanctioning the fight. This might be a state athletic commission or an organization such as the World Boxing Association (WBA), the International Boxing Federation (IBF), the World Boxing Council (WBC), or others.

Some Ring Announcers may use their own unique sayings before a fight card begins. Others just give the information and announce the fights.

After a bout ends, the Ring Announcer gathers the scorecards from the judges. The individual must know the boxing terminology used. For example, he or she may be calling a split decision, a unanimous decision, or a draw. If one of the opponents is knocked out, the Ring Announcer must indicate the round and exact time into that round that the fight was stopped. In states hosting athletic commissions, the M.C. may be required to give the official scorecards to a member of the commission before making announcements of the decision.

The M.C. announces to the audience how each official judged the fight and then announces the winner. He or she continues on through the entire boxing card in the same manner. After all the bouts, the individual may thank everyone for coming and then end the event.

Announcing is usually done in the center of the boxing ring. The M.C. must be able to get in the ring before each bout and out of it after each announcement.

Ring Announcers may work for one promoter or many. Individuals are responsible directly to the promoter with whom they are working at the time.

Salaries

Ring Announcers are paid fees for each bout they announce. These fees may have a wide range depending on the individual's experience, prestige, and personal demand.

Fees may range from $100 to $15,000 plus per bout. The average fee for Ring Announcers working major bouts is $2,000 per show. Announcers for club bouts earn less. Annual earnings depend on the number of bouts that the individual is contracted to announce each year.

Employment Prospects

Employment prospects are fair for individuals who are willing to work for smaller promoters. Prospects are fair for individuals aspiring to work as Ring Announcers for major promoters and televised events.

It should be noted that many Ring Announcers do this as a part-time profession.

Advancement Prospects

Advancement prospects are poor. Individuals may advance their career by obtaining additional jobs as Ring Announcers or by securing more prestigious assignments working for major promoters or televised events.

Some individuals climb the career ladder by becoming familiar with both athletes and their backgrounds in the boxing industry and then move on to television reporting or boxing commentating.

Education and Training

There are no formal educational requirements for Ring Announcers.

Special Requirements

Individuals working in states with athletic commissions governing boxing may have to be licensed to be Ring Announcers. In some states this license is a written application; in other states written or oral tests may be required.

Experience, Skills, and Personality Traits

Ring Announcers should be comfortable speaking in front of large groups of people as well as into a microphone. Individuals should be articulate in their verbal communication skills and have a pleasant speaking voice. A good command of the English language is helpful. Announcers should be well-groomed individuals. They should be able to carry themselves with confidence.

Announcers need to gather information on the fighters quickly and accurately. They also have to be able to present the information clearly.

A knowledge and enjoyment of the sport is helpful, as the individual will be attending many boxing shows. Contacts in the boxing industry, or the ability to make them, are essential to the success of the Ring Announcer in obtaining jobs during his or her career.

Unions and Associations

There is no specific trade organization for Boxing Ring Announcers. Individuals may be members of state athletic commissions or sanctioning bodies, such as the WBA, the WBC or the IBF. Depending on the individual's other skills, he or she may also belong to the Boxing Writers' Association (BWA).

Tips for Entry

1. Obtain experience speaking in front of groups of people.
2. Volunteer to act as Master of Ceremonies for an amateur entertainment benefit.
3. Watch both live and televised boxing events to see the various Ring Announcers' work and styles.
4. Find the local boxing gyms in your area and visit them on a regular basis. Talk to the fighters,

managers, and trainers. You will learn about boxing and make important contacts.

5. Make a demo tape of your voice and send it with your résumé and a cover letter to promoters. Try sending it to promoters holding smaller, local shows instead of the major promoters. Send it, wait a few days, and call up to make sure it was received. Ask for an interview. If they tell you there are no openings, wait a few months and try again. Persistence may pay off.

PROFESSIONAL WRESTLING REFEREE

CAREER PROFILE

Duties: Controlling a wrestling match; calling counts and breaks between opponents

Alternate Title(s): Ref

Salary Range: $300 daily to $500,000+ annually

Employment Prospects: Poor

Advancement Prospects: Poor

Best Geographical Location(s) for Position: Areas hosting professional wrestling leagues

Prerequisites:

Education or Training—Training in officiating wrestling matches

Experience—Experience officiating matches

Special Skills and Personality Traits—Ability to take punches, blows, and falls; good physical and medical shape; small stature; good showperson; knowledge of sport

Special Requirements—State licensing may be required

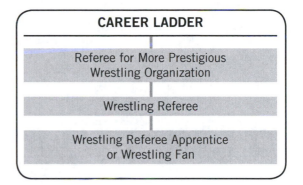

CAREER LADDER

Referee for More Prestigious Wrestling Organization

Wrestling Referee

Wrestling Referee Apprentice or Wrestling Fan

Position Description

Within the past few years, professional wrestling has increased dramatically in popularity. Fans used to be able to attend live wrestling shows only on a limited basis. Today wrestling fans can attend live bouts in almost every corner of the country. Wrestling exhibitions are now shown on network television in prime time as well as on pay-per-view television, cable, local, and regional networks.

In professional wrestling, the official in the ring is called the Referee, or Ref. The function of this individual is to control the wrestling match from start to finish. Matches may last from 15 minutes to one hour in length.

The Referee is in charge of officiating during the entire match. It is the Ref's duty to tell the timekeeper when to start the match and when to end it. While the Referee does no judging, he gives counts to the wrestlers. Counts determine the number of seconds a wrestler has before he or she must release an illegal hold. Counts also determine the end of a match. The Referee must, therefore, be knowledgeable about the different counts that may be called. The Referee is also in charge of calling breaks between opponents during the match.

Due to the nature of professional wrestling, the Referee often gets bumped and banged around by the wrestlers during the match. He or she must be able to take these bumps without getting seriously injured. The individual must also learn how to fall—falling frequently is all in a day's work in this sport.

The Referee is part of the action in professional wrestling. The better the showperson, the more excited the crowd will become.

Professional Wrestling Referees may travel extensively in the course of their work. Shows may be held anywhere in the country or abroad depending on the specific league the Ref is involved with.

Referees may be called on to officiate at any type of match, for any sex or size wrestler. Individuals may officiate at world-class wrestling events, shows featuring women wrestlers, or others.

Individuals may work full or part time. Some Referees work 200 days a year. Others may work a couple days a month. It all depends on whether or not they have other jobs and how much they are in demand. The individuals are usually directly responsible to the promoter of the show or president of the league.

Salaries

There is a tremendous salary range for Professional Wrestling Referees. Differences in compensation depend on many things, including the type of bout in which the Referee officiates, the level of the league, and whether the show is being televised. Another variable might be the Referee's activity in the ring during the bout. The more action that occurs during a bout, the higher the individual's salary. Salaries are also dependent on the seniority of the official and whether he works full or part time.

Compensation for Professional Referees can be extremely lucrative. Earnings can run from $300 daily to $100,000 plus annually. Some officials earn salaries of $500,000 and more.

Traveling expenses, meals, and lodging for Professional Referees are covered when they work on the road.

Employment Prospects

Employment prospects are poor for Professional Wrestling Referees. Even with the increase of wrestling shows, individuals may have a difficult time finding employment in this area. The major reason for this is that professional wrestling appears to be a closed business. In order to become a Professional Wrestling Referee, an individual needs training and experience. As a rule, the only way to obtain this training and experience is to find a sponsor who will teach the individual the business. Many Referees are wary of giving out this information because it threatens their jobs.

Individuals who aspire to be Professional Wrestling Referees will have a better chance if they find a low-level wrestling league or one that is just starting out. These are located throughout the country.

Advancement Prospects

Advancement prospects are determined by the Referee's drive and determination. To move to the top of this business, the individual must do two things: officiate at bouts put on by the top wrestling league in the world, the World Wrestling Entertainment (WWE), and officiate at bouts televised nationally and abroad.

Wrestling crowds enjoy action and like to see both the wrestlers and the Referee take chances in the ring. Individuals who take these chances will catch the eye of the fans and promoters and become more in demand.

It may take a Professional Wrestling Referee three to four years from the beginning of his career to reach this point. Some may never get there professionally.

Education and Training

While there is no formal educational requirement for this position, Professional Wrestling Referees must be fully trained before being appointed as officials. Unfortunately, as noted previously, most of this training is available only through other Professional Referees and wrestlers and not through classes or seminars. Those seeking training must locate a skilled professional who will teach them the ropes of the business.

Special Requirements

Professional Wrestling Referees must generally be licensed by the state athletic commission.

Experience, Skills, and Personality Traits

The most employable Professional Wrestling Referees are individuals of small stature. The smaller an individual appears in the ring, the larger the Wrestler will seem. Referees must be in good physical shape. Those who are not will have short careers.

Referees working televised bouts must be comfortable in front of a camera. They must also have a basic knowledge of the television industry. It is important that the Ref officiating at a televised bout know where to stand and be familiar with TV cameras to know which camera is picking up the action. If not, the Ref may block the wrestlers from camera view.

Successful Wrestling Referees must be good showpeople. Although professional wrestling is recognized as a sport, a good part of the action is its entertainment value. The Referee must be able and willing to take chances in the ring. Being thrown out of a ring by a wrestler, being chased and almost caught, and so on are actions that excite and entertain crowds.

Knowledge of the counts used in wrestling is essential. A love of the sport is necessary to work successfully in this area.

Unions and Associations

Professional Wrestling Referees belong to the various wrestling leagues throughout the country and abroad.

Tips for Entry

1. This is one type of job where you have to be in the right place at the right time to get in. Keep plugging away. Don't let a few disappointments get you down.
2. If you have any contacts at all in the professional wrestling industry, use them. You will have to prove yourself once you make the initial contact. However, it is a way to get your foot in the door.
3. Look through wrestling magazines to locate small wrestling leagues. Contact them, one by one, to try to find someone willing to teach you the ropes.
4. Watch as much professional wrestling as possible. Try to see live shows as well as televised

bouts. This will help give you a perspective on the industry.

5. Try to find gyms where professional wrestlers train. Consider a job doing anything in the gym, from maintenance to sweeping the floors or answering the phones. This will be your best way to make needed contacts.

RACING

JOCKEY

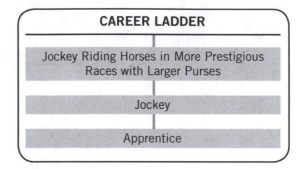

Position Description

There are two popular varieties of horse racing. One is called harness racing. This is where the horse pulls a two-wheeled cart called a sulky with a driver seated in the cart and guiding it. The other is called thoroughbred or flat racing. This is the type of race where a man or woman called a Jockey rides the horse during a competition.

Jockeys' responsibilities may vary depending on the situation. Their main function, however, is to ride horses in competitions at racetracks. These individuals are often crucial to the success of a horse in a race.

Because Jockeys sit on the horse's back when racing, it is important they keep their body weight down. The lighter they are, the better. Their average weight is around 100 pounds.

Most Jockeys begin their careers working in the stables taking care of horses. Individuals must learn how to care for the animals, how to feed them, clean them, and get them ready for exercising. Aspiring Jockeys help trainers exercise and train the horses on a daily basis. When they are 18 years old, they can apply for an apprentice license.

Jockeys often travel extensively in the course of their job. Racing at many tracks is seasonal. Individuals may work at one track for a couple of months and then move on. They may also travel between tracks when a horse is being raced at a number of tracks during a season.

When racing a horse, the Jockey must be strong enough to control the animal. He or she must also know how to guide and motivate the horse into a winning position. The Jockey must know the specific horse well enough to know what its strengths, weaknesses, and abilities are. In this way he or she can develop a strategy to race the horse. To accomplish this, individuals must know if a horse is a slow starter, quick starter, quick finisher, and so on.

A lot of this knowledge and understanding comes from the Jockey working with the horse. He or she may help with the daily training of the animals as well as with their general conditioning.

Jockeys are responsible to either the horse owner or trainer, depending on who hired the individual. This may be a stressful job. If the horse does not win, the Jockey is often the one blamed. To stay successful in the industry, he or she must constantly have winners. Jockeys must also be concerned with injuries. Working with animals is unpredictable. Jockeys may be bitten, kicked, or thrown off horses and injured. For those who love horses and the exciting life of racing, however, none of these drawbacks is overwhelming.

Salaries

Earnings for Jockeys vary greatly depending on a number of factors. These include the experience and skills of the individual and the type of race he or she is riding in. Other variables include how often the Jockey rides and the number of winners he or she has. Salaries also depend on the type of financial arrangement the Jockey has made. He or she may be under contract with a trainer or owner and/or may also earn various percentages of winning purses.

Individuals may earn from $40 to $250 or more every time they ride in a race. Jockeys may also earn a percentage of the winning purse. Although percentages vary, an average may be 10% of the purse if the horse a Jockey rides comes in first. If it comes in second or third, their Jockey's share may be only 5%.

For Jockeys riding in races with major purses, earnings can be quite high. Some individuals in this field earn only $23,000 a year, while others earn $500,000 or more.

Employment Prospects

Employment prospects are good for skilled Jockeys. Individuals usually are hired by horse owners. They may be under contract with the owners or may ride on a freelance basis. Jockeys who have proven themselves in a number of races have no problem finding work. Racetracks are located around the country. However, many tracks located in colder climates are seasonal.

Advancement Prospects

Advancement prospects are good for Jockeys who are willing to learn their craft and really want to make it in the horse racing industry. Climbing the career ladder for a Jockey might mean that he or she obtains a position riding a champion in a major race. Other paths the Jockey may take to career advancement include riding more prestigious horses or in more prestigious races, or obtaining a greater number of horses to ride.

As Jockeys often receive a percentage of winning purses, riding winners in races with big purses can mean large earnings.

Education and Training

There are no formal educational requirements for Jockeys. Individuals must, however, have a complete knowledge of horses and experience working with them. Some individuals attend Jockey school.

Special Requirements

Individuals must be licensed to be Jockeys. To obtain a license, the Jockey must first go through an apprenticeship program. Programs may be administered by the state or by organizations, depending on the specific state.

Individuals must be at least 18 years old to apply for an apprentice license. They may obtain a freelance apprentice certificate or a contract apprentice license. The former means that the individual can ride for any trainer at any stable, while the latter means that he or she can ride only for one specific stable. As an apprentice, the individual rides in races, getting experience. After riding a number of winners in races, an individual can become a full-fledged Jockey and receive his or her journeyman's license. Licensing may be done by individual organizations or the state, depending on the location.

Experience, Skills, and Personality Traits

Most successful Jockeys are small and lightweight. Individuals must know how to ride horses expertly. In order for Jockeys to be successful, they must also love horses. Like many other domestic animals, horses are sensitive to people who deal with them. They can instinctively tell if a Jockey is comfortable doing his or her job.

Jockeys must be dependable, honest, and trustworthy. They must not use any type of stimulants or illegal drugs on the animals. Not only could this endanger the horse's health, but the Jockey could lose his or her license for life.

Individuals must be able to deal with the pressure of people wanting them to win constantly. They also must recognize that when a horse does not win, they may be made to feel it is their fault.

Unions and Associations

Jockeys may belong to a number of local, state, and national organizations and associations that bring members of the profession together. One of the most prominent in the field is the Jockey's Guild, Inc. (JGI).

Tips for Entry

1. Get a job working at a racetrack or in a local stable. This will give you on-the-job experience and help you make important contacts in the field.
2. Locate trainers and Jockeys to talk with about your aspirations. They are usually glad to offer advice and help.
3. Go to a racetrack and watch the races. Get a feel for what Jockeys do and how they handle the horses.
4. Go to the library and get some books on horse racing. The more you know about the industry, the better chance you will have to be successful in it.

HARNESS DRIVER

Duties: Racing horses; training horses

Alternate Title(s): Driver; Harness Race Driver

Salary Range: $23,000 to $1.5 million+

Employment Prospects: Fair

Advancement Prospects: Fair

Best Geographical Location(s) for Position: Areas hosting harness racetracks

Prerequisites:

Education or Training—No formal educational requirement; licensing necessary

Experience—Experience as a groom or trainer's assistant required

Special Skills and Personality Traits—Knowledge of horse care and training; ability to drive sulkies;

enjoy working with horses; self-confident; quick reflexes

Special Requirements—State licensing and licensing through the USTA are necessary

Position Description

In harness racing, horses pull carts competitively around a track. These carts, called sulkies, are guided by skilled individuals known as Harness Drivers. Individuals may be Harness Drivers or Harness Driver/Trainers. The latter train the horses and race them. In order to drive professionally, individuals must be licensed.

There are two varieties of harness races, one for trotters and the other for pacers. Drivers may work in either type of race.

The road to becoming a Harness Driver is much like that of becoming a jockey. Individuals usually begin working at jobs in racetrack stables. They become grooms and help trainers work with the horses, feeding them, brushing them, and cleaning and exercising them.

After gaining some experience working with horses as a groom or a trainer's assistant, aspiring Harness Drivers may apply for a license. The first license many Drivers obtain is the matinee license. This license is valid only for matinee meets that do not involve wagering or purses.

The next license individuals may apply for is a qualifying license for extended pari-mutuel meets. In order to obtain this license, Drivers are required to take a written exam as well as a practical test demonstrating their ability to drive. They have to demonstrate to those giving the test that they are safe, talented drivers. Individuals must also provide references before they are issued such a license.

Drivers hold their qualifying license for six months and must participate in at least 12 satisfactory drives with a licensed pari-mutuel judge watching. They must then obtain the approval of both the judge and the local district track committee in their area.

After these requirements are met, they obtain their provisional license. Now they are similar to apprentices. Drivers who hold a provisional license for a year must then drive either 25 satisfactory drives and obtain the same approvals as noted above or hold the license for less than a year and drive 50 satisfactory extended pari-mutuel drives. They must also then obtain judge and committee approvals. Individuals who complete these requirements are then granted a full or A license. Once this license is obtained, they can drive in any track in the country.

Harness Drivers may travel from track to track to race horses. Some are under contract with a stable or trainer, driving only for those people. Others, called Catch Drivers, are not under contract. These individuals drive for hire, for any stable or trainer.

Individuals who have made a name for themselves often are asked to drive various horses in the same race. As Drivers often are paid on a percentage of the money earned by the horse (or purse), they will likely choose the horse that appears to have the best chance to win. Harness Drivers may travel extensively to race horses in tracks across the country.

Harness Drivers may prefer just to drive in races or may also train the horses. Those who act as trainers must also have a trainer's license. Trainers spend a great many hours training and driving horses that are destined to become winners. Crossing the finish line a winner makes all of the work that has been put into the animal worth it.

Salaries

Salaries vary greatly for Harness Drivers depending on a number of factors. These include the driver's experience level and the number of races he or she drives in. Other determining factors include the tracks the individuals is racing at and the amount of the purse for each horse the individual drives.

Drivers earn a percentage of the purse when the horse comes in first through fifth. If the individual is a Driver-Trainer, he or she earns 10% of the purse. If, however, the Driver is not helping with the training, the percentage is split. The Driver receives 5% and the trainer receives 5%.

In a major competition with a large purse, Drivers can win a great deal of money.

Annual earnings for Drivers who are racing full time may range from $23,000 to $750,000 plus. Those who drive and train can double that amount.

Employment Prospects

Employment prospects are fair for Harness Drivers. There is a great deal of competition in this industry, but there is always room for skilled Drivers. Individuals must be dedicated and committed to the sport to make it in harness racing. One of the best ways to obtain work is to find owners who are interested in having their horses trained and raced. If owners are impressed with the skills of a Driver, they often purchase other horses for the Driver/Trainer to work with.

Advancement Prospects

Drivers who do their job well will have no trouble advancing their careers. Individuals can climb the career ladder by driving horses in more prestigious races that have larger purses. As Drivers begin to win races and show that they can drive well, owners and others will seek out their services.

Education and Training

There are no formal educational requirements necessary to become a Harness Race Driver. Individuals must, however, be trained in working with horses and driving a sulky in races. This skill usually comes from experience working as an apprentice to a trainer and/or Driver.

Special Requirements

Harness Drivers must be licensed in order to work. Licensing is handled through the United States Trotting Association (USTA). Drivers may have a variety of licenses from matinee to qualifying to provisional. Most states also require state licensing as well.

Experience, Skills, and Personality Traits

In order to become a Harness Driver or Driver/Trainer, individuals usually obtain experience by becoming an apprentice to an established Driver or Driver/Trainer. They should have experience training and jogging horses.

Harness Drivers and Driver/Trainers must like to work around horses. They must have a feel for the the way the animals think, act, and behave. Individuals must have a complete knowledge of maintaining horses as well as of training and racing them.

Drivers should be confident in their abilities. They must have quick reflexes. Driving a sulky is not as easy as it looks. Individuals must have a feel for driving.

Drivers usually are required to wear helmets and to observe safety measures. However, as in other sports, accidents in horse racing do occur. While driving, the individual cannot express any fear. If he or she does, the horse can often sense this fear and will not perform well.

Unions and Associations

The major association for those involved in this industry is the USTA. This organization licenses Drivers and offers guidance and support to those in the industry.

Tips for Entry

1. Go to a harness race track and watch Drivers in action.

2. Consider a part-time or summer job in a stable or at a racetrack to give you the feel for harness racing. It will also give you a good opportunity to get your foot in the door of the industry and make important contacts. You have to make a major commitment to be involved in horse racing. This experience will help you decide if it is the career for you.

3. Contact the U.S. Trotting Association for more information on getting into harness driving and licensing requirements.

4. When you are ready to begin your career, try to find an established Trainer or Driver whom you like and respect. You will be spending a great deal of time with this individual. Learn as much as you can from your mentor.

HARNESS RACING JUDGE

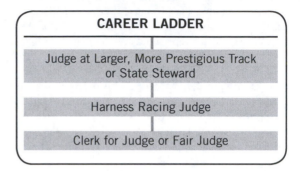

Position Description

In horse racing, as in all sports, officials preside over each race. The officials in horse racing are known as either Judges or Stewards.

For each race there are Patrol Judges, Associate Judges, Presiding Judges, and State Stewards. While they are all Judges, they may perform different duties. The main function of these Judges is to supervise all racing activity at the particular track to which they are assigned. The Judges also preside over the actual running of races. They must make sure that all track rules and regulations are followed. They oversee the actual racetrack as well as the areas where the horses are kept, where the drivers stay, and where patrons bet.

Judges' duties vary depending on the type of Judge they are and what work they are assigned to do. Judges inspect horses to make sure that they are in compliance with all commission rules. They may also confer with veterinarians about the fitness of horses on the race card.

Stewards are the highest level of Judges at the track. They and the other Judges serve on judiciary boards that make decisions about occurrences at the racetrack. Judges may receive written or verbal complaints on any number of issues, from a driver not agreeing with the order of horses finishing a race to a trainer accused of injecting a horse with an illegal substance. The Judges must determine the validity of the complaints and then decide how to deal with them. The Steward is responsible for writing reports on all complaints, actions taken, and penalties imposed and then filing them with the state's racing commission.

Some Judges are responsible for inspecting the equipment of horses and their drivers in the paddock before a race. This is done to make sure that equipment meets regulations. Other individuals observe the races to determine if there are any infractions or fouls committed. In order to get a good view, Judges watch the race from elevated stands. They may also view videos and use photographs of the race to determine infractions.

If, during a race, a driver feels that another driver or trainer has done something against the rules, he or she can bring the matter to the attention of the Judges. The Judges then must determine if the complaint is valid.

Judges preside over the entire racing community. When a rule is broken or there is a regulation infraction, the Judge or Steward has the power to take action. Individuals may suspend or fine participants for violations of the rules. Their powers, however, are limited by state regulations. Some states have more lenient fines and suspension policies than others. For example, one state may have a limit of a 15-day suspension for an infraction while in another state the limit might be as high as 90 days.

Racing is a highly regulated industry. A major function of Judges is the approval of licenses for all individuals involved at the track, from the drivers and trainers to the grooms and mutual clerks.

Judges are also responsible for determining the order of the winning horses at the finish line. Before the racetrack announcer tells patrons the order of the winners in a race, often he or she must wait for the Judges to determine which horse came in first. To do this, the Judges may look at photographs and videos taken at the finish line. A photo finish occurs when two horses appear to reach the finish line at the same moment. The video or photograph allows the Judges to make an accurate decision.

It is the Judge's duty to protect the interest of the state, the betting public, the track owners, and the actual participants. To accomplish this, Judges are responsible for many of the day-to-day activities at the track.

Judges and Stewards often work split shifts. That means that they will perform some of their duties in the morning and the rest in the evening hours.

Salaries

Earnings for Judges and Stewards vary depending on a number of factors. These include the individual's experience and education as well as the size and location of the track. Individuals are usually paid on a per-day basis.

A Patrol Judge can earn from $100 to $250 plus a day. Associate Judges may earn from $150 to $450 plus per day. Presiding Judges or State Stewards may earn $200 to $750 or more per day.

Employment Prospects

While there is a great deal of competition for these positions, talented, skilled Judges are always in demand. Individuals who are educated and experienced in the racing industry and who are willing to relocate to areas requiring Judges will have an easier time finding work.

In some situations, Judges are state employees. Others are appointed by the specific track they are working at.

Advancement Prospects

Individuals advance their careers in judging by obtaining experience and education in the field. Individuals

can move up from the position of a Paddock Judge to become a Patrol Judge. They can then climb the career ladder to the next step, which is Associate Judge and then Presiding Judge. The top level of officials are called State Stewards.

Education and Training

A college degree is not required to become a Judge in the racing industry, but it does help. As there is so much competition for these jobs, individuals who are the most qualified will get the positions.

Special Requirements

All Judges must be licensed. The organization licensing individuals is the the United States Trotting Association (USTA). Individuals must pass a written examination in order to be licensed. The USTA offers an intensive weeklong course covering information needed to pass the test. This organization also offers a great deal of other education and school opportunities for those interested in becoming Judges or advancing their careers.

Experience, Skills, and Personality Traits

Two of the most important traits officials should have are good judgment and common sense. They should also be fair and consistent.

Individuals should have a high self-esteem and be confident in their decisions. Judges often work under a great deal of pressure. They should be able to function in stressful situations.

A racing background is necessary to perform this job well. Some individuals grew up in the racing industry. Others had family or friends who were involved with it. Still other individuals worked at tracks or in the racing profession in other capacities.

Communication skills, both written and verbal, are necessary for this job.

Unions and Associations

Judges and Stewards in the racing industry can be members of the North American Judges and Stewards Association (NAJSA). Individuals may also be members of the USTA. These organizations provide educational and professional guidance and support.

Tips for Entry

1. Contact the USTA to learn more about licensing requirements.
2. It is also a good idea to inquire about the classes, seminars, and other educational programs available.

3. Remember that you are going to have to start at the lowest level and advance your career from there.
4. A background in the racing industry is necessary. Consider a part-time or summer job at a race-track in some capacity to help you learn more about racing.
5. Look in your library for books on the subject. Read as much as you can about the racing industry.

RACING SECRETARY

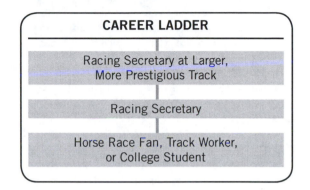

Position Description

A Racing Secretary works at a horse racing track. His or her function is to make sure that the horses in each race are competitive with each other. The individual in this position is responsible for arranging the daily race card for the racetrack. Depending on the particular track, this schedule may be from seven to 11 races.

There are a certain number of stalls available for horses at each racetrack. Owners and trainers apply for these stalls so that their horses can train and compete at the track. The Racing Secretary prepares for races by scrutinizing stall applications. He or she decides which horses will be given stall space by determining the individual animal's qualifications and potential.

The Racing Secretary reviews data from the animal's past workout and performance records. He or she prepares a condition sheet based on an evaluation of the horses already on the grounds. The individual strives to put together a race card of horses that are competitively matched with each other.

In some situations, the Racing Secretary may handicap horses for races using criteria such as the animal's age and sex. Other data that may be used include the horse's past money winnings and the distance of the races won.

The individual then must classify horses for the proper type of race; these include claiming, condition, and stake races. Races may be classified by money earn-ings or by the type of horse, such as mares, fillies, or geldings.

In order to do his or her job properly, the Racing Secretary must know as much as possible about each horse's background. After the preliminary work is completed, the individual plans the races that will be run. The Racing Secretary may also be responsible for determining the purse, or amount of money to be won, for each of those races. The Secretary uses his or her research and data on the horses scheduled to participate in the race to determine the purse. Patrons and fans use the race card to place bets on the races.

Functions of the Racing Secretary may also include registering and keeping track of the names of people who have a financial interest in each horse and changes in ownership. He or she may also be required to obtain the entrance and application fees for races from owners.

The individual is ultimately responsible for racing information that is supplied to newspapers, racing forms, and daily racing programs. Depending on the specific position, the Racing Secretary may supervise the individuals who compile the racing information. He or she is also required to keep records of the results of each horse in every race.

While most of the work of the Racing Secretary is accomplished prior to the actual races, he or she is usually on hand during the races too. At this time, the individual might verify the specific selection of entries in the race as well as the shape, form, and ability of the animals taking part in the competition.

The Racing Secretary is usually responsible to the track's owner or general manager. Hours can be long in this job. The individual might put in a full day preparing for the races and then, as noted, be required to be at the track for the entire card. It must also be noted that many racetracks are seasonal. Race Secretaries may work at one track during the spring and summer and another during the fall and winter.

Salaries

Salaries for Racing Secretaries vary widely depending on a number of variables, including the size and prestige of the track and the length of its season. Earnings will also be dependent on the experience level of the individual.

Some Racing Secretaries are paid by the draw or race day for which they have drawn up the race card. Others are paid by the week. Salaries for Racing Secretaries can range from $30,000 for individuals working at smaller tracks around the country to $150,000 plus for those working at larger, more prestigious tracks.

Employment Prospects

Employment prospects are poor for Racing Secretaries. As a rule, each track needs the services of only one individual for this position. As there is only a limited number of racetracks in the country and their number is dwindling, it is extremely difficult to find jobs.

Those who aspire to be Racing Secretaries might find it easier to break into the field by trying to locate positions with smaller tracks. Then as the individual gains experience, he or she will be able to move up in the ranks to larger tracks.

Advancement Prospects

In order for the Racing Secretary to climb the career ladder, he or she must usually find a similar position at a larger, more prestigious racetrack. This will lead to higher earnings.

Other Racing Secretaries advance their careers by becoming officials at the tracks.

Education and Training

There usually is no formal educational requirement for this position. However, a college degree might be helpful in attaining a position.

There are Racing Secretaries with degrees in everything from communications to animal science. Training and any type of background in horsemanship is extremely useful. Seminars and workshops are often offered through racing associations.

Special Requirements

Individuals may be required to hold various racing licenses depending on the specific job.

Experience, Skills, and Personality Traits

Racing Secretaries must be able to deal with constant stress and tension. With each race that they classify, there can be only one winner. Owners and trainers of horses that did not win often try to place blame on the person who did the classifying.

Individuals in this position should have good memories. The Race Secretary must read about horses constantly and must be able to remember the data. In this way, he or she is able to put horses that belong together in the same races.

The Racing Secretary should have good communication skills, both written and verbal. He or she needs to be able to deal well with a variety of people. Experience dealing with horses and in horsemanship is essential to the success of the Racing Secretary.

Unions and Associations

Racing Secretaries working at horse racing tracks may belong to a number of trade associations, including the American Harness Racing Secretaries (AHRS) and the United States Trotting Association (USTA). These organizations offer meetings, symposiums, conventions, and workshops that bring together those interested in working in the sport. The associations also offer training, professional guidance, and support.

Tips for Entry

1. Consider a summer or part-time job at a local racetrack. While working as a clerk or an assistant to a Racing Secretary would be ideal, experience in any facet of racing will prove helpful.
2. Try to obtain an intern position with the Racing Secretary of a racetrack. This too will provide valuable experience and on-the-job training.
3. Contact relevant trade associations for help in training and professional guidance.
4. Attend workshops, seminars, and symposiums on horsemanship. You will make a lot of contacts and gain valuable information.
5. Send your résumé and a cover letter to racetracks where you might want to work. Ask that your résumé be kept on file if there is no current opening.

RACETRACK ANNOUNCER

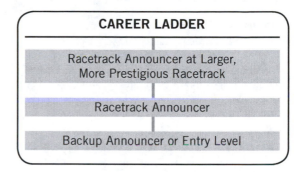

Position Description

A Racetrack Announcer works at either a horse or a dog racetrack. He or she is responsible for announcing the races as they occur. The Racetrack Announcer's main function is to let the track patrons know what is going on before, during, and after each race.

The individual is required to announce races as they occur, beginning with the number of each race. He or she then usually gives the name and number of the horse or dog in each race and often the odds as the animals parade around the track. On occasion, the Announcer gives the track fans other information, such as the name of the jockey, driver, or trainer. He or she might also tell patrons in what position the animal finished the last time it raced.

The Racetrack Announcer tells patrons how many minutes there are until post time (the time the race starts). He or she may give updates during this prerace period on the various odds that are on the specific horses or dogs.

The individual announces the beginning of each race. He or she then monitors the race and tells fans about the progress of each horse or dog. He or she is expected to do this quickly and accurately. Before the race, the Announcer must memorize the color each horse, dog, driver, and/or jockey is wearing and the number accompanying each color. In this way he or she can tell what is happening as the race progresses.

As the race gets close to the finish line, the Announcer tells the fans who is in first, second, and third positions and who is moving up. Successful track announcers can make a race even more exciting.

The Racetrack Announcer is the track representative who tells patrons which horse or dog has won a race. He or she also announces the numbers and names of the winning, place, and show animals. The individual then tells patrons the official race results or, in the case of a photo finish, instructs fans to hold their tickets until the track judges make a final decision.

Once race results are official, the individual may announce the cash winnings in each category. The racing process then begins again until all races on the card are run.

Sometimes the Racetrack Announcer may also be required to make other types of announcements. These might include broadcasting the names of people or businesses visiting the track, indicating the celebrities who are attending, and previewing special events that will be taking place at the track.

Racetrack Announcers may work in the morning, afternoon, or evenings, depending on the specific track's racing schedule. Most Announcers work a full card, which may run anywhere from seven to 11 races. They do a lot of talking. For people who enjoy the sport of racing and like to comment on its activities, this can be a very interesting career.

Racetrack Announcers may be responsible to the track general manager, assistant manager, or owner, depending on the specific situation.

Salaries

Salaries for Racetrack Announcers vary from job to job. Some tracks pay their Announcers weekly, while others compensate Announcers on a per-day basis. Earnings can range from $100 to $350 plus a day. Those paid on a weekly basis may earn from $15,000 to $50,000 or more a year.

Most tracks are seasonal and do not operate all year. In some situations, where the Announcer has built a reputation over the years, he or she is compensated throughout the year, even when not working. In other situations, the individual has to work part of the year in one area of the country and another part of the year in a different area.

Employment Prospects

Employment prospects are poor for those who seek positions as Racetrack Announcers. There are only a limited number of racetracks in the country. Once an individual gets a job as a track Announcer, he or she often stays in that position for years.

Individuals who aspire to be Racetrack Announcers may be more successful obtaining jobs at smaller tracks. Once they gain some experience, Racetrack Announcers can often become substitute or backup Announcers at larger tracks.

Advancement Prospects

Advancement prospects can be poor to fair depending on a number of variables. These include the speaking personality of the individual and his or her experience level. Advancement also depends on a certain amount of luck and contacts, and the individual being at the right place at the right time.

Those who climb the career ladder in this profession do so by obtaining jobs at larger, more prestigious tracks or by becoming the track's main Announcer.

Education and Training

Some tracks have no formal educational requirement for their Announcers other than a high school diploma. Others prefer or require individuals to have a college degree or background. Knowledge about using the track's P.A. (public address) system is useful but can usually be learned in a short time.

Seminars about the sport of horse racing or dog racing may help the individual understand more about the sport and the industry.

Experience, Skills, and Personality Traits

Some racetracks do not require Racetrack Announcers to have any experience. Others require that applicants have had prior announcing experience at tracks. The amount of experience required is dependent on the specific position and racetrack.

It is important that the Racetrack Announcer have a pleasant speaking voice, free of speech impediments. He or she should be both articulate and understandable. The Announcer should either have or be able to develop an announcing personality or voice that distinguishes him or her from other announcers.

The Racetrack Announcer must have a good memory. He or she must memorize the colors that the jockeys, horses, and/or dogs are wearing before the race in order to accurately announce the race's progress. While Announcers often use binoculars and/or cameras to see the horses and/or dogs clearly, it helps to remember the relationship of color to number on each animal.

Unions and Associations

While there are no specific associations for Racetrack Announcers, individuals may belong to a number of organizations and associations related to the racing industry. These might include the International Trotting and Pacing Association (ITPA) and the Racing Fans Club of America.

Tips for Entry

1. Send your résumé and a demo tape of your voice calling a race to the personnel director of racetracks that you are interested in working with.
2. Call up racetracks and ask if they have any openings for backup announcers.
3. Get experience speaking into a microphone. You might consider working at your school radio station.
4. If you are in school, see if you can get a summer or part-time job working at a racetrack in some capacity. This will help you make important contacts and give you an understanding of the way a track works.
5. On occasion, openings are advertised in local newspaper display and classified sections. Look under heading classifications of "Announcer," "Racetrack Announcer," "Horse Racing," "Dog Racing," or "Broadcaster."

WHOLESALING AND RETAILING

MANUFACTURER'S REPRESENTATIVE (SPORTING GOODS OR EQUIPMENT COMPANY)

Position Description

A Manufacturer's Representative working for a sporting equipment company is responsible for selling the company's line of products at a wholesale level. The individual may handle a single line of goods and products or may represent diversified or several lines. The Manufacturer's Representative may also be called a Rep or Sales Representative.

The Manufacturer's Representative may sell products to sporting goods stores or departments, professional teams, amateur, college and high school teams, and others. The Manufacturer's Rep may work for the manufacturer of any type of sporting equipment, supplies, accessories, machines, and/or sports clothing.

Individuals are usually assigned a territory. The territory is an area, region, or district consisting of a few cities, counties, states, or an entire section of the country. When assigned a territory, Reps try to sell their product line in the specific area and that area only. If a store outside that territory wants to purchase company goods, a different Rep is responsible for the sale. Sizes and locations of sales zones may vary depending on the size of the company, company policy, product sold, and salesperson.

While it is not imperative to know everything about sports and athletics in this line of work, the Manufacturer's Rep must have a complete knowledge of the product or equipment sold. He or she should also know as much as possible about both competitors' products and those of his or her own company. Knowing the similarities and differences will help the Manufacturer's Rep speak to store buyers knowledgeably and honestly concerning comparisons. For the same reason, it is important that the Manufacturer's Rep be aware of both the strengths and weaknesses of all competitive products. Being knowledgeable about the line will help the individual develop a good, strong sales pitch to use when trying to sell products.

Manufacturer's Reps use a number of methods to sell goods. They may work from the office making sales calls on the phone and mailings to distribute literature. Individuals might also make "cold" sales calls in person, actually visiting shop owners or store buyers. Most successful Manufacturer's Reps use a combination of the two systems.

The Rep might visit established accounts to see what goods and equipment have moved since the last sales call and what sales support is needed. The individual also discusses any problems that might have developed regarding the product, such as defective pieces, returns, or warranties.

The Rep discusses with the store buyer or owner new trends and developments in the sporting goods industry and the way they relate to new equipment or products the company manufacturers. In this manner, the Rep develops a good client rapport and obtains orders for products.

The Manufacturer's or Sales Rep generally seeks out new customers or accounts. To do this he or she may call to set up appointments, send correspondence, product brochures, and other mailings, or just drop in at a potential new customer's place of business. While he or she may not get an order on that first call, persistence usually pays off.

The Manufacturer's Representative is responsible for demonstrating the use of products, pointing out salable features, and answering relevant questions regarding the product.

Representatives must build good, honest working relationships with their customers. Buyers must feel comfortable with both the salesperson and the manufacturing company or they will not continue placing orders.

Depending on the Rep's territory, he or she may visit schools, colleges, or professional teams to try to sell his or her products. The Rep constantly strives to create and develop new markets for the product.

The Rep must handle a great deal of paperwork. He or she is expected regularly to send mailings, letters, spec sheets, and brochures about products to both new and established accounts. The Rep must also keep accurate records regarding orders, callbacks, and customers. Not following this procedure could mean a forgotten order, an invoice unbilled, or a dissatisfied customer.

The Manufacturer's Representative is usually responsible to either the district or sales manager of the company. If the Rep has a large territory, he or she may be required to travel extensively. The individual must set up appointments at the convenience of the buyer. He or she must also put in a number of office hours making calls and keeping records.

Salaries

Manufacturer's Representatives may be paid straight salaries, commissions, or a combination of the two.

Reps are also often rewarded with bonuses for outstanding sales.

Salaries vary extensively depending on the company the individual is working for, the product or products sold, territories, experience, and sales ability. Earnings for Manufacturer's Representatives of sporting goods and products may range from $24,000 to $150,000 and up.

One of the most exciting things about being paid on any type of commission basis is that the sky is the limit in relation to earnings.

Employment Prospects

Employment prospects are excellent for those aspiring to Manufacturer's Representatives positions. Individuals must be good salespeople who are highly motivated with a lot of drive and determination. Companies are constantly on the lookout for people who fit this mold.

Prospective manufacturers may be located throughout the country.

Advancement Prospects

Advancement prospects are usually determined by sales ability. The individual advances by meeting and exceeding sales quotas, developing good relationships with customers, and opening up new accounts.

Manufacturer's Reps may advance their careers by locating similar positions in larger, more prestigious companies, obtaining better sales territories, or by becoming sales managers.

Education and Training

Educational requirements differ with each position. Many companies just require their Manufacturer's Reps to have high school diplomas. Others prefer or require college graduates.

Seminars and workshops in all aspects of selling and salesmanship will be useful in both obtaining a position and being successful with it.

Experience, Skills, and Personality Traits

Manufacturer's Representatives must have sales ability. They must be able to develop good sales pitches and deliver them to potential customers. It is essential that individuals be motivated, driven, and aggressive without being pushy.

Reps should be organized and detail oriented. The ability to keep clear, concise records is necessary. Writing skills may be necessary for some positions.

Some Reps working for manufacturers of sporting goods and equipment have had experiences in either retail or wholesaling positions. For others, the Rep position is entry level.

The Rep should have good verbal communication skills and be comfortable talking to a variety of people. The individual should be as articulate communicating on the phone as he or she is in person. The Rep should have a neat and well-groomed appearance.

Unions and Associations

Manufacturer's Representatives may belong to any number of professional trade organizations specifically relevant to the type of product or products represented. Individuals might also be members of the Manufacturer's Agents National Association (MANA) or the Sporting Goods Agents Association (SGAA). Both organizations provide training and professional guidance to their members.

Tips for Entry

1. Consider getting some experience working with sporting goods and equipment prior to seeking a Manufacturer's Representative position. Find a job in a retail sporting goods shop or department. An added bonus might be meeting and talking with Reps who come in the store.
2. When you do apply for a job, try to learn as much as possible about the company and its products.

It is also helpful to know about competing products. In this manner, you can discuss the company knowledgeably with your interviewer.

3. Manufacturer's Representative positions are often advertised in the newspaper display or classified sections. Look under heading classifications of "Sales," "Salesperson," "Manufacturer's Reps," "Sporting Goods," "Wholesale," "Athletics," or "Sports Equipment."
4. If there are specific companies you would like to work with, obtain their addresses by checking their product packaging, asking for the information in a sporting goods store, or looking up the data in *Standard & Poor's*, a directory found in most libraries.
5. Look in the yellow pages of the phone book to locate sporting goods and equipment manufacturers. Send your résumé with a cover letter requesting an interview or information on job openings.
6. Positions may be located on the Internet. Search various career and job sites as well as sporting goods and equipment manufacturers' sites.

SPORTS STORE MANAGER

CAREER PROFILE

Duties: Managing sporting goods, athletic equipment, or general sports store; overseeing operation of store; supervising employees; handling customers' problems

Alternate Title(s): Sporting Goods Store Manager; Athletic Equipment Store Manager

Salary Range: $24,000 to $85,000+

Employment Prospects: Excellent

Advancement Prospects: Good

Best Geographical Location(s) for Position: Positions located throughout the country

Prerequisites:

    Education or Training—Minimum educational requirement is high school diploma; some positions may require or prefer college background or degree

Experience—Experience working in retail sales necessary

Special Skills and Personality Traits—Supervisory skills; administrative skills; detail oriented; honest; dependable; communication skills; knowledgeable about sporting goods and athletic equipment

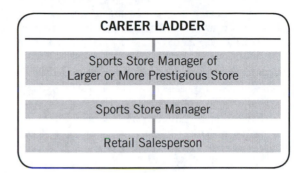

CAREER LADDER

Sports Store Manager of Larger or More Prestigious Store

Sports Store Manager

Retail Salesperson

Position Description

Every city and many small towns throughout the country have at least one if not more sporting goods and athletic equipment shops. These stores sell everything from inexpensive fishing lines to costly exercise equipment. For individuals who have an interest in the sport and athletic industries as well as some retail or business experience, becoming a Sports Store Manager is a good way to get involved in an interesting and lucrative career.

Sports Store Managers may work in various settings. These include the all-purpose sporting goods shop or the specialized sporting goods store. Managers also may work in sports store chains that are located throughout the country. Shops may sell equipment, machines, accessories, and clothing for exercise, camping, recreation, and other sporting goods. Store Managers have varied duties depending on the specific job and store they are working for.

The Store Manager is responsible for the operation of the entire store. An important function of the Manager is hiring personnel. The individual may be responsible for placing advertisements in the paper, notifying employment agencies, or putting up signs in the store window in order to find staff. He or she is also expected to interview potential employees. The Store Manager must be sure that the staff he or she hires is competent, trustworthy, and dependable.

In this position, the Store Manager needs supervisory skills. Depending on the size of the store, he or she may be in charge of a large number of employees. These staff people may include salespeople, clerks, cashiers, stock people, maintenance people, and bookkeepers.

He or she must make sure that they are trained in all phases of the operation, from running the cash register to helping a customer choose an expensive piece of sports equipment. In some situations, the Store Manager must run training sessions for new employees. In others, the Manager may train each new employee personally as he or she comes on the job or assign another staff member to the task.

The Store Manager is responsible for scheduling staff members in an effective manner. This is often a difficult job, because the store must always be fully staffed. The Manager must also make contingency plans in case someone calls in sick or there is an emergency.

The Manager must be totally knowledgeable about all the store's stock. He or she must become an expert on everything in the store. The Store Manager must know about different types of exercise equipment, recreational equipment, and sporting supplies that the store stocks. He or she also must know how the various machines and equipment work in order to demonstrate it to both staff and buyers. It also helps if the Manager has a knowledge of competitors' products.

The Store Manager oversees everything and everybody. At times, the individual may assume the duties of a salesperson, clerk, or cashier. The Manager may be responsible for approving checks and making sure large bills are not counterfeit. He or she may also be responsible for arranging layaways and putting through credit card purchases.

An important role of the Store Manager is to handle customer service problems. When a customer has a problem, the Store Manager is expected to find a solution. For example, a customer may return an expensive rowing machine after the warranty has expired because it fell apart. To keep goodwill between the customer and the store, the Manager may authorize an exchange or may fix the piece of equipment at no charge. The Store Manager is also expected to handle any problems arising between employees and patrons. The successful Store Manager's motto is usually "The customer is always right."

Another major function of the Store Manager may be acting as the buyer of the store. The individual may talk with various representatives of sporting goods and equipment companies about their products. When ordering merchandise, he or she also listens to the needs of customers who come into the store. The Manager gets price quotes and writes orders.

In some situations, such as a large sporting good chain store, he or she may not do the purchasing. Instead, the individual reports stock deficiencies to the main office. Headquarters, in turn, sends needed equipment from the main warehouse.

The Manager is expected to check inventory on a regular basis. In this way, he or she knows what items are low in stock or have sold out completely. The Manager may assign this duty to an assistant or to a salesperson.

When stock arrives at the store, the Manager is responsible for making sure every piece is accounted for. He or she may count and sort merchandise and verify the receipt of items on invoices personally or assign this duty to an assistant or salesperson. The individual must also make sure that all items are priced for sale.

In some situations, the Manager is responsible for advertising store specials. In others, he or she receives advertising circulars from a main office. The Manager must be sure that all items advertised are available in the store and sale priced.

Another duty of the Manager is to keep stock arranged attractively and samples of the product line assembled for customers to see and try out. If a customer was purchasing an exercise bicycle or treadmill, he or she would not only want to look at the product when it was assembled but would probably want to try it out too.

In most situations the Store Manager is responsible for obtaining time sheets and work hours of employees for payroll purposes. He or she may then be expected to personally draw up payroll checks or may give the information to the store owner or district manager.

The Sports Store Manager may be responsible to the owner of the store or, in chain stores, to the regional manager. The individual may often work overtime if an employee calls in sick, there is an emergency, a shipment of stock comes in, or there is work to be completed.

Salaries

Earnings for Sports Store Managers vary depending on the experience of the individual, his or her responsibilities, the size of the store, and the geographical location. Salaries can range from $24,000 to $85,000 plus per year.

Individuals with little experience working in smaller stores may earn from $24,000 to $26,000. Those with a modest amount of experience in a larger store setting may have annual salaries from $25,000 to $35,000. Earnings for Store Managers with a great deal of experience and responsibilities working in a large sports store in a major city may range between $24,000 and $85,000 plus.

Employment Prospects

Employment prospects are currently excellent for Sports Store Managers. Positions are located throughout the country in sporting goods and athletic equipment stores. Individuals may work in large or small stores.

Advancement Prospects

Advancement prospects are good for Sports Store Managers. The next rung on the career ladder for the Sports Store Manager is to locate a similar position in a larger, more prestigious sports store. This usually results in increased responsibilities and higher earnings. As there is quite a bit of mobility in all aspects of the retail market, jobs open up frequently.

Education and Training

Educational requirements vary depending on the specific position. Almost all sports stores require their Managers to hold at least a high school diploma. Many either require or prefer Managers to have either a college background or a four-year college degree.

A college degree in almost any major will be useful. Good choices for those interested in this field might include sports administration, business, marketing, communications, retailing, or liberal arts.

Experience, Skills, and Personality Traits

Sports Store Managers need to be informed about the stock level in the store. Any experience working with sporting equipment, athletic equipment, athletic shoes, or clothing is useful. The more sports and athletic oriented the individual is, the more successful he or she will be in this position.

The Store Manager should have supervisory and administrative skills. He or she is responsible for the organization, administration, and running of the store. The ability to organize and handle many details at one time is necessary.

Honesty and dependability are important traits. Communication skills are imperative. The Store Manager should not only like working with people but be good with them as well.

Store Managers need experience in retail sales. While it helps to have experience in retail sales in a sports store, it is not always necessary. Some Store Managers landed their position after a stint as an assistant manager, while others moved up from a sales position.

Unions and Associations

There are no associations geared specifically toward Managers of sports stores.

Tips for Entry

1. Positions as Sports Store Managers may often be located in the display or classified section of the newspaper. Look under heading classifications of "Retail Sales," "Sales Manager," "Sports Store," or "Athletic Equipment."

2. Malls and shopping centers also advertise management positions in their store windows. Visit these areas and browse looking for signs.

3. You might consider sending your résumé and a cover letter to some of the sporting goods, athletic equipment, or sports stores in your area. Ask that your résumé be kept on file if there are no current openings. As noted previously, there is a great deal of mobility in retail jobs. If your résumé is on file, you may get a call. Get names and addresses of stores by looking in the yellow pages of the phone book.

4. Carry copies of your résumé with you when job hunting. Make sure that they are neat, clean, and well put together. If you do not type yourself, have someone else type your résumé for you. Bring it to a quick print shop to have copies made.

5. Job opportunities may be located on the World Wide Web. Search popular job and career sites as well as the sites of major chain sporting goods stores.

SPORTING GOODS SALESPERSON

CAREER PROFILE

Duties: Selling sporting equipment, machines, accessories, supplies, and clothing; acting as cashier; taking inventory; arranging merchandise

Alternate Title(s): Sporting Equipment Salesperson; Sales Associate

Salary Range: $18,000 to $45,000+

Employment Prospects: Excellent

Advancement Prospects: Excellent

Best Geographical Location(s) for Position: Positions located throughout the country

Prerequisites:

Education or Training—Minimum of a high school diploma required for full-time position

Experience—Experience working with public helpful but not necessary in many positions

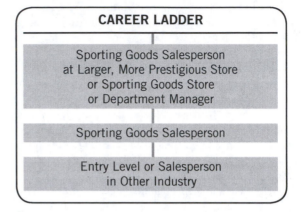

CAREER LADDER

Sporting Goods Salesperson at Larger, More Prestigious Store or Sporting Goods Store or Department Manager

Sporting Goods Salesperson

Entry Level or Salesperson in Other Industry

Special Skills and Personality Traits—Sales skills; dependable; ability to work well with people; personable; articulate; good communication skills

Position Description

The trend toward attaining health and fitness is increasing today. With the importance placed on health and fitness, sports equipment shops and departments are becoming more common.

As more shops open up throughout the country and additional department stores begin carrying fuller lines of sports equipment, informed, knowledgeable Salespeople have become increasingly necessary. Sporting Goods Salespeople are responsible for selling sports-oriented equipment, supplies, accessories, machines, and clothing.

The Salesperson must know how the various machines and equipment work so that he or she can demonstrate their functions to buyers. The individual must also be able to explain the differences between brands of the same types of equipment. The Salesperson may specialize in one type of equipment or may be required to be fully informed about all of the store's merchandise. For example, one Salesperson may specialize in exercise machines, while another may be knowledgeable about recreational equipment.

Other functions of the Salesperson may include serving as a cashier, closing sales, totaling up customers' purchases, arranging for layaways, putting through credit card purchases, taking payments for products, and giving change to customers.

Good Salespeople try to find out exactly what the customers' needs are. When a customer comes into a store asking about purchasing an exercise bicycle, rowing machine, cross-country ski machine, or treadmill, the Salesperson must try to determine certain things. He or she accomplishes this by talking and questioning: What is the price range? What brands would the buyer consider? What types of options are desired? How long has the customer been exercising? How many people will be using the machine? Approaching the sale in this way, the Salesperson can assist the customer in making a wise purchase.

In some shops, the Salesperson may repair or assemble equipment. The individual might also explain directions concerning assembly or instructions for repair to customers. The Salesperson in some stores must also help carry and load equipment into customers' cars after purchase.

Others duties of the Salesperson might include counting and sorting merchandise and verifying the receipt of items on invoices. The individual checks that stock arriving is the merchandise that was ordered. He or she may stamp, mark, or attach price tags to equipment and other products in the stores.

The Salesperson may be required to stock shelves, set up advertising displays, and arrange merchandise under the supervision of the store manager.

Depending on the situation, the Salesperson may be responsible for checking inventory and reporting to store management items that have sold out or are low in stock. The individual may order special items for customers if the store does not have specific items in stock.

Salespeople may work in various settings. These include all-purpose sporting goods shop, specialized sporting goods shop, or sports department in a department store. Individuals may sell equipment, machines, accessories, and clothing for exercise, camping, recreation, and any other sporting goods carried by the store.

The Salesperson is directly responsible to the manager of the sporting equipment shop or department. Hours vary depending on the shift the individual works. He or she may or may not work overtime, depending on the specific job.

Salaries
Earnings for Salespeople working in sporting goods and equipment stores or departments vary, depending on the experience of the person, the size of the store, the geographical location, and method of payment. Salaries can range from $18,000 to $45,000 plus per year.

Salespeople may be compensated in a number of different ways. The individual may receive a straight salary, a commission on equipment sold, or a combination of the two.

Employment Prospects
Employment prospects are currently excellent in every facet of retail sales, and sporting equipment sales is no exception. Individuals aspiring to work in sporting equipment shops or departments may find positions throughout the country.

Virtually anyone can enter the sports industry as a Sporting Goods Salesperson. With hard work, an individual can also advance quickly.

Advancement Prospects
Advancement prospects are excellent for Sporting Goods Salespersons. There are two methods of career advancement. The individual might find a similar position in a larger, more prestigious sporting goods store. This could result in added responsibilities and higher earnings. The other option for climbing the career ladder is for the Salesperson to become a sporting goods store or department manager.

Both paths are wide open at this time. There is a growing need for personnel in all areas of retail sales. An individual with drive and determination will have no problem moving up in this type of job.

Education and Training
Salespeople working full time in sporting goods stores or department must usually hold at least a high school diploma. Part-timers may still be attending school. Some stores now require a college background or degree. A college background may be necessary for advancement.

Experience using any sporting goods or equipment is helpful in both attaining a job and achieving success in it.

Experience, Skills, and Personality Traits
While sales skills are necessary for this type of position, the most important trait an individual can have is to be a personable, likable individual who works well with the public. The Salesperson needs to make customers feel comfortable when purchasing equipment and other items from the store. He or she should be able to make customers feel they are important. The individual should know how to talk to customers without being pushy and pressuring them into a purchase.

The more informed a Salesperson is about the products being sold, the more successful he or she will be. The individual needs to be able to give concise, honest information about equipment and other products.

The Salesperson should be dependable, articulate, and have good communication skills. He or she should be neat, clean, and well groomed.

Any experience in retail sales or dealing with the public will be helpful.

Unions and Associations
Many stores are represented by bargaining unions that negotiate minimum salaries and working conditions. Employees including the Sports Equipment Salesperson may be members of these organizations.

If the Salesperson is working in a store specializing in selling equipment or uniforms to schools or colleges, he or she may be a member of the Athletic Goods Team Distributors (AGTD).

Tips for Entry
1. One of the easiest ways to find a sales position is to look in the newspaper. Look in the display or classified section under heading classifications of "Sales," "Selling," "Salesperson," "Sales Associate," "Retail," "Athletics," "Fitness," "Sports," or "Exercise."
2. Another method of locating a sales job in a sports equipment shop is to visit malls and shopping centers in your area and look in store windows. There will often be signs stating "Help Wanted,"

"Salesperson Wanted," or "Sales Associate Wanted." All you have to do is go into the store, ask to speak to the manager, fill out an application, and wait to be called for an interview.

3. It is always a good idea to carry copies of your résumé with you when job hunting. Make sure that they are neat, clean, and well put together.

4. Once you have a résumé put together, think about sending it out to sports shops in your area with a cover letter inquiring about openings. You can obtain names and addresses by looking in the yellow pages of the phone book or online.

You can also get leads by looking through the local newspaper. Sports shops often advertise sales and specials. Their addresses are usually somewhere in the advertisement.

5. If you cannot find a job right away working in a sport equipment shop, consider getting a sales job in another field until a suitable position opens up. This will give you good hands-on experience working with people.

6. Positions may be located on the Internet. Search popular job and career sites.

SPORTS MEDICINE

ATHLETIC TRAINER

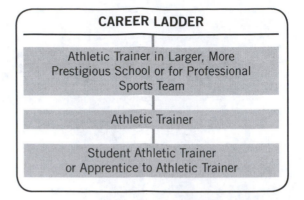

Position Description

Athletic Trainers may work in amateur or professional sports. Individuals in this position have a number of duties. Their main responsibility is to work with athletes in an effort to prevent injuries. Once injuries do occur, the Athletic Trainer is required to evaluate the problem and get the athlete the proper medical treatment. He or she also makes sure that athletes are physically ready and able to play after an injury.

Athletic Trainers often work with team coaches in the development and implementation of programs that can be used to help athletes get in the best possible physical condition. This is important because athletes who are in good condition will have fewer injuries. Athletes are also interested in conditioning; they know their performance will peak with proper training and good conditioning.

Athletic Trainers also work with the equipment manager to make sure that playing and training areas are in working order. Depending on the situation, the Athletic Trainer requests from the equipment manager or head coach supplies he or she needs to do the job. These items might include braces, bandages, cold packs, and the like. The Athletic Trainer is responsible for recommending the types of supplies he or she needs and making sure that they are available as required.

One of the major functions of the Athletic Trainer occurs during games and practice sessions. He or she is on the sidelines watching the athletes. As soon as someone looks injured or does not look quite right after a move, the Athletic Trainer rushes out on the field to evaluate the injury. Sometimes injuries are slight and just need a simple treatment, such as an ice application. The Trainer must determine if the athlete needs medical attention and, if so, must get it for him or her immediately.

Another of the Athletic Trainer's duties is to work with the physician in a rehabilitation program for injured players. The Trainer discusses prognoses with the physician and with the athletes. The Trainer is then responsible for developing and implementing a program that will help the athletes regain use of the injured body part. This program may include prescribed exercises, heat treatments, whirlpools, or massages.

The Trainer must keep records of each athlete's progress throughout his or her injury and rehabilitation. Good record keeping of all injuries is necessary. Often an injury does not seem serious at first but can cause problems later. Records must indicate when an athlete was injured, where, what the injury was, the prognosis, prescribed rehabilitation, and progress.

The Athletic Trainer is responsible for deciding when an athlete's injuries have healed sufficiently for the individual to get back to the game. This may be difficult because athletes usually do not like to miss games. They have been known to tell Trainers they are no longer in pain, when in reality they still are. The Trainer may also have to deal with coaches who want players back in games before they are ready.

Individuals working in a school setting may have additional responsibilities. Athletic Trainers in these situations may be responsible for teaching classes, working in health centers, or coaching sports teams, or some combination of these jobs.

Individuals work long hours preparing playing and practice areas, keeping records, attending games and practice sessions, evaluating and taking care of injuries, supervising rehabilitation, and soothing players who are frightened that an injury might end their careers. Their job is extremely important. Most Athletic Trainers and athletes are aware that their expertise can mean the difference between a permanent injury and one that can be rehabilitated.

Salaries
Salaries vary greatly depending on the specific setting in which the Athletic Trainer works. Athletic Trainers working in schools or colleges may earn salaries ranging from $35,000 to $65,000 plus. The range depends on the type and size of the school, the importance the administration puts on sports programs and teams, prestige, and location. Earnings are also based on the duties and responsibilities of the individual and his or her experience.

Athletic Trainers working for professional teams earn from $35,000 to $150,000 plus. These salaries too depend on the type of team, its prestige, and the responsibilities and experience of the individual Trainer.

Employment Prospects
Employment prospects are excellent for Athletic Trainers. Individuals may find employment throughout the country in a variety of different settings. Athletic Trainers are hired in public and private high schools, junior colleges, four-year colleges and universities, and professional sports teams. One or more Athletic Trainers may be required.

Advancement Prospects
Advancement prospects are excellent for Athletic Trainers. An individual might begin his or her career working in a high school situation and advance to the college level. The Athletic Trainer might then climb the career ladder by locating a position in a larger college or university that puts more emphasis on its sports and athletic teams.

The next level of advancement, with professional teams, becomes more difficult to reach. This is not to say that advancement is impossible. Athletic Trainers who have proven themselves in the field may advance to pro levels.

Education and Training
Most positions for Athletic Trainers require the individual to have a four-year college degree. While many jobs do not require an individual be certified as an Athletic Trainer, it might be useful. Individuals who wish to be certified should consider a college accredited by the National Athletic Trainer's Association (NATA). Others may obtain a degree with a major in physical education. Certain positions may also require graduate degree.

Good course choices might include those in anatomy, exercise physiology, kinesiology, nutrition, physics, chemistry, first aid, coaching, and psychology.

Athletic Trainers who want to be certified but who have not attended one of NATA's accredited colleges, may take part in an apprenticeship program.

Workshops, seminars, and courses in athletic training, coaching, and health education are also useful to the individual in this profession. Continuing education may be required for some positions.

Special Requirements
Voluntary certification is available through the National Athletic Trainer's Association (NATA).

Experience, Skills, and Personality Traits
Athletic Trainers need the ability to get along well with people. Individuals will be interacting with all the athletes on the team as well as coaches and physicians. Those who are not people oriented and personable are usually not successful in this type of job.

Athletic Trainers need to feel comfortable working with injured people. This is not the job for individuals who feel faint at the sight of blood. Athletic Trainers should be able to deal well in crisis situations. Individuals need to know basic first aid procedures. They should also be able to do preliminary evaluations of injured athletes.

Athletic Trainers must understand the psychology of both team athletes and coaches. Some athletes who want to get back to a game say that their injuries are not serious or have healed when they really have not. The Trainer must have a sixth sense in such matters. Sending an individual back to a game before he or she is ready might cause permanent injury.

Trainers must have good communication skills. They deal with a variety of people. Individuals are also responsible for written reports dealing with team injuries.

It is helpful for the Athletic Trainer to have an understanding and enjoyment of sports. He or she must attend a great many games. Trainers who are not sports fans may not be able to enjoy their work fully, while those who are fans will be very happy.

Unions and Associations

Athletic Trainers may belong to the National Athletic Trainers Association (NATA). NATA offers education, training, certification programs, and career guidance. It also brings people in this profession together to maintain high standards. This group also sponsors student memberships.

Tips for Entry

1. Become a student member of NATA. This will give you constant, up-to-date information about the profession and help you make important contacts in the field.
2. Volunteer to work with your school team. If your school has an Athletic Trainer, ask if you can assist him or her. If not, talk to the head coach or athletic director.
3. Learn the proper first aid procedures. You will need to know them when you get a job.
4. Look for and attend seminars in athletic training, advanced first aid, sports injuries, sports medicine, and the like. These will give you additional training and help you make more contacts.
5. Read books and periodicals on the subject of athletic training.
6. Subscribe to trade journals. These will suggest other relevant reading material and may advertise job opportunities.
7. There are a number of workshops, clinics, and camps around the country for student Athletic Trainers. Attending one of these will be very valuable to an individual for training purposes and to instill added confidence. It will also look good on your résumé.

PHYSICAL THERAPIST

Position Description

A Physical Therapist is a registered professional. In many states the Physical Therapist must be licensed by the state. He or she is responsible for a variety of functions, including assessing physical therapy needs, performing initial patient evaluations, performing physical therapy procedures, and revising patient's therapeutic plan of care. The individual in this position may also assist in directing physical therapy ancillary personnel.

The Physical Therapist may work with athletes or nonathletes. Physical therapy is an adjunct to the growing field of sports medicine. At one time or another during their careers, many professional sportsmen and women use the services of a Physical Therapist.

Physical Therapists develop therapies and exercise treatments for their patients. These therapies can help patients ease pain, recover from injuries or illness, or regain use of body parts.

Individuals become patients as a result of accidents or, in the case of athletes, sports-related injuries. People may also be born with physical disabilities or may become disabled through an illness, such as a stroke, heart attack, polio, or other diseases.

Physical therapy is very important to athletes who have been injured whether or not they are professionals. Almost any type of athlete, from an amateur runner to a professional ballplayer, may become a physical therapy patient. Physical therapy may also be used by handicapped individuals who would like to excel or just participate in some type of physical activity.

The Physical Therapist works with a variety of rehabilitative personnel, including physiatrists and physical therapy assistants. Specific duties depend on the situation and the specific job.

One of the first things a Physical Therapist does with a new patient is evaluate the individual and develop a rehabilitation plan. The Therapist may put the individual through a battery of tests to determine the extent of his or her injuries.

The individual must know which type of procedures and treatments will help ease a patient's pain and be therapeutic. He or she must set realistic rehabilitation goals for all patients.

The Physical Therapist may instruct and supervise physical therapy assistants in all phases of their work. He or she is required to instruct the assistant on how to run tests and how to keep proper documentation on each patient.

The Physical Therapist is responsible for reevaluating patients after a series of treatments have been completed. After the reevaluation, the individual revises the patient's therapy accordingly.

Records and documentation are extremely important in this field. In some situations, the Physical

Therapist may be responsible for all paperwork and documentation of a patient's progress, therapy, reactions, and so on. In other situations, the individual passes this responsibility on to an assistant.

Depending on the situation, the Physical Therapist may be required to participate in patient care conferences with individuals in the nursing or social services department, or even with families of the patient.

Often the individual must know about all aspects of the patient's medical care. The Therapist is also responsible for instructing family members, coaches, and trainers in the patient's physical therapy program.

Depending on the requirements of the job, the Physical Therapist may be required to perform additional duties, including ordering equipment, scheduling daily workloads, assessing departmental needs, and assisting in the maintenance of the physical environment of the therapy department.

The Physical Therapist may be responsible to any number of people, depending on the institution in which he or she works. The individual may report directly to the head physical therapist, physical therapist supervisor, physiatrist, or director of rehabilitative services.

He or she usually works normal or fairly normal hours. While most hospitals and health care facilities usually schedule physical therapy sessions during the day, some facilities keep Physical Therapists on staff during all hours. During an emergency, Physical Therapists may be called in and asked to work beyond normal working hours.

Salaries

Salaries for Physical Therapists vary greatly depending on a number of variables, including geographical location of the facility and its size and prestige.

Earnings also depend on the individual's education, experience, and responsibilities. The Physical Therapist can earn from $25,000 to $85,000 plus annually. In addition, compensation is also usually augmented by liberal fringe benefit packages.

Employment Prospects

A nationwide shortage of qualified individuals makes employment prospects excellent for Physical Therapists. Positions may be located throughout the country in sports medicine clinics, independent physical therapy centers, hospitals, rehabilitation centers, nursing homes, and other health care facilities.

Advancement Prospects

Advancement prospects are good for Physical Therapists. Individuals can advance their career by becoming supervisors or by locating positions in larger, more prestigious facilities.

Education and Training

While Physical Therapists must hold a minimum of a master's degree from an accredited physical therapy program, more and more positions are currently requiring doctoral degrees. With this in mind, individuals might want to look into all options before choosing a program. At this time there are more than 40 accredited master's programs and more than 160 doctoral programs.

Special Requirements

Physical Therapists must be licensed by the state in which they work. In order to practice, individuals must pass both national and state certification exams.

Experience, Skills, and Personality Traits

The Physical Therapist should genuinely like to help others. Compassion and empathy are also traits that will help the individual to excel in his or her career.

The Physical Therapist should be articulate. He or she may be required to explain procedures and therapies to both patients and their families, coaches, and trainers. He or she should be able to give directions to others in a way they understand. Physical Therapists must be able to supervise others, including assistants and aides.

The individual should be positive, personable, and enthusiastic so that he or she can motivate patients to help themselves.

The Physical Therapist must also have both the physical and the mechanical ability to use equipment relevant to the job, such as wheelchairs, stretchers, lifts, geriatric chairs, whirlpools, and traction equipment.

Unions and Associations

Physical Therapists working in health care facilities may or may not belong to a variety of unions that represent workers in hospitals or health care facilities.

Individuals may also belong to trade associations, including the American Physical Therapy Association (APTA). This organization provides educational guidance and support for those working in the physical therapy field.

Tips for Entry

1. Locate sports medicine clinics and private physical therapy centers in the area by looking in the yellow pages of the phone book.
2. Positions are often advertised in the display or classified section of the newspaper. Look under

heading classifications of "Health Care," "Hospitals," "Physical Therapy," "Sports Medicine," or "Therapists."

3. Consider sending your résumé to hospitals or health care facilities with a cover letter. Ask that your résumé be kept on file if a position is not currently available.

4. Call the personnel director of hospitals and health care facilities in the areas where you want to work to try to set up an appointment for an interview.

5. If you are still in school or taking part in an accredited training program, contact the job placement office for job possibilities.

6. Employment agencies located throughout the country specialize in jobs in the health care industry. Check to see who pays the fee if you do get a job (you or the employer) before getting involved.

PHYSICAL THERAPY ASSISTANT

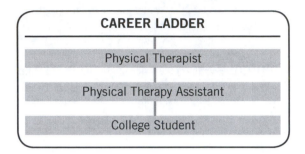
Position Description

A Physical Therapy Assistant is a paraprofessional who is responsible for providing direct patient care under immediate direction and supervision. He or she is also required to assist the physical therapist, physiatrist, and/or other rehabilitation specialist in any procedure or function, including those not related to direct patient care when directed to do so.

The individual may work with athletes or nonathletes depending on the situation. Physical therapy is an adjunct to the growing field of sports medicine.

Physical Therapy Assistants or Physical Therapist Assistants, as they may be called, provide patients with various therapies and exercise modalities developed by the physical therapist. These therapies help the patient ease pain, recover from an injury or illness, or regain use of a body part.

Individuals become patients as a result of accidents or, in the case of athletes, game-related injuries. People may also be born with physical disabilities or may become disabled through an illness, such as a stroke, heart attack, polio, or other diseases.

Physical therapy is very important to athletes who have been injured whether or not they are professionals. Almost any type of athlete, from an amateur runner to a professional ballplayer, may become a physical therapy patient. Physical therapy may also be used by handicapped individuals who would like

to excel or just participate in some type of physical activity.

The Physical Therapy Assistant takes orders from the head physical therapist, physiatrist, or other rehabilitation specialist. Duties depend on the situation and the specific job.

The Physical Therapy Assistant may work with the physical therapist or physiatrist in evaluating a new patient and implementing a care or rehabilitation plan. For example, if an athlete comes in after a sports-related injury, the Assistant may be instructed on which particular tests to put him or her through. In physical therapy treatment it is important to know the extent of injuries.

The Assistant may be asked to do tests, such as checking the amount of weight an athlete can put on his or her leg or how far the individual can bend. The Assistant may help the patient walk, climb stairs or inclines, or perform other exercises to regain mobility. If the Assistant does not do his or her job correctly, a patient may have a treatment that is too strenuous or not strenuous enough to help.

In many cases, the Physical Therapy Assistant helps a patient not only ease the pain but also learn how to deal with pain. He or she may, for example, assist the patient by providing heat therapy, hydrotherapy, such as whirlpool baths or wet packs, massages, and so on.

In some cases, the Assistant helps the physical therapist reevaluate patients after a series of treatments have been completed. The Physical Therapy Assistant often must do a great deal of the paperwork documentation, from making original records of a patient's problems, capabilities, and so on to evaluating his or her current capabilities and progress.

The Physical Therapy Assistant often builds a close bond with his or her patients. It is exciting to watch someone who couldn't walk take his or her first step after a major injury.

Physical Therapy Assistants are responsible directly to the head physical therapist, physiatrist, or rehabilitation specialist, depending on the institution they are working in. They usually work normal or fairly normal hours. While most hospitals and health care facilities usually schedule physical therapy sessions during the day, some facilities keep both physical therapists and Assistants on staff at all hours.

Salaries

Salaries for Physical Therapy Assistants vary greatly depending on a number of variables, including the geographical location of the facility and its size and prestige.

Earnings also depend on the individuals' education, experience, and responsibilities. The Physical Therapy Assistant's annual earnings can range from $23,000 to $35,000 or more. In addition, compensation is also usually augmented by liberal fringe benefit packages.

Employment Prospects

Employment prospects are excellent for Physical Therapy Assistants as there is currently a nationwide shortage of qualified individuals. There are many opportunities in hospitals, rehabilitation centers, nursing homes, and other health care facilities. Physical Therapy Assistants may also work in sports medicine clinics, which are springing up throughout the country, or in independent physical therapy centers. One of the good things about this position is that jobs may be found in almost any geographical location.

While some institutions only have one or two people in this position, many hire a number of Physical Therapy Assistants. Part-time work as a Physical Therapy Assistant in a variety of different health care facilities is also available.

Advancement Prospects

Advancement prospects are excellent for Physical Therapy Assistants. Individuals can advance their career by becoming full-fledged physical therapists. In order to climb the career ladder, however, the Physical Therapy Assistant must take additional training. This usually includes at least another two years of schooling in an institution that has an accredited program in physical therapy.

Education and Training

Physical Therapy Assistants are required to hold an Associate's degree from an accredited two-year college that offers a physical therapy or physical therapy assistants' program.

Special Requirements

Physical Therapy Assistants must be either licensed or registered in most states. Generally this requires obtaining a degree from an accredited program, fieldwork, and taking and passing a licensing exam.

Experience, Skills, and Personality Traits

The Physical Therapy Assistant should have a great deal of patience. This is important because the individual often works with patients who can't do very much. A small step by a patient may be a major accomplishment, and it may take a long time to achieve.

The Assistant should be a giving person who genuinely likes to help others. Compassion and empathy are also traits that will help the individual excel in his or her career.

The Physical Therapy Assistant should be articulate. He or she should be able to follow directions and explain them to others in a way they understand. The Assistant should also be positive, personable, and enthusiastic so that he or she can motivate patients to help themselves. Many patients who work with the Assistant are under severe emotional and physical strain. A smiling face at a therapy session can sometimes make the difference between success and failure.

If the individual is working in a health care facility, he or she must be able to handle the situation both physically and emotionally.

Unions and Associations

Many Physical Therapy Assistants working in health care facilities do not belong to unions. Others may belong to a variety of unions that represent workers in hospitals or health care facilities.

The individual may belong to trade associations, including the American Physical Therapy Association (APTA). This organization provides educational guidance and support for those working in the physical therapy field.

Tips for Entry

1. Positions can often be located in display or classified advertisements in the newspaper. Look

under heading classifications of "Health Care," "Hospitals," "Physical Therapy," "Sports Medicine," or "Therapists."

2. You might want to send your résumé to hospitals or health care facilities with a cover letter. Ask that your résumé be kept on file if a position is not currently available.

3. You might also consider calling the personnel director of hospitals and health care facilities in the areas where you want to work to set up an appointment for an interview.

4. If you are still in school or taking part in an accredited training program, contact the job placement office for job possibilities.

5. Check out openings online. Start with sites like monster.com and hotjobs.yahoo.com and go from there.

SPORTS AND FITNESS NUTRITIONIST

Duties: Analyzing nutritional needs of individuals; planning nutritious, healthful meals for athletes; counseling athletes on nutritional problems

Alternate Title(s): Nutritionist; Sports Nutritionist; Sports Nutrition Counselor

Salary Range: $24,000 to $125,000+

Employment Prospects: Good

Advancement Prospects: Fair

Best Geographical Location(s) for Position: Positions may be located throughout the country

Prerequisites:

Education or Training—Educational requirements vary from one-year program through master's degree in nutritional science

Experience—Experience in nutrition and fitness helpful

CAREER LADDER

Director of Sports Nutrition
or Sports and Fitness Nutritionist
for More Prestigious Team or Facility

Sports and Fitness Nutritionist

College Student

Special Skills and Personality Traits—Complete knowledge of nutrition; understanding of exercise, athletics, and fitness; personable; communication skills; understanding; compassionate

Position Description

It is important to both professional and amateur athletes to be physically fit and healthy. This is accomplished by exercising, sleeping a sufficient number of hours, living an appropriate and healthy lifestyle, and eating correctly. The field of sports nutrition is becoming more popular as people realize the importance of good nutrition to athletes. Studies have shown that an athlete's performance can often increase if he or she eats balanced and nutritious meals. The Sports Nutritionist is the individual called on to develop nutritional programs for individual athletes or athletic teams and organizations.

The Sports Nutritionist can work in a variety of settings. He or she may work with professional sports teams, collegiate or amateur teams, individual athletes, sports training camps, hospitals, health clubs, or sports clinics. The individual's responsibilities vary depending on the specific job. Many of the responsibilities of the Sports and Fitness Nutritionist also depend on the level of education the individual has secured.

The main function of the Sports and Fitness Nutritionist is to plan nutritious, healthful meals and menus for athletes. To do this, the Nutritionist may talk to the athlete to determine what type of diet he or she has

been following, foods currently on his or her menus, and so on. The Nutritionist determines the physical activities that the athlete does routinely and his or her height, weight, and other factors.

The individual then analyzes the nutritional requirements of the athlete and plans meals around this information. The Nutritionist must understand the athlete's food likes and dislikes as well as eating routines and schedules. Planning a nutritious food program is useless unless someone can and will follow it. The Sports and Fitness Nutritionist may be expected to explain the correlation between eating correctly and potential athletic performance to many of his or her clients.

The individual may work on a one-on-one basis with athletes helping them learn what foods will be most beneficial to their performance level. He or she may also develop a nutritional analysis for a team or group of people and use this analysis to plan meals and menus. The Nutritionist may be required to develop food budgets and keep within set dollar limits when putting together menus.

The Sports and Fitness Nutritionist may, for example, work for a professional sports team at a training camp. The individual is expected to plan meals to be prepared and served to the athletes during the training camp.

The individual may also be expected to counsel athletes about what they should eat after leaving training camp. He or she is expected to keep records of client needs, prescribed programs, and progress. In some cases, athletes may have to either take off or put on weight. The Sports and Fitness Nutritionist works with these individuals prescribing diets to help them attain their goals.

At times, the Sports and Fitness Nutritionist may be required to lecture groups of athletes on nutrition and healthy eating patterns. He or she may also explain how various foods can affect their athletic performance. The individual may also offer cooking lessons to either athletes or chefs. This is done to help explain how to prepare nutritious food when away from camp or out of the Nutritionist's jurisdiction.

The individual may work long hours analyzing dietary needs. However, watching an athlete excel because of a suggested change in his or her diet can be exciting and fulfilling for the Nutritionist.

Salaries
Earnings for Sports Nutritionists may range from $24,000 to $125,000 plus per year. Variables affecting salaries include the experience, education, responsibilities, and duties of the individual as well as the specific job.

Individuals with a master's degree or higher earn considerably more than a person with less education.

Employment Prospects
Employment prospects for Sports and Fitness Nutritionists are good and steadily increasing. As more and more people begin to realize the importance of nutrition in relation to athletic performance, there is a greater need for individuals working in the field. Jobs may be located throughout the country.

Sports and Fitness Nutritionists may be on staff with professional sports teams as well as scholastic and/or amateur teams. They may also work on a consulting basis for teams or individual athletes.

Sports medicine clinics are also beginning to utilize the services of Sports and Fitness Nutritionists. Many health and fitness clubs have individuals in this capacity on staff.

Advancement Prospects
Advancement prospects are fair for Sports and Fitness Nutritionists. Individuals may climb the career ladder by locating a position with a more prestigious, well-known team or athlete. Sports and Fitness Nutritionists might also advance their careers by becoming directors of sports nutrition for a team or a clinic.

For many individuals, career advancement may be attained by obtaining additional education.

Education and Training
Educational requirements vary for Sports and Fitness Nutritionists. While some jobs require a minimum of a one-year program in nutrition or a two-year associate's degree in food and nutrition, most require at least a four-year college degree with a major in food and nutrition. Many professional sports teams and sports medicine clinics may prefer individuals with advanced degrees, such as a master's in nutrition.

Continuing education in the form of classes, seminars, and symposiums on athletics, fitness, exercise, nutrition, and food will be helpful.

Many jobs also require an individual to be a registered member of the American Dietetic Association (ADA).

Experience, Skills, and Personality Traits
Sports and Fitness Nutritionists should enjoy working with people. They should be able to relate to individuals on a variety of levels. The Nutritionist should be understanding, compassionate, and nonjudgmental. It is often difficult for people to change their dietary patterns even if their professional career depends on it.

Nutritionists should have a complete knowledge of nutrition and food and its effect on the body. They should be healthy, fit people themselves with an understanding of exercise and fitness.

Individuals should be easy to talk to and personable. They should have good communication skills, both verbal and written.

Unions and Associations
There are no specific trade associations for Sports and Fitness Nutritionists. Individuals may, however, be members of the ADA.

Tips for Entry
1. Get as much education as you can in this field. The better your educational background, the better chance you will have of obtaining a job and advancing your career.
2. Contact health and fitness clubs about openings. If the clubs do not have a staff Nutritionist, try to create a position for yourself. You may have to work part time at a couple of clubs in order to get your career started.

3. If you can't find a job in sports and fitness and you have the educational requirements, consider a job in a hospital dietary department. This will give you hands-on experience working with nutrition. You can then move on to the sports and fitness fields.

4. Jobs may be advertised in the newspaper's classified or display section. Look under heading classifications of "Nutritionist," "Sports Nutritionist," "Fitness," or "Dietary."

5. You may also search for job openings on the Internet. Go to any of the popular job sites and search by using keywords such as "nutritionist" or "nutrition counselor."

SPORTS WEB JOBS

SPORTS TEAM WEBMASTER

and layout skills; knowledge and understanding of specific sport; good verbal and written communications skills

  Special Requirements—Voluntary certification available

Position Description

In order to create a presence on the World Wide Web, most sports teams today have their own Web sites. These sites are an important way to promote and market the team, its members, games, and events. They also are an information resource for fans and the media.

The individual responsible for creating, putting together, and maintaining the Web site is called the Webmaster. The Webmaster may work alone or may assign tasks to assistants, content producers, copywriters, graphic artists, etc.

If the site is new, one of the first things the Webmaster must do is find a host for the site. In order for a sports team (or any company) to have a Web site, they must rent a space or location on the Web. This may be done by obtaining a host. The sports team pays the host for the right to place its site online on the host's space. In some instances, the team and the host are one and the same. This may occur, for example, if the team buys the space instead of renting it.

Web sites must have Web addresses so fans and other individuals are able to locate the sports team online. This Web address is called the domain name. If the team is a new one or it recently changed the team name, the Webmaster may need to work with team management to develop a Web address that people can

easily remember and that is available. Most often, the Web address is the sports team name or a derivative.

Sports Team Webmaster's duties depend to a great extent on the size and structure of the team, and the importance it puts on the Web site. Duties also will be dependent on whether or not the Web site has already been set up or whether it needs to be revamped.

The Webmaster is expected to determine the direction the sports team wants the Web site to take and the goals of the Web site. This is accomplished through communication with team management. Does the management just want a Web site to maintain a Web presence? Do they want people to have the ability to buy tickets? Do they want to have a Web store where fans can buy team-branded merchandise? Do they want people to be able to join a loyalty program online? Will there be separate sites for the major league and minor league teams? Does the team want to sell advertising to other companies to increase revenue? How does the team want to market itself? Once the Webmaster understands what the team management wants, he or she can get to work.

The Webmaster may be responsible for developing and creating the team's Web site on the World Wide Web. He or she must design the site so that it is exciting and easy to navigate and use. The Webmaster must be sure that each Web page on the site opens easily and quickly. If they do not, people may get frustrated and will often leave the site and surf to another location.

The Webmaster is expected to develop the site by adding photos, videos, animations, other graphics, and sound. Much of this information comes from the Web content producer and marketing department. In creating the site, the Webmaster may need to manipulate images to the proper size and format. If this is not done correctly, an image may either be too large, slowing down the loading of a Web page, or too small, making it difficult to see clearly. In some cases, the team may already have a site but need or want to have it revamped and redesigned.

The Sports Team Webmaster is expected to develop the site's search function so that people can search for something specific on the site quickly and easily. He or she may program pop-up windows, shopping carts, secure payment systems, the ability to see videos of team action, sweepstakes entries, and a variety of other functions. The Webmaster may also build in technology so that sports team management can find how long people stay on a specific Web page, which part of the site is most popular, how many hits the site gets, etc.

To keep the Web site fresh and timely, the Webmaster may frequently change the home page and update other parts of the site. Sometimes the site content changes daily; sometimes the site might change hourly or by even by the minute. For example, the Webmaster may program the site so game scores can be shown in real time or pictures of the game are shown immediately after the action occurs.

As part of the job, the Webmaster must make changes and remove out-of-date content. The individual is expected, for example, to take content off old news, past events, and promotions. He or she must also take off the names of team members and management who have left and add in the names and information of any new team personnel.

Developing and designing the Web site is just one part of the job of the Webmaster. He or she is additionally responsible for the continued management and maintenance of the site.

Web sites are created in special languages so they can be displayed on the Internet. Text, for example, is converted into a language called HTML, or hypertext markup language. Other languages may be used as well. The Webmaster must know how to format the special languages. Part of the job of the Webmaster is to monitor the site on a continuing basis. Every time new content or a link is added, the individual or one of his or her assistants must be sure everything on the site is working and all links are accurate. This is often accomplished by testing each link.

The Sport Team Webmaster is expected to make sure that the site is user-friendly. When there are problems with the site, the individual is responsible for handling them. This may include responding to inquiries from browsers having problems with the site.

At times, the Webmaster may find software bugs that cause either the site or specific Web pages to have problems. The individual is responsible for repairing these bugs so the site is working perfectly.

On occasion, the Webmaster may find that the security of the site has been breached, or there are other security issues. The individual must be able to track down the problem and fix it so that site visitors can experience safe browsing.

Salaries

Earnings for Sports Team Webmasters can vary from approximately $32,000 to $86,000 or more. Factors affecting earnings include the specific team for which the individual works, as well as the size and importance to the team of their Web site.

Other factors affecting earnings include the responsibilities, professional reputation, and experience of the individual. Webmasters who are responsible for handling more than one Web site, such as those who may be in charge of handling major league and minor league teams, will generally earn more than their counterparts who are responsible only for one site.

Employment Prospects

Employment prospects are good for Sports Team Webmasters. While some teams just have one Webmaster, teams with larger sites often have more than one individual in this position. Individuals may find employment with major league teams and minor league teams in a variety of sports. They may also find employment with amateur or collegiate sports teams.

Some employers may allow their Webmasters to telecommute all or part of the time. Individuals may also find part-time or consulting positions.

Advancement Prospects

Advancement prospects are fair for Sports Team Webmasters. The most common method for advancement is to find similar positions handling the Web sites for more prestigious teams. This will result in increased responsibilities and earnings.

Some individuals advance their careers by becoming senior Webmasters for more prestigious teams. Others may become Webmasters for more than one team, resulting in responsibility for a number of sites. Some Webmasters also decide to strike out on their own and begin consulting firms.

Education and Training

Education and training requirements vary for Sports Team Webmasters. Some positions may require a formal education such as a bachelor's degree with a major in computer science or a related field. Others may not have formal educational requirements as long as individuals can demonstrate competence.

Some Webmasters are self-taught. Some have taken classes. Others have college backgrounds or degrees in computers, programming, languages, graphics, Web authoring, and the Internet.

However it is learned, Webmasters must know HTML. It is also necessary to know other programming languages such as Cold Fusion, PERL, and Active Server Pages. Knowing how to integrate databases is a plus. It is essential that Webmasters update their skills by study and/or classes, seminars, and workshops to keep up with changes in technology.

Special Requirements

Voluntary Certified Web Professional (CWP) certification is available from various industry organizations. This certification demonstrates that individuals have attained professional status in their field.

Experience, Skills, and Personality Traits

Those seeking positions with major league teams will generally be required to have a minimum of two to three years' experience either as a Webmaster or in Web application development or administration. These teams will generally also want their Webmasters to have a proven track record and experience.

Creativity is essential to the success of Webmasters. Individuals should also have excellent written and verbal communication skills. A total knowledge and understanding of computer technology is vital. An understanding of the specific sport to which the Web site is aimed is also useful.

Unions and Associations

Individuals interested in learning more about careers in the field may obtain additional information by contacting the Internet Professionals Association (IPA), the International Webmasters Association (IWA), and the World Organization of Webmasters (WOW)

Tips for Entry

1. Positions may be advertised in the classified section of newspapers in areas hosting sports teams. Look under headings such as "Webmaster," "Sports Teams," "Web Careers," and so on. In some situations, the specific team may also take out box ads in the classified section advertising many different jobs.
2. Most sports teams now have job openings posted on their Web sites. Look for sections such as "Employment," "Jobs," or "Work for Us."
3. Don't forget other online searches. Check out traditional job sites such as monster.com and hotjobs.yahoo.com. You might also want to check out some of the career sites dedicated to the sports industry or even Internet jobs.
4. Get experience by volunteering to put Web sites together for not-for-profit organizations or civic groups. Remember to add your name as the creator and Webmaster.
5. If you are still in school, look for internships. These will give you on-the-job training, experience, and the opportunity to make important contacts. Contact sports team human resource departments to see what they offer.
6. Send your résumé and a short cover letter to the human resource department of sports teams in which you might be interested in working. You never know when an opening might exist.

SPORTS TEAM WEB SITE CONTENT PRODUCER

Position Description

Almost every company today has realized the power of the Internet, and sports teams are no exception. Web sites give teams an important presence on the Web that is necessary for all sports and entertainment-based organizations.

Sports teams, like others in the sports and entertainment industry, have begun using Web sites as marketing tools. Depending on the specific team and its popularity, a Web site can get potentially thousands of hits a day. Attracting visitors to a site once is not all that difficult. Keeping them coming back on a regular basis can be a challenge.

In order to keep fans engaged, informed, and, most important, returning to the site, most teams retain Web Site Content Producers. These individuals are responsible for creating and maintaining the content of the team's Web site.

In order to be successful, Web Site Content Producers must constantly come up with fresh, innovative content that makes fans want to keep coming back to the site. As part of the job, individuals are expected to develop and execute a strategic online content plan.

Sports teams use Web sites for a number of reasons. To begin with, as noted previously, Web sites give teams the necessary presence on the Web. This presence makes it easy for fans to obtain general information on teams as well as to stay informed about timely team news and game dates. Team Web sites also give teams a simple way to sell and promote team-branded merchandise such as hats, mugs, T-shirts, jackets, and so on.

Web sites also are instrumental in helping teams build communities of fans. These communities can often dramatically help teams increase their popularity and sell tickets to games and other events.

Team Web sites also mean that if the media or anyone else needs information, it is available with a click of the mouse. In a world where people want information *now*, this can be priceless.

Web Site Content Producers are responsible for the content of every aspect of the Web site. It is essential that the team Web site is full of great information, is user-friendly, and makes people want to keep coming back. Individuals in this position are responsible for researching and writing engaging stories and articles in a variety of areas and categories. Their job is similar to that of a combination of a print journalist and editor.

Web Site Content Producers are expected to develop a variety of stories for the Web site that are of interest to fans of the team. These articles might be about the entire team, team members, sports news in general, or other news that may simply interest those visiting the site.

Sometimes these articles are short blurbs. Other times, they might be longer. The Web Site Content Producer must be sure each article will both catch the eye of those visiting the site and keep visitors' attention.

The home page is the location where most people start at the team's Web site and is the one that should entice visitors to keep exploring the site. The Web Site Content Producer must be sure the home page stays fresh and is constantly updated. No fan wants to go to a team's Web site to see what is happening and find that the news on the page is six months old.

The home page may include breaking news about the team or team members, announcements of game dates, upcoming special events and promotions, photos, and links to other information.

Other pages on the site might include bios or profiles of the team members, feature stories, reprints of interviews, stats, sports news, forums, photos, and videos. The Web Site Content Producer must be sure all copy is interesting and easy to read.

In an effort to increase interest in the team as well as giving fans a reason to visit the site, Web Site Content Producers may develop blogs, Webcasts, chats, and podcasts. These techniques help get fans involved. This in turn often leads to the opportunity to solicit positive reviews or user comments.

Web Site Content Producers often find ways to develop mailing lists of fans. They may accomplish this by using a variety of methods, including developing "contact us" forms, surveys, sweepstakes, or fan clubs. These mailing lists can be extremely valuable to sports teams. They can be used to get news out quickly, let fans know about special events, team member appearances, and so on.

Some Web Site Content Producers develop e-mail blasts that they send out to fans of the team. These may be used to get news out quickly as well.

Depending on the size, structure, and extent of the team's Web site, there may be more than one Content Producer. One may be a senior or executive Web Site Content Producer who oversees the entire site. Another may develop and monitor blogs. Still another may develop podcasts.

Some Web Site Content Producers are responsible for researching and writing feature stories, articles about the team, or doing interviews. Everything really depends on the specific team and its popularity as well as the size of the site and how comprehensive team management wants it to be.

Web Site Content Producers are often responsible for overseeing staff copywriters, photographers, and graphic artists. Some Content Producers are also responsible for finding and retaining freelancers to write articles on specific subjects or specific areas.

The Content Producer is responsible for getting all stories, editing them when necessary, and giving them to the Webmaster to put online. He or she may also be expected to arrange for photos and obtain other information such as downloads that might make interesting online stories.

One of the exciting things about the Internet is that it can be interactive. The Content Producer may develop surveys, questionnaires, or other pieces to involve those visiting the site. In some instances, the interactive part of the site may be related to promotions, games, or other happenings.

The Web Site Content Producer is often responsible for finding pictures, animation, and other graphics to make the content more appealing. He or she may use the services of graphic artists, photographers, or others to accomplish this task. The individual may work with the Webmaster, finding images that are appropriate and will look good but not affect the ease of opening the site. The Web Site Content Producer may also use videos of a winning basket, a winning home run, or even one of the team members being interviewed.

In order to keep fans coming back, it is essential that the Web Site Content Producer keep the site fresh. This is often done with daily updates. These might include game times, information on television or radio interviews, and personal appearances and promotions.

Salaries

Sports Team Web Site Content Producers can earn between $25,000 and $75,000 or more annually. Factors affecting earnings include experience, responsibilities, and the professional reputation of the individual, as well as the popularity and level of the specific team. Other variables include the size of the Web site and the importance team management places on the particular Web site.

Web Site Content Producers working for major league teams with fairly extensive Web sites will generally earn more than their counterparts handling similar duties for minor league teams.

Individuals working on a consulting basis may be paid a monthly fee ranging from $2,000 to $5,000 or more. Some are also compensated on a per project basis.

Employment Prospects

Employment prospects are fair for Web Site Content Producers. Individuals may work for professional major or minor league teams in almost every sport. These might include among others baseball, football, hockey, soccer, and basketball. Some individuals may also be employed by colleges or universities that have large prestigious sports departments.

Web Site Content Producers may also work on a consulting basis.

Advancement Prospects

Advancement prospects are fair for Web Site Content Producers working on Web sites for sports teams. Advancement prospects depend, to a great extent, on the individual's level is in his or her career.

Web Site Content Producers handling the Web sites for an amateur or collegiate sports team, for example, can climb the career ladder by finding similar positions with professional sports teams. This generally results in increased responsibilities and earnings. Those handling Web sites for minor league teams may climb the career ladder by finding similar positions with major league teams.

Some individuals become senior Web Site Content Producers.

Education and Training

While there might be exceptions, most positions require or prefer individuals to hold have a four-year college degree. Good choices for majors include journalism, communications, English, public relations, marketing, sports management or administration, or liberal arts.

Courses, workshops, and seminars in public relations, writing, promotion, journalism, the sports industry, and Web journalism will be helpful in honing skills and making new contacts.

Experience, Skills, and Personality Traits

Experience requirements for Sports Team Web Site Content Producers depend on the specific team and its popularity as well as the importance it puts on its Web site. More prestigious major league teams generally will require individuals to have more experience than those seeking positions with smaller minor league teams. Major league teams often prefer that individuals have a proven track record and a minimum of two or three years of experience developing, creating, editing, and managing Web and interactive content.

Writing and editing experience will be useful whether or not it is Web related. Web Site Content Producers need to be innovative, creative, and orga-nized. An excellent command of the English language is necessary, as are excellent communication skills, both written and verbal.

Web Site Content Producers need to be able to multitask effectively. A full understanding and working knowledge of the sports industry and its lingo are essential. Individuals must also be Internet savvy. While it may not be required, individuals who know HTML (a programming language) may have a leg up on other candidates.

Unions and Associations

Sports Team Web Site Content Producers may belong to a number of trade associations related directly to the area of sports in which they are working. Individuals may also belong to the Internet Professionals Association (IPA).

Tips for Entry

1. Positions may be advertised in the classified section of newspapers in cities hosting professional sports teams. Look under headings such as "Web Site Content Producer," "Web Site Content Manager," "Sport Team—Web Sites," "Web Sites," "Web Careers," and so on. Remember to look under the name of the specific sports teams located in the area.
2. This is the perfect type of job to look for online. Start with some of the more popular job sites such as www.hotjobs.yahoo.com and www.monster.com and go from there.
3. Jobs openings may also be located on career sites specific to the sports industry and Internet jobs.
4. Get as much experience writing as you can. If you are still in school, get involved in your school newspaper and/or Web site.
5. If you are still in school, offer to put together a Web site for your school or school's sports team. It will give you good experience and give you a line to add on your résumé.
6. Consider a part-time job for a local newspaper to get some writing experience and to build up your contacts.
7. Look for internships with sport teams. These will give you on-the-job training, experience, and the opportunity to make important contacts. Contact the human resource department to see what they offer.
8. Many sports teams advertise their openings on their Web site. Look for the section of the Web site that says "employment opportunities," "work for us," "exciting opportunities," or "jobs."

SPORTS TEAM WEB SITE MARKETING DIRECTOR

Position Description

The Internet has changed the way most of us live our lives. When we need information, most of us today look it up on the Web. To do research, we look on the Web. Information that might have taken days to locate can now be found almost instantaneously. The Internet has also changed the way companies throughout the world do business. Sports teams are no exception.

With a click of the mouse, sports fans can now easily find news, scores, stats, and more about their favorite team. They can buy tickets, shop for team merchandise, and join online communities of fans. As a result, teams not only have a Web presence, they need it to compete and market their team effectively. Individuals responsible for handling the marketing of these sites are called Web Site Marketing Directors.

Responsibilities of individuals in this position will vary depending on the specific team as well as the importance it puts on its Web site. The Sports Team Web Site Marketing Director is expected to develop the concepts and campaigns that determine how the site will be marketed and how people will be attracted. He or she is responsible for determining the most effective

techniques and programs to market the site and its contents and then find ways to implement them.

As part of the job, the Sports Team Web Site Marketing Director plans and coordinates the site's marketing goals and objectives. How will people know the Web site is online? How will they know the Web address? How will they find it? Who is the site being marketed to? What will bring them there?

Sports Team Web Site Marketing Directors may use traditional marketing techniques or may come up with innovative methods and techniques to promote and market the team's Web Site. For a very creative Web Site Marketing Director, the sky can be the limit on marketing activities.

The Sports Team Web Site Marketing Director is expected to find innovative ways to get the Web address known so that when people think of the specific sports team they can easily find it on the Web. This might be done through promotions, advertising, and/or public relations.

The Web Site Marketing Director must be sure that the team's Web address, or URL, is added to all television commercials, print advertisements, brochures, billboards, stationery, products, and branded merchandise, etc. This is important to keep the team's name and Web address in the public eye as often as possible.

The Sports Team Web Site Marketing Director will often use various forms of e-mail marketing and e-mail blasts to get people to visit the site. The individual must additionally find ways to track visitors to the site so that he or she knows what areas of the Web site people are visiting, how long they are staying, and what brought them there.

The Sports Team Web Site Marketing Director may work with the team's public relations department sending out press releases to develop ways to attract media attention that will help garner the attention of the general public. Once again, the more places the public sees the Web address, the more likely they are to remember it and visit it to see what is happening on the site.

The Web Site Marketing Director works with the team's general marketing director to coordinate marketing efforts. These might include advertisements, promotions, and publicity efforts.

Depending on the situation, the Web Site Marketing Director may decide it is advantageous to advertise the team's Web site on other Web sites. This is often done with banner ads. When an individual clicks on one of these banner ads, he or she is taken to the site of the advertiser. The individual may, for example, advertise the team's site on a local newspaper, television, or radio Web site.

The Web Site Marketing Director is expected to perform research in order to obtain information about visitors to the site. He or she may do this by preparing questionnaires or surveys placed strategically on the site. In order to entice people to answer questionnaires as well as to attract new visitors to the site, the Sports Team Web Site Marketing Director may offer gifts, discounted game tickets, or entry into sweepstakes.

The Sport Team Web Site Marketing Director may work with either internal or external promotion companies developing these contests, sweepstakes, and other promotions that can be entered online. This gives people an extra incentive to go to the team's Web site. The more people who visit the Web site, the more hits the site gets. This is important not only to increase traffic, but because many teams also charge other companies to put their online advertisements on their site.

Many Sports Team Web Site Marketing Directors also find that sweepstakes are an excellent way to build mailing lists. When people enter sweepstakes, they generally are asked to provide their name, address, phone number, age, and e-mail address. In many cases, with the enticement of possibly winning a prize, people are also often enticed to give additional information they might not normally give out.

This information is useful to the Web Site Marketing Director for a variety of reasons. It can help target what potential visitors to the site want. It can also help build information for e-mail lists, which in turn can be used for informing people about site changes, team promotions, specials on ticket sales, team news, promotions, and more.

Sports Team Web Site Marketing Directors who come up with innovative and creative ideas often get the attention of media personnel who are doing articles or television or radio pieces. If the Sports Team Web Site Marketing Director is lucky, these media pieces can literally generate hundreds of thousands of Web site hits. These hits then may turn into fans who buy game tickets or branded merchandise. These promotions can also help generate positive media exposure.

Sweepstakes or contests with large prizes, for example, may garner the attention of the media. For instance, the Sports Team Web Site Marketing Director may develop an online sweepstakes where the prize is $1 million if the winner can land a basket from a certain location on the basketball court. This promotion might grab the attention of local or regional radio, television, and print news, giving the team positive exposure. If the winner actually lands the basket, the promotion and the team stand a good chance of getting national media coverage.

One of the newer functions of Sports Team Web Site Marketing Directors is creating online communities. These may include fan forums, blogs, fan connections, chats, and more. These online communities help the team attract new fans and keep the ones they have. The trickle-down effect can mean thousands of dollars in ticket sales, merchandise sales, media exposure, and more. The individual may work on this with a Web site content producer or an individual who is specifically responsible for solely handling the online fan community.

Depending on the specific team and structure, the Web Site Marketing Director may be responsible to the team's general marketing director or VP of marketing. In some situations, he or she may handle both the responsibilities of the team's traditional and online marketing. This is often the case, for example, with a smaller minor league team. Sometimes the Sports Team Web Site Marketing Director may also be responsible for handling the marketing activities of all of the team franchise's Web sites.

Salaries

Earnings of Sports Team Web Site Marketing Directors can range from approximately $35,000 to $75,000 or more annually. Factors affecting earnings include the specific team for which the individual works, its popularity, and the importance that team puts on its Web site. Other variables include the experience, reputation, and responsibilities of the Web Site Marketing Director.

Individuals who are responsible for more than one site will generally earn more than their counterparts handling the marketing activities of only one site. Those working for popular major league teams will also have higher earnings than those working for minor league, collegiate, or amateur teams.

Employment Prospects

Employment prospects are fair for Sports Team Web Site Marketing Directors. Individuals may find employment with major league, minor league, amateur, and collegiate sports teams throughout the country.

Positions with collegiate or amateur teams may be part time. It should also be noted that in some situations, the duties of the Web Site Marketing Director may be outsourced.

Positions may be located throughout the country in areas hosting sports teams. Individuals working for major league sports teams may be required to work in the corporate office. Some jobs may also allow the Web Site Marketing Directors to telecommute all or part of the time.

Advancement Prospects

Advancement prospects for Sport Team Web Site Marketing Directors are fair. Individuals may climb the career ladder in a number of ways depending on their career aspirations. Some may find similar positions with larger or more prestigious sports teams. Others are promoted to the general marketing directors or VP of marketing for larger sports teams.

Individuals may also climb the career ladder by finding similar positions in other industries. Some individuals may also strike out on their own and start their own marketing firms.

Education and Training

Sports Team Web Site Marketing Directors generally are required to hold a minimum of a four-year college degree. Good choices for majors include marketing, public relations, advertising, journalism, liberal arts, English, communications, business, sports admin-

istration, or a related field. Classes, seminars, and workshops in general marketing, promotion, Web marketing, sports marketing, publicity, and public relations will be helpful in honing skills and making important contacts.

Experience, Skills, and Personality Traits

Experience requirements for Sports Team Web Site Marketing Directors vary depending on the specific position. Major league teams generally require their Web Site Marketing Directors to have more experience than other teams do.

Individuals working as Sports Team Web Site Marketing Directors need to have the same skills as traditional marketing directors and an understanding of Web marketing. In order to be successful, they need to be creative, innovative, ambitious, articulate, and highly motivated. Excellent written and verbal communications skills are also essential. A full knowledge of publicity, promotion, public relations, advertising, and research techniques is necessary. The ability to multitask without getting flustered is needed.

An understanding of the specific sport to which the Web site is targeted is essential.

Unions and Associations

Sports Team Web Site Marketing Directors may belong to a number of trade associations, including the Web Marketing Association (WMA), the American Marketing Association (AMA), the Marketing Research Association (MRA), and the Public Relations Society of America (PRSA). These organizations provide professional support to members and often offer networking opportunities. Individuals may also belong to associations geared to the specific sports their Web site targets.

Tips for Entry

1. Positions are often advertised in the classified section of newspapers in areas hosting sports teams. Look under headings such as "Marketing," "Marketing Director," "Marketing Manager," "Website Marketing," "Website Marketing Director," "Sports Teams," or "Sports Team Web Site Marketing Director."
2. Positions may also be located online. Start off by checking out some of the more popular career sites such as monster.com and hotjobs.yahoo.com as well as career sites specific to the sports industry and the Web.
3. Remember to check out sports teams Web sites. Many post openings.

4. Search firms, headhunters, and recruiters specific to the sports industry, marketing, and Web industries.
5. Look for seminars, workshops, and courses in marketing, promotion, public relations, publicity, Web marketing, and the sports industry. These are good opportunities to help you hone skills as well as making valuable contacts.

ADVERTISING ACCOUNT EXECUTIVE—SPORTS-ORIENTED WEB SITE

CAREER PROFILE

Duties: Selling advertising on sports-oriented Web site; meeting with potential customers; sending out advertising and rate kits; developing promotions to help sell more advertising; preparing buy orders; keeping records of sales

Alternate Title(s): Account Executive; Advertising Account Representative; Rep.; Sales Rep; Advertising Rep; Sales Representative

Salary Range: $25,000 to $100,000+

Employment Prospects: Good

Advancement Prospects: Good

Best Geographical Location(s) for Position: Positions may be located throughout country

Prerequisites:

   Education or Training—Educational requirements vary; minimum of high school diploma; college background or degree required or preferred by many employers; see text

CAREER LADDER

Sales Manager or Advertising Account Executive for Larger, More Prestigious Sports-Oriented Web Site

↑

Advertising Account Executive— Sports-Oriented Web Site

↑

Entry Level or Sales Position in Other Industry

Experience—Experience in sales helpful but not always required

Special Skills and Personality Traits—Persuasiveness; articulate; self-motivated; aggressiveness; personable; outgoing nature; understanding of area of sports industry Web site targets

Position Description

The World Wide Web has created an array of opportunities for businesses. Every day more and more sports-oriented companies are getting a presence there. Some of these are established businesses that just want to be sure that they have an important Internet presence. Others are companies and businesses that were created solely for the Internet. There are large companies, small companies, and everything in between.

Some Web sites sell merchandise such as sports memorabilia, sporting goods, fitness equipment, magazines, books, and so on. Other Web sites sell tickets to games or tournaments. Some sell sports-branded merchandise such as T-shirts, jackets, or hats. Some Web sites are informational.

Virtually every sports team has its own Web site. So do sports-oriented radio stations, television and cable stations, and sports-oriented television programs. There are superstar sports Web sites, fan sites, and more. Many sports agents, promoters, management companies, agencies, and other companies also have their own

sites. So do sports-oriented trade associations, leagues, and other organizations.

Whether a Web site is selling merchandise or services, promoting its company, or providing information, many are now finding additional ways to use their site to generate income by selling advertising space on the site.

The individual in charge of selling advertising on the Web site is called the Advertising Account Executive. He or she may also be referred to as an account rep, salesperson, sales rep, advertising account rep, or advertising rep. Depending on the size and structure of the specific Web site, there may be one or more Advertising Account Executives selling ads on the site.

The Advertising Account Executive may be assigned accounts or may be expected to find potential advertisers on his or her own. In some cases, the Web site itself may have a banner or text inviting potential companies to advertise.

If the sports-oriented Web site is well known, potential advertisers often contact the site itself to get information about advertising opportunities. They may inquire about the site, demographics, and advertising rates. Depending on the structure of the Web site, calls may go directly to a sales manager or marketing manager who in turn will refer them to the appropriate Account Executive.

Advertising Account Executives working for sports-oriented Web sites have a number of responsibilities. They are responsible for selling advertising. Selling advertising on Web sites may have certain challenges other Advertising Account Executives may not have. The individuals in these cases must be able to prove to potential advertisers the popularity of the site and how many hits it gets. This is often a difficult task.

Advertising Account Executives must also be able to demonstrate to potential advertisers the demographics of the people who visit their site. They must be able to prove the exposure that the Web site gets and what that exposure can give to a potential advertiser.

Web Site Advertising Account Executives specializing in the sports industry use a variety of methods to sell ads on their Web site. Some set up meetings and go to visit potential advertisers in person. Others call advertisers. Still others use the Internet and e-mail to prospect for advertisers. For example, many Account Executives selling space on sports-oriented Web sites send out e-mail blasts trying to solicit advertisers. Some e-mail reader surveys or even articles to potential clients on how advertising on the particular site has increased another advertiser's business.

If the site is very well known, selling advertising is often easier. For example, if the Web site is that of an established television sports channel or sports show, the Advertising Account Executive is selling a known commodity. Other advertisers know people interested in sports visit those sites. If the site is not very well known, the Advertising Account Executive needs to find ways to prove the importance of the site to advertisers.

Once the Advertising Account Executive contacts potential advertisers, he or she is responsible for sending out advertising or rate kits. This may be done via traditional mail or through e-mail. These kits may contain things like rate cards, informational sheets on the Web site, demographics, testimonials from other advertisers, etc.

Advertising Account Executives often schedule appointments with potential clients to discuss advertising needs. Because advertisers on the World Wide Web might be almost anywhere, meetings may be in person, on the phone, or via e-mail. Depending on the specific advertiser, the Advertising Account Executive may deal directly with a client or may deal with the client's advertising agency.

A major function of a Sports-Oriented Web Site Advertising Account Executive is bringing in new business. The individual may make what are known as cold calls to potential advertisers. These calls are made to people who have not advertised on the site. After identifying him- or herself and the site's affiliation, the Account Executive attempts to set up an appointment to tell the potential advertiser more about the Web site and advertising opportunities. Not every call will result in an appointment. The Advertising Account Executives must have the ability to accept rejection without taking it personally.

Advertising Account Executives must have a complete knowledge of the Web site. He or she must know the demographics of the visitors to the site, how long the site has been in existence, other advertisers, competitive sites, and so on. This information can help the Advertising Account Executive illustrate how advertising on his or her site can benefit a potential advertiser.

In order to entice new advertisers to try advertising on the Web site, the Advertising Account Executive may offer a variety of promotions and discounts. The individual may also offer specials, promotions, and discounts to established accounts in order to tempt them to advertise more as well.

Some of these promotions are developed by the sales manager or the marketing manager. In other cases, the Account Executive may help develop marketing and advertising ideas for current or potential customers. These may include sweepstakes or co-op ads. Individuals also often brainstorm with clients to come up with effective advertising ideas. The more effective ads are, the more advertising customers will purchase in the future.

It is essential that Advertising Account Executives be aware of all the promotions and stay up to date on various rates, discounts, and advertising packages offered. He or she must also be able to explain all of these to advertisers.

To be a successful Web Site Advertising Account Executive the individual must find ways to not only sell an advertiser one ad, but to build a lasting business relationship. He or she can do this by explaining promotions, putting together the best package possible, and servicing the account. The individual also must continually check with clients to be sure they are happy with their ads and are being billed properly.

Sports-Oriented Web Site Advertising Account Executives are expected to keep accurate records of advertisements sold, billings, and so on. Individuals are responsible for writing orders and making sure that they get to the appropriate department at the Web site.

Unlike some traditional print ads, Web advertising often has limitations and options. In some cases, the Web Site Advertising Account Executive may offer suggestions to advertisers for copy, ad content, or design. As large graphics may slow down a site, the Advertising Account Executive may, for example, suggest ad graphics be specially sized and created to allow the Web site and the ad to open quickly.

Depending on the situation and the site, the individual may sometimes suggest a banner ad on the site. With this type of ad, a visitor need only hit the banner on the site to be taken to the advertiser's site.

One of the responsibilities of the Web Site Advertising Account Executive is to determine how long an advertiser wants to run a specific ad. He or she may also help establish when the advertiser wants his or her ad changed. With Web advertising, it is relatively easy to change online ads quickly. It is up to the Advertising Account Executive to know which ads need to be put up on the site and when.

Salaries

Annual earnings for Web Site Advertising Account Executives working for a sports-oriented company can range from $25,000 to $100,000 or more depending on a number of variables. These include the size, prestige, and popularity of the Web site. Other variables include the sales ability of the Advertising Account Executive. Individuals who sell more earn more. The reason many people love this type of job so much is that the sky is the limit on earnings. Most Advertising Account Executives are paid on a commission basis. This means that for every dollar of advertising that an individual sells, he or she receives a percentage as part of his or her salary. Percentages can vary from company to company and generally range from 10% to 20%, with the average commission about 15%.

Some companies offer a weekly or monthly draw against salary for the Advertising Account Executive. They do this for a number of reasons. It is helpful for beginning Advertising Account Executives to get into the swing of selling. It also adjusts the take-home pay of individuals in case they had a bad week or month.

Employment Prospects

Employment prospects are good for Web Site Advertising Account Executives who want to work with sports-oriented Web sites and are getting better all the time as more and more sites open. Individuals who are sales-oriented, pleasantly aggressive, and hardworking are always in demand for sales positions.

Jobs may be located throughout the country. In some cases, companies allow people in this job to telecommute either all or part of the time.

Advancement Prospects

Advancement prospects are good for aggressive, hardworking Advertising Account Executives. Some individuals climb the career ladder by selling more advertisements, increasing their earnings. Others find similar positions working for larger, more prestigious and more popular sports-oriented Web sites. Some become sales managers. Still others move into selling either print advertising or advertising in another industry.

Education and Training

Educational requirements vary from job to job for Advertising Account Executives working for sports-oriented Web sites. Generally, companies require a minimum of a high school diploma or GED. Many prefer or require a college degree or background. Educational requirements are often waived by the employer if the applicant is eager, aggressive, and shows potential for selling.

Courses that might prove useful in selling include advertising, sales, business, English, psychology, sociology, writing, and communications. Seminars and workshops in selling and various areas of the sports industry may also be helpful.

Experience, Skills, and Personality Traits

Experience requirements vary from company to company. Some Web sites will hire individuals with no experience but who illustrate a desire to sell. Other Web sites require their Advertising Account Executives to have some sales experience.

Advertising Account Executives selling for a sports-oriented Web site need to understand the area of the sports industry for which the site is geared. Sales skills are critical. Individuals should be articulate with excellent verbal and written communications skills. An understanding of Web sites, the Internet, graphics, types, etc., is also necessary.

Advertising Account Executives need to be personable, outgoing, and pleasantly aggressive. Self-motivation and the ability to work without constant supervision are mandatory.

Advertising Account Executives must be able to plan out their workday, make appointments and calls, and go to appointments without someone looking over their shoulders. The ability to work with numbers is helpful in figuring out costs and rates of ads and packages.

Unions and Associations

Advertising Account Executives selling ads for a sports-oriented Web site may belong to a trade association specific to the area of the sports industry for which the site is focused. Individuals may also get additional career information from the American Advertising Federation (AAF).

Tips for Entry

1. Many sports-oriented Web sites offer internships. Internships give you on-the-job training, experience, and the opportunity to make important contacts.

2. Many Web sites advertise job openings themselves. Check them out.

3. Send your résumé and a short cover letter to sports-oriented Web sites asking about job openings. Request that your résumé be kept on file if there are no current openings.

4. Remember to check traditional job sites such as monster.com and hotjobs.yahoo.com as well as job sites specific to the sports industry and sales jobs for openings.

5. Jobs may also be located in traditional newspaper classified ads. Look under heading classifications such as "Account Executive," "Web Site Jobs," "Sales," "Sports Industry," and "Advertising Account Executive."

APPENDIXES

APPENDIX I
DEGREE PROGRAMS

A. COLLEGES AND UNIVERSITIES OFFERING DEGREES IN SPORTS ADMINISTRATION

The following is a selected listing of four-year schools granting degrees in sports administration and management. They are grouped by state. School names, addresses, phone numbers, Web addresses, and e-mail addresses are included when available.

The author does not endorse any one school over another. Use this list as a beginning. Check the reference section of libraries or guidance counseling centers for additional schools offering degrees in this field.

ALABAMA

Columbia Southern University
25326 Canal Road
Orange Beach, AL 36561
Phone: (251) 981-3771
Fax: (251) 224-0540
E-mail: admissions@columbia
    southern.edu
http://www.columbiasouthern.edu

Faulkner University
5345 Atlanta Highway
Montgomery, AL 36109
Phone: (334) 386-7200
Fax: (334) 386-7137
http://www.faulkner.edu

Huntingdon College
1500 East Fairview Avenue
Montgomery, AL 36106
Phone: (334) 833-4497
Fax: (334) 833-4347
E-mail: admiss@huntingdon.edu
http://www.huntingdon.edu

Troy University
111 Adams Administration Building
Troy, AL 36082
Phone: (334) 670-3179
http://www.troy.edu

ARIZONA

Grand Canyon University
3300 West Camelback Road
P.O. Box 11097
Phoenix, AZ 86017
Phone: (800) 486-7085
http://www.gcu.edu

ARKANSAS

Arkansas State University
P.O. Box 1630
State University, AR 72467
Phone: (870) 972-3024
Fax: (870) 910-3406
E-mail: admissions@astate.edu
http://www.astate.edu

Harding University
P.O. Box 12255
Searcy, AR 72149
Phone: (501) 279-4407
Fax: (501) 279-4129
E-mail: admissions@harding.edu
http://www.harding.edu

Henderson State University
1100 Henderson Street
P.O. Box 7560
Arkadelphia, AR 71999
Phone: (870) 230-5028
Fax: (870) 230-5066
E-mail: hardwrv@hsu.edu
http://www.hsu.edu

CALIFORNIA

Fresno Pacific University
1717 South Chestnut Avenue
Fresno, CA 93727
Phone: (800) 660-6089
Fax: (559) 453-2007
E-mail: ugadmis@fresno.edu
http://www.fresno.edu

National University
11255 North Torrey Pines Road
La Jolla, CA 92037
Phone: (858) 628-8648
E-mail: advisor@nu.edu
http://www.nu.edu

Saint Mary's College of California
P.O. Box 4800
Moraga, CA 94556
Phone: (925) 631-4224
Fax: (925) 376-7193
E-mail: smcadmit@stmarys-ca.edu
http://www.stmarys-ca.edu

COLORADO

Fort Lewis College
1000 Rim Drive
Durango, CO 81301
Phone: (970) 247-7184
http://www.fortlewis.edu

Mesa State College
1100 North Avenue
Grand Junction, CO 81501
Phone: (970) 248-1802
Fax: (970) 248-1973
E-mail: admissions@mesastate.edu
http://www.mesastate.edu

Western State College of Colorado
600 North Adams Street
Gunnison, CO 81231
Phone: (800) 876-5309
E-mail: admissions@western.edu
http://www.western.edu

CONNECTICUT

Eastern Connecticut State University
83 Windham Street
Willimantic, CT 06336
Phone: 860-465-5286
Toll-free: 877-353-3278
Fax: 860-465-5544
E-mail: admissions@easternct.edu
http://www.easternct.edu

Mitchell College
437 Pequot Avenue
New London, CT 06320
Phone: (800) 443-2811
Fax: (860) 444-1209
E-mail: admissions@mitchell.edu
http://www.mitchell.edu

Sacred Heart University
5151 Park Avenue
Fairfield, CT 06825
Phone: (203) 371-7880
E-mail: guastellek@sacredheart.edu
http://www.sacredheart.edu

DELAWARE

Delaware State University
1200 North DuPont Highway
Dover, DE 19901-2277
Phone: (302) 857-6351
Fax: (302) 857-6908
E-mail: gcheatha@desu.edu
http://www.desu.edu

University of Delaware
116 Hullihen Hall
Newark, DE 19716
Phone: (302) 831-8123
Fax: (302) 831-6905
E-mail: admissions@udel.edu
http://www.udel.edu

Wilmington University
320 North DuPont Highway
New Castle, DE 19720
Phone: (302) 356-6745
Fax: (302) 328-5902
http://www.wilmu.edu

FLORIDA

Barry University
11300 Northeast Second Avenue
Miami Shores, FL 33161
Phone: (305) 899-3100
Fax: (305) 899-2971
E-mail: admissions@mail.barry.edu
http://www.barry.edu

Flagler College
P.O. Box 1027
St. Augustine, FL 32085
Phone: (904) 819-6220
Fax: (904) 819-6466
http://www.flagler.edu

Florida State University
Tallahassee, FL 32306
Phone: (850) 644-2525
E-mail: admissions@admin.fsu.edu
http://www.fsu.edu

Northwood University, Florida Campus
2600 North Military Trail
West Palm Beach, FL 33409
Phone: (561) 478-5500
E-mail: fladmit@northwood.edu
http://www.northwood.edu

Nova Southeastern University
3301 College Avenue
Fort Lauderdale, FL 33314
Phone: (954) 262-8000
E-mail: admissions@nova.edu
http://www.nova.edu/admissions

Saint Leo University
P.O. Box 6665
Saint Leo, FL 33574
Phone: (352) 588-8283
Fax: (352) 588-8257
E-mail: admission@saintleo.edu
http://www.saintleo.edu

Stetson University
Unit 8378
Griffith Hall
DeLand, FL 32723
Phone: (386) 822-7100
Fax: (386) 822-7112
E-mail: admissions@stetson.edu
http://www.stetson.edu

University of Florida
P.O. Box 114000
Gainesville, FL 32611
Phone: (352) 392-3261
E-mail: freshman@ufl.edu
http://www.ufl.edu

University of Miami
P.O. Box 248025
Coral Gables, FL 33124
Phone: (305) 284-2211
E-mail: admission@miami.edu
http://www.miami.edu

University of North Florida
4567 St. Johns Bluff Road South
Jacksonville, FL 32224
Phone: (904) 620-2624
Fax: (904) 620-2014
E-mail: admissions@unf.edu
http://www.unf.edu

University of Tampa
401 West Kennedy Boulevard
Tampa, FL 33606
Phone: (813) 253-6211
Fax: (813) 254-4955
E-mail: admissions@ut.edu
http://www.ut.edu

Webber International University
1201 North Scenic Highway
P.O. Box 96
Babson Park, FL 33827
Phone: (863) 638-2910
E-mail: admissions@webber.edu
http://www.webber.edu

GEORGIA

Georgia Southern University
Forest Drive
Statesboro, GA 30460

Phone: (912) 681-5391
Fax: (912) 486-7240
E-mail: admissions@
    georgiasouthern.edu
http://www.georgiasouthern.edu

Kennesaw State University
1000 Chastain Road
Kennesaw, GA 30144
Phone: (770) 423-6300
Fax: (770) 420-4435
E-mail ksuadmit@ksumail.
    kennesaw.edu
http://www.kennesaw.edu

Reinhardt College
7300 Reinhardt College Circle
Waleska, GA 30183
Phone: (770) 720-5526
Fax: (770) 720-5602
E-mail: admissions@mail.reinhardt.
    edu
http://www.reinhardt.edu/

University of Georgia
Athens, GA 30602
Phone: (706) 542-8776
Fax: (706) 542-1466
E-mail: undergrad@admissions.
    uga.edu
http://www.uga.edu

IDAHO

College of Idaho
2112 Cleveland Boulevard
Caldwell, ID 83605
Phone: (208) 459-5689
http://www.collegeofidaho.edu

ILLINOIS

Elmhurst College
190 Prospect Avenue
Elmhurst, IL 60126
Phone: (630) 617-3400
E-mail: admit@elmhurst.edu
http://www.elmhurst.edu

Judson University
1151 North State Street
Elgin, IL 60123
Phone: (847) 695-2522

Fax: (847) 628-2526
E-mail: bdean@judsoncollege.edu
http://wwwjudsoncollege.edu

Lewis University
One University Parkway
Romeoville, IL 60446
Phone: (800) 897-9000
E-mail: admissions@lewisu.edu
http://www.lewisu.edu

Millikin University
1184 West Main Street
Decatur, IL 62522
Phone: (217) 424-6210
Fax: (217) 425-4669
E-mail: admis@millikin.edu
http://www.millikin.edu

North Central College
30 North Brainard Street
Naperville, IL 60540
Phone: (630) 637-5800
Fax: (630) 637-5819
E-mail: ncadm@noctrl.edu
http://www.northcentralcollege.edu

Olivet Nazarene University
One University Avenue
Bourbonnais, IL 60914
Phone: (800) 648-1463
E-mail: admissions@olivet.edu
http://www.olivet.edu

Quincy University
Quincy, IL 62301
Phone: (217) 228-5210
E-mail: admissions@quincy.edu
http://www.quncy.edu

**University of Illinois—Urbana-
    Champaign**
901 West Illinois
Urbana, IL 61801
Phone: (217) 333-1000
E-mail: admissions@oar.uiuc.edu
http://www.uiuc.edu

INDIANA

Ball State University
2000 University Avenue
Muncie, IN 47306

Phone: (765) 285-8300
E-mail: askus@bsu.edu
http://www.bsu.edu

Bethel College
1001 West McKinley Avenue
Mishawaka, IN 46545
Phone: (574) 257-3339
Fax: (574) 257-3335
E-mail: admissions@bethelcollege.
    edu
http://www.bethelcolleg.edu

Grace College
200 Seminary Drive
Winona Lake, IN 46590
Phone: (574) 372-5100
Fax: (574) 372-5120
http://www.grace.edu

**Indiana University
    Bloomington**
300 North Jordan Avenue
Bloomington, IN 47405
Phone: (812) 855-0661
Fax: (812) 855-5102
E-mail: iuadmit@indiana.edu
http://www.indiana.edu

Marian College
3200 Cold Spring Road
Indianapolis, IN 46222
Phone: (317) 955-6300
Fax: (317) 955-6401
E-mail: admissions@marian.edu
http://www.marian.edu

Taylor University
236 West Reade Avenue
Upland, IN 46989
Phone: (765) 998-5511
E-mail: admissions@taylor.edu
http://www.taylor.edu

Trine University
One University Avenue
Angola, IN 46703
Phone: (260) 665-4100
E-mail: admit@trine.edu
http://trine.edu

University of Evansville
1800 Lincoln Avenue

Evansville, IN 47722
Phone: (812) 488-2468
Fax: (812) 488-4076
E-mail: admission@evansville.edu
http://www.evansville.edu

University of Indianapolis
1400 East Hanna Avenue
Indianapolis, IN 46227
Phone: (317) 788-3216
Fax: (317) 788-3300
E-mail: admission@uindy.edu
http://uindy.edu

Valparaiso University
Valparaiso, IN 46383
Phone: (219) 464-5011
Fax: (219) 464-6898
E-mail: undergrad.admissions@
valpo.edu
http://www.valpo.edu

IOWA

Buena Vista University
610 West Fourth Street
Storm Lake, IA 50588
Phone: (712) 749-2235
E-mail: admissions@bvu.edu
http://www.bvu.edu

Clarke College
1550 Clarke Drive
Dubuque, IA 52001
Phone: (563) 588-6316
Fax: (319)588-6789
E-mail: admissions@clarke.edu
http://www.clarke.edu

Iowa Wesleyan College
601 North Main Street
Mount Pleasant, IA 52641
Phone: (319) 385-6230
Fax: (319) 385-6240
http://www.iwc.edu

Loras College
1450 Alta Vista
Dubuque, IA 52004
Phone: (563) 588-7829
Fax: (563) 588-7119
http://www.loras.edu

Simpson College
701 North C Street
Indianola, IA 50125
Phone: (515) 961-1624
E-mail: admiss@simpson.edu
http://www.simpson.edu

St. Ambrose University
518 West Locust Street
Davenport, IA 52803
Phone: (563) 333-6300
E-mail: admit@sau.edu
http://www.sau.edu

University of Iowa
Iowa City, IA 52242
Phone: (319) 335-3847
Fax: (319) 335-1535
E-mail: admissions@uiowa.edu
http://www.uiowa.edu

Wartburg College
100 Wartburg Boulevard
P.O. Box 1003
Waverly, IA 50677
Phone: (319) 352-8264
Fax: (319) 352-8579
E-mail: admissions@wartburg.edu
http://www.wartburg.edu

William Penn University
201 Trueblood Avenue
Oskaloosa, IA 52577
Phone: (641) 673-1012
Fax: (641) 673-2113
http://www.wmpenn.edu

KENTUCKY

Alice Lloyd College
100 Purpose Road
Pippa Passes, KY 48144
Phone: (606) 368-6036
Fax: (606) 368-6215
http://www.alc.edu

Asbury College
Wilmore, KY 40390
Phone: (859) 858-3511
Fax: (859) 858-3921
http://www.asbury.edu

Kentucky Wesleyan College
3000 Frederica Street
Owensboro, KY 42301
Phone: (270) 852-3120
Fax: (270) 852-3133
http://www.kwc.edu

Midway College
512 East Stephens Street
Midway, KY 40347
Phone: (859) 846-5799
http://www.midway.edu

Morehead State University
100 Admissions Center
Morehead, KY 40351
Phone: (606) 783-2000
Fax: (606) 783-5038
http://www.moreheadstate.edu

Northern Kentucky University
Highland Heights, KY 41099
Phone: (859)572-5220
E-mail: admitnku@nku.edu
http://www.nku.edu

Thomas More College
333 Thomas More Parkway
Crestview Hills, KY 41017
Phone: (859) 344-3332
E-mail: billy.sarge@thomasmore.
edu
http://www.thomasmore.edu

Union College
310 College Street
Barbourville, KY 40906
Phone: (606) 546-1222
Fax: (606) 546-1667
http://www.unionky.edu

University of Louisville
2211 South Brook
Louisville, KY 40292
Phone: (502) 852-6531
Fax: (502) 852-4776
http://louisville.edu

Western Kentucky University
1906 College Heights Boulevard
Bowling Green, KY 42101
Phone: (270) 745-2551
Fax: (270) 745-6133

E-mail: admission@wku.edu
http://www.wku.edu

LOUISIANA

Louisiana State University and Agricultural and Mechanical College
Baton Rouge, LA 70803
Phone: (225) 578-1175
http://louisiana.stateuniversity.com

MAINE

Husson College
One College Circle
Bangor, ME 04401
Phone: (207) 941-7100
Fax: (207) 941-7935
E-mail: admit@husson.edu
http://www.husson.edu

Saint Joseph's College of Maine
278 Whites Bridge Road
Standish, ME 04084
Phone: (207) 893-7746
Fax: (207) 893-7862
E-mail: admissions@sjcme.edu
http://www.sjcme.edu

Thomas College
180 West River Road
Waterville, ME 04901
Phone: (207) 859-1101
Fax: (207) 859-1114
E-mail: its@thomas.edu
http://www.thomas.edu

University of New England
Hills Beach Road
Biddeford, ME 04005
Phone: (207) 283-0170
Fax: (207)602-5900
http://www.une.edu

MARYLAND

Coppin State University
2500 West North Avenue
Baltimore, MD 21216
Phone: (410) 951-3600
Fax: (410) 523-7351
http://www.coppin.edu

Frostburg State University
101 Braddock Road
Frostburg, MD 21532
Phone: (301) 687-4201
Fax: (301) 687-7074
E-mail: fsuadmissions@frostburg.edu
http://www.frostburg.edu

Morgan State University
Cold Spring Lane and Hillen Road
Baltimore, MD 21251
Phone: (443) 885-3000
http://www.morgan.edu

Mount St. Mary's University
16300 Old Emmitsburg Road
Emmitsburg, MD 21727
Phone: (301) 447-5214
Fax: (301) 447-5860
http://www.msmary.edu

Towson University
8000 York Road
Towson, MD 21252
Phone: (410) 704-2113
Fax: (410) 704-3030
http://www.towson.edu

MASSACHUSETTES

Anna Maria College
Box O, Sunset Lane
Paxton, MA 01612
Phone: (508) 849-3360
Fax: (508) 849-3362
E-mail: admissions@annamaria.edu
http://www.annamaria.edu

Becker College
61 Sever Street
Worcester, MA 01609
Phone: (508) 791-9241
Fax: (508) 890-1500
E-mail: admissions@beckercollege.edu
http://www.beckercollege.edu

Bridgewater State College
Bridgewater, MA 02325
Phone: (508) 531-1237
Fax: (508) 531-1746

E-mail: admission@bridgew.edu
http://www.bridgew.edu

Endicott College
376 Hale Street
Beverly, MA 01915
Phone: (978) 921-1000
Fax: (978) 232-2520
E-mail: admissio@endicott.edu
http://www.endicott.edu

Fitchburg State College
160 Pearl Street
Fitchburg, MA 01420
Phone: (978) 665-3140
Fax: (978) 665-4540
http://www.fsc.edu

Mount Ida College
777 Dedham Street
Newton, MA 02459
Phone: (617) 928-4553
http://www.mountida.edu

Nichols College
124 Center Road
Dudley, MA 01571
Phone: (508) 213-2203
Fax: (508) 943-9885
http://www.nichols.edu

Salem State College
352 Lafayette Street
Salem, MA 01970
Phone: (978) 542-6200
Fax: (978) 542-6893
http://www.salemstate.edu

Springfield College
263 Alden Street
Box M
Springfield, MA 01109
Phone: (413) 748-3136
Fax: (413) 748-3694
E-mail: admissions@spfldcol.edu
http://www.spfldcol.edu

University of Massachusetts, Amherst
37 Mather Drive
Amherst, MA01003
Phone: (413) 545-0222
Fax: (413) 545-4312
http://www.umass.edu

Western New England College
1215 Wilbraham Road
Springfield, MA 01119
Phone: (413) 782-1321
Fax: (413) 782-1777
E-mail: ugradmis@wnec.edu
http://www.wnec.edu

MICHIGAN

Calvin College
3201 Burton Street, SE
Grand Rapids, MI 49546
Phone: (616) 526-6106
Fax: (616) 526-6777
E-mail: admissions@calvin.edu
http://www.calvin.edu

Central Michigan University
Mount Pleasant, MI 48859
Phone: (989) 774-3076
E-mail: cmuadmit@cmich.edu
http://www.cmich.edu

Lake Superior State University
650 West Easterday Avenue
Sault Saint Marie, MI 49783
Phone: (906) 635-2231
Fax: (906) 635-6669
E-mail: admissions@lssu.edu
http://www.lssu.edu

Madonna University
36600 Schoolcraft Road
Livonia, MI 48150
Phone: (734) 432-5317
Fax: (734) 432-5393
E-mail: muinfo@madonna.edu
http://www.madonna.edu

Northern Michigan University
1401 Presque Isle Avenue
Marquette, MI 49855
Phone: (906) 227-2650
Fax: (906) 227-1747
E-mail: admiss@nmu.edu
http://www.nmu.edu

Olivet College
320 South Main Street
Olivet, MI 49076
Phone: (269)749-7635
http://www.olivetcollege.edu

Rochester College
800 West Avon Road
Rochester Hills, MI 48307
Phone: (248) 218-2190
Fax: (248) 218-2035
http://www.rc.edu

Siena Heights University
1247 East Siena Heights Drive
Adrian, MI 49221
Phone: (517) 264-7180
E-mail: sjohnson@sienaheights.edu
http://www.sienaheights.edu

Spring Arbor University
106 East Main Street
Spring Arbor, MI 49283
Phone: (517) 750-1200
Fax: (517) 750-6620
E-mail: admissions@arbor.edu
http://www.arbor.edu

University of Michigan
515 East Jefferson
Ann Arbor, MI 48109
Phone: (734) 764-7433
Fax: (734) 936-0740
E-mail: ugadmiss@umich.edu
http://www.umich.edu

MINNESOTA

Crown College
8700 College View Drive
St. Bonifacius, MN 55375
Phone: (952) 446-4144
Fax: (952) 446-4149
http://www.crown.edu

Minnesota State University, Mankato
122 Taylor Center
Mankato, MN 56001
Phone: (507) 389-6670
Fax: (507) 389-1511
E-mail: admissions@mnsu.edu
http://www.mnsu.edu

Minnesota State University, Moorhead
Owens Hall
Moorhead, MN 56563
Phone: (218) 477-2161

Fax: (218) 477-4374
E-mail: dragon@mnstate.edu
http://www.mnstate.edu

North Central University
910 Elliot Avenue
Minneapolis, MN 55404
Phone: (612) 343-4460
Fax: (612) 343-4146
E-mail: admissions@northcentral.edu
http://www.northcentral.edu

University of Minnesota, Crookston
2900 University Avenue
Crookston, MN 56716
Phone: (218) 281-8569
Fax: (218) 281-8575
E-mail: info@UMCrookston.edu
http://www.crk.umn.edu

Winona State University
P.O. Box 5838
Winona, MN 55987
Phone: (507) 457-5100
Fax: (507) 457-5620
E-mail: admissions@winona.edu
http://www.winona.edu

MISSISSIPPI

Belhaven College
150 Peachtree Street
Jackson, MS 39202
Phone: (601) 968-5940
Fax: (601) 968-8946
E-mail: admission@belhaven.edu
http://www.belhaven.edu

Mississippi College
P.O. Box 4026
200 South Capitol Street
Clinton, MS 39058
Phone: (601) 925-3800
Fax: (601) 925-3804
E-mail: enrollment-services@mc.edu
http://www.mc.edu

MISSOURI

Culver-Stockton College
Canton, MO 63435

Phone: (800) 537-1883
E-mail: enrollment@culver.edu
http://www.culver.edu

Drury University
900 North Benton
Springfield, MO 65802
Phone: (417) 873-7205
Fax: (417) 866-3873
E-mail: druryad@drury.edu
http://www.drury.edu

Fontbonne University
6800 Wydown Boulevard
St. Louis, MO 63105
Phone: (314) 889-1400
Fax: (314) 889-1451
E-mail: pmusen@fontbonne.edu
http://www.fontbonne.edu

Lindenwood University
209 South Kings Highway
St. Charles, MO 63301
Phone: (636) 949-4949
Fax: (636) 949-4989
http://www.lindenwood.edu

Maryville University of Saint Louis
650 Maryville University Drive
St. Louis, MO 63141
Phone: (314) 529-9350
Fax: (314) 529-9927
http://www.maryville.edu

Missouri Baptist University
One College Park Drive
St. Louis, MO 63141
Phone: (877) 434-1115
Fax: (314) 434-7596
http://www.mobap.edu

Northwest Missouri State University
800 University Drive
Maryville, MO 64468
Phone: (660) 562-1146
E-mail: admissions@nwmissouri.edu
http://www.nwmissouri.edu

Southeast Missouri State University
MS 3550

Cape Girardeau, MO 63701
Phone: (573) 651-2590
Fax: (573) 651-5936
http://www.semo.edu

MONTANA

Montana State University
P.O. Box 172190
Bozeman, MT 59717
Phone: (406) 994-2452
Fax: (406) 994-1923
E-mail: admissions@montana.edu.
http://www.montana.edu

Montana State University— Billings
1500 University Drive
Billings, MT 59101
Phone: (406) 657-2158
Fax: (406) 657-2302
E-mail: admissions@msubillings.
edu
http://www.subillings.edu

NEBRASKA

Concordia University
800 North Columbia Avenue
Seward, NE 68434
Phone: (402) 643-7233
Fax: (402) 643-4073
E-mail: admiss@cune.edu
http://www.cune.edu

Dana College
2848 College Drive
Blair, NE 68008
Phone: (402) 426-7220
Fax: (402) 426-7386
E-mail: admissions@dana.edu
http://www.dana.edu

Hastings College
710 North Turner Avenue
Hastings, NE 68901
Phone: (402) 461-7320
Fax: (402) 461-7490
E-mail: mmolliconi@hastings.edu
http://www.hastings.edu

Nebraska Wesleyan University
5000 Saint Paul Avenue

Lincoln, NE 68504
Phone: (402) 465-2218
Fax: (402) 465-2177
E-mail: admissions@nebrwesleyan.
edu
http://www.nebrwesleyan.edu

Union College
3800 South 48th Street
Lincoln, NE 68506
Phone: (402) 486-2504
Fax: (402) 486-2566
E-mail: ucenroll@ucollege.edu
http://www.ucolle.edu

University of Nebraska at Kearney
905 West 25th Street
Kearney, NE 68849
Phone: (308) 865-8702
Fax: (308) 865-8987
http://www.unk.edu

Wayne State College
1111 Main Street
Wayne, NE 68787
Phone: (402) 375-7234
Fax: (402) 375-7204
E-mail: admit1@wsc.edu
http://www.wsc.edu

York College
1125 East 8th Street
York, NE 68467
Phone: (402) 363-5627
Fax: (402) 363-5623
E-mail: enroll@york.edu
http://www.york.edu

NEVADA

University of Nevada, Las Vegas
P.O. Box 451021
4505 Maryland Parkway
Las Vegas, NV 89154
Phone: (702) 774-UNLV
Fax: (702) 774-8008
http://www.unlv.edu

NEW HAMPSHIRE

Colby-Sawyer College
541 Main Street

New London, NH 03257
Phone: (603) 526-3700
Fax: (603) 526-3452
E-mail: admissions@colby-sawyer.edu
http://www.colby-sawyer.edu

Daniel Webster College
20 University Drive
Nashua, NH 03063
Phone: (800) 325-6876
Fax: (603) 577-6001
E-mail: admissions@dwc.edu
http://www.dwc.edu

Franklin Pierce University
40 University Drive
Rindge, NH 03461
Phone: (603) 899-4050
Fax: (603) 899-4394
E-mail: admissions@franklinpierce.edu
http://www.franklinpierce.edu

New England College
102 Bridge Street
Henniker, NH 03242
Phone: (800) 521-7642
Fax: (603) 428-3155
E-mail: admission@nec.edu
http://www.nec.edu

Southern New Hampshire University
2500 North River Road
Manchester, NH 03106
Phone: (603) 645-9611
Fax: (603) 645-9693
http://www.snhu.edu

NEW JERSEY

Centenary College
400 Jefferson Street
Hackettstown, NJ 07840
Phone: (908) 852-1400
Fax: (908) 852-3454
E-mail: admissions@centenarycollege.edu
http://www.centenarycollege.edu

Seton Hall University
400 South Orange Avenue
South Orange, NJ 07079
Phone: (800) THE-HALL (843-4255)
E-mail: thehall@shu.edu
http://www.shu.edu

NEW YORK

Cazenovia College
Cazenovia, NY 13035
Phone: (315) 655-7208
Fax: (315) 655-4860
E-mail: admission@cazenovia.edu
http://www.cazenovia.edu

College at Brockport-State University of New York
350 New Campus Drive
Brockport, NY 14420
Phone: (585) 395-2751
Fax: (585) 395-5452
http://www.brockport.edu

Globe Institute of Technology
291 Broadway
New York, NY 10007
Phone: (212) 349-4330
E-mail: admissions@globe.edu
http://www.globe.edu

Ithaca College
100 Job Hall
Ithaca, New York 14850
Phone: (607) 274-3124
Fax: (607) 274-1900
E-mail: admission@ithaca.edu
http://www.ithaca.edu

Medaille College
Buffalo, NY 14214
Phone: (716) 880-2200
Fax: (716) 880-2007
http://www.medaille.edu

New York University
22 Washington Square North
New York, NY 10011
Phone: (212) 998-4500
http://admissions.nyu.edu

Niagara University
630 Bailo Hall
Niagara University, NY 14109
Phone: (716) 286-8700

Fax: (716) 286-8710
E-mail: admissions@niagara.edu
http://www.niagara.edu

St. John Fisher College
3690 East Avenue
Rochester, NY 14618
Phone: (585) 385-8064
Fax: (585) 385-8386
E-mail: admissions@sjfc.edu
http://www.sjfc.edu/admissions

St. John's University
8000 Utopia Parkway
Queens, NY 11439
Phone: (718) 990-2000
Fax: (718) 990-2160
E-mail: admhelp@stjohns.edu
http://www.stjohns.edu

State University of New York—Oswego
229 Sheldon Hall
Oswego, NY 13126
Phone: (315) 312-2250
Fax: (315) 312-3260
E-mail: admiss@oswego.edu
http://www.oswego.edu

NORTH CAROLINA

Barton College
P.O. Box 5000
Wilson, NC 27893
Phone: (252) 399-6317
Fax: (252) 399-6572
E-mail: enroll@barton.edu
http://www.barton.edu

Campbell University
P.O. Box 546
Buies Creek, NC 27506
Phone: (910) 893-1320
E-mail: adm@mailcenter.campbell.edu
http://www.campbell.edu

Chowan University
200 Jones Drive
Murfreesboro, NC 27855
Phone: (252) 398-6298
E-mail: admissions@chowan.edu
http://www.chowan.edu

Elon University
Elon, NC 27244
Phone: (336) 278-3566
E-mail: admissions@elon.edu
http://www.elon.edu

Gardner-Webb University
Boiling Springs, NC 28017
Phone: (704) 406-4GWU
E-mail: admissions@gardner-webb.
edu
http://www.gardner-webb.edu

Greensboro College
815 West Market Street
Greensboro, NC 27401
Phone: (800) 346-8226
Fax: (336) 378-0154
E-mail: admissions@gborocollege.
edu
http://ww.gborocollege.edu

Guilford College
5800 West Friendly Avenue
Greensboro, NC 27410
Phone: (336) 316-2100
E-mail: admission@guilford.edu
http://www.guilford.edu

High Point University
833 Montlieu Avenue
High Point, NC 27262
Phone: (336) 841-9216
E-mail: admiss@highpoint.edu
http://www.highpoint.edu

Johnson C. Smith University
100 Beatties Ford Road
Charlotte, NC 28216
Phone: (704) 378-1010
Fax: (704) 378-1242
E-mail: admissions@jcsu.edu
http://www.jcsu.edu

Lenoir-Rhyne College
P.O. Box 7227
Hickory, NC 28603
Phone: (828) 328-7300
Fax: (828) 328-7378
E-mail: admission@lrc.edu
http://www.lrc.edu

Mars Hill College
Mars Hill, NC 28754

Phone: (828) 689-1201
Fax: (828) 689-1473
E-mail: admissions@mhc.edu
http://www.mhc.edu

North Carolina State University
P.O. Box 7103
Raleigh, NC 27695
Phone: (919) 515-2434
Fax: (919) 515-5039
http://www.ncsu.edu

Pfeiffer University
P.O. Box 960
Highway 52 North
Misenheimer, NC 28109
Phone: (704) 463-1360
Fax: (704) 463-1363
E-mail: admiss@pfeiffer.edu
http://www.pfeiffer.edu

Western Carolina University
Cullowhee, NC 28723
Phone: (828) 227-7317
Fax: (828) 227-7319
E-mail: admiss@wcu.edu
http://www.poweryourmind.com

Wingate University
Wingate, NC 28174
Phone: (704) 233-8200
Fax: (704) 233-8110
E-mail: admit@wingate.edu
http://www.wingate.edu

Winston-Salem State University
601 South Church Street
Winston-Salem, NC 27101
Phone: (336) 721-2621
E-mail: admissions@wssu.edu
http://www.wssu.edu

NORTH DAKOTA

Minot State University
500 University Avenue West
Minot, ND 58707
Phone: (701) 858-3126
Fax: (701) 858-3825
E-mail askmsu@minotstateu.edu
http://www.minotstateu.edu

North Dakota State University
P.O. Box 5454
Fargo, ND 58105
Phone: (701) 231-8643
Fax: (701) 231-8802
E-mail: ndsu.admission@ndsu.edu
http://www.ndsu.edu

OHIO

Baldwin-Wallace College
275 Eastland Road
Berea, OH 44017
Phone: (440) 826-2222
Fax: (440) 826-3830
E-mail: info@bw.edu
http://www.bw.edu

Bluffton University
1 University Drive
Bluffton, OH 45817
Phone: (419) 358-3254
Fax: (419) 358-3081
E-mail: admissions@bluffton.edu
http://www.bluffton.edu

Bowling Green State University
Bowling Green, OH 43403
Phone: (419) 372-BGSU
E-mail: choosebgsu@bgnet.bgsu.edu
http://www.bgsu.edu

Cedarville University
251 North Main Street
Cedarville, OH 45314
Phone: (800) 233-2784
E-mail: admissions@cedarville.edu
http://www.cedarville.edu

Cleveland State University
2121 Euclid Avenue
Cleveland, OH 44115
Phone: (216) 687-2100
Fax: (216) 687-9210
http://www.csuohio.edu

Defiance College
701 North Clinton Street
Defiance, OH 43512
Phone: (419) 783-2365
E-mail: admissions@defiance.edu
http://www.defiance.edu

Malone University
515 25th Street, NW
Canton, OH 44709
Phone: (330) 471-8145
E-mail: admissions@malone.edu
http://www.malone.edu

Miami University
Oxford, OH 45056
Phone: (513) 529-5040
E-mail: admissions@muohio.edu
http://www.miami.muohio.edu

Mount Union College
1972 Clark Avenue
Alliance, OH 44601
Phone: (330) 823-2590
E-mail: admissn@muc.edu
http://www.muc.edu

Mount Vernon Nazarene University
800 Martinsburg Road
Mount Vernon, OH 43050
Phone: (740) 392-6868
Fax: (740) 393-0511
E-mail: admissions@mvnu.edu
http://www.mvnu.edu

Notre Dame College
4545 College Road
South Euclid, OH 44121
Phone: (216) 373-5355
Fax: (216) 373-5278
E-mail: admissions@ndc.edu
http://www.NotreDameCollege.edu

Ohio Northern University
Ada, OH 45810
Phone: (888) 408-4668
Fax: (419) 772-2821
E-mail: admissions-ug@onu.edu
http://www.onu.edu

Ohio University
Athens, OH 45701-2979
Phone: (740) 593-4100
Fax: (740) 593-0560
E-mail: admissions@ohio.edu
http://www.ohio.edu

Otterbein College
One Otterbein College

Westerville, OH 43081
Phone: (614) 823-1500
E-mail: uotterb@otterbein.edu
http://www.otterbein.edu

Shawnee State University
940 Second Street
Portsmouth, OH 45662
Phone: (740) 351-3610
http://www.shawnee.edu

Tiffin University
155 Miami Street
Tiffin, OH 44883
Phone: (419) 448-3423
Fax: (419) 443-5006
E-mail: admiss@tiffin.edu
http://www.tiffin.edu

University of Akron
277 East Buchtel Avenue
Akron, OH 44325
Phone: (330) 972-6427
Fax: (330) 972-7022
E-mail: admissions@uakron.edu
http://www.uakron.edu

University of Dayton
300 College Park
Dayton, OH 45469
Phone: (937) 229-4411
E-mail: admission@udayton.edu
http://www.udayton.edu

Wilmington College
251 Ludovic Street
Wilmington, OH 45177
Phone: (937) 382-6661
Fax: (937) 382-7077
E-mail: admission@wilmington.edu
http://www.wilmington.edu

Xavier University
3800 Victory Parkway
Cincinnati, OH 45207-5311
Phone: (513) 745-2941
http://www.xavier.edu

OKLAHOMA

Oklahoma Baptist University
P.O. Box 61174
Shawnee, OK 74804

Phone: (405) 878-2033
Fax: (405) 878-2046
E-mail: admissions@mail.okbu.edu
http://www.okbu.edu

Rogers State University
1701 West Will Rogers Boulevard
Claremore, OK 74017
Phone: (918) 343-7545
Fax: (918) 343-7595
http://www.rsu.edu

Southern Nazarene University
6729 Northwest 39th Expressway
Bethany, OK 73008
Phone: (405) 491-6324
Fax: (405) 491-6320
E-mail: admis@snu.edu
http://www.snu.edu

University of Tulsa
800 South Tucker Drive
Tulsa, OK 74104
Phone: (918) 631-2307
Fax: (918) 631-5003
E-mail: admission@utulsa.edu
http://www.utulsa.edu/admission

OREGON

Concordia University
2811 Northeast Holman
Portland, OR 97211
Phone: (503) 493-6526
Fax: (503) 280-8531
E-mail: admissions@cu-portland.edu
http://www.cu-portland.edu

Corban College
5000 Deer Park Drive, SE
Salem, OR 97301
Phone: (503) 375-7115
Fax: (503) 585-4316
E-mail: admissions@corban.edu
http://www.corban.edu

PENNSYLVANIA

Alvernia University
Reading, PA 19607
Phone: (888) 258-3764
Fax: (610) 790-2873

E-mail: admissions@alvernia.edu
http://www.alvernia.edu

DeSales University
2755 Station Avenue
Center Valley, PA 18034
Phone: (610) 282-1100
E-mail: admiss@desales.edu
http://www.desales.edu

Edinboro University of Pennsylvania
Academy Hall
200 East Normal Street
Edinboro, PA 16444
Phone: (814) 732-2761
Fax: (814) 732-2420
http://www.edinboro.edu

Gannon University
109 University Square
Erie, PA 16541
Phone: (814) 871-7240
Fax: (814) 871-5803
E-mail: admissions@gannon.edu
http://www.gannon.edu

Keystone College
One College Green
La Plume, PA 18440
Phone: (570) 945-8111
E-mail: admissions@keystone.edu
http://www.keystone.edu

Lock Haven University of Pennsylvania
Akeley Hall
Lock Haven, PA 17745
Phone: (570) 484-2027
Fax: (570) 484-2201
http://www.lhup.edu/

Mercyhurst College Admissions
501 East 38th Street
Erie, PA 16546
Phone: (814) 824-2202
E-mail: admissions@mercyhurst.
edu
http://www.mercyhurst.edu

Messiah College
P.O. Box 3005
One College Avenue

Grantham, PA 17027
Phone: (717) 691-6000
Fax: (717) 796-5374
E-mail: admiss@messiah.edu
http://www.messiah.edu

Neumann College
One Neumann Drive
Aston, PA 19014
Phone: (610) 558-5616
E-mail: neumann@neumann.edu
http://www.neumann.edu

Robert Morris University
6001 University Boulevard
Moon Township, PA 15108
Phone: (800) 762-0097
http://www.rmu.edu

University of Pittsburgh at Bradford
300 Campus Drive
Bradford, PA 16701
Phone: (814) 362-7555
http://www.upb.pitt.edu

University of the Sciences in Philadelphia
600 South 43rd Street
Philadelphia, PA 19104
Phone: (215) 596-8810
Fax: (215) 596-8821
E-mail: admit@usp.edu
http://www.usp.edu

Slippery Rock University of Pennsylvania
1 Morrow Way
Slippery Rock, PA 16057
Phone: (724) 738-2015
http://www.sru.edu

York College of Pennsylvania
York, PA 17405
Phone: (717) 849-1600
Fax: (717) 849-1607
E-mail: admissions@ycp.edu
http://www.ycp.edu

SOUTH CAROLINA

Coastal Carolina University
P.O. Box 261954

Conway, SC 29528
Phone: (843) 349-2037
http://www.coastal.edu

Coker College
300 East College Avenue
Hartsville, SC 29550
Phone: (843) 383-8050
Fax: (843) 383-8056
E-mail: : admissions@coker.edu
http://www.coker.edu

Limestone College
1115 College Drive
Gaffney, SC 29340
Phone: (864) 488-4554
Fax: (864) 488-8206
E-mail: admiss@limestone.edu
http://www.limestone.edu

North Greenville University
P.O. Box 1892
Tigerville, SC 29688
Phone: (864) 977-7052
http://www.ngu.edu

Southern Wesleyan University
P.O. Box 1020
907 Wesleyan Drive
Central, SC 29630
Phone: (864) 644-5149
Fax: (864) 644-5901
http://www.southernwesleyanu.com

Winthrop University
Rock Hill, SC 29733
Phone: (803) 323-2191
E-mail: admissions@winthrop.edu
http://www.winthrop.edu

University of South Carolina
Columbia, SC 29208
Phone: (803) 777-7700
E-mail: admissions-ugrad@sc.edu
http://www.sc.edu

SOUTH DAKOTA

Augustana College
2001 South Summit Avenue
Sioux Falls, SD 57197
Phone: (605) 274-5516
Fax: (605) 274-5518

E-mail: admission@augie.edu
http://www.audie.edu

Black Hills State University
1200 University ST USB 9502
Spearfish, SD 57799
Phone: (605) 642-6343
Fax: (605) 642-6254
E-mail: admissions@bhsu.edu
http://www.bhsu.edu

TENNESSEE

King College
1350 King College Road
Bristol, TN 37620-2699
Phone: (423) 652-4861
Fax: (423) 652-4727
http://www.king.edu

Lambuth University
705 Lambuth Boulevard
Jackson, TN 38301
Phone: (731) 425-3223
E-mail: admit@lambuth.edu
http://www.lambuth.edu

Southern Adventist University
P.O. Box 370
Collegedale, TN 37315
Phone: (423) 236-2844
Fax: (423) 236-1844
https://www.southern.edu

Trevecca Nazarene University
333 Murfreesboro Road
Nashville, TN 37210
Phone: (615) 248-1320
Fax: (615) 248-7406
E-mail: admissions_und@trevecca.
edu
http://www.trevecca.edu

Tusculum College
P.O. Box 5047
Greeneville, TN 37743
Phone: (423) 636-7300
Fax: (423) 798-1622
http://www.tusculum.edu

Union University
1050 Union University Drive
Jackson, TN 38305

Phone: (800) 33-UNION
E-mail: info@uu.edu
http://www.uu.edu

University of Memphis
101 John Wilder Tower
Memphis, TN 38152
Phone: (901) 678-2169
http://www.memphis.edu

University of Tennessee
1331 Circle Park
Knoxville, TN 37996
Phone: (865) 974-2184
Fax: (865) 974-6341
E-mail: admissions@utk.edu
http://www.utk.edu

TEXAS

Abilene Christian University
ACU Box 29000
Abilene, TX 79699
Phone: (325) 674-2650
Fax: (325) 674-2130
http:// www.acu.edu

Howard Payne University
1000 Fisk Avenue
Brownwood, TX 76801
Phone: (325) 649-8027
Fax: (325) 649-8901
E-mail: enroll@hputx.edu
http://www.hputx.edu

LeTourneau University
P.O. Box 7001
Longview, TX 75607-7001
Phone: (903) 233-3400
Fax: (903) 233-3411
E-mail: admissions@letu.edu
http://www.letu.edu

Midwestern State University
Wichita Falls, TX 76308
Phone: (940) 397-4334
Fax: (940) 397-4672
E-mail: admissions@mwsu.edu
http://www.mwsu.edu

Schreiner University
2100 Memorial Boulevard
Kerrville, TX 78028

Phone: (830) 792-7217
http://www.schreiner.edu

Texas Lutheran University
1000 West Court Street
Seguin, TX 78155
Phone: (830) 372-8050
E-mail: admissions@tlu.edu
http://www.tlu.edu

**Texas State University—San
Marcos**
601 University Drive
San Marcos, TX 78666
Phone: (512) 245-2364
http://www.txstate.edu

Texas Wesleyan University
1201 Wesleyan Street
Fort Worth, TX 76105
Phone: (817) 531-4422
Fax: (817) 531-7515
E-mail: freshman@txwesleyan.edu
http://www.txwesleyan.edu

**University of Mary Hardin-
Baylor**
UMHB Station Box 8004
900 College Street
Belton, TX 76513
Phone: (254) 295-4520
Fax: (254) 295-5049
http://www.umhb.edu

University of Texas at Austin
P.O. Box 8058
Austin, TX 78713
Phone: (512) 475-7440
Fax: (512) 475-7475
http://www.utexas.edu

VERMONT

Johnson State College
337 College Hill
Johnson, VT 05656
Phone: (802) 635-1219
Fax: (802) 635-1230
http://www.jsc.vsc.edu

Lyndon State College
P.O. Box 919
Lyndonville, VT 05851

Phone: (800) 225-1998
Fax: (802) 626-6335
E-mail: admissions@lyndonstate.edu
http://www.lyndonstate.edu

VIRGINIA

Averett University
420 West Main Street
Danville, VA 24541
Phone: (434) 791-4996
E-mail: admit@averett.edu
http://www.averett.edu

Eastern Mennonite University
1200 Park Road
Harrisonburg, VA 22802
Phone: (540) 432-4118
Fax: (540) 432-4444
E-mail: admiss@emu.edu
http://www.emu.edu

Ferrum College
Spilman-Daniel House
P.O. Box 1000
Ferrum, VA 24088
Phone: (540) 365-4290
Fax: (540) 365-4266
http://www.ferrum.edu

Hampton University
Hampton, VA 23668
Phone: (757) 727-5328
Fax: (757) 727-5095
E-mail: admit@hamptonu.edu
http://www.hamptonu.edu

Liberty University
1971 University Boulevard
Lynchburg, VA 24502
Phone: (434) 592-3054
Fax: (800) 542-2311
E-mail: admissions@liberty.edu
http://www.liberty.edu

Longwood University
Farmville, VA 23909
Phone: (434) 395-2060
Fax: (434) 395-2332
E-mail: admit@longwood.edu
http://www.longwood.edu

Lynchburg College
1501 Lakeside Drive

Lynchburg, VA 24501
Phone: (434) 544-8300
Fax: (434) 544-8653
E-mail: admissions@lynchburg.edu
http://www.lynchburg.edu

Marymount University
2807 North Glebe Road
Arlington, VA 22207
Phone: (703) 284-1500
E-mail: prospectivestudents@
    marymount.edu
http://www.marymount.edu

Old Dominion University
108 Rollins Hall
Norfolk, VA 23529
Phone: (757) 683-3685
E-mail: admit@odu.edu
http://www.odu.edu

Virginia Intermont College
1013 Moore Street
Campus Box D-460
Bristol, VA 24201
Phone: (276) 466-7856
Fax: (276) 466-7885
http://www.vic.edu

WASHINGTON

Central Washington University
400 East University Way
Ellensburg, WA 98926
Phone: (509) 963-1211
Fax: (509) 963-3022
E-mail: cwuadmis@cwu.edu
http://www.cwu.edu

Gonzaga University
Spokane, Washington 99258
Phone: (800) 322-2584
E-mail: admissions@gu.gonzaga.
    edu
http://www.gonzaga.edu

Walla Walla College
204 South College Avenue
College Place, WA 99324
Phone: (509) 527-2327
Fax: (509) 527-2397
E-mail: info@wwc.edu
http://www.wwe.edu

Washington State University
French Administration Building
Pullman, WA 99164
Phone: (509) 335-5586
Fax: (509) 335-7468
E-mail: admiss@wsu.edu
http://www.wsu.edu

WEST VIRGINIA

**American Public University
    System**
322-C West Washington Street
Charles Town, WV 25414
Phone: (703) 330-5398
Fax: (304) 724-3788
E-mail: admissions@apus.edu
http://www.apus.edu

Bethany College
Bethany, WV 26032
Phone: (304) 829-7611
Fax: (304) 829-7142
http://www.bethanywv.edu

Davis & Elkins College
100 Campus Drive
Elkins, WV 26241
Phone: (304) 637-1230
E-mail: admiss@davisandelkins.edu
http://www.davisandelkins.edu

Glenville State College
200 High Street
Glenville, WV 26351
Phone: (304) 462-4128
Fax: (304) 462-8619
http://www.glenville.wvnet.edu

Salem International University
P.O. Box 500
Salem, WV 26426
Phone: (304) 326-1359
Fax: (304) 326-1592
E-mail: admissions@salemu.edu
http://www.salemu.edu

West Virginia University
P.O. Box 6009
Morgantown, WV 26506
Phone: (304) 293-2124
Fax: (304) 293-3080
http://www.wvu.edu

West Virginia Wesleyan College
59 College Avenue
Buckhannon, WV 26201
Phone: (304) 473-8510
E-mail: admission@wvwc.edu
http://www.wvwc.edu

WISCONSIN

Carthage College
2001 Alford Park Drive
Kenosha, WI 53140

Phone: (262) 551-6000
E-mail: admissions@carthage.edu
http://www.carthage.edu

Concordia University Wisconsin
12800 North Lake Drive
Mequon, WI 53097
Phone: (262) 243-4305
http://www.cuw.edu

Marian College of Fond du Lac
45 South National Avenue
Fond du Lac, WI 54935

Phone: (800) 262-7426
Fax: (920) 923-8755
E-mail: admit@mariancollege.edu
http://www.mariancollege.edu

B. COLLEGES AND UNIVERITIES OFFERING DEGREES IN PHYSICAL EDUCATION

The following is a selected listing of four-year schools granting degrees in physical education. They are grouped by state. School names, addresses, phone numbers, Web addresses, and e-mail addresses are included when available.

The author does not endorse any one school over another. Use this list as a beginning. Check the reference section of libraries or guidance counseling centers for additional schools offering degrees in this field.

ALABAMA

Alabama Agricultural and Mechanical University
P.O. Box 908
Normal, AL 35762
Phone: (256) 372-5245
Fax: (256) 851-9747
http://www.aamu.edu

Alabama State University
915 South Jackson Street
Montgomery, AL 36104
Phone: (334) 229-4291
E-mail: mpettway@alasu.edu
http://www.alasu.edu

Athens State University
300 North Beaty Street
Athens, AL 35611
Phone: (256) 233-8217
Fax: (256) 233-6565
http:// www.athens.edu

Auburn University
202 Martin Hall
Auburn University, AL 36849
Phone: (334) 844-4080

E-mail: admissions@auburn.edu
http://www.auburn.edu

Faulkner University
5345 Atlanta Highway
Montgomery, AL 36109
Phone: (334) 386-7200
Fax: (334) 386-7137
http://www.faulkner.edu

Jacksonville State University
700 Pelham Road North
Jacksonville, AL 36265
Phone: (256) 782-5363
Fax: (256) 782-5291
http://www.jsu.edu

Oakwood University
7000 Adventist Boulevard, NW
Huntsville, AL 35896
Phone: (256) 726-7354
Fax: (256) 726-7154
http://www.oakwood.edu

Samford University
Birmingham, AL 35229
Phone: (205) 726-3673
E-mail: admission@samford.edu
http://www.samford.edu

Stillman College
P.O. Drawer 1430
3600 Stillman Boulevard
Tuscaloosa, AL 35403
Phone: (205) 366-8837
Fax: (205) 366-8941
http://www.stillman.edu

Troy University
134 Adams
Troy, AL 36082
Phone: (334) 670-3243
Fax: (334) 670-3733
http://www.troy.edu

University of Alabama
P.O. Box 870132
Tuscaloosa, AL 35487
Phone: (205) 348-5666
Fax: (205) 348-9046
E-mail: admissions@ua.edu
http://www.ua.edu

University of South Alabama
307 University Boulevard
Mobile, AL 36688
Phone: (251) 460-6141
www.southalabama.edu

University of West Alabama
Station 4
Livingston, AL 35470
Phone: (205) 652-3581
Fax: (205) 652-3522
http://www.uwa.edu

ALASKA

University of Alaska, Anchorage
3211 Providence Drive
Anchorage, AK 99508
Phone: (907) 786-1480
Fax: (907) 786-4888
http://www.uaa.alaska.edu

ARIZONA

Grand Canyon University
3300 West Camelback Road
Phoenix, AZ 85017
Phone: (800) 486-7085
E-mail: admissionsground@gcu.edu
http://www.gcu.edu

Prescott College
220 Grove Avenue
Prescott, AZ 86301
Phone: (928) 350-2100
E-mail: admissions@prescott.edu
http://www.prescott.edu

University of Arizona
P.O. Box 210040
Tucson, AZ 85721
Phone: (520) 621-3237
Fax: (520)621-9799
E-mail: appinfo@arizona.edu
http://www.arizon.edu

ARKANSAS

Arkansas State University
P.O. Box 1630
State University, AR 72467
Phone: (870) 972-3024
Fax: (870) 910-3406
E-mail: admissions@cicsaw.astate.
    edu
http://www.astate.edu

Arkansas Tech University
L.L. "Doc" Bryan Student Services
    Building

Russellville, AR 72801-2222
Phone: 479-968-0343
Fax: 479-964-0522
E-mail: tech.enroll@mail.atu.edu
http://www.atu.edu

Henderson State University
1100 Henderson Street
P.O. Box 7560
Arkadelphia, AR 71999
Phone: (870) 230-5028
Fax: (870) 230-5066
http://www.hsu.edu

Ouachita Baptist University
OBU Box 3776
Arkadelphia, AR 71998
Phone: (870) 245-5110
Fax: (870) 245-5500
http://www.obu.edu

**Southern Arkansas University–
    Magnolia**
100 East University
Magnolia, AR 71753
Phone: (870) 235-4040
http://www.saumag.edu

**University of Arkansas at
    Monticello**
Monticello, AR 71656
Phone: (870) 460-1026
http://www.uamont.edu

**University of Arkansas at Pine
    Bluff**
UAPB Box 17
1200 University Drive
Pine Bluff, AR 71601
Phone: (870) 575-8487
Fax: (870) 543-2021
http://www.uaphb.edu

University of Central Arkansas
201 Donaghey Avenue
Conway, AR 72035
Phone: (501) 450-5371
E-mail: admissions@mail.usa.edu
http://www.uca.edu

University of the Ozarks
415 North College Avenue
Clarksville, AR 72830

Phone: (479) 979-1227
Fax: (479) 979-1417
E-mail: admiss@ozarks.edu
http://www.ozarks.edu

CALIFORNIA

Azusa Pacific University
901 East Alosta Avenue
P.O. Box 7000
Azusa, CA 91702
Phone: (626) 812-3016
Fax: (626) 812-3096
http://www.apu.edu

Biola University
13800 Biola Avenue
La Mirada, CA 90639
Phone: (800) 0K-BIOLA
E-mail: admissions@biola.edu
http://www.biola.edu

California Lutheran University
60 West Olsen Road
Thousand Oaks, CA 91360
Phone: (805) 493-3135
Fax: (805) 493-3114
E-mail: admissions@callutheran.
    edu
http://www.callutheran.edu

**California State University,
    Chico**
400 West First Street
Chico, CA 95929
Phone: (800) 542-4426
Fax: (530) 898-6456
E-mail: info@csuchico.edu
http://www.csuchico.edu

**California State University,
    East Bay**
25800 Carlos Bee Boulevard
Hayward, CA 94542
Phone: (510) 885-3248
Fax: (510) 885-4059
E-mail: admissions@csueastbay.
    edu
http://www.csueastbay.edu

**California State University,
    Fresno**
5150 North Maple Avenue

Fresno, CA 93740
Phone: (559) 278-6115
Fax: (559) 278-4812
E-mail: yolandad@csufresno.edu
http://www.csufresnu.edu

California State University, Long Beach
1250 Bellflower Boulevard
Long Beach, CA 90840
Phone: (562) 985-4641
http://www.csulb.edu

Fresno Pacific College
1717 South Chestnut Avenue
Fresno, CA 93702
Phone: (559) 453-2069
Fax: (559) 453-5501
http://www.fresno.edu

Pacific Union College
One Angwin Avenue
Angwin, CA 94508
Phone: (707) 965-6425
Fax: (707) 965-6432
E-mail: enroll@puc.edu
http://www.puc.edu

Pepperdine University
24255 Pacific Coast Highway
Malibu, CA 90263
Phone: (310) 506-4392
Fax: (310) 506-4861
E-mail: admission-seaver@
    pepperdine.edu
http://www.pepperdine.edu

San Diego State University
5500 Campanile Drive
San Diego, CA 92182
Phone: (619) 594-6886
Fax: (619) 594-1250
E-mail: admissions@sdsu.edu
http://www.sdsu.edu

San Jose State University
One Washington Square
San Jose, CA 95192
Phone: (408) 924-1000
E-mail: contact@sjsu.edu
http://www.sjsu.edu

Sonoma State University
1801 East Cotati Avenue
Rohnert Park, CA 94928
Phone: (707) 664-2778
http://www.sonoma.edu

University of San Francisco
2130 Fulton Street
San Francisco, CA 94117
Phone: (415) 422-6563
Fax: (415) 422-2217
E-mail: admission@usfca.edu
http://www.usfca.edu

University of Southern California
University Park
Los Angeles, CA 90089
Phone: (213) 740-1111
E-mail: admitusc@usc.edu
http://www.usc.edu

Westmont College
Office of Admission
955 La Paz Road
Santa Barbara, CA 93108
Phone: (800) 777-9011
Fax: (805) 565-6234
E-mail: admissions@westmont.edu
http://www.westmont.edu

Whittier College
P.O. Box 634
Whittier, CA 90608
Phone: (562) 907-4238
Fax: (562) 907-4870
E-mail: admission@whittier.edu
http://www.whittier.edu

COLORADO

Fort Lewis College
1000 Rim Drive
Durango, CO 81301
Phone: (970) 247-7184
http://www.fortlewis.edu

Western State College of Colorado
600 North Adams Street
Gunnison, CO 81231
Phone: (800) 876-5309
E-mail: admissions@western.edu
http://www.western.edu

CONNECTICUT

Central Connecticut State University
1615 Stanley Street
New Britain, CT 06050
Phone: (860)832-CCSU
E-mail: admissions@ccsu.edu
http://www.ccsu.edu

Eastern Connecticut State University
83 Windham Street
Willimantic, CT 06226
Phone: (860) 465-5286
Fax: (860) 465-5544
E-mail: admissions@easternct.edu
http://www.easternct.edu

Mitchell College
437 Pequot Avenue
New London, CT 06320
Phone: (800) 443-2811
Fax: (860) 444-1209
E-mail: admissions@mitchell.edu
http://www.mitchell.edu

University of Connecticut
2131 Hillside Road, U-88
Storrs, CT 06269
Phone: (860) 486-3137
Fax: (860) 486-1476
http://www.uconn.edu

DELAWARE

Delaware State University
1200 North DuPont Highway
Dover, DE 19901
Phone: (302) 857-6351
Fax: (302) 857-6908
E-mail: gcheatha@desu.edu
http://www.desu.edu

University of Delaware
Newark, DE 19716
Phone: (302) 831-8123
Fax: (302) 831-6905
E-mail: admissions@udel.edu
http://www.udel.edu

Wesley College
120 North State Street
Dover, DE 19901

Phone: (302) 736-2400
Fax: (302) 736-2382
E-mail: admissions@wesley.edu
http://www.wesley.edu

DISTRICT OF COLUMBIA

University of the District of Columbia
4200 Connecticut Avenue, NW
Washington, DC 20008
Phone: (202) 274-6110
Fax: (202) 274-5553
http://www.udc.edu

Gallaudet University
800 Florida Avenue, NE
Washington, DC 20002-3625
Phone: 202-651-5750
http://www.gallaudet.edu

Howard University
2400 Sixth Street, NW
Washington, DC 20059-0002
Phone: (202) 806-2700
http://www.howard.edu

FLORIDA

Barry University
11300 Northeast Second Avenue
Miami Shores, FL 33161
Phone: (305)899-3100
Fax: (305) 899-2971
E-mail: admissions@mail.barry.edu
http://www.barry.edu

Bethune-Cookman College
640 Dr. Mary McLeod Bethune
   Boulevard
Daytona Beach, FL 32114
Phone: (386) 255-1401
E-mail: admissions@cookman.edu
http://www.bethune.cookman.edu

Clearwater Christian College
3400 Gulf-to-Bay Boulevard
Clearwater, FL 33759-4595
Phone: (727) 726-1153
http://www.clearwater.edu

Edward Waters College
1658 Kings Road

Jacksonville, FL 32209
Phone: (904) 366-2715
http://www.ewc.edu

Florida Agriculture and Mechanical University
Lee Hall Suite 303
Tallahassee, FL 32307
Phone: (850) 599-3000
http://www.famu.edu

Florida International University
University Park
Miami, FL 33199
Phone: (305) 348-2000
E-mail: admiss@fiu.edu
http ://ww w.fiu .edu

Florida Memorial University
15800 Northwest 42 Avenue
Miami, FL 33054
Phone: (305) 626-3600
http://www.fmuniv.edu

Florida Southern College
111 Lake Hollingsworth Drive
Lakeland, FL 33801
Phone: (800) 274-4131
E-mail: fscadm@flsouthern.edu
http://www.flsouthern.edu

Florida State University
Tallahassee, FL 32306
Phone: (850) 644-2525
E-mail: admissions@admin.fsu.
   edu
http://www.fsu.edu

Jacksonville University
2800 University Boulevard North
Jacksonville, FL 32211
Phone: (904) 744-3950
E-mail: admission@ju.edu
http://www.ju.edu

Palm Beach Atlantic College
P.O. Box 24708
West Palm Beach, FL 33416
Phone: (561) 803-2000
E-mail: admit@pbac.edu
http://www.pbac.edu

University of Central Florida
4000 Central Florida Boulevard
Orlando, FL 32816-0111
Phone: (407) 823-2000
E-mail: admission@mail.ucf.edu
http://www.ucf.edu

University of Florida
201 Criser Hall
Gainesville, FL 32611
Phone: (352) 392-3261
http://www.ufl.edu

University of North Florida
4567 St. Johns Bluff Road
Jacksonville, FL 32224-2645
Phone: (904) 620-1000
http://www.unf.edu

University of South Florida
4202 East Fowler Avenue
Tampa, FL 33620
Phone: (813) 974-3350
Fax: (813) 974-9689
http://www.usf.edu

Warner Southern College
13895 US 27
Lake Wales, FL 33853
Phone: (863) 638-1426
E-mail: admission@warner.edu
http://www.warner.edu

GEORGIA

Albany State University
504 College Drive
Albany, GA 31705
Phone: (229) 430-4645
Fax: (229) 430-3936
E-mail: fsuttles@asurams.edu
http://www.potentialrealized.org

Armstrong State College
11935 Abercorn Street
Savannah, GA 31419
Phone: (912) 927-5211
http://www.armstrong.edu

Augusta State University
2500 Walton Way
Augusta, GA 30904
Phone: (706) 737-1632

Fax: (706) 667-4355
E-mail: admissions@aug.edu
http://www.aug.edu

Berry College
2277 Martha Berry Highway
Mount Berry, GA 30149-0159
Phone: (706) 232-5374
E-mail: admissions@berry.edu
http://www.berry.edu

Clayton State University
2000 Clayton State Boulevard
Morrow, GA 30260
Phone: (678) 466-4115
Fax: (678) 466-4149
E-mail: csu-info@clayton.edu
http://www.clayton.edu

Columbus State University
4225 University Avenue
Columbus, GA 31907-5645
Phone: (706) 568-2001
E-mail: admissions@colstate.edu
http://www.colstate.edu

Fort Valley State University
1005 State University Drive
Fort Valley, GA 31030
Phone: (478) 825-6307
E-mail: admissap@mail.fvsu.edu
http://www.fvsu.edu

Georgia College & State University
231 West Hancock Street
Milledgeville, GA 31061
Phone: (478) 445-2774
Fax: (478) 445-1914
E-mail: info@gcsu.edu
http://www.gcsu.edu

Georgia Southern University
Forest Drive
Statesboro, GA 30460
Phone: (912)681-5391
Fax: (912) 486-7240
E-mail: admissions@gasou.edu
http://www.gasou.edu

Georgia Southwestern State University
800 Wheatley Street

Americus, GA 31709
Phone: (229) 928-1273
Fax: (229) 931-2983
E-mail: gswapps@canes.gsw.edu
http://www.gsw.edu

Kennesaw College
1000 Chastain Road
Kennesaw, GA 30144-5591
Phone: (770) 423-6000
E-mail: ksuadmit@kennesaw.edu
http://www.kennesaw.edu

North Georgia College and State University
Dahlonega, GA 30597
Phone: (706) 864-1400
E-mail: admissions@ngcsu.edu
http://www.ngcsu.edu

Reinhardt College
7300 Reinhardt College Circle
Waleska, GA 30183
Phone: (770) 720-5526
Fax: (770) 720-5602
E-mail: admissions @ mail.
reinhardt.edu
http://www.reinhardt.edu

University of Georgia
Athens, GA 30602
Phone: (706) 542-3000
E-mail: undergrad@admissions.
uga.edu
http://www.uga.edu

Valdosta State College
1500 North Patterson Street
Valdosta, GA 31698
Phone: (229) 333-5800
E-mail: admissions@valdosta.edu
http://www.valdosta.edu

HAWAII

Brigham Young University-Hawaii
55-220 Kulanui Street
Laie, HI 96762
Phone: (808) 293-3211
E-mail: admissions@byuh.edu
http://www.byuh.edu

University of Hawaii at Manoa
2600 Campus Road
Honolulu, HI 96822
Phone: (808) 956-8975
Fax: (808) 956-4148
http://www.uhm.hawaii.edu

IDAHO

Boise State University
1910 University Drive
Boise, ID 83725
Phone: (208) 426-1101
E-mail: bsuinfo@boisestate.edu
http://www.boisestate.edu

College of Idaho
2112 Cleveland Boulevard
Caldwell, ID 83605
Phone: (208) 459-5689
http://www.collegeofidaho.edu

Idaho State University
741 South Seventh Avenue
Pocatello, ID 83209
Phone: (208)282-0211
E-mail: info@isu.edu
http://www.isu.edu

Lewis-Clark State College
500 Eighth Avenue
Lewiston, ID 83501
Phone: (208) 792-2210
Fax: (208) 792-2876
E-mail: admissions@lcsc.edu
http ://www.lcsc.edu

University of Idaho
P.O. Box 442282
Moscow, ID 83844
Phone: (208) 885-6111
E-mail: admappl@uidaho.edu
http://www.uidaho.edu

ILLINOIS

Augustana College
639 38th Street
Rock Island, IL 61201
Phone: (309) 794-7000
E-mail: admissions@augustana.edu
http://www.augustana.edu

Aurora University
347 South Gladstone Avenue
Aurora, IL 60506
Phone: (630) 844-5533
E-mail: admissions@aurora.edu
http://www.aurora.edu

Blackburn College
700 College Avenue
Carlinville, IL 62626
Phone: (217) 854-3231
Fax: (217) 854-3713
E-mail: admit@mail.blackburn.edu
http://www.blackburn.edu

Chicago State University
9501 South King Drive
Chicago, IL 60628
Phone: (773) 995-2000
http://www.csu.edu

Concordia University
7400 Augusta Street
River Forest, IL 60305
Phone: (708) 209-3100
Fax: (708) 209-3473
E-mail: crfadmis@curf.edu
http://www.curf.edu

DePaul University
1 East Jackson Boulevard
Chicago, IL 60604
Phone: (312) 362-8300
E-mail: admission@depaul.edu
http://www.depaul.edu

Eastern Illinois University
600 Lincoln Avenue
Charleston, IL 61920
Phone: (217) 581-5000
http://www.eiu.edu

Elmhurst College
190 Prospect Avenue
Elmhurst, IL 60126-3296
Phone: (630) 617-3500
http://www.elmhurst.edu

Eureka College
300 College Avenue
Eureka, IL 61530
Phone: (309) 467-6350
E-mail: admissions@eureka.edu
http://www.eureka.edu

Greenville College
315 East College Avenue
Greenville, IL 62246
Phone: (618) 664-2800
http://www.greenville.edu

Illinois College
1101 West College
Jacksonville, IL 62650
Phone: (217) 245-3030
Fax: (217) 245-3034
http://www.ic.edu

Illinois State University
Normal, IL 61790
Phone: (309) 438-2181
Fax: (309) 438-3932
E-mail: ugradadm@ilstu.edu
http://www.ilstu.edu

Judson College
1151 North State Street
Elgin, IL 60123
Phone: (847) 695-2500
http://www.judsoncollege.edu

Lincoln College–Normal
715 West Raab Road
Normal, IL 61761
Phone: (309) 452-0500
E-mail: ncadmissionsinfo@
  lincolncollege.edu
http://www.lincolncollege.edu/normal

MacMurray College
447 East College Avenue J
Jacksonville, IL 62650-2590
Phone: (217) 479-7000
http://www.mac.edu

Millikin University
1184 West Main Street
Decatur, IL 62522
Phone: (217) 424-6211
E-mail: admis@mail.millikin.edu
http://www.millikin.edu

**Northeastern Illinois
  University**
5500 North St. Louis Avenue
Chicago, IL 60625
Phone: (773) 583-4050
http://www.neiu.edu

Northern Illinois University
DeKalb, IL 60115
Phone: (815) 753-1000
E-mail: admission-info@niu.edu
http://www.niu.edu

North Park University
3225 West Foster Avenue
Chicago, IL 60625
Phone: (773) 244-6200
http://www.northpark.edu

Quincy University
1800 College Avenue
Quincy, IL 62301
Phone: (217) 228-5210
E-mail: admissions@quincy.edu
http://www.quincy.edu

Trinity Christian College
6601 West College Drive
Palos Heights, IL 60463
Phone: (708) 597-3000
E-mail: adm@trnty.edu
http://www.trnty.edu

Trinity International University
2065 Half Day Road
Deerfield, IL 60015
Phone: (847) 317-7000
Fax: (847) 317-8097
E-mail: tcadmissions@tiu.edu
http://www.tiu.edu

**University of Illinois at
  Urbana–Champaign**
901 West Illinois
Urbana, IL 61801
Phone: (217) 333-0302
Fax: (217) 244-4614
E-mail: ugradadmissions@uiuc.edu
http://www.uinc.edu

Western Illinois University
900 West Adams Street
Macomb, IL 61455
Phone: (309) 295-1414
E-mail: wiuadm@wiu.edu
http://www.wiu .edu

INDIANA

Anderson University
1100 East Fifth

Anderson, IN 46012
Phone: (765) 649-9071
E-mail: info@anderson.edu
http://www.anderson.edu

Ball State University
2000 University Avenue
Muncie, IN 47306-0855
Phone: (765) 285-8300
E-mail: askus@ball.edu
http://www.bsu.edu

Bethel College
1001 West McKinley Avenue
Mishawaka, IN 46545
Phone: (574) 257-3319
Fax: (574) 257-3335
E-mail: admissions @ bethelcollege.
    edu

DePauw University
101 East Seminary Street
Greencastle, IN 46135
Phone: (765) 658-4006
Fax: (765) 658-4007
E-mail: admission@depauw.edu
http://www.depauw.edu

Franklin College
101 Branigin Boulevard
Franklin, IN 46131
Phone: (317) 738-8062
Fax: (317) 738-8274
E-mail: admissions@franklincollege.
    edu
http://admissions.franklincollege.edu

Goshen College
1700 South Main Street
Goshen, IN 46526
Phone: (574) 535-7000
E-mail: admissions@goshen.edu
http://www.goshen.edu

Grace College
200 Seminary Drive
Winona Lake, IN 46590
Phone: (219) 372-5100
E-mail: enroll@grace.edu
http://www .grace.edu

Hanover College
P.O. Box 108

Hanover, IN 47243
Phone: (800) 213-2178
Fax: (812) 866-2164
E-mail: admission@hanover.edu
http://www.hanover.edu

Huntington University
2303 College Avenue
Huntington, IN 46750
Phone: (260) 356-6000
Fax: (260) 356-9448
E-mail: admissions@huntington.
    edu
http://www.huntington.edu

Indiana State University
Terre Haute, IN 47809
Phone: (812) 237-2121
E-mail: admissions@indstate.edu
http://www.indstate.edu

Indiana University
    Bloomington
300 North Jordan Avenue
Bloomington, IN 47405
Phone: (812) 855-0661
Fax: (812) 855-5102
E-mail: iuadmit@indiana.edu
http://www.indiana.edu

Indiana University—Purdue,
    University of Indianapolis
535 West Michigan Street
Indianapolis, IN 46202
Phone: (317) 278-2014
http://www.iupui.edu

Indiana Wesleyan University
4201 South Washington Street
Marion, IN 46953
Phone: (866) GO TO IWU
Fax: (765) 677-2333
http://www.indwes.edu

Manchester College
604 East College Avenue
North Manchester, IN 46962
Phone: (260) 982-5000
http://www.manchester.edu

Marian College
3200 Cold Spring Road
Indianapolis, IN 46222

Phone: (317) 955-6300
Fax: (317) 955-6401
E-mail: admissions@marian.edu
http://www.marian.edu

Oakland City College
143 North Lucretia Street
Oakland City, IN 47660
Phone: (812)749-4781
http://www.oak.edu

Purdue University
475 Stadium Mall Drive
West Lafayette, IN 47907
Phone: (765) 494-1776
E-mail: admissions@purdue.cdu
http://www.purdue.ed

Taylor University
236 West Reade Avenue
Upland, IN 46989
Phone: (765) 998-5511
E-mail: admissions@taylor.edu
http://www.taylor.cdu

University of Evansville
1800 Lincoln Avenue
Evansville, IN 47722
Phone: (812) 488-2468
Fax: (812) 488-4076
E-mail: admission@evansville.edu
http://www.evansville.edu

University of Indianapolis
1400 East Hanna Avenue
Indianapolis, IN 46227
Phone: (317) 788-3216
Fax: (317) 788-3300
E-mail: admissions@uindy.edu
http://www.uindy.edu/

University of Southern Indiana
8600 University Boulevard
Evansville, IN 47712
Phone: (812) 464-8600
E-mail: enroll@usi.edu
http://www.usi.edu

Valparaiso University
1700 Chapel Drive
Valparaiso, IN 46383
Phone: (219) 464-5011
Fax: (219) 464-6898

E-mail: undergrad.admissions@
valpo.edu
http://www.valpo.edu

IOWA

Briar Cliff University
3303 Rebecca Street
Sioux City, IA 51106
Phone: (712) 279-5200
Fax: (712) 279-1632
E-mail: admissions@briarcliff.edu
http://www.briarcliff.edu

Buena Vista College
610 West Fourth Street
Storm Lake, IA 50588
Phone: (712) 749-2400
http://www.bvu.edu

Clarke College
1550 Clarke Drive
Dubuque, IA 52001
Phone: (563) 588-6300
E-mail: admissions@clarke.edu
http://www.clarke.edu

Coe College
1220 First Avenue, NE
Cedar Rapids, IA 52402
Phone: : (319) 399-8500
Fax: (319) 399-8816
E-mail: admission@coe.edu
http://www.coe.edu

Dordt College
498 Fourth Avenue
Northeast Sioux Center, IA 51250
Phone: (712)722-6000
E-mail: admission@dordt.edu
http://www.dordt.edu

Graceland College
1 University Place
Lamoni, IA 50140
Phone: (866) 472-2352
http://www.graceland.edu

Luther College
700 College Drive
Decorah, IA 52101
Phone: (563) 387-2000
http://www.luther.edu

St. Ambrose University
518 West Locust Street
Davenport, IA 52803
Phone: (563) 333-6300
E-mail: admit@sau.edu
http://www.sau.edu

University of Dubuque
2000 University Avenue
Dubuque, IA 52001
Phone: (563) 589-3000
E-mail: admssns@dbq.edu
http://www.dbq.edu

University of Northern Iowa
1227 West 27th Street
Cedar Falls, IA 50614
Phone: (319) 273-2311
http://www.uni.edu

Upper Iowa University
P.O. Box 1859
Fayette, IA 52142
Phone: (563) 425-5393
Fax: (563) 425-5323
E-mail: admission@uiu.edu
http://www.uiu.edu

Waldorf College
106 South 6th Street
Forest City, IA 50436
Phone: (641) 585-8119
E-mail: admissions@waldorf.edu
http://www.waldorf.edu

Wartburg College
100 Wartburg Boulevard
P.O. Box 1003
Waverly, IA 50677
Phone: (319) 352-8264
Fax: (319) 352-8579
E-mail: admissions@wartburg.edu
http://www.wartburg.edu

William Penn College
201 Trueblood Avenue
Oskaloosa, IA 52577
Phone: (641) 673-1012
E-mail: admissions@wmpenn.edu
http://www.wmpenn.edu

KANSAS

Benedictine College
1020 North Second Street

Atchison, KS 66002
Phone: (913) 367-5340
Fax: (913) 367-5462
E-mail: bcadmiss@benedictine.
edu
http://www.benedictine.edu

Bethany College
421 North First Street
Lindsborg, KS 67456
Phone: (785) 227-3311
Fax: (785) 227-8993
E-mail: admissions@bethanylb.edu
http://www.bethanylb.edu

Fort Hays State University
600 Park Street
Hays, KS 67601
Phone: (785) 628-5830
E-mail: tigers@fhsu.edu
http://www.fhsu.edu

Friends University
2100 University
Wichita, KS 67213
Phone: (316)295-5000
http://www.friends.edu

Kansas Wesleyan University
100 East Claflin Avenue
Salina, KS 67401
Phone: (785) 827-5541
Fax: (785) 827-0927
E-mail: admissions@kwu.edu
http://www.kwu.edu

McPherson College
P.O. Box 1402
McPherson, KS 67460-
Phone: (620)241-0731
http://www.mcpherson.edu

MidAmerica Nazarene University
2030 East College Way
Olathe, KS 66062
Phone: (913) 791-3380
Fax: (913) 791-3481
E-mail: admissions@mnu.edu
http://www.mnu.edu

Pittsburg State University
Pittsburg, KS 66762

Phone: (620) 235-4251
Fax: (620) 235-6003
E-mail: psuadmit@pittstate.edu
http://www.pittstate.edu

Ottawa University
1001 South Cedar #17
Ottawa, KS 66067
Phone: (785) 242-5200
E-mail: admiss@ottawa.edu
http://www.ottawa.edu

Sterling College
P.O. Box 98
Sterling, KS 67579-0098
Phone: (620) 278-2173
http://www.sterling.edu

Tabor College
400 South Jefferson
Hillsboro, KS 67063
Phone: (620) 947-3121
Fax: (620) 947-6276
E-mail: rustya@tabor.edu

University of Kansas
Room 448 Murphy Hall
1530 Naismith Drive
Lawrence, KS 66045
Phone: (785) 864-9635
http://www.ku.edu

Wichita State University
1845 North Fairmount
Wichita, KS 67260
Phone: (316) 978-3085
Fax: (316) 978-3174
E-mail: admissions@wichita.edu
http://www.wichita.edu

KENTUCKY

Alice Lloyd College
100 Purpose Road
Pippa Passes, KY 41844
Phone: (606) 368-2101
Fax: (606) 368-6215
E-mail: admissions@alc.edu
http://www.alc.edu

Asbury College
Wilmore, KY 40390
Phone: (859) 858-3511

Fax: (859) 858-3921
http://www.asbury.edu

Campbellsville College
One University Drive
Campbellsville, KY 42718
Phone: (270) 789-5000
http://www.campbellsvil.edu

Eastern Kentucky University
521 Lancaster Avenue
Richmond, KY 40475
Phone: (859) 622-2106
Fax: (859) 622-8024
E-mail: admissions@eku.edu
http://www.eku.edu

Kentucky State University
400 East Main Street
Frankfort, KY 40601
Phone: (502) 597-6000
http ://www.ky su .edu

Kentucky Wesleyan College
3000 Frederica Street
Owensboro, KY 42302
Phone: (270) 926-3111
http ://www.kwc .edu

Morehead State University
University Boulevard
Morehead, KY 40351
Phone: (606) 783-2221
http://www.moreheadstate.edu

Murray State University
P.O. Box 9
Murray, KY 42071
Phone: (270) 762-3035
Fax: 270) 762-3050
E-mail: admissions@murraystate.
edu
http://www.murraystate.edu

Northern Kentucky University
Highland Heights, KY 41099
Phone: : (859) 572-5220
E-mail: admitnku@nku.edu
http://www.nku.edu

Transylvania University
300 North Broadway
Lexington, KY 40508

Phone: (859) 233-8242
E-mail: admissions@transy.edu
http://www.transy.edu

Union College
310 College Street
Barbourville, KY 40906
Phone: (606) 546-1222
Fax: (606) 546-1667
http://www.unionky.edu

University of Kentucky
100 W.D. Funkhouser Building
Lexington, KY 40506
Phone: (859) 257-2000
E-mail: admissio@uky.edu
http://www.uky.edu

University of the Cumberlands
Williamsburg, KY 40769
Phone: (606) 539-4241
E-mail: admiss@ucumberlands.edu
http://www.ucumberlands.edu

Western Kentucky University
One Big Red Way
Bowling Green, KY 42101
Phone: (270) 745-2551
Fax: (270) 745-6133
E-mail: admission@wku.edu
http://www.wku.edu

LOUISIANA

Centenary College of Louisiana
P.O. Box 41188
Shreveport, LA 71134
Phone: (318) 869-5011
http://www.centenary.edu

Dillard University
2601 Gentilly Boulevard
New Orleans, LA 70122
Phone: (504) 816-4670
Fax: (504) 816-4895
E-mail: mreed@dillard.edu
http://www.dillard.edu

Grambling State University
100 Main Street
Grambling, LA 71245
Phone: (318)274-3811
http://www.gram.edu

Louisiana College
1140 College Drive
Pineville, LA 71359
Phone: (318)487-7011
http://www.lacollege.edu

Louisiana State University and Agricultural and Mechanical College
University Station
Baton Rouge, LA 70803
Phone: (225) 388-3202
http://www.lsu.edu

McNeese State University
4100 Ryan Street
Lake Charles, LA 70609
Phone: (337) 475-5000
http://www.mcneese.edu

Nicholls State University
P.O. Box 2009
Thibodaux, LA 70310
Phone: (985)446-8111
http ://ww w.nicholls .edu

Southeastern Louisiana University
SLU 10752
Hammond, LA 70402
Phone: (985) 549-2066
Fax: (985) 549-5632
E-mail: admissions@selu.edu
http://www.selu.edu

Southern University and Agricultural and Mechanical College
P.O. Box 9901
Baton Rouge, LA 70813
Phone: (225) 771-2430
Fax: (225) 771-2500
http://www.subr.edu

University of Louisiana at Lafayette
P.O. Drawer 41210
Lafayette, LA 70504
(337) 482-6473
Fax: (337) 482-1317
E-mail: admissions@louisiana.edu
http://www.louisiana.edu

University of New Orleans
103 Administration Building
2000 Lakeshore Drive
New Orleans, LA 70148
Phone: (504) 280-6000
http://www.uno.edu

Xavier University of Louisiana
1 Drexel Drive
New Orleans, LA 70125
Phone: (504)486-7411
http://www.xula.edu

MAINE

Saint Joseph's College of Maine
278 Whites Bridge Road
Standish, ME 04084
Phone: (207) 893-7746
Fax: (207) 893-7862
E-mail: admission@sjcme.edu
http://www.sjcme.edu

University of Maine
5713 Chadbourne Hall
Orono, ME 04469
Phone: (207) 581-1561
Fax: (207) 581-1213
E-mail: um-admit@maine.maine.edu
http://www.go.umaine.edu

University of Maine at Presque Isle
181 Main Street
Presque Isle, ME 04769
Phone: (207) 768-9536
Fax: (207) 768-9777
E-mail: adventure@umpi.maine.edu
http://www.umpi.maine.edu

MARYLAND

Frostburg State University
101 Braddock Road
Frostburg, MD 21532
Phone: (301) 687-4201
Fax: (301) 687-7074
E-mail: fsuadmissions@frostburg.edu
http://www.frostburg.edu

Morgan State University
Cold Spring Lane and Hillen Road
Baltimore, MD 21251
Phone: (443) 885-3000
http://www.morgan.edu

Salisbury University
1200 Camden Avenue
Salisbury, MD 21801
Phone: (410) 543-6161
Fax: (410) 546-6016
E-mail: admissions@salisbury.edu
http://www.salisbury.edu

University of Maryland— College Park
College Park, MD 20742
Phone: (301) 405-1000
http://www.umd.edu

University of Maryland— Eastern Shore
Backbone Road
Princess Anne, MD 21853
Phone: (410) 651-2200
http://www.umes.edu

MASSACHUSETTS

Boston University
121 Bay State Road
Boston, MA 02215
Phone: (617) 353-2000
E-mail: admissions@bu.edu
http://www.bu.edu

Bridgewater State College
Bridgewater, MA 02325
Phone: (508) 531-1237
Fax: (508) 531-1746
E-mail: admission@bridgew.edu
http://www.bridgew.edu

Eastern Nazarene College
23 East Elm Avenue
Quincy, MA 02170
Phone: (800) 883-6288
Fax: (617) 745-3992
E-mail: admissions@enc.edu
http://www.enc.edu

Endicott College
376 Hale Street
Beverly, MA 01915
Phone: (978) 921-1000

Fax: (978) 232-2520
http://www.endicott.edu

Salem State College
352 Lafayette Street
Salem, MA 01970
Phone: (978) 542-6200

Springfield College
263 Alden Street
Springfield, MA 01109
Phone: (413) 748-3136
E-mail: admissions@spfldcol.edu
http://www.springfieldcollege.edu

University of Massachusetts—Boston
100 Morrissey Boulevard
Boston, MA 02125
Phone: (617) 287-6000
Fax: (617) 287-5999
E-mail: enrollment.info@umb.edu
http://umb.edu

MICHIGAN

Albion College
611 East Porter Street
Albion, MI 49224
Phone: (800) 858-6770
Fax: (517) 629-0569
E-mail: admissions@albion.edu
http://www.albion.edu

Alma College
614 West Superior Street
Alma, MI 48801
Phone: (800) 321-ALMA (toll-free)
E-mail: admissions@alma.edu
http://www.alma.edu

Aquinas College
1607 Robinson Road, SE
Grand Rapids, MI 49506
Phone: (616) 632-2900
E-mail: admissions@aquinas.edu
http://www.aquinas.edu

Calvin College
3201 Burton Street, SE
Grand Rapids, MI 49546
Phone: (616) 526-6106
Fax: (616) 526-6777

E-mail: admissions@calvin.edu
http://www.calvin.edu

Central Michigan University
Mt. Pleasant, MI 48859
Phone: (989) 774-3076
Fax: (989) 774-7267
E-mail: cmuadmit@cmich.edu
http://www.cmich.edu

Concordia University
4090 Geddes Road
Ann Arbor, MI 48105
Phone: (734) 995-7450
Fax: (734) 995-4610
http://www.cuaa.edu

Cornerstone University
1001 East Beltline Avenue, NE
Grand Rapids, MI 49525
Phone: (616) 222-1426
Fax: (616) 222-1400
http://www.cornerstone.edu

Eastern Michigan University
Ypsilanti, MI 48197
Phone: (734)487-1849
http://www.emich.edu

Grand Valley State University
One Campus Drive
Allendale, MI 49401
Phone: (616) 895-6611
E-mail: go2gvsu@gvsu.edu
http://www.gvsu.edu

Hillsdale College
Hillsdale, MI 49242
Phone: (517) 607-2327
E-mail: admissions@hillsdale.edu
http://www.hillsdale.edu

Hope College
P.O. Box 9000
Holland, MI 49422
Phone: (616) 395-7000
http://www.hope.edu

Michigan State University
250 Administration Building
East Lansing, MI 48824
Phone: (517) 355-8332
Fax: (517) 353-1647

E-mail: admis@msu.edu
http://www.msu.edu

Northern Michigan University
1401 Presque Isle Avenue
Marquette, MI 49855
Phone: (906) 227-2650
Fax: (906) 227-1747
E-mail: admiss@nmu.edu
http://www.nmu.edu

Saginaw Valley State University
7400 Bay Road
University Center, MI 48710
Phone: (989) 964-4000
http://www.svsu.edu

Spring Arbor University
106 East Main Street
Spring Arbor, MI 49283
Phone: (517) 750-1200
Fax: (517) 750-6620
E-mail: admissions@arbor.edu
http://www.arbor.edu

University of Michigan—Ann Arbor
Ann Arbor, MI 48109
Phone: (734) 764-1817
http://www.umich.edu

Wayne State University
656 West Kirby Street
Detroit, MI 48202
Phone: (313) 577-2424
http://www.wayne.edu

Western Michigan University
1903 West Michigan Avenue
Kalamazoo, MI 49008
Phone: (269) 387-2000
http://www.wmich.edu

MINNESOTA

Augsburg College
2211 Riverside Avenue
Minneapolis, MN 55454
Phone: (612) 330-1273
E-mail: admissions@augsburg.edu
http://www.augsburg.edu

Bemidji State University
1500 Birchmont Drive, NE
Bemidji, MN 56601
Phone: (218)755-3732
http://www.bemidji.state.edu

Bethel University
3900 Bethel Drive
St. Paul, MN 55112
Phone: (651) 638-6242
Fax: (651) 635-1490
E-mail: BUadmissions-cas@bethel.edu
http://www.bethel.edu

Concordia College
901 South Eighth Street
Moorhead, MN 56562-9981
Phone: (218) 299-4000
http://www.concordiacollege.edu

Concordia University
275 Syndicate North
St. Paul, MN 55104
Phone: (651) 641-8230
Fax: (651) 659-0207
E-mail: admiss@csp.edu
http://www.csp.edu

Crown College
8700 College View Drive
St. Bonifacius, MN 55375
Phone: (952) 446-4144
Fax: (952) 446-4149
http://www.crown.edu

Gustavus Adolphus College
800 West College Avenue
St. Peter, MN 56082
Phone: (507) 933-7676
Fax: (507) 933-7474
http://www.gustavus.edu

Hamline University
1536 Hewitt Avenue
St. Paul, MN 55104
Phone: (651) 523-2800
http://www.hamline.edu

Minnesota State University, Mankato
Mankato, MN 56001
Phone: (507) 389-6670

Fax: (507) 389-1511
E-mail: admissions@mnsu.edu
http://www.mnsu.edu

Minnesota State University, Moorhead
Owens Hall
Moorhead, MN 56563
Phone: (218) 477-2161
Fax: (218) 477-4374
E-mail: dragon@mnstate.edu
http://www.mnstate.edu

Northwestern College
3003 Snelling Avenue North
St. Paul, MN 55113
Phone: (651) 631-5209
Fax: (651) 631-5680
E-mail: admissions@nwc.edu
http://www.nwc.edu

Southwest Minnesota State University
1501 State Street
Marshall, MN 56258
Phone: (507) 537-6286
Fax: (507) 537-7145
E-mail: shearerr@southwestmsu.edu
http://www.southwestmsu.edu

St. Cloud State University
720 Fourth Avenue South
St. Cloud, MN 56301
Phone: (320) 308-2244
Fax: (320) 308-2243
http://www.stcloudstate.edu/

University of Minnesota
2106 Fourth Street South
Minneapolis, MN 55455
Phone: (612) 624-1091
E-mail: admissions@tc.umn.edu
http://www.umn.edu

Winona State University
P.O. Box 5838
Winona, MN 55987
Phone: (507) 457-5100
Fax: (507) 457-5620
E-mail: admissions@winona.edu
http://www.winona.edu

MISSISSIPPI

Alcorn State University
1000 ASU Drive
Alcorn State, MS 39096
Phone: (601) 877-6100
http://www.alcorn.edu

Blue Mountain College
P.O. Box 160
Blue Mountain, MS 38610-0160
Phone: (662) 685-4771
http://www.bmc.edu

Delta State University
Highway 8 West
Cleveland, MS 38733
Phone: (662) 846-3000
http://www.deltast.edu

Jackson State University
1400 John R. Lynch Street
Jackson, MS 39217
Phone: (601) 979-2121
http://www.jsums.edu

Mississippi State University
P.O. Box 6334
Mississippi State, MS 39762
Phone: (662) 325-2323
http://www.msstate.edu

Mississippi Valley State University
14000 Highway 82
West Itta Bena, MS 38941
Phone: (601) 254-9041
http://www.mvsu.edu

University of Southern Mississippi
Southern Station 5011
Hattiesburg, MS 39406
Phone: (601) 266-4111
http://www.usm.edu

University of St. Thomas
2115 Summit Avenue
St. Paul, MN 55105
Phone: (651) 962-6150
Fax: (651) 962-6160
E-mail: admissions@stthomas.edu
http://www.stthomas.edu

William Carey College
498 Tuscan Avenue
Hattiesburg, MS 39401
Phone: (601) 318-5051
http://www.wmcarey.edu

MISSOURI

Central Methodist College
411 Central Methodist Square
Fayette, MO 65248
Phone: (660) 248-3391
http://www.cmc.edu

College of the Ozarks
P.O. Box 17
Point Lookout, MO 65726
Phone: (417) 334-6411
Fax: (417) 335-2618
E-mail: admiss4@cofo.edu
http://www.cofo.edu

Culver-Stockton College
One College Hill
Canton, MO 63435
Phone: (800) 537-1883
E-mail: admissions@culver.edu
http://www.culver.edu

Hannibal-LaGrange College
2800 Palmyra Road
Hannibal, MO 63401
Phone: (573) 629-2278
http://www.hlg.edu

Lincoln University
820 Chestnut
Jefferson City, MO 65102
Phone: (573) 681-5000
http://www.lincolnu.edu

Lindenwood University
209 South Kings Highway
St. Charles, MO 63301
Phone: (636) 949-4949
Fax: (636) 949-4989
http://www.lindenwood.edu

Missouri State University
901 South National
Springfield, MO 65804
Phone: (417) 836-5517

Fax: (417) 836-6334
http://www.missouristate.edu

Missouri Valley College
500 East College
Marshall, MO 65340
Phone: (660) 831-4125
Fax: (660) 831-4233
http://www.moval.edu

Northwest Missouri State University
800 University Drive
Maryville, MO 64468
Phone: (660) 562-1146
Fax: (660) 562-1121
E-mail: admissions@nwmissouri. edu
http://www.nwmissouri.edu

Southeast Missouri State University
One University Plaza
Cape Girardeau, MO 63701
Phone: (573) 651-2000
http://www.semo.edu

Southwest Baptist University
1600 University Avenue
Bolivar, MO 65613-2597
Phone: (417) 328-5281
http://www.sbuniv.edu

University of Central Missouri
1400 Ward Edwards
Warrensburg, MO 64093
Phone: (660) 543-4170
Fax: (660) 543-8517
E-mail: admit@ucmo.edu
http://www.ucmo.edu

University of Missouri—St. Louis
8001 Natural Bridge Road
St. Louis, MO 63121
Phone: (314) 516-5000
http://www.umsl.edu

William Jewell College
500 College Hill
Liberty, MO 64068
Phone: (816) 781-7700
http://www.jewell.edu

William Woods University
1 University Avenue
Fulton, MO 65251
Phone: : (573) 592-4221
E-mail: admissions@williamwoods. edu
http://www.williamwoods.edu

MONTANA

Carroll College
1601 North Benton Avenue
Helena, MT 59625
Phone: (406) 447-4384
E-mail: admit@carroll.edu
http://www.carroll.edu

Montana State University— Billings
1500 University Drive
Billings, MT 59101
Phone: (406) 657-2158
Fax: (406) 657-2302
E-mail: admissions@msubillings. edu
http://www.subillings.edu

University of Montana—Western
710 South Atlantic Street
Dillon, MT 59725
Phone: (406) 683-7331
Fax: (406) 683-7493
E-mail: admissions@umwestern. edu
http://www.umwester.edu

NEBRASKA

Bellevue University
1000 Galvin Road South
Bellevue, NE 68005
Phone: (800) 756-7920
E-mail: infocenter@bellevue.edu
http://www.bellevue.edu

Chadron State College
1000 Main Street
Chadron, NE 69337
E-mail: inquire@csc.edu
http://www.csc.edu

Concordia University
800 North Columbia Avenue

Seward, NE 68434
Phone: (402) 643-7233
Fax: (402) 643-4073
E-mail: admiss@cune.edu
http://www.cune.edu

Doane College
1014 Boswell Avenue
Crete, NE 68333
Phone: (402) 826-8222
Fax: (402) 826-8600
http://www.doane.edu

Hastings College
710 North Turner Avenue
Hastings, NE 68901
Phone: (402) 461-7320
Fax: (402) 461-7490
E-mail: mmolliconi@hastings.edu
http://www.hastings.edu

Midland Lutheran College
Fremont, NE 68025
Phone: (402) 941-6504
Fax: (402) 941-6513
E-mail: admissions@admin.mlc.
edu
http://www.mlc.edu

Nebraska Wesleyan University
5000 Saint Paul Avenue
Lincoln, NE 68504
Phone: (402) 465-2218
Fax: (402) 465-2177
E-mail: admissions@nebrwesleyan.
edu
http://www.nebrwesleyan.edu

Peru State College
P.O. Box 10
Peru, NE 68421
Phone: (402) 872-2221
Fax: (402) 872-2296
E-mail: mwillis@oakmail.peru.ed
http://www.peru.edu

Union College
3800 South 48th Street
Lincoln, NE 68506
Phone: (402) 486-2504
Fax: (402) 486-2566
E-mail: ucenroll@ucollege.edu
http://www.ucolle.edu

**University of Nebraska—
Kearney**
905 West 25th Street
Kearney, NE 68849
Phone: (308) 865-8702
Fax: (308) 865-8987
http://www.unk.edu

**University of Nebraska—
Lincoln**
1410 Q Street
Lincoln, NE 68588
Phone: (402) 472-2023
Fax: (402) 472-0670
E-mail: admissions@unl.edu
http://www.unl.edu

Wayne State College
1111 Main Street
Wayne, NE 68787
Phone: (402) 375-7234
Fax: (402) 375-7204
E-mail: admit1@wsc.edu
http://www.wsc.edu

York College
1125 East Eighth Street
York, NE 68467
Phone: (402) 363-5627
Fax: (402) 363-5623
E-mail: enroll@york.edu
http://www.york.edu

NEVADA

University of Nevada, Las Vegas
P.O. Box 451021
4505 Maryland Parkway
Las Vegas, NV 89154
Phone: (702) 774-UNLV
Fax: (702) 774-8008
http://www.unlv.edu

University of Nevada, Reno
Reno, NV 89557
Phone: (775) 784-4700
E-mail: asknevada@unr.edu
http://www.unr.edu

NEW HAMPSHIRE

Keene State College
Elliot Hall

Keene, NH 03435
Phone: (603) 358-2276
Fax: (603) 358-2767
E-mail: admissions@keene.edu
http://www.keene.edu

New England College
26 Bridge Street
Henniker, NH 03242
Phone: : (800) 521-7642
Fax: (603) 428-3155
E-mail: admission@nec.edu
http://www.nec.edu

NEW JERSEY

College of New Jersey
P.O. Box 7718
Ewing, NJ 08628
Phone: (609) 771-2131
http://www.tcnj.edu

Kean University
1000 Morris Avenue
Union, NJ 07083
Phone: (908) 737-7100
Fax: (908) 737-7105
E-mail: admitme@kean.edu
http://www.kean.edu

Montclair State University
1 Normal Avenue
Upper Montclair, NJ 07043
Phone: (973) 655-5268
http://www.montclair.edu

Rowan University
Glassboro, NJ 08028
Phone: (856) 256-4200
E-mail: admissions@rowan.edu
http://www.rowan.edu

**William Paterson University of
New Jersey**
Wayne, NJ 07470
Phone: (973) 720-2125
E-mail: admissions@wpunj.edu
http://www.wpunj.edu

NEW MEXICO

Eastern New Mexico University
Station #7 ENMU

Portales, NM 88130
Phone: (505) 562-2178
Fax: (505) 562-2118
http://www.enmu.edu

New Mexico Highlands University
P.O. Box 9000
Las Vegas, NM 87701
Phone: (505) 454-3566
http://www.nmhu.edu/

New Mexico State University
P.O. Box 30001, MSC 3A
Las Cruces, NM 88003
Phone: (575) 646-3121
Fax: (575) 646-6330
http://wwwnmsu.edu

University of New Mexico
P.O. Box 4895
Albuquerque, NM 87196
Phone: (505) 277-2447
Fax: (505) 277-6686
http://www.unm.edu

Western New Mexico University
College Avenue
Silver City, NM 88062
Phone: (505) 538-6106
Fax: (505) 538-6127
http://www.wnmu.edu

NEW YORK

Adelphi University
Garden City, NY 11530
Phone: : (800) ADELPHI
E-mail: admissions@adelphi.edu
http://www.adelphi.edu

Brooklyn College of the City University of New York
2900 Bedford Avenue
Brooklyn, NY 11210
Phone: (718) 951-5001
E-mail: adminqry@brooklyn.cuny.
edu
http://www.brooklyn.cuny.edu/pug

Canisius College
2001 Main Street
Buffalo, NY 14208

Phone: (716) 888-2200
Fax: (716) 888-3230
E-mail: admissions@canisius.edu
http://www.canisius.edu/admissions

Hofstra University
100 Hofstra University
Hempstead, NY 11549
Phone: (516) 463-6700
Fax: (516) 463-5100
http://www.hofstra.edu

Houghton College
P.O. Box 128
Houghton, NY 14744
Phone: (585) 567-9353
Fax: (585) 567-9522
E-mail: admission@houghton.edu
http://www.houghton.edu

Hunter College of the City University of New York
695 Park Avenue
New York, NY 10065
Phone: (212) 772-4490
Fax: (212) 650-3336
E-mail: WelcomeCenter@hunter.
cuny.edu
http://www.hunter.cuny.edu

Ithaca College
100 Job Hall
Ithaca, NY 14850
Phone: (607) 274-3124
Fax: (607) 274-1900
http://www.ithaca.edu/admission

Long Island University, Brooklyn Campus
1 University Plaza
Brooklyn, NY 11201
Phone: (718) 488-1011
Fax: (718) 797-2399
E-mail: admissions@brooklyn.liu.
edu
http://www.brooklyn.liu.edu

Long Island University, C.W. Post Campus
720 Northern Boulevard
Brookville, NY 11548
Phone: (516) 299-2900
Fax: (516) 299-2137

E-mail: enroll@cwpost.liu.edu
http://www.liu.edu

Manhattan College
Riverdale, NY 10471
Phone: (718) 862-7200
E-mail: admit@manhattan.edu
http://www.manhattan.edu

Queens College of the City University of New York
65-30 Kissena Boulevard
Flushing, NY 11367
Phone: (718) 997-5600
E-mail: admissions@qc.edu
http://www.qc.edu

State University of New York at Brockport
350 New Campus Drive
Brockport, NY 14420
Phone: (585) 395-2751
Fax: (585) 395-5452
E-mail: admit@brockport.edu

State University of New York at Cortland
P.O. Box 2000
Cortland, NY 13045
Phone: (607) 753-4711
Fax: (607) 753-5998
http://www.cortland.edu/

Syracuse University
Syracuse, NY 13244
Phone: (315) 443-3611
http://admissions.syr.edu
http://www.syr.edu

NORTH CAROLINA

Appalachian State University
Boone, NC 28608
Phone: (828) 262-2000
E-mail: admissions@appstate.edu
http://www.appstate.edu

Barton College
P.O. Box 5000
Wilson, NC 27893
Phone: (252) 399-6317
Fax: (252) 399-6572
E-mail: enroll@barton.edu
http://www.barton.edu

Campbell University
P.O. Box 546
Buies Creek, NC 27506
Phone: (910) 893-1320
E-mail: adm@mailcenter.campbell.
edu
http://www.campbell.edu

Catawba College
Salisbury, NC 28144
Phone: (704) 637-4402
E-mail: admissions@catawba.edu

Chowan University
200 Jones Drive
Murfreesboro, NC 27855
Phone: (252) 398-6298
http://www.chowan.edu

East Carolina University
Greenville, NC 27858
Phone: (252) 328-6640
Fax: (252) 328-6945
E-mail: admis@mail.ecu.edu
http://www.ecu.edu

Elon University
Elon, NC 27244
Phone: (336) 278-3566
E-mail: admissions@elon.edu
http://www.elon.edu

Fayetteville State University
1200 Murchison Road
Fayetteville, NC 28301
Phone: (910) 486-1371
http://www.uncfsu.edu

Gardner-Webb University
Boiling Springs, NC 28017
Phone: (704) 406-4GWU
http://www.gardner-webb.edu

Greensboro College
815 West Market Street
Greensboro, NC 27401
Phone: (800) 346-8226
E-mail: admissions@gborocollege.
edu
http://ww.gborocollege.edu

High Point University
833 Montlieu Avenue

High Point, NC 27262
Phone: (336) 841-9216
E-mail: admiss@highpoint.edu
http://www.highpoint.edu

Lenoir-Rhyne College
P.O. Box 7227,
Hickory, NC 28603
Phone: (828) 328-7300
Fax: (828) 328-7378
E-mail: admission@lrc.edu
http://www.lrc.edu

Mars Hill College
Mars Hill, NC 28754
Phone: (828) 689-1201
Fax: (828) 689-1473
E-mail: admissions@mhc.edu
http://www.mhc.edu

Meredith College
3800 Hillsborough Street
Raleigh, NC 27607
Phone: (919) 760-8581
Fax: (919) 760-2348
E-mail: admissions@meredith.edu
http://www.meredith.edu

Methodist University
5400 Ramset Street
Fayetteville, NC 28311
Phone: (910) 630-7027
http://www.methodist.edu

**North Carolina Agricultural
and Technical State
University**
Greensboro, NC 27411
Phone: (336) 334-7946
http://www.ncat.edu

**North Carolina Central
University**
P.O. Box 19717
Durham, NC 27707
Phone: (919) 530-6298
Fax: (919) 530-7625
E-mail: admissions@nccu.edu
http://www.nccu.edu

Pfeiffer University
P.O. Box 960
Highway 52 North

Misenheimer, NC 28109
Phone: (704) 463-1360
Fax: (704) 463-1363
E-mail: admiss@pfeiffer.edu
http://www.pfeiffer.edu

**University of North Carolina at
Pembroke**
One University Drive
Pembroke, NC 28372
Phone: (910) 521-6262
Fax: (910) 521-6497
E-mail: admissions@uncp.edu
http://www.uncp.edu

**University of North Carolina at
Wilmington**
601 South College Road
Wilmington, NC 28403
Phone: (910) 962-4198
Fax: (910) 962-3038
E-mail: admissions@uncwil.edu
http://www.uncwil.edu

Western Carolina University
Cullowhee, NC 28723
Phone: (828) 227-7317
Fax: (828) 227-7319
E-mail: admiss@wcu.edu
http://www.poweryourmind.com

NORTH DAKOTA

Dickinson State University
Dickinson, ND 58601
Phone: (701) 483-2175
http://www.dickinsonstate.edu

Jamestown College
6081 College Lane
Jamestown, ND 58405
Phone: (701) 252-3467
Fax: (701) 253-4318
E-mail: admissions@jc.edu
http://www.jc.edu

Minot State University
500 University Avenue West
Minot, ND 58707
Phone: (701) 858-3126
Fax: (701) 858-3825
E-mail askmsu@minotstateu.edu
http://www.minotstateu.edu

North Dakota State University
P.O. Box 5454
Fargo, ND 58105
Phone: (701) 231-8643
Fax: (701) 231-8802
E-mail: ndsu.admission@ndsu.edu
http://www.ndsu.edu

University of North Dakota
P.O. Box 7125
Grand Forks, ND 58202
Phone: (701) 777-2828
Fax: (701) 777-2721
E-mail: enrollmentservices@mail.
   und.nodak.edu
http://www.und.nodak.edu

Valley City State University
101 College Street Southwest
Valley City, ND 58072
Phone: (701) 845-7204
Fax: (701) 845-7299
http://www.vcsu.edu

OHIO

Ashland University
Ashland, OH 44805
Phone: (419) 289-5052
Fax: (419) 289-5999
E-mail: enrollme@ashland.edu
http://www.Ashland.edu

Bowling Green State University
Bowling Green, OH 43403
Phone: (419) 372-BGSU
E-mail: choosebgsu@bgnet.bgsu.
   edu
http://www.bgsu.edu

Capital University
1 College and Main
Columbus, OH 43209
Phone: (614) 236-6101
Fax: (614) 236-6926
E-mail: admissions@capital.edu
http://www.capital.edu

Cleveland State University
1806 East 22nd Street
Cleveland, OH 44114
Phone: (216) 687-2100
Fax: (216) 687-9210

E-mail: admissions@csuohio.edu
http://csuohio.edu

Denison University
Granville, OH 43023
Phone: (740) 587-6276
E-mail: admissions@denison.edu
http://www.denison.edu

Heidelberg College
310 East Market Street
Tiffin, OH 44883
Phone: (419) 448-2330
Fax: (419) 448-2334
E-mail: adminfo@heidelberg.edu
http://www.heidelberg.edu

John Carroll University
University Heights, OH 44118
Phone: (216) 397-4294
E-mail: admission@jcu.edu
http://www.jcu.edu

Kent State University
P.O. Box 5190
Kent, OH 44242
Phone: (330) 672-2444
E-mail: kentadm@kent.edu
http://www.kent.edu

Miami University
Oxford, OH 45056
Phone: (513) 529-5040
http://www.miami.muohio.edu

Miami University Hamilton
1601 Peck Boulevard
Hamilton, OH 45011
Phone: (513) 785-3111
Fax: (513) 785-1807
http://www.ham.muohio.edu

Mount Union College
1972 Clark Avenue
Alliance, OH 44601
Phone: (330) 823-2590
E-mail: admissn@muc.edu
http://www.muc.edu

Muskingum College
163 Stormont Street
New Concord, OH43762
Phone: (740) 826-8137

Fax: (740) 826-8100
E-mail: adminfo@muskingum.edu
http://www.muskingum.edu

Ohio Northern University
Ada, OH 45810
Phone: (888) 408-4668
Fax: (419) 772-2821
E-mail: admissions-ug@onu.edu
http://www.onu.edu

Ohio University
Athens, OH 45701-2979
Phone: (740) 593-4100
Fax: (740) 593-0560
E-mail: admissions@ohio.edu
http://www.ohio.edu

Ohio Wesleyan University
Delaware, OH 43015
Phone: (740) 368-3020
Fax: (740) 368-3314
E-mail: owuadmit@owu.edu
http://www.owu.edu

Otterbein College
One Otterbein College
Westerville, OH 43081
Phone: (614) 823-1500
E-mail: uotterb@otterbein.edu
http://www.otterbein.edu

University of Akron
277 East Buchtel Avenue
Akron, OH 44325
Phone: (330) 972-6427
Fax: (330) 972-7022
E-mail: admissions@uakron.edu
http://www.uakron.edu

University of Cincinnati
P.O. Box 210091
Cincinnati, OH 45221
Phone: (513) 556-1100
Fax: (513) 556-1105
E-mail: admissions@uc.edu
http://www.uc.edu

University of Dayton
300 College Park
Dayton, OH 45469
Phone: (937) 229-4411
E-mail: admission@udayton.edu
http://www.udayton.edu

University of Findlay
1000 North Main Street
Findlay, OH 45840
Phone: (419) 434-4732
E-mail: admissions@findlay.edu
http://www.findlay.edu

University of Rio Grande
P.O. Box 500
Rio Grande, OH 45674
Phone: (740) 245-7208
Fax: (740)245-7260
E-mail: admissions@rio.edu
http://www.rio.edu

University of Toledo
2801 West Bancroft
Toledo, OH 43606
Phone: (419) 530-5728
Fax: (419) 530-5872
E-mail: enroll@utnet.utoledo.edu
http://www.utoledo.edu

Walsh University
2020 East Maple Street, NW
North Canton, OH 44720
Phone: (330) 492-7172
Fax: (330) 490-7165
E-mail: admissions@walsh.edu
http://www.walsh.edu

Wilmington College
251 Ludovic Street
Wilmington, OH 45177
Phone: (937) 382-6661
Fax: (937) 382-7077
E-mail: admission@wilmington.
edu
http://www.wilmington.edu

Wright State University
Dayton, OH 45435
Phone: (937) 775-5700
E-mail: admission@wright.edu
http://www.wright.edu

Youngstown State University
One University Plaza
Youngstown, OH 44555
Phone: (330) 941-2000
Fax: (330) 941-3674
E-mail: enroll@ysu.edu
http://www.ysu.edu

OKLAHOMA

East Central University
1100 East 14th Street
Ada, OK 74820
Phone: (580) 310-5233
E-mail: pdenny@ecok.edu
http://www.ecok.edu

Langston University
P.O. Box 728
Langston, OK 73120
Phone: (405) 466-2984
Fax: (405) 466-3391
http://www.lunet.edu

Northeastern State University
601 North Grand
Tahlequah, OK 74464
Phone: (918) 444-2211
Fax: (918) 458-2342
E-mail: cain@nsuok.edu
http://www.nsuok.edu

Northwestern Oklahoma State University
709 Oklahoma Boulevard
Alva, OK 73717
Phone: (580) 327-8550
Fax: (580) 327-8699
E-mail: smmurrow@nwosu.edu
http://www.nwosu.edu

Oklahoma Baptist University
P.O. Box 61174
Shawnee, OK 74804
Phone: (405) 878-2033
Fax: (405) 878-2046
E-mail: admissions@mail.okbu.edu
http://www.okbu.edu

Oklahoma Christian University
P.O. Box 11000
Oklahoma City, OK 73136
Phone: (405) 425-5050
Fax: (405) 425-5208
E-mail: info@oc.edu
http://www.oc.edu

Oklahoma City University
2501 North Blackwelder
Oklahoma City, OK 73106
Phone: (405) 521-5050

E-mail: mlockhart@okcu.edu
http://www.okcu.edu

Oklahoma State University
Stillwater, OK 74078
Phone: (405) 744-6858
Fax: (405) 744-5285
E-mail: admit@okstate.edu
http://www.okstate.edu

Oral Roberts University
7777 South Lewis Avenue
Tulsa, OK 74171
Phone: (918) 495-6518
Fax: (918) 495-6222
E-mail: admissions@oru.edu
http://www.oru.edu

Southeastern Oklahoma State University
1405 North Fourth Avenue
Durant, OK 74701
Phone: (580) 745-2060
Fax: (580) 745-7502
E-mail: admissions@sosu.edu
http://www.sosu.edu

Southwestern Oklahoma State University
100 Campus Drive
Weatherford, OK 73096
Phone: (580) 774-3009
Fax: (580) 774-3795
E-mail: ropers@swosu.edu
http://www.swosu.edu

University of Central Oklahoma
100 North University Drive
Edmond, OK 73034
Phone: (405) 974-2338
Fax: (405) 341-4964
E-mail: admituco@ucok.edu
http://ucok.edu

OREGON

Concordia University
3811 Northeast Holman Street
Portland, OR 97211
Phone: (503) 493-6526
Fax: (503)280-8531
E-mail: admission@cu-portland.edu
http://www.cu-portland.edu

Corban College
5000 Deer Park Drive, SE
Salem, OR 97301
Phone: (503) 375-7115
Fax: (503) 585-4316
E-mail: admissions@corban.edu
http://www.corban.edu

Eastern Oregon University
One University Boulevard
La Grande, OR 97850
Phone: (541) 962-3085
Fax: (541) 962-3418
E-mail: admissions@eou.edu
http://www.eou.edu

George Fox University
Newberg, OR 97132
Phone: (800) 765-4369
E-mail: admissions@georgefox.edu
http://www.georgefox.edu

Oregon State University
104 Kerr Administration Building
Corvallis, OR 97331
Phone: (800) 291-4192
Fax: (541) 737-2482
E-mail: osuadmit@oregonstate.edu
http://oregonstate.edu/admissions

Southern Oregon University
1250 Siskiyou Boulevard
Ashland, OR 97520
Phone: (541) 552-6411
Fax: (541) 552-6614
E-mail: admissions@sou.edu
http://www.sou.edu

Warner Pacific College
2219 Southeast 68th Avenue
Portland, OR 97215
Phone: (503) 517-1000
http://www.warnerpacific.edu

PENNSYLVANIA

East Stroudsburg University of Pennsylvania
200 Prospect Street
East Stroudsburg, PA 18301
Phone: (570) 422-3542
Fax: (570) 422-3933
http://www.esu.edu

Gettysburg College
300 North Washington Street
Gettysburg, PA 17325
Phone: (717) 337-6100
Fax: (717) 337-6145
http://www.gettysburg.edu

Indiana University of Pennsylvania
1011 South Drive
Indiana, PA 15705
Phone: (724) 357-2230
Fax: (724) 357-6281
E-mail: admissions-inquiry@iup.edu
http://www.iup.edu/admissions

Lock Haven University of Pennsylvania
Lock Haven, PA 17745
Phone: (570) 484-2027
Fax: (570) 484-2201
E-mail: admissions@lhup.edu
http://www.lhup.edu

Messiah College
P.O. Box 3005
One College Avenue
Grantham, PA 17027
Phone: (717) 691-6000
Fax: (717) 796-5374
E-mail: admiss@messiah.edu

Slippery Rock University of Pennsylvania
1 Morrow Way
Slippery Rock, PA 16057
Phone: (724) 738-2447
Fax: (724) 738-2913
E-mail: asktherock@sru.edu
http://www.sru.edu

Temple University
1801 North Broad Street
Philadelphia, PA 19122
Phone: (215) 204-7200
E-mail: tuadm@temple.edu
http://www.temple.edu

University of Pittsburgh
4227 Fifth Avenue
First Floor, Alumni Hall
Pittsburgh, PA 15260
Phone: (412) 624-7488

Fax: (412) 648-8815
E-mail: oafa@pitt.edu
http://www.pitt.edu

University of Pittsburgh at Bradford
300 Campus Drive
Bradford, PA 16701
Phone: (814) 362-7555
http://www.upb.pitt.edu

RHODE ISLAND

Rhode Island College
600 Mount Pleasant Avenue
Providence, RI 02908
Phone: (401) 456-8234
Fax: (401) 456-8817
E-mail: admission@ric.edu
http://www.ric.edu

University of Rhode Island
14 Upper College Road
Kingston, RI 02881
Phone: (401) 874-7000
E-mail: admission@uri.edu
http://www.uri.edu

SOUTH CAROLINA

Anderson College
316 Boulevard
Anderson, SC 29621
Phone: (864) 231-2030
Fax: (864) 231-2033
http://www.ac.edu

Charleston Southern University
9200 University Boulevard
P.O. Box 118087
Charleston, SC 29423
Phone: (843) 863-7050
http://www.charlestonsouthern.edu

Coker College
300 East College Avenue
Hartsville, SC 29550
Phone: (843) 383-8050
Fax: (843) 383-8056
E-mail: admissions@coker.edu
http://www.coker.edu

Erskine College
2 Washington Street
Due West, SC 29639
Phone: (864) 379-2131
http://www.erskine.edu

Lander University
320 Stanley Avenue
Greenwood, SC 29649
Phone: (864) 388-8307
Fax: (864) 388-8125
http://www.lander.edu

Limestone College
1115 College Drive
Gaffney, SC 29340
Phone: (864) 488-4554
Fax: (864) 488-8206
E-mail: admiss@limestone.edu
http://www.limestone.edu

Newberry College
2100 College Street
Newberry, SC 29108
Phone: (803) 321-5127
E-mail: admissions@newberry.edu
http://www.newberry.edu

South Carolina State University
300 College Street Northeast
Orangeburg, SC 29117
Phone: (803) 536-8408
Fax: (803) 536-8990
E-mail: admissions@scsu.edu
http://www.scsu.edu

**University of South Carolina—
Columbia**
Columbia, SC 29208
Phone: (803) 777-7000
E-mail: admissions-ugrad@sc.edu
http://www.sc.edu

**University of South Carolina—
Upstate**
800 University Way
Spartanburg, SC 29303
Phone: (864) 503-5280
Fax: (864) 503-5727
http://www. upstate.edu

Voorhees College
P.O. Box 678

Denmark, SC 29042
Phone: (803) 703-1049
http://www.voorhees.edu/

Winthrop University
Rock Hill, SC 29733
Phone: (803) 323-2191
E-mail: admissions@winthrop.edu
http://www.winthrop.edu

SOUTH DAKOTA

Augustana College
2001 South Summit Avenue
Sioux Falls, SD 57197
Phone: (605) 274-5516
Fax: (605) 274-5518
http://www.augustana.edu

Dakota State University
820 North Washington
Madison, SD 57042
Phone: (605) 256-5139
Fax: (605) 256-5020
http://www.dsu.edu

Northern State College
1200 South Jay Street
Aberdeen, SD 57401
Phone: (605) 626-3011
http://www.northern.edu

University of South Dakota
414 East Clark Street
Vermillion, SD 57069
Phone: (605) 677-5434
Fax: (605) 677-6753
http://www.sdstate.edu

TENNESSEE

Belmont University
1900 Belmont Boulevard
Nashville, TN 37212,
Phone: (615) 460-6785
Fax: (615) 460-5434
E-mail: buadmission@mail.
belmont.edu
http://www.belmont.edu

Bryan College
P.O. Box 7000
Dayton, TN 37321

Phone: (423) 775-2041
Fax: (423) 775-7199
E-mail: admissions@bryan.edu
http://www.bryan.edu

Carson-Newman College
Jefferson City, TN 37760
Phone: (865) 471-3223
E-mail: thuebner@cn.edu
http://www.cn.edu

Cumberland University
One Cumberland Square
Lebanon, TN 37087
Phone: (615) 444-2562 Ext. 1280
Fax: (615) 444-2569
E-mail: admissions@cumberland.
edu
http://www.cumberland.edu

Freed-Hardeman University
158 East Main Street
Henderson, TN 38340
Phone: (731) 989-6651
Fax: (731) 989-6047
E-mail: admissions@fhu.edu
http://www.fhu.edu

Lambuth University
705 Lambuth Boulevard
Jackson, TN 38301
Phone: (731) 425-3223
E-mail: admit@lambuth.edu
http://www.lambuth.edu

Lee College
P.O. Box 3450
Cleveland, TN 37311
Phone: (423) 614-8000
http://www.leeuniversity.edu

Lincoln Memorial University
Cumberland Gap Parkway
Harrogate, TN 37752
Phone: (423) 869-6280
E-mail: admissions@lmuuet.edu
http://www.lmunet.edu

Maryville College
502 East Lamar Alexander Parkway
Maryville, TN 37804
Phone: (865) 981-8092
Fax: (865) 981-8005

E-mail: admissions@maryville
college.edu
http://www.maryvillecollege.edu

Union University
1050 Union University Drive
Jackson, TN 38305
Phone: (731) 661-5100
E-mail: info@uu.edu
http://www.uu.edu

University of Memphis
101 John Wilder Tower
Memphis, TN 38152
Phone: (901) 678-2169
http://www.memphis.edu

TEXAS

Abilene Christian University
ACU Box 29100
Abilene, TX 79699
Phone: (915) 674-2000
http://www.acu.edu

Baylor University
One Bear Place #97056
Waco, TX 76798
Phone: (254) 710-3435
http://www.baylor.edu

Dallas Baptist University
3000 Mountain Creek Parkway
Dallas, TX 75211
Phone: (214) 333-5360
Fax: (214) 333-5447
E-mail: admiss@dbu.edu
http://www.dbu.edu

East Texas Baptist University
1209 North Grove
Marshall, TX 75670
Phone: (903) 935-7963
http://www.etbu.edu

Hardin-Simmons University
P.O. Box 16050
Abilene, TX 79698
Phone: (325) 670-5890
Fax: (325) 671-2115
E-mail: breynolds@hsutx.edu
http://www.hsutx.edu

Howard Payne University
1000 Fisk Avenue
Brownwood, TX 76801
Phone: (325) 649-8027
Fax: (325) 649-8901
E-mail: enroll@hputx.edu
http://www.hputx.edu

Huston-Tillotson College
900 Chicon Street
Austin, TX 78702
Phone: (512) 505-3027
http://www.htc.edu

Jarvis Christian College
P.O. Box 1470
Hawkins, TX 75765
Phone: (903) 769-5700
http://www.jarvis.edu

Lamar University
Lamar University Station
Beaumont, TX 77705
Phone: (409) 880-8888
http://www.lamar.edu

Midland College
3600 North Garfield
Midland, TX 79705
Phone: (432) 685-5502
Fax: (432) 685-6401
http://www.midland.edu

Sam Houston State University
P.O. Box 2418
Huntsville, TX 77341
(936) 294-1111
E-mail: admissions@shsu.edu
http://www.shsu.edu

Tarleton State University
Tarleton Station
Stephenville, TX 76402
Phone: (254) 968-9125
Fax: (254) 968-9951
E-mail: uadm@tarleton.edu
http://www.tarleton.edu

Texas A&M University
Texas A&M International
University
5201 University Boulevard
Laredo, TX 78041-1900

Phone: (956) 326-2270
http://www.tamiu.edu/

Texas Christian University
2800 South University Drive
Fort Worth, TX 76129
Phone: (817) 257-7490
Fax: (817) 257-7268
E-mail: frogmail@tcu.edu
http://www.tcu.edu

Wiley College
711 Wiley Avenue
Marshall, TX 75670
Phone: (903) 927-3222
Fax: (903) 923-8878
E-mail: ajones@wileyc.edu
http://www.wileyc.edu

UTAH

Southern Utah University
351 West Center Street
Cedar City, UT 84720
Phone: (801) 586-7740
Fax: (435) 865-8223
E-mail: adminfo@suu.edu
http://www.suu.edu

Utah State University
Logan, UT 84322
Phone: (435) 797-1079
Fax: (435) 797-3708
E-mail: admit@cc.usu.edu
http://www.usu.edu

Utah Valley State College
800 West University Parkway
Orem, UT 84058
Phone: (801) 863-8460
Fax: (801) 225-4677
E-mail: info@uvsc.edu
http://www.uvsc.edu

Weber State University
3748 Harrison Boulevard
Ogden, UT 84408
Phone: (801) 626-6050
Fax: (801) 626-6744
E-mail: admissions@weber.edu
http://www.weber.edu

VERMONT

Castleton State College
Castleton, VT 05735
Phone: (802) 468-1213
Fax: (802) 468-1476
E-mail: info@castleton.edu
http://www.castleton.edu

Johnson State College
337 College Hill
Johnson, VT 05656
Phone: (802) 635-1219
Fax: (802) 635-1230
http://www.jsc.vsc.edu

Lyndon State College
P.O. Box 919
Lyndonville, VT 05851
Phone: (800) 225-1998
Fax: (802) 626-6335
E-mail: admissions@lyndonstate.edu
http://www.lyndonstate.edu

University of Vermont
194 South Prospect Street
Burlington, VT 05401
Phone: (802) 656-3370
Fax: (802) 656-8611
E-mail: admissions@uvm.edu
http://www.uvm.edu

VIRGINIA

Bluefield College
3000 College Drive
Bluefield, VA 24605
Phone: (276) 326-4214
Fax: (276) 326-4288
E-mail: admissions@mail.bluefield.
edu
http://www.bluefield.edu

George Mason University
4400 University Drive
Fairfax, VA 22030
Phone: (703) 993-2398
E-mail: admissions@gmu.edu
http://www.gmu.edu

Hampton University
Hampton, VA 23668
Phone: (757) 727-5328

Fax: (757) 727-5095
E-mail: admit@hamptonu.edu
http://www.hamptonu.edu

Liberty University
1971 University Boulevard
Lynchburg, VA 24502
Phone: (434) 582-2000
http://www.liberty.edu

Longwood University
Farmville, VA 23909
Phone: (434) 395-2060
Fax: (434) 395-2332
E-mail: admit@longwood.edu
http://www.longwood.edu

Old Dominion University
108 Rollins Hall
Norfolk, VA 23529
Phone :(757) 683-3685
E-mail: admit@odu.edu
http://www.odu.edu

Shenandoah University
1460 University Drive
Winchester, VA 22601
Phone: (540) 665-4581
Fax: (540) 665-4627
E-mail: admit@su.edu
http://www.su.edu

WASHINGTON

Central Washington University
400 East University Way
Ellensburg, WA 98926
Phone: (509) 963-1211
Fax: (509) 963-3022
E-mail: cwuadmis@cwu.edu
http://www.cwu.edu

Gonzaga University
Spokane, WA 99258
Phone: (800) 322-2584
E-mail: mcculloh@gu.gonzaga.edu
http://www.gonzaga.edu

Seattle Pacific University
3307 Third Avenue West, Suite 115
Seattle, WA 98119
Phone: (206) 281-2021

E-mail: admissions@spu.edu
http://www.spu.edu

Walla Walla College
204 South College Avenue
College Place, WA 99324
Phone: (509) 527-2327
Fax: (509) 527-2397
E-mail: info@wwc.edu
http://www.wwc.edu

Washington State University
Pullman, WA 99164
Phone: (509) 335-5586
Fax: (509) 335-7468
E-mail: admiss@wsu.edu
http://www.wsu.edu

Western Washington University
516 High Street
Bellingham, WA 98225
Phone: (360) 650-3440
Fax: (360) 650-7369
E-mail: admit@wwu.edu
http://www.wwu.edu

Whitworth College
West 300 Hawthorne Road
Spokane, WA 99251
Phone: (509) 777-3212
E-mail: admission@whitworth.edu
http://www.whitworth.edu

WEST VIRGINIA

Alderson-Broaddus College
Philippi, WV 26416
Phone: (800) 263-1549 (toll-free)
E-mail: admissions@ab.edu
http://www.ab.edu

Concord University
1000 Vermillion Street
Athens, WV 24712
Phone: (304) 384-5248
Fax: (304) 384-9044
E-mail: admissions@concord.edu
http://www.concord.edu

Davis & Elkins College
100 Campus Drive
Elkins, WV 26241
Phone: (304) 637-1230

E-mail: admiss@davisandelkins.edu
http://www.davisandelkins.edu

Fairmont State University
1201 Locust Avenue
Fairmont, WV 26554
Phone: (304) 367-4892
E-mail: fscinfo@mail.fscwv.edu
http://www.fscwv.edu

West Virginia State University
Campus Box 197
P.O. Box 1000
Institute, WV 25112
Phone: (304) 766-3032
Fax: (304) 766-4158
E-mail: : sweeneyt@wvstateu.edu
http://www.wvstateu.edu

West Virginia Wesleyan College
59 College Avenue
Buckhannon, WV 26201
Phone: (304) 473-8510
E-mail: admission@wvwc.edu
http://www.wvwc.edu

West Virginia University
P.O. Box 6009
Morgantown, WV 26506
Phone: (304) 293-2124
Fax: (304) 293-3080
E-mail: go2wvu@mail.wvu.edu
http://www.wvu.edu

WISCONSIN

Carroll University
100 North East Avenue
Waukesha, WI 53186
Phone: (262) 524-7221
Fax: (262) 524-7139
http://www.cc.edu

Carthage College
2001 Alford Park Drive
Kenosha, WI 53140
Phone: (262) 551-8500
http://www.carthage.edu

Concordia University Wisconsin
12800 North Lake Drive
Mequon, WI 53097
Phone: (262) 243-4305
http://www.cuw.edu

Ripon College
300 Seward Street
P.O. Box 248
Ripon, WI 54971
Phone: (800) 94RIPON
E-mail: adminfo@ripon.edu
http://www.ripon.edu

University of Wisconsin—La Crosse
1725 State Street
La Crosse, WI 54601
Phone: (608) 785-8939
Fax: (608)785-8940
http://www.uwlax.edu

University of Wisconsin—Madison
716 Langdon Street
Madison, WI 53706
Phone: (608) 262-3961
Fax: (608) 262-7706
E-mail: on.wisconsin@admissions.wisc.edu
http://www.wisc.edu

University of Wisconsin—Oshkosh
800 Algoma Boulevard
Oshkosh, WI 54901
Phone: (920) 424-0202

E-mail: oshadmuw@uwosh.edu
http://www.uwosh.edu

University of Wisconsin—River Falls
410 South Third Street
River Falls, WI 54022
Phone: (715) 425-3500
Fax: (715) 425-0676
E-mail: admit@uwrf.edu
http://www.urf.edu

University of Wisconsin—Stevens Point
2100 Main Street
Stevens Point, WI 54481
Phone: (715) 346-0123
http://www.uwsp.edu

University of Wisconsin—Superior
Belknap Catlin
P.O. Box 2000
Superior, WI 54880
Phone: (715) 394-8101
http://www.uwsuper.edu

University of Wisconsin—Whitewater
800 West Main Street
Whitewater, WI 53190
Phone: (262) 472-1440
Fax: (262) 472-1515
http://www.uww.edu

WYOMING

University of Wyoming
1000 East University Avenue
Laramie, WY 82071
Phone: (307) 766-5160
E-mail: why-wyo@uwyo.edu
http://www.uwyo.edu

APPENDIX II
PROGRAMS IN SPORTS OFFICIATING

The following is a selected listing of schools, training camps, and other programs developed or sponsored by organizations that train officials for various sports. Write, call, or e-mail to obtain information.

Use these names to get started. This is not a complete listing by any means. Contact associations and organizations relevant to the sport you are interested in officiating to locate additional programs. Inclusion or exclusion on this list does not indicate the recommendation or endorsement by the author of one company over another.

Amateur Softball Association of America (ASA)
2801 Northeast 40th Street
Oklahoma City, OK 73111
Phone: (405) 424-5266
Fax: (405) 424-3855
E-mail: bmccall@softball.org
http://www.softball.org

Eastern College Athletic Conference (ECAC)
P.O. Box 3
Centerville, MA 02632
Phone: (508) 771-5060
E-mail: cserajin@ecac.org
http://www.ecac.org

Harry Wendelstedt Umpire School
88 South Street & Andrews Drive
Ormond Beach, FL 32174
Phone: (800) 818-1690
http://www.umpireschool.com

International Association of Approved Basketball Officials (IAABO)
P.O. Box 1300
Germantown, MD 20875
Phone: (301) 540-5180

Fax: (301) 540-5182
E-mail: jacky_loube@verizon.net
http://www.iaabo.org

Jim Evans Academy of Professional Umpiring
200 South Wilcox Street, #508
Castle Rock, CO 80104
Phone: (303) 290-7411
http://www.umpireacademy.com

Major League Baseball Umpire Camp
245 Park Avenue
New York, NY 10167
Phone: (212) 931-7537
E-mail: mlbumpirecamps@mlb.com
http://mlb.mlb.com/mlb/official_info/umpires/camp

National Association of Sports Officials (NASO) (various sports)
2017 Lathrop Avenue
Racine, WI 53405
Phone: (262) 632-5448
Fax: (262) 632-5460
E-mail: cservice@naso.org
http://www.naso.org

National Gymnastics Judges Association (NGJA)
c/o Butch Zunich, President
2302 Sand Point
Champaign, IL 61822
Phone: (217) 359-4866
(217) 384-8517
Fax: (217) 384-8550
E-mail: zunich@ngja.org
http://www.ngja.org

National Intercollegiate Soccer Officials Association (NISOA)
541 Woodview Drive
Longwood, FL 32779
Phone: (407) 862-3305
Fax: (407) 862-8545
E-mail: information@nisoa.com
http://www.nisoa.com

Professional Association of Volleyball Officials
P.O. Box 780
Oxford, KS 67119
Phone: (888) 791-2074
E-mail: pavo@pavo.org
http://www.pavo.org

APPENDIX III
WORKSHOPS, SEMINARS, AND SYMPOSIUMS

The following is a listing of workshops, seminars, courses, and symposiums, including what general subject matter is covered. This is by no means a complete listing. Many associations, schools, companies, and organizations offer other workshops. As subject matter changes frequently, a number of people running these workshops and seminars did not wish to have their programs listed. You may want to contact associations related to the area of employment in which you are interested to obtain more information on programs not listed here.

This listing is provided for informational purposes. The author does not recommend or endorse any one program over another.

American Athletic Trainers Association and Certification Board (AATA)
146 East Duarte Road
Arcadia, CA 91006
Phone: (626) 445-1978
Fax: (626) 574-1999
E-mail: americansportsmedicine@hotmail.com
The American Athletic Trainers Association and Certification Board (AATA) hold an annual conference as well as conducting continuing training for athletic trainers.

American Baseball Coaches Association (ABCA)
108 South University Avenue
Suite 3
Mount Pleasant, MI 48858
Phone: (989) 775-3300
Fax: (989)775-3600
E-mail: abca@abca.org
http://www.abca.org
The American Baseball Coaches Association offers coaching clinics to coaches working in schools, colleges, and universities.

American Sportscasters Association (ASA)
225 Broadway
New York, NY 10007
Phone: (212) 227-8080
Fax: (212) 571-0556
E-mail: lschwa8918@aol.com
http://www.americansportscasters online.com
The American Sportscasters Association offers seminars, clinics, and workshops to individuals aspiring to enter the sportscasting field.

American Youth Soccer Organization (AYSO)
12501 South Isis Avenue
Hawthorne, CA 90250
Phone: (310) 643-6455
Fax: (310) 643-5310
E-mail: suitup@ayso.org
http://www.soccer.org
The American Youth Soccer Organization offers a number of regional training conferences as well as an annual business conference for those interested in the sport.

Athletic Equipment Managers Association (AEMA)
460 Hunt Hill Road
Freeville, NY 13068
Phone: (607) 539-6300
Fax: (607) 539-6340
E-mail: dec13@cornell.edu
http://www.aema1.com
The AEMA holds an annual convention in Reno, Nevada. The organization also offers a number of workshops and clinics throughout the year to equipment managers and those who purchase equipment who work in amateur or professional sports.

De-Stress Express Stress Management Seminars
P.O. Box 711
Monticello, NY 12701
Phone: (845)794-7312
http://www.shellyfield.com
The De-Stress Express offers stress management seminars and personal coaching for athletes, sports teams, sports stars, celebrities, and corporate executives.

Eastern College Soccer Association (ECSA)
P.O. Box 3
Centerville, MA 02632
Phone: (508) 771-5060
Fax: (508) 771-9481
E-mail: pbuttafuoco@ecac.org
http://www.ecac.org
The Eastern College Soccer Association (ECSA) sponsors annual clinics and workshops for soccer officials.

International Association of Approved Basketball Officials (IAABO)
P.O. Box 1300
Germantown, MD 20875
Phone: (301) 540-5180
Fax: (301) 540-5182

E-mail: jacky_loube@verizon.net
http://www.iaabo.org
The IAABO holdsannual workshops and conferences for basketball officials.

International Association of Dive Rescue Specialists (IADRS)

201 North Link Lane
Fort Collins, CO 80524
Phone: (970) 482-1562
Fax: (970) 482-0893
E-mail: swatson@iadrs.org
http://www.iadrs.org
The International Association of Dive Rescue Specialists holds conferences and seminars that address a variety of topics relating to water rescue and recovery.

National Association of Sports Officials (NASO)

2017 Lathrop Avenue
Racine, WI 53405
Phone: (262) 632-5448
Fax: (262) 632-5460
E-mail: cservice@naso.org
http://www.naso.org
The National Association of Sports Officials organizes seminars, clinics, and camps for sports officials.

National Exercise Trainers Association (NETA)

5955 Golden Valley Road
Minneapolis, MN 55422
Phone: (763) 545-2505
Fax: (763) 545-2524
E-mail: neta@netafit.org
http://www.ndeita.com
NETA offers workshops for aerobic teaching certification.

National Gymnastics Judges Association (NGJA)

c/o Butch Zunich, President
2302 Sand Point
Champaign, IL 61822
Phone: (217) 359-4866
Fax: (217) 384-8550
E-mail: zunich@ngja.org
http://www.ngja.org

The NGJA provides training, certification, and refresher courses for individuals in this field. They also hold semiannual conferences and workshops.

National Health Club Association

640 Plaza Drive
Highlands Ranch, CO 80129
Phone: (303) 753-6422
Fax: (303) 986-6813
http://www.nhcainsurance.com
The National Health Club Association offers certification courses for fitness instructors and sponsors programs on fitness, sports medicine, and nutrition.

National Strength and Conditioning Association (NSCA)

1885 Bob Johnson Drive
Colorado Springs, CO 80906
Phone: (719) 632-6722
Fax: (719) 632-6367
E-mail: nsca@nsca-lift.org
http://www.nsca-lift.org
The National Strength and Conditioning Association holds an annual conference and trade show for members as well as developing clinics and workshops throughout the country for coaches, athletic trainers, and others in the field of sports medicine.

Professional Football Athletic Trainers Society (PFATS)

13655 Broncos Parkway
Englewood, CO 80112
Phone: (303) 649-9000
E-mail: contact@pfats.com
http://www.edblock.com
Professional Football Athletic Trainers Society holds seminars, workshops, and continuing education courses for members on various aspects of the profession.

Professional Ski Instructors of America (PSIA)

133 South Van Gordon Street
Lakewood, CO 80228

Phone: (303) 987-9390
Fax: (303) 988-3005
E-mail: psia@psia.org
http://www.psia.org
PSIA sponsors clinics and management seminars in the field of ski instruction.

Public Relations Society of America (PRSA)

33 Maiden Lane
New York, NY 10038
Phone: (212) 460-1400
Fax: (212) 995-0757
E-mail: exec@prsa.org
http://www.prsa.org
The PRSA offers seminars and educational courses throughout the year in a variety of public relations subjects.The organization also hold an annual conference for professionals in the industry.

Sporting Goods Agents Association (SGAA)

P.O. Box 998
Morton Grove, IL 60053
Phone: (847) 296-3670
Fax: (847) 827-0196
E-mail: sgaa998@aol.com
http://www.sgaaonline.org
The Sporting Goods Agents Association offers training seminars to manufacturers' agents.

Stress Busters Sports Seminars and Programs

P.O. Box 711
Monticello, NY 12701
Phone: (845) 794-7312
http://www.shellyfield.com
Stress Busters Sports Seminars and Programs offer stress reduction and management programs throughout the country to professional and collegiate athletes and teams as well as corporate executives.

Succeeding in Sports Seminars

P.O. Box 711
Monticello, NY 12701
Phone: (845)794-7312
http://www.shellyfield.com

Succeeding in Sports Seminars offers programs throughout the country for those interested in exploring sports-oriented careers and individuals seeking to succeed in the sports industry.

United States Association of Independent Gymnastic Clubs (USAIGC)

c/o Paul Spadaro, Vice President
450 North End Avenue
Suite 20F
New York, NY 10282
Phone: (212) 227-9792
Fax: (212) 227-9793
E-mail: usaigcpsny2@aol.com
http://www.usaigc.com
The USAIGC offers a number of national and regional gymnastic clinics in a variety of subjects, from business management to coaching techniques.

United States Youth Soccer Association

9220 World Cup Way
Frisco, TX 75034
Phone: (972) 334-9300
Fax: (972) 334-9960
E-mail: troby@usyouthsoccer.org
http://www.usyouthsoccer.org
This organization sponsors clinics on the officiating and administration of soccer.

U.S.A. Wrestling

6155 Lehman Drive
Colorado Springs, CO 80918
Phone: (719)598-8181
Fax: (719) 598-9440
http://www.themat.com
This organization holds clinics for officials, coaches, and amateur wrestlers on various subjects of interest to those working in amateur wrestling.

Women in Sports Careers

E-mail: info@wiscnetwork.com
http://www.womenssportscareers.com
Women in Sports has special networking events in various cities throughout the country as well as a variety of seminars and workshops aimed at women who want to work in the sports industry.

APPENDIX IV
TRADE ASSOCIATIONS, UNIONS, AND OTHER ORGANIZATIONS

The following is a listing of associations and unions discussed in this book as well as other associations that may be useful to you.

Names, addresses, phone and fax numbers, e-mail addresses, and Web sites have been included when available to help make it easier for you to contact any of the organizations for further information.

Many of the organizations have branch offices located throughout the country. Organization head-quarters can provide you with the contact information of branches closest to you.

Academy of Television Arts and Sciences (ATAS)
5220 Lankershim Boulevard
North Hollywood, CA 91601
Phone: (818) 754-2800
Fax: (818) 761-2827
E-mail: vint@emmys.org
http://www.emmys.org

Advertising Council (AC)
1203 19th Street, NW
Washington, DC 20036
Phone: (202) 331-9135
Fax: (202) 331-9790
E-mail: info@adcouncil.org
http://www.adcouncil.org

Aerobics and Fitness Association of America (AFAA)
15250 Ventura Boulevard
Sherman Oaks, CA 91403
Phone: (877) 968-7263
Fax: (818) 990-5468
E-mail: contactafaa@afaa.com
http://www.afaa.com

Amateur Athletic Union (AAU)
P.O. Box 22409
Lake Buena Vista, FL 32830
Phone: (407) 934-7200
Fax: (407) 934-7242
E-mail: bdodd@aausports.org
http://www.aausports.org

Amateur Softball Association of America (ASAA)
2801 NE 50th Street
Oklahoma City, OK 73111
Phone: (405) 424-5266
Fax: (405) 424-3855
E-mail: info@softball.org
http://www.softball.org

American Alliance for Health, Physical Education, Recreation and Dance (AAHPERD)
1900 Association Drive
Reston, VA 20191
Phone: (703)476-3400
Fax: (703) 476-9527
E-mail: info@aahperd.org
http://www.aahperd.org

American Amateur Baseball Congress
100 West Broadway
Farmington, NM 87401
Phone: (505) 327-3120
Fax: (505) 327-3132
E-mail: aabc@aabc.us
http://www.aabc.us

American Amateur Karate Federation (AAKF)
1930 Wilshire Boulevard
Los Angeles, CA 90057
Phone: (213) 483-8262

Fax: (213) 483-4060
E-mail: aakf@aakf.org
http://www.aakf.org

American Association for Active Lifestyles and Fitness (AAALF)
1900 Association Drive
Reston, VA 20191
Phone: (703) 476-3472
Fax: (703) 476-9527
E-mail: cneumann@aahperd.org
http://www.aahperd.org/aapar

American Association for the Improvement of Boxing (AAIB)
86 Fletcher Avenue
Mount Vernon, NY 10552
Phone: (914) 664-4571
Fax: (914) 664-3164
E-mail: aaib@worldnet.att.net
http://www.aaib.org

American Athletic Trainers Association and Certification Board (AATACB)
146 East Duarte Road
Arcadia, CA 91006 USA
Phone: (626) 445-1978
Fax: (626) 574-1999
E-mail: americansportsmedicine@ hotmail.com

American Auto Racing Writers and Broadcasters Association (AARWBA)
922 North Pass Avenue
Burbank, CA 91505
Phone: (818) 842-7005
Fax: (818) 842-7020
E-mail: aarwba@compuserve.com
http://www.aarwba.org

American Baseball Coaches Association (ABCA)
108 South University Avenue
Mount Pleasant, MI 48858
Phone: (989) 775-3300
Fax: (989) 775-3600
E-mail: abca@abca.org
http://www.abca.org

American Federation of Teachers (AFT)
555 New Jersey Avnue, NW
Washington, DC 20001
Phone: (202) 879-4400
Fax: (202) 879-4545
E-mail: online@aft.org
http://www.aft.org

American Federation of Television and Radio Artists (AFTRA)
260 Madison Avenue
New York, NY 10016
Phone: (212) 532-0800
Fax: (212) 532-2242
E-mail: info@aftra.com
http://www.aftra.com

American Football Coaches Association (AFCA)
100 Legends Lane
Waco, TX 76706
Phone: (254) 754-9900
Fax: (254) 776-3744
E-mail: info@afca.com
http://www.afca.com

American Guild of Variety Artists (AGVA)
363 Seventh Avenue
New York, NY 10001
Phone: (212) 675-1003
Fax: (212) 633-0097
http://www.agva.com

American Hockey Coaches Association (AHCA)
c/o Joe Bertagna, Executive Director
7 Concord Street
Gloucester, MA 01930
Phone: (781) 245-4177
Fax: (781) 245-2492
E-mail: jbertagna@ hockeyeastonline.com
http://www.ahcahockey.com

American Hockey League (AHL)
1 Monarch Place
Springfield, MA 01144
Phone: (413) 781-2030
Fax: (413) 733-4767
E-mail: info@theahl.com
http://www.theahl.com

American Legion Baseball (ALB)
700 North Pennsylvania Street
Indianapolis, IN 46204
Phone: (317) 630-1213
Fax: (317) 630-1369
E-mail: acy@legion.org
http://www.baseball.legion.org

American Marketing Association (AMA)
311 South Wacker Drive
Chicago, IL 60606
Phone: (312)542-9000
Fax: (312)542-9001
http://www.marketingpower.com

American Medical Athletic Association (AMAA)
4405 East-West Highway
Bethesda, MD 20814
Phone: (301) 913-9517
Fax: (301) 913-9520
E-mail: bbaldwin@ americanrunning.org
http://www.amaasportsmed.org

American Physical Therapy Association (APTA)
4405 East-West Highway
Bethesda, MD 20814
Phone: (301) 913-9517

Fax: (301) 913-9520
E-mail: bbaldwin@ americanrunning.org
http://www.amaasportsmed.org

American Sportscasters Association (ASA)
225 Broadway
New York, NY 10007
Phone: (212) 227-8080
Fax: (212) 571-0556
E-mail: lschwa8918@aol.com
http://www.americansportscasters online.com

American Swimming Coaches Association (ASCA)
5101 Northwest 21st Avenue
Fort Lauderdale, FL 33309
Phone: (954) 563-4930
Fax: (954) 563-9813
E-mail: asca@swimmingcoach.org
http://www.swimmingcoach.org

American Tennis Association (ATA)
1100 Mercantile Lane
Largo, MD 20774
Phone: (301) 583-4631
E-mail: info@atanational.com
http://www.atanational.com

American Turners (AT)
1127 East Kentucky Street
P.O. Box 4216
Louisville, KY 40204
Phone: (502) 636-2395
Fax: (502) 636-1935
E-mail: natlturner@aol.com

American Women in Radio and Television (AWRT)
8405 Greensboro Drive
McLean, VA 22102
Phone: (703) 506-3290
Fax: (703) 506-3266
E-mail: info@awrt.org
http://www.awrt.org

American Youth Soccer Organization (AYSO)
12501 South Isis Avenue
Hawthorne, CA 90250

Phone: (310) 643-6455
Fax: (310) 643-5310
E-mail: suitup@ayso.org
http://www.soccer.org

Associated Press Broadcasters (APB)

c/o AP Broadcast News Center
1825 K Street, NW
Washington, DC 20006
Phone: (202) 736-1100
Fax: (202) 736-1107
E-mail: info@abroadcaster.org
http://www.apbroadcast.com

Association for Women in Communications (AWC)

3337 Duke Street
Alexandria, VA 22314
Phone: (703) 370-7436
Fax: (703) 370-7437
E-mail: info@womcom.org
http://www.womcom.org

Association for Women in Sports Media

P.O. Box F
Bayville, NJ 08721
E-mail: vmichaelis@usatoday.com
http://www.awsmonline.org

Association of National Advertisers (ANA)

708 Third Avenue
New York, NY 10017
Phone: (212) 697-5950
Fax: (212) 661-8057
E-mail: rliodice@ana.net
http://www.ana.net

Association of Professional Ball Players of America (APBPA)

1820 West Orangewood Avenue
Orange, CA 92868
Phone: (714) 935-9993
http://www.apbpa.org

Athletic Equipment Managers Association (AEMA)

460 Hunt Hill Road
Freeville, NY 13068
Phone: (607) 539-6300

Fax: (607) 539-6340
E-mail: dec13@cornell.edu
http://www.aema1.com

Athletic Goods Team Distributors (AGTD)

1601 Feehanville Drive
Mount Prospect, IL 60056
Phone: (847) 296-6742
Fax: (847) 391-9827
E-mail: info@nsga.org
http://www.nsga.org

Athletic Institute (AI)

c/o Sporting Goods Manufacturers Association
1150 17th Street, NW
Washington, DC 20036
Phone: (202) 775-1762
Fax: (202) 296-7462
E-mail: info@sgma.com
http://www.sgma.com

Athletic Success Institute (ASI)

c/o William J. Winslow, Director
1933 Winward Point
Discovery Bay, CA 94514
Phone: (925) 516-8686
E-mail: winslow@athleticsuccess.org
http://www.athleticsuccess.org

Babe Ruth Baseball League

c/o Cory George, President
40575 California Oaks Road
Murrieta, CA 92562
Phone: (909) 677-2882
E-mail: baberuthca@hotmail.com

Babe Ruth Baseball/Softball (BRB)

Babe Ruth League, Inc.
1770 Brunswick Pike
P.O. Box 5000
Trenton, NJ 08638
Phone: (609) 695-1434
Fax: (609) 695-2505
E-mail: info@baberuthleague.org
http://www.baberuthleague.org

Boating Writers International (BWI)

108 Ninth Street

Wilmette, IL 60091
Phone: (847) 736-4142
E-mail: info@bwi.org
http://www.bwi.org

Bowling Writers Association of America (BWAA)

8501 North Manor Lane
Fox Point, WI 53217
Phone: (414) 351-6085
E-mail: sjames2652@wi.rr.com
http://www.bowlingwriters.com

Business Marketing Association (BMA)

400 North Michigan Avenue.
Chicago, IL 60611
Phone: (312)822-0005
Fax: (312) 822-0054
E-mail: bma@marketing.org
http://www.marketing.org

Central Intercollegiate Athletic Association (CIAA)

303 Butler Farm Road
P.O. Box 7349
Hampton, VA 23666
Phone: (757) 865-0071
Fax: (757) 865-8436
E-mail: theciaa@aol.com
http://www.theciaa.com

Club Managers Association of America (CMAA)

1733 King Street
Alexandria, VA 22314
Phone: (703) 739-9500
Fax: (703) 739-0124
E-mail: cmaa@cmaa.org
http://www.cmaa.org

College Athletic Business Management Association (CABMA)

c/o Pat Manak, Assistant Secretary
P.O. Box 16428
Cleveland, OH 44116
Phone: (440) 892-4000
Fax: (440) 892-4007
E-mail: pmanak@nacda.com
http://nacda.ocsn.com/cabma/nacda-cabma.html

College Sports Information Directors of America (COSIDA)
c/o Jeff Hodges, Secretary
University of North Alabama
P.O. Box 5038
Florence, AL 35632
Phone: (256) 765-4595
Fax: (256) 765-4659
E-mail: sportsinformation@una.edu
http://www.cosida.com

College Swimming Coaches Association of America (CSCAA)
P.O. Box 63285
Colorado Springs, CO 80962
Phone: (719) 266-0064
Fax: (719) 266-6844
E-mail: swimco@aol.com
http://www.cscaa.org

Collegiate Commissioners Association (CCA)
2201 Richard Arrington Boulevard
Birmingham, AL 35242
Phone: (205) 458-3000
Fax: (205) 458-3031
http://www.secsports.com

Consolidated Athletic Commission (CAS)
851 North Leavitt Street
Chicago, IL 60622

Continental Basketball Association (CBA)
195 Washington Avenue
Albany, NY 12210
Phone: (518) 694-7160
Fax: (518) 694-8291
E-mail: info@cbahoopsonline.com
http://www.cbahoopsonline.com

Cosmopolitan Soccer League (CSL)
115 River Road
Edgewater, NJ 07020
Phone: (201) 943-3390
Fax: (201) 943-3394
E-mail: info@cslny.com
http://www.newyorksoccer.com

Eastern College Athletic Conference (ECAC)
1311 Craigville Beach Road
Centerville, MA 02632
Phone: (508) 771-5060
Fax: (508) 771-9481
E-mail: sbamford@ecac.org
http://www.ecac.org

Eastern College Soccer Association
P.O. Box 3
Centerville, MA 02632
Phone: (508) 771-5060
Fax: (508) 771-9481
E-mail: pbuttafuoco@ecac.org
http://www.ecac.org

Employee Services Management Association (ESMA)
568 Spring Road
Elmhurst, IL 60126
Phone: (630) 559-0020
Fax: (630) 559-0025
E-mail: esmahq@esmassn.org
http://www.esmassn.org

Football Writers Association of America (FWAA)
c/o Steve Richardson, Executive Director
18652 Vista Del Sol Drive
Dallas, TX 75287
Phone: (972) 713-6198
E-mail: tigerfwaa@aol.com
http://www.sportswriters.net/fwaa

George Khoury Association of Baseball Leagues (GKABL)
5400 Meramec Bottom Road
St. Louis, MO 63128
Phone: (314) 849-8900
Fax: (314) 849-8901

Golf Writers Association of America (GWAA)
c/o Melanie Hauser, Secretary/Treasurer
10210 Greentree Road
Houston, TX 77042
Phone: (713) 782-6664
Fax: (713) 781-2575

E-mail: golfwritersinc@aol.com
http://www.gwaa.com

Harness Horsemen International (HHI)
64 Route 33
Manalapan, NJ 07726
Phone: (609) 259-3717
Fax: (732) 683-1578

Harness Horse Youth Foundation (HHYF)
16575 Carey Road
Westfield, IN 46074
Phone: (317) 867-5877
Fax: (317) 867-5896
E-mail: ellen@hhyf.org
http://www.hhyf.org

Harness Racing Museum and Hall of Fame
P.O. Box 590
Goshen, NY 10924
Phone: (845) 294-6330
Fax: (845) 294-3463
E-mail: hrm@frontiernet.net
http://www.harnessmuseum.com

Harness Tracks of America (HTA)
4640 East Sunrise
Tucson, AZ 85718
Phone: (520) 529-2525
Fax: (520) 529-3235
E-mail: info@harnesstracks.com
http://www.harnesstracks.com

Hockey North America (HNA)
P.O. Box 78
Sterling, VA 20167
Phone: (703) 430-8100
Fax: (703) 421-9205
E-mail: hnasupport@aol.com
http://www.hna.com

IDEA, Health and Fitness Association
10455 Pacific Center Court
San Diego, CA 92121
Phone: (858) 535-8979
Fax: (858) 535-8234
E-mail: contact@ideafit.com
http://www.ideafit.com

Intercollegiate Association of Amateur Athletes of America (IAAAA)
c/oEastern College Athletic
Conference
1311 Craigville Beach Road
Centerville, MA 02632
Phone: (508) 771-5060
Fax: (508) 771-9486
E-mail: stevebartold@aol.com
http://www.ecac.org

Intercollegiate Tennis Association (ITA)
c/o David A. Benjamin, Executive
Director
174 Tamarack Circle
Skillman, NJ 08558
Phone: (609) 497-6920
Fax: (609) 497-9766
E-mail: itatennis2@aol.com
http://www.itatennis.com

International Academy of Television Arts and Sciences (IATAS)
888 Seventh Avenue
New York, NY 10019
Phone: (212) 489-6969
Fax: (212) 489-6557
E-mail: info@iemmys.tv
http://www.iemmys.tv

International Association of Dive Rescue Specialists (IADRS)
201 North Link Lane
Fort Collins, CO 80524
Phone: (970) 482-1562
Fax: (970) 482-0893
E-mail: swatson@iadrs.org
http://www.iadrs.org

International Basketball Federation (IBF)
Federation Internationale de
Basketball
53, avenue Louis Casai
Cointrin
CH-1216 Geneva, Switzerland
Phone: 41 22 5450000
Fax: 41 22 5450099
E-mail: info@fiba.com
http://www.fiba.com

International Boxing Federation (IBF)
516 Main Street
East Orange, NJ 07018
Phone: (973) 414-0300
Fax: (973) 414-0307
E-mail: mmuhammad@ibfboxing.
com
http://www.ibf-usba-boxing.com

International Boxing Hall of Fame Museum (IBHFM)
1 Hall of Fame Drive
Canastota, NY 13032
Phone: (315) 697-7095
Fax: (315) 697-5356
http://www.ibhof.com

International Federation of Associated Wrestling Styles (FILA)
Fédération Internationale des Luttes
Associées
6, rue du Chateau
1804 Vevey, Switzerland
Phone: 41 21 3128426
Fax: 41 21 3236073
E-mail: fila@fila-wrestling.com
http://www.fila-wrestling.com

International Female Boxers Association (IFBA)
50B Peninsula Center Drive
Rolling Hills Estates, CA 90274
Phone: (310) 428-1402
Fax: (310) 541-9708
E-mail: info@ifba.com
http://www.ifba.homestead.com

International League of Professional Baseball Clubs (ILPBC)
55 South High Street
Dublin, OH 43017
Phone: (614) 791-9300
Fax: (614) 791-9009
E-mail: office@ilbaseball.com

International Physical Fitness Association (IPFA)
415 West Court Street
Flint, MI 48503
Phone: (810) 239-2166

Fax: (810) 239-9390
E-mail: contact@ipfa.us
http://www.ipfa.us

International Public Relations Association (IPRA)
1 Dunley Hill Court
Ranmore Common
Dorking
Surrey RH5 6SX, United Kingdom
Phone: 44 1483 280130
Fax: 44 1483 280131
E-mail: iprasec@btconnect.com
http://www.ipra.org

International Society of Sports Psychology (ISSP)
c/o Judy Van Raalte, Vice President
Psychology Department
263 Alden Street
Springfield, MA 01109
Phone: (413) 748-3388
Fax: (413) 748-3854
E-mail: jvanraal@spfldcol.edu
http://www.issponline.org

International Trotting and Pacing Association (ITPA)
60 Gulf Road
Gouverneur, NY 13642
Phone: (315) 287-2294
Fax: (315) 287-5010
E-mail: ldenesha@twcny.rr.com
http://www.trottingbreds.com

International Veteran Boxers Association (IVBA)
35 Brady Avenue
New Rochelle, NY 10805
Phone: (914) 235-6820
Fax: (914) 654-9785

Jockeys' Guild (JG)
P.O. Box 150
Monrovia, CA 91017
Phone: (626) 305-5605
Fax: (626) 305-5615
E-mail: info@jockeysguild.com
http://www.jockeysguild.com

Knights Boxing Team International
12086 Flat Shoals Road

Covington, GA 30016
Phone: (770) 787-3131
E-mail: hmw3@flash.net

Ladies Professional Golf Association (LPGA)
100 International Golf Drive
Daytona Beach, FL 32124
Phone: (386) 274-6200
Fax: (386) 274-1099
E-mail: feedback@lpga.com
http://www.lpga.com

Little League Baseball and Softball
P.O. Box 3485
Williamsport, PA 17701
Phone: (570) 326-1921
Fax: (570) 326-1074
E-mail: cdowns@littleleague.org
http://www.littleleague.org

Manufacturers' Agents National Association (MANA)
c/o Joe Miller, President
1 Spectrum Pointe
Lake Forest, CA 92630
Phone: (949) 859-4040
Fax: (949) 855-2973
E-mail: mana@manaonline.org
http://www.MANAonline.org

Marketing Agencies Association Worldwide (MAA)
460 Summer Street
Stamford, CT 06901
Phone: (203) 978-1590
Fax: (203) 969-1499
E-mail: keith.mccracken@maaw.org
http://www.maaw.org

National Academy of Sports (NAS)
220 East 63rd Street
New York, NY 10021
Phone: (212) 838-2980
Fax: (212) 838-3980

National Academy of Television Arts and Sciences (NATAS)
5220 Lankershim Boulevard
North Hollywood, CA 91601

Phone: (818) 754-2810
Fax: (818) 761-2827
E-mail: pprice@emmyonline.tv
http://www.emmyonline.org

1375 Broadway
New York, NY 10018
Phone: (212) 459-3630
Fax: (212) 459-9772
E-mail: jgonzalez@nyemmys.org
http://www.nyemmys.org

National Advertising Division Council of Better Business Bureaus (NAD)
70 West 36th Street
New York, NY 10018
Phone: (212) 705-0120
E-mail: sharris@nad.bbb.org
http://www.nadreview.org

National Alliance for Youth Sports (NAYS)
2050 Vista Parkway
West Palm Beach, FL 33411
Phone: (561) 684-1141
Fax: (561) 684-2546
E-mail: nays@nays.org
http://www.nays.org

National Amateur Baseball Federation (NAFB)
c/o Charles M. Blackburn Jr.,
    Executive Director
P.O. Box 705
Bowie, MD 20715
Phone: (301) 464-5460
Fax: (301) 352-0214
E-mail: nabf1914@aol.com
http://www.nabf.com

National Association for Girls and Women in Sports (NAGWS)
c/o American Alliance for Health,
    Physical Education, Recreation
    and Dance
1900 Association Drive
Reston, VA 20191
Phone: (703) 476-3400
Fax: (703) 476-4566
E-mail: nagws@aahperd.org
http://www.aahperd.org/nagws

National Association for Sports and Physical Education(NASPE)
1900 Association Drive
Reston, VA 20191
Phone: (703) 476-3400
Fax: (703) 476-8316
E-mail: naspe@aahperd.org
http://www.naspeinfo.org

National Association for Stock Car Auto Racing (NASCAR)
1801 West InternationalSpeedway
    Boulevard
P.O. Box 2875
Daytona Beach, FL 32120
Phone: (386) 253-0611
Fax: (386) 258-7646
E-mail: nascar@turner.com
http://www.nascar.com

National Association of Athletic Development Directors (NAADD)
P.O. Box 16428
Cleveland, OH 44116
Phone: (440) 892-4000
Fax: (440) 892-4007
E-mail: mcleary@nacda.com
http://nacda.ocsn.com/naadd/
    nacda-naadd.html

National Association of Basketball Coaches (NABC)
1111 Main Street
Kansas City, MO 64105
Phone: (816) 878-6222
Fax: (816) 878-6223
E-mail: jim@nabc.com
http://nabc.cstv.com

National Association of Broadcasters (NOA)
1771 N Street, NW
Washington, DC 20036
Phone: (202) 429-5300
Fax: (202) 429-4199
E-mail: nab@nab.org
http://www.nab.org

National Association of Collegiate Directors of Athletics (NACDA)
P.O. Box 16428
Cleveland, OH 44116
Phone: (440) 892-4000
Fax: (440) 892-4007
E-mail: mcleary@nacda.com
http://nacda.cstv.com

National Association of Collegiate Gymnastics Coaches/Women (NACGCW)
c/o Mike Lorenzen, President
120 Indian Hill Road
Boalsburg, PA 16827
Phone: (814) 404-4686
E-mail: mlorenzen@
woodwardcamp.com
http://www.collegegymnast.com

National Association of Collegiate Women Athletic Administrators (NACWAA)
4701 Wrightsville Avenue
Oak Park
Building 1
Wilmington, NC 28403
Phone: (910) 793-8244
Fax: (910) 793-8246
E-mail: jalley@nacwaa.org
http://www.nacwaa.org

National Association of Intercollegiate Athletics (NAIA)
23500 West 105th Street
P.O. Box 1325
Olathe, KS 66051
Phone: (913) 791-0044
Fax: (913) 791-9555
E-mail: eeastep@naia.org
http://www.naia.org

National Association of Professional Baseball Leagues (NAPBL)
P.O. Box A
St. Petersburg, FL 33731
Phone: (727) 822-6937
Fax: (727) 821-5819

E-mail: admin@minorleague
baseball.com
http://www.minorleaguebaseball.com

National Association of Schools of Dance (NASD)
11250 Roger Bacon Drive
Reston, VA 20190
Phone: (703) 437-0700
Fax: (703) 437-6312
E-mail: info@arts-accredit.org
http://nasd.arts-accredit.org

National Association of Sporting Goods Wholesalers (NASGW)
c/o Wayne Smith, President
P.O. Box 881525
Port St. Lucie, FL 34988
Phone: (772) 621-7162
Fax: (772) 264-3233
E-mail: wsmith@nasgw.org
http://www.nasgw.org

National Association of Sports Officials (NASO)
2017 Lathrop Avenue
Racine, WI 53405
Phone: (262) 632-5448
Fax: (262) 632-5460
E-mail: cservice@naso.org
http://www.naso.org

National Athletic Trainers Association (NATA)
2952 Stemmons Freeway
Dallas, TX 75247
Phone: (214) 637-6282
Fax: (214) 637-2206
E-mail: ebd@nata.org
http://www.nata.org

National Baseball Congress (NBC)
P.O. Box 1420
Wichita, KS 67201
Phone: (316) 267-3372
Fax: (316) 267-3382
E-mail: jerry@wichitawranglers.com
http://www.nbcbaseball.com

National Baseball Hall of Fame and Museum
25 Main Street

Cooperstown, NY 13326
Phone: (607) 547-0330
Fax: (607) 547-4094
E-mail: research@
baseballhalloffame.org
http://baseballhalloffame.org

National Basketball Athletic Trainers Association
c/o Rollin Mallernee
400 Colony Square
Atlanta, GA 30361
Phone: (404) 875-4000
Fax: (404) 892-8560
E-mail: rmallernee@mallernee-
branch.com
http://www.nbta.info

National Basketball Players Association (NBPA)
2 Penn Plaza
New York, NY 10121
Phone: (212) 655-0880
Fax: (212) 655-0881
E-mail: info@nbpa.com
http://www.nbpa.com

National Collegiate Athletic Association (NCAA)
P.O. Box 6222
700 West Washington Street
Indianapolis, IN 46206
Phone: (317) 917-6222
Fax: (317) 917-6888
E-mail: pmr@ncaa.org
http://www2.ncaa.org

National Dance Association (NDA)
1900 Association Drive
Reston, VA 20191
Phone: (703) 476-3464
Fax: (703) 476-9527
E-mail: nda@aahperd.org
http://www.aahperd.org/nda

National Dance Education Association (NDEA)
c/o Jane Bonbright, Executive Director
4948 St. Elmo Avenue
Bethesda, MD 20814

Phone: (301) 657-2880
Fax: (301) 657-2882
E-mail: info@ndeo.org
http://www.ndeo.org

**National Dance Teachers
    Association (NDTA)**
c/o Ronnie Gardner, President
2309 East Atlantic Boulevard
Pompano Beach, FL 33062
Phone: (954) 782-7760
E-mail: rg_ndta@comcast.net
http://www.nationaldanceteachers.
    org

**National Exercise Trainers
    Association (NETA)**
5955 Golden Valley Road
Minneapolis, MN 55422
Phone: (763) 545-2505
Fax: (763) 545-2524
E-mail: neta@netafit.org
http://www.ndeita.com

**National Federation Officials
    Association (NFOA)**
P.O. Box 690
Indianapolis, IN 46206
Phone: (317) 972-6900
Fax: (317) 822-5700
http://www.nfhs.org

**National Federation of Press
    Women (NFPW)**
P.O. Box 5556
Arlington, VA 22205
Phone: (703) 812-9487
Fax: (703) 812-4555
E-mail: presswomen@aol.com
http://www.nfpw.org

**National Football Foundation
    and College Hall of Fame
    (NFF)**
22 Maple Avenue
Morristown, NJ 07960
Phone: (973) 829-1933
Fax: (973) 829-1737
E-mail: membership@
    footballfoundation.com
http://www.footballfoundation.com

**National Football League
    (NFL)**
280 Park Avenue
New York, NY 10017
Phone: (212) 655-5665
E-mail: customer_service@nflshop.
    com
http://www.nfl.com

**National Football League
    Alumni**
3696 North Federal Highway
Fort Lauderdale, FL 33308
Phone: (954) 630-2100
Fax: (954) 630-2535
E-mail: contact@nflahq.org
http://www.nflalumni.org

**National Football League
    Players Association
    (NFLPA)**
2021 L Street, NW
Washington, DC 20036
Phone: (202) 463-2200
Fax: (202) 857-0380
E-mail: webmaster@nflplayers.com
http://www.nflpa.org

**National Gymnastics Judges
    Association (NGJA)**
c/o Butch Zunich, President
2302 Sand Point
Champaign, IL 61822
Phone: (217) 359-4866
Fax: (217) 384-8550
E-mail: zunich@ngja.org
http://www.ngja.org

**National Health Club
    Association (NHCA)**
640 Plaza Drive
Highlands Ranch, CO 80129
Phone: (303) 753-6422
Fax: (303) 986-6813
http://www.nhcainsurance.com

**National High School Athletic
    Coaches Association
    (NHSACA)**
c/o Gary Makowicki
305 Broadway

Norwich, CT 06360
Phone: (860) 425-5512
Fax: (860) 204-9606
E-mail: office@hscoaches.org
http://www.hscoaches.org

**National Hockey League
    Booster Clubs Association
    (NHLBCA)**
P.O. Box 805
St. Louis, MO 63188
Phone: (314) 895-9466
E-mail: blueliners@aol.com

**National Hockey League
    Player's Association
    (NHLPA)**
777 Bay Street
P.O. Box 121
Toronto, ON, Canada M5G 2C8
Phone: (416) 313-2300
Fax: (416) 313-2301
http://www.nhlpa.com

**National Intercollegiate Soccer
    Officials Association
    (NISOA)**
541 Woodview Drive
Longwood, FL 32779
Phone: (407) 862-3305
Fax: (407) 862-8545
E-mail: information@nisoa.com
http://www.nisoa.com

**National Interscholastic
    Swimming Coaches
    Association of America
    (NISCA)**
c/o Arvel McElroy
Olathe South High School
Olathe, KS 66062
Phone: (913) 780-7160
Fax: (913) 780-7170
E-mail: president@nisca.net
http://www.nisca.net

**National Intramural
    Recreational Sports
    Association (NIRSA)**
4185 Southwest Research Way
Corvallis, OR 97333

Phone: (541) 766-8211
Fax: (541) 766-8284
E-mail: nirsa@nirsa.org
http://www.nirsa.org

National Junior Baseball League (NJBL)
c/o Jan Rosenblum
2800 Coyle Street
Brooklyn, NY 11235
Phone: (631) 582-5191
E-mail: njbl@optonline.net
http://www.nationaljunior.com

National Junior College Athletic Association (NJCAA)
1755 Telstar Drive
Colorado Springs, CO 80920
Phone: (719) 590-9788
Fax: (719) 590-7324
E-mail: wbaker@njcaa.org
http://www.njcaa.org

National Press Club (NPC)
National Press Building
529 14th Street, NW
Washington, DC 20045
Phone: (202) 662-7500
Fax: (202) 662-7512
E-mail: info@press.org
http://www.press.org

National Press Photographers Association (NPPA)
3200 Croasdaile Drive
Durham, NC 27705
Phone: (919) 383-7246
Fax: (919) 383-7261
E-mail: info@nppa.org
http://www.nppa.org

National Soccer Coaches Association of America (NSCAA)
6700 Squibb Road
Mission, KS 66202
Phone: (913) 362-1747
Fax: (913) 362-3439
E-mail: info@nscaa.com

National Sporting Goods Association (NSGA)
1601 Feehanville Drive
Mount Prospect, IL 60056
Phone: (847) 296-6742
Fax: (847) 391-9827
E-mail: info@nsga.org
http://www.nsga.org

National Sports and Fitness Association (NSFA)
1945 Palo Verde Avenue
Long Beach, CA 90815
Phone: (562) 799-8333
Fax: (562) 799-3355
E-mail: info@nsfa-online.com

National Sportscasters and Sportswriters Association (NSSA)
323 North Main Street
Salisbury, NC 28144
Phone: (704) 633-4275
Fax: (704) 633-2027
E-mail: nssa@nssahalloffame.com
http://www.nssahalloffame.com

National Strength and Conditioning Association (NSCA)
1885 Bob Johnson Drive
Colorado Springs, CO 80906
Phone: (719) 632-6722
Fax: (719) 632-6367
E-mail: nsca@nsca-lift.org
http://www.nsca-lift.org

National Women Bowling Writers Association (NWBW)
c/o Barbara Spencer, Treasurer
225 Love Avenue
Greenwood, IN 46142
E-mail: bspencerlm@sbcglobal.net
http://www.nwbw.freeservers.com/index.htm

National Wrestling Coaches Association (NWCA)
P.O. Box 254
Manheim, PA 17545
Phone: (717) 653-8009

Fax: (717) 653-8270
E-mail: mmoyer@nwca.cc
http://www.nwcaonline.com

National Youth Sports Safety Foundation (NYSSF)
1 Beacon Street
Boston, MA 02108
Phone: (617) 367-6677
Fax: (617) 722-9999
E-mail: nyssf@aol.com
http://www.nyssf.org

Newspaper Association of America (NAA)
1921 Gallows Road
Vienna, VA 22182
Phone: (703) 902-1600
Fax: (703) 917-0636
E-mail: schij@naa.org
http://www.naa.org

North America Boxing Federation (NABF)
c/o Ed Pearson, Vice President
2020 105th Street
Edmonton, AB, Canada T6J 5J2
Phone: (780) 435-5907
Fax: (780) 435-5909
E-mail: epearson@canadianboxing.com
http://www.nabfnews.com

North American Boxing Federation (NABF)
c/o Rex Ross Walker, Presisent
3300 Airport Road
Boulder, CO 80301
Phone: (303) 442-0258
Fax: (303) 442-0380
E-mail: info@nabfnews.com
http://www.NABFNews.com

Pony Baseball and Softball
P.O. Box 225
Washington, PA 15301
Phone: (724) 225-1060
Fax: (724) 225-9852
E-mail: info@pony.org
http://www.pony.org

Pop Warner Football (PWF)
586 Middletown Boulevard
Langhorne, PA 19047
Phone: (215) 752-2691
Fax: (215) 752-2879
E-mail: football@popwarner.com
http://www.popwarner.com

Professional Football Athletic Trainers Society (PFATS)
c/o Steve Antonopulos, President
13655 Broncos Parkway
Englewood, CO 80112
Phone: (303) 649-9000
E-mail: contact@pfats.com
http://www.edblock.com

Professional Football Researchers Association (PFRA)
12870 Route 30
North Huntingdon, PA 15642
E-mail: bob2296@comcast.net
http://www.footballresearch.com

Professional Golfers' Association of America (PGA)
100 Avenue of the Champions
Palm Beach Gardens, FL 33410
Phone: (561) 624-8400
Fax: (561) 624-8430
E-mail: info@pga.com
http://www.pga.com

Professional Hockey Writers' Association (PHWA)
c/o Sherry L. Ross
1480 Pleasant Valley Way
West Orange, NJ 07052
Phone: (973) 669-8607

Professional Photographers of America
229 Peachtree Street, NE
Atlanta, GA 30303
Phone: (404) 522-8600
Fax: (404) 614-6400
E-mail: csc@ppa.com
http://ppa.com

Professional Ski Instructors of America (PSIA)
133 South Van Gordon Street

Lakewood, CO 80228
Phone: (303) 987-9390
Fax: (303) 988-3005
E-mail: psia@psia.org
http://www.psia.org

Public Relations Society of America (PRSA)
33 Maiden Lane
New York, NY 10038
Phone: (212) 460-1400
Fax: (212) 995-0757
E-mail: exec@prsa.org
http://www.prsa.org

Radio Advertising Bureau (RAB)
1320 Greenway Drive
Irving, TX 75038
Phone: (972) 753-6822
Fax: (972) 753-6727
E-mail: dareeder@rab.com
http://www.rab.com

Radio and Television News Directors' Association (RTNDA)
1600 K Street, NW
Washington, DC 20006
Phone: (202) 659-6510
Fax: (202) 223-4007
E-mail: rtnda@rtnda.org
http://rtnda.org

Radio and Television News Directors' Association— Canada (RTNDA)
2175 Sheppard Avenue East
Toronto, ON, Canada M2J 1W8
Phone: (416) 756-2213
Fax: (416) 491-1670
E-mail: info@rtndacanada.com
http://www.rtndacanada.com

Society for American Baseball Research (SABR)
812 Huron Road
Cleveland, OH 44115
Phone: (216) 575-0500
Fax: (216) 575-0502
E-mail: info@sabr.org
http://www.sabr.org

Sporting Goods Agents Association (SGAA)
P.O. Box 998
Morton Grove, IL 60053
Phone: (847) 296-3670
Fax: (847) 827-0196
E-mail: sgaa998@aol.com
http://www.sgaaonline.org

Sporting Goods Manufacturers Association International (SGMA)
1150 17th Street, NW
Washington, DC 20036
Phone: (202) 775-1762
Fax: (202) 296-7462
E-mail: info@sgma.com
http://www.sgma.com

Synchro Swimming U.S.A.
201 South Capitol
Indianapolis, IN 46225
Phone: (317) 237-5700
Fax: (317) 237-5705
E-mail: webmaster@usasynchro.org
http://www.usasynchro.org

Tennis Industry Association (TIA)
117 Executive Center
Hilton Head Island, SC 29928
Phone: (843) 686-3036
Fax: (843) 686-3078
E-mail: info@tennisindustry.org
http://www.tennisindustry.org

Thoroughbred Club of America (TCA)
P.O. Box 8098
Lexington, KY 40533
Phone: (859) 254-4282
Fax: (859) 231-6131
E-mail: info@thoroughbredclubof america.com
http://www.thoroughbredclubof america.com

United States Association of Independent Gymnastic Clubs (USAIGC)
c/o Paul Spadaro, Vice President
450 North End Avenue
New York, NY 10282

Phone: (212) 227-9792
Fax: (212) 227-9793
E-mail: usaigcpsny2@aol.com
http://www.usaigc.com

United States Basketball Writers Association (USBWA)

1818 Chouteau Avenue
St. Louis, MO 63103
Phone: (314) 421-0339
Fax: (314) 421-3505
E-mail: mitch@mvc.org
http://www.sportswriters.net/
    usbwa

United States College Athletic Association (USCAA)

c/o Dave Schmidt, Commissioner
P.O. Box 16364
Loves Park, IL 61132
Phone: (419) 733-4957
E-mail: info@theuscaa.com
http://www.theuscaa.com

United States Cross Country Coaches Association (USCCCA)

c/o Walt Drenth, President
Michigan State University
Jenison Fieldhouse
East Lansing, MI 48824
Phone: (517) 355-1640
Fax: (517) 432-3339
E-mail: admin@usccca.org
http://www.usccca.org

United States Curling Association (USCA)

1100 Center Point Drive
P.O. Box 866
Stevens Point, WI 54481
Phone: (715) 344-1199
Fax: (715) 344-2279
E-mail: info@usacurl.org
http://www.usacurl.org

United States Deaf Ski and Snowboard Association (USDSSA)

c/o Edward Ingham, President
709 8th Street, NE
Washington, DC 20002

E-mail: president@usdssa.org
http://www.usdssa.org

United States Fencing Association (USFA)

1 Olympic Plaza
Colorado Springs, CO 80909
Phone: (719) 866-4511
Fax: (719) 632-5737
E-mail: info@usfencing.org
http://www.usfencing.org

United States Harness Writers' Association (UUSHWA)

c/o Jerry Connors, Secretary
P.O. Box 1314
Mechanicsburg, PA 17055
Phone: (717) 651-5889
E-mail: ushwa@paonline.com
http://www.ustrotting.com

United States Judo (USJ)

1 Olympic Plaza
Colorado Springs, CO 80909
Phone: (719) 866-4730
Fax: (719) 866-4733
E-mail: drrontripp@aol.com
http://www.usjudo.org

United States Judo Association (USJA)

21 North Union Boulevard
Colorado Springs, CO 80909
Phone: (719) 633-7750
Fax: (719) 633-4041
E-mail: usja@usja-judo.org
http://www.usja-judo.org

United States Lifesaving Association (USLA)

P.O. Box 322
Avon-by-the-Sea, NJ 07717
Phone: (866) FOR-USLA
E-mail: guard4life@aol.com
http://www.usla.org

United States Masters Swimming (USMS)

P.O. Box 322
Avon-by-the-Sea, NJ 07717
Phone: (866) FOR-USLA
E-mail: guard4life@aol.com
http://www.usla.org

United States of America Boxing (USAB)

1 Olympic Plaza
Colorado Springs, CO 80909
Phone: (719) 866-4506
Fax: (719) 632-3426
E-mail: ljones@usaboxing.org
http://www.usaboxing.org

United States Racquetball Association (USRA)

1 Olympic Plaza
Colorado Springs, CO 80909
Phone: (719) 866-4506
Fax: (719) 632-3426
E-mail: ljones@usaboxing.org
http://www.usaboxing.org

United States Rowing Association (USRA)

2 Wall Street
Princeton, NJ 08540
Phone: (609) 751-0700
Fax: (609) 924-1578
E-mail: members@usrowing.org
http://www.usrowing.org

United States Ski and Snowboard Association (USSSA)

P.O. Box 100
1500 Kearns Boulevard
Park City, UT 84060
Phone: (435) 649-9090
Fax: (435) 649-3613
E-mail: info@ussa.org
http://www.ussa.org

United States Sports Academy (USSA)

1 Academy Drive
Daphne, AL 36526
Phone: (251) 626-3303
Fax: (251) 625-1035
Toll-free: 800-223-2668
E-mail: academy@ussa.edu
http://www.ussa.edu

United States Tennis Association (USTA)

c/o Iris Kenworthy, Executive
    Director
1414 Rhorer Road

Bloomington, IN 47401
Fax: (812) 336-7376
E-mail: usdta@sbcglobal.net
http://www.dentaltennis.org

United States Trotting Association (USTA)
750 Michigan Avenue
Columbus, OH 43215
Phone: (614) 224-2291
Fax: (614) 224-4575
E-mail: customerservice@ustrotting.com
http://www.ustrotting.com

United States Water Polo (USWP)
1631 Mesa Avenue
Colorado Springs, CO 80906
Phone: (719) 634-0699
Fax: (719) 634-0866
E-mail: ntprograms@usawaterpolo.org
http://www.usawaterpolo.com

United States Youth Soccer Association (USYSA)
9220 World Cup Way
Frisco, TX 75034
Phone: (972) 334-9300
Fax: (972) 334-9960
E-mail: troby@usyouthsoccer.org
http://www.usyouthsoccer.org

USA Baseball (USAB)
Durham Bulls Athletic Park
403 Blackwell Street
Durham, NC 27701
Phone: (919) 474-8721
Fax: (919) 474-8822
E-mail: info@usabaseball.com
http://mlb.mlb.com/NASApp/mlb/usa_baseball/index.jsp

U.S.A. Basketball (USA—Basketball)
5465 Mark Dabling Boulevard
Colorado Springs, CO 80918
Phone: (719) 590-4800
Fax: (719) 590-4811
E-mail: fanmail@usabasketball.com
http://www.usabasketball.com

U.S.A. Gymnastics (USA—GYM)
Pan American Plaza
201 South Capitol Avenue
Indianapolis, IN 46225
Phone: (317) 237-5050
Fax: (317) 237-5069
E-mail: rebound@usa-gymnastics.org
http://www.usa-gymnastics.org

U.S.A. Hockey (USAH)
1775 Bob Johnson Drive
Colorado Springs, CO 80906
Phone: (719) 576-8724
Fax: (719) 538-1160
E-mail: usah@usahockey.org
http://www.usahockey.com

USA Swimming (USS)
1 Olympic Plaza
Colorado Springs, CO 80909
Phone: (719) 866-4578
Fax: (719) 866-4669
E-mail: media@usaswimming.org
http://www.usswim.org

U.S.A Wrestling (USAW)
6155 Lehman Drive
Colorado Springs, CO 80918
Phone: (719) 598-8181
Fax: (719) 598-9440
E-mail: hthompson@usawrestling.org
http://www.themat.com

U.S. Field Hockey Association (USFHA)
1 Olympic Plaza
Colorado Springs, CO 80909
Phone: (719) 866-4567
Fax: (719) 632-0979
E-mail: usfha@usfieldhockey.com
http://www.usfieldhockey.com

U.S. Soccer (USSF)
1801-1811 South Prairie Avenue
Chicago, IL 60616
Phone: (312) 808-1300
Fax: (312) 808-1301
E-mail: dflynn@ussoccer.org
http://www.ussoccer.com

Western Winter Sports Representatives Association (WWSRA)
726 Tenacity Drive
Longmont, CO 80504
Phone: (303) 532-4002
Fax: (303) 512-6162
E-mail: info@wwsra.com
http://www.wwsra.com

Women's Basketball Coaches Association (WBCA)
4646 Lawrenceville Highway
Lilburn, GA 30047
Phone: (770) 279-8027
Fax: (770) 279-8473
E-mail: wbca@wbca.org
http://www.wbca.org

Women's Sports Foundation (WSF)
Eisenhower Park
East Meadow, NY 11554
Phone: (516) 542-4700
Fax: (516) 542-4716
E-mail: info@womenssportsfoundation.org
http://www.womenssportsfoundation.org

Women's Sports Foundation (WSF)
Victoria House
Bloomsbury Square
London WC1B 4SE, United Kingdom
Phone: 44 20 72731740
E-mail: info@wsf.org.uk
http://www.wsf.org.uk

World Aquatic Babies Congress
190-112th Avenue North
St. Petersburg, FL 33716
E-mail: info@wabcswim.com
http://www.wabcswim.com

World Boxing Association (WBA)
P.O. Box 377
Maracay 2101
Estado Aragua -Venezuela -
Phone: (0244) 663-15-84

Fax: (0244) 663-31-77
http://www.wbaonline.com

World Boxing Council (WBC)
Consejo Mundial de Boxeo
Cuzco 872

Colonia Lindavista
07300 Mexico City, Federal District,
    Mexico
Phone: 52 55 51195276
E-mail: info@wbcboxing.com
http://www.wbcboxing.com

**World Umpires Association
    (WUA)**
P.O. Box 394
Neenah, WI 54957
http://www.worldumpires.com

APPENDIX V
MAJOR LEAGUE BASEBALL CLUBS

The following is a listing of the clubs in Major League Baseball, as well as related organizations. Names, addresses, phone numbers, and Web sites are included for each. Use them to obtain general information, locate internships, and/or to send your résumé for job possibilities.

Major League Baseball (MLB) Players Association
12 East 49th Street
New York, NY 10017
Phone: (212) 826-0808
http://www.MLBPlayers.com

Office of the Commissioner of Baseball
245 Park Avenue
31st Floor
New York, NY 10167
Phone: (212) 931-7800
http://mlb.mlb.com

AMERICAN LEAGUE OF PROFESSIONAL BASEBALL CLUBS (AL)

Baltimore Orioles
Oriole Park at Camden Yards
333 West Camden Street
Baltimore, MD 21201
Phone: (410) 685-9800
http://www.orioles.com

Boston Red Sox
Fenway Park
4 Yawkey Way
Boston, MA 02215-3496
Phone: (617) 226-6740
http://www.redsox.com

Chicago White Sox
U.S. Cellular Field
333 West 35th Street
Chicago, IL 60616
Phone: (312) 674-1000
http://www.whitesox.com

Cleveland Indians
Progressive Field
2401 Ontario Street
Cleveland, OH 44115
Phone: (216) 420-4200
http://www.indians.com

Detroit Tigers
Comerica Park
2100 Woodward
Detroit, MI 48201
Phone: (313)471-2000
http://www.tigers.com

Kansas City Royals
P.O. Box 419969
Kansas City, MO 64141
Phone: (816) 921-8000
http://www.royals.com

Los Angeles Angels of Anaheim
P.O. Box 2000
Anaheim, CA 92803
Phone: (714) 940-2000
http://losangeles.angels.mlb.com

Minnesota Twins
34 Kirby Puckett Place
Minneapolis, MN 55415
Phone: (612) 375-1366
http://www.twinsbaseball.com

New York Yankees
Yankee Stadium
One East 161st Street
Bronx, NY 10451
Phone: (718) 293-4300
http://www.yankees.com

Oakland Athletics
Oakland-Alameda County Coliseum
7000 Coliseum Way
Oakland, CA 94621
Phone: (510) 638-4900
http://www.oaklandathletics.com

Seattle Mariners
Safeco Field
P.O. Box 4100
Seattle, WA 98104
Phone: (206) 346-4000
http://www.mariners.com

Tampa Bay Rays
Tropicana Field
One Tropicana Drive
St. Petersburg, FL 33705
Phone: (727) 825-3137
http://www.raysbaseball.com

Texas Rangers
Rangers Ballpark in Arlington
1000 Ballpark Way
Arlington, TX 76011
Phone: (817) 273-5222
http://www.texasrangers.com

Toronto Blue Jays
Rogers Centre
1 Blue Jays Way
Suite 3200
Toronto, Ontario,
Canada M5V1J1
Phone: (416) 341-1000
http://www.bluejays.com

NATIONAL LEAGUE OF PROFESSIONAL BASEBALL CLUBS (NL)

Arizona Diamondbacks
Chase Field
401 East Jefferson Street
Phoenix, AZ 85001
Phone: (602) 462-6500
http://www.dbacks.com

Atlanta Braves
Turner Field
755 Hank Aaron Drive
Atlanta, GA 30315
Phone: (404) 522-7630
http://www.braves.com

Chicago Cubs
Wrigley Field
1060 West Addison
Chicago, IL 60613
Phone: (773) 404-2827
http://www.cubs.com

Cincinnati Reds
Great American Ball Park
100 Main Street
Cincinnati, OH 45202
Phone: (513) 765-7000
http://www.reds.com

Colorado Rockies
Coors Field
2001 Blake Street
Denver, CO 80205
Phone: (303) 292-0200
http://www.colorado.rockies.com

Florida Marlins
Dolphin Stadium
2269 Dan Marino Boulevard
Miami, FL 33056
Phone: (305) 626-7400
http://www.marlins.com

Houston Astros
Minute Maid Park
501 Crawford Street
Houston, TX 77002
Phone: (713) 259-8000
http://www.astros.com

Los Angeles Dodgers
Dodger Stadium
1000 Elysian Park Avenue
Los Angeles, CA 90012
Phone: (323) 224-1500
http://www.dodgers.com

Milwaukee Brewers
Miller Park
One Brewers Way
Milwaukee, WI 53214
Phone: (414) 902-4400
http://www.brewers.com

New York Mets
Citi Field
Flushing, NY 11368
Phone: (718) 507-6387
http://www.mets.com

Philadelphia Phillies
Citizens Bank Park
One Citizens Bank Way
Philadelphia, PA 19148
Phone: (215) 463-6000
http://www.phillies.com

Pittsburgh Pirates
PNC Park
115 Federal Street
Pittsburgh, PA 15212
Phone: (412) 323-5000
http://www.pirates.com

San Diego Padres
PETCO Park
100 Park Boulevard
San Diego, CA 92101
Phone: (619) 795-5000
http://www.padres.com

San Francisco Giants
AT&T Park
24 Willie Mays Plaza
San Francisco, CA 94107
Phone: (415) 972-2000
http://www.sfgiants.com

St. Louis Cardinals
Busch Stadium
700 Clark Street
St. Louis, MO 63102
Phone: (314) 345-9600
http://www.stlcardinals.com

Washington Nationals
1500 South Capitol Street, SE
Washington, DC 20003
Phone: (202) 349-0400
http://www.nationals.com

APPENDIX VI
NATIONAL ASSOCIATION OF PROFESSIONAL BASEBALL LEAGUES MEMBERS

The following is a listing of the members of the National Association of Professional Baseball Leagues, Inc., provided courtesy of Minor League Baseball. This list will help you find the various clubs in the minor leagues. Names, addresses, phone numbers, and Web sites are included for each as well as the club affiliation and association.

Use them to obtain general information, locate internships, and/or to send your résumé for job possibilities.

Minor League Baseball Directory
National Association of Professional Baseball Leagues, Inc. (NAPBL)
P.O. Box A
St. Petersburg, FL 33731
Phone: (727) 822-6937
Fax: (727) 821-5819
E-mail: admin@minorleaguebaseball. com
http://web.minorleaguebaseball.com

TRIPLE-A International League
International League
55 South High Street
Suite 202
Dublin, OH 43017
Phone: (614) 791-9300
Fax: (614) 791-9009
http://www.ilbaseball.com

Buffalo Bisons
(New York Mets)
275 Washington Street
Buffalo, NY 14203
Phone: (716) 846-2000
Fax: (716) 852-6530
http://web.minorleaguebaseball. com/clubs/index.jsp?cid=t422

Charlotte Knights
(Chicago White Sox)
2280 Deerfield Drive
Fort Mill, SC 29715

Phone: (704) 357-8071
Fax: (704) 329-2155
http://web.minorleaguebaseball. com/clubs/index.jsp?cid=t422

Columbus Clippers
(Cleveland Indians)
1155 West Mound Street
Columbus, OH 43223
Phone: (614) 462-5250
Fax: (614) 462-3271
http://web.minorleaguebaseball. com/clubs/index.jsp?cid=t445

Durham Bulls
(Tampa Bay Rays)
P.O. Box 507
Durham, NC 27702
Phone: (919) 687-6500
Fax: (919) 687-6560
http://web.minorleaguebaseball. com/clubs/index.jsp?cid=t234

Gwinnett Braves
(Atlanta Braves)
1735 North Brown Road
Lawrenceville, GA 30043
Phone: (678) 277-0300
Fax: (678) 277-0338
http://web.minorleaguebaseball. com/index.jsp?sid=t431

Indianapolis Indians
(Pittsburgh Pirates)

501 West Maryland Street
Indianapolis, IN 46225
Phone: (317) 269-3542
Fax: (317) 269-3541
http://web.minorleaguebaseball. com/index.jsp?sid=t484

Lehigh Valley IronPigs
(Philadelphia Phillies)
1050 IronPigs Way
Allentown, PA 18109
Phone: (610) 435-3001
Fax: (610) 435-3088
http://web.minorleaguebaseball. com/clubs/ip_index. jsp?sid=milb&cid=t1410

Louisville Bats
(Cincinnati Reds)
401 East Main Street
Louisville, KY 40202
Phone: (502) 212-2287
Fax: (502) 515-2255
http://web.minorleaguebaseball. com/index.jsp?sid=t416

Norfolk Tides
(Baltimore Orioles)
150 Park Avenue
Norfolk, VA 23510
Phone: (757) 622-2222
Fax: (757) 624-9090
http://web.minorleaguebaseball. com/index.jsp?sid=t568

Pawtucket Red Sox
(Boston Red Sox)
P.O. Box 2365
Pawtucket, RI 02861
Phone: (401) 724-7300
Fax: (401) 724-2140
http://web.minorleaguebaseball.
    com/index.jsp?sid=t533

Rochester Red Wings
(Minnesota Twins)
One Morrie Silver Way
Rochester, NY 14608
Phone: (585) 454-1001
Fax: (585) 454-1056
http://web.minorleaguebaseball.
    com/index.jsp?sid=t534

Scranton/Wilkes-Barre Yankees
(New York Yankees)
235 Montage Mountain Road
Moosic, PA 18507
Phone: (570) 969-2255
Fax: (570) 963-6564
http://web.minorleaguebaseball.
    com/index.jsp?sid=t531

Syracuse Chiefs
(Washington Nationals)
One Tex Simone Drive
Syracuse, NY 13208
Phone: (315) 474-7833
Fax: (315) 474-2658
http://web.minorleaguebaseball.
    com/index.jsp?sid=t552

Toledo Mud Hens
(Detroit Tigers)
406 Washington Street
Toledo, OH 43604
Phone: (419) 725-4367
Fax: (419) 725-4368
http://web.minorleaguebaseball.
    com/clubs/ip_index.
    jsp?sid=milb&cid=t512

TRIPLE-A Pacific Coast League
Pacific Coast League
630 Southpointe Court
Suite 106
Colorado Springs, CO 80906
Phone: (719) 636-3399
Fax: (719) 636-1199

Albuquerque Isotopes
(Los Angeles Dodgers)
1601 Avenida Cesar Chavez, SE
Albuquerque, NM 87106
Phone: (505) 924-2255
Fax: (505) 242-8899
http://web.minorleaguebaseball.
    com/index.jsp?sid=t342

Colorado Springs Sky Sox
(Colorado Rockies)
4385 Tutt Boulevard
Colorado Springs, CO 80922
Phone: (719) 597-1449
Fax: (719) 597-2491
http://web.minorleaguebaseball.
    com/index.jsp?sid=t551

Fresno Grizzlies
(San Francisco Giants)
1800 Tulare Street
Fresno, CA 93721
Phone: (559) 320-4487
Fax: (559) 264-0795
http://web.minorleaguebaseball.
    com/index.jsp?sid=t259

Iowa Cubs
(Chicago Cubs)
One Line Drive
Des Moines, IA 50309
Phone: (515) 243-6111
Fax: (515) 243-5152
http://web.minorleaguebaseball.
    com/index.jsp?sid=t451

Las Vegas 51s
(Toronto Blue Jays)
850 Las Vegas Boulevard North
Las Vegas, NV 89101
Phone: (702) 386-7200
Fax: (702) 386-7214
http://web.minorleaguebaseball.
    com/index.jsp?sid=t400

Memphis Redbirds
(St. Louis Cardinals)
175 Toyota Plaza, Suite 300
Memphis, TN 38103
Phone: (901) 721-6000
Fax: (901) 527-1642
http://web.minorleaguebaseball.
    com/index.jsp?sid=t235

Nashville Sounds
(Milwaukee Brewers)
534 Chestnut Street
Nashville, TN 37203
Phone: (615) 242-4371
Fax: (615) 256-5684
http://web.minorleaguebaseball.
    com/clubs/ip_index.
    jsp?sid=milb&cid=t556

New Orleans Zephyrs
(Florida Marlins)
6000 Airline Drive
Metairie, LA 70003
Phone: (504) 734-5155
Fax: (504) 731-5118
http://web.minorleaguebaseball.
    com/index.jsp?sid=t588

Oklahoma City RedHawks
(Texas Rangers)
2 South Mickey Mantle Drive
Oklahoma City, OK 73104
Phone: (405) 218-1000
Fax: (405) 218-1001
http://web.minorleaguebaseball.
    com/index.jsp?sid=t238

Omaha Royals
(Kansas City Royals)
1202 Bert Murphy Avenue
Omaha, NE 68107
Phone: (402) 734-2550
Fax: (402) 734-7166
http://web.minorleaguebaseball.
    com/index.jsp?sid=t541

Portland Beavers
(San Diego Padres)
1844 Southwest Morrison
Portland, OR 97205
Phone: (503) 553-5400
Fax: (503) 553-5405
http://web.minorleaguebaseball.
    com/clubs/ip_index.
    jsp?sid=milb&cid=t248

Reno Aces
(Arizona Diamondbacks)
50 West. Liberty Street, Suite 1040
Reno, NV 89501
Phone: (775) 334-4700
Fax: (775) 334-4701

http://web.minorleaguebaseball.
com/index.jsp?sid=t2310

Round Rock Express

(Houston Astros)
3400 East Palm Valley Boulevard
Round Rock, TX 78665
Phone: (512) 255-2255
Fax: (512) 255-1558
http://web.minorleaguebaseball.
com/clubs/ip_index.
jsp?sid=milb&cid=t102

Sacramento River Cats

(Oakland A's)
400 Ballpark Drive
West Sacramento, CA 95691
Phone: (916) 376-4700
Fax: (916) 376-4710
http://web.minorleaguebaseball.
com/clubs/ip_index.
jsp?sid=milb&cid=t105

Salt Lake Bees

(Los Angeles Angels of Anaheim)
77 West 1300 South
Salt Lake City, UT 84115
Phone: (801) 350-6900
Fax: (801) 485-6818
http://web.minorleaguebaseball.
com/index.jsp?sid=t561

Tacoma Rainiers

(Seattle Mariners)
3560 Bridgeport Way West, Suite 3E
University Place, WA 98466
Phone: (253) 752-7707
Fax: (253) 752-7135
http://web.minorleaguebaseball.
com/index.jsp?sid=t529

AA Eastern League

Eastern League
30 Danforth Street
Suite 208
Portland, ME 04101
Phone: (207) 761-2700
Fax: (207) 761-7064
http://www.easternleague.com

Akron Aeros

(Cleveland Indians)
300 South Main Street

Akron, OH 44308
Phone: (330) 253-5151
Fax: (330) 253-3300
http://web.minorleaguebaseball.
com/clubs/ip_index.jsp?sid=
milb&cid=t402

Altoona Curve

(Pittsburgh Pirates)
P.O. Box 1029
Altoona, PA 16603
Phone: (814) 943-5400
Fax: (814) 943-9050
http://web.minorleaguebaseball.
com/clubs/ip_index.jsp?sid=
milb&cid=t452

Binghamton Mets

(New York Mets)
P.O. Box 598
Binghamton, NY 13902
Phone: (607) 723-6387
Fax: (607) 723-7779
http://web.minorleaguebaseball.
com/clubs/ip_index.jsp?sid=
milb&cid=t505

Bowie Baysox

(Baltimore Orioles)
4101 Northeast Crain Highway
Bowie, MD 20716
Phone: (301) 805-6000
Fax: (301) 464-4911
http://web.minorleaguebaseball.
com/clubs/ip_index.jsp?sid=
milb&cid=t418

Connecticut Defenders

(San Francisco Giants)
14 Stott Avenue
Norwich, CT 06360
Phone: (860) 887-7962
Fax: (860) 886-5996
http://web.minorleaguebaseball.
com/index.jsp?sid=t514

Erie SeaWolves

(Detroit Tigers)
110 East 10th Street
Erie, PA 16501
Phone: (814) 456-1300
Fax: (814) 456-7520

http://web.minorleaguebaseball.
com/index.jsp?sid=t106

Harrisburg Senators

(Washington Nationals)
P.O. Box 15757
Harrisburg, PA 17105
Phone: (717) 231-4444
Fax: (717) 231-4445
http://web.minorleaguebaseball.
com/index.jsp?sid=t547

New Britain Rock Cats

(Minnesota Twins)
P.O Box 1718
New Britain, CT 06050
Phone: (860) 224-8383
Fax: (860) 225-6267
http://web.minorleaguebaseball.
com/clubs/ip_index.jsp?sid=
milb&cid=t538

New Hampshire Fisher Cats

(Toronto Blue Jays)
One Line Drive
Manchester, NH 03101
Phone: (603) 641-2005
Fax: (603) 641-2055
http://web.minorleaguebaseball.
com/clubs/ip_index.jsp?sid=
milb&cid=t463

Portland Sea Dogs

(Boston Red Sox)
P.O Box 636
Portland, ME 04104
Phone: (207) 874-9300
Fax: (207) 780-0317
http://web.minorleaguebaseball.
com/index.jsp?sid=t546

Reading Phillies

(Philadelphia Phillies)
P.O. Box 15050
Reading, PA 19612
Phone: (610) 375-8469
Fax: (610) 373-5868
http://web.minorleaguebaseball.
com/clubs/ip_index.jsp?sid=
milb&cid=t522

Trenton Thunder

(New York Yankees)

One Thunder Road
Trenton, NJ 08611
Phone: (609) 394-3300
Fax: (609) 394-9666
http://web.minorleaguebaseball.
    com/clubs/ip_index.
    jsp?sid=milb&cid=t567

AA Southern League
Southern League
2551 Roswell Road
Suite 330
Marietta, GA 30062
Phone: (770) 321-0400
Fax: (770) 321-0037
http://www.southernleague.com

Birmingham Barons
(Chicago White Sox)
P.O. Box 360007
Birmingham, AL 35236
Phone: (205) 988-3200
Fax: (205) 988-9698
http://web.minorleaguebaseball.
    com/index.jsp?sid=t247

Carolina Mudcats
(Cincinnati Reds)
P.O. Drawer 1218
Zebulon, NC 27597
Phone: (919) 269-2287
Fax: (919) 269-4910
http://web.minorleaguebaseball.
    com/index.jsp?sid=t249

Chattanooga Lookouts
(Los Angeles Dodgers)
P.O. Box 11002
Chattanooga, TN 37401
Phone: (423) 267-2208
Fax: (423) 267-4258
http://web.minorleaguebaseball.
    com/index.jsp?sid=t498

Huntsville Stars
(Milwaukee Brewers)
P.O. Box 2769
Huntsville, AL 35804
Phone: (256) 882-2562
Fax: (256) 880-0801
http://web.minorleaguebaseball.
    com/clubs/index.jsp?cid=t559

Jacksonville Suns
(Florida Marlins)
P. O. Box 4756
Jacksonville, FL 32201
Phone: (904) 358-2846
Fax: (904) 358-2845
http://web.minorleaguebaseball.
    com/clubs/index.jsp?cid=t564

Mississippi Braves
(Atlanta Braves)
P.O. Box 97389
Pearl, MS 39288
Phone: (601) 932-8788
Fax: (601) 936-3567
http://web.minorleaguebaseball.
    com/clubs/index.jsp?cid=t430

Mobile BayBears
(Arizona Diamondbacks)
755 Bolling Brothers Boulevard
Mobile, AL 36606
Phone: (251) 479-2327
Fax: (251) 476-1147
http://web.minorleaguebaseball.
    com/clubs/index.jsp?cid=t417

Montgomery Biscuits
(Tampa Bay Rays)
200 Coosa Street
Montgomery, AL 36104
Phone: (334) 323-2255
Fax: (334) 323-2225
http://web.minorleaguebaseball.
    com/clubs/index.jsp?cid=t421

Tennessee Smokies
(Chicago Cubs)
3540 Line Drive
Kodak, TN 37764
Phone: (865) 286-2300
Fax: (865) 523-9913
http://web.minorleaguebaseball.
    com/clubs/index.jsp?cid=t553

West Tenn Diamond Jaxx
(Seattle Mariners)
4 Fun Place
Jackson, TN 38305
Phone: (731) 988-5299
Fax: (731) 988-5246
http://web.minorleaguebaseball.
    com/clubs/index.jsp?cid=t104

AA Texas League
Texas League
2442 Facet Oak
San Antonio, TX 78232
Phone: (210) 545-5297
Fax: (210) 545-5298
http://www.texas-league.com

Arkansas Travelers
(Kansas City Royals)
P.O. Box 55066
Little Rock, AR 72215-5066
Phone: (501) 664-1555
Fax: (501) 664-1834
http://web.minorleaguebaseball.
    com/clubs/index.jsp?cid=t1350

Corpus Christi Hooks
(Houston Astros)
734 East Port Avenue
Corpus Christi, TX 78401
Phone: (361) 561-4665
Fax: (361) 561-4666
http://web.minorleaguebaseball.
    com/clubs/index.jsp?cid=t482

Frisco RoughRiders
(Texas Rangers)
7300 RoughRiders Trail
Frisco, TX 75034
Phone: (972) 334-1900
Fax: (972) 334-5355
http://web.minorleaguebaseball.
    com/clubs/index.jsp?cid=t540

Midland RockHounds
(Oakland A's)
5514 Champions Drive
Midland, TX 79706
Phone: (432) 520-2255
Fax: (432) 520-8326
http://web.minorleaguebaseball.
    com/clubs/index.jsp?cid=t237

Northwest Arkansas Naturals
(Kansas City Royals)
P.O. Box 6817
Springdale, AR 72766
Phone: (479) 927-4900
Fax: (479) 756-8088
http://web.minorleaguebaseball.
    com/clubs/index.jsp?cid=t1350

San Antonio Missions

(San Diego Padres)
5757 US Highway 90 West
San Antonio, TX 78227
Phone: (210) 675-7275
Fax: (210) 670-0001
http://web.minorleaguebaseball.
    com/clubs/index.jsp?cid=t510

Springfield Cardinals

(St. Louis Cardinals)
955 East Trafficway
Springfield, MO 65802
Phone: (417) 863-2143
Fax: (417) 863-0388
http://web.minorleaguebaseball.
    com/clubs/index.jsp?cid=t440

Tulsa Drillers

(Colorado Rockies)
4802 East 15th Street
Tulsa, OK 74112
Phone: (918) 744-5998
Fax: (918) 747-3267
http://web.minorleaguebaseball.
    com/clubs/index.jsp?cid=t260

A California League

California League
P.O. Box 9503
Greensboro, NC 27429
Phone: (336) 691-9030
Fax: (336) 691-9070
http://www.carolinaleague.com

Bakersfield Blaze

(Texas Rangers)
P.O. Box 10031
Bakersfield, CA 93389
Phone: (661) 716-4487
Fax: (661) 322-6199
http://web.minorleaguebaseball.
    com/clubs/index.jsp?cid=t423

High Desert Mavericks

(Seattle Mariners)
12000 Stadium Way
Adelanto, CA 92301
Phone: (760) 246-6287
Fax: (760) 246-3197
http://web.minorleaguebaseball.
    com/clubs/index.jsp?cid=t504

Inland Empire 66ers of San Bernardino

(Los Angeles Dodgers)
280 South E Street
San Bernardino, CA 92401
Phone: (909) 888-9922
Fax: (909) 888-5251
http://web.minorleaguebaseball.
    com/clubs/index.jsp?cid=t401

Lake Elsinore Storm

(San Diego Padres)
P.O. Box 535
Lake Elsinore, CA 92531
Phone: (951) 245-4487
Fax: (951) 245-0305
http://web.minorleaguebaseball.
    com/clubs/index.jsp?cid=t103

Lancaster JetHawks

(Houston Astros)
45116 Valley Central Way
Lancaster, CA 93536
Phone: (661) 726-5400
Fax: (661) 726-5406
http://web.minorleaguebaseball.
    com/clubs/index.jsp?cid=t491

Modesto Nuts

(Colorado Rockies)
P.O. Box 883
Modesto, CA 95353
Phone: (209) 572-4487
Fax: (209) 572-4490
http://web.minorleaguebaseball.
    com/clubs/index.jsp?cid=t515

Rancho Cucamonga Quakes

(Los Angeles Angels of Anaheim)
P.O. Box 4139
Rancho Cucamonga, CA 91729
Phone: (909) 481-5000
Fax: (909) 481-5005
http://web.minorleaguebaseball.
    com/clubs/index.jsp?cid=t526

San Jose Giants

(San Francisco Giants)
P.O. Box 21727
San Jose, CA 95151
Phone: (408) 297-1435
Fax: (408) 297-1453
http://web.minorleaguebaseball.
    com/clubs/index.jsp?cid=t476

Stockton Ports

(Oakland A's)
404 West Fremont Street
Stockton, CA 95203
Phone: (209) 644-1900
Fax: (209) 644-1931
http://web.minorleaguebaseball.
    com/clubs/index.jsp?cid=t524

Visalia Rawhide

(Arizona Diamondbacks)
440 North Giddings Street
Visalia, CA 93291
Phone: (559) 625-0480
Fax: (559) 739-7732
http://web.minorleaguebaseball.
    com/clubs/index.jsp?cid=t516

A Carolina League

Carolina League
P.O. Box 9503
Greensboro, NC 27429
Phone: (336) 691-9030
Fax: (336) 691-9070
http://www.carolinaleague.com

Frederick Keys

(Baltimore Orioles)
P.O. Box 3169
Frederick, MD 21705
Phone: (301) 662-0013
Fax: (301) 662-0018
http://web.minorleaguebaseball.
    com/clubs/index.jsp?cid=t493

Kinston Indians

(Cleveland Indians)
P.O. Box 3542
Kinston, NC 28502
Phone: (252) 527-9111
Fax: (252) 527-0498
http://web.minorleaguebaseball.
    com/clubs/index.jsp?cid=t485

Lynchburg Hillcats

(Pittsburgh Pirates)
P.O. Box 10213
Lynchburg, VA 24506
Phone: (434) 528-1144
Fax: (434) 846-0768
http://web.minorleaguebaseball.
    com/clubs/index.jsp?cid=t481

Myrtle Beach Pelicans
(Atlanta Braves)
1251 21st Avenue North
Myrtle Beach, SC 29577
Phone: (843) 918-6000
Fax: (843) 918-6001
http://web.minorleaguebaseball.
    com/clubs/index.jsp?cid=t521

Potomac Nationals
(Washington Nationals)
P.O. Box 2148
Woodbridge, VA 22195
Phone: (703) 590-2311
Fax: (703) 590-5716
http://web.minorleaguebaseball.
    com/clubs/index.jsp?cid=t436

Salem Red Sox
(Boston Red Sox)
P.O. Box 842
Salem, VA 24153
Phone: (540) 389-3333
Fax: (540) 389-9710
http://web.minorleaguebaseball.
    com/clubs/index.jsp?cid=t414

Wilmington Blue Rocks
(Kansas City Royals)
801 Shipyard Drive
Wilmington, DE 19801
Phone: (302) 888-2015
Fax: (302) 888-2032
http://web.minorleaguebaseball.
    com/clubs/index.jsp?cid=t426

Winston-Salem Dash
(Chicago White Sox)
926 Brookstown Avenue
Winston-Salem, NC 27101
Phone: (336) 714-2287
Fax: (336) 714-2288
http://web.minorleaguebaseball.
    com/clubs/index.jsp?cid=t580

A Florida State League
Florida State League
P.O. Box 349
Daytona Beach, FL 32115
Phone: (386) 252-7479
Fax: (386) 252-7495
http://www.fslbaseball.com

Brevard County Manatees
(Milwaukee Brewers)
5800 Stadium Parkway, Suite 101
Viera, FL 32940
Phone: (321) 633-9200
Fax: (321) 248-0292
http://web.minorleaguebaseball.
    com/clubs/index.jsp?cid=t503

Charlotte Stone Crabs
(Tampa Bay Rays)
2300 El Jobean Road
Port Charlotte, FL 33948
Phone: (941) 206-4487
Fax: (941) 206-3599
http://web.minorleaguebaseball.
    com/clubs/index.jsp?cid=t2730

Clearwater Threshers
(Philadelphia Phillies)
601 North Old Coachman Road
Clearwater, FL 33765
Phone: (727) 467-4457
Fax: (727) 712-4498
http://web.minorleaguebaseball.
    com/clubs/index.jsp?cid=t566

Daytona Cubs
(Chicago Cubs)
105 East Orange Avenue
Daytona Beach, FL 32114
Phone: (386) 257-3172
Fax: (386) 257-3382
http://web.minorleaguebaseball.
    com/clubs/index.jsp?cid=t450

Dunedin Blue Jays
(Toronto Blue Jays)
373 Douglas Avenue #A
Dunedin, FL 34698
Phone: (727) 733-9302
Fax: (727) 734-7661
http://web.minorleaguebaseball.
    com/clubs/index.jsp?cid=t424

Fort Myers Miracle
(San Diego Padres)
14400 Six Mile Cypress Parkway
Ft. Myers, FL 33912
Phone: (239) 768-4210
Fax: (239) 768-4211
http://web.minorleaguebaseball.
    com/clubs/index.jsp?cid=t584

Jupiter Hammerheads
(Florida Marlins)
4751 Main Street
Jupiter, FL 33458
Phone: (561) 775-1818
Fax: (561) 691-6886
http://web.minorleaguebaseball.
    com/clubs/index.jsp?cid=t479

Lakeland Flying Tigers
(Detroit Tigers)
2125 North Lake Avenue
Lakeland, FL 33805
Phone: (863) 686-8075
Fax: (863) 688-9589
http://web.minorleaguebaseball.
    com/clubs/index.jsp?cid=t570

Palm Beach Cardinals
(St. Louis Cardinals)
4751 Main Street
Jupiter, FL 33458
Phone: (561) 775-1818
Fax: (561) 691-6886
http://web.minorleaguebaseball.
    com/clubs/index.jsp?cid=t279

Sarasota Reds
(Cincinnati Reds)
1090 North Euclid Ave.
Sarasota, FL 34237
Phone: (941) 955-6501
Fax: (941) 955-6365
http://web.minorleaguebaseball.
    com/clubs/index.jsp?cid=t535

St. Lucie Mets
(New York Mets)
525 Northwest Peacock Boulevard
Port St. Lucie, FL 34986
Phone: (772) 871-2100
Fax: (772) 878-9802
http://web.minorleaguebaseball.
    com/clubs/index.jsp?cid=t507

Tampa Yankees
(New York Yankees)
One Steinbrenner Drive
Tampa, FL 33614
Phone: (813) 875-7753
Fax: (813) 673-3174
http://web.minorleaguebaseball.
    com/clubs/index.jsp?cid=t587

A Midwest League

Midwest League
P.O. Box 936
Beloit, Wisconsin 53512-0936
Phone: (608) 364-1188
Fax: (608) 364-1913
http://www.midwestleague.com

Beloit Snappers

(Minnesota Twins)
P.O. Box 855
Beloit, WI 53512
Phone: (608) 362-2272
Fax: (608) 362-0418
http://web.minorleaguebaseball.
   com/clubs/index.jsp?cid=t554

Burlington Bees

(Kansas City Royals)
P.O. Box 824
Burlington, IA 52601
Phone: (319) 754-5705
Fax: (319) 754-5882
http://web.minorleaguebaseball.
   com/clubs/index.jsp?cid=t420

Cedar Rapids Kernels

(Los Angeles Angels of Anaheim)
P.O. Box 2001
Cedar Rapids, IA 52406
Phone: (319) 363-3887
Fax: (319) 363-5631
http://web.minorleaguebaseball.
   com/clubs/ip_index.jsp?sid=
   milb&cid=t492

Clinton LumberKings

(Seattle Mariners)
P.O. Box 1295
Clinton, IA 52733
Phone: (563) 242-0727
Fax: (563) 242-1433
http://web.minorleaguebaseball.
   com/index.jsp?sid=t500

Dayton Dragons

(Cincinnati Reds)
P.O. Box 2107
Dayton, OH 45401
Phone: (937) 228-2287
Fax: (937) 228-2284
http://web.minorleaguebaseball.
   com/clubs/ip_index.
   jsp?sid=milb&cid=t459

Fort Wayne TinCaps

(San Diego Padres)
1616 East Coliseum Boulevard
Fort Wayne, IN 46805
Phone: (260) 482-6400
Fax: (260) 471-4678
http://web.minorleaguebaseball.
   com/clubs/ip_index.
   jsp?sid=milb&cid=t584

Great Lakes Loons

(Los Angeles Dodgers)
825 East Main Street
Midland, MI 48640
Phone: (989) 837-2255
Fax: (989) 837-8780
http://web.minorleaguebaseball.
   com/index.jsp?sid=t456

Kane County Cougars

(Oakland A's)
34W002 Cherry Lane
Geneva, IL 60134
Phone: (630) 232-8811
Fax: (630) 232-8815
http://web.minorleaguebaseball.
   com/clubs/ip_index.
   jsp?sid=milb&cid=t446

Lansing Lugnuts

(Toronto Blue Jays)
505 East Michigan Avenue
Lansing, MI 48912
Phone: (517) 485-4500
Fax: (517) 485-4518
http://web.minorleaguebaseball.
   com/clubs/ip_index.
   jsp?sid=milb&cid=t499

Peoria Chiefs

(Chicago Cubs)
730 Southwest Jefferson Avenue
Peoria, IL 61602
Phone: (309) 680-4000
Fax: (309) 680-4080
http://web.minorleaguebaseball.
   com/index.jsp?sid=t443

Quad Cities River Bandits

(St. Louis Cardinals)
P.O. Box 3496
Davenport, IA 52808
Phone: (563) 324-3000

Fax: (563) 324-3109
http://web.minorleaguebaseball.
   com/index.jsp?sid=t565

South Bend Silver Hawks

(Arizona Diamondbacks)
P.O. Box 4218
South Bend, IN 46634
Phone: (574) 235-9988
Fax: (574) 235-9950
http://web.minorleaguebaseball.
   com/index.jsp?sid=t550

West Michigan Whitecaps

(Detroit Tigers)
P.O. Box 428
Comstock Park, MI 49321
Phone: (616) 784-4131
Fax: (616) 784-4911
http://web.minorleaguebaseball.
   com/clubs/ip_index.
   jsp?sid=milb&cid=t582

Wisconsin Timber Rattlers

(Milwaukee Brewers)
P.O. Box 7464
Appleton, WI 54912
Fax: (920) 733-8032
Phone: (920) 733-4152
http://web.minorleaguebaseball.
   com/index.jsp?sid=t572

A South Atlantic League

South Atlantic League
111 Second Avenue, NE, Suite 335
St. Petersburg, FL 33701
Phone: (727) 456-1240
Fax: (727) 499-6853
http://www.southatlanticleague.com

Asheville Tourists

(Colorado Rockies)
McCormick Field, 30 Buchanan
   Place
Asheville, NC 28801
Phone: (828) 258-0428
Fax: (828) 258-0320
http://web.minorleaguebaseball.
   com/index.jsp?sid=t573

Augusta GreenJackets

(San Francisco Giants)
P.O. Box 3746

Augusta, GA 30914
Phone: (706) 736-7889
Fax: (706) 736-1122
http://web.minorleaguebaseball.
   com/clubs/ip_index.
   jsp?sid=milb&cid=t478

Bowling Green Hot Rods
(Tampa Bay Rays)
P.O. Box 929
Bowling Green, KY 42102
Phone: (270) 901-2121
http://web.minorleaguebaseball.
   com/index.jsp?sid=t2498

Charleston RiverDogs
(New York Yankees)
P.O. Box 20849
Charleston, SC 29413
Phone: (843) 723-7241
Fax: (843) 723-2641
http://web.minorleaguebaseball.
   com/clubs/ip_index.
   jsp?sid=milb&cid=t233

Delmarva Shorebirds
(Baltimore Orioles)
P.O. Box 1557
Salisbury, MD 21802
Phone: (410) 219-3112
Fax: (410) 219-9164
http://web.minorleaguebaseball.
   com/index.jsp?sid=t548

Greensboro Grasshoppers
(Florida Marlins)
408 Bellemeade Street
Greensboro, NC 27401
Phone: (336) 268-2255
Fax: (336) 273-7350
http://web.minorleaguebaseball.
   com/clubs/ip_index.
   jsp?sid=milb&cid=t477

Greenville Drive
(Boston Red Sox)
945 South Main Street
Greenville, SC 29601
Phone: (864) 240-4500
Fax: (864) 240-4501
http://web.minorleaguebaseball.
   com/clubs/ip_index.
   jsp?sid=milb&cid=t428

Hagerstown Suns
(Washington Nationals)
274 East Memorial Boulevard
Hagerstown, MD 21740
Phone: (301) 791-6266
Fax: (301) 791-6066
http://web.minorleaguebaseball.
   com/clubs/ip_index.
   jsp?sid=milb&cid=t563

Hickory Crawdads
(Texas Rangers)
P.O. Box 1268
Hickory, NC 28603
Phone: (828) 322-3000
Fax: (828) 322-6137
http://web.minorleaguebaseball.
   com/index.jsp?sid=t448

Kannapolis Intimidators
(Chicago White Sox)
P.O. Box 64
Kannapolis, NC 28082
Phone: (704) 932-3267
Fax: (704) 938-7040
http://web.minorleaguebaseball.
   com/index.jsp?sid=t487

Lake County Captains
(Cleveland Indians)
35300 Vine Street
Eastlake, OH 44095
Phone: (440) 975-8085
Fax: (440) 975-8958
http://web.minorleaguebaseball.
   com/index.jsp?sid=t437

Lakewood BlueClaws
(Philadelphia Phillies)
2 Stadium Way
Lakewood, NJ 08701
Phone: (732) 901-7000
Fax: (732) 901-3967
http://web.minorleaguebaseball.
   com/clubs/ip_index.
   jsp?sid=milb&cid=t427

Lexington Legends
(Houston Astros)
207 Legends Lane
Lexington, KY 40505
Phone: (859) 252-4487
Fax: (859) 252-0747

http://web.minorleaguebaseball.
   com/index.jsp?sid=t495

Rome Braves
(Atlanta Braves)
P.O. Box 1915
Rome, GA 30162
Phone: (706) 368-9388
Fax: (706) 368-6525
http://web.minorleaguebaseball.
   com/index.jsp?sid=t432

Savannah Sand Gnats
(New York Mets)
P.O. Box 3783
Savannah, GA 31414
Phone: (912) 351-9150
Fax: (912) 352-9722
http://web.minorleaguebaseball.
   com/index.jsp?sid=t543

West Virginia Power
(Pittsburgh Pirates)
601 Morris Street, Suite 201
Charleston, WV 25301
Phone: (304) 344-2287
Fax: (304) 344-0083
http://web.minorleaguebaseball.
   com/index.jsp?sid=t525

**SHORT-A New York—Penn
League**
New York—Penn League
One Progress Plaza
200 Central Avenue
St. Petersburg, FL 33701
Phone: (727) 576-6300
Fax: (727) 822-3768

Aberdeen IronBirds
(Baltimore Orioles)
873 Long Drive
Aberdeen, MD 21001
Phone: (410) 297-9292
Fax: (410) 297-6653
http://web.minorleaguebaseball.
   com/clubs/ip_index.
   jsp?sid=milb&cid=t488

Auburn Doubledays
(Toronto Blue Jays)
130 North Division Street
Auburn, NY 13021

Phone: (315) 255-2489
Fax: (315) 255-2675
http://web.minorleaguebaseball.
com/index.jsp?sid=t458

Batavia Muckdogs
(St. Louis Cardinals)
299 Bank Street
Batavia, NY 14020
Phone: (585) 343-5454
Fax: (585) 343-5620
http://web.minorleaguebaseball.
com/index.jsp?sid=t511

Brooklyn Cyclones
(New York Mets)
1904 Surf Avenue
Brooklyn, NY 11224
Phone: (718) 449-8497
Fax: (718) 449-6368
http://web.minorleaguebaseball.
com/clubs/ip_index.jsp?sid=
milb&cid=t453

Hudson Valley Renegades
(Tampa Bay Rays)
P.O. Box 661
Fishkill, NY 12524
Phone: (845) 838-0094
Fax: (845) 838-0014
http://web.minorleaguebaseball.
com/clubs/ip_index.jsp?sid=
milb&cid=t537

Jamestown Jammers
(Florida Marlins)
P.O. Box 638
Jamestown, NY 14702
Phone: (716) 664-0915
Fax: (716) 664-4175
http://web.minorleaguebaseball.
com/index.jsp?sid=t489

Lowell Spinners
(Boston Red Sox)
450 Aiken Street
Lowell, MA 01854
Phone: (978) 459-2255
Fax: (978) 459-1674
http://web.minorleaguebaseball.
com/index.jsp?sid=t558

Mahoning Valley Scrappers
(Cleveland Indians)
111 Eastwood Mall Boulevard

Niles, OH 44446
Phone: (330) 505-0000
Fax: (330) 505-9696
http://web.minorleaguebaseball.
com/index.jsp?sid=t545

Oneonta Tigers
(Detroit Tigers)
95 River Street
Oneonta, NY 13820
Phone: (607) 432-6326
Fax: (607) 432-1965
http://web.minorleaguebaseball.
com/index.jsp?sid=t571

State College Spikes
(Pittsburgh Pirates)
112 Medlar Field at Lubrano Park
University Park, PA 16802
Phone: (814) 272-1711
Fax: (814) 272-1718
http://web.minorleaguebaseball.
com/clubs/ip_index.
jsp?sid=milb&cid=t1174

Staten Island Yankees
(New York Yankees)
75 Richmond Terrace
Staten Island, NY 10301
Phone: (718) 720-9265
Fax: (718) 273-5763
http://web.minorleaguebaseball.
com/clubs/ip_index.
jsp?sid=milb&cid=t586

Tri-City ValleyCats
(Houston Astros)
P.O. Box 694
Troy, NY 12180
Phone: (518) 629-2287
Fax: (518) 629-2299
http://web.minorleaguebaseball.
com/index.jsp?sid=t577

Vermont Lake Monsters
(Washington Nationals)
1 King Street Ferry Dock
Burlington, VT 05401
Phone: (802) 655-4200
Fax: (802) 655-5660
http://web.minorleaguebaseball.
com/index.jsp?sid=t462

Williamsport Crosscutters
(Philadelphia Phillies)
P.O. Box 3173
Williamsport, PA 17701
Phone: (570) 326-3389
Fax: (570) 326-3494
http://web.minorleaguebaseball.
com/clubs/ip_index.
jsp?sid=milb&cid=t449

SHORT-A Northwest League
Northwest League
P.O. Box 1645
Boise, ID 83701
Phone: (208) 429-1511
Fax: (208) 429-1525
http://www.northwestleague.com

Boise Hawks
(Chicago Cubs)
5600 Glenwood Street
Boise, ID 83714
Phone: (208) 322-5000
Fax: (208) 322-6846
http://web.minorleaguebaseball.
com/clubs/ip_index.
jsp?sid=milb&cid=t480

Eugene Emeralds
(San Diego Padres)
P.O. Box 5566
Eugene, OR 97405
Phone: (541) 342-5367
Fax: (541) 342-6089
http://web.minorleaguebaseball.
com/index.jsp?sid=t461

Everett AquaSox
(Seattle Mariners)
3802 Broadway
Everett, WA 98201
Phone: (425) 258-3673
Fax: (425) 258-3675
http://web.minorleaguebaseball.
com/index.jsp?sid=t403

Salem-Keizer Volcanoes
(San Francisco Giants)
P.O. Box 20936
Keizer, OR 97307
Phone: (503) 390-2225
Fax: (503) 390-2227

http://web.minorleaguebaseball.
com/clubs/ip_index.
jsp?sid=milb&cid=t578

Spokane Indians
(Texas Rangers)
P.O. Box 4758
Spokane, WA 99220
Phone: (509) 535-2922
Fax: (509) 534-5368
http://web.minorleaguebaseball.
com/clubs/ip_index.
jsp?sid=milb&cid=t486

Tri-City Dust Devils
(Colorado Rockies)
6200 Burden Boulevard
Pasco, WA 99301
Phone: (509) 544-8789
Fax: (509) 547-9570
http://web.minorleaguebaseball.
com/index.jsp?sid=t460

Vancouver Canadians
(Oakland A's)
4601 Ontario Street
Vancouver, BC, Canada V5V 3H4
Phone: (604) 872-5232
Fax: (604) 872-1714
http://web.minorleaguebaseball.
com/clubs/ip_index.
jsp?sid=milb&cid=t435

Yakima Bears
(Arizona Diamondbacks)
P.O. Box 483
Yakima, WA 98907
Phone: (509) 457-5151
Fax: (509) 457-9909
http://web.minorleaguebaseball.
com/index.jsp?sid=t419

ROOKIE Appalachian League
Appalachian League
283 Deerchase Circle
Statesville, NC 28625
Phone: (704) 873-5300
Fax: (704) 873-4333

Bluefield Orioles
(Baltimore Orioles)
P.O. Box 356
Bluefield, WV 24701

Phone: (276) 326-1326
Fax: (276) 326-1318
http://web.minorleaguebaseball.
com/index.jsp?sid=t517

Bristol White Sox
(Chicago White Sox)
P.O. Box 1434
Bristol, VA 24203
Phone: (276) 669-6859
Fax: (276) 669-7686
http://web.minorleaguebaseball.
com/index.jsp?sid=t557

Burlington Royals
(Kansas City Royals)
P.O. Box 1143
Burlington, NC 27216
Phone: (336) 222-0223
Fax: (336) 226-2498
http://web.minorleaguebaseball.
com/index.jsp?sid=t420

Danville Braves
(Atlanta Braves)
P.O. Box 378
Danville, VA 24543
Phone: (434) 797-3792
Fax: (434) 797-3799
http://web.minorleaguebaseball.
com/clubs/index.jsp?cid=t429

Elizabethton Twins
(Minnesota Twins)
136 South Sycamore
Elizabethton, TN 37643
Phone: (423) 547-6441
Fax: (423) 547-6442
http://web.minorleaguebaseball.
com/clubs/index.jsp?cid=t576

Greeneville Astros
(Houston Astros)
P.O. Box 5192
Greeneville, TN 37743
Phone: (423) 638-0411
Fax: (423) 638-9450
http://web.minorleaguebaseball.
com/clubs/index.jsp?cid=t413

Johnson City Cardinals
(St. Louis Cardinals)
P.O. Box 179

Johnson City, TN 37605
Phone: (423) 461-4866
Fax: (423) 461-4864
http://web.minorleaguebaseball.
com/clubs/index.jsp?cid=t438

Kingsport Mets
(New York Mets)
P.O. Box 1128
Kingsport, TN 37662
Phone: (423) 378-3744
Fax: (423) 392-8538
http://web.minorleaguebaseball.
com/clubs/index.jsp?cid=t506

Princeton Rays
(Tampa Bay Rays)
P.O. Box 5646
Princeton, WV 24740
Phone: (304) 487-2000
Fax: (304) 487-8762
http://web.minorleaguebaseball.
com/clubs/index.jsp?cid=t455

Pulaski Mariners
(Seattle Mariners)
P.O. Box 676
Pulaski, VA 24301
Phone: (540) 440-0578
http://web.minorleaguebaseball.
com/clubs/index.jsp?cid=t425

ROOKIE Pioneer League
Pioneer League
Steam Plant Square
157 South Lincoln Street
Spokane, WA 99201
Phone: (509) 456-7615
Fax: (509) 456-0136
http://www.pioneerleague.com

Billings Mustangs
(Cincinnati Reds)
P.O. Box 1553
Billings, MT 59103
Phone: (406) 252-1241
Fax: (406) 252-2968
http://web.minorleaguebaseball.
com/clubs/index.jsp?cid=t513

Casper Ghosts
(Colorado Rockies)

P.O. Box 1293
Casper, WY 82602
Phone: (307) 232-1111
Fax: (307) 265-7867
http://web.minorleaguebaseball.
    com/clubs/index.jsp?cid=t539

Great Falls Voyagers
(Chicago White Sox)
P.O. Box 1621
Great Falls, MT 59403
Phone: (406) 452-5311
Fax: (406) 454-0811
http://web.minorleaguebaseball.
    com/clubs/index.jsp?cid=t581

Helena Brewers
(Milwaukee Brewers)
P.O. Box 6756
Helena, MT 59604

Phone: (406) 495-0500
Fax: (406) 495-0900
http://web.minorleaguebaseball.
    com/clubs/index.jsp?cid=t433

Idaho Falls Chukars
(Kansas City Royals)
P.O. Box 2183
Idaho Falls, ID 83403
Phone: (208) 522-8363
Fax: (208) 522-9858
http://web.minorleaguebaseball.
    com/clubs/index.jsp?cid=t444

Missoula Osprey
(Arizona Diamondbacks)
412 West Alder Street
Missoula, MT 59802
Phone: (406) 543-3300
Fax: (406) 543-9463

http://web.minorleaguebaseball.
    com/clubs/index.jsp?cid=t518

Ogden Raptors
(Los Angeles Dodgers)
2330 Lincoln Avenue
Ogden, UT 84401
Phone: (801) 393-2400
Fax: (801) 393-2473
http://web.minorleaguebaseball.
    com/clubs/index.jsp?cid=t530

Orem Owlz
(Los Angeles Angels of Anaheim)
970 West University Parkway
Orem, UT 84058
Phone: (801) 377-2255
Fax: (801) 377-2345
http://web.minorleaguebaseball.
    com/clubs/index.jsp?cid=t519

APPENDIX VII
NATIONAL BASKETBALL ASSOCIATION (NBA) TEAMS

The following is a listing of the teams in the National Basketball Association (NBA). Names, addresses, phone numbers, and Web sites are included for each (when available). Use this list to contact teams for additional information, locate internships, and/or to send your résumé for job possibilities.

National Basketball Association (NBA)
645 Fifth Avenue
New York, NY 10022
Phone: (212) 407-8000
http://www.nba.com

Atlanta Hawks
Centennial Tower
101 Marietta Street, NW
Suite 1900
Atlanta, GA 30303
Phone: :(404) 878-3800
http://www.nba.com/hawks

Boston Celtics
226 Causeway Street
Boston, MA 02114
Phone: (617) 523-3030
http://www.nba.com/celtics

Charlotte Bobcats
333 East Trade Street
Charlotte, NC 28202
Phone: (704) 688-8600
Fax: (704) 688-8727
E-mail: info@bobcats.com
http://www.nba.com/bobcats

Chicago Bulls
United Center
1901 West Madison Street
Chicago, IL 60612
Phone: (312) 455-4000
Fax: (312) 455-4189
http://www.nba.com/bulls

Cleveland Cavaliers
One Center Court

Cleveland, OH 44115
Phone: (216) 420-2000
http://www.nba.com/cavaliers

Dallas Mavericks
The Pavilion
2909 Taylor Street
Dallas, TX 75226
Phone: (214) 747-MAVS
http://www.nba.com/mavericks

Denver Nuggets
1000 Chopper Circle
Denver, CO 80204
Phone: (303) 405-1100
E-mail: nuggetsmail@pepsicenter.com.
http://www.nba.com/nuggets

Detroit Pistons
5 Championship Drive
Auburn Hills, MI 48326
Phone: (248) 377-0100
http://www.nba.com/pistons

Golden State Warriors
1011 Broadway
Oakland, CA 94607
Phone: (510) 986-2200
http://www.nba.com/warriors

Houston Rockets
1510 Polk Street
Houston, TX 77002
Phone: (713) 627-3865
http://www.nba.com/rockets

Indiana Pacers
125 South Pennsylvania Street

Indianapolis, IN 46204
Phone: (317) 917-2500
Fax: (317) 917-2599
E-mail: PacersInsider@Pacers.com
http://www.nba.com/pacers

Los Angeles Clippers
Staples Center
1111 South Figueroa Street
Los Angeles, CA, 90015
Phone: (213) 742-7500
http://www.nba.com/clippers

Los Angeles Lakers
555 North Nash Street
El Segundo, CA 90245
Phone: (310) 426-6000
http://www.nba.com/lakers

Memphis Grizzlies
191 Beale Street
Memphis, TN 38103
Phone: (901) 888-4667
Fax: (901) 201-1235
http://www.nba.com/grizzlies

Miami Heat
AmericanAirlines Arena
601 Biscayne Boulevard
Miami, FL 33132
Phone: (786) 777-1000
http://www.nba.com/heat

Milwaukee Bucks
1001 North Fourth Street
Milwaukee, WI 53203
Phone: (414) 227-0599
http://www.nba.com/bucks

Minnesota Timberwolves
600 First Avenue North
Minneapolis, MN 55403
Phone: (612) 673-1600
http://www.nba.com/timberwolves

New Jersey Nets
390 Murray Hill Parkway
East Rutherford, NJ 07073
Phone: (201) 935-8888
http://www.nba.com/nets

New Orleans Hornets
1250 Poydras Street
New Orleans, LA 70113
Phone: (504) 593-4700
http://www.nba.com/hornets

New York Knicks
Madison Square Garden
Two Pennsylvania Plaza
New York, NY 10121
Phone: (212) 465-6471
http://www.nba.com/knicks

Oklahoma City Thunder
Two Leadership Square
211 North Robinson Avenue
Oklahoma City, OK 73102
Phone: (405) 208-4800
http://www.nba.com/thunder

Orlando Magic
8701 Maitland Summit Boulevard
Orlando, FL 32810
Phone: (407) 916-2400
http://www.nba.com/magic

Philadelphia 76ers
3601 South Broad Street
Philadelphia, PA 19148
Phone: (215) 339-7676
http://www.nba.com/sixers

Phoenix Suns
201 East Jefferson Street
Phoenix, AZ 85004
Phone: (602) 379-7900
Fax: (602) 379-7990
http://www.nba.com/suns

Portland Trail Blazers
One Center Court
Suite 200
Portland, OR 97227
Phone: (503) 234-0201
http://www.nba.com/blazers

Sacramento Kings
ARCO Arena
One Sports Parkway
Sacramento, CA 95834
Phone: (916) 928-0000

Fax: (916) 928-0727
http://www.nba.com/kings

San Antonio Spurs
One AT&T Center
San Antonio, TX 78219
Phone: (210) 444-500
http://www.nba.com/spurs

Toronto Raptors
Air Canada Centre
40 Bay Street
Suite 400
Toronto, Ontario M5J 2x2
Phone:
http://www.nba.com/raptors

Utah Jazz
301 West South Temple
Salt Lake City, UT 84101
Phone: (801) 325-2500
http://www.nba.com/jazz

Washington Wizards
601 F Street, NW
Washington DC 20004
Phone: (202) 661-5050
http://www.nba.com/wizards

APPENDIX VIII
WOMEN'S NATIONAL BASKETBALL ASSOCIATION (WNBA) TEAMS

The following is a listing of the teams in the Women's National Basketball Association (WNBA). Names, addresses, phone and fax numbers, and Web sites have been included for each. Use these resources to obtain general information, locate internships, and/or to send your résumé for possible jobs.

Atlanta Dream
83 Walton Street, NW
Suite 500
Atlanta, GA 30303
Phone: (404) 604-2626
Fax: (404) 954-6666
http://www.wnba.com/dream

Chicago Sky
20 West Kinzie Street
Suite 1010
Chicago, IL 60654
Phone: (312) 828-9550
http://www.wnba.com/sky

Connecticut Sun
One Mohegan Sun Boulevard
Uncasville, CT 06382
Phone: (860) 862-4000
Fax: (860) 862-4010
http://www.connecticutsun.com
http://www.wnba.com/sun

Detroit Shock
5 Championship Drive
Auburn Hills, MI 48326
Phone: (248) 377-0100
http://www.wnba.com/shock

Indiana Fever
Conseco Fieldhouse
One Conseco Court
125 South Pennsylvania Street
Indianapolis, IN 46204
Phone: (317) 917-2500
http://www.wnba.com/fever

Los Angeles Sparks
888 South Figueroa Street
Suite 2010
Los Angeles, CA 90017
Phone: (213) 929-1300
Fax: (213) 929-1325
http://www.wnba.com/sparks

Minnesota Lynx
600 First Avenue North
Minneapolis, MN 55403
Phone: (612) 673-1600
http://www.wnba.com/lynx

New York Liberty
Madison Square Garden
Two Pennsylvania Plaza, 14th Floor
New York, NY 10121
Phone: (212) 564-9622
Fax: (212) 465-6250
http://www.wnba.com/liberty

Phoenix Mercury
201 East Jefferson Street
Phoenix, AZ 85004
Phone: (602) 514-8333
Fax: (602) 514-8303
http://www.wnba.com/mercury

Sacramento Monarchs
ARCO Arena
One Sports Parkway
Sacramento, CA 95834
Phone: (916) 928-0000
Fax: (916) 928-0727
http://www.wnba.com/monarchs

San Antonio Silver Stars
One AT&T Center
San Antonio, TX 78219
Phone: (210) 444-5050
http://www.wnba.com/silverstars

Seattle Storm
3421 Thorndyke Avenue West
Seattle, WA 98119
Phone: (206) 217-WNBA
http://www.wnba.com/storm

Washington Mystics
Verizon Center
601 F Street, NW
Washington, DC 20004
Phone: (202) 527-7540
Fax: (202) 527-7539
http://www.wnba.com/mystics

APPENDIX IX
NATIONAL FOOTBALL LEAGUE (NFL) TEAMS

The following is a listing of the teams and organizations in the National Football League (NFL). Those in the American Football Conference (AFC) are listed first, and those in the National Football Conference (NFC) follow.

Names, addresses, phone numbers, and Web sites are included for each (when available). Use them to obtain general information, locate internships, and/or to send your résumé for job possibilities.

National Football League (NFL)
280 Park Avenue
New York, NY 10017
Phone: (212) 450-2000
Fax: (212) 681-7599
http://www.nfl.com

NFL (National Football League) Players Association
1133 20th Street, NW
Washington, DC 20036
Phone: (202) 463-2200
http://www.nflplayers.com

AMERICAN FOOTBALL CONFERENCE (AFC)

Baltimore Ravens
11001 Owings Mills Boulevard
Owings Mills, MD 21117
Phone: (410) 701-4000
http://www.baltimoreravens.com

Buffalo Bills
One Bills Drive
Orchard Park, NY 14127
Phone: (716) 648-1800
Fax: (716)649-6446
http://www.buffalobills.com

Cincinnati Bengals
One Paul Brown Stadium
Cincinnati, OH 45202
Phone: (513) 621-3550
Fax: (513) 621-3570
http://www.bengals.com

Cleveland Browns
76 Lou Groza Boulevard
Berea, OH 44017
Phone: (440) 891-5000
Fax: (440) 891-5009
http://www.clevelandbrowns.com

Denver Broncos
13655 Broncos Parkway
Englewood, CO 80112
Phone: (303) 649-9000
Fax: (303) 649-0562
http://www.denverbroncos.com

Houston Texans
Reliant Stadium
Two Reliant Park
Houston, TX 77054
Phone: (832) 667-2000
Fax: (832) 667-2100
http://www.houstontexans.com

Indianapolis Colts
7001 West 56th Street
Indianapolis, IN 46254
Phone: (317) 297-2658
Fax: (317) 297-8971
http://www.colts.com

Jacksonville Jaguars
One Stadium Place
Jacksonville, FL 32202
Phone: (904) 633-6000
http://www.jaguars.com

Kansas City Chiefs
One Arrowhead Drive
Kansas City, MO 64129

Phone: (816) 920-9300
http://www.kcchiefs.com

Miami Dolphins
7500 Southwest 30th Street
Davie, FL 33314
Phone: (954) 452-7000
http://www.miamidolphins.com

New England Patriots
CMGI Field
Foxboro, MA 02035
Phone: (508) 543-8200
Fax: (508) 543-9053
http://www.patriots.com

New York Jets
1 Jets Drive
Florham Park, NJ 07932
Phone: (973) 549-4800
http://www.newyorkjets.com

Oakland Raiders
1220 Harbor Bay Parkway
Alameda, CA 94502
Phone: (510) 864-5000
http://www.raiders.com

Pittsburgh Steelers
3400 South Water Street
Pittsburgh, PA 15203
Phone: (412) 432-7800
Fax: (412) 432-7878
http://www.steelers.com

San Diego Chargers
4020 Murphy Canyon Road
San Diego, CA 92123

Phone: (858) 874-4500
http://www.chargers.com

Tennessee Titans
460 Great Circle Road
Nashville, TN 37228
Phone: (615) 565-4000
Fax: (615) 565-4105
http://www.titansonline.com

NATIONAL FOOTBALL CONFERENCE (NFC)

Arizona Cardinals
P.O. Box 888
Phoenix, AZ 85001
Phone: (602) 379-0101
Fax: (602) 379-1821
http://www.azcardinals.com

Atlanta Falcons
4400 Falcon Parkway
Flowery Branch, GA 30542
Phone: (770) 965-3115
Fax: (770) 965-3185
http://www.atlantafalcons.com

Carolina Panthers
800 South Mint Street
Charlotte, NC 28202
Phone: (704) 358-7000
http://www.panthers .com

Chicago Bears
Halas Hall at Conway Park
1000 Football Drive
Lake Forest, IL 60045
Phone: (847) 295-6600
Fax: (847) 295-8986
http://www.chicagobears.com

Dallas Cowboys
Cowboys Center
One Cowboys Parkway
Irving, TX 75063
Phone: (972) 556-9900
Fax: (972) 556-9304
http://www.dallascowboys.com

Detroit Lions
222 Republic Drive
Alien Park, MI 48101
Phone: (313) 216-4000
Fax: (313) 216-4226
http://www.detroitlions.com

Green Bay Packers
1265 Lombardi Avenue
Green Bay, WI 54304
Phone: (920) 569-7500
http://www.packers.com

Minnesota Vikings
9520 Viking Drive
Eden Prairie, MN 55344
Phone: (952) 828-6500
http://www.vikings .com

New Orleans Saints
5800 Airline Highway
Metairie, LA 70003
Phone: (504) 733-0255
Fax: (504) 731-1888
http://www.neworleanssaints.com

New York Giants
Giants Stadium
East Rutherford, NJ 07073
Phone: (201) 935-8111
http://www.giants.com

Philadelphia Eagles
NovaCare Complex
One NovaCare Way
Philadelphia, PA 19145
Phone: (215) 463-2500
Fax: (215) 339-5464
http://www.philadelphiaeagles.com

San Francisco 49ers
4949 Centennial Boulevard
Santa Clara, CA 95054
Phone: (408) 562-4949
Fax: (408) 727-2760
http://www.sf49ers.com

Seattle Seahawks
12 Seahawks Way
Renton, WA 98056
Phone: (425) 203-8000
http://www.seahawks.com

St. Louis Rams
One Rams Way
St. Louis, MO 63045
Phone: (314) 982-7267
Fax: (314) 770-9261
http://www.stlouisrams.com

Tampa Bay Buccaneers
One Buccaneer Place
Tampa, FL 33607
Phone: (813) 870-2700
http://www.buccaneers.com

Washington Redskins
21300 Redskin Park Drive
Ashburn, VA 20147
Phone: (703) 726-7000
Fax: (703) 726-7086
http://www.redskins.com

APPENDIX X
CANADIAN FOOTBALL LEAGUE (CFL) TEAMS

The following is a listing of the teams in the Canadian Football League (CFL). Names, addresses, phone numbers, and Web sites are included for each when available. Use them to obtain general information, to locate internships, and/or to send your résumé for possible employment. When sending mail from the United States to Canada, remember to check postage rates.

Canadian Football League
50 Wellington Street East
Toronto, Ontario M5E 1C8,
    Canada
Phone: (416) 322-9650
Fax: (416) 322-9651
http://www.cfl.ca

EAST DIVISION

Hamilton Tiger Cats
1 Jarvis Street
Hamilton, ON
L8R 3J2
Phone: (905) 547-2287
Fax: (905) 547-8423
http://www.ticats.ca

Toronto Argonauts
355 King Street West
Toronto, ON
M5V 1J6
Phone: (416) 341-2700
Fax: (416) 341-2714
http://www.argonauts.ca

Montreal Alouettes
1260, rue University

Montreal, Quebec - H3B 3B9
Phone: (514) 871-2266
E-mail: info@montrealalouettes.com
http://www.montrealalouettes.com

Winnipeg Blue Bombers
1465 Maroons Road
Winnipeg, MB R3G 0L6
Phone: (204) 784-2583
Fax: (204 783-5222
E-mail: bbombers@bluebombers.com
http://www.bluebombers.com

WESTERN DIVISION

B.C. Lions
10605 - 135th Street
Surrey, BC
V3T 4C8
Phone: (604) 930-5466
Fax: (604) 583-7882
E-mail: communityrelations@
    bclions.com
http://www.bclions.com

Calgary Stampeders
McMahon Stadium
1817 Crowchild Trail, NW

Calgary, AB T2M 4R6, Canada
Phone: (403) 282-2044
http://www.stampeders.com

Edmonton Eskimos
9023 - 111 Avenue
Edmonton, AB T5B 0C3
Phone: (780) 448-1525
Fax: (780) 429-3452
http://www.esks.com

Saskatchewan Roughriders
Mosaic Stadium
1910 Piffles Taylor Way
P.O. Box 1966
Regina, SK
S4P 3E1
Phone: (306) 569-2323
Fax: (306) 566-4280
http://www.riderville.com

APPENDIX XI
NATIONAL HOCKEY LEAGUE (NHL) TEAMS

The following is a listing provided by the National Hockey League (NHL) of teams in the NHL. Use this list to obtain general information, locate internships, and/or to send your résumé for possible jobs.

National Hockey League
1185 Avenue of the Americas
New York, NY 10036
Phone: (212) 789-2000
http://www.nhl.com

Anaheim Ducks
Honda Center
2695 East Katella Avenue
Anaheim, CA 92806
Phone: (877) 945-3946
http://ducks.nhl.com

Atlanta Thrashers
Centennial Tower
101 Marietta Street, NW
Suite 1900
Atlanta, GA 30303
Phone: (404) 878-3800
http://thrashers.nhl.com

Boston Bruins
TD Banknorth Garden
100 Legends Way
Boston, MA 02114
Phone: (617) 624-1900
http://bruins.nhl.com

Buffalo Sabres
HSBC Arena
One Seymour H. Knox III Plaza
Buffalo, NY 14203
Phone: (716) 855-4100
http://sabres.nhl.com

Calgary Flames
Pengrowth Saddledome
P.O. Box 1540, Station M
Calgary, AB T2P 3B9

Phone: (403) 777-2177
http://flames.nhl.com

Carolina Hurricanes
RBC Center
1400 Edwards Mill Road
Raleigh, NC 27607
Phone: (919) 467-7825
http://hurricanes.nhl.com

Chicago Blackhawks
United Center
1901 West Madison
Chicago, IL 60612
Phone: (312) 455-7000
http://blackhawks.nhl.com

Colorado Avalanche
Pepsi Center
1000 Chopper Circle
Denver, CO 80204
Phone: (303) 405-1100
http://avalanche.nhl.com

Columbus Blue Jackets
Nationwide Arena
200 West Nationwide Boulevard
Columbus, OH 43215
Phone: (614) 246-4625
http://bluejackets.nhl.com

Dallas Stars
Dr Pepper StarCenter
2601 Avenue of the Stars
Frisco, TX 75034
Phone: (214) 387-5500
http://stars.nhl.com

Detroit Red Wings
Joe Louis Arena

600 Civic Center Drive
Detroit, MI 48226
Phone: (313) 983-6606
http://redwings.nhl.com

Edmonton Oilers
Rexall Place
7424-118 Avenue
Edmonton, AB T5B 4M9
Phone: (780) 414-4000
http://oilers.nhl.com

Florida Panthers
BankAtlantic Center
One Panther Parkway
Sunrise, FL 33323
Phone: (954) 835-7000
http://panthers.nhl.com

Los Angeles Kings
Toyota Sports Center
555 North Nash Street
El Segundo, CA 90245
Phone: (213) 742-7100
http://kings.nhl.com

Minnesota Wild
317 Washington Street
St. Paul, MN 55102
Phone: (651) 602-6000
http://wild.nhl.com

Montréal Canadiens
Bell Centre
1260, de la Gauchetiere Street West
Montreal, Quebec H3B 5E8
Phone: (514) 932-2582
http://canadiens.nhl.com

Nashville Predators
Sommet Center
501 Broadway
Nashville, TN 37203
Phone: (615) 770-2355
http://predators.nhl.com

New Jersey Devils
Prudential Center
165 Mulberry Street
Newark, NJ 07102
Phone: (973) 757-6100
http://devils.nhl.com

New York Islanders
1535 Old Country Road
Plainview, NY 11803
Phone: (516) 501-6700
http://islanders.nhl.com

New York Rangers
Madison Square Garden
Two Pennsylvania Plaza
New York, NY 10121
Phone: (212) 465-6000
http://rangers.nhl.com

Ottawa Senators
Scotiabank Place
1000 Palladium Drive
Ottawa, ON K2V 1A5
Phone: (613) 599-0250
http://senators.nhl.com

Philadelphia Flyers
Wachovia Center
3601 South Broad Street
Philadelphia, PA 19148
Phone: (215) 465-4500
http://flyers.nhl.com

Phoenix Coyotes
6751 North Sunset Boulevard #200
Glendale, AZ 85305
Phone: (623) 772-3200
http://coyotes.nhl.com

Pittsburgh Penguins
Mellon Arena
66 Mario Lemieux Place
Pittsburgh, PA 15219
Phone: (412) 642-1300
http://penguins.nhl.com

San Jose Sharks
HP Pavilion at San Jose
525 West Santa Clara Street
San Jose, CA 95113
Phone: (408) 287-7070
http://sharks.nhl.com

St. Louis Blues
Scottrade Center
1401 Clark Avenue
St. Louis, MO 63103
Phone: (314) 622-2500
http://blues.nhl.com

Tampa Bay Lightning
St. Pete Time Forum
401 Channelside Drive
Tampa, FL 33602
Phone: (813) 301-6500
http://lightning.nhl.com

Toronto Maple Leafs
Air Canada Centre
40 Bay Street
Suite 400
Toronto, ON M5J 2X2
Phone: (416) 815-5700
http://mapleleafs.nhl.com

Vancouver Canucks
General Motors Place
800 Griffiths Way
Vancouver, BC V6B 6G1
Phone: (604) 899-7400
http://canucks.nhl.com

Washington Capitals
Kettler Capitals Iceplex
627 North Glebe Road
Suite 850
Arlington, VA 22203
Phone: (202) 266-2200
http://capitals.nhl.com

APPENDIX XII
AMERICAN HOCKEY LEAGUE (AHL) TEAMS

The following, provided by the NHL, is a listing of the teams in the American Hockey League. Names, addresses, phone numbers, and Web sites have been included as well as the NHL affiliation. Use this list to find general information, locate internships, and/or to send your résumé for possible jobs.

American Hockey League (AHL)
One Monarch Place
Suite 2400
Springfield, MA 01144
Phone: (413) 781-2030
Fax: (413) 733-4767
http://www.theahl.com

Albany River Rats
51 South Pearl Street
Albany, NY 12207
Phone: (518) 487-2244
NHL affiliation: Carolina Hurricanes
http://www.albanyriverrats.com

Binghamton Senators
One Stuart Street, 3rd floor
Binghamton, NY 13901
Phone: (607) 722-SENS
NHL affiliation: Ottawa Senators
http://www.binghamtonsenators.com

Bridgeport Sound Tigers
600 Main Street
Bridgeport, CT 06604
Phone: (203) 334-GOAL
NHL affiliation: New York Islanders
http://www.soundtigers.com

Chicago Wolves
2301 Ravine Way
Glenview, IL 60025
Phone: (847) 724-GOAL
NHL affiliation: Atlanta Thrashers
http://www.chicagowolves.com

Grand Rapids Griffins
130 West Fulton
Suite 111
Grand Rapids, MI 49503
Phone: (616) 774-4585
NHL affiliation: Detroit Red Wings
http://www.griffinshockey.com

Hamilton Bulldogs
101 York Boulevard
Hamilton, ON L8R 3L4
Phone: (905) 529-8500
NHL affiliation: Montreal Canadiens
http://www.hamiltonbulldogs.com

Hartford Wolf Pack
One Civic Center Plaza
Hartford, CT 06103
Phone: (860) 249-6333
NHL affiliation: New York Rangers
http://www.hartfordwolfpack.com

Hershey Bears
950 West Hersheypark Drive
Hershey, PA 17033
Phone: (717) 534-3380
NHL affiliation: Washington Capitals
http://www.hersheybears.com

Houston Aeros
1221 Lamar Street
Suite 1100
Houston, TX 77010
Phone: (713) 974-PUCK
NHL affiliation: Minnesota Wild
http://www.aeros.com

Iowa Chops
833 5th Avenue
Des Moines, IA 50309
Phone: (515) 564-8700
NHL affiliation: Anaheim Ducks
http://www.iowachops.com

Lake Erie Monsters
Quicken Loans Arena
One Center Ice
Cleveland, OH 44115
Phone: (216) 420-0000
NHL affiliation: Colorado Avalanche
http://www.lakeeriemonsters.com

Lowell Devils
Paul E. Tsongas Arena
300 Martin Luther King Jr. Way
Lowell, MA 01852
Phone: (978) 458-PUCK
NHL affiliation: New Jersey Devils
http://www.lowelldevilshockey.com

Manchester Monarchs
555 Elm Street
Manchester, NH 03101
Phone: (603) 626-PUCK
NHL affiliation: Los Angeles Kings
http://www.manchestermonarchs.com

Manitoba Moose
260 Hargrave Avenue
Winnipeg, MB R3C 5S5
Phone: (204) 987-PUCK
NHL affiliation: Vancouver Canucks
http://www.moosehockey.com

Milwaukee Admirals
1001 North Fourth Street
Milwaukee, WI 53203
Phone: (414) 227-0550
NHL affiliation: Nashville Predators
http://www.milwaukeeadmirals.com

Norfolk Admirals
201 East Brambleton Avenue
Norfolk, VA 23510
Phone: (757) 640-1212
NHL affiliation: Tampa Bay
    Lightning
http://www.norfolkadmirals.com

Philadelphia Phantoms
3601 South Broad Street
Philadelphia, PA 19148
Phone: (215) 465-4522
NHL affiliation: Philadelphia Flyers
http://www.phantomshockey.com

Portland Pirates
94 Free Street
Portland, ME 04101
Phone: (207) 828-HOOK
NHL affiliation: Buffalo Sabres
http://www.portlandpirates.com

Providence Bruins
1 LaSalle Square
Providence, RI 02903
Phone: (401) 273-5000
NHL affiliation: Boston Bruins
http://www.providencebruins.com

Quad City Flames
1201 River Drive
Moline, IL 61265
Phone: (309) 764-PUCK

NHL affiliation: Calgary Flames
http://www.qcflames.com

Rochester Americans
1 War Memorial Square
Rochester, NY 14614
Phone: (585) 454-5335
NHL affiliation: Florida Panthers
http://www.amerks.com

Rockford Icehogs
300 Elm Street
Rockford, IL 61101
Phone: (815) 986-6465
NHL affiliation: Chicago Blackhawks
http://www.icehogs.com

San Antonio Rampage
One AT&T Center
San Antonio, TX 78219
Phone: (210) 444-5000
NHL affiliation: Phoenix Coyotes
http://www.sarampage.com

Springfield Falcons
45 Falcons Way
Springfield, MA 01103
Phone: (413) 739-3344
NHL affiliation: Edmonton Oilers
http://www.falconsahl.com

Syracuse Crunch
800 South State Street

Syracuse, NY 13202
Phone: (315) 473-4444
NHL affiliation: Columbus Blue
    Jackets
http://www.syracusecrunch.com

Toronto Marlies
100 Princes' Boulevard
Toronto, ON M6K 3C3
Phone: (416) 263-3900
NHL affiliation: Toronto Maple
    Leafs
http://www.torontomarlies.com

**Wilkes-Barre/Scranton
    Penguins**
670 North River Street
Suite 210
Wilkes-Barre, PA 18705
Phone: (570) 208-PENS
NHL affiliation: Pittsburgh
    Penguins
http://www.wbspenguins.com

Worcester Sharks
50 Foster Street
Worcester, MA 01608
Phone: (508) 929-0500
NHL affiliation: San Jose Sharks
http://www.sharksahl.com

APPENDIX XIII
MAJOR LEAGUE SOCCER (MLS) CLUBS

The following is a listing of the clubs provided by Major League Soccer (MLS). Names, addresses, fax and phone numbers, as well as Web sites are included (when available) for each. Use them to obtain general information, to locate internships, and/or to send your résumé for job possibilities.

Major League Soccer
420 Fifth Ave
New York, NY 10018
Phone: (212) 450-1200
Fax: (212) 450-1300
http://web.mlsnet.com

EASTERN DIVISION

Chicago Fire
Toyota Park
7000 South Harlem Avenue
Bridgeview, IL 60455
Phone: (708) 594-7200
Fax: (708) 496-6050
http://chicago.fire.mlsnet.com

Columbus Crew
Columbus, OH 43211
Phone: (614) 447-2739
Fax: (614) 447-4109
http://columbus.crew.mlsnet.com

D.C. United
2400 East Capitol Street, SE
Washington, DC 20003
Phone: (202) 587-5000
Fax: (202) 587-5400
http://www.dcunited.com

Kansas City Wizards
8900 State Line Road
Leawood, KS66206
Phone: (913) 387-3400
Fax: (913) 387-3401
http://kc.wizards.mlsnet.com

New England Revolution
One Patriot Place
Foxborough, MA 02035
Phone: (508) 543-8200
Fax: (508) 549-0405
http://www.revolutionsoccer.net

Red Bull New York
One Harmon Plaza
Secaucus, NJ 07094
Phone: (201) 583-7000
Fax: (201) 583-7055
http://redbull.newyork.mlsnet.com

Toronto FC
BMO Field
Exhibition Place
170 Princes Boulevard
Toronto, Ontario, Canada M6K 3C3
Phone: (416) 263-5700
http://toronto.fc.mlsnet.com

WESTERN CONFERENCE

Club Deportivo Chivas USA
18400 Avalon Blvd
Suite 500
Carson, CA 90746
Phone: (310) 630-4550
http://web.mlsnet.com/t120

Colorado Rapids
6000 Victory Way
Commerce City, CO 80022
Phone: (303) 727-3500
Fax: (303) 727-3536
http://www.coloradorapids.com

FC Dallas
9200 World Cup Way
Frisco, TX 75034
Phone: (214) 705-6700
Fax: (214) 705-6799
http://fc.dallas.mlsnet.com

Houston Dynamo
1415 Louisiana St
Suite 3400
Houston, TX 77002
Phone: (713) 276-7500
Fax: (713) 276-7572
http://houston.mlsnet.com

Los Angeles Galaxy
18400 Avalon Boulevard
Carson, CA 90746
Phone: (310) 630-2200
Fax: (310) 630-2250
http://la.galaxy.mlsnet.com

Real Salt Lake
9256 South State Street
One Rio Tinto Way
Sandy, UT 84070
Phone: (801) 727-2701
Fax: (801) 727-1459
http://real.saltlake.mlsnet.com

San Jose Earthquake
451 El Camino Real
Santa Clara, CA 95050
Phone: (408) 556-7700
Fax: (408) 260-6802
http://sjearthquakes.mlsnet.com

Seattle Sounders FC
Qwest Field
Suite 100
800 Occidental Avenue South
Seattle, WA 98134
Phone: (206) 381-7555
http://www.soundersfc.com

The following is a listing of harness racing tracks in the United States. Harness racing uses a specific breed of horse called standardbred. In harness racing, a driver is pulled behind the horse in a two-wheeled cart called a sulky. The sulky is attached via a harness.

Some tracks hold racing year-round. Others only have racing dates during specific times of the year. Some of the most well known harness races include the Hambletonian in the Meadowlands, the Kentucky Futurity in Lexington, and the Yonkers Trot in Yonkers, New York.

Tracks are listed by state. Names, addresses, phone numbers, and Web sites are included for each (when available). Use this list to obtain general information, locate internships, and/or to send your résumés for job possibilities.

CALIFORNIA

Cal Expo Horse Racing
1600 Exposition Way
Sacramento, CA 95852
Phone: (916) 239-4040
http://www.colonialdowns.com

Los Alamitos Race Course
4961 East Katella Avenue
Los Alamitos, CA 90720
Phone: (714) 236-4400
http://www.losalamitos.com/laqhr

DELAWARE

Dover Downs
1131 North DuPont Highway
Dover, DE 90720
Phone: (302) 674-4600
http://www.doverdowns.com

Harrington Raceway
U.S. Route 13
Harrington, DE 19952
Phone: (302) 398-7223
http://www.harringtonraceway.com

FLORIDA

Pompano Park
1800 Southwest Third Street
Pompano Beach, FL 33069
Phone: (954) 972-2000
http://pompano-park.isleofcapri
    casinos.com/racing.aspx

ILLINOIS

Balmoral Park
26325 South Dixie Highway
Crete, IL 33069
Phone: (708) 672-7544
http://www.balmoralpark.com

DuQuin State Fair (Racing dates during fair)
P.O. Box 19281
Springfield, IL 62702
Phone: (618) 542-9373
http://www.agr.state.il.us

Fairmont Park
9301 Collinsville Road
Collinsville, IL 62234
Phone: (618) 345-4300
http://www.fairmountpark.com

Hawthorne Race Course
3501 South Laramie Avenue
Cicero, IL 60803
Phone: (708) 780-3700
http://www.hawthorneracecourse.com

Marywood Park Raceway
8600 West North Avenue
Marywood, IL 60153
Phone: (708) 343-4800
http://www.maywoodpark.com

Springfield (Racing dates during Illinois State Fair)
P.O. Box 19281
Springfield, IL 62794
Phone: (217) 782-4321
http://www.illinoisstatefair.info

INDIANA

Hoosier Park
4500 Dan Patch Circle
Anderson, IN 46013
Phone: (765) 642-7223
http://www.hoosierpark.com

Indiana Downs
4200 North Michigan Road
Shelbyville, IN 46176
Phone: (317) 421-0000
http://www.indianadowns.com

Indiana State Fair (Racing dates during Indiana State Fair)
1202 East 38th Street
Indianapolis, IN
Phone: (317) 927-7500
http://www.in.gov/statefair

IOWA

Prairie Meadows Racetrack
One Prairie Meadow Drive
Altoona, IA 50009
Phone: (515) 967-1000
http://www.prairiemeadows.com

KENTUCKY

The Red Mile
1200 Red Mile Road

Lexington, KY 40504
Phone: (859) 255-0752
http://www.theredmile.com

Thunder Ridge
164 Thunder Road
Prestonburg, KY 41653
Phone: (606) 886-7223

MAINE

Bangor Raceway
100 Dutton Street
Bangor, ME 04401
Phone: (207) 561-6068
http://www.bangorraceway.net

Cumberland Fair (Racing dates during Cumberland Fair)
6 Crossing Brook Road
Cumberland, ME 04021
Phone: (207) 829-6647
http://www.cumberlandfair.com

Oxford County Fair (Racing dates during Oxford County Fair)
P.O. Box 223
Norway, ME 04268
Phone: (207) 743-9594
http://www.oxfordcountyfair.com

Scarborough Downs
P.O. Box 468
Scarborough, ME 04070
Phone: (207) 883-4331
http://www.scarboroughdowns.com

Skowhegan Fair (Part of Fair)
P.O. Box 39
Skowhegan, ME 04976
Phone: (207) 474-2947
http://www.skowheganstatefair.com

MARYLAND

Ocean Downs
P.O. Box 11
Berlin, MD 21811
Phone: (641) 0600
http://www.oceandowns.com

Rosecroft Raceway
6336 Rosecroft Drive

Fort Washington, MD 20744
Phone: (301) 567-4000
http://www.rosecroft.com

MASSACHUSETTS

Plainridge Racecourse
301 Washington Street
Plainville, MA 02762
Phone: (508) 643-2500
http://www.prcharness.com

MICHIGAN

Hazel Park Harness Raceway
1650 East Ten Mile Road
Hazel Park, MI 48030
Phone: (248) 398-1000
http://hazelparkraceway.com

Jackson Raceway
P.O. Box 881
Jackson, MI 49204
Phone: (517) 788-4500
http://www.jacksonharnessraceway.com

Northville Downs
301 South Center Street
Northville, MI 48167
Phone: (248) 349-1000
http://www.northvilledowns.com

Saginaw Harness Raceway
2701 East Genesee Street
Saginaw, MI 48601
Phone: (987) 755-3451

Sports Creek Raceway
4920 Morrish Road
Swartz Creek, MI 48473
Phone: (810) 653-3333
http://sportscreek.com

MINNESOTA

Running Acres
15201 Zurich Street
Forest Lake, MN 55025
Phone: (651) 925-4600
http://www.runningacesharness.com

NEW HAMPSHIRE

Rockingham Park
P.O. Box 47
Salem, NH 03079
Phone: (603) 898-2311
http://www.rockinghampark.com

NEW JERSEY

Freehold Raceway
P.O. Box 6249
Freehold, NJ 07728
Phone: (732) 462-3800
http://www.freeholdraceway.com

Meadowlands Racetrack
50 State Route 120
East Rutherford, NJ 07073
Phone: (201) 935-8500
http://www.thebigm.com

NEW YORK

Batavia Downs
8315 Park Road
Batavia, NY 14020
Phone: (585) 343-3750
http://www.batavia-downs.com

Buffalo Raceway
5600 McKinley Parkway
Hamburg, NY 14075
Phone: (716) 649-1280
http://www.buffaloraceway.com

Historic Park-Goshen
P.O. Box 192
Goshen, NY 10924
Phone: (845) 294-5333

Monticello Raceway
Route 17 & 17B
Raceway Road
Monticello, NY 12701
Phone: (845) 794-4100
http://www.monticelloraceway.com

Saratoga Raceway
P.O. Box 356
Saratoga Springs, NY 12866
Phone: (518) 584-2110
http://www.saratogaraceway.com

Syracuse Mile (Part of New York State Fair)
P.O. Box 860
Vernon, NY 13476
Phone: (315) 829-2201
http://nysfair.org

Tioga Downs
2384 West River Road
Nichols, NY 13812
Phone: (888) 946-8464
http://nysfair.org/home.php

Vernon Downs
P.O. Box 860
Vernon, NY 13476
Phone: (315) 829-2201
http://www.vernondowns.com

Yonkers Raceway
810 Central Avenue
Yonkers, NY 10704
Phone: (914) 968-4200
http://www.yonkersraceway.com

OHIO

Delaware Ohio Fair (Racing dates during fair)
239 Pennsylvania Avenue
Delaware, OH 43015
Phone: (740) 363-6000
http://www.littlebrownjug.com

Lebanon Raceway
P.O. Box 58
Lebanon, OH 45036
Phone: (513) 932-4936
http://www.lebanonraceway.com

Northfield Park
P.O. Box 374
Northfield, OH 44067
Phone: (330) 467-4101
http://www.northfieldpark.com

Raceway Park
5700 Telegraph Road
Toledo, OH 43612
Phone: (419) 476-7751
http://www.racewayparktoledo.com

Scioto Downs
6000 South High Street
Columbus, OH 43207
Phone: (614) 491-2515
http://www.sciotodowns.com

PENNSYLVANIA

The Meadows
P.O. Box 499
Meadow Lands, PA 15357
Phone: (724) 225-9300
http://www.themeadowsracing.com

Pocono Downs
1280 Highway 315
Wilkes-Barre, PA 18702
Phone: (570) 825-6681
http://www.poconodowns.com

VIRGINIA

Colonial Downs
P.O. Box 228
New Kent, VA 23124
Phone: (804) 966-7223
http://www.colonialdowns.com

APPENDIX XV
U.S. THOROUGHBRED RACETRACKS

The following is a listing of thoroughbred racetracks in the United States. Thoroughbreds are a specific breed of horse. In thoroughbred racing, a jockey rides the saddled horse.

Some of the more popular thoroughbred races held annually include the Kentucky Derby at Churchill Downs in Lexington, Kentucky, the Belmont Stakes at Belmont Race Park in Elmont, New York, the Preakness Stakes at Pimlico in Baltimore, Maryland, and the Travers Stakes at Saratoga in Saratoga Springs, New York.

Some tracks hold racing year-round. Others only have racing dates during specific times of the year.

Tracks are listed by state. Names, addresses, phone numbers, and Web sites are included for each (when available). Use this list to obtain general information, locate internships, and/or to send your résumés for job possibilities

ARIZONA

Apache @ St. John's (Racing dates during fair)
Apache County Fair
West Fourth Street North
St. John's, AZ 85936
Phone: (928) 337-2621

Cochise @ Douglas (Racing dates during fair)
Cochise County Fair
P.O. Box 782
Douglas, AZ 85608
Phone: (520) 364-3819
http://www.cochisecountyfair.
50megs.com

Coconino County Horse Races (Racing dates during fair)
Fort Tuthill Downs
Flagstaff, AZ 86001
Phone: (928) 774-5139

Gila County Fair (Racing dates during fair)
P.O. Box 2193
Globe, AZ 88502
Phone: (928) 425-2772
http://gilafair.net

Graham @ Safford (Racing dates during fair)
Graham County Fair
527 East Armory Road
Safford, AZ 85546
Phone: (928) 428-6240

Greenlee County Fair and Racing (Racing dates during fair)
P.O. Box 123
Duncan, AZ 85533
Phone: (928) 359-2032
http://www.co.greenlee.
az.us/FairRacing/
FairRacingHomePage.aspx

Mohave County Fair (Racing dates during fair)
2600 Fairgrounds Boulevard
Kingman, AZ 86401
Phone: (928) 753-2636
http://www.mcfafairgrounds.org

Prescott Downs Race Track
P.O. Box 26557
Prescott Valley, AZ 86312
Phone: (928) 775-8000
http://www.amdest.com/az/
prescott/pd/prescottdowns.
html

Rillito Park
4502 North First Avenue
Tucson, AZ 85718
Phone: (520) 293-5011
http://www.thepepper.com/tucson_
horse_racing.html

Santa Cruz County Horse Races (Racing dates during fair)
Santa Cruz County Fair
P.O. Box 85
Sonoita, AZ 85637
Phone: (520) 455-5553
http://www.sonoitafairgrounds.com

Turf Paradise
1501 West Bell Road
Phoenix, AZ 85023
Phone: (602) 942-1101
http://www.turfparadise.com

Yavapai Downs
P.O. Box 26557
Prescott Valley, AZ 86312
Phone: (928) 775-8000
http://www.yavapaidownsatpv.com

ARKANSAS

Oaklawn Jockey Club
P.O. Box 699
Hot Springs, AR 71902
Phone: (501) 623-4411
http://www.oaklawn.com

CALIFORNIA

Alameda County Fair (Racing dates during fair)
4501 Pleasanton Avenue
Pleasanton, CA 94566

Phone: (925) 426-7600
http://www.alamedacountyfair.com

Bay Meadows
P.O. Box 5050
San Mateo, CA 94402
Phone: (650) 574-7223
http://www.baymeadows.com

California Exposition
1600 Exposition Boulevard
Sacramento, CA 95815
Phone: (916) 263-3000

Del Mar Thoroughbred Club
P.O. Box 700
Del Mar, CA 92014
Phone: (858) 755-1141
http://www.delmarracing.com

Fairplex Park
P.O. Box 2250
Pomona, CA 91769
Phone: (909) 623-3111
http://www.fairplex.com/fp

Ferndale (Racing dates during fair)
P.O. Box 637
Ferndale, CA 95536
Phone: (707) 786-9511

Fresno Fair (Racing dates during fair)
1121 Chance Avenue
Fresno, CA 93702
Phone: (559) 650-3247

Golden Gate Fields
P.O. Box 6027
Albany, CA 94706
Phone: (510) 559-7330
http://www.goldengatefields.com

Hollywood Park
P.O. Box 369
Inglewood, CA 90306
Phone: (310) 419-1500
http://www.hollywoodpark.com

Los Alamitos
4961 East Katella Avenue
Los Alamitos, CA 90720

Phone: (714) 820-2800
http://www.losalamitos.com/laqhr

Santa Anita Park
P.O. Box 60014
Arcadia, CA 91066
Phone: (626) 574-7223
http://www.santaanita.com

Santa Rosa (Racing dates during fair)
Sonoma County Fairgrounds
P.O. Box 1536
Santa Rosa, CA 95402
Phone: (707)545-4200

Solano County Fair (Racing dates during fair)
900 Fairgrounds Drive
Vallejo, CA 94589
Phone: (707) 551-2000
http://www.scfair.com/sc

Stockton(Racing dates during fair)
San Joaquin County Fair
1658 South Airport Way
Stockton, CA 95205
Phone: (209) 466-5041

COLORADO

Arapahoe Park
26000 East Quincy Avenue
Aurora, CO 80016
Phone: (303) 690-2400
http://www.mihiracing.com/
arapahoe_park.shtml

FLORIDA

Calder Race Course
P.O. Box 1808
Miami, FL 33055
Phone: (800) 333-3227
http://www.calderracecourse.com

Gulfstream Park
901 South Federal Highway
Hallandale, FL 33009
Phone: (954) 454-7000
http://www.gulfstreampark.com

Hialeah Park
P.O. Box 158
Hialeah, FL 33011
Phone: (954) 305-8000

Tampa Bay Downs
P.O. Box 2007
Tampa, FL 34677
Phone: (813) 855-4401
http://www.tampabaydowns.com

IDAHO

Blackfoot (Racing dates during fair)
P.O. Box 250
Blackfoot, ID 83221
Phone: (208) 785-2480
http://www.funatthefair.com

Burley (Racing dates during fair)
Cassia County Fair
P.O. Box 1222
Burley, ID 83318
Phone: (208) 678-8610

Emmett (Racing dates during fair)
Gem County Fairboard
Box 443
Emmett, ID 83617
Phone: (208) 365-6828

Jerome (Racing dates during fair)
Jerome County Fair
P.O. Box 414
Jerome, ID 83338
Phone: (208) 324-7057

Les Bois Park
5610 Glenwood Road
Boise, ID 83714
Phone: (208) 321-0222
http://www.lesboisracing.com

Malad(Racing dates during fair)
Oneida County Fair
P.O. Box 13
Malad City, ID 83252
Phone: (208) 766-4706

Pocatello Downs
P.O. Box 0248
Pocatello, ID 83202
Phone: (208) 238-1721

Rupert Downs, Inc.
P.O. Box 263
Rupert, ID 83350
Phone: (208) 436-3109

Sandy Downs
3665 North 15th East
Idaho Falls, ID 83401
Phone: (208) 529-0671

ILLINOIS

Arlington Park
2200 West Euclid
Arlington Heights, IL 60006
Phone: (847) 255-4300
http://www.arlingtonpark.com

Fairmont Park
9301 Collinsville Road
Collinsville, IL 62234
Phone: (618) 345-4300
http://www.fairmountpark.com

Hawthorne Race Course
3501 South Laramie Avenue
Cicero, IL 60804
Phone: (708) 780-3700
http://www.hawthorneracecourse.
    com

Sportsman's Park
3301 Laramie Avenue
Cicero, IL 60804
Phone: (708)780-3700
http://www.sportsmanspark.com

KENTUCKY

Churchill Downs
700 Central Avenue
Louisville, KY 40208
Phone: (502) 636-4400
http://www.churchilldowns.com

Ellis Park
P.O. Box 33
Henderson, KY 42419

Phone: (812) 425-1456
http://www.ellisparkracing.com

Keeneland
P.O. Box 1690
Lexington, KY 40592
Phone: (859) 254-3412
http://www.keeneland.com

Kentucky Downs
P.O.Box 405
Franklin, KY 42135
Phone: (270) 586-7778
http://www.kentuckydowns.com

Turfway Park
P.O. Box 8
Florence, KY 41022
Phone: (606) 371-0200
http://www.turfway.com

LOUISIANA

Delta Downs
P.O. Box 175
Vinton, LA 70668
Phone: (800) 589-7441
http://www.deltadowns.com

Evangeline Downs
2235 Creswell Lane
Opelousas, LA 70570
Phone: (337) 594-3000
http://www.evangelinedowns.com

Fairgrounds Racecourse
P.O. Box 52529
New Orleans, LA 70152
Phone: (504) 944-5515
http://www.fairgroundsracecourse.
    com

Louisiana Downs
P.O. Box 5519
Bossier City, LA 71171
Phone: (318) 742-5555
http://www.harrahslouisianadowns.
    com

MARYLAND

Laurel Park
P.O. Box 130

Laurel, MD 20725
Phone: (301) 725-0400
http://www.laurelpark.com

Pimlico
5201 Park Heights Avenue
Baltimore, MD 21215
Phone: (410) 542-9400
http://www.pimlico.com

Timonim (Racing dates during fair)
Maryland State Fair
2200 Block York Road
Timonium, MD 21094
Phone: (410) 252-0200

MASSACHUSETTS

Northampton (Racing dates during fair)
P.O. Box 305
Northampton, MA 01061
Phone: (413) 584-2237

Suffolk Downs
111 Waldemar Avenue
East Boston, MA 02128
Phone: (617) 567-3900
http://www.suffolkdowns.com

MICHIGAN

Detroit Race Course
28001 Schoolcraft
Livonia, MI 48150
Phone: (734) 525-7300

Mount Pleasant Meadows
P.O. Box 220
Mt. Pleasant, MI 48858
Phone: (517) 773-0012

Pinnacle Racetrack
18000 Vining Road
New Boston, MI 48164
Phone: (734) 753-2000
http://www.pinnacleracecourse.com

MINNESOTA

Canterbury Park
1100 Canterbury Road

Shakopee, MN 55379
Phone: (612) 445-7223
http://www.canterburypark.com

MONTANA

Great Falls (Racing dates during fair)
Montana State Fair
P.O. Box 1524
Great Falls, MT 59403
Phone: (406) 727-8900
http://www.montanastatefair.com/
horseracing.htm

Kalispell (Racing dates during fair)
Northwest Montana Fair
256 North Meridian Road
Kalispell, MT 59801
Phone: (406) 758-5810
http://www.nwmtfair.com/default.
htm

Missoula (Racing dates during fair)
Western Montana Fair
1101 South Avenue West
Missoula, MT 59801
Phone: (406) 721-3247

Yellowstone Downs
5035 Alkaki Creek Road
Billings, MT 59106
Phone: (406) 256-2449
http://www.yellowstonedowns.com

NEBRASKA

Columbus Races
Platte County Agricultural Society
P.O. Box 1335
Columbus, NE 68601
Phone: (402) 564-0133
http://www.agpark.com

Fonner Park
P.O. Box 490
Grant Island, NE 68802
Phone: (308) 382-4515
http://www.fonnerpark.com

Horseman's Park
6303 "Q" Street
Omaha, NE 68117
Phone: (402) 731-2900
http://www.horsemenspark.com

Lincoln State Fair
P.O. Box 81233
Lincoln, NE 68501
Phone: (402) 474-5371
http://www.statefair.org/
statefairpark

NEVADA

Elko County Fair (Racing dates during fair)
557 West Silver Street
Elko, NV 89801
Phone: (775) 738-7191
http://www.elkocountyfair.com

Winnemucca
Tri-County Fair & Stampede
50 West Winnemuca Boulevard
Winnemuca, NV 89445
Phone: (775) 623-5071
http://www.winnemucca.nv.us

NEW JERSEY

Atlantic City Race Course
4501 Black Horse Pike
Mays Landing, NJ 08330
Phone: (609) 641-2190
http://www.acracecourse.com

Garden State Park
P.O. Box 4274
Cherry Hill, NJ 08034
Phone: (856) 488-8400

Meadowlands Racetrack
50 State Route 120
East Rutherford, NJ 07073
Phone: (201) 843-2446
http://www.thebigm.com

Monmouth Park
175 Oceanport Avenue
Oceanport, NJ 07757
Phone: (732) 222-5100
http://www.monmouthpark.com

NEW MEXICO

Downs at Albuquerque
P.O. Box 8510
Albuquerque, NM 87198
Phone: (505) 266-5555
http://www.abqdowns.com

Ruidoso Downs
P.O. Box 449
Ruidoso Downs, NM 88346
Phone: (505) 378-4431
http://www.ruidownsracing.com

Sunland Parks
1200 Futurity Drive
Sunland Park, NM 88063
Phone: (505) 874-5200
http://www.sunland-park.com

Sun Ray Park
39 Route 5568
Farmington, NM 87401
Phone: (505) 566-1200
http://www.sunraygaming.com

Zia Park
3901 West Millen Drive
Hobbs, NM 88240
Phone: (888) ZIA PARK

NEW YORK

Aqueduct Raceway
110-00 Rockaway Boulevard
Jamaica, NY 11417
Phone: (718) 641-4700
http://nyra.com/index_aqueduct.
html

Belmont Park
P.O. Box 90
Jamaica, NY 11417
Phone: (718) 641-4700
http://www.nyra.com/index_
belmont.html

Finger Lakes
P.O. Box 25250
Farmington, NY 14425
Phone: (585) 924-3232
http://www.fingerlakesracetrack.com

Saratoga
Union Ave
Saratoga Springs, NY 12866
Phone: (518) 584-6200
http://www.nyra.com/index_
　saratoga.html

NORTH DAKOTA

Belcourt
Sky Dancer Hotel and Casino
P.O. Box 900
Highway 5 West
Belcourt, ND 58316
Phone: (701) 244-2400
http://www.skydancercasino.com

North Dakota Horse Park
5180 19th Avenue North
Fargo, ND 58102
Phone: (701) 277-8027

OHIO

Beulah Park
P.O. Box 850
Grove City, OH 43123
Phone: (614) 871-9600
http://www.beulahpark.com

River Downs
P.O. Box 30286
Cincinnati, OH 45230
Phone: (513) 232-8000
http://www.riverdowns.com

Thistledown
21501 Emery Road
North Randall, OH 44128
Phone: (216) 662-8600
http://www.thistledown.com

OKLAHOMA

Blue Ribbon Downs
P.O. Box 489
Sallisaw, OK 74955
Phone: (918)775-7771
http://www.blueribbondowns.net

Fair Meadows
P.O. Box 4735
Tulsa, OK 74159

Phone: (918) 743-7223
http://www.exposquare.com/fm/
　index.asp

Remington Park
One Remington Place
Oklahoma City, OK 73111
Phone: (405) 424-1000
http://www.remingtonpark.com

Will Rogers Downs
20900 South 4200 Road
Claremore, OK 74919
Phone: (918) 283-8800

OREGON

Grants Pass
P.O. Box 282
Grants Pass, OR 97526
Phone: (541) 476-3215
http://www.grantspassdowns.com

Portland Meadows
1001 North Schmeer Road
Portland, OR 97217
Phone: (503) 285-9144
http://www.portlandmeadows.
　com

Prineville (Racing dates during fair)
P.O. Box 507
Prineville, OR97754
Phone: (541) 447-6575
http://www.crookcountyfairgrounds.
　com

Tillamook (Racing dates during fair)
Tillamook County Fair
P.O. Box 455
Tillamook, OR 97141
Phone: (503) 842-2272
http://www.tillamookfair.com

Union (Racing dates during fair)
P.O. Box 4092
Union, OR 97883
Phone: (541) 562-5768

PENNSYLVANIA

Penn National
P.O. Box 32
Grantville, PA 17028
Phone: (717) 469-2211
http://www.pennnational.com

Philadelphia Park
P.O. Box 1000
Bensalem, PA 19020
Phone: (215) 639-9000
http://www.philadelphiapark.com

Presque Isle Downs
8199 Perry Highway
Erie, PA 16509
Phone: (866) 374-3386
http://www.presqueisledowns.com

SOUTH DAKOTA

Brown County
216 Northwest 24th Avenue
Aberdeen, SD 57401
Phone: (605) 626-7110
http://www.thebrowncountyfair.
　com

South Dakota Horse Racing
P.O. Box 426
Fort Pierre, SD 57532
Phone: (605) 223-2178
http://www.sdhorseracing.com

TEXAS

Gillespie
P.O. Box 526
Fredericksburg, TX 78624
Phone: (830) 997-2359
http://www.gillespiefair.com

Lone Star
1000 Lone Star Parkway
Grand Prairie, TX 75050
Phone: (972) 263-7223
http://www.lonestarpark.com

Manor Downs
P.O. Box 141309
Austin, TX 78714

Phone: (512) 272-5581
http://www.manordowns.com

Retama Park
P.O. Box 47535
San Antonio, TX 78265
Phone: (210) 651-7000
http://www.retamapark.com

Sam Houston Race Park
7575 North Sam Houston Parkway West
Houston, TX 77064
Phone: (281) 807-8700
http://www.shrp.com

UTAH

Dixie Downs
P.O. Box 444
Washington, UT 84780
Phone: (435) 673-4932

VIRGINIA

Colonial Downs
P.O. Box 228
New Kent, VA 23124
Phone: (804) 966-7223
http://www.colonialdowns.com

WASHINGTON

Dayton (Racing dates during fair)
Columbia County Fairgrounds
P.O. Box 264
Dayton, WA 99328
Phone: (509) 382-2370
http://www.columbiafair.com

Emerald Downs
P.O. Box 617
Auburn, WA 98071
Phone: (253) 288-7000
http://www.emdowns.com

Sun Downs
P.O. Box 6662
Kennewick, WA 99336
Phone: (509) 582-5434

Waitsburg (Racing dates during fair)
Waitsburg Fairgrounds
P.O. Box 391
Waitsburg, WA 99361
Phone: (509) 337-6241

Walla Walla (Race dates during fair)
Southeast Washington Fairgrounds

P.O. Drawer G
Walla Walla, WA 99362
Phone: (509) 527-3247
http://www.whrc.wa.gov/page4.htm

WEST VIRGINIA

Charles Town Races
P.O. Box 551
Charles Town, WV 25414
Phone: (304) 725-7001
http://www.ctownraces.com

Mountaineer Racetrack
P.O. Box 358
Chester, WV 26034
Phone: (800) 804-0468
http://www.mtrgaming.com/index.php

WYOMING

Wyoming Downs
P.O. Box 1607
Evanston, WY 82930
Phone: (307) 789-0511
http://www.wyomingdowns.com

APPENDIX XVI
BOXING SANCTIONING BODIES

The following is a selected listing of boxing sanctioning bodies. Names, addresses, phone numbers, and Web sites have been included when available. This list may be useful when looking for information regarding professional boxing.

International Boxing Association (IBA)
9505 West Smithville-Western Road
Wooster, OH 44691
Phone: (330) 264-5423
Fax: (330) 262-2476
http://www.ibamensboxing.com

Intercontinental Boxing Council(IBC)
12200 Shelbyville Road
Louisville, KY 40243
Phone: (502) 245-8164

International Boxing Federation (IBF)
516 Main Street
East Orange, NJ 07018
Phone: (973) 414-0300
Fax: (973) 414-0307
E-mail: mmuhammad@ibfboxing. com
http://www.ibf-usba-boxing.com

International Boxing Organization (IBO)
328 Minorca Avenue
Coral Gables FL 33134
Phone: (305) 446-0684
Fax: (305) 446-2973
http://www.iboboxing.com

North American Boxing Federation (NABF)
2020 105th Street
Edmonton, AB, Canada T6J 5J2
Phone: (780) 435-5907
Fax: (780) 435-5909
E-mail: epearson@canadianboxing. com
http://www.nabfnews.com

National Boxing Association (NBA)
P.O. Box 262636
Tampa, FL 33685
Phone: (813) 884-7711
Fax: (813) 890-0099
E-mail: nbaboxing@aol.com
http://www.nbaboxing.com

Women's International Boxing Federation (WIBF)
2445 Flamingo Place 3
Miami Beach, FL 33140
Phone: (305) 531-0380
http://www.wibf-champions.com

World Boxing Association (WBA)
P.O. BOX 377
Maracay 2101
Estado Aragua, Venezuela

Phone: (0244) 663-15-84
Fax: (0244) 663-31-77
http://www.wbanews.com

World Boxing Council (WBC)
Consejo Mundial de Boxeo
Cuzco 872
Colonia Lindavista
07300 Mexico City, Federal District, Mexico
Phone: 52 55 51195276
E-mail: info@wbcboxing.com
http://www.wbcboxing.com

World Boxing Federation (WBF)
1305 Baxter Street
Jackson City, TN 17601
Phone: (423) 926-8821
Fax: (423) 538-4933
http://www.worldboxingfederation. org

World Boxing Organization (WBO)
1056 Muñoz Rivera Avenue
San Juan, P.R. 00927
Phone: (787) 765-4444
Fax: (787) 758-9053
E-mail: info@wbo-int.com
http://www.wbo-int.com

APPENDIX XVII
BOXING AND WRESTLING PROMOTERS AND PROMOTION COMPANIES

The following is a listing of boxing and wrestling promoters and promotion companies. Use this list as a beginning. There are many more. Due to space limitations, all promoters and promotion companies have not been included. Inclusion or exclusion on this list does not indicate the recommendation or endorsement of one company over another.

All Pro Wrestling
21063 Cabot Boulevard # 1
Hayward, CA 94545
Phone: (510) 785-8397
http://www.allprowrestling.com

Art of Boxing Promotions
Phone: (818) 521-2373
Fax: (818) 550-9959
E-mail: info@artofboxingpromotions.com
http://www.artofboxingpromotions.com

BAM Promotions
23 Packard Drive
Millville, NJ 08332
Phone: (609) 319-4400
Fax: (856) 765-0119
http://bampromotions.com

Banner Promotions
1231 Bainbridge Street
Philadelphia, PA 19147
Phone: (215) 670-2220
http://www.banner-promotions.com

Butch Lewis Productions
250 West 57th Street
New York, NY 10107
Phone: (212) 582-4344

Don King Productions, Inc.
501 Fairway Drive
Deerfield Beach, FL 33441
Phone: (954) 418-5800
http://www.donking.com

8 Count Productions
410 North Oakley Boulevard
Phone: (312) 226-5800
Fax: (312) 226-5801
E-mail: count8@aol.com
http://www.8countproductions.com

Gary Shaw Productions, LLC
555 Preakness Avenue
Totowa, NJ 07512
Phone: (973) 904-0008
Fax: (973) 904-1250
http://www.garyshawproductions.com

Golden Boy Promotions
626 Wilshire Boulevard
Los Angeles, CA 90017
Phone: (213) 489-5631
Fax: (213) 489-9048
http://www.goldenboypromotions.com

Gotham Boxing
1414 Avenue of the Americas
New York, NY 10021
Phone: (646) 912-5547
E-mail: cedkushner@aol.com
http://www.gothamboxing.com

Let's Get It On Promotions
P.O. Box 3584
Reno, NV 89505
http://www.letsgetitonboxing.com

Main Events
772 Union Boulevard
Totowa, NJ 07512
Phone: (973) 890-7730
http://www.1.mainevents.operationdistort.com

Star Boxing
991 Morris Park Avenue
Bronx, NY 10462
Phone: (718) 823-2000
Fax: (718) 823-6330
http://www.starboxing.com

Sycuan Ringside Promotions
1400 Hill Street
El Cajon, CA 92020
Phone: (619) 590-2030
Fax: (619) 590-2220
http://www.sycuan.com

Thompson Boxing Promotions
282 South Anita Drive
Orange, CA 92868
Phone: (714) 935-0900
Fax: (714) 935-0600
http://www.thompsonboxing.com

Top Rank, Inc.
3980 Howard Hughes Parkway
Las Vegas, NV 89109
Phone: (702) 732-2717
Fax: (702) 733-8232
E-mail: contact@toprank.com
http://www.toprank.com

WWE
1241 East Main Street
Stamford, CT 06902
Phone: (203) 352-8600
http://www.wwe.com

The following is a listing of some of the larger cable stations and network television sports departments. Your local TV guide or the Internet may provide you with additional information on other stations or channels in your area. Use this list to obtain general information, location of internships, and/or to send your résumé for possible jobs.

ABC Sports
47 West 66th Street
New York, NY 10023
Phone: (212) 456-7777
Fax: (212) 456-2930
http://www.abcsports.com

CBS Sports
51 West 52nd Street
New York, NY 10019
Phone: (212) 975-4321
http://www.cbssportsonline.com

CNN Sports
Cable News Network
1 CNN Center
P.O.Box 105366
Atlanta, GA 30348
Phone: (404) 827-1500
http://www.cnn.com/sports

ESPN
935 Middle Street
Bristol, CT 06010
Phone: (860) 585-2000
http://espn.go.com

ESPN 2
935 Middle Street
Bristol, CT 06010
Phone: (860) 585-2000
http://espn.go.com

Fox Sports Networks
10201 West Pico Boulevard # 10
Los Angeles, CA 90064
Phone: (310) 369-6000
http://msn.foxsports.com

Golf Channel
7580 Commerce Center Drive
Orlando, FL 32819
Phone: (407) 355-4653
http://www.thegolfchannel.com

HBO Sports
1100 Avenue of the Americas
New York, NY 10036
Phone: (212) 512-1000
http://www.hbo.com/sports

Madison Square Garden (MSG) Network
Madison Square Garden
Two Penn Plaza
New York, NY 10021
Phone: (212) 563-1968
http://www.msg.com/msg

MSNBC
1 MSNB Plaza
Secaucus, NJ 07094
Phone: (201) 583-5000
http://www.msnbc.com

NBC Sports
30 Rockefeller Plaza
New York, NY 10112
Phone: (212) 664-4444
http://www.nbc.com

Prime Sportschannel Network
http://primesportsnetwork.com

Showtime Sports
1633 Broadway
New York, NY 10019
Phone: (212) 708-1600
http://sports.sho.com

Turner Network Television Sports
1050 Techwood Drive, NW
Atlanta, GA 30318
Phone: (404) 885-2402
http://www.tnt.tv/sports

USA Network
1230 Avenue of the Americas
New York, NY 10020
Phone: (212) 408-9100
http://www.usanetwork.com/sports

APPENDIX XIX
SPORTS CAREER WEB SITES

The following is a listing of both sports and general job Web sites. Use it as a beginning to help you in your job search. There are many other sites on the Internet.

This listing is provided for informational purposes. The author does not endorse or recommend any one site over another.

CareerBuilder.com
http://www.careerbuilder.com

Coaching Jobs
http://www.coachingjobs.com

ESPN Career Center
http://espn.go.com/mediakit/demo/monster

FILCRO Sports Jobs
http://www.filcro.com/sports-jobs.html

Flipdog.com
http://www.flipdog.com/jobs/usa/sports

HoopCoach.org
http://www.hoopcoach.org

HotJobs.com
http://www.hotjobs.com

ICoachUSA.com
http://www.icoachusa.com

Job Bank USA
http://www.jobbank.com

Jobs.com
http://www.jobs.com

Jobs in Sports
http://www.jobsinsports.com

Just Golf Jobs
http://golfsurfin.com

MLB and Its Teams Job Board
http://baseballjobs.teamworkonline.com

Monster.com
http://www.monster.com

National Athletic Trainers' Association Career Center
http://www.nata.org/careercenter

NBA/WNBA League Teams Job Board
http://nbateamjobs.teamworkonline.com

NFL Teams Jobs
http://footballjobs.teamworkonline.com

NHL Hockey Jobs.com
http://hockeyjobs.nhl.com

PGA Employment Center
http://pgajobfinder.pgalinks.com

Sports Job Board
http://www.sportsjobboard.com

Sports Career Finder
http://www.sportscareerfinder.com

Sports Careers.com
http://www.sportscareers.com

Sports Casting Jobs
http://www.sportscastingjobs.com

TazSport
http://www.tazsport.com

Team Work Online's Sports Jobs
http://www.teamworkonline.com

TopUSAJobs.com
http://www.topusajobs.com

Women in Sports Careers
http://www.wiscfoundation.org

Women Sports Jobs
http://www.sportsjobwire.com

Women Sports Jobs
http://womensportsjobs.monster.com

Work in Sports
http://www.workinsports.com

GLOSSARY

The following is a list of abbreviations, acronyms, and terms that will prove helpful to individuals interested in the sports industry. Entries are listed alphabetically.

AAABA American Amateur Baseball Association

AABC American Amateur Baseball Congress

AAF American Advertising Federation

AAHPERD American Alliance for Health, Physical Education, Recreation and Dance

AARWBA American Auto Racing Writers and Broadcasters Association

AATACB American Athletic Trainers Association and Certification Board

AAU Amateur Athletic Union of the United States

AAU/USA JO Amateur Athletic Union/U.S.A. Junior Olympics

ABAUSA Amateur Basketball Association of the United States of America

ABCA American Baseball Coaches Association

ABO Affiliated Boards of Officials

AC Advertising Council

AEMA Athletic Equipment Managers Association

AFA American Fitness Association

AFAA Aerobics and Fitness Association of America

AFB Association for Fitness in Business

AFCA American Football Coaches Association

Affiliate A broadcast station that belongs to a network. For example, WABC in New York and KABC in Los Angeles are both affiliates of the ABC network.

AFM American Federation of Musicians

AFT American Federation of Teachers

AFTRA American Federation of Television and Radio Artists

AGMA American Guild of Musical Artists

AGTD Athletic Goods Team Distributors

AGVA American Guild of Variety Artists

AHAUS Amateur Hockey Association of the United States

AHCA American Hockey Coaches Association

AHL American Hockey League

AI Athletic Institute

AISA American Indoor Soccer Association

AJA American Judges Association

AL American League

ALB American Legion Baseball

All-Star game An exhibition game played annually between the best players in the American League and the National League.

AMA American Management Association

AMA American Marketing Association

AMAA American Medical Athletic Association

Amateur An athlete who does not receive money for competing in a sport.

American League One of the professional baseball leagues in the United States.

ANA Association of National Advertisers, Inc.

APB Associated Press Broadcasters

APBPA Association of Professional Ball Players of America

APFC Association of Physical Fitness Centers

APTA American Physical Therapy Association

ARF Advertising Research Foundation

ARFA American Running and Fitness Association

ARPA Association of Representatives of Professional Athletes

ASA Amateur Softball Association of America

ASA American Sportscasters Association

ASCA American Swimming Coaches Association

ASTVC American Society of TV Cameramen

AT American Turners

ATA American Tennis Association

ATAS Academy of Television Arts and Sciences

AWRT American Women in Radio and Television

AYSO American Youth Soccer Organization

B & W glossy Used by publicists, press agents, and public relations people when putting together press kits. It is an 8- × 10-inch glossy photograph of a client that can be used for reproduction purposes in newspapers or magazines.

B/PAA Business/Professional Advertising Association

Ballgame A baseball game.

Ballpark The area where baseball games are played.

Banner ad A graphic Web advertising unit

Basket The hoop in a basketball game.

Batter The player who is at bat in a baseball game.

BBWAA Baseball Writers Association of America

Bell A gong, buzzer, or bell used to indicate the start and finish of a round in boxing.

BHFCBV Baseball Hall of Fame Committee on Baseball Veterans

Bio   A biography put together by press agents, publicists, public relations people, etc., on a client.

Blow   A punch used in boxing.

BRB   Babe Ruth Baseball

BWA   Boxing Writers Association

BWAA   Bowling Writers Association of America

BWI   Boating Writers International

CABA   Canadian Amateur Boxing Association

CABMA   College Athletic Business Managers Association

CAC   Consolidated Athletic Commission

Calendar listing   Dated listings sent to the media by publicists regarding upcoming events and programs. They are designed to bring the events to the attention of the public, the media, and other editors.

Campaign (advertising)   A series of advertisements used to promote and publicize a product or group of products.

Campaign (public relations)   A public relations concept used to promote a client.

CBA   Continental Basketball Association

CCA   Collegiate Commissioners Association

CFA   College Football Association

CIAA   Central Intercollegiate Athletic Association

Circulation   The number of distributed copies of a newspaper or magazine.

Combination   Two or more punches used quickly in combination with each other in boxing.

Counterpunch   A boxing blow thrown after one opponent hits another.

Course   Golf course; area where people play golf.

Court   A basketball court; the playing area in basketball.

CPRBLS   Cardiopulmonary resuscitation and basic life support.

CSCA   College Swimming Coaches Association of America

CSIDA   College Sports Information Directors of America

CSL   Cosmopolitan Soccer League

CSS   Center for Sports Sponsorship

Dateline   Location information provided at the beginning of a news release indicating the specific town, city, etc., where the press or news release originated. In some instances the date may also be included.

Defense tackle   One of the positions played in football.

Doubleheader   Two games played consecutively on the same day.

Draft   A system where teams get to choose athletes from a list of amateur players who want to become professionals.

ECBA   Eastern College Basketball Association

ECHA   Eastern College Hockey Association

ECSA   Eastern College Soccer Association

EIGL   Eastern Intercollegiate Gymnastic League

E-mail   Mail transmitted electronically via modems and telephone lines.

EWABL/AAU   Eastern Women's Amateur Basketball League of the AAU

FCC   Federal Communications Commission

Five Ws   The Who, What, When, Where, and Why used by journalists to gather and write the basic news story.

Forward pass   A play in football.

Foul   An illegal move or an infraction of rules.

FPA   Federation of Professional Athletes

Free throw   A shot in basketball.

FTA   Fitness Trade Associations

FWAA   Football Writers Association of America

GGAA   Golden Gloves Association of America

GKABL   George Khoury Association of Baseball Leagues

Golden Gloves   The Golden Gloves Association of America sponsors amateur boxing tournaments, across the country.

Golf pro   Golf professional.

Gross income   Total income before expenses and taxes are deducted

Group sales   Tickets sold in blocks to groups of people.

GWAA   Golf Writers Association of America

Halftime   The break after the first half of the game has been played in a football game.

Harness racing   Type of horse racing using a specific breed of horse called a standardbred; harness racing drivers follow behind the horse in sulkys.

Heavy bag   Bag used to develop boxer's punch.

HHI   Harness Horsemen International

HHYF   Harness Horse Youth Foundation

Hook   A boxing blow.

HTA   Harness Tracks of America

Hype   Extensive publicity used to promote people, products, events, etc. Hype is not always true.

IAABO   International Association of Approved Basketball Officials

IABA   International Amateur Boxing Association

IADRS   International Association of Dive Rescue Specialists

IBA   International Baseball Association

IBC   International Boxing Council

IBF   International Boxing Federation

IBHF   International Boxing Hall of Fame

IBRO   International Boxing Research Organization

IBWA   International Boxing Writers Association

ICAAA   Intercollegiate Association of Amateur Athletes of America

ICAEO   International Center for Athletic and Educational Opportunities

ICF   International Cheerleading Foundation

ICNATAS   International Council—National Academy of Television Arts and Sciences

ICSF   International Collegiate Sports Foundation

IDEA   International Dance-Exercise Association

ILPBC   International League of Professional Baseball Clubs

INHL   International Hockey League

IPFA   International Physical Fitness Association

IPRA   International Public Relations Association

ISAA   Intercollegiate Soccer Association of America

ISSP   International Society of Sports Psychology

ITCA   Intercollegiate Tennis Coaches Association

ITPA   International Trotting and Pacing Association

IVBA   International Veteran Boxing Association

Jab   A blow used in boxing.

JGI   Jockey's Guild, Inc.

Jockey   The person who rides a horse in a race.

Judge   An official who scores and judges sporting events.

Jump shot   A shot in basketball.

KBTI   Knights Boxing Team International

Key man clause   A contract provision allowing clients to terminate a contract if a specific person integral to the individual's career leaves the company; may apply to management contracts, booking agency contracts, publishing contracts, etc.

KO   Knockout. Used to indicate when a boxer is knocked out.

Lead   The opening lines of a news release or feature designed to attract reader interest.

LLB   Little League Baseball

Low blow   In boxing, an illegal punch delivered below the waist.

LPGA   Ladies Professional Golf Association of America

Making weight   A term used in boxing; boxers are weighed before a fight to make sure they are within the limits of a specific weight category.

MANA   Manufacturer's Agents National Association

Market   Refers to a geographical location in television or radio; may refer to a specific size or style of audience market such as small market radio, major market television, etc.

Men in blue   Umpires

Mike   Microphone

Minor League   Professional leagues other than the major leagues.

MLBBPA   Major League Baseball Players Association; union representing major league baseball players.

MLBPA   Major League Baseball Players Association

MLUA   Major League Umpires Association

Mouthpiece   A plastic guard used in boxing to protect a fighter's mouth and teeth.

MVP   Most Valuable Player

NAB   National Association of Broadcaster

NAB   National Association of Broadcasting

NAB   Newspaper Advertising Bureau

NABC   National Association of Basketball Coaches of the United States

NABET   National Association of Broadcast Employees and Technicians

NABF   National Amateur Baseball Federation

NABF   North American Boxing Federation

NABR   National Association of Basketball Referees

NACDA   National Association of Collegiate Directors of Athletics

NACGC   National Association of Collegiate Gymnastics Coaches

NAIA   National Association of Intercollegiate Athletics

NAJSA   North American Judges and Stewards Association

NALUS   National Association of Leagues, Umpires and Scorers

NAPBL   National Association of Professional Baseball Leagues

NAS   National Academy of Sports

NASCAR   National Association for Stock Car Auto Racing

NASF   North American Soccer Foundation

NASGW   National Association of Sporting Goods Wholesalers

NASLP   North American Soccer League Players Association

NASO   National Association of Sports Officials

NASPE   National Association for Sport and Physical Education

NATA   National Athletic Trainers Association

NATAS   National Academy of Television Arts and Sciences

National League   A professional baseball league.

NAYSI   North American Youth Sport Institute

NBA National Basketball Association

NBC National Baseball Congress

NBPA National Basketball Players Association

NBPRS National Black Public Relations Society

NCAA National Collegiate Athletic Association

NCBWA National Collegiate Baseball Writers Association

NCFA National Collegiate Football Association

NCSA National Club Sports Association

NDA National Dance Association

NDEITA National Dance-Exercise Instructor's Training Association

NEA National Education Association

NEJA National Entertainment Journalists Association

NESRA National Employee Services and Recreation Association

Net The Internet

Network A group of TV or radio stations affiliated and interconnected for simultaneous broadcast of the same programming.

Neutral corners Corners of a boxing ring that are not used during rest periods between rounds.

NFF National Fitness Foundation

NFICA National Federation Interscholastic Coaches Association

NFIOA National Federation Interscholastic Officials Association

NFL National Football League

NFLPA National Football League Players Association

NFPW National Federation of Press Women

NFSHSA National Federation of State High School Associations

NFT National Federation of Teachers

NGJA National Gymnastics Judges Association

NHL National Hockey League

NHLPA National Hockey League Player's Association

NHSACA National High School Athletic Coaches Association

NIRSA National Intramural-Recreational Sports Association

NISCA National Interscholastic Swimming Coaches Association of America

NISOA National Intercollegiate Soccer Officials Association

NJCAA National Junior College Athletic Association

NL National League of Professional Baseball Clubs

NLC National Lifeguard Championships

NLCAA National Little College Athletic Association

NPC National Press Club

NPPA National Press Photographers Association

NSCA National Strength and Conditioning Association

NSCAA National Soccer Coaches Association of America

NSGA National Sporting Goods Association

NSL National Soccer League

NSPBA National Semi-Professional Baseball Association

NSSA National Sportscasters and Sportswriters Association

NVBA National Veterans Boxers Association

NWBW National Women Bowling Writers Association

NWCA National Wrestling Coaches Association

NYSCA National Youth Sports Coaches Association

OBUD Office for Baseball Umpire Development

Official A referee or judge of an athletic game.

OFPCP Organization of Fitness and Personal Care Professionals

Olympics Games and tournaments held every four years for amateur events in a variety of sports.

On-line Connected to the Internet

Out of bounds Out of the playing area.

Overtime Extra time needed to complete a game.

P.E. Physical Education

PR Public Relations

PAC Public Affairs Council

Pacers Horses trained to pace instead of trot.

PB Pony Baseball

PBWAA Professional Basketball Writers Association of America

PFATS Professional Football Athletic Trainers Society

PFRA Professional Football Referees Association

PFRA Professional Football Researchers Association

PFWA Professional Football Writers of America

PGA Professional Golfers Association of America

Photo caption The story line accompanying a photograph, identifying the people in the photo and/or telling the story about the photo.

PHWA Professional Hockey Writers' Association

Pitcher The athlete who throws or pitches the ball in baseball.

Play ball Begin playing the game or restart game.

PMAA Promotion Marketing Association of America

PPA Professional Photographers of America

Press kit A promotion kit containing publicity, photographs, and other promotional materials used by publicists, press agents, and public relations people to help publicize a client.

Pro   Professional

Pro   Professional Athlete

Professional   An athlete who receives compensation for competing in sporting events.

Promo   Promotion

PRSA   Public Relations Society of America

PRSSA   Public Relations Student Society of America

PSIA   Professional Ski Instructors of America

Purse (boxing)   The amount of money a boxer is paid for fighting.

Purse (racing)   The amount of money a horse earns if it wins.

PWF   Pop Warners Football

RAB   Radio and Advertising Bureau

Rate card   A card listing rates for space or time and providing mechanical requirements for advertisements.

Ref   Referee

Retail sports store   A store in which consumers buy sports equipment or products.

RTNDA   Radio Television News Directors Association

SABR   Society for American Baseball Research

SAG   Screen Actors Guild

Scale   Minimum wages that can be paid to a union member.

Search the Net   Look for information on the Internet.

SEG   Screen Extras Guild

SF   Sports Foundation

SGAA   Sporting Goods Agents Association

SGMA   Sporting Goods Manufacturers Association

Shoot   Throw a basketball.

Shortstop   A defensive player in baseball.

Site   Web site.

Standardbred racing   A type of horse racing also known as harness racing

Stats   Statistics.

STD   Sports Therapy Division

Sulky   Two-wheeled cart connected to a horse via a harness used in harness racing

Surf the Net   Going on-line, visiting various sites on the Internet.

TAC/USA   The Athletics Congress of the U.S.A.

Tennis Pro   Tennis professional.

Thoroughbred   Breed of horse.

Thoroughbred racing   Type of horse racing where a jockey rides a horse.

Trades   Magazines and newspapers that deal with specific industries.

Trotters   Horses that race at a trot instead of a gallop.

Ump   Umpire.

Umpire   Official who enforces the rules of a game.

USAA   United States Athletes Association

USAABF   U.S.A. Amateur Boxing Federation

USAFHA   U.S.A. Field Hockey Association

USAIGC   United States Association of Independent Gymnastics Clubs

USAWF   United States Amateur Wrestling Foundation

USBF   United States Baseball Federation

USBF   United States Boxing Federation

USBWA   United States Basketball Writers Association

USCCCA   United States Cross Country Coaches Association

USGF   United States Gymnastics Federation

USHWA   United States Harness Writers' Association

USL   United Soccer League

USLA   United States Lifesaving Association

USS   United States Swimming, Inc.

USSA   United States Ski Association

USSA   United States Sports Academy

USSCA   U.S. Ski Coaches Association

USSF   United States Soccer Federation

USSF   United States Swimming Foundation

USSWA   United States Ski Writers Association

USTA   United States Tennis Association or United States Trotting Association

USWTCA   United States Women's Track Coaches Association

USYSA   United States Youth Soccer Association

WABA   Women's American Basketball Association

WBA   World Boxing Association

WBC   World Boxing Council

WBCA   Women's Basketball Coaches Association

WBF   World Boxing Federation

WBO   World Boxing Organization

Web   The World Wide Web.

Website   A place on the World Wide Web.

WEPR   Women Executives in Public Relations

WIC   Women In Communications, Inc.

WIS   Women In Soccer

WNBA   Women's National Basketball Association

WSF   Women's Sports Foundation

WWSRA   Western Winter Sports Representatives Association

WWW   World Wide Web

BIBLIOGRAPHY

A. BOOKS

There are thousands of books written on all aspects of the sports industry. The books listed below are separated into general categories. The subject matter of many of the books overlaps.

These books can be found in bookstores and libraries. If your local library does not have the one you want, ask your librarian to order them through the Intralibrary loan system.

This list should be used only as a starting point. For other books that might interest you, look in the sports section of bookstores and libraries. You can also check *Books in Print* for other books on the subject. *Books in Print* may be located in your local library or online.

BASEBALL AND BASKETBALL

Canfield, Jack. *Chicken Soup for the Soul: Inside Basketball: 101 Great Hoop Stories from Players, Coaches and Fans.* Cos Cob, Conn.: Chicken Soup for the Soul®, 2009.

Castle, George. *Sweet Lou and the Cubs: A Year Inside the Dugout.* Guilford, Conn.: Globe Pequot Press, 2009.

Cohen, Marilyn. *No Girls in the Clubhouse: The Exclusion of Women from Baseball.* Jefferson, N.C.: McFarland, 2009.

Davis, Seth. *When March Went Mad: The Game That Transformed Basketball.* New York: Henry Holt, 2009.

Fountain, Charles. *Under the March Sun: The Story of Spring Training.* New York: Oxford University Press, 2009.

Gratz, Alan M. *The Brooklyn Nine.* New York: Penguin, 2009.

Harris, E. Lynn. *Basketball Jones.* New York: Knopf, 2009.

Herzog, Brad. *The Book of Basketball History and Trivia.* New York: Rosen, 2009.

Kuska, Bob. *Cinderella Ball: A Look Inside Small-College Basketball in West Virginia.* Lincoln: University of Nebraska Press, 2009.

Leslie, Lisa, and Larry Burnett. *Don't Let the Lipstick Fool You.* New York: Kensington, 2009.

Lupica, Mike. *The Big Field.* New York: Penguin, 2009.

Maddox, Jake. *Hoop Hotshot.* Minneapolis, Minn.: Stone Arch Books, 2009.

Muschett, Jim. *Citi Field: The Mets' New World-Class Ballpark.* New York: Universe, 2009.

Nelson, Kadir. *We Are the Ship: The Story of Negro League Baseball.* Salon, Ohio: Findaway World, 2009.

Nelson, Murry R. *The National Baseball League.* Jefferson, N.C.: McFarland, 2009.

Philadelphia Inquirer. *Champions!: A Look Back at the Phillies' Triumphant 2008 Season.* Philadelphia: Camino Books, 2009.

Stewart, Mark. *The Los Angeles Clippers.* Chicago: Norwood House, 2009.

Sutter, L. M. *Ball, Bat and Bitumen: A History of Coalfield Baseball in the Appalachian South.* Jefferson, N.C.: McFarland, 2009.

Swaine, Rick. *The Integration of Major League Baseball: A Team by Team History.* Solon, Ohio: Findaway Publishing: 2009.

Szalontai, James. *Teenager on First, Geezer at Bat, 4-F on Deck: Major League Baseball in 1945.* Jefferson, N.C.: McFarland, 2009.

Torre, Joe. *The Yankee Years.* New York: Random House: 2009.

Tully, Gregory J. *Nine College Nines: A Closeup View of Campus Baseball Programs Today.* Jefferson, N.C.: McFarland, 2009.

Wilson, John. *Jackie Robinson and the American Dilemma.* East Rutherford, N.J.: Prentice Hall, 2009.

Woods, Mark. *Basketball Legends.* Saint Catharines, Ontario: Crabtree, 2009.

Zaremba, Alan Jay. *The Madness of March: Bonding and Betting with the Boys in Las Vegas.* Lincoln: University of Nebraska Press, 2009.

BOXING

Berardinelli, David J. *From Good Hands to Boxing Gloves: The Dark Side of Insurance.* Portland, Ore.: Trial Guides LLC, 2009.

Cerasini, Marc. *Cinderella Man.* New York: HarperCollins, 2009.

Ezra, Michael. *Muhammad Ali: The Making of an Icon.* Philadelphia: Temple University Press, 2009.

Holyfield, Evander. *Becoming Holyfield: A Fighter's Journey*. New York: Simon & Schuster, 2008.

Paxton, Bill. *The Fearless Harry Greb: Biography of a Tragic Hero of Boxing*. Jefferson, N.C.: McFarland, 2009.

Rodriguez, Robert G. *The Regulation of Boxing: A History and Comparative Analysis of Policies among American States*. Jefferson, N.C.: McFarland, 2009.

Satterwhite, Al. *Titans: Muhammas Ali and Arnold Schwarzenegger*. Deerfield, Ill.: Dalton Watson Fine Books, 2009.

Scott, David. *The Art and Aesthetics of Boxing*. Lincoln: University of Nebraska Press, 2009.

Shone, Rob. *Muhammad Ali: The Life of a Boxing Hero*. New York: Rosen, 2009.

Torres, José. *Sting Like a Bee: The Muhammad Ali Story*. Lincoln: University of Nebraska Press, 2009.

COACHING

Brichford, Maynard. *Bob Zuppke: The Life and Football Legacy of the Illinois Coach*. Jefferson, N.C.: McFarland, 2009.

Browning, Earl. *2008 Coach of the Year Clinics Football Manual*. Monterey, Calif.: Coaches Choice, 2008.

Dietzel, Paul, F. *Call Me Coach: A Life in College Football*. Baton Rouge: Louisiana State University Press, 2009.

Ellis, Doris M. *Going out a Champion: The Coach Joe Ellis Story*. Bloomington, Ind.: Authorhouse, 2008.

Goldstein, Sidney. *The Basketball Coach's Bible: A Comprehensive and Systematic Guide to Coaching*. Philadelphia: Golden Aura, 2008.

Gutman, Dan. *Coach Hyatt Is a Riot!* New York: HarperCollins, 2009.

Harkins, Harry L. *Shuffle Offenses for Men's and Women's Basketball*. Montery, Calif.: Coaches Choice, 2008.

NBA Coaches Association. *NBA Coaches Playbook: Techniques, Tactics, and Teaching Points*. Champaign, Ill.: Human Kinetics, 2008.

Nelson, Shawn. *Basketball Coaches' Guide to Advanced Offensive Skill Development*. Monterey, Calif.: Coaches Choice, 2008.

Robinson, Paul. *Foundations of Sports Coaching*. New York: Routledge, 2009.

Schreck, Vic. *The Making of Champions: Coaching Youth Football*. Frederick, Md.: PublishAmerica, 2009.

Tarwater, Mark. *So You Want to Be a Football Coach: How to Coach Little League*. Frederick, Md.: PublishAmerica, 2007.

Thompson, Peter J. L. *Introduction to Coaching Theory*. Garsington, Great Britain: Meyer & Meyer Sport, 2009.

———. *Run! Jump! Throw!: The Official IAAF Guide to Teaching Athletics*. Garsington, Great Britain: Meyer & Meyer Sport, 2009.

Ulloa, Edward. *27: A Football Coach's Memoirs*. Frederick, Md.: PublishAmerica, 2009.

Wallace, Francis. *Knute Rockne: The Story of the Greatest Football Coach Who Ever Lived*. Whitefish, Mont.: Kessinger, 2007.

Wojnarowski, Adrian. *Jimmy V: The Life and Death of Jim Valvano*. New York: Penguin, 2008.

COLLEGE SPORTS, RECRUITING, AND ATHLETIC SCHOLARSHIPS

Britz, Pat. *Athletic Scholarships for Dummies*. Hoboken, N.J.: John Wiley, 2007.

Feldman, Bruce. *Meat Market: Inside the Smash-Mouth World of College Football Recruiting*. New York: ESPN, 2007.

Radford, Jerry. *Superscout Women's Basketball Recruiting Guide: An In-Depth Look at the Entire Recruiting Process for High School Basketball Players and Parents*. Bloomington, Ind.: Authorhouse, 2007.

Richter, Laurie A. *Put Me in, Coach: A Parent's Guide to Winning the Game of College Recruiting*. Lincolnshire, Ill.: Right Fit Press, 2009.

Spainhour, Dan. *How to Get Your Child an Athletic Scholarship: The Parent's Ultimate Guide to Recruiting*. Winston-Salem, N.C.: Educational Coaching & Business Communications, 2007.

Tully, Gregory J. *Nine College Nines: A Closeup View of Campus Baseball Programs Today*. Jefferson, N.C.: McFarland, 2009.

Yaeger, Don. *Tarnished Heisman: Did Reggie Bush Turn His Final College Season into a Six-Figure Job?* New York: Simon & Schuster, 2008.

EQUIPMENT MANAGER

Dodson, Steve. *Golf Maintence Equipment Manager*. Raleigh, N.C.: Lulu, 2009.

FITNESS

Dugdill, Lindsey. *Physical Activity and Health Promotion: Evidence-Based Approaches to Practice*. Hoboken, N.J.: John Wiley, 2009.

Dumas, Andy. *Knockout Fitness: Boxing Workouts to Get You in the Best Shape of Your Life*. New York: Skyhorse, 2009.

Kennedy-Armbruster, Carol. *Methods of Group Exercise Instruction*. Champaign, Ill.: Human Kinetics, 2009.

Ransdell, Lynda B. *Developing Effective Physical Activity Programs*. Champaign, Ill.: Human Kinetics, 2009.

Wilson, Gregory S. *Exploring Exercise Science*. New York: McGraw-Hill, 2009.

FOOTBALL

Bearport Publishing. *Football Heroes Making a Difference*. New York: Bearport Publishing, 2009.

Bradley, John. *It Never Rains in Tiger Stadium*. New York: Random House, 2009.

Daly, Charles Dudley. *American Football*. Charleston, S.C.: BiblioBazaar, 2009.

Edwards, William H. *Football Days*. New York: Moffat, Yard and Co., 2009.

Haughton, Percy Duncan. *Football and How to Watch It*. Whitefish, Mont.: Kessinger, 2009.

Koestler-Grack, Rachel A. *Tom Brady*. New York: Facts On File, 2009.

Pervin, Lawrence A. *Football's New York Giants: A History*. Jefferson, N.C.: McFarland, 2009.

Sandler, Michael. *Brett Favre*. New York: Bearport Publishing, 2009.

Sterngass, Jon. *Jerry Rice*. New York: Facts On File, 2009.

St John, Allen. *The Billion Dollar Game: Behind the Scenes of the Greatest Day in American Sport—Super Bowl Sunday*. New York: Doubleday, 2009.

Worth, Richard. *Donovan Mcnabb*. New York: Facts On File, 2009.

GOLF

Baltz, Tripp. *The Pro's Pro: Warren Smith, Golf Professional—Lessons on Life and Golf from the Ol' Pro at Cherry Hills Country Club*. Parker, Colo.: Outskirts Press, 2008.

Hansen, Mark Victor. *Chicken Soup for the Woman Golfer's Soul: Stories about Trailblazing Women Who've Changed the Game Forever*. Deerfield Beach, Fla.: Health Communications, 2007.

Hicks, Betty. *My Life: From Fairway to Airway*. Bloomington, Ind.: iUniverse, 2006.

Lake, Brian. *Putt Like a Pro: Master the Ground Game Stroke That's Right for You*. New York: McGraw-Hill, 2008.

Loebs, Timothy. *Magical Golf—A Tale of Transformation: How to Achieve Mental and Emotional Control over Your Golf Game*. North Charleston, S.C.: BookSurge, 2009.

Smiley, Bob. *Follow the Roar: Tailing Tiger for All 604 Holes of His Most Spectacular Season*. New York: HarperCollins, 2009.

Thorp, David. *Missing the Cut: The Highs and Lows of a Golf Pro on the Edge of the Big Time*. Bloomington, Ind.: Authorhouse, 2008.

HOCKEY

Daccord, Brian. *Hockey Goaltending*. Champaign, Ill.: Human Kinetics, 2008.

Gilbert, John. *Herb Brooks: The Inside Story of a Hockey Mastermind*. Stillwater, Minn.: Voyageur Press, 2009.

Goodman, Robert. *Forged on Ice: Freemasons within the Hershey Bears and the Hockey Hall of Fame*. North Charleston, S.C.: BookSurge, 2009.

Hotchkiss, Harley. *Hat Trick: A Life in the Hockey Rink, Oil Patch and Community*. Toronto, Ontario: Dundurn Group, 2009.

Pecknold, Rand. *Hard Core Hockey: Essential Skills, Strategies, and Systems from the Sport's Top Coaches*. New York: McGraw-Hill, 2009.

Podnieks, Andrew. *The Complete Hockey Dictionary: More Than 12,000 Words and Phrases and Their Specific Hockey Definitions*. Toronto: Key Porter Books, 2008.

Sports Illustrated. *Montreal Canadiens: One Hundred Years*. New York: Time, 2009.

Turowetz, Allan. *Lions in Winter*. Hoboken, N.J.: John Wiley, 2009.

HORSE RACING

Brodowsky, Pamela K. *Two Minutes to Glory: The Official History of the Kentucky Derby*. New York: HarperCollins, 2009.

Conley, Kevin. *Stud: Adventures in Breeding*. New York: Bloomsbury, 2008.

Estep, Maggie. *Bloodlines: A Horse Racing Anthology*. New York: Knopf, 2009.

Simpson, Joseph Cairn. *Horse Portraiture: Embracing Breeding, Rearing and Training Trotters; with Their Management in the Stable and on the Track and Preparation for Races*. Whitefish, Mont.: Kessinger, 2008.

Splan, John. *Life with the Trotters*. Whitefish, Mont.: Kessinger, 2008.

OFFICIATING

American Sport Education Program. *Officiating Volleyball*. Champaign, Ill.: Human Kinetics, 2007.

Ashford, Adrienne Cherie. *Strrr-Ike!!: Emmett Ashford, Major League Umpire*. Bloomington, Ind.: Authorhouse, 2004.

Breban, Shmuel. *Laws of the Ring*. Bloomington, Ind.: iUniverse, 2007.

Garlett, Kyle. *The Worst Call Ever!: The Most Infamous Calls Ever Blown by Referees, Umpires, and Other Blind Officials*. New York: HarperCollins, 2008.

Johnson, Harry. *Standing the Gaff: The Life and Hard Times of a Minor League Umpire*. Tuscaloosa: University of Alabama Press, 2005.

Wargo, John. *What Now?: The Essential Guide for New Soccer Referees*. North Charleston, S.C.: BookSurge, 2007.

PHYSICAL EDUCATION

Neide, Joan. *Teaching Self-Defense in Secondary Physical Education*. Champaign, Ill.: Human Kinetics, 2009.

Pangrazi, Robert P. *Dynamic Physical Education for Elementary School Children*. San Francisco, Calif.: Benjamin-Cummings, 2009.

Summerford, Cathie. *Action-Packed Classrooms, K–5: Using Movement to Educate and Invigorate Learners*. Thousand Oaks, Calif.: Corwin Press, 2009.

PUBLIC RELATIONS, PUBLICITY, PROMOTION, AND MARKETING

Basic Books Staff. *Stylebook and Briefing on Media Law*. New York: Basic Books, 2007.

Beasley, Jerry. *7 Steps to Success: How to Market Your Martial Arts School, Seminar and Summer Camp*. Palm Coast, Fla.: Black Belt, 2008.

Davis, John. *The Olympic Games Effect: How Sports Marketing Builds Strong Brands*. Edison, N.J.: John Wiley: 2009.

Desbordes, Michel. *Marketing and Football: An International Perspective*. Burlington, Mass. Elsevier, 2009.

Favorito, Joseph. *Sports Publicity: A Practical Approach*. Burlington, Mass.; Elsevier, 2009.

Ferrand, Alain. *Marketing the Sports Organization: Building Networks and Relationships*. New York: Routledge, 2008.

Field, Shelly. *Career Opportunities in Advertising and Public Relations*. New York: Facts On File, 2005.

Fullerton, Sam. *Sports Marketing*. New York: McGraw-Hill, 2009.

Funk, Daniel C. *Consumer Behavior in Sport and Events: Marketing Action*. Burlington, Mass.: Elsevier, 2008.

Irwin, Richard R. *Sport Promotion and Sales Management*. Champaign, Ill.: Human Kinetics, 2008.

Wakefield, Kirk L. *Team Sports Marketing*. Burlington, Mass.: Elsevier, 2009.

Yudkin, Marcia. *Six Steps to Free Publicity*. Franklin Lakes, N.J.: Career Press, 2008.

SCOUTING

Allen, George. *How to Scout Football*. Mansfield Center, Conn.: Martino, 2009.

SPORTS ADMINISTRATION AND MANAGEMENT

Appenzeller, Herb. *Successful Sports Management*. Durham, N.C.: Carolina Academic Press, 2008.

Girginov, Vassil. Management of Sports Development. Burlington, Mass.: Elsevier, 2008.

Hoye, Russell. *Sport Management*. Burlington, Mass.: Elsevier, 2009.

Humphreys, Brad R. *The Business of Sports*. Westport, Conn.: Greenwood, 2008.

Hums, Mary A. *Governance and Policy in Sport Organizations*. Scottsdale, Ariz.: Holcomb Hathaway, 2009.

Lussier, Robert. *Applied Sport Management Skills*. Champaign, Ill.: Human Kinetics, 2009.

SPORTS CAREERS

Field, Shelly. *Ferguson Career Coach: Managing Your Career in the Sports Industry*. New York: Facts On File, 2008.

SPORTS JOURNALISM, REPORTING, AND COMMUNICATIONS

Collins, Jerome. *On the Sidelines: 100 Years of the Best in Local Sports Reporting*. Buffalo, N.Y.: Bates Jackson, 2006.

Conrad, Mark. *The Business of Sports: A Primer for Journalists*. New York: Routledge, 2008.

Fatsis, Stefan. *A Few Seconds of Panic: A 5-Foot-8, 170-Pound, 43-Year-Old Sportswriter Plays in the NFL*. New York: Penguin, 2008.

Jack, Zachary Michael. *Inside the Ropes: Sportswriters Get Their Game On*. Lincoln, Neb.: Bison Books, 2008.

Price, S. L. *Far Afield: A Sportswriting Odyssey*. Guilford, Conn.: Globe Pequot, 2007.

Reilly, Rick. *The Life of Reilly: The Best of Sports Illustrated's Rick Reilly*. New York: Time, 2008.

Reinardy, Scott. *Sports Writing*. New York: Routledge, 2008.

———. *Game On!: An Introduction to Sports Reporting and Writing*. New York: Routledge, 2008.

———. *Essentials of Sports Reporting and Writing*. New York: Routledge, 2009.

SPORTS MEDICINE

Kummer, Patricia K. *Athletic Trainer*. Ann Arbor, Mich.: Cherry Lake, 2009.

Rich, Brent. *Tarascon Sports Medicine Pocketbook*. Sudbury, Mass.: Jones and Bartlett, 2009.

McKeag, Douglas B. *ACSM's Primary Care Sports Medicine*. Philadelphia: Lippincott, Williams and Wilkins, 2007.

McMahon, Patrick J. *Current Diagnosis and Treatment in Sports Medicine*. New York: McGraw-Hill, 2006.

National Academy of Sports Medicine Staff. *Nasm's Therapeutic Exercise*. Philadelphia: Lippincott, Williams and Wilkins, 2009.

SPORTS NUTRITION

Driskell, Judy A. *Nutrition and Exercise Concerns of Middle Age*. Boca Raton, Fla.: C R C Press, 2009.

Williams, Melvin. *Nutrition for Health, Fitness and Sport*. New York: McGraw-Hill, 2009.

WOMEN & SPORTS

Baker, Christine A. *Why She Plays: The World of Women's Basketball*. Lincoln: University of Nebraska Press, 2008.

Chatman, Pokey. *Winning Women's Basketball*. Champaign, Ill.: Human Kinetics, 2007.

Grundy, Pamela. *Shattering the Glass: The Remarkable History of Women's Basketball*. Chapel Hill: University of North Carolina Press, 2007.

Ikard, Roberto. *Just for Fun: The Story of AAU Women's Basketball*. Fayetteville: University of Arkansas Press, 2008.

Melnick, Ralph. *Senda Berenson: The Unlikely Founder of Women's Basketball*. Amherst: University of Massachusetts Press, 2007.

Radford, Jerry. *Superscout Women's Basketball Recruiting Guide: An in-Depth Look at the Entire Recruiting Process for High School Basketball Players and Parents*. Bloomington, Ind.: Authorhouse, 2008.

Women's Basketball Coaches Association. *The Women's Basketball Drill Book*. Champaign, Ill.: Human Kinetics Publishers, 2007.

WRESTLING

Caprio, Robert. *Are We There Yet? Tales From the Never Ending Travels of WWE Superstars*. New York: Simon & Schuster, 2005.

Davidson, Tom. *Wrestling the ABC's*. Northville, Mich.: Nelson, 2009.

Gorman, Jacqueline Laks. *Dwayne the Rock Johnson*. Stongsville, Ohio: Gareth Stevens, 2007.

Payan, Michael. *In the Ring with Kevin Nash*. New York: Rosen, 2009.

B. PERIODICALS

Magazines, newspapers, membership bulletins, and newsletters may be helpful in finding information about a specific job category, locating a job in a specific field, or giving you insight into what certain jobs entail.

As with the books in the previous section, this list should serve as a starting point only. Due to space limitations, there are many periodicals that are not listed. Periodicals also tend to come and go. Look in your local library, on the Internet, or in newspaper/magazine shops for other periodicals of interest.

ATHLETES

ACC Sports Journal
P.O. Box 4323
Chapel Hill, NC 27515
Phone: (800) 447-7667

Amateur Athlete
Eliot Wineberg Publisher
7840 North Lincoln Avenue

Skokie, IL 60077
Phone: (847) 675-0200
Fax: (847) 675-2903

Athletes in Action
651 Taylor Drive
Xenia, OH 45385
Phone: (513) 933-2421
Fax: (513) 933-2424
E-mail: aiacom@aol.com
http://www.athletesinaction.org

AUTO RACING

Auto Racing Digest
Century Publishing, Inc.
990 Grove Street
Evanston, IL 60201
Phone: (847) 491-6440
Fax: (847) 491-6203
http://www.centurysports.net

National Speedway Directory
P.O. Box 448
Comstock, MI 49321
Phone: (616) 785-0340
Fax: (616) 785-0346
E-mail: speedways@dnx.net
http://www.speedwaysonline.com

NASCAR

Street & Smith's Sports Group
120 West Morehead Street
Charlotte, NC 28202
Phone: (704) 973-1300
Fax: (704) 973-1576
E-mail: annuals@streetandsmiths.com
http://www.streetandsmiths.com

BASEBALL

Amateur Baseball News
American Amateur Baseball Congress, Inc.
100 West Broadway
Farmington, NM 87401
Phone: (269) 781-2002
Fax: (269) 781-2060

Baseball
Tellstar Productions
2660 Petersbourg
Herndon, VA 20171

Baseball America
201 West Main Street
Durham, NC 27701
Phone: (919) 682-9635
Fax: (919) 682-2880
E-mail: letters@baseballamerica.com
http://www.baseballamerica.com

Baseball Digest
Century Publishing, Inc.
P.O. Box 730
Coeur d'Alene, ID 83816
Phone: (208) 765-6300
Fax: (208) 667-2856
E-mail: bb@centruysports.net
http://www.centurypublishing.com

Baseball Handbook
National Research Bureau
320 Valley Street
Burlington, IA 52601

Baseball Illustrated
Dorchester Media
P.O. Box 6640
Wayne, PA 19087
Phone: (212) 725-8811
http://www.dorchesterpub.com

Baseball Research Journal
Society for American Baseball Research, Inc.
812 Huron Road
Cleveland, OH 44115
Phone: (216) 575-0500
Fax: (216) 575-0502
E-mail: info@sabr.org
http://www.sabr.org

Baseball Umpires Manual
National Federation of State High School Associations
P.O. Box 690
Indianapolis, IN 46206
Phone: (317) 972-6900
Fax: (317) 822-5700
E-mail: info@nfhs.org
http://www.nfhs.org

Beckett Baseball Card Plus
Beckett Media LP
4635 McEwen Road
Dallas, TX 75244
Phone: (972) 991-6657
Fax: (972) 991-8930
http://www.beckett.com

Collegiate Baseball: The Voice of Amateur Baseball
Collegiate Baseball Newspaper, Inc.
50566, Tucson, AZ 85703
E-mail: cbn@baseballnews.com
http://www.baseballnews.com

Junior Baseball: America's Youth Baseball Magazine
2 D Publishing
22026 Gault Street
Canoga Park, CA 91303
Phone: (818) 710-1234
Fax: (818) 710-1877
E-mail: editor@juniorbaseball.com
http://www.juniorbaseball.com

P O N Y Baseball—Softball Express
P O N Y Baseball, Inc.
1951 Pony Place

P.O. Box 225
Washington, PA 15301
Phone: 724-225-1060
Fax: 724-225-9852
E-mail: info@pony.org
http://www.pony.org

Reds Report
Columbus Sports Publications
1350 West Fifth Avenue
Columbus, OH 43212
Phone: (614) 486-2202

S A B R Review of Books: A Forum of Baseball Literary Opinion
Society for American Baseball Research, Inc.
812 Huron Road
Cleveland, OH 44115
E-mail: info@sabr.org

Sporting News Ultimate Baseball Scouting Guide
America City Business Journals, Inc.
120 West Morehead Street
Charlotte, NC 28202
Phone: (704) 973-1001
http://www.acbj.com

USA Today Sports Weekly
1000 Wilson Boulevard
Arlington, VA 2229
Phone: (703) 854-3400
Fax: (703) 854-2034
http://cgi.usatoday.com

BASKETBALL

Basketball Digest Annual Guide
Century Publishing, Inc.
East 5710 Seltice Way
Post Falls, ID 83854
Phone: (208) 765-6300
Fax: (208) 676-8476
http://www.centurypublishing.com

Basketball Records
National Collegiate Athletic Association
700 West Washington Street
P.O. Box 6222
Indianapolis, IN 46206
Phone: (317) 917-6222
Fax: (317) 917-6888
E-mail: esummers@ncaa.org
http:;//www.ncaa.org

Court Awareness
Jan Travers Publishing
2177 Carol Drive
Harrisburg, PA 17110
Phone: (717) 545-7429

NCAA News
National Collegiate Athletic Association
700 West Washington Street
P.O. Box 6222
Indianapolis, IN 46206
Phone: (317) 917-6222
Fax: (317) 917-6888
E-mail: esummers@ncaa.org
http://www.ncaa.org

Sporting News Official NBA Guide
American City Business Journals, Inc.
120 Morehead Street
Charlotte, NC 28202
Phone: (704) 973-1000
Fax: (704) 973-1001
http://www.acbj.com

Women's Basketball
Goldman Group, Inc.
4125 Gunn Highway
Tampa, FL 33618
Phone: (813) 264-2772
Fax: (813) 264-2343
E-mail: todd@ggpubs.com
http://www.ggpubs.com

BOWLING

Bowling Center Management
Luby Publishing
122 South Michigan Avenue
Chicago, IL 60603
Phone: (312) 341-1110
Fax: (312) 341-1180
E-mail: email@lubypublishing.com
http://www.lubypublishing.com

Bowling News
Bowling News, Inc.
2606 West Burbank Boulevard
Burbank, CA 91505
Phone: (818) 849-4664
Fax: (818) 845-6321

BOXING

Boxing USA
United States Amateur Boxing, Inc.
One Olympic Plaza
Colorado Springs, CO 80909
Phone: (719) 578-4506
Fax: (719) 632-3426

Electronic Boxing Weekly
Comp-U-Sports
571 South Gosser Hill Road
Leechburgh, PA 15656
Phone: (724) 845-9775
Fax: (724) 639-8514
http://www.boxmag.com

In the Ring
Michigan Suburbs Alliance
300 East Nine Mile Road
Ferndale, MI 48220
Phone: (248) 546-2380
Fax: (248) 546-2369
http://michigansuburbsalliance.org

Ring Rhetoric
American Association for the Improvement of Boxing, Inc.
86 Fletcher Avenue
Mount Vernon, NY 10533
Phone: (914) 664-4571

The Ring: The Bible of Boxing
Sports and Entertainment Publications, LLC
6198 Butler Pike
Bell, PA 19422
Phone: (215) 461-0583
Fax: (215) 643-3176

COACHING AND TRAINING

American Swimming Coaches Association World Clinic Yearbook
American Swimming Coaches Association
5101 Northwest 21st Avenue
Fort Lauderdale, FL 33309
Phone: (954) 563-4930
Fax: (954) 563-9813
E-mail: asca@swimmingcoach.org
http://www.swimmingcoach.org

Coach and Athletic Director
Scholastic Inc.
557 Broadway
New York, NY 10012
Phone: (212) 343-6100
Fax: (212) 343-4808
http://www.scholastic.com

Journal of Strength and Conditioning Research
National Strength and Conditioning Association
1885 Bob Johnson Drive
Colorado Springs, CO 80906
Phone: (719) 632-6722
Fax: (719) 632-6367
E-mail: nsca@nsca-lift.org
http://www.nsca-lift.org

National Strength and Conditioning Association Bulletin
National Strength and Conditioning Association
1885 Bob Johnson Drive
Colorado Springs, CO 80906
Phone: (719) 632-6722
Fax: (719) 632-6367
E-mail: nsca@nsca-lift.org
http://www.nsca-lift.org

Swimming World magazine
Sports Publications, Inc.
P.O. Box 20337
Sedona, AZ 86341
Phone: (928) 284-4005
Fax: (928) 284-2477

CYCLING

Adventure Cyclist
Adventure Cycling Association
150 East Pine Street
P.O. Box 8308
Missoula, MT 59807
Phone: (406) 721-1776
Fax: (406) 721-8754

Cycle News
Cycle News Publishing Group
3505-M Cadillac Avenue
Costa Mesa, CA 92626
Phone: (714) 751-7433
Fax: (714) 435-436-9573

League of American Bicyclists Magazine
1612 K Street, NW
Washington, DC 20006
Phone: (202) 822-1333
Fax: (202) 822-1334

USA Cycling
One Olympic Plaza
Colorado Springs, CO 80909
Phone: (719) 866-4581
Fax: (719) 866-4628
http://www.usacycling.org

FITNESS

ACE Fitness Matters
American Council on Exercise
4851 Paramount Drive
San Diego, CA 92123
Phone: (858) 279-8227
Fax: (858) 279-8064
http://www.acefitness.org

A C S M's Health & Fitness Journal
Lippincott Williams & Wilkins
351 West Camden Street
Baltimore, MD 21201
Phone: (410) 528-4000
http://www.lww.com

Aerobic Beat
7985 Santa Monica
Los Angeles, CA 90046
Phone: (310) 659-2503
Fax: (213) 655-5223

Chiropractic Wellness and Fitness Magazine
910 Via Rodeo
Placentia, CA 92870
Phone: (714) 996-2229
Fax: (714) 996-2223
http://www.cwfmonline.com

Club Industry's Fitness
Penton Media, Inc.
9800 Metcalf Avenue
Overland Park, KS 66212
Phone: (913) 341-1300
Fax: (913) 967-1898
http://www.penton.com

Course Conductor News
Canadian Society for Exercise Physiology
185 Somerset Street West
Ottawa, ON K2P OJ2 Canada
Phone: (613) 234-3755
Fax: (613) 234-3565
http://www.csep.ca

Diet and Fitness Magazine
Frederick Fell Publishers, Inc.
2131 Hollywood Boulevard
Hollywood, CA 33020
Phone: (954) 925-0555
Fax: (954) 925-5244
http://www.fellpub.com

Exercise and Health
Harris Publications, Inc.
1115 Broadway
New York, NY 10010
Phone: (212) 807-7100
Fax: (212) 807-1479
http://ww.harris-pub.com

Fitness
Meredith Corporation
125 Park Avenue
New York, NY 10017
Phone: (212) 557-6600
Fax: (212) 455-1345
http://www.meredith.com

Fitness Management
Leisure Publications, Inc.
4160 Wilshire Boulevard
Los Angeles, CA 90010
Phone: (323) 964-4835
Fax: (323) 964-4800

Fit Pregnancy
A M I—Weider Publications
1 Park Avenue
New York, NY 10016
Phone: (212) 545-4800
Fax: (212) 448-9890
http://www.amilink.com

IDEA Health and Fitness Source
I D E A Health & Fitness Association
10455 Pacific Center Court
San Diego, CA 82121
Phone: (858) 535-8979
Fax: (858) 535-8234
http://www.ideafit.com

Living Fit
Weider Publications
One Park Avenue
New York, NY 10016
Phone: (212) 545-4800
Fax: (212) 532-1013

Men's Exercise
Pumpkin Press, Inc.
350 Fifth Avenue
New York, NY 10118
Phone: (212) 947-4322
Fax: (212) 563-4774

Men's Fitness
AMI Weider Publications
21100 Erwin Street
Woodland Hills, CA 91367
Phone: (818) 595-0589
Fax: (818) 884-6910
http://www.americanmediainc.com

Shape
AMI Weider Publications
21100 Erwin Street
Woodland Hills, CA 91367
Phone: (818) 595-0589
Fax: (818) 884-6910
http://www.americanmediainc.com

24: Everyday Fitness for Everyday Body
12647 Alcosta Boulevard
San Ramon, CA 94583
Phone: (818) 783-7945
Fax: (818) 783-2387
http://www.24hourfitness.com

**University of California, Berkeley, Wellness Letter:
    The Newsletter of Nutrition, Fitness, and Stress
    Management**
Health Letter Associates
P.O. Box 412
Prince Street Station
New York, NY 10012
Phone: (510) 642-8061
Fax: (510) 505-5462

FOOTBALL

Athlon's Pro Football
Athlon Sports Communications, Inc.
220 25th Avenue North
Nashville, TN 37203
Phone: (615) 327-0747
Fax: (615) 327-1149
http://www.athlonsports.com

College and Pro Football Newsweekly
Sports Publications Production

18 Industrial Park Drive
Port Washington, NY 11050
Phone: (516) 484-3300

GamePlan Pro Football Annual
113 East Taft Road
North Syracuse, NY 13212
Phone: (315) 452-0518
Fax: (315) 452-1504
E-mail: info@gameplanmagazines.com
http://www.gameplanmagazines.com

High School Football
American City Business Journals, Inc.
120 Morehead Street
Charlotte, NC 28202
Phone: (704) 973-1000
Fax: (704) 973-1001
http://www.acbj.com

Pro Football Action
Sports Publications Production
18 Industrial Park Drive
Port Washington, NY 11050
Phone: (516) 484-3300

Pro Football Weekly
Source Interlink Companies
302 Saunders Road
Riverwoods, IL 60015
Phone: (847) 940-1100
http://www.sourceinterlinkmedia.com

Sporting News College Football Yearbook
American City Business Journals, Inc.
120 Morehead Street
Charlotte, NC 28202
Phone: (704) 973-1000
Fax: (704) 973-1001
http://www.acbj.com

**Touchdown Illustrated: College Football Game
    Day Programs**
Professional Sports Publications
519 Eighth Avenue
New York, NY 10019
Phone: (212) 697-1460
http://www.pspsports.com

GENERAL INTEREST

Sporting News
America City Business Journals, Inc.

120 W Morehead Street
Charlotte, NC 28202
Phone: (704) 973-1001
http://www.acbj.com

Sports Illustrated

Sports Illustrated Group
135 West 50th Street
New York, NY 10020
Phone: (212) 522-1212
Fax: (212) 522-0392

Sports Illustrated for Kids

Sports Illustrated Group
135 West 50th Street
New York, NY 10020
Phone: (212) 522-1212
Fax: (212) 522-0392

GOLF

AA Golf

559 West Diversey Parkway
Chicago, IL 60614
Phone: (888) 458-8889
E-mail: info@aagolfmag.com
http://www.aagolfmag.com

Amazing Golf Newsletter

Kleban Technologies, Inc.
1733 H Street
Blaine, WA 98230
Phone: (604) 803-7272
Fax: (604) 984-7922
E-mail: webmaster@winninggoffers.com

Athlon Sports Golf

Athlon Sports Communications, Inc.
220 25th Avenue North
Nashville, TN 37203
Phone: (615) 327-0747
Fax: (615) 327-1149
E-mail: info@athlonsports.com
http://www.ww.athonlsports.com

Best of Golf Tips

Werner Publishing Corporation
12121 Wilshire Boulevard
Los Angeles, CA 90025
Phone: (310) 820-1500
Fax: (310) 826-5008
http://www.wernerpublishing.com

Best of Northeast Golf

Divot Communication Corporation
5197 Main Street
Waitsfield, VT 05673
Phone: (802) 496-7575
Fax: (802) 496-7585
E-mail: info@playnortheastgolf.com
http://www.playnortheastgolf.com

California Golf Course Superintendents Association Magazine

California Golf Course Superintendents Association
221 West Palm Avenue
Reedly, CA 93654
Phone: (866) 643-8707
Fax: (559) 643-8707

Callaway Golf

MacDuff Publishing, LLC
2000 RiverEdge Park
Atlanta, GA 30328
Phone: (770) 859-9600
Fax: (770) 859-9686
http://www.macduffpublishing.com

Colorado Golf Magazine

Pade Publishing, LLC.
559 East Second Avenue
Castle Rock, CO 80104
Phone: (800) 858-9677
http://www.coloradogolf.com

Golf Magazine Living

Time, Inc.
1271 Avenue of the Americas
New York, NY 10020
Phone: (212) 522-1212
http://www.timeinc.com

Golf Market Today

National Golf Foundation
1150 South U.S. Highway 1
Jupiter, FL 33477
Phone: (561) 744-6006
Fax: (561) 744-6107
http://www.ngf.org

Golf Marketing and Operations

Cypress Magazines, Inc.
5715 Kerny Villa Road
San Diego, CA 92123
Phone: (858) 503-7588
Fax: (858) 503-7588
http://www.cypressmagazines.com

Golf Today
25101 Bear Valley Road
PMB 90
Tehachapi, CA 93561
Phone: (661) 823-7842
Fax: (661) 823-7942

Golf World
The Golf Digest Companies
20 Westport Road
Wilton, CT 06897
Phone: (203) 761-5100
Fax: (203) 761-5129

HOCKEY

**American Hockey League Official Guide and
Record Book**
American Hockey League
1 Monarch Place
Springfield, MA 01144
Phone: (413) 781-2030
Fax: (413) 733-4767
E-mail: info@thenhl.com
http://wwwthenhl.com

Beckett Hockey
Beckett Media LP
4635 McEwen Road
Dallas, TX 75244
Phone: (972) 991-6657
Fax: (972) 991-8930
E-mail: customerservice@beckett.com
http://www.beckett.com

Beckett Hockey Card Plus
Beckett Media LP
4635 McEwen Road
Dallas, TX 75244
Phone: (972) 991-6657
Fax: (972) 991-8930
E-mail: customerservice@beckett.com
http://www.beckett.com

Hockey News
United States Field Hockey Association
USFHA National Office
One Olympic Plaza
Colorado Springs, CO 80909
Phone: (719) 578-4567
Fax: (719) 632-0979
E-mail: usfha@usfieldhockey.com
http://www.usfieldhockey.com

Hockey News
Transcontinental Media, Inc.
25 Sheppard Avenue West
Toronto, ON M2N 6S7 Canada
Phone: (416) 733-7600
Fax: (416) 218-3544
E-mail: info@transcontinental.ca
http://www.transcontinental-gtc.com/en/home.html

Hockey Preview
American City Business Journals, Inc.
120 West Morehead Street
Charlotte, NC 28202
Phone: (704) 973-1000
Fax: (704) 973-1001
http://www.acbj.com

Hockey Weekly
Castine Communications
33425 Grand River Avenue
Farmington, MI 48335
Phone: (313) 563-9130
Fax: (313) 563-9538
http://www.amateurhockey.com

HORSE RACING

Daily Racing Form
Daily Racing Form LLC
1634 West 139th Street
Los Angeles, CA 90249
Phone: (310) 768-8907
Fax: (31) 768-1045

Hoof Beats
United States Trotting Association
750 Michigan Avenue
Columbus, OH 43215
Phone: (614) 224-2291
Fax: (614) 222-6791
http://www.ustrotting.com

Horse Illustrated
Bow Tie, Inc.
2401 Beverly Boulevard
P.O. Box 57900
Los Angeles, CA 90057
Phone: (213) 385-2222
Fax: (213) 385-8565
E-mail: adtraffic@bowtieoinc.com
http://www.bowtieinc.com

National Horseman
16101 North 82nd Street
Scottsdale, AZ 85260
Phone: (480) 922-5202
http://www.tnhl865.com

Thoroughbred Times
Thoroughbred Times Co, Inc.
2008 Mercer Road
Lexington, KY 40511
Phone: (859) 260-9800
Fax: (859) 260-9812
http://www.thoroughbredtimes.com

MARKETING

Direct Marketing
Hoke Communications, Inc.
224 Seventh Street
Garden City, NY 11530
Phone: (516) 746-6700
Fax: (516) 294-8141

Journal of Marketing
American Marketing Association
311 South Wacker Drive
Chicago, IL 60606
Phone: (312) 542-9000
Fax: (312) 542-9001
E-mail: info@ama.org
http://www.marketingpower.com

MEDIA

Bacon's Media Calendar
Cision US, Inc.
332 South Michigan Avenue
Chicago, IL 60604
Phone: (866) 639-5087
E-mail: info.us@cision.com
http://www.us.cision.com

Broadcasting and Cable
Reed Business Information
360 Park Avenue South
New York, NY 10010
Phone: (646) 746-6400
Fax: (646) 746-7131
http://www.reedbusiness.com

Contacts: The Media Pipeline for Public Relations People
MerComm, Inc.

500 Executive Boulevard
Ossining, NY 10562
Phone: (914) 923-9400
Fax: (914) 923-9484

PartyLine: The Weekly Roundup of Media Placement Opportunities
PartyLine Publishing
35 Sutton Place
New York, NY 10022
http://www.partylinepublishing.com

OFFICIATING

Referee
Referee Enterprises, Inc.
P.O. Box 161
Franksville, WI 53126
Phone: (262) 632-8855
Fax: (262) 632-5460

PHYSICAL EDUCATION

Journal of Physical Education, Recreation and Dance
American Alliance for Health, Physical Education, Recreation, and Dance
1900 Association Drive
Reston, VA 20191
Phone: (703) 476-3400
Fax: (703) 476-9527
E-mail: info@aahperd.org
http://www.aahperd.org

Journal of Teaching in Physical Education
Human Kenetics
P.O. Box 5076
Champaign, IL 61825
Phone: (217) 351-5076
Fax: (217) 351-2674
http://www.humankinetics.com

PHYSICAL THERAPY

Journal of Physical Therapy Education
American Physical Therapy Association
1111 North Fairfax Street
Alexandria, VA 22314
Phone: (703) 684-2782
Fax: (703) 684-7343
http://www.apta.org

PUBLIC RELATIONS AND PUBLICITY

Bulldog Reporter Business Media

InfoCom Group
124 Linden Street
Oakland, CA 94607
Phone: (510) 596-9300
E-mail: bulldog@infocomgroup.com
http://www.bulldogreporter.com

Community Relations Report

Joe Williams Communications, Inc.
P.O. Box 924
Bartlesville, OK 74005
Phone: (918) 336-2267

Lifestyle Media Relations Reporter

InfoCom Group
124 Linden Street
Oakland, CA 94607
Phone: (510) 596-9300
E-mail: bulldog@infocomgroup.com
http://www.infocomgroup.com

PR Reporter

Lawrence Ragan Communications, Inc.
111 East Wacker Drive
Chicago, IL 60601
Phone: (312) 861-3592

PR Week

Haymarket Media, Inc.
114 West 26th Street
New York, NY 10001
Phone: (646) 638-6000
Fax: (646) 638-6114
http://www.haymarket.com

Ragan's Public Relations Review

Lawrence Ragan Communications, Inc.
111 East Wacker Drive
Chicago, IL 60601
Phone: (312) 960-4106
Fax: (312) 960-4106
http://www.ragan.com

RETAIL/WHOLESALE

Cost of Doing Business for Retail Sporting Goods Stores

National Sporting Goods Association
1601 Feehanville Drive
Mount Prospect, IL 60056
Phone: (847) 296-6742

Fax: (847) 391-9827
E-mail: info@nsga.org
http://www.nsga.org

S G B: The National News Magazine of the Sporting Goods Industry

SportsOneSource Group
P.O. Box 480156
Charlotte, NC 28269
Phone: (704) 987-3450
Fax: (704) 987-3455
E-mail: info@sportonesource.com
http://www.sportsonesource.com

Sporting Goods Dealer

Nielsen Business Publications
770 Broadway
New York, NY 10003
Phone: (646) 654-4500
Fax: (646) 654-4949
E-mail: bmcomm@nielsen.com
http://www.nielsenbusinessmedia.com

Sport Shop News

P.O. Box 566
Stratford, CT 06615
Phone: (203) 279-0149

RUNNING

Fodor's Sports: Running

Fodor's Travel Publications
1745 Broadway
New York, NY 10019
Phone: (212) 572-2313
http://www.fodors.com

Runner's World

Rodale Publishing
33 East Minor Street
Emmaus, PA 18098
Phone: (610) 967-5171
Fax: (610) 967-8963
E-mail: info@rodale.com
http://www.rodale.com

SKATING

International Figure Skating

Madavor Media, LLC
420 Boylston Street
Boston, MA 02116
Phone: (617) 536-0100
Fax: (617) 536-0102

E-mail: info@madavor.com
http://www.madavor.com

SOCCER

Soccer America
Soccer America Communications LLC
P.O. Box 23704
Oakland, CA 94623
Phone: (510) 420-3640
Fax: (510) 420-3655

SOFTBALL

Let's Play Softball
Let's Play, Inc.
2721 East 42nd Street
Minneapolis, MN 55406
Phone: (612) 729-0023
Fax: (612) 729-0259

SPORTS BUSINESS AND ADMINISTRATION

Encyclopedia of Sports Business Contacts: The Sports Networking Reference Guide
Global Sports Productions Ltd.
1223 Broadway
Santa Monica, CA 90404
Phone: (310) 454-9480
Fax: (310) 454-6500

Sports Business Daily
Street & Smith's Sports Group
120 West Morehead Street
Charlotte, NC 28202
Phone: (704) 973-1300
Fax: (704) 973-1576
http://www.streetandsmiths.com

SPORTS COLLECTING

Sports Collector's Digest
Krause Publications, Inc.
700 East State Street
Iola, WI 54990
Phone: (715) 445-2214
Fax: (715) 445-2164
http://www.krause.com

Tuff Stuff's Sports Collector's Monthly
Krause Publications, Inc.
700 East State Street
Iola, WI 54990
Phone: (715) 445-2214
Fax: (715) 445-2164
http://www.krause.com

SPORTS MANAGEMENT

International Journal of Sport Management
American Press
28 State Street
Boston, MA 02109
E-mail: ampress@flash.net
http://www.americanpresspublishers.com

Journal of Sport Management
Human Kinetics
P.O. Box 5076
Champaign, IL 61825
Phone: (217) 351-5076
Fax: (217) 351-2764
http://www.humankinetics.com

SPORTS MARKETING

Sports Marketing Quarterly
Fitness Information Technology, Inc.
P.O. Box 6116
Morgantown, WV 26506
Phone: (304) 293-6888
Fax: (304) 293-6658
E-mail: fit@fitint
http://www.fitinfotech.com

SPORTS MEDICINE

American Journal of Sports Medicine
Sage Science Press
2455 Teller Road
Thousand Oaks, CA 91320
Phone: (805) 499-0721
Fax: (805) 499-0871
E-mail: info@sagepub.com
http://www.sagepub.com

Physician and Sportsmedicine
J T E Multimedia, LLC
1235 Westlakes Drive
Berwyn, PA 19312
Phone: (610) 889-3730
Fax: (610) 889-3731

SPORTS RESEARCH

Research in Sports Medicine: An International Journal
Taylor & Francis, Inc.
325 Chestnut Street
Philadelphia, PA 19016
Phone: (215) 625-8900

Fax: (215) 625-8914
http://www.taylorandfrancis.com

Research Quarterly for Exercise and Sport
American Alliance for Health, Physical Education,
     Recreation, and Dance
1900 Association Drive

Reston, VA 20191
Phone: (703) 476-3400
Fax: (703) 476-9527
E-mail: info@aahperd.org
http://www.aahperd.org

INDEX

ABOUT THE AUTHOR

Shelly Field is a nationally recognized motivational speaker, career expert, stress management specialist, personal career and life coach, and author of over 35 best-selling books in the business and career fields.

Her books help people find careers in a wide variety of areas, including the music, sports, hospitality and communications industries, casinos and casino hotels, advertising and public relations, theater, the performing arts, entertainment, animal rights, heath care, writing, and art. She is a frequent guest on local, regional, and national radio, cable, and television talk, information, and news shows and has been the subject of numerous print interviews for articles and news stories.

Field is a featured speaker at conferences, conventions, expos, corporate functions, spouse programs, employee training and development sessions, career fairs, casinos, and events nationwide. A former comedienne, she adds a humorous spin whether speaking on empowerment, motivation, stress management, staying positive, the power of laughter, careers, attracting, retaining and motivating employees, or customer service. Her popular presentations, "STRESS BUSTERS: Beating the Stress in Your Work and Your Life" and "The De-Stress Express" are favorites around the country.

A career consultant to businesses, educational institutions, employment agencies, women's groups, and individuals, Field is sought out by executives, celebrities, and sports figures for personal life and career coaching and stress management.

In her role as a corporate consultant to businesses throughout the country, she provides assistance with human resources issues such as attracting, retaining, and motivating employees, customer service training, and stress management in the workplace.

The president and CEO of The Shelly Field Organization, a public relations, marketing and management firm handling national clients, she has represented celebrities in the sports, music, and entertainment industries as well as authors, businesses, and corporations.

For media inquiries, information about personal appearances, seminars, or workshops, stress management, or personal coaching, please contact The Shelly Field Organization at P.O. Box 711, Monticello, NY, 12701, or visit Shelly on the Web at www.shellyfield.com.